A Sonata Theory Handbook

A Sonata Theory Handbook

JAMES HEPOKOSKI

OXFORD

UNIVERSITY PRESS

OXFORD
UNIVERSITY PRESS

Oxford University Press is a department of the University of Oxford. It furthers
the University's objective of excellence in research, scholarship, and education
by publishing worldwide. Oxford is a registered trade mark of Oxford University
Press in the UK and certain other countries.

Published in the United States of America by Oxford University Press
198 Madison Avenue, New York, NY 10016, United States of America.

© Oxford University Press 2021

Library of Congress Cataloging-in-Publication Data
Names: Hepokoski, James A. (James Arnold), 1946– author.
Title: A sonata theory handbook / James Hepokoski.
Description: New York : Oxford University Press, 2021. |
Includes bibliographical references and index.
Identifiers: LCCN 2020031917 (print) | LCCN 2020031918 (ebook) |
ISBN 9780197536810 (hardback) | ISBN 9780197536827 (paperback) |
ISBN 9780197536841 (epub)
Subjects: LCSH: Sonata form. | Instrumental music—
18th century—Analysis, appreciation. | Instrumental music—19th century—Analysis,
appreciation. | Symphony—18th century. | Symphony—19th century. |
String quartet—18th century. | String quartet—19th century.
Classification: LCC MT62 .H47 2020 (print) | LCC MT62 (ebook) |
DDC 784.18/301—dc23
LC record available at https://lccn.loc.gov/2020031917
LC ebook record available at https://lccn.loc.gov/2020031918

DOI: 10.1093/oso/9780197536810/001.0001

3 5 7 9 8 6 4 2

Paperback printed by Marquis, Canada
Hardback printed by Bridgeport National Bindery, Inc., United States of America

What the naïve, uninstructed, childlike, or illusion-ridden viewer accepts as "real" a more knowledgeable and emancipated one sees to be a carefully planned show, and planned within the framework of a . . . convention.

—Northrop Frye[1]

The aesthetic attitude demands that the distanced object be not merely contemplated disinterestedly, the viewer should also participate in producing it as an imaginary object—like the world of play into which one enters as a fellow player.

—Hans Robert Jauss.[2]

Rather than looking behind the text—for its hidden causes, determining conditions, and noxious motives—we might place ourselves in front of the text, reflecting on what it unfurls, calls forth, makes possible . . . the text's status as coactor: as something that makes a difference, that helps make things happen . . . reading as a coproduction between actors [the reader and the text] rather than an unraveling of manifest meaning, a form of making rather than unmaking.

—Rita Felski[3]

Thought's depth depends on how deeply it penetrates its object, not on the extent to which it reduces it to something else.

—Theodor W. Adorno[4]

Contents

Acknowledgments

Most readers will recognize this book as a follow-up, some 15 years later, to the 2006 publication of *Elements of Sonata Theory*, which I coauthored with Warren Darcy. But what kind of follow-up is it? And was a follow-up needed? For the first decade after the book's publication, I resisted the idea, determined to let the *Elements* stand as is. Above all, I resisted, and continue to resist, the idea of producing an undergraduate-classroom textbook that simplifies and regularizes Sonata Theory with step-by-step, dutiful, rule-bound exercises. Such a book would run counter to the spirit of the theory, which thrives on analytical nuance, historical understanding, and a commitment to blend the practicalities of analysis with responsible hermeneutic interpretation.

And yet a great deal of cardinal importance within form theory emerged after 2006—along with other trends and concerns in the protean and fast-moving world of musical scholarship. By 2015 or 2016 it was becoming clear that a broad, varied, and sometimes surprising wake of reception had become part of what that book was. It was time to revisit the basics of Sonata Theory—better, to re-*present* those basics—in a different way from that found in the earlier book, one also attuned, I hoped, to where the field was at present. And so, encouraged by the able Suzanne Ryan of Oxford University Press (thank you, Suzanne!), in late 2015 I found myself setting aside other plans and drifting toward the writing of another Sonata Theory–centered book, a second, updated run at laying out this interpretive approach.

My ideas for the book ran along two complementary lines. In the first, I decided to draw on my experience of introducing Sonata Theory in my own classes at Yale University—most obviously in my regularly offered graduate and undergraduate seminars on it but also in those on Late Beethoven, on late-nineteenth-century symphonic nationalism, and on the historical movement of "early modernism," Gustav Mahler, and Richard Strauss. The intention was to write a book that replicated, to the extent possible in such a different format, how I introduced Sonata Theory in my seminars—which is to say, through neither abstract principles nor a lockstep marching through the *Elements* but rather through an ordered showing of how the method worked through the analysis of multiple, complete movements, one after another, growing in complexity, each with its own challenges. First and foremost, then, I am grateful to the many students in those seminars over the years, who not only consistently helped me to find ever clearer ways to present the theory but also taught me time and again what "worked" pedagogically and what didn't.

Complementary to this was the rapidly changing, highly charged world of music scholarship with which I found myself immediately engaged. I am indebted to the several invitations to present workshops and papers on Sonata Theory and to participate in often-robust panel discussions or round tables on issues and problems within current views of musical form. In the past dozen or more years, new ideas and theories, challenging views and concepts, have been cropping up on all sides. Many of these were deeply relevant to my own concerns, on the one hand inviting enhancements to the Sonata Theory project, broadening it, I hope, to a more generous inclusivity, and, on the other hand, showing me the areas in it—soft spots or blind spots (all theories have them)—that would profit by clarification or correction. I have learned much from my professional colleagues within the larger field, not least from those whose approach to sonata form differs from that of mine.

Over the past several years many individual conversations with colleagues, perhaps even the most casual conversations, have also left their mark on this book. I think first of my faculty colleagues and friends at Yale, and particularly my fellow Long Branchians, Patrick McCreless, Daniel Harrison, Ian Quinn, Richard Cohn, Brian Kane, Gary Tomlinson, Gundula Kreuzer, and Anna Zayaruznaya. In the early years of the writing of this book, I sent drafts of the first two or three chapters to Sumanth Gopinath (University of Minnesota) and Vasili Byros (Northwestern University) for use in their own graduate seminars. The resulting feedback from each of them, and from their students, was enormously helpful.

In such an analytically detailed book as this one, the risk for errors or oversights, unintended misrepresentations or simplifications of other points of view, and issues of tone and presentation is large. I owe huge debts of thanks to Andrew Schartmann, Liam Hynes, and Ethan Edl, each of whom read carefully through the entire book in its penultimate version and provided me with helpful commentary and advice from three different readers' perspectives. I am also grateful for the responses of the two anonymous readers for Oxford University Press, whose insightful comments and suggestions spurred me into an eleventh-hour, multi-month flurry of tweakings and expansions of the final version. The book's figures (diagrams and musical examples) and tables were prepared by Kai Yin Lo at the University of Minnesota, and shepherding me through the publication process was Sean Decker of Oxford University Press. While one's work along these lines is never done, at some point one can only draw the line, cross one's fingers, publish the book, and hope for the best.

Finally, I thank my wife, Barbara, for her unflagging support and encouragement. As I finished out my years at Yale, it was she who made this book possible is so many ways. In that effort she and I were happily bolstered by our two daughters, Joanna Wing and Laura Nirider, and their families. Writing now in the onslaught of the 2020 pandemic, family is more important than ever.

Overture

Sonata form and "the new *Formenlehre*"

This is a book about sonata form, particularly as treated in the half-century of canonically foundational works by Haydn, Mozart, Beethoven, and Schubert, though its final chapter is devoted to Brahms. It provides an updated *entrée* to many of the central features of Sonata Theory, and it does so largely through close readings of individual works, illustrating that approach's procedures and principles in analytical practice.

Readers of this book will already have general ideas, perhaps even very specific ones, about the workings of sonata form. Those ideas usually result from having adopted or having been taught a particular way of approaching sonatas, whether through the generalized blends typical of undergraduate classroom instruction or through the more individualized, if diverging, approaches explored by writers on musical form. These latter include the Tovey/Rosen "classical-style" view of sonata form; the Schoenberg/Réti/Dahlhaus "generative-processual" view; the Schenker long-range *Ursatz* view; the Ratner "historical-theorist" view; and Caplin's more recent "form-functional" view. These varied approaches are *hermeneutic genres*: contrasting styles and modes of professional-discipline analysis and explication. Sonata Theory is another, and it has a number of methodological differences specific to itself.

Sonata Theory is a participant in "the new form theory" ("the new *Formenlehre*") that arose within the Anglophone academy in the later 1990s and early 2000s. This was a discipline-wide rekindling of interest in matters of musical form after several decades of relative neglect. Warren Darcy and I devised this new approach during those years, and we laid out our summary of how far we had gotten into that inquiry in our book from 2006, *Elements of Sonata Theory* (referred to throughout this book as the *Elements* or abbreviated as *EST*). Sonata Theory's capital letters are not intended to single out this approach for special merit but only to identify it as a particular analytical style within an array of contrasting though often complementary "sonata theories."

The *Elements* is a large volume addressed to music theorists, musicologists, and graduate students in music. That said, Darcy and I—and others—have used parts or all of it in undergraduate classes or seminars, typically by helping students to cut through the book's technical underbrush to emphasize its main lines of thought, largely through close analyses of individual works. Now, more than a dozen years after the publication of the *Elements*, it seems appropriate to provide an updated review and reframing of its leading ideas, along with extended illustrations of the analytical practice in action.

The book's aims

While the points foregrounded here are treated in greater detail in *EST*, the present book has three main goals. First, it hopes to demonstrate how a Sonata Theory analysis can illuminate not only individual sections of works but also entire movements, with the hope of making evident the analytical style's conceptual and hermeneutic payoff. Second, through clarification and occasional emendation along the way, it responds to some concerns and misunderstandings that have arisen upon the earlier book's publication. Third, in both the analyses and the more generalized chapters it updates some of the ideas in *EST* by integrating the ideas advanced by a number of form-theory and related studies that have emerged since 2006, including some of the language and insights of cognitive research into music perception and the more generalized concerns of conceptual metaphor theory. While this book provides a review of many of Sonata Theory's mainsprings, it aspires to be more than a repackaging of earlier ideas. Combining aspects of an introduction, a synopsis, and a supplement to the *Elements*, it hopes to move the conceptual ball forward.

What follows is not a beginner's book about sonata form. Instead, it's an upper-level handbook offered to students of musical form and to those who teach and write professionally about sonata analysis. Some readers of this book may already be familiar with Sonata Theory through its presentation in the *Elements*. For those readers my intention is to review and exemplify much of it from refreshed, more inclusive angles. I do this both to convey how my own thought about Sonata Theory has advanced since 2006 and to show what kinds of close readings this method, blended with features of other new or revitalized approaches, makes possible. For those who have little or no prior acquaintance with Sonata Theory, I hope that the book provides a comprehensible sample of its tone and feel.

A seminar in Sonata Theory

In this book I have tried to present Sonata Theory's core principles in a way that resembles how I have dealt with them in seminars. Sonata Theory's strengths and flexibilities are most productively absorbed through concrete examples of its application in practice—close analytical discussions of complete pieces. In fact, that is the purpose of the theory: the explication and interpretation of entire pieces as wholes (or large sections of them), not merely as brief extracts.

With that in mind I have given over the lion's share of chapters to close analyses of individual sonata-form movements from the classical and romantic eras. Eight of the chapters (2, 3, 5, 6, 7, 9, 10, and 12) provide readings of eight movements: two each by Mozart, Haydn, and Beethoven and one each by Schubert and Brahms. The first four of these composers furnished the most influential models for later generations, and before long the study and perpetuation of their works became normative practice in nineteenth- and twentieth-century conservatories and universities. As has been shown in separate studies, many of Sonata Theory's principles for the high-classical and early-romantic eras are extendable, albeit with appropriate modifications and nuances (see the end of chapter 11 and the initial sections of chapter 12), to later composers working in the self-conscious, historicist wake of that earlier tradition: Mendelssohn, Chopin, Schumann, Liszt, Wagner, Brahms, Tchaikovsky, Bruckner, Strauss, Mahler, Sibelius, Elgar, Rachmaninoff, and others, including several twentieth-century composers who blazed trails in more modernist styles.

Mozart, Haydn, Beethoven, Schubert, and Brahms are five very different composers, uncommonly gifted adepts projecting five distinct musical personalities. Each was schooled in the prototypical conventions of his place and time but realized them in individualized ways—and for different kinds of audiences. As a group they represent successive generations of Austro-Germanic sonata composition. Each came of age in a different cultural, political, and musical milieu: Haydn was born in 1732; Mozart in 1756; Beethoven in 1770; Schubert in 1797; Brahms in 1833. (That Mozart is treated first in this book—chapters 2 and 3—is a matter of analytical convenience. His works, and certainly the ones chosen here, are the most symmetrically lucid with regard to sonata-form prototypes, and I have written both chapters as step-by-step introductions to the Sonata Theory system for those who have had little or no experience with it.) Following the Mozart chapters, the two Haydn chapters, 5 and 6, deal with works composed after Mozart's death in 1791 and wade into more analytically complex issues, as do the later chapters. Each later-generation master was aware of the achievements of his chronologically overlapping predecessors, not so much through an anxiety of influence—though the pressure must have been intense—but through the sheer fact of being woven into an honorific and competitive dialogue with a musical tradition that each was embodying and extending. Viewed as a group, these five composers' sonata movements are sufficiently alike in their awareness of the prototypical but ever-advancing norms of their respective eras. Yet in their individualized particularities (one might even say eccentricities), their differences also loom large and must never be minimized.

Along the way these analytical chapters introduce, reintroduce, and reinforce most of Sonata Theory's basic concepts. At the same time they show, when such questions arise, how it deals with challenging or potentially ambiguous situations, approaching the problems *as problems*, then showing what it can mean to think our way through them. Since scores of these eight pieces are readily available online and elsewhere, I have not included them here, though a few music examples do appear in the book to call attention to specific issues in particular passages. As will be apparent, however, none of these chapters will be comprehensible without a score (with numbered measures) in hand.

As complements to the analytical chapters, four others (1, 4, 8, and 11) zoom out to provide generalized considerations of Sonata Theory's conceptual terrain and interests, particularly as viewed now, a decade or two after its initial conceptualization. Chapter 1, a broad portal, introduces the concepts and style of thought specific to Sonata Theory and the methodological inclusivity that it encourages. (Some readers might prefer to start with chapter 2—the Mozart analysis—before launching into the more conceptual chapter 1, sampling Sonata Theory first through a concrete analysis that provides a preliminary feel for the system and defines many of its basic terms. My ordering of those first two chapters—both of them introductory, though in different ways—has switched back and forth in response to differing suggestions of early readers.) The nuts-and-bolts chapter 4 lays out many of the technical fundamentals of this approach to sonata form. Chapter 8 zeroes in on issues specific to the minor-mode sonata and responds to Matthew Riley's monograph, *The Viennese Minor-Key Symphony in the Age of Haydn and Mozart* (2014). Chapter 11 revisits what Sonata Theory designates as the Type 2 sonata—by 1800 a far less frequent but by no means obsolete format, and one that has sometimes been misconstrued by analysts of form. A brief appendix glances at two other sonata types: Type 4 (sonata-rondo) and Type 5 (concerto-sonata).

As one moves through the 12 chapters, Sonata Theory's interpretive aspects are increasingly underscored, for at bottom this is a hermeneutic project in pursuit of issues of musical and cultural meaning. For the most part I have tried to keep the text as free as possible from diversions into the weeds of current analytical debates, though from time to time it has been necessary to reply to specific, individual controversies that have arisen with regard to certain features of Sonata Theory as laid out in 2006. More advanced commentary is confined to the endnotes, which are addressed to specialist readers.

With all this in mind—let's begin!

1

What Is Sonata Theory?

Sonata Theory is a twenty-first-century approach to understanding how individual sonata-form compositions work. While grounded in "the classical style," the general approach, suitably nuanced, is extendable beyond the music of that era. Its central concern is the analytical interpretation of movements as wholes: close readings of entire pieces or at least substantial sections of them. Flexible, musically intuitive, and historically sensitive, it can enable listeners, performers, and commentators to come to more robust interpretations of an individual piece's particulars. Its hope is to awaken such pieces from their slumbers, to recognize living tissue within pieces deadened to us through the numbing familiarity of their rote-rehearsal and repetition. It seeks to recognize and hear once again their surprises, their unusual twists and turns, their bold strokes, their audacious moves—and also, just as often, to register the pleasure of experiencing their capable fashionings of generic normalities.

Sonata Theory sports a generous number of its own ways of framing analytical issues, fortified by an arsenal of freshly devised, method-specific terms and technical concepts. And yet it is characterized by openness and eclecticism, a willingness to integrate insights from other analytical methods and fields of study. Above all, it seeks to combine the mechanisms of text-adequate form analysis with the aesthetic feel of personal experience with the music as music. This latter falls into the domain of what cognitive theorists and philosophers of mind call phenomenological *qualia*, an individual's immediate, subjective responses of feeling and affect to the world of sensory experience, which includes music's most basic attributes: contours, colors, rhythms, syntax, dynamics, and the like. Shuttling between individualized response and technical observation, then trying to fuse them, this aspect of Sonata Theory is easier to convey in public presentations than it is through the distanced mediation of written words or diagrams, which can settle into entrenched patterns of neutralized abstraction.

Analysis and interpretation are acts of personal commitment. "You are the music / While the music lasts," wrote T. S. Eliot in "The Dry Salvages" from *Four Quartets*. This is a much-cited line among music-cognition specialists, and as their research into musical perception and embodied cognition has shown, musical immersion— attending aesthetically to music—is accompanied by the psychological impression of identifying subjectively with it, that is, through what Hatten (2018) elaborates as an "imaginatively interactive participation" with the "virtual agency" implicit in the music and in the backdrop of musical force fields within which an individual piece is carried out. It is as if we ourselves are enacting the music, moving with it in

A Sonata Theory Handbook. James Hepokoski, Oxford University Press (2021). © Oxford University Press.
DOI: 10.1093/oso/9780197536810.003.0001.

"mimetic engagement" (Cox 2016), or that, conversely, it is enacting us, shaping us in its ways. In a very real sense, the bodies and minds of both receptively engaged and casual listeners are being "played by the music" (Margulis 2014).[1] This is an automatic process, much of which is carried out at our brain's deepest levels, below the threshold of consciousness.[2]

Acknowledging all this, Sonata Theory is open to personalized description and imaginative metaphor. To write about music is to write of our own experiences with it. Even while the end products of such analyses are objectively grounded in close attention to the pieces' structural facts, in the end they remain individualized readings of works. Rather than brandishing any claim to being definitive solutions, such readings are no more—and no less—than offerings of how the writer hears and processes what he or she has heard, offerings recounted, one hopes, in historically plausible, musically inviting ways. This chapter is devoted to some of the conceptual wellsprings of Sonata Theory, those that distinguish it from other, more traditional approaches.

Dialogic form

Sonata Theory's core concept is that of *dialogic form*. This means that each sonata movement that we encounter (most likely a piece from the post-1750 past that has persisted as part of the standard performing repertory) can be grasped as having been set by the composer into a dialogue with the contextually relevant, normative expectations of a once-in-place, taken-for-granted genre. From the complementary standpoint of the present-day analyst this can be restated as: "For the purposes of structural analysis [a piece of music] exists most substantially in the ongoing dialogue that it may be understood to pursue with its stated or implied genre—a dialogue that may be recreated (more accurately, proposed as a reading) in the mind of the informed listener. . . . Therefore the central task of analysis is to reanimate this implicit dialogue in a way that is historically and musically sensitive" (*EST*, 605).

A genre is a complex set of ever-ready possibilities or flexible guidelines for the production of individual works, a constellation of norms and traditions that may be regarded as historically fluid conceptual forces that are culturally situated "social actions," systems-in-motion (Artemeva 2004). An essential aspect of all genres is that each of its exemplars is a token of a general type, just as each individual detective story or game of chess, no matter how eccentric or unusual, is a token of its genre. To draw on Wittgenstein's construal of such issues, however much individual tokens might differ from each other in their particulars, they still share certain overlapping "family resemblances" or "family likenesses" that enable them to be grasped under a set of flexible yet describable regulative guidelines.

As cultural constructions, genres are shot through with social implications, riddled with the aspirations, complicities, and problematic social tensions of their eras. They arise and flourish because of the cultural work that they do within the production/reception systems of their historical moments. As such, genres, qua genres, are open to broader questions of analysis and critique, and we may wish to pursue questions about their embeddedness within once-taken-for-granted worldviews, about the way, for instance, that their drives toward containment and resolution might resonate with aspects of then-existing social power and/or exclusion.[3] In many cases, perhaps most, those force-fields of cultural authority will differ from those that we imagine to be in play in our own world.

Yet when we attend to any of a genre's exemplars as a singularity—*that* particular detective story; *that* particular chess game—our interest can shift to the aesthetic. Each invites us to become attentive to the sway of that specific realization: the expertise of its "madeness" or *poiesis*.[4] This is why it is reductive to suppose that an individual exemplar's meaning should be diagnosed primarily as a symptom of the historically compromised genre or worldview in which it participates.[5] Even so, what remains culturally telling in each are its entanglements both with the complex social world that initially gave rise to its broader genre and with the ever-changing reception worlds that continued to sustain it until that singularity arrives at our own culturally fraught doorstep, tugging at our sleeves to beckon for attention.

From this perspective, any individual work is shot through with two aspects: the expectations of its genre and the internal realization of that genre as an aesthetic or presentational singularity, a quality of individual craft or expertise. As it is put in *Elements of Sonata Theory* (*EST*, 607),

> Beethoven was by no means the only composer of the *Eroica*: he cannot lay exclusive claim to the totality of the work's implications. Many of the compositional features of that piece are more accurately regarded as dramatized affirmations of (or dialogues with) pre-existing, culturally produced norms that were external to Beethoven. . . . Because the tacit societal aspects inscribed within a genre-constellation were also given and accepted as self-evident, they cannot be made subject to an act of personal intentionality.

Our discussions of those works depend on which aspect we foreground and for which purposes we do so.

No matter the sonata type at hand (chapters 4, 11, and the appendix), as a genre it sets the terms under which the piece asks us to register what happens, dialogically, inside it. Under these terms there is an implicit generic contract between the composer and the implied listener or performer.[6] Cognizant of the wide range of normative options within that genre (knowing how to write that detective story or how to play chess), the master composer rings changes on those conventions to fashion an individualized work. Reciprocally, text-adequate listeners are invited to use their knowledge of the genre to interpret that musical message. We should not seek to grasp an individual work on its internal terms alone, as though the work were autonomously self-generated. To be sure, considering the internal coherence and ongoing implications within an individual piece is a vital thing to do, but it is also important to compare what happens moment by moment (or sometimes what does *not* happen) with our generically conditioned expectations of how sonatas in that period and by that composer generally behave.

As a genre, sonata form is a socially shared, historically grounded complex of commonly understood guidelines. We might regard sonata form, as grasped by any knowledgeable group or person in his or her historical setting, as an inductively learned *schema*, a quasi-standardized mode of organizing certain kinds of musical space. For the listener this corresponds (from the field of cognitive theory) to Huron's description of a schema as "an expectational 'set.' A schema provides an encapsulated behavioral or perceptual model that pertains to some situation or context" (2006, 204). The appropriate model is psychologically triggered within the experienced and participatory listener who has learned to frame what he or she hears on the basis of the music's "context cueing" (204) interacting with his or her anticipation of what sorts of things are most likely to happen next, grounded in an internalized sense of probabilities. An informed listener proceeds through a temporally flowing work with an ongoing schematic expectation (225) that the music will proceed to satisfy, delay, thwart, or undermine. This idea, also explored by Byros (2009, 2012, 2015), corresponds well with Sonata Theory's point of view.[7] Any single work traces out an individualized path through a culturally given schematic space, one that we now call sonata form.

Alternatively, we might construe the schema of sonata form from the perspective of *prototype theory*, whereby a set of ready-to-hand illustrations—prototypes—can provide tacit guidelines for how the most normative sonata-form compositions are typically constructed. This model is not a set of stringent rules demanding that all composers treat sonata form in the same way. Quite the opposite: built into it—one of the attractions of the sonata game—is the freedom, within some limits, to alter individual aspects of the sonata. The strongest composers customized for themselves the socially shared genre's guidelines, the most normative things to do, in order to fashion a personalized style, an arresting manner of tracing engaging pathways through the schema.[8]

For some composers that drive toward individual adaptation was uncommonly strong. A classic case is the ever-inventive Haydn, who delighted in the unpredictable, turning virtually each of his sonata forms into a unique yet internally coherent product. Thus Haydn's often-quoted remark to Griesinger, his biographer, concerning the isolation of his decades-long employment at Esterháza: "As head of an orchestra I was able to make experiments, observe what makes a [good] effect and what weakens it, and thus revise, expand, cut, take chances; I was cut off from the world, nobody around me could upset my self-confidence, and so I had to become original" (as quoted in Webster 2005a, 36). Paradoxically, Haydn adopted the non-normative principles of ongoing idiosyncrasy and unpredictable exceptionality to become his own norm, one also driven by his superior mastery of technique vis-à-vis his 1760s and 1770s contemporaries.

To adapt Waltham-Smith's recent (2017) construction of this aspect of Haydn, the composer's often-playful originality not infrequently relies on the treating of socially shared, conventional figures and formal structures in unexpected, unaccustomed, or purposefully "misused" ways. (Well-known, highly localized instances of such "misuses" include the opening of the quartet, op. 33 no. 5, with a two-bar closing figure and the non-motivated *forte* chord, the "surprise," in the second movement of Symphony No. 94.) Haydn often writes into his music unusual, pointedly asymmetrical, or seemingly misplaced features, whose intended effects must presuppose the likely communities of listeners' ability to perceive such moments as deviant from their shared understanding of the normative high-galant (or classical) style. "This music is from the outset oriented outward, composed to have a calculated effect on its listeners. . . . This music anticipates its listener in its own composition" (16).[9]

Thus while Haydn's mature works certainly invite consideration under the terms of the individualized style that he had customized for himself (his "surprises" are less surprising when assessed only within the norms of his own practice, concerned with crafting singular coherences and internal relationships within each work), he did not devise that style out of nothing, siloed away from the relatively more orthodox practice of his contemporaries. Even such customizations as we find in Haydn are to be understood as personalized figures against the larger background of the socially shared genre—or, if one prefers, as ever more habitualized, personalized swerves away from the established genre's less adventurous prototypes. Relishable in themselves, Haydn's "experiments" are set in highest relief when understood as interactions with the more typical, more commonly shared expectations of the time, the very existence of which permits the composer's originality to be perceived as such. Conversely, Haydn's penchant for frequent, whimsical deviations from more prototypical phrase shapes and sonata practices can project into high relief the evaded regularities themselves: those normative aspects that he does not realize in standardized ways.

We should not confuse any set of generalized guidelines with the individualities of actual practice. Sonata Theory would never wish to collapse the delicious particularities of a work's microworld into a neutralized, exchangeable token of its genre, nor to reduce it to only a symptom of the social conflicts of its era. It bears repeating: composers place each of their works into a dialogue with the wide range of the options and expectations offered by its genre. As a distinctive singularity, no individual work is under any obligation to fit all of the generalities of this or that generic or prototypical norm, nor are we under any obligation to make it fit in order to suit our theories. To try to do so would miss the point of dialogic form. We value individual sonatas because of the unique realizations that they present, even as each remains in dialogue with the normative practice of its specific place and era. The freedom of the generic principle encourages the creation of particularized exemplars that modify, refashion, or even violate the more commonly accepted norms of this or that portion of the genre in which they participate.

Sonata form is no static, unmodifiable thing at all times and in all places. While the core of its mid- and late-eighteenth-century guidelines remained in place as a pedagogical regulative idea for well over a century, as the decades progressed it accrued a number of on-the-ground modifications, new options, and localized updates, and composers treated it with increasing expansiveness and freedom. Many of the compositional practices that had been statistically normative for Mozart or relatable late-eighteenth-century composers were regularly transgressed or overridden in later decades in order to produce dramatic or distinctively personalized effects—as we find already in early Beethoven. Nonetheless, as I treat at more length at the end of chapter 11 and in chapter 12, its status as a high-prestige cluster of referential norms and options lingered throughout nineteenth- and early-twentieth-century art music as a persistent yet malleable prototype with which individualized compositions were set into dialogue—something along the lines of a culturally shared conceptual backdrop or interpretive code. Keeping the classical prototypes in mind is the best facilitator of locating and interpreting difference in later compositions.

Sonata Theory lays out the set of norms and types—and their flexibilities—implicit in the sonata-form genre, particularly as evidenced in or contextually inferable from the works, here, of Haydn, Mozart, and early-to-middle-period Beethoven, with whom we see, from the very start, the impulse to tweak traditional sonata practices with non-generic swerves in order to produce quirky or dramatic effects. (Obviously, the dozens or hundreds of lesser masters of the period introduced or favored their own personal variants, but the more general guidelines of the current approach still seem sturdy.) The usual compositional options within the various points of the late-eighteenth-century sonata are called the normative *default procedures*. Even in those decades these defaults were not ironclad rules that had to be obeyed. Even the strongest of them were only the customary choices, the modes of procedure most immediately offered by the genre at this or that compositional moment. Exceptions could abound.

While composers produced creative realizations of the familiar defaults in the course of a sonata—standardized theme types and textural signs, generically normative cadences, and the like—from time to time they overrode customary procedures for special, individualized effects. As performers or listeners, we want to perceive when something exceptional is happening. Extraordinary effects, purposeful distortions, or uncommonly staged sonata events sometimes fall into the subjective category called *deformations*. One should not misunderstand this term. In this limited, form-technical context it is never intended to carry any connotation of the unpleasantly misshapen or ugly. Nor is it meant to suggest the projection of a disability. It means not only that the composer has chosen not to do any of the normative things at that moment of the piece but also that what the composer has done at musical point X is extravagantly uncommon, something strikingly unusual that we as listeners should attend to and interpret with particular care. To lessen the risk of a potentially negative connotation, in proper Sonata Theory parlance we do not say that this or that event is "deformed" but rather that "it has been subjected to a deformation" (*EST*, 614–21).

Any piece or section thereof will provide evidence of an answer to any question that we might wish to ask of it. More adequate questions draw forth more adequate answers. The trick is to learn how to ask more productive questions. Sonata Theory is not a system that claims, once its analytical apparatus has processed an individual work's formal layout, that that work's content has been fully grasped. That apparatus is better understood as a particularized but flexible way of thinking that can help us to ask better questions of that layout.

When confronted with an unusual or idiosyncratic work, for instance, it is an error to ask the reductive question, "Is this piece in sonata form?" expecting to get a simple yes or no answer that puts the matter to rest. Rather, as I have suggested elsewhere (2009a, 71–75), the proper question is, "Does this piece invite us to use the normative or prototypical guidelines of sonata form in order to understand the composer's moment-to-moment, phrase-to-phrase choices within it?" In most cases this question is easy to answer, as with most of the Allegro first movements (and often some subsequent movements) of later-eighteenth-century sonatas, chamber music, symphonies, concertos, and with many overtures as well. To come to an understanding with any individual composition is to make a connection with the way in which that exemplar activates or modifies the normative expectations of the historical state of its genre in its own time and place. The critical question: Why and to what expressive effect did the composer choose to situate *that* musical module *there*?

Successive action zones within a musically narrative journey

We are all familiar with the larger sectional divisions of the most common types of sonata form, those sections that English speakers call the exposition, the development, and the recapitulation. Sonata Theory regards these as broad *action zones* (or *action spaces*) within which certain generically expected thematic and tonal things are supposed to happen—and in a certain order. More often, though, we use the term *action zone* to refer to subdivisions within the larger zones, especially to those smaller, successive zones that build up the exposition and the corresponding recapitulation. In the most common format for expositions (the two-part format, in which the two parts are separated by an important break or gap called the *medial caesura*) we encounter four action spaces that are usually closed off with terminal (structural) cadences. These are:

- the *primary-theme zone* (P), beginning the sonata process;
- the *transition zone* (TR), accepting P and proceeding further into the process, normatively ending with a reinforced, breath-like break, the *medial caesura* (MC), concluding part 1;

- a newly launched *secondary-theme zone* (S), which opens part 2 and drives toward a cadential close in the new key (the point of *essential expositional closure* or EEC);
- and the *closing zone* (C)—if one is present at all—which houses any differing, additional material following the EEC, material that serves to confirm the new key and expand or round off the whole. (As will be noted in chapters 2 and 4, the thematic materials of S and C can also be grouped together as an *S/C thematic complex*, a coherent "narrative" or rhetorical succession in its own right, extending beyond the EEC that closes S space.)

In Sonata Theory's shorthand, the expositional action-zone succession is indicated by P TR ' S / C, in which P TR ' comprises part 1 and S / C comprises part 2. The apostrophe, or breath mark, represents the MC, the medial caesura separating the exposition's two parts; the slash (/) represents the EEC, the cadential point of essential expositional closure. The most elementary steps in understanding an ongoing sonata form are, first, to realize which action zone is currently being set into motion and, second, to compare what one is hearing with what kinds of activity—thematic, textural, rhetorical, and cadential—are generically expected to be carried out within that zone. A closer outline of the compositional options within zones of the two-part exposition is provided in chapter 4.

While the flow of music is temporal, a forward-moving stream in ongoing, linear time, the effect of the successive action zones can be metaphorically spatial, as each zone is progressively filled, sealed off, and experienced as a conceptual CONTAINER.[10] Still, even while conceptualized spatially ("from the top down"), each zone is to be filled ("from the bottom up") with propulsive, bar-to-bar musical material vectored toward an expected cadence. The composer's task was to move through the successive action zones, filling each with ingenious and engaging realizations of the familiar, ready-to-hand schemata (standardized voice-leading patterns appropriate for various phases of the composition), topics, styles, poses, and affects. In the mid-eighteenth century the modest goal was to do this in tasteful, galant, entertaining ways. As the decades advanced into the late eighteenth century and beyond, the task was being modified into that of realizing the action zones in more original, complex, dramatic, or deeply moving ways: the stylistic norms and options were becoming less schematic, more open to personalized variants and enrichments.

To feel this music musically—to identify with this music as music—is to monitor the moment-to-moment tensions of the drives toward the succession of boundary cadences. Each action space has a different functional role to play. The effect of moving through a sonata is like coursing one's way through a pre-planned relay or like that of building a bridge, girder by girder, a bridge thrown out into time and musical space until it securely reaches the other side—the end of the piece or movement. As it is put in *EST*, "In the hands of most composers, constructing a sonata-form movement was a task of *modular assembly*: the forging of a succession of short, section-specific musical units [action spaces] linked together into an on-going linear chain—pressing down and connecting one appropriately stylized musical tile after another" (15–16).

This is not to say that a composer could not simultaneously seek to provide the impression of a process of motivic growth and networked diversification as one action zone gives way to another. The separate zones can be and not infrequently are musically interrelated, as if the one zone grows into the next in an ongoing process of elaboration. This can create the complementary but no less important impression of an internally generative form, of form as process or quasi-organic growth, even at the moment-to-moment level, as is frequently the case in Haydn and Beethoven (think of the Fifth Symphony).

Within Germanic scholarship, as James Webster reminds us (2009, 123), distinctions have been made between the concepts of *Form* and *Formung*: "between form-as-shape (balance, symmetry, proportions, architecture), and form-as-process (the dynamic development of musical ideas through time)." The idea is easily clarified if one imagines parallel instances in literature. Sonnet form, for example, prescribes 14 poetic lines grouped and rhymed in specific ways. On the other hand, each individual sonnet pursues and intensifies its own trajectories of thought from line 1 into line 2, then into line 3, and so on, through line 14—and even in prescribed line-groupings of, say, 8+6 (Petrarchan) or 4+4+4+2 (in either the Spenserian or Shakespearean formats). As each of its lines proceeds to the next through idea-patterns also swayed by convention, one could say, from a certain perspective, that any individual poem's language and imagery can also be construed as its personalized internal "form." One understands the point at once, though it entails a different construal of the word "form," perhaps a metaphorical construal, since the internal process works itself out in a dialogic interaction with the pre-given expectations of "what a sonnet is."

Claims on behalf of musical form as most essentially a process of becoming have been especially marked in discussions of Haydn and Beethoven. Among the latter's achievements, in Dahlhaus's carefully worded assessment (1991, 41), is to have invited his listeners to understand "form" also, or perhaps even centrally, as "an aesthetic process" rather than as a schematic arrangement. "Aesthetically, the decisive factor is the outcome of the process that works itself out in the form." Dahlhaus's remark, in which the term "aesthetically" is the key qualifier, was also relayed by Schmalfeldt (2011, 34), whose book explores music "in the process of becoming" and devotes sustained chapters to the historical course of "the Beethoven-Hegelian tradition" and "the processual legacy of the late eighteenth century."

This impression of processual form is carried out with admirable single-mindedness in many sonata movements, and in subsequent chapters I appeal to it especially in my discussions of Haydn, Beethoven, and Brahms. Still, notwithstanding its presence within this or that sonata, the boundaries of the underlying action zones (P TR ' S / C) are nearly always apparent. More than that, they are compositionally prior as generic givens, conceptually present before the act of composition starts. Even when the music that fills and connects them is emphatically processual, as it often is, they still mark the pre-established succession of generically prescribed CONTAINERS that the composer is treating in a certain way. By these lights, the generative aspects of the musical contents are secondary to the de facto roles of the action zones, though in another sense they are crucially important to the creative work that turns each piece into a dramatized singularity. In short, a work's internal musical process does not "create the form" in the normative sense of that phrase—or at least not in Sonata Theory's way of using it—but rather fashions the particulars of the piece's content to articulate its progress along a pre-established set of stations of departure and arrival.[11]

One final caveat: as Schmalfeldt has also noted (2011, 9 and passim), expositions that actively pursue "the process of [a continuous] becoming" can sometimes occasion us, *en route*, to revise our initial sense of where we are in the action-zone succession. What we might first have taken to be an onset of TR, for instance, might subsequently be shown to be incorporated into a broader P space, occasioning us to revise our initial impression (TR? ==> still P!). Such reassessments are common in the listening experience and nearly always help us to interpret the musical point of what is happening in this or that work. Far from undermining the centrality of the generic action zones, perceiving any such localized ambiguity is possible only when one has an awareness of the expectations associated with what turn out to be imaginatively bounded action spaces.

Trajectories toward generically normative cadences (cadential spans)

"At the heart of [Sonata Theory] is the recognition and interpretation of *expressive/ dramatic trajectories toward generically obligatory cadences*" (*EST*, 13). Because a composer can soften or even withhold the realizations of certain moments of cadential closure, I have altered the wording in the preceding heading to "generically *normative* cadences." But the concept remains: any sonata form consists of a succession of *cadential spans*, and the various action zones of a sonata are traversed through in order to attain and articulate their appropriate cadences before proceeding to the next zone.

In order of increasing closural strength, the available structural cadences—those most capable of closing off an action zone—are the half cadence (HC), the imperfect authentic cadence (IAC, with scale degree $\hat{3}$ or $\hat{5}$ in the upper voice), and the perfect authentic cadence (PAC, with $\hat{1}$ or $\hat{8}$ in the upper voice). That said, one should be aware that the historical concept of what qualifies as a cadence is a complicated issue that has been the topic of much recent historical and theoretical work. What had seemed clear in recent decades—that to qualify as a genuine "authentic cadence," for instance, one needs to be dealing with root-position chords, not inversions—has been unsettled by historical research into eighteenth-century (and earlier) theoretical treatises, which are more flexible with regard to various degrees of cadential strength and classification.[12] While at deeper levels of inquiry these scholarly investigations are of prime importance, warning us away from inordinately rigid cadential pronouncements, their pursuit here would lead us down a slippery slope of harmonic and voice-leading gradations that would be counterproductive in the present volume. In analysis of the classical and romantic repertories, the pragmatic solution is the most workable one. Thus within Sonata Theory the term "cadence" normally implies one of the three structural-cadence types (or terminal-cadence types) mentioned earlier: these are the HC (ending on V in root position) and the two root-position-oriented authentic cadences (V-I, often concluding a more complete cadential progression of tonic, predominant, dominant, and tonic), the IAC and the PAC.[13]

In the later eighteenth century the theorist Heinrich Christoph Koch, describing smaller binary-format works from earlier decades, outlined what we now call a major-key sonata's exposition as a harmonic journey that touches, in order, on four cadential stations ("resting points of the spirit"): an authentic cadence in the tonic (I:AC), a half cadence in the tonic (I:HC), a half cadence in the dominant (V:HC), and an authentic cadence in the dominant (V:AC, usually a V:PAC), which may or may not be followed by an "appendix" or "clarifying period" to further ground the dominant key.[14] Koch was not writing in terms of what we now hear as action spaces, and his view allows more flexibility than it might initially seem, but from our vantage point it is clear that by the 1750s or 1760s the generic, *de facto* spatial zones (P TR ' S / C) succeeded each other in order to articulate, even dramatically enhance, such harmonic journeys.

A cadential span covers the trajectory of any passage of music that leads immediately upon or just after the previous cadence (or its cadential extension) to the next one. Cadential spans may be brief, such as a four-bar antecedent or consequent, or quite lengthy, as when expected cadences are avoided or undermined throughout an extended section of music. One of the first tasks of analysis is to identify where and in which key the successive cadences occur. In the majority of cases no action zone should be regarded as beginning in the middle of a cadential span. In turn this means that the analyst must have a clear conception of both what a cadence is and the varieties of their realizations—a seemingly elementary matter that in recent decades, as noted above has been the subject of much debate. This is particularly the case with regard to the half cadence, some potential instances of which form-functional theory has persuasively downgraded into a structurally significant but non-cadential *dominant arrival*—a simple landing on an active V chord that nonetheless concludes its preceding phrase. Nonetheless, for most practical sonata-form analyses, the usual definitions of the various cadence types will suffice.

Keys, tonal layout, and tonal confirmation

Consider the most commonly encountered situation in high-galant sonata forms: those with two-part/four-zone expositions and corresponding, full recapitulations beginning with P in the tonic key. In that situation the strong norm is that all or most of the post-medial-caesura material in the exposition (S/C, presented and cadentially confirmed in a non-tonic key) will reappear in the tonic key ("be resolved") in the recapitulation. This has been dubbed the "sonata principle," though in the past that principle was often overstated. Exceptions to expansive versions of it are not difficult to find, especially in Haydn's works with their often substantially recrafted recapitulations. Even so, the norm is that the exposition's out-of-tonic S and C modules (or their similarly situated equivalents in continuous expositions) will return in the tonic, usually in full, in the recapitulation. This creates a complementary, symmetrical balance with their expositional appearance: historically understood, a prolonged, extended end-rhyme with the later blocks of the exposition (Greenberg 2017). Sonata Theory calls this later tonic-centering of the once-off-tonic S/C zones the *tonal resolution*. (Anticipating a later discussion, I note that while one of the five sonata types, the Type 2 sonata, does not have what Sonata Theory calls a recapitulation, it most definitely features a tonal resolution: see chapter 11. And the overview of recapitulatory practice in chapter 4 will look at non-normative situations in which the tonal resolution either deviates from the proper key or fails to achieve decisive closure with a cadence.)

One should distinguish between keys that are cadentially confirmed with an IAC or PAC and those that are not. Keys confirmed with only an HC are established as governing keys but are not yet fully secured, remaining open until closed with an authentic cadence. One can seem to be obviously "in" a key at a thematic or modular outset, but that key is present only as a local, tonal promise or proposition to be ratified and secured with an authentic cadence; in fact, it may fail to be ratified, moving on instead to a different key. This issue can emerge with the exposition's P-theme. How grounded is that tonic? Does it present us only with a I:HC (or perhaps not even that) before moving elsewhere? Is it fully secured with a I:PAC before moving on to the perhaps-elided TR action zone? Or does it give us two or more different ideas each of which ends with a I:PAC, in which case, P is *tonally overdetermined*? Or consider the situation within developments, where instability of key is the norm, the shifting from one *tonal color* to another. The larger question is: in the developmental process which of these tonal colors is cadentially secured? When an implicit, localized new key is secured with a cadence, we can speak appropriately of a modulation to that key; short of that, a non-confirmed tonal color is a tonicization. To this one might add the fundamental importance of the affectively different colors (the qualia) of the major and minor modes—a vitally important modal dualism, analogous to light and shadow, that runs through the entire repertory. I deal with specific issues surrounding the minor mode in chapter 8.

Themes and their ordered successions: rotations

Quite differently from most form-theory orthodoxies in recent memory, Sonata Theory restores attention to the structural importance and local characters of musical themes and especially to the order in which they are presented in the various phases of the composition. Themes matter: this is one of the cardinal features of the approach. In the past half-century or more there has been a downplaying of the structural roles of themes within sonatas, subordinating these foregrounded ideas and their topical or gestural implications to background harmonic or contrapuntal processes. In some respects this is understandable, especially within current academic contexts: Koch's late-eighteenth-century outline of an exposition's typical cadential journey could also be adduced as a reinforcement of such a view, and no one would think of downplaying the central role that tonal and harmonic processes have within sonata form.

Nonetheless, it is the striking, moment-to-moment immediacy of the thematic material—the sounding surface of music as it being played or listened to—that beguiles us and captures our attention. And there can be no doubt that the creation of enticing sonic surfaces and their subsequent entailments, elaborations, and contrasts was a front-and-center concern for the composer. To make a mark, one had to craft successions of compelling musical ideas. As I hope will be clear from the analysis chapters that follow, while by no means steering clear of longer-range goals within the music (most especially, trajectories toward generically normative cadences), Sonata Theory encourages close attentiveness to the affective, topical, and gestural connotations of themes at the moments in which they are experienced. These are not mere sonic markers to be passed through in search of deep-structural processes or other, less audible implications that are then presented to us as what should be the central items for our attention. This aspect of Sonata Theory can be understood as participating in the *restoration of the surface* called for in some recent musical (and literary) quarters: a rebalancing of conceptual, longer-range generic goals with the claims of the immediate—what one is literally apprehending in the here and now.[15]

What Sonata Theory challenges are the claims that a piece's "real form" is (take your choice) strictly harmonic, or the cumulative outcome of only "local harmonic progression[s]," or most essentially the product of a generative process of sub-thematic, motivic-cellular development, or the result of long-range, background, coherence-governing middle-ground contrapuntal arcs, while the themes on the audible surface and the manner in which they are arrayed are devalued to the lower-rung status of "design" or incidental "arrangement." While much attention has been paid in the past half-century to the local implications of commonly encountered thematic styles and shapes, that attention has been mostly relevant to what I call these themes' *vertical* or on-the-spot implications (how the themes might be characterized in isolation or in the abstract), regardless of where and to what larger end they are situated *horizontally* within the linear-structural flow. Here one thinks of such things as:

- *topic theory*, grounded in common thematic stylizations of the era, pointing semiotically toward external social or natural-world implications (march, gavotte, minuet, fanfare, hunt, pastoral, battle, storm, ombra, learned style, bells, clockwork, flowing water, sunrises, birdsong, and the like);[16]
- *rhetoric theory*, comparing the postures and placements of themes to long-established manners of classical rhetorical delivery (*exordium, antithesis, anaphora, circumlocutio, apostrophe, aposiopesis, peroratio*, and so on);
- *form-functional theory*'s classifications of common thematic shapes (sentence and period, along with various compound-enlargements and hybrids of the two).

Still, such important work has not restored a large-scale *structural* role to themes *per se*. Sonata Theory does not privilege thematic presentation and ordering above harmonic process. Rather, it considers the two as equal partners working together, thereby generating a synoptic view of a piece's structure: its "real form."[17]

This is most evident in Sonata Theory's concept of musical *rotations*: the compositional tendency to lay out an ordered succession of musical units (or *modules*)—like modules A, B, C, D, and so on—and then to return to that ordering or parts thereof to alter, expand, or treat it once again, perhaps quite differently, in the next rotational cycle (*EST*, 611–14). The metaphor called upon here is that of a circular or motion or cycle, like that traversed by a 12-hour clock. At 11:59:59 the clock hands' next move is to return to the beginning, 12:00:00 (or 0:00:00), and to start the round once again. To illustrate: all strophic songs are rotational, with each stanza comprising one rotation. The last bar of each stanza is followed by the first bar of the next. The same is true of compositions over ostinato basses, from folias, passacaglias, and chaconnes to the blues, in which cases, of course, it is the bassline or recurring harmonic pattern, not the ever-varied upper-voice melodic material, that generates the rotations.

Typically, returning to the initial module of a cycle—a *rotation initiator*—after one has gone elsewhere is the signal that a new rotation is beginning: a new, probably modified trip through the cycle. In a baroque concerto each statement of a ritornello or tutti head-motive could be heard as starting a new rotation, one usually spinning off into its own unique direction. The same might be said of fugues. In sonata form the P-idea is the normative rotation initiator. Rotation patterns sometimes also feature a final module capable of serving as the most definitive *rotation concluder*.

Sonata form is grounded in the principle of thematic/modular rotation (a flexible concept of ordered modular recurrence) that works in tandem with but on another axis of meaning from that of tonality. Since rotations are only about thematic/modular ordering, issues of harmony, key, and tonality are irrelevant from the rotational point of view. Most obviously, the recapitulation is another, somewhat varied rotation of the musical modules arrayed in the exposition. As such, the recapitulation may also be called the *recapitulatory rotation*. Developments also often have important rotational or half-rotational implications in the ordered selection of modules that are being treated. While this is by no means invariable, developments most frequently begin with an off-tonic sounding of at least the incipit of P, the rotation initiator, a feature that we also find in extended codas.

The expositional ordering of its parts is the *referential layout* for the selection and appearance of the thematic modules in all the subsequent rotations. This means that as the exposition passes through its normative action zones, P TR ' S / C, it also establishes a fixed order of thematic/modular events to which later sections of music are to be compared. Whenever a subsequent main section begins (a development, a recapitulation, or a coda), if P material appears at all, it is normally to be treated before TR material, TR before S, and S before C. In a development section the composer need not allude to all of the action zones; it can suffice to select only one or two of them. One might find workings-out of only P and C, for example, or even S and C, but the norm still remains to treat them in rotational order. As with all generic norms, exceptions can occur—non-rotational developments—and they should be noted as such.

As we shall see in the next chapter with Mozart, K. 333/i, the expositional rotation is sometimes divisible into *subrotations*: smaller varied cycles within the larger, referential cycle. If TR starts off with the P-idea, for instance, it can be heard as launching a *subrotation* of P. Analogously, Haydn's attraction to beginning many of his S zones with the basic idea or incipit of P, the rotation initiator (resulting in a "P-based S"), divides the exposition into two differing *subrotations* at the point of the medial caesura that precedes S. The same principle applies to our understanding of the materials presented in the development or recapitulation.

To observe the rotational principle at work in sonata form—its thematically cyclical aspect—is not to reduce that structure to one of reiterative stasis, in the manner, say, of the circular recurrences of mythical time. Other aspects of sonata form are emphatically linear, vectored; they push forward in our linear-temporal imaginations toward specific generic signposts and specific tonal goals. What we find in sonatas are variable applications of the rotational principle, operating at overlapping levels of structure, counterpointed against the nonrepeatable linear flow of time and goal-oriented tonal process. Just as one does not step twice into the same river, as Heraclitus famously insisted, even the most literal recurrence of a thematic rotation—the repeat of the exposition—is conceptually non-identical to its first sounding for at least three reasons: (1) it occupies a different space of onward-flowing linear time; (2) it should be contextualized as retracing something already heard, therefore construed in relation to our memory of what we have just experienced; and (3) it is a commonly encountered feature of the genre—indeed, we may have been predicting its appearance during the first presentation of the exposition—which means that as we hear the repeat we situate its formal meaning in terms of its role in the succession of the larger action spaces (exposition, development, recapitulation) regulated by the relevant generic norms.

Sonata Theory and other analytical or descriptive methodologies

Rather than closing other interpretive doors, Sonata Theory aims to make available another one that can be uncommonly rich, opening new encounters with freshly defamiliarized musical worlds. What has become evident by now is that no single analytical or descriptive methodology can claim—or (thankfully) will ever be able to claim—an exclusive purchase on the study of this repertory. The daunting nature of the analytical enterprise must be admitted from the start. It is a humbling truth that "texts always take place on the level of their reader's abilities."[18] At each point in its history sonata composition was entangled in a web of concerns and interests, a network of subsystems that a composer was obliged to coordinate, however habitually or intuitively: generic/technical norms, cultural functions, acceptable manipulations of the quasi-formulaic musical topics or tropes of the era, anticipated interactions with historically specific audiences' expectations, self-placement and presentation within the state of the historical tradition and its arbiters of success or failure, and all the rest. No analytical or descriptive method can deal with all of these at the same time.

We, too, are caught up in our own webs, swept up in the blinding contextual flow of our own present. At stake, then, is the larger issue: how might we come to an understanding with the language of this endlessly varied and complex music from the past, music that comes to us like a precious historical gift, an undeserved inheritance, from a horizon of social practices different from those of our own? How can we come to recognize yet somehow also come to terms with the strangeness of it all?

Such questions can be addressed from multiple directions. Some of the most promising work today is integrative, selecting and blending the interests of the varied practices found in the current toolbox of analytical approaches. This is not to take the benign position that all methodologies are always and everywhere compatible, much less that anything goes and that as a consequence debates about subjective readings are futile. There are differences among them in important points and emphases. Still, sharply different readings of individual works can help to deepen our sense of the challenges with which these works confront us—how they can say such different things to different persons, how this feature of it, or now that one, or perhaps still another, might be drawn forth for hitherto unnoticed attention, thereby altering our perception of how that display object now appears to us.

All form theories are encouragements to adjust our perceptions of works in order to privilege certain features within them. As Wittgenstein put it in the *Philosophical Investigations*, when a new aspect of something is presented to us, or even occurs to us, "I *see* that [that thing or object] has not changed; and yet I see it differently. I call this experience 'noticing an aspect.'"[19] This act of *seeing-as* or *seeing-in* (to use art historian Richard Wollheim's much-noted term) is of course subject to the potentials opened up or closed in any historically specific time and place.[20] But in the analysis of musical form the relevant point is that becoming attuned to other methods' or other eras' differences of aspect-perception can be a productive thing. Absorbing those differences in good faith can deepen the questions and responses that each of us has when engaging with this music.

So let's be clear on this point. To become engaged with Sonata Theory does not mean to shrug off other modes of inquiry. Three of the most recent and influential form-analytical methods, all of which make appearances in this book, are:

1. *Form-functional theory*, as laid out in 1998 in William E. Caplin's *Classical Form* and in his subsequent textbook from 2013, *Analyzing Classical Form: An Approach for the Classroom*. Both books are indispensable contributions to the new *Formenlehre*. Since much of what follows is devoted to close analyses, the reader will come across frequent identifications of the formal structures of individual themes: often *sentences* or *periods* of different sizes or occasional *hybrids* thereof. (Sonata Theory's distinctiveness, recall, lies in its theory of larger, action-zone or rotational norms, not of the structures of their smaller thematic constituents.) The analytical challenge is that, valorizing different criteria, diverse analytical traditions have characterized the familiar thematic shapes in differing ways. As Brody has reminded us (2016, 97–102)—and he is by no means alone—there has been little consensus among theorists with regard, for instance, to how strenuously, or how flexibly, to define a thematic period, which in turn depends on definitions of its two constituent parts, an *antecedent* and a *consequent*. This is not a simple matter. It involves decisions about foundational matters, debates that to this day are not settled, particularly those concerning the question of what is and what is not to be considered a cadence in the era(s) under consideration.

   And yet consistency demands that we base our descriptions in something. In this book I not only ground my phrase descriptions in Caplin's terminology but I also assume an awareness of that terminology, along with his distinctions among the various types of cadences. Caplin's taxonomic categories have the advantage of obliging us to look at themes in a fine-grained way, charging us to examine the constituent parts and harmonic actions of music's smallest building-blocks—often two-, four-, and eight-bar units—with rigorously defined terms. The relevant classifications are to be made by parsing a theme's internal *formal functions*, including but not limited to beginning, middle, and ending functions.[21] While I sometimes adapt or modify some of Caplin's concepts and terminology, I generally adhere to them, and in seminars I ask that students become versed in them, realizing also that some thematic configurations can ask us to apply them more flexibly.

What is most often at issue is the classification of individual themes that divide into two distinct halves, with the sense that the second half responds to, continues, or completes the first.[22] (Not all "classical" themes are divisible in this manner, though a great number of them are.) For purposes of classification we regard the normative length for such a two-part, short theme to be eight measures long and subdivisible into two parts, 4+4. The first part may or may not end with a cadence, strictly considered; the second part, however, will: it may be a half cadence (HC), an imperfect authentic cadence (IAC), or a perfect authentic cadence (PAC)—listed here in ascending order of closural strength. Moreover, the second part may or may not be similar in content to the first part. As a whole, the theme may either prolong the initial tonic (ending, for example, I:PAC), or it may modulate to a different key, as in a modulatory period or a modulatory sentence.

While frequently modified in the repertory, this 4+4 norm serves best as a ready-to-hand prototype with which most encountered exemplars may be set into dialogue. In practice the normative length is often altered by *compression, expansion,* or *extension*—or by the visual effect of the notation or literal barring of the passage. Thus the 4+4 norm is not always embraced, and one commonly finds asymmetrical or irregular variants (4+6, 5+6, and the like). Nonetheless, the 4+4 norm is heuristically useful in classification schemes, suggesting as it does the two parts of the theme in question, each of which has a different functional role to play.

In brief, within form-functional theory the standard options are:

- The normative eight-bar *period*, consisting of an antecedent and a non-elided, parallel consequent. Each of these, antecedent and consequent, usually houses a smaller, two-bar *basic idea* followed by a two-bar *contrasting idea* (b.i. + c.i.) that *ends with a cadence*. To qualify as an antecedent, its cadence must be lighter (or "weaker," less fully closed: an HC or an IAC) than that of the consequent, which will end with an IAC or, more often, a PAC. (If both similar phrases end with a PAC, what we have is not a period but rather a repeated phrase adopting the statement-response "feel" of a period.)[23] To qualify as a period the consequent must start with either the same basic idea as the antecedent or a closely related variant of it. Within form-functional theory, if what might seem to be a potential antecedent of a period does not end with a half cadence or imperfect authentic cadence, strictly considered—and this is not always an easy call—then it is regarded not as an antecedent but rather as a *compound basic idea* (still b.i. + c.i), and the larger 4+4 structure is no longer regarded as a period. Under that condition, as noted below, the whole is classified as a hybrid.

- The normative eight-bar *sentence*, constructed as an aab or aa'b structure. In its short and simplest realizations we find four bars of *presentation*, 2+2 (aa or aa', that is, a two-bar basic idea [b.i.] and its repetition or complementary recasting), and four more of *continuation* (b), ending with a cadence

(HC, IAC, or PAC).[24] A postulate of form-functional theory is that, by definition, the first part of such a theme, the 2+2, b.i. + b.i.' presentation, should not be construed as ending with a cadence, even if mm. 3 and 4, for instance, provide us with a root-position dominant-to-tonic motion. In part, this is because these presentational bars stake out the propositional beginning of something larger—the whole sentence—not an initial musical passage that itself executes an ending function. The structural cadence and the thematic closure that it connotes are thus postponed until the completion of the entire sentence, and they are triggered by the ending-function music most immediately leading up to that completion.

While all of this seems clear enough, it bears observing that orthodox form-functional theory holds that a prototypical continuation combines (or sometimes fuses) a *continuation function* (the destabilizing role of "being-in-the-middle" through fragmentation, harmonic acceleration, faster surface rhythm, and harmonic sequence [Caplin 1998, 41–42; 2013, 705]) with a *cadential function*. Notice, then, the misunderstanding that can arise: the term "continuation" can apply not only to the entire post-presentation unit (Caplin's "continuation phrase"), but also to only the first of its potential subparts, the passage of "continuation function" preceding the onset of a cadential idea. In what follows, the reader will note that, departing somewhat from strict form-functional usage, my shorthand use of the term "continuation" sometimes refers only to the "continuation-function" portion of the post-presentation material, the whole of which is now construed as "continuation + cadence." Moreover, my own preference is to label the parts of the sentence not as aab or aa'b but as ααβ or αα'β (alpha, alpha-prime, beta), reserving Greek letters as indications of sentential subparts. In addition, following my previous caveat, in some continuations—especially ones longer than four bars and in which the "continuation function" and cadential idea are clearly distinguishable—I find it clarifying to subdivide β, form-functional theory's more generalized "continuation phrase," into β + γ (beta-plus-gamma), thereby distinguishing the continuation function proper from the cadential unit. (In even longer continuations, one might extend this into β + γ + δ, in which the cadential unit is signified by δ, delta.)

- Any of four *hybrids* related to the preceding options. Hybrids 1 and 2 are the categories in which an antecedent (b.i. + c.i., ending with an HC or an IAC) is not responded to with a parallel consequent (beginning with the same or similar b.i.). Instead, the response begins with a musical idea different from that of the antecedent. (These are situations that other systems have referred to as contrasting periods.) Hybrids 1 and 2 are similar, the distinction being that the first is an antecedent plus a *continuation* (which latter comprises a middle function followed by a cadential function), while the second is an antecedent plus a *cadence* (in which the entire second part is occupied by an elaborated cadential formula, such as a *complete* or *expanded cadential progression*, prototypically a $\hat{3}$-$\hat{4}$-$\hat{5}$-$\hat{1}$ motion in the bass supporting a I^6–IV [or ii^6]–V–I succession). Hybrids 3 and 4 are reserved for situations in which the first four bars are parsed as b.i. + c.i. (that is, not as a presentational b.i. + b.i.') but do not end with a cadence. Denied antecedent status on these grounds, the first four bars are then regarded as a *compound basic idea* (*c.b.i*). Hybrid 3—the loosest of the categories— covers themes in which a c.b.i. is followed by a *continuation*, that is, by differing music that soon leads to a cadence. Hybrid 4 covers themes in which a c.b.i. is followed by a parallel *consequent* (beginning with the same b.i.). In other words, Hybrid 4 can also be thought of as a period in which the "antecedent's" music does not end with what form-functional theory considers to be a cadence: it is neither an HC nor an IAC, strictly considered. Hybrid 4 cases, for instance, would cover situations in which the first phrase, b.i. + c.i., might end with a V^6 chord, which that theory would not regard as sufficiently cadential. Such a phrase would be in obvious dialogue with the prototypical antecedent but would not fully articulate its more common, root-position dominant ending.

- And the larger, sixteen or more–bar *compound* expansions of these basic types: *compound sentence, compound period*, and so on. Consider the case of the larger, 8+8 compound period. Here we find an eight-bar *compound antecedent* and an eight-bar *compound consequent* that, to be a true consequent, must begin as had the antecedent. Each eight-bar unit is subdivisible into 4+4. Thus the prototypical sixteen bars subdivide as (4+4) + (4+4). To qualify as a compound antecedent the first 4+4 complex must end with a weak cadence (an HC or IAC, as form-functional theory defines them), and the second 4+4 with a stronger one (nearly always a PAC). (In this respect the sixteen-bar compound period is similar to what has traditionally been called the "double period," a term that form-functional theory avoids.) We then ask, do the compound antecedent's first four bars also end with a cadence or not—creating an *en route*, internal cadence at the end of the fourth bar on the way to the more decisive structural cadence in the eighth bar? It may be that they do not. In that situation it is often the case that the composer has built that 4+4 compound antecedent as a sentence (2+2+4, b.i. + b.i. + continuation): this is the commonly encountered *sentential antecedent*. In other cases, the compound antecedent might have been built differently. Each case merits individual examination and assessment.

2. *Schema theory*, identifying formulaic, eighteenth-century voice-leading patterns, as introduced in Robert O. Gjerdingen's *Music in the Galant Style* (2007). It is possible and often instructive to provide any movement with a succession of schema-labels, but that is not my goal here. In this handbook, references to Gjerdingen's work are sporadic and limited mostly to

observations that help to reinforce a particular passage's identity or function through a specific catchphrase or now-standard label. In my analytical work I am particularly interested in noting:

- various "opening-gambit" schemata (DO-RE-MI, SOL-FA-MI, ROMANESCA, and a few others), when recognizing them can reinforce the identification of an initiatory function;
- prototypes and variants of the (continuation-function) MONTE schema: the familiar ascending 5–6 sequence, especially when chromatically intensified (effecting the "lift," for example, of the two-event chord-succession, G [or G^6], C – A [or A^6], d);
- prototypes and variants of the FONTE schema, a chromatically inflected descending-fifth sequence alternating root positions and first inversions.
- schemata that characterize stylized authentic or half-cadence realizations ("galant cadence," "converging half cadence");
- and the frequently encountered, versatile, and immediately recognizable QUIESCENZA figure (rotary linear motion away from the tonic and back to it, sounding a melodic figure, $\hat{8}$-$\flat\hat{7}$-$\hat{6}$-$\natural\hat{7}$-$\hat{8}$, often against a tonic pedal).

Sonata Theory takes an expansive view of such schemata, noting instances of their deviations from their prototypical patterns. In general, the individual patterns are better regarded as flexible *schema families*, the background voice-leading ideas of which can inform non-standard realizations. A recognizable use of the MONTE family, for example, might not support a standard sequential replication of the melody in its second event-pair. Perhaps most frequently, I invoke a broadly inclusive QUIESCENZA family whose various instantiations—including fully harmonized and considerably expanded ones, dispensing with the tonic pedal—can play ingenious roles.[25]

3. The *process theory* elaborated in Janet Schmalfeldt's *In the Process of Becoming* (2011): a construal of "form" as an ongoing process of self-generation. As mentioned earlier, one of Schmalfeldt's many useful observations has to do with the phenomenology of the on-the-spot assessments of the music's process as it flows past us. It sometimes happens that, on the basis of the evidence that we have been hearing thus far, we might initially interpret a passage to be accomplishing one functional role ("I think that this must be the transition") only retrospectively, as the music proceeds further along, to revise our understanding ("Oh, I see: it's still part of the primary theme"). Such revised assessments are common features of the music in question here, and as such this book calls attention to them more than once. It is worth reminding ourselves that, following Schmalfeldt (9), the analytical symbol for this *en route* interpretive revision is the symbol ==>, meaning "becomes" or, more specifically, "retrospectively reinterpreted as." The symbol for the preceding reassessment, for instance, a presumed transition that we later realize is still housed within the primary-theme action zone, is either TR==>P^2 or TR?==>P^2.

Facets of the preceding methods, along with those of others, also surface or are implicit from time to time in the discussions that follow. Among these are topic theory and semiotics, Schenkerian theory, historically oriented theory, embodied cognitive theory (including Hatten's "theory of virtual agency"), conceptual metaphor theory, and the philosophical tradition of hermeneutics. The Sonata Theory project is eager to learn from and apply ideas from other approaches whenever those approaches can help to clarify or sharpen our larger aim of analytical and hermeneutic understanding. I have tried to make this clear from the opening pages of the next chapter, where, to make the point, Sonata Theory concerns are juxtaposed with observations typical also of Schenkerian analysis, schema theory, and form-functional theory. Subsequent chapters, less explicit in this regard, bring up such observations only for the purposes of enhanced clarification.

What Sonata Theory is not

The Achilles heel of any form-analytical method is that it congeals all too readily into a routinized exercise: applying a rule-bound system that pretends to explain everything by identifying the proper label for it and then setting aside more telling questions of musical expression and purpose. The analysis of musical form should not be reduced to acts of taxonomical labeling. Yes, Sonata Theory does offer up an abundance of labels and acronyms, but those identifiers should be understood as tools to be used for larger interpretive purposes. Sometimes there are no unequivocally correct answers to analytical questions, and opinions can legitimately differ about how to read a given passage of music. Ambiguous cases are frequently encountered. When they are, the analyst's calling is not dogmatically to insist upon the "right answer." Instead, as often stated in *Elements of Sonata Theory*, the preferable approach is to *explicate the ambiguity* and then to relate it to the musical processes into which that problematic moment is embedded.

Pointing especially to the idiosyncratic practice of Haydn (but not only Haydn), Sonata Theory's critics sometimes characterize it as an ahistorical, broad-brush system of universalized norms that are expected to be frictionlessly applicable to all late-eighteenth- and nineteenth-century composers. That is not the case. Sonata Theory is no fixed template or unalterable grid to be imposed on individual compositions from before and after the late eighteenth century. (There can be no doubt that the compositional reality on the ground was messier, freer, than any current system can capture if it seeks to go beyond the broadest generalizations.) Instead, Sonata Theory tries to outline a complex set of loosely shared, often-tacit, and ever-developing norms and options—aspects of a culturally shared, multifaceted genre—that emerged and became relatively stabilized in the eighteenth century's last several decades, even as it happily admits local, temporal, and personally customized variants and exceptions. And its continued utility in confronting the freer sonata-form practices throughout the nineteenth century will be addressed in later chapters of this handbook.

Sonata Theory's detailed manner of presentation responds to the analytical conversations characteristic of our own time. It is the product of an attempt inductively to reconstruct for twenty-first-century specialists, and in twenty-first-century language, an extraordinarily rich, historical world of musical practice. It, too, has been historically conditioned, generated within an academic context shot through with its own constraining force-fields of professionalized, disciplinary practice. Yet even while acknowledging the potential fallibility or blind spots of aspects of the enterprise, it tries to do this with the hope that the historical actors of earlier periods might at least have recognized the sorts of things that it proposes, even if they would never have articulated it in this way. And it does so with the hope that this twenty-first-century construct can encourage us, today, to listen carefully to the varied ways that past composers seem to have implicitly utilized, and often individualized, this ever-developing generic complex's shared options and potential overrides.

Despite its plethora of MCs, EECs, ESCs, TMBs, and other notational descriptors, Sonata Theory is not a self-contained, mechanistic system. On the contrary, it aspires to be a mode of reflection that can help us to ask better questions of music. It participates little or not at all in closed-shop, mathematical, or systemic certainty. It is an approach, a style, a supple way of thinking about music.[26] It harbors no claim to provide a ready-made answer to everything about every moment of every sonata form. Whether the reader of this book is a student, a performer, a knowledgeable listener, or a professional music scholar in academia, I urge you to stop whenever your reading of a piece becomes routine, an act of workaday labeling or a clever decoding for decoding's sake. Stop! And reconsider what you are doing and why. Analysis should never be an exercise in sterile formalism. It should be a musically sensitive art, a hermeneutic art in search of musical and human meaning, not the academic grinding of yet another piece of music through the system. The utility of an analytical method depends on its power to call a composition back into life, to provide, at least from time to time, those wonderful eye-and-ear-opening moments: "Aha!"; "Yes!"; "Oh, now I see!"

And so we confront the two sides of the interpretive challenge. On the one hand, it should be expected that professionally oriented commentators on music ground their readings in well-honed, up-to-date analytical skills—ably grasping what is specifically musical about the music under consideration. As it is put in *EST* (603), "In any discussion of music, insufficient or defective analysis undermines the legitimacy of broader interpretive claims and calls the commentator's competence into question; cultural readings of individual works unsupported by adequate music analysis are all too easily produced and ring hollow." On the other hand, "Even though analysis, with all of its technical terminology and lumber-room mechanisms, looms large at the initial stage of one's inquiry, that first stage is no end in itself. Rather, all analysis should [ultimately] be directed toward the larger goal of a hermeneutic understanding of music as a communicative system, a cultural discourse implicated in issues of humanness, worldview, and ideology, widely construed."

2

Mozart, Piano Sonata in B-flat,
K. 333/i (Allegro)

On the occasions when I have had the opportunity to lead seminars in Sonata Theory, whether at the undergraduate or graduate level, I have begun by selecting two or three exemplary movements by Mozart: listening to them and talking our way through every moment of them, section by section, with score in hand. Which aspects of each are especially worth drawing forth for our attention? As the music moves through time and through us (or, from a reversed perspective, as we move through the music), what should we be perceiving? Composed of a succession of individual parts, themes, and sections, why does it seem to make sense at all? How can we understand it as a coherent structure? The music under review must be vividly in our ears—recently heard and felt—before any discussion of it is worthwhile, and that discussion should never be abstract but should correlate with our musically intuitive responses to what we have just heard or played.

The goal has always been twofold: first, to illustrate the characteristic procedures and terminology of Sonata Theory, which in addition to its classificatory language's professional tone is also committed to describing a personalized encounter with music in terms of metaphor and expressive gesture; second, to show how each of a composition's phrases, once we come to recognize what its musical and structural role is, can come alive, even startle us with its directness and purpose. A Sonata Theory analysis seeks to be an aesthetically receptive, interactive dialogue with an individual work. Even in its most language-technical moments it tries to integrate methodical observation with a personal sensitivity to the affective contours and colors of music *as music*.

What is needed at the outset is a relatively straightforward example or two of sonata form, and in my Sonata Theory seminars the first session is always devoted to this. My usual choices have been the first movements of three lesser-known Mozart works: String Quartet in F, K. 168; Symphony No. 28 in C, K. 200; and Symphony No. 30 in D, K. 202. For this book, though, it seems prudent to select a better-known, frequently performed first movement, one, moreover, that has been a staple of classroom form analysis: that of Mozart's Piano Sonata in B-flat, K. 333. What follows is an illustration of the sorts of observations that I would bring to such a seminar—or, alternatively, of the sorts of things that I would encourage the participants to notice on their own in an ongoing exchange of question and answer.

As noted in the preceding chapter, my aim is not to "solve" a piece once and for all. Sonata Theory harbors no such delusions. Rather, my aim is to arrive at a

A Sonata Theory Handbook. James Hepokoski, Oxford University Press (2021). © Oxford University Press.
DOI: 10.1093/oso/9780197536810.003.0002.

historically plausible, robust reading of that piece, one which can claim to be no more (and no less) than a personalized reading. In this chapter, as well as in the succeeding analytical chapters, I assume that the reader has a close aural familiarity with this movement as well as a score of it, with numbered measures, close at hand. We'll start off with another of this handbook's features, that of preceding the analytical reading proper with some historical and biographical contextualization, along with some remarks about the problems with which such a work can present us.

Backdrop

Throughout much of the nineteenth and twentieth centuries the date, and even the year, in which Mozart composed K. 333 had been unclear due to a seeming absence of unequivocal documentary evidence. While the triptych of the three piano sonatas, K. 330–332, and K. 333 itself were published in Vienna in 1784 (K. 330–332 by Artaria and K. 333 by Toricella, along with the Violin Sonata K. 454 and the Piano Sonata K. 284), it had long been supposed that they must all have been composed a half decade before, in 1778 or 1779, perhaps during the composer's trip to Paris—that is, two or three years before Mozart's move from Salzburg to Vienna in 1781. In the last quarter of the twentieth century, however, this view has been set aside in favor of the later date of 1783 or 1784 (Irving 1997, 66–72).

The most compelling argument on behalf of K. 333's date of composition was made by Alan Tyson. Following a painstaking study of the "unusual paper" on which Mozart wrote it (along with meticulous research into its little-known manufacturer), Tyson was "inclined to place the writing of the sonata in the middle of November [1783]—at any rate after the *Akademie* at Linz on 4 November, for which he had to write a new symphony, K. 425, at breakneck speed" (1987, 80). At that time Mozart and his wife Constanze were returning to Vienna from Salzburg, where they had visited his father for three months, and the Linz *Akademie* was a hastily arranged affair. Still, Mozart's time in and around Linz proved a plausible possibility for Tyson, who suggested—albeit questioningly—that it was reasonable to think of K. 333 as the "Linz" Sonata. At present, Tyson's dating seems the most likely one. This adjusts our view of K. 333 (and perhaps also its predecessors, K. 330–332) to make it generally contemporaneous with the Symphony No. 36 in C, K. 425, "Linz," and not, as some of the earlier datings would have had it, with the "Paris" Symphony, No. 31 in D, K. 297, from 1778.

With K. 333, then, we are dealing not with "early Mozart" but rather with the mature composer in the full stride of his compositional powers. This brings us to two questions. The first: for which purposes would Mozart have written this work? Tyson summarizes the composer's likely concerns during that return trip from Salzburg: "His mind was already on Vienna and on the material that he needed for teaching and for private concerts and soirées. . . . Between its composition in

November 1783 and its publication in the summer of 1784 Mozart is likely to have made much use of the Sonata in B-flat" (1987, 81).

The second question leads us into issues of late-eighteenth-century aesthetics and expression. What we may expect from Mozart in his piano sonatas, several of which were probably written for didactic purposes within a marketplace that also sought to attract amateur musicians? Here we are dealing neither with the quest for metaphysical depth nor the projection of an urgent, existential drama. Much less, as Mark Evan Bonds has argued, should we be looking for that sense of autobiographical subjectivity, personal confession, expression of self, or even the authentically stamped "sincerity" or "oracularity" that we might wish to project onto the sonatas of later, romantic composers: "In an era that conceived of music as a rhetorical art, [eighteenth-century] composers repeatedly described the creative process as a means of moving listeners, not as an externalization of their own inner emotions" (2020, 22).

It might be profitable, then, to recalibrate some of our framings of these "classical-era" piano sonatas, now so comfortably assimilated into our own, current marketplace of advocacy and cultural prestige. The "classical style" in such works is better characterized as "the high-galant style," the earlier, mid-century galant style now exquisitely wrought and brought at every turn to a perfection in dazzlingly imaginative ways. Mozart's piano sonatas display brilliant realizations not only of the standardized musical topics, moods, and manners that suffuse the galant era's music, but also of its numerous ready-to-hand, standardized musical figures—ringing changes on those decades' familiar patterns and "stock musical phrases," those contrapuntal patterns that we now identify as *schemata*—all processed ingeniously through the action zones of the sonata.[1] From this perspective the high polish of Mozart's workmanship, consummately finished in every detail, remains breathtaking. And that is more than enough.

Exposition (mm. 1–63)

In addition to its well-known harmonic requirements (to move from the initial tonic key to a non-tonic one and to secure that non-tonic key with a perfect authentic cadence) one of the *rhetorical* charges of any exposition is to lay out an ordered succession of musical ideas to which the orderings of the materials of the subsequent sections—development, recapitulation, and coda (if any)—are to be compared. The exposition establishes the *referential layout* of ideas against whose succession those later sections should be read. We can also refer to the referential layout as the *expositional rotation*, that is, the first rotation or cycle through the referential layout. (The recapitulation is a later rotation through these same materials.) In most cases from the later eighteenth century an exposition's materials move through four *action zones* or *action spaces*. Sonata Theory identifies these as the primary theme, the transition, the secondary theme, and the closing zone.

Primary theme (P, mm. 1–10)

Announcing the tonic key of the movement, the primary theme (P) of any sonata occupies the exposition's initial *action zone* and is that sonata's principal or leading idea. The mere laying-out of P proposes that a sonata can be, or is to be, built on its premises. P is normally a theme-like construction of shorter ideas, or *modules*, brought at its end to a cadence that marks the conclusion of that zone. (In Sonata Theory the generalized term "modules" often refers to smaller units or constituent parts of a theme—thematic fragments, one might say—though it can also be used to suggest larger aggregates of these particles, such as a complete phrase or thematic unit.)[2]

In the case of K. 333/i, P's boundaries could hardly be clearer. At a modest Allegro tempo it spans mm. 1–10 and is closed with a tonic-key perfect authentic cadence (I:PAC) in m. 10. All listeners will hear that what had begun with a lyrical, gracefully fluid character in mm. 1–4 stalls in mm. 5–8 and finally rises upward to cadence in a tenser, higher register in m. 10 with the high $B\flat_5$ in the top voice. This $B\flat_5$ is followed by tension-releasing octave-drops to $B\flat_4$ and $B\flat_3$, this last merging with an uprising tonic arpeggiation in the bass. Listeners might also notice that a prominent expressive feature of the theme is that most of its measures' downbeats are dissonant, non-chordal tones: tender pushes or yearning throbs with sentimental or amorously melancholic connotations. It's all very clear. But the ease and elegance of the theme belies the high craft that has put it together as a coherent, exquisite whole.

Consider the theme's opening move, mm. 1–4. This is a four-bar unit, a songlike, cantabile flow set into motion by the downward-cascading upbeat preceding and falling into bar 1, all over an arpeggiated bass whose gentle, forward-rolling propulsion is furthered by the downbeat rests in the bass.[3] How might we hear these four bars? Sonata Theory does not have its own procedures for the analysis of individual themes or their constituent parts. Instead, its approach with regard to thematic structure is eclectic, drawing on a variety of different ways of reading themes. For expository purposes, we can demonstrate this by taking the unusually thorough step of considering mm. 1–4 from three analytical perspectives: form-functional theory, schema theory, and Schenkerian theory. The point is to demonstrate the degree to which these different approaches can be mutually reinforcing, with each angle of perception deepening and strengthening the others.

We begin with form-functional theory, which would have us notice that mm. 1–2 and 3–4, while different, are paired with each other as a statement and a response. This 2+2 pair is regarded as the set of complementary, tonic-prolonging modules that lay out the *presentation* (αα'), the initiatory gesture, of a now-begun *sentence* that will end at m. 10: αα'β (alpha-alpha-prime-beta), the whole 10 bars comprising a presentation, a continuation, and a cadence (which last, should we wish to isolate the cadential-function module, could be indicated as γ, gamma).

What form-functional theory regards as the *beginning function* always executed by a sentence's presentation (2+2, αα') may be buttressed through an appeal to the

Figure 2.1. One version of the SOL-FA-MI schema.

standpoint of recent schema theory, concerned with the era's formulaic, commonly employed bass-treble voice-leading patterns. Here we recognize mm. 1–4 as a decorated realization of the generic SOL-FA-MI schema (Gjerdingen 2007, 253–62, 463). As its name implies, it is characterized by a $\hat{5}$-$\hat{4}$-($\hat{4}$)-$\hat{3}$ melodic descent in the upper voice (notated in schema theory as ❺❹[❹]❸) underpinned by $\hat{1}$-$\hat{2}$-$\hat{7}$-$\hat{1}$ (①-②-⑦-①) or $\hat{1}$-$\hat{2}$-$\hat{5}$-$\hat{1}$ (①②⑤①) in the bass. Figure 2.1 shows the background schema in play here, producing the I-ii-V⁷-I succession that guides these four bars. More to the point, as Gjerdingen demonstrates, the SOL-FA-MI schema is a typical opening gambit—which underscores the initiating role that form-functional theory assigns to a sentence's presentation modules.

From here it is a short step to Schenkerian-grounded observations. As just noted, schema theory has us observe that mm. 1–4's leading upper voice-line (or guiding thread) is F_5, $E\flat_5$, D_5. What we can hear, then, is a richly decorated $\hat{5}$-$\hat{4}$-($\hat{4}$)-$\hat{3}$ descent in the melody, with graceful, undulating sweeps below these schema-tones. Those familiar with Schenkerian analysis will also recognize that the melodic voice traces through a style-basic *linear progression* or *Zug*, "stepwise motion in one direction between two tones [here $\hat{5}$ and $\hat{3}$] that are related to each other harmonically" (Schachter 2016, 1). M. 4's $\hat{3}$, D_5, is approached not from above but from below and is enhanced with a lower shadow of thirds at the moment of attainment. The preceding $\hat{5}$ (F_5) is decorated with an unprepared upper neighbor ($\hat{6}$), G_5 (perhaps a foreshadowing of the later downbeat dissonances?), which triggers the right-hand anacrusis-cascade before m. 1 and is touched upon again in mm. 1 and 2. Thus the $\hat{5}$-$\hat{4}$-$\hat{3}$ descent might be rendered as ($\hat{6}$)-$\hat{5}$-$\hat{4}$-$\hat{3}$. This linear descent proves critical in all that follows.

For the moment, though, let's turn to another issue. Crucial to any consideration of musical form and meaning is the identification of cadences. Preceded by a predominant (ii, m. 2) and a dominant (V⁷, m. 3), should m. 4 be considered an imperfect authentic cadence (I:IAC)? Opinions will differ on this, depending on how narrowly or how broadly one defines a cadence. Form-functional theory would deny a genuine cadential status to m. 4, reading mm. 1–4 as a short-range tonic prolongation or a brief chordal oscillation around a tonic. This view has much to commend it. In general, the presentation modules of any sentence (here, mm. 1–2, 3–4, αα′) are best understood as the beginning of something larger (αα′β), not as a complete, self-standing unit. Moreover, as a familiar schema of beginning, the underlying SOL-FA-MI schema reinforces this initiatory function. However we read it, whatever light cadential effect that we might feel at m. 4 (its localized chordal possession of *cadential content* [Caplin 2004, 81–85]) can be subordinate to our awareness that we are dealing with a presentation that is about to branch off into a continuation. The rule of thumb: be hesitant to ascribe an authentic or imperfect cadence to the end of a compact presentation. Mm. 1–10 are better seen as a 10-bar whole containing only one terminal (or structural) cadence, that is, one not only containing a cadential content but also completing a manifestly cadential or ending function.

The remainder of P, the sentence's continuation modules, mm. 5–10 (β, or if one prefers to distinguish between the internally fused continuational and cadential functions, βγ, beta-gamma), is easily dealt with. While mm. 1–4 had presented the descending upper line, $(\hat{6})$-$\hat{5}$-$\hat{4}$-$\hat{3}$, mm. 5–8 seek to complete it with $\hat{2}$-$\hat{1}$, C_5-$B\flat_4$—and insistently so, with the left hand now sounded on the downbeat and the right hand sounding wistfully repeated syncopations. But mm. 5–6 do not produce a structural cadence: scale degree $\hat{1}$ is sounded above a first-inversion tonic. Back up, then, and retry: mm. 7–8. But again: no closure, only the I^6 chord. Change of strategy: a flight to the upper register—and gathering rhythmic momentum—to produce a decisive I:PAC in m. 10 (with the bass now reaching its lowest register so far, $B\flat_2$). That PAC's high $B\flat_5$ is then transferred to its proper register on beat 2, $B\flat_4$, while the left hand provides an ingratiating confirmation with its own climb to $B\flat_3$, elegantly merging on beat 3 with yet another implicit octave descent in the upper voice to produce the final member of the triple-stroke finishes so common to unequivocal endings in this repertory.

As a whole, P traces not only a trajectory of structure but also a trajectory of gesture and affect that simulates the fluidly narrative experience of an implied subject, or what Hatten calls a "virtual agent," one that can be "fictionalized as an actor in a dramatic trajectory and even internalized as part of a subjectivity, akin to an active stream of consciousness" (2018, 2). The opening amorous melancholy proceeds into hesitations at mm. 5–9 and decision in mm. 9–10. Throughout the theme the dissonant downbeats, signs of sighing, gradually give way to more forthright consonant downbeats in mm. 6, 8, 9, and 10—indications of a mounting resolve. More than that, the initial anacrusis-cascade into m. 1, the compressed fall, $(\hat{6}\text{-})\hat{5}$-$\hat{4}$-$\hat{3}$-$\hat{2}$-$\hat{1}$, is revisited throughout all of mm. 1–10 as the governing framework for the whole. (Here we are observing a more extended *linear progression* or *Zug*, this time moving through passing tones from $\hat{5}$ to $\hat{3}$ to $\hat{1}$, that is, a melodic outlining of the tonic triad. While noting this is resonant with orthodox procedures of Schenkerian analysis, the musical impression at hand is readily perceptible aurally without an appeal to that analytical apparatus.) The opening six-note fall is a bud that blossoms into the 10-bar whole: the guiding line of that whole is sounded embryonically in the anacrusis. Bringing forth the presence of these 10 bars can be an act of connoisseurship, like coming to cherish an exquisitely wrought detail or a perfectly executed little patch of yellow wall in a painting by Vermeer.

Transition (TR, mm. 11–22)

P now completed, m. 11 opens onto the next action zone, the transition (TR). Relay-like, this zone's goal is to move the structure onward, thereby showing P's *acceptance* as the onset of a sonata. TR then surges ahead, most commonly (by the 1770s and in Mozart) to the medial caesura (MC, here at m. 22), the break or breath that divides the exposition into two distinct parts. Composers have many options for beginning TR. In this case Mozart gives us a TR of the *dissolving-restatement* type: m. 11 replicates the start of m. 1, down an octave, suggesting a more earnest tone, but soon diverges from its model with an expressive octave-leap upward to $B\flat_4$ followed by a dissonant sigh on the downbeat of m. 12. Harmonically, m. 12 tilts onto C^7, an applied V^7 of V, and so in this transition it seems that the plan is to modulate to the dominant. (Not all transitions modulate.)

This modulation is nearly complete by the F-chord in m. 14 (it could still resolve back to the tonic) but is more fully secured with the $B\natural_3$ in m. 17 (the middle member of a left-hand $\hat{4}$-$\sharp\hat{4}$-$\hat{5}$ push), producing a *converging half cadence* in the dominant at m. 18 (V:HC, $V^{[7]}$/V). As often happens, once that active dominant is attained (m. 18), it is prolonged with a *dominant-lock*, here of five bars (mm. 18–22) decoratively treated in the left hand. The V-lock keeps the force of m. 18's V:HC alive, and, taking advantage of the momentum gained, the music glides forward to the literal break of the medial-caesura gap, the structurally crucial MC, at m. 22. Thus we say that this MC is *built around* a half cadence in the key of the dominant. Sonata Theory notates m. 22 as a V:HC MC, even though the actual time-point at which the HC occurs is earlier, at m. 18. A nice touch in this dominant-lock is the progressive cleansing-away of the $B\flat_5$: chipping away at the chord-seventh through m. 20's hammeringly repetitive $B\natural_5$-C_6 figures, replied to and reinforced with m. 21's left-hand flurry, and finally pushing through the B♭-B♮ tussle to arrive at a pure dominant chord, without seventh, at the MC, m. 22. (The $B\flat_5$-$B\natural_5$ alternations, of course, had been in play from m. 15 onward.) That MC (literally m. 22, beat 4), is signaled with an elaboration of the triple-hammerstroke figure (♩[♩]♩)—a common way of sounding it, here with the familiar change of octave. In this case the figure is complementary to the one that had ended P in m. 10.

Reflecting on TR as a whole, we see that its musical material is a recast version of P, module for module. Mm. 11–14 are a recomposed version of P's presentation, αα', mm. 1–4; mm. 15–16 vary the figuration of the repetitive continuation, β, from mm. 5–8; and the push into and through the dominant-lock and MC, mm. 17–22, reworks and extends models found in mm. 9–10. This TR recycles the modules of P but reshapes them to the new action-zone task of TR. Considering the whole exposition as a broad *referential rotation* of materials that will be recycled through, with some changes, in the recapitulatory rotation and perhaps elsewhere, we see that this TR can be construed as a *subrotation* of P, a smaller rotation of materials within the larger expositional rotation.

Secondary thematic zone (S, mm. 23–38)

An MC both brings TR to a close and, like an elevator arriving at a higher floor, reopens the door onto a style-appropriate secondary theme (S) in a non-tonic key, V in a major-mode sonata from this period. S is the exposition's *second launch* (P being the first), the beginning of its second part and its third action zone. Mandated by the implicit generic contract of sonata construction, S's harmonic and structural goal is to unfold an attractive musical space vectored toward securing at least one perfect authentic cadence in the new, non-tonic key (here, a V:PAC). When that first V:PAC is not followed by a mere repetition of all or part of S but either closes the exposition or goes on to new, differing material, that perfect authentic cadence marks the point of *essential expositional closure*, the EEC, Sonata Theory's term for the end-boundary of S-space. For now, I'll note only that the "essential" aspect of the EEC resides in its fulfillment of the minimal generic expectation for non-tonic closure (here a V:PAC) within an exposition. Much more material can follow that V:PAC: additional themes leading to their own V:PACs, as is the case in this movement. Sonata Theory considers those events to be housed within the subsequent action zone, *closing space*. (Once we get to that point in this piece, I'll return to the analytical question of multiple themes and multiple cadences in post-MC space.)

As is the case with TR, composers have a variety of options for treating S. Mozart usually gives us the sense of a new, contrasting theme at this point, and that is what we find at m. 22, now in F major (V). It begins with the jolt of a ramrod-plucky, thick opening chord, re-calling us to attention. For all of its sense of newness, S reworks materials from P (also noted in Kinderman 2006, 54). M. 23 gives us the generating head-motive idea of $(\hat{6}-)\hat{5}-\hat{4}-\hat{3}-\hat{2}-\hat{1}$, returning at once in m. 24 to $\hat{6}$, an unmistakable intervallic reference back to P, just as the repetitive syncopations of mm. 25, 29, and 33 hark back to those in mm. 5 and 7; and the similar SOL-FA-MI schema of mm. 23–26 could hardly be clearer. (Notice also how S's C_5-F_4 fifth has been sonically prepared by the C_6-F_5 spans of mm. 15–17.) While more varied from P in content than is TR, this S theme is still another, reworked *subrotation* of P. More technically, this kind of S is one produced via the tactic of *contrasting derivation*: a motivic sense of P is present, but its recasting produces a different thematic effect. Considering the subrotations P, TR, and S together, we see that as the action zones unfold, we move further away from the thematic model provided in P, as if the gravitational pull of P, its sway over what follows, were being left increasingly behind. This is part of the strategy of coherence behind this exposition as a whole.

Mozart shapes this S as a large period: an eight-bar antecedent ending with a half cadence (V:HC, m. 30) and a paired eight-bar consequent ending with the V:PAC at m. 38 (the EEC). It is therefore a *compound period*, 8+8, not 4+4. More specifically, the 8+8 compound antecedent and compound consequent subdivide into (4+4) + (4+4). Unlike the forward-driving sentence format, any period, small or large, is a stable, balanced structure, even a somewhat static one, even though its temporal motion is still drawn (as we are with it) to the cadential station of the EEC at m. 38. Obviously, mm. 31–34 are an only slightly varied restatement of mm. 23–26. To be noted, though, is the Mozartian sigh in m. 34, the characteristic chromatic descent, here from $\hat{5}$ to $\hat{3}$, a hand-on-heart fingerprint of the composer. Mm. 35–38 provide a newly composed, rippling drive toward the V:PAC (the EEC).

As for S's cadential material, we should notice a few things. To begin with, the tonic sonority at m. 36, beat 3, begins a four-stage formulaic move toward the cadence that form-functional theory identifies as a *complete cadential progression*, the "complete functional sequence" of tonic/predominant/dominant/tonic (or T-P-D-T; Caplin 1998, 27–29; 2004, 54; 2013, 14–15). The cadential intention becomes even clearer with the fourth beat of m. 36, where the I^6 more emphatically initiates a standard cadential formula: $\hat{3}$-$\hat{4}$-$\hat{5}$-($\hat{5}$)-$\hat{1}$ in the bass. Listeners and performers should be aware that reaching such a crucially placed I^6 is a signal that one of a small handful of fashionable "galant clausulae" or "galant cadences" has been triggered (Gjerdingen 2007, 141–55). (Compare this with the similar, emphatically striding $\hat{1}$-$\hat{4}$-$\hat{5}$-$\hat{1}$ in the bassline of mm. 9–10.) Moreover, in this case, the upper voice above that $\hat{3}$-$\hat{4}$-$\hat{5}$-($\hat{5}$)-$\hat{1}$ bassline sparkles down an octave descent from $\hat{7}$ to $\hat{1}$. This is "the most famous [upper-voice line] of galant cadences" (Gjerdingen 2007, 146–49), a stereotyped descent from $\hat{8}$ with an often-emphatic $\hat{3}$-$\hat{2}$-$\hat{1}$ at its end: MI-RE-DO, where MI is sounded above a $^6_4$ chord. Gjerdingen labels this familiar upper-voice formula the "Cudworth cadence" in honor of its first musicological identifier. Finally, that "Cudworth" descent in m. 37 recalls the anacrusis figuration that launched m. 1's P theme, while the final trill into the tonic recalls figuration from m. 26. With the finality of that cadence, the EEC, this action zone, S, is brought to a close.

Closing zone (C, mm. 39–63)

With the new, non-tonic key now secured, the role of any *closing zone* (C) is to confirm that key, with either one or more new themes or, at least, briefer, key-stabilizing modules. When present, the C-zone can be considered an add-on appendix that follows an EEC. The term "closing zone" (or "closing space") should not be understood as suggesting that the things that occur in it are unimportant (less rhetorically telling than S proper, for instance) nor that they do not have important roles to play in the exposition. When Sonata Theory identifies a theme or module as belonging to closing space, this is only an indication that a perfect authentic cadence in the new key has already been reached (the EEC, the only non-tonic PAC called for by the genre) and that we are moving on to different material. The C-zone can vary in length and melodic content, ranging from a mere codetta to a series of elaborated themes differing from yet complementing S and carrying the exposition's part 2 to its conclusion. The breadth of C is typically relatable to the expected proportions of an exposition. An early EEC can invite a longer string of C themes or modules;

a late one none at all, or perhaps only a brief codetta. In K. 333/i the EEC occurs rather early, in m. 38 of what turns out to be a 63-bar exposition, retrospectively, some 60 percent of the way through it. Were the exposition to end at m. 38, it would give the impression of an awkward foreshortening. As a consequence, a number of C ideas follow it.

Multiple C themes are common in Mozart's works. With his ability to set forth stunning successions of ever-new ideas, he often composed a string of post-MC (part-2) themes, each of which ends with a non-tonic PAC—as happens in this movement. The abundance of new ideas and multiple V:PACs gives rise to what some analysts have called "the Mozart problem," namely, which of these is best regarded as the most decisive with regard to closure? The first one? The last one? The strongest one? The question can be debated at length: *EST* devotes several pages to it (120–24 and 147–49). Some insist that it is intuitively the case that since all such non-tonic themes hang together, additively, they are best understood as a "subordinate theme group," noting that the last theme proper often produces the most forceful cadence (for example, an emphatic trill cadence, one of the strongest markers of finality in the compositional toolbox). This perception of a continued successional affinity past the EEC cannot be casually set aside, and to it one should add that the most manifestly conjoined themes are those linked by elided cadences, where the cadential end of one phrase simultaneously sets off the beginning of the next.

The debate's questions are terminological: How do we best describe this perception of post-MC thematic grouping? And what do we mean by "closure"? Sonata Theory agrees that the differing materials in any S/C grouping cohere in some successional sense that drives the exposition toward its strongly articulated end. That is not at issue. Rather, the question is whether one prefers to identify all of these themes with S terminology, concluding that they must all be members of a "subordinate theme group"—in which case "closure" might imply "the closure of all of the post-MC expositional themes within a coherently shaped group." This is not, however, Sonata Theory's preference. Instead of to a "subordinate theme group," the present approach refers instead to an *S/C thematic complex*, a term new to this book.[4] In most cases the differing descriptions observe the same thing—the coherence and continued purpose of the thematic succession—but Sonata Theory prefers to distinguish the C themes as "closing themes" in order to notice that they appear after the generic guideline of producing at least one non-tonic PAC has been fulfilled. While these post-EEC (post-first-non-tonic-cadence) themes may continue other types of ongoing intensification or other important activities begun by S, from the tonal/generic perspective they are "extras" or additionally clarifying ideas that complement and reinforce the attainment of the already secured first non-tonic PAC/ EEC. I take up this issue at greater length in chapter 4, in the discussion introducing Figure 4.2.

Returning now to K. 333/i, we start our look at this closing space by noting, first, that it is *non-elided* to S (a break at m. 38 effects a clear separation between S and

C), and, second, by locating the perfect authentic cadences within it. Here there are four such cadences, at mm. 50, 54, 59, and 63. Of these, three, mm. 50, 59, and 63, are preceded by new material, while mm. 54–59 are a varied repetition of mm. 50–54. We therefore call the three divergent musical ideas driving to those cadences C^1 (mm. 39–50), C^2 (mm. 50–54, 54–59), and C^3 (mm. 59–63). Superscript integers are used in any action zone when a PAC in its interior goes on to differing material housed within the same zone (for example, P^1, P^2; TR^1, TR^2; C^1, C^2). Any label C^2, for instance, tells us that an earlier, differing C module, C^1, had already produced a PAC and that the music has now gone on with new material either seeking its own PAC or content to confirm the one just attained in some other way (such as one or more "non-thematic" codettas). If there is only one PAC or closural equivalent within an action zone we might not need to use superscript numerals, and I have not yet done so within P, TR, and S in K. 333/i. Should we wish to differentiate smaller, internal modules within any such thematic space, however—before its PAC—they may be indicated by *decimal designators*, such as $P^{1.1}$, $P^{1.2}$ (we could have labeled mm. 1–4, α, as $P^{1.1}$ and 5–10, β, as $P^{1.2}$), $TR^{1.1}$, $TR^{1.2}$, $S^{1.1}$, $S^{1.2}$, $C^{1.1}$, $C^{1.2}$, $C^{1.3}$, and so on.

C^1, mm. 39–50, is led into with a bar of vigorously regenerating left-hand fill in m. 38. That fill again outlines the $(\hat{6}\text{-})\hat{5}\text{-}\hat{4}\text{-}\hat{3}\text{-}\hat{2}\text{-}\hat{1}$ figure first heard as the tumbling fall into m. 1. Moreover, in the upper voice of mm. 39–42 the insistent pushing through $B\flat_5$ into $B\natural_5$ and C_6 recalls the similar events of mm. 19–22. Is C^1, then, a *fourth* subrotation, as S had been a third? Perhaps so, but by this point the back-references to earlier action zones are less overt, suggesting again that the further we get away from P, the weaker its force to shape thematic events.

Mozart structures C^1 as a sentence. The brash, aggressive mm. 39–42 comprise the presentation (αα)—call it $C^{1.1}$—and mm. 43–46 (β or $C^{1.2}$) the continuation to the expected cadence. With its hammering *fortepiano* blows, the aggressive $C^{1.1}$ prepares the way for a special-effect surprise: a *piano*-dynamic $C^{1.2}$, mm. 43–44, like a leap into the air, a sudden release, a floating hypermeasure at half-speed—an *alla breve*—featuring m. 44's tart cross-relation of the right hand's octave B♭s against the left hand's $B\natural_3$. Sixteenth-note motion is restored for the drive to cadence at m. 45. Here we should notice the familiar $(\hat{6})\text{-}\hat{5}\text{-}\hat{4}\text{-}\hat{3}\text{-}\hat{2}\text{-}\hat{1}$ fall from D_6, m. 43, to the expected, but not sounded, F_5 on the downbeat on m. 46. The absence of that downbeat F_5 results not in an unequivocal V:PAC (though almost one) but rather what Sonata Theory calls an *attenuated* or *evaded cadence* that is not yet satisfactory for closure. This is because Mozart undercuts the predicted cadence in order to present the spotlighted, special-effect $C^{1.2}$ bars "one more time" (to use Schmalfeldt's now-familiar term for such local cadential evasions and immediate repetitions: 1992; 2011, 48). This time around, though, they are varied with a delicious patch of chromatic color (more easily characterized retrospectively once we get to C^3 later) coupled with expressive upper-voice octave leaps. In addition, the module is expanded by a measure, as if hovering in the air even longer, floating through a set of gently descending fifths (mm. 47–48, D_5^6, g, C_5^6, F)—an imaginative realization of what Gjerdingen calls the FONTE schema (2007, 61–71)—even as those bars drift inexorably to the V:PAC at m. 50, completing C^1.

A second C module, C^2, follows at m. 50. Its goal is more clearly that of near-immediate cadential confirmation, like the broad sweep of a cadential hand from m. 50 to m. 54. Mm. 50–51 can be heard as a re-energized, scalar pathway to the expanded cadential progression (ECP), triggered by the I^6 at the downbeat of m. 52 and reaching its V:PAC goal at m. 54. As often happens in C zones, C^2 is shot through with subdominant inflections: not only the repeated chromatic sighs in the inner voice of mm. 50 and 51 ($E\natural_4$-$E\flat_4$-D_4, or $\natural\hat7$-$\flat\hat7$-$\hat6$; compare these with the single languid sigh in m. 34) but also the $E\flat_5$ twice rushed through in the rapid sixteenth-note runs of mm. 51 and 52. Once the cadence at m. 54 is touched upon, Mozart gives us a varied, bravura repetition of C^2, invading again the instrument's highest register that had been attained only once before, within P at mm. 8–9. All this sets up an even rhetorically stronger ECP launched by the I^6 at m. 56 and carried through to the end with that ultra-conclusive signal of finality, the trill-cadence ending (m. 58), driving the V:PAC home at m. 59. If we assess the strengths of the three expanded cadential progressions heard up to this point (concluding in mm. 38, 54, and 59), we see that Mozart has made each of them stronger, more emphatic. As mentioned earlier, there is thus a secondary trajectory of "narrative" coherence drawing S, C^1, and C^2 together as a common-purpose rhetorical grouping—an *S/C thematic complex* that brings its series of intensifications to a close at m. 59.

With that accomplished, the final module, C^3, serves as tension-lowering aftermath, a codetta (which could also be labeled as C^{cod}). The grounding formula behind it is the voice-leading pattern that Gjerdingen has dubbed the QUIESCENZA (2007, 181–95). The telltale sign of a QUIESCENZA, a much-favored gesture of both openings and conclusions, is its rotary motion around the tonic, $\hat8$-$\flat\hat7$-$\hat6$-$\natural\hat7$-$\hat8$, often against a tonic pedal in another voice, usually the bass, though the schema can also be decorated, expanded, or harmonized. Figure 2.2 illustrates a prototypical version of the pattern, including the tonic pedal. In effect, it circumscribes a quasi-ritualized, chromatic tour around the tonic, holding it in place notwithstanding its subdominant-inflected coloration. In turn, this can induce the sensation of personally cycling around a fixed, stable tonic pitch. In C^3 we hear two decorated cycles through the $\hat8$-$\flat\hat7$-$\hat6$-$\natural\hat7$-$\hat8$ pattern. The first, with sighing chromatic enhancements, is presented in mm. 59–61 (F_4-$E\flat_4$-D_4-$E\natural_4$-F_4). The second, mm. 61–63, does away with the tonic pedal and presents the pattern split between two different voices: we first hear, in the bass, F_3, $E\flat_3$, and D_3, whereupon, in m. 62, the music converts into a more straightforward cadential process, with the completion of the QUIESCENZA pattern now shifted to the upper voice ($E\natural_4$-F_4) to complete the final V:PAC— and the exposition—at m. 63. (Once we can recognize more basic types of the QUIESCENZA pattern, we are prepared to revisit mm. 46–48 within C^1 to observe a much more enriched realization of it.) The commonly found expositional repeat at

Figure 2.2. A prototypical QUIESCENZA ($\hat{8}$-♭$\hat{7}$-$\hat{6}$-♮$\hat{7}$-$\hat{8}$, notated here in C).

m. 63 sends us back to the beginning to experience another cycle or rotation of the four action zones that comprise the exposition's *referential layout*.

Development (mm. 64–86/93)

K. 333/i's development (or developmental space) opens by sounding a variant of P in the dominant, F major, the key in which the exposition had ended. While beginning a development by sounding a version of P or a P-fragment in a non-tonic key relatable in some way to that of the exposition's end is by no means the invariable practice within developments, it is the most customary thing to do (the *first-level default*). As such, the impression given in this *entry zone* of the development is that of starting another rotation or thematic cycle, set off once again by P. The development's version of P (mm. 64–71) replicates its model's sentential structure (αα′β, with β beginning at m. 68), though this variant of it is more unstable (no longer serving as a tonic prolongation), anxiety-ridden, and worryingly tinged with the risk of collapsing into the minor mode. And that is what happens: with its perfect authentic cadence at m. 71, P's F-major onset falls into the snares of F minor, a negatively valenced, "lights-out" effect common in this repertory.

What follows is this development's *central action space*, in this case the outburst of a contrasting, modulatory *episode* (mm. 71–86), here a plunge into the era's familiar storm or *tempesta* topic. While the episode's thrashing, Alberti-bass sixteenth-notes recall those of C^1 (mm. 39–42), the impression given by the wide-ranging right-hand wails and syncopations is that of something new, unforeseen, and dire—a casting into a tonally unstable squall. (Kinderman 2006, 55, aptly describes it as a region of "surprising turbulence and drama" within "this graceful, Apollonian work," perhaps even, as an early commentator had suggested, "an eruption of anger.") Quite apart from the driven figuration, much of the drama is set forth by means of expressive tonal colors and modulations. The stormy F minor (mm. 71–72) is soon yanked to a G^7 chord, V^7 of C minor (mm. 73–74, with a despairing ninth, A♭$_5$, in m. 74). A dark chromatic shift through a passing e♭^{6} chord that starts a second, complementary module, m. 76, lands on a potentially hopeful F^7, mm. 77–78 (V^7 of the tonic), recapturing and converting the lost F-bass from m. 71. But in vain: m. 79's D^6_5 throws us into G-minor color (vi of the tonic B-flat) and ratifies that color by casting us via an augmented sixth chord onto an emphatic half cadence in G minor (vi:HC, m. 81). The dominant of G minor is now sustained as a dominant-lock (with upper-neighbor oscillations) from m. 81 to m. 86. From the affective/illustrative perspective, this is the dying-down of the tempest. From another, m. 86 is the end of both the episode and developmental space proper, but the situation here, not an uncommon one at the end of high-galant developments, is that the development ends not on the more usual V of I but on the less frequent V of vi (here V of G minor). Even while the V/vi is a still-familiar alternative to more normative V of I, it is still, in a sense, a "wrong-key" preparation for the onset of the recapitulation.

M. 87–93 are best construed as an extended link or harmonized fill, conveying us from V of vi, the end of the development proper at m. 86, to the correct dominant, F^7, of B-flat major. This is not the more standard retransition procedure (RT) that we often find at the end of developments: it is more of a separate, corrective or recovery link (with an RT function, of course), leading from the hard break that closes the development's end to the moment of recapitulation. V^7 of B-flat major, F^7, emerges as early as m. 88. That too is fixed as a dominant-lock through m. 92, albeit with pointed mixtures from B-flat minor (embellishing the dominant with an ominous ♭$\hat6$ upper-neighbor, as had happened with the V-lock in mm. 81–86—backing up to the earlier idea, perhaps, in order to correct it). Above this we are given the sense that the P-idea "protagonist" (the "virtual agent" or *narrative subject*) is in the process of re-formation, pulling itself together after the pummeling of the storm. Mm. 92 and 93 revert to single-voice *caesura-fill*, and finally, at m. 94, now fully recovered, the music slips effortlessly into the recapitulation.

Recapitulation (mm. 94–165)

In confronting any recapitulation the analyst's task is to compare it, bar-for-bar, to the exposition. As with all recapitulations, the expectation is that the exposition's off-tonic S and C will be resolved into the tonic, but the larger burden is to observe any other significant alterations from the expositional model: localized recompositions, deletions, or expansions. Mozart's normal preference is that most of the recapitulation's thematic/rhetorical content (setting aside the issue of the usual transposition of S and C) will be identical or nearly identical with those in the exposition's referential layout, resulting in an impression of extensive symmetry and retracing. In other words, most of the recapitulatory rotation will consist of *correspondence measures*: here, m. 94 = m. 1; m. 95 = m. 2, and so on. Similarly, within S, m. 119 = m. 23 (now a fifth lower, in the tonic); m. 120 = m. 24, and so on. Yet a few passages might contain telling differences. We need to discern which bars are correspondence measures and which are not. Which passages have been recomposed and to what end? And the same question might be asked of the passages that have been retained.

The recapitulation's P is identical to that of the exposition: mm. 94–103 = mm. 1–10. The modifications begin with the end of the first bar of the recapitulatory transition, m. 104, which slips off track from the expositional model. This is no surprise. Recompositions are common in recapitulatory TRs, since the MC that it is charged to produce has to set up a tonic-key entry of S, not a dominant-key one. The aimed-for MC, in other words, is likely to be a I:HC MC (as it is in m. 118, with the half cadence proper attained in m. 114), not the original V:HC MC (m. 22).

One of the easiest ways to accomplish this is to drift early on in TR toward the subdominant (because the imminent S is to be produced down a fifth or up a fourth) and then to rejoin the drive to the MC with correspondence measures down a fifth or up a fourth. In this TR, Mozart alters m. 105 with the now-familiar chromatic sigh figure, $B\flat_4$-A_4-$A\flat_4$, producing a subdominant-leaning $B\flat^7$ chord, V of IV, in mm. 105–6. The suggestion of an E-flat to come, though, is derailed at m. 107 (G_5^6, V_5^6/ii), and we are led through three more recomposed bars of characteristically Mozartian, minor-mode-tinged wistfulness, mm. 108–10. By m. 110, B-flat major is recovered, and at m. 111 the music shifts back on track with correspondence measures to the exposition, down a fifth: mm. 111–18 = mm. 15–22. We call the moment where TR rejoins the expositional model the *crux* (m. 111 = m. 15), and the preceding bars where the recapitulation had deviated from the expositional model the *pre-crux alterations* (mm. 105–10). As a result of the pre-crux alterations, the recapitulatory TR is longer than the expositional TR: 15 bars as opposed to 12.

With the entry of the tonic-key S at m. 119—down a fifth from the exposition, a darker, more sober statement—we enter the post-MC part 2 of the recapitulation, the broad section that we designate as the *tonal resolution*. In principle, once the recapitulatory crux has been attained (here, m. 111), the composer could simply copy out a transposition of the expositional model, shifting melodic register when desired or necessary: compositional thought could largely stop, yielding to sonata-form ideals of balance and symmetry. Any significant modifications made after the crux, then, are products of conscious compositional intervention—*post-crux alterations*—and the most notable of them demand our attention.

With one major exception, K. 333/i's tonal resolution, S and C, is built from correspondence measures: for the most part one could map the exposition's S and C bars onto those of the recapitulation's. Here and there one finds small, affective melodic alterations (m. 126) or a shift of register (m. 127), but the impression given is largely identical. The exposition's EEC moment (m. 38), for instance, is paralleled with the important moment of *essential structural closure* (ESC) at m. 134, the generically obligatory first point of tonal resolution.

The prominent exception—and a spectacular one—occurs at the end of the recapitulation's C¹. We recall that the exposition's C¹ was marked by the special-effect C^{1.2} leap into a quasi-hypermetrical weightlessness, two bars of it in mm.

43–44 followed by three more in mm. 46–48. Here in the recapitulation we find a display-expansion of that special effect. First, we notice that the octaves-reinforcement of the *fortepiano* third and fourth bars of $C^{1.1}$, mm. 137–38, provide for a more urgently prepared running-start before the subsequent grand leap. Two bars of leap, mm. 139 and 140, are still presented as correspondence measures, though with a yawningly wide registral displacement, and the anticipated cadence at m. 142 is again attenuated (evaded) with the intention of returning to an expanded, now higher-register version of the special-effect leap. With m. 142, though, we find that the subsequent passage is recomposed and the hovering in the air much expanded. Noting that the model, mm. 47–48, had articulated a series of descending fifths (D_5^6, g, C_5^6, F), Mozart now prolongs the descending-fifth "floating" for several more bars. This starts with correspondence measures (or at least referential measures): mm. 47–48 are replicated up a compound fourth, with right-hand variants, in mm. 143–44 (G_5^6, c, F_5^6, B♭). But in the post-crux alterations that begin in m. 145, the fifth-descent is made to continue: $E♭_5^6$, a°, D_5^6, g, and C_5^6 (at m. 147). Nor is the recomposition yet finished. The music pushes onward for several more bars, finally reaching its I:PAC and yielding to C^2 at m. 152. Mozart has recomposed and expanded one bar of exposition, m. 49, into a hold-your-breath seven, mm. 147–52, a *coup de théâtre*.

At m. 152, C^2, Mozart reverts to correspondence measures for the remainder of the exposition (mm. 152–65 = mm. 50–63, C^2, C^2, C^3). Notwithstanding the slight upper-voice modification in m. 158, their effect is that of a relaxed relief, a gratified rounding after the sensationalism of the altered end of C^1. The trill cadence ending the repetition of C^2 (I:PAC, m. 161) sounds all the more emphatic and final in this context, and the subsequent, circular relaxation provided by the twofold QUIESCENZA figure in C^3 (mm. 161–65) brings the movement to a satisfying close. Once the recapitulation has made its way to the equivalent of the exposition's end (m. 165 = m. 63), no more music follows. There is no appended coda.

3

Mozart, Symphony No. 34 in C, K. 338/ii
(Andante di molto più tosto Allegretto)

Before proceeding into an overview of Sonata Theory as a systematic approach (chapter 4), we should experience the analytical system in action once again, now applied to a different piece. As noted in the previous chapter, this mirrors the procedure that I follow in seminars, where I try to make more real the rudiments of Sonata Theory's conceptual style and sometimes unfamiliar terminology by introducing them through concrete examples and applications. Getting an adequate feel for the approach requires putting it to work in differing musical environments. Since each piece confronts us with new situations and challenges, it is only after unwrapping several of them that we get a clearer sense of how this approach is productively applied in practice. Beyond this, providing an *entrée* into the method through illustrative analyses can show its exegetical advantages. Sonata Theory's aim is not to provide only another competing academic analysis—whether for oneself, for the classroom, or for publication—but rather to awaken a composition from the sleep of canonic familiarity, to shake off its schoolroom dust.

And so, still in this introductory mode, we turn to a second composition by Mozart. The slow movement from his Symphony No. 34, K. 338, can strike us as simpler, more transparent than the one set forth in the previous chapter. Yet for that very reason it affords us the opportunity to reinforce core concepts already pressed into service. While many of the basic principles of Sonata Theory will resurface here, the choice of this movement permits us to advance our study by introducing two additional aspects of it: the concerns brought to the analytical table by all slow movements; and the deployment of a different, less common sonata format, that lacking a development section and consisting of only an unrepeated exposition and a recapitulation. As we shall see in chapter 4 and beyond, Sonata Theory calls this format the *Type 1 sonata* (*EST*, 345–49). (The more familiar arrangement, exposition-development-recapitulation, as in K. 333/i, is called the *Type 3 sonata*, and outlining its norms is the central topic of the next chapter. The other sonata types, 2, 4, and 5, are treated in chapter 11 and the appendix.)

Global tonics, slow movements, and keys

Slow movements from the Mozartian era are often written in a key or mode other than that of the multimovement whole's *global tonic* (here, C major, the key of the

A Sonata Theory Handbook. James Hepokoski, Oxford University Press (2021). © Oxford University Press.
DOI: 10.1093/oso/9780197536810.003.0003.

outer movements). When this happens, it takes place in a temporary *escape key* away from that tonic. In major-mode works the most common alternative key—the *first-level default*—is the subdominant, and this is what we find in K. 338/ii (F major). Other alternatives include the dominant and the parallel minor, and later decades would explore more adventurous choices. (*EST*, 323–29 provides a more exhaustive list and discussion.) Accordingly, the slow movement can enact *a swinging-away from the global tonic*, which will be returned to in the final movement or movements. In turn this implies at least two additional things that are frequently overlooked in discussions of slow movements. First, the key of any such slow movement is to be heard in relation to the global-tonic movements that surround it. Second, any appearance of the global tonic in the otherwise off-tonic slow movement is a notable event.

Consider, then, the diverging situations in this respect between a sonata-form slow movement in the subdominant key and one in the dominant. In the subdominant slow movement the exposition's normative secondary key will be that of its dominant, which turns out to be the global tonic, establishing a resonance with it but with an important difference: the key that had been *primary* in the first movement is now relegated to a locally provisional, *secondary* status, approached from its darker, more relaxed subdominant below. On the other hand, in the dominant-key slow movement, the primary tonality is that of the secondary key of the first movement's exposition, and its own secondary key will be a fifth higher. In these instances the global tonic does not appear in the exposition and the movement as a whole effects a shift into a brighter, more intense expressive realm.

Backdrop

Mozart was 24 years old when he composed the three-movement C-major Symphony, K. 338. This "last of the Salzburg symphonies" (Brown 2002, 393) was completed in late August 1780 and first performed at the Salzburg court in early September. The next month Mozart left Salzburg for Munich, now composing the opera *Idomeneo* for that city and, as Solomon reminds us (1995, 229–30), bringing this new symphony and a few other compositions with him in his portfolio "to bolster his prospects" of gaining a position there—which turned out not to materialize. The following year the composer would move to Vienna, a decisive move both in his life and in the history of European music. We are concerned here with K. 338's middle movement. In the autograph it is marked as Andante di molto, though in a lead part-book for a performance in Donaueschingen, Mozart added three words to this description, expanding it to Andante di molto più tosto allegretto ("Andante di molto, [but] rather Allegretto"), which suggests that he did not wish this movement to be played too slowly (Zaslaw 1989, 364).

Many of Mozart's slow movements from the later 1770s and early 1780s not only feature a remarkable simplicity of means and clarity of thought but also radiate a wondrously luminous glow that lights up their interiors. This movement provides a perfect example of that, and beyond any Sonata Theory action-zone parsing of it— an easy task—close readings are also invited to attend to the particulars of the piece's meticulously wrought details, that is, to the phenomenology of what it can mean knowledgeably to experience (or to *feel*) those moment-to-moment particulars as they move through us (or we through them) in the flow of time. This will occasion Sonata Theory's attention to musical motion and gesture to come more to the fore: its openness to affective-cognitive response, virtual agency, and conceptual metaphor.[1]

While the first movement had been scored for a full orchestra, including trumpets and timpani, this gauzy, intimate second movement pares down the texture to strings alone plus a two-bassoon doubling of the lowest line in the cellos and double basses: a galant-style reduction of forces characteristic also of several of the composer's earlier Salzburg symphonies. Mozart's attunement to the sensuousness of orchestral sonority is heard both in his dividing of the viola parts (Viola I and II, imparting a warm fullness of motion to the middle voices) and in his careful markings of dynamics, articulations, and other special effects, such as the *sotto voce* opening.

Exposition (mm. 1–81)

Primary theme (P, mm. 1–30)

When we open the score to begin our study of the exposition's first part (the premedial-caesura material), the most basic first step is to scan the opening section to determine whether there exist any tonic-key perfect authentic cadences in it and if there are, to locate the last of them, which will almost surely be the conclusion of the primary-theme zone, P. (For instances in which there are no I:PACs, see chapter 4.) In the case of K. 338/ii we find only a single I:PAC, and this occurs at m. 30. This suggests that P occupies mm. 1–30, and from there we can predict that the transition zone (TR) begins with the upbeat to m. 31. This initial overview frames our expectation of how the exposition's first two action spaces are laid out. We now need to look at the details of P, and then TR, either to confirm or to alter our predictions.

Our next step is the technical one of theme-type classification. It's obvious that the span of P, mm. 1–30, subdivides into two quasi-parallel units, statement and response, that together articulate a broad parallel period (classifiable as a *compound period* because of its length and more complex internal organization). This familiar format is built from a *compound antecedent* ending with a half cadence (mm. 1–14, concluding I:HC), balanced by a slightly longer *compound consequent* ending with a perfect authentic cadence (mm. 15–30, concluding I:PAC). As is often the case with compound periods, both mm. 1–14 and 15–30 are *sentential*—structured as *compound sentences*, each propelled toward its phrase-concluding cadence. Mm.

1–4/5–8 initiate the sentence's presentation (αα', alpha/alpha prime, with the eight-bar whole outlining an F-major tonic prolongation), mm. 9–12 the artfully compressed beginning of the continuation (β, beta) and its conclusion in mm. 13–14 with the half cadence (γ, gamma). Mm. 15–30 replicate the compound sentence's format pattern, only with extended continuation (mm. 28–29 are a varied repeat of mm. 26–27), and a final I:PAC at m. 30. In sum, P's layout is that of a *compound period* built from a *sentential compound antecedent* followed by a gracefully balancing, though extended and intensified, *sentential compound consequent*. Once we recognize the theme's structure, which can be regarded as its schematically preformatted CONTAINER (see chapter 1), we can proceed to consider the specific content that flows into and fills it. The musical interest of all this resides in the affective stirrings of its particulars: the pathway of expressive gestures, contours, registers, and textures with which Mozart lights up this galant-standardized theme-format.

Consider the initial sentence presentation, mm. 1–4/5–8, a yearning musical idea gently whispered *sotto voce*, like a tentative, intimately amorous avowal or confession. The upper line in the first violin begins with an anacrusis-climb from C_5 to F_5 to C_6, a stretching upward toward an apex pitch as its goal, that lingeringly caressed C_6, scale degree $\hat{5}$: listeners or performers are invited to feel this gesture of upward tightening. Mozart provides the anacrusis-ascent with an added, tender spur via the pseudo-imitation an octave lower in the second violin, tracking in parallel tenths with the upper voice. Once the upper-voice C_6 is touched in m. 2, its poised repetitions lean forward into the quarter-note C_6 in m. 3, as the lower voices now join in. Thus the anacrusis begun at the opening stretches all the way from the upbeat to m. 1 to the downbeat-arrival of m. 3, whereupon, in m. 4, the now-salient apex pitch C_6 starts its gentle fall back to the tonic with a sighing, stepwise descent to $B\flat_5$ (approached by a neighboring A_5 below). This is the beginning of an extended $\hat{5}$-$\hat{4}$-$\hat{3}$-$\hat{2}$-$\hat{1}$ descent found in the upper line of mm. 1–9 (and beyond).

Reinforcing the downbeat C_6 in bar 3 with an upwelling of sentiment, the first full chord of the movement is not a diatonic chord of F major but rather a relatively bright, altered chord, D^7 or V^7/ii. And when, exhaling like a wistful sigh, the upper-voice C_6 falls to $B\flat_5$ in bar 4, that pitch is supported by a G-minor chord, ii of F. The first harmonic move thus shades fleetingly into a melancholy, minor-chord hue, enhanced by the interior, parallel-third rustlings in the *divisi* violas in m. 4, which bridge the gap between the two presentation modules. When that upper-voice $B\flat_5$ is projected once again in mm. 6–7, it is now recaptured as the seventh of a different sonority, C^7, and that $B\flat_5$ falls to a tonic-colored A_5 in m. 8 (approached from below by a neighboring G_5). Looking at mm. 1–8 as a presentational whole, 4+4 (αα', a model and slightly varied sequence), we can see that the upper-voice $\hat{5}$-$\hat{4}$-$\hat{3}$ descent (the SOL-FA-MI schema settling on A_5 in m. 8) has been harmonically illuminated by a set of falling fifths: from the initial tonic in mm. 1–2, we have had D^7 (m. 3), g (m. 4), C^7 (mm. 5–7), and back to F (m. 8). The gently modulated descent from the downbeat high C_6 in m. 3 is complemented by the falling of the harmonic fifths. M. 8 is not to be regarded as an imperfect authentic cadence (IAC): not only does it mark the end of the sentence's presentation (which is normally not to be considered a structural cadence), but it is also the endpoint of the series of languorously descending fifths that had begun with the plush D^7 in m. 3.

Proceeding now into the sentence's *continuation* module (β, mm. 9–12), we find an instance of the fragmentation strategy so characteristic of continuations. Should we wish, we could label this as $P^{1.2}$—a second, interior module of P before any final cadence has been reached—relabeling m. 1 as $P^{1.1}$. In the $P^{1.2}$ continuation we see that the presentation's $\hat{5}$-$\hat{4}$-$\hat{3}$ seeks repeatedly to complete itself with a $\hat{3}$-$\hat{2}$-$\hat{1}$ descent to the tonic (A_5-G_5-F_5). These $\hat{3}$-$\hat{2}$-$\hat{1}$ descents are more urgent than the preceding music, pressing forward toward a conclusion. A finalizing completion of the descent, though, could occur only when the $\hat{2}$-$\hat{1}$ is secured with a tonic PAC. But within the broader phrase the $\hat{2}$-$\hat{1}$ descent is sounded "too soon." Over a more rapidly moving but oscillating harmonic pattern, the potential finality of the upper-voice $\hat{2}$-$\hat{1}$ is thwarted, as the $\hat{1}$ is supported not with a tonic in root position but with a I^6 chord (F^6).[2] We experience this in four iterations (mm. 9–11), compressing the falling thirds of mm. 3 and 7 from quarters to eighths, then to sixteenths, suggesting a growing frustration intensified by a crescendo.

At the same time the compression-and-crescendo sway in m. 11, like a mounting resolve, also serves as an energy-gaining anacrusis, springing free and upward in a surging, syncopated figure, *forte*, to m. 12's C_6 ($\hat{5}$) and Bb_5 ($\hat{4}$). This casts the linear descent back up to $\hat{5}$ and $\hat{4}$ (overshooting the proper chord tone, the C_6 is now an unprepared, quasi-exclamatory upper neighbor to Bb_5) and also, though only for a beat, shifts the harmonic cycle back to the G minor sonority (here a ii^7) heard in m. 4. M. 11's dynamically enhanced syncopated figure (which we hear repeatedly throughout this movement) projects a characteristically Mozartian onrush of emotion: the stylized press of hand on heart. The sentiment that had been restrained in the preceding measures now gushes forth before being brought back in check. In turn, the pullback triggers a realization, *piano*, that this opening phrase will not resolve with a PAC after all, and certainly not in this wide-eyed high register. What follows is the sentential antecedent's *cadential-function module* (γ, mm. 13–14): the stepwise descent to G_4, and with it, suggesting an air of resignation, a half cadence ending the antecedent phrase with the broadest of sighs. One learns here, then, that mm. 1–14's attempted $\hat{5}$-$\hat{4}$-$\hat{3}$-$\hat{2}$-$\hat{1}$ descent is kept from reaching I:PAC finality. Instead, it settles for what amounts to a $\hat{5}$-$\hat{4}$-$\hat{3}$-$\hat{2}$ descent and the half cadence that it produces to conclude a compound antecedent.

If one has attended to the affective pathway of mm. 1–14, it is evident that instead of presenting a single, relatively stable emotion, Mozart has invited us to trace out the delicate shades of an affective experience in flux, tinged at every turn with subtle nuances. With the emergence of the parallel-consequent response to it—the modified restatement leading into a more finalized completion (mm. 15–30)—we experience essentially the same thematic/harmonic pathway but with some telling differences. First, the first-violin melody is now placed an octave lower than before, re-sounded in a warmer, richer lower register (more grounded in a normative human-voice register, more earnestly heartfelt), and the widely spaced parallel tenths heard earlier (mm. 1–3, 5–7) are now more richly blended as parallel thirds (mm. 15–17, 19–21). Second, the sixteenth-note fill figures from mm. 4 and 8 now stream forth as eighth-note, descending counterpoints, flowing rivulets of sentiment that enrich the musical phrase's presentation modules (αα′, mm. 15–22). The result is a sumptuous version of the material, tinged with the sentimental pang of the augmented second, $F\sharp_5$-$E\flat_5$, in m. 17's G-minor oriented descent. Third, the continuation (β, mm. 23–28) is not only intensified with interior chromatic sighs (the D_4-$D\flat_4$-C_4 and $D\flat_4$-C_4 motion in mm. 23–24) but is also extended by two bars by leaping upward to the *forte* $\hat{5}$ (C) not only once (as in m. 12) but twice (mm. 26, 28), the second time vaulting up a compound sixth to regain the earlier C_6 register. Doing so allows the cadential module (γ, mm. 29–30) to accomplish and finalize in its original register the long-implied $\hat{5}$-$\hat{4}$-$\hat{3}$-$\hat{2}$-$\hat{1}$ descent, coming to rest—and ending P—with the I:PAC supporting F_5 (1) in m. 30.

Transition (TR, mm. 31–44)

Any P theme can be imagined as a *proposition* to build a sonata. The subsequent transition (TR) can be construed as an *acceptance* of that proposition by moving forthrightly into the next action zone. In most cases from this era, TR will be an intensifying or energy-gaining space with its sights set on producing a medial-caesura hard break as its end-boundary. In this case Mozart shapes TR as another sentence, and its *piano*-dynamic presentation modules (αα′, mm. 31–32, 33–34), along with the tiptoeing staccato figures in the middle voices, give the impression of setting forth on a new task. To what extent is this new material? Obviously, some of it recalls gestures within P. The A_5-$B\flat_5$-C_6 upbeat-ascent in the melody, for instance (with repeated C_6), retraces the same $\hat{3}$-$\hat{4}$-$\hat{5}$ ascent heard in mm. 1–2, and the inner-voice staccato-sixteenths figure, if we start our reckoning with beat 2 of m. 30, replicate the pitches of the *divisi* violas' fill figure in mm. 8. Nonetheless, the impression most likely provided at m. 31 is less likely to strike us as the onset of a subrotation (as was the case with K. 333/i) than as the start of a new idea. As such, we might prefer to think of mm. 31–44 as a largely *independent transition*, albeit one that fleetingly looks back to certain gestures within P, as if adapting certain earlier figurations to new purposes.

The first four bars (2+2, mm. 31–32, 33–34) suggest an F major leaning heavily toward its dominant, C major (V): notice the recurrent B♭s (mm. 30 and 32) with local inflections to B♮ in mm. 31 and 33. While mm. 32 and 34 are still likely to be heard as dominant chords within F major, the continuation that follows (mm. 35ff—also sustaining a C_4 interior pedal in the second violin) is better read as a prolonged predominant (ii$^6_5$) of C major (the symphony's *global tonic*), treating that key as the newly operative tonal center. The sentence's continuation also proceeds in differing but concatenated 2+2 units (mm. 35–36, 37–38; mm. 39–40, 41–42), additionally shot through with dynamic upheavals. Expanding on the tiptoeing-staccato figure, the first 2+2 set *rhetorically* (even though not harmonically) suggests the start of a new sentence. Consequently, Sonata Theory regards this as a *sentential continuation* (a continuation that starts with the modular pairings typical of a sentence)—one could label it TR$^{1.2}$—and the overall phrase from m. 31 onward can be regarded as a *sentence chain* or a *nested sentence*. In addition, mm. 35–38 rework certain gestures heard in P: its parallel-sixth figuration can suggest the analogous parallel motions in the primary theme, and the crescendo-swells in mm. 35 and 37 can remind us of those in mm. 11 and 25.

At m. 39, initiating the next 2+2 module (TR$^{1.3}$, still sustaining its predominant-chord function), the cautious, staccato tiptoeing gives way to smooth, legato slides: slow-motion, crescendo glides toward the imminent medial caesura. Adding throbbing pangs to the mix is the fourfold return, *sforzando-piano* each time, of the syncopated figure (mm. 39, 40, 41, 42) from m. 12. Additionally, at m. 39 the strictly parallel voicings are enriched with contrary-motion voice exchanges between the violas and the bass line. At mm. 41 and 42, the F♮ of the prolonged ii$^6_5$ predominant is altered to F♯, changing the expressive quality of the chord to an expectant V$^6_5$ of V. By the second half of m. 42 the process darkens with yearning, melancholy mixtures from the minor mode. While m. 42 begins as V$^4_3$ of V, the inflection onto the E♭$_5$ in the first violin and in the bass's chromatic slippage downward, through A♭, transforms the sonority into an augmented-sixth chord, pressing over the barline into the local C-*minor* half cadence at m. 43—simultaneously enhanced with a beseeching groan, the E♭$_5$-D$_5$ suspension in the top voice (a drawn-out variant of the preceding syncopated figure). This half cadence serves as the medial caesura (v:HC MC), which occurs after the first beat of m. 44. The conceptual hard break at m. 44, dividing the two parts of the exposition, is bridged with sixteenth-note *caesura-fill* (CF), and we are now prepared to enter the next action zone, and the exposition's second part, in the key of the dominant major—the global tonic, C major, of K. 338 as a whole.

Secondary thematic zone (S, mm. 45–77)

Secondary-theme space opens in m. 45 with a decisive tonic chord on the downbeat that lays down the new key as a pillar of security, one whose bass, C, will be fixed in place as a tonic pedal in mm. 47 and 49. Sonata Theory understands m. 45 as an "S^0" gesture that sets the accompaniment pattern into motion but is only preparatory to the theme proper (complementarily construable as "S^1" or "S$^{1.1}$"), which begins with the upbeat to m. 46.

We see at once that this theme is a brief, eight-bar (4+4) unit that starts at m. 46 and ends with a V:PAC at m. 53. Were this V:PAC to mark the point of essential expositional closure (the EEC), and thus the conclusion of S-space, that space could strike us as too brief, too perfunctory, in proportion to what we have heard so far.

But that cadence is followed by a repetition of the theme, extending S-space further. That means that m. 53 cannot be considered as the EEC, because that moment is defined as the first PAC in the new key that goes on to differing material. Any repetition of S, as here, undoes the closural effect of that first V:PAC, deferring the EEC down the road to the next V:PAC (provided that that, in turn, goes on to differing material).

Mozart shapes the theme proper, mm. 46–53, as a paradigmatic sentence ($\alpha\alpha'\beta$, or $\alpha\alpha'\beta\gamma$). Its reiterated tonic pedal in mm. 47 and 49 insists on the solidity of the new key, C major, and the hold of that pedal is released only for the cadential progression at the end (γ, mm. 52–53). Moreover, the rising aspects of the upper-voice theme outline the pitches of the C-major chord: C_5 (mm. 45–47), E_5 (mm. 48–49), and G_5-C_6-G_5 (mm. 49–51)—and *en route* we might notice how consistently C_6 is being treated as the apex pitch of all the action zones.

In a number of respects the sentence's presentation ($\alpha\alpha'$, $S^{1.1}$, mm. 46–47, 48–49) and continuation/cadence ($\beta\gamma$, $S^{1.2}$, mm, 50–53) present us with a restrained, formalized stiffness, an expressive contrast with what we have been hearing in P and TR. What emerges, albeit playfully, is the projection of a mechanized clockwork or a carefully groomed precision. What topic or image might be being suggested? The regulated, ultra-formalized dance steps lightly executed on a courtly dance floor (perhaps a gavotte?)—and in that sense continuing the galant orientation of the ruffled-sleeve, rouge-cheeked amorous play that may have been suggested in the music up to this point? Or, alternatively, the image of a mechanical, wind-up-and-gear-driven toy, like a drawing-room music box—perhaps playing a miniaturized march, as with that of figurine soldiers? Notice in particular Mozart's carefully marked articulations: daintily ticking staccatos in mm. 45–46, 48, and 50, pushing into the downbeat dissonances of the legato slides (galant bows?) of mm. 47, 49, and (at least in the upper voice) 51. In m. 51, with the cadential end in sight, we hear again the now-familiar *forte-piano* alternations, which press directly into the formulaic (quasi-"Cudworth") galant cadence (γ, $S^{1.3}$), completing the phrase by emptying out into mm. 53. While this eight-bar theme is likely to strike us as new, certain local effects of P and TR reappear in it: the C_6 apex pitch; the extended reliance on parallel motion (parallel $\frac{6}{3}$s, as in mm. 46 and 48, and parallel tenths in m. 50); and the ephemeral *forte* surges at unexpected moments (m. 51).

From the point of view of Sonata Theory the nearly complete repetition of this theme is instructive. All such repetitions involve the aesthetic game in which the listener can be lulled into thinking (or pretending) that the repetition is going to be literal. And in some instances that proves to be the case. One of Mozart's favorite devices, however, is to begin what seems to be a literal repetition but then to alter, expand, or extend it in one way or another, a technique of *phrase expansion*, often with wondrously brilliant effect, through a delicious (or perhaps spectral) florification of what had been only a local detail or through any of a number of other ingenious ways of delaying its cadence. In this case Mozart presents all of this theme as a literal repetition up through its penultimate bar (m. 60 = m. 52). He brings us to the brink of cadence-completion (and what would be the EEC) but at the very last moment (m. 61) fails to deliver the cadence. What we get instead at the downbeat of m. 61 is a "loud rest" (to adopt the term in London 1993 and 2012), a sixteenth-rest registering the absence of what had been so strongly anticipated. One viscerally feels this silence. Its effect is all the more salient because of the quasi-mechanized nature of both the theme and its repetition.

Instead of the expected downbeat cadence at m. 61 we are given a new, four-bar idea (call it, perhaps, $S^{1.4}$) that reapproaches the thwarted cadence even more methodically, through the start of a complete cadential progression (m. 64, starting on I^6)—but the cadence is interrupted a second time with another "loud rest" at the downbeat of m. 65. At this point the composer restarts the $S^{1.4}$ idea, quasi-mechanically, as a second try ("one more time") for the still-unsounded cadence, only now to enrich it with a characteristically broad, Mozartian expansion/florification. This one begins by passing briefly through the chromatic shadow-*frisson* of the minor mode (starting with the blurry diminished-seventh chord of m. 67 and the first inversion of the C-minor chord in m. 68). This triggers a six-bar, phantasmal drift in slow-motion, restoring C-major color along the way and ultimately clarifying into the reassurance of the invigorated arrival $^6_4$ in m. 73 ($S^{1.5}$). That arrival is marked not only with the return of the *forte* surge but also with the affectively charged syncopated figure, now spread into three different voices, *sforzando* (m. 73, recalling mm. 12, 26, 28, and 39–42). But even here, the cadence is evaded once again: mm. 75–76 produce instead only a stammering return to the cadential $^6_4$ that, finally—*finally*—tips into the V:PAC at m. 77 to articulate the arrival of the EEC. What had started out in m. 45/46 as a straightforward, short-winded S theme has in its latter stages been extended through the techniques of cadence evasion and coloristic, expansive recomposition.

Closing zone (C, mm. 78–81)

In the context of the expected proportions of the exposition up to this point, all that is required is a galant rounding-off of the exposition. Mozart provides this with a brief codetta of cadential reinforcement (C or C^{cod}), a single module and its elided repetition (mm. 77–79, 79–81), in which the quasi-mechanized motion is restored as a gesture of completion. (Compare the rhythmic staccatos of mm. 78 and 80 with the complete-cadential-progression lead-in in m. 64.)

Retransition (RT, mm. 81–84)

Since the recapitulation begins with m. 85 (= m. 1), there is no development. It is at this point that we realize that Mozart cast this movement as a *Type 1 sonata* (that with an unrepeated exposition and recapitulation only) and linked the exposition to the recapitulation with a four-bar retransition (RT).[3] The RT converts the C-major tonic of the exposition's part 2 into an active V (V_A) of the movement's tonic, F major. It does so by returning to the dotted-rhythm anacrusis figuration and parallel tenths of m. 1 and using them to climb to the chordal ninth (m. 83), a tense D_6. With its feel of having stretched upward with maximal exertion—or like a rewinding of the spring that makes possible what must follow—the D_6 is a new apex pitch, the highest pitch so far in this movement. (Throughout the exposition C_6 has repeatedly served as the upper-limit boundary pitch.) As the last gesture of the RT, the strained tension of m. 83's dominant-ninth chord rearranges its inner voice and relaxes—another broad sigh—before entering the reprise. In the process, the D_6 falls down a seventh to E_5, the top voice of V^7 of F major and an expectant leading-tone that will bridge the harmonic interruption at the end of m. 84 to the F_5 downbeat of m. 85, launching of the recapitulation.

Recapitulation (mm. 85–167)

To revisit a point laid out in chapter 2, confronting a recapitulation (or recapitulatory rotation) is a matter of comparing each of its bars with those of the expositional layout (the *referential rotation*). Which measures are exactly (or nearly exactly) replicated here, either in the same tonic key (in pre-MC part 1) or resolved into the tonic (in post-MC part 2)? Those bars are the *correspondence measures* (or *referential measures*, if their local alterations are better construed as compositional variants). As a symmetrical double-rotation movement with few complications (a middle-galant, straightforward Type 1 sonata), K. 338/ii presents few challenges along these lines. The recapitulation's entire P-space is a set of correspondence measures (mm. 85–114 = mm. 1–30). To be sure, we do hear a few new, but small, decorative touches (for instance, mm. 101, 105, second violin, while the upper voice of mm. 110 and 112 is slightly modified—affectively intensified—to produce that characteristically Mozartian chromatic sigh on the *forte* surges), but the overall effect is one of close replication.

The only significant deviation from the expositional layout occurs at the opening bars of TR (m. 115–20), the onset of *pre-crux alterations*. Here the original mm. 31–34, which had leaned toward a tonicization of V, are discarded and recomposed. Mozart replaces a four-bar passage with a differing, six-bar one that begins by tilting instead toward the subdominant (B♭ or IV, m. 115–16) and passing through a G minor chord (vi of B♭, ii of F, mm. 117–18) in order to land squarely on an F chord (V of B♭, I of F, mm. 119–20). With the upbeat to m. 121, the *crux*, Mozart places the music back onto the expositional-layout track (only now in F, of course, not in the original C), and with only a few upper-voice variants (mm. 130, 154, 156–57) the remainder of the recapitulation consists of correspondence measures (mm. 121–67 = mm. 35–81), either down a fifth from the expositional model, producing a more earnest, resonantly middle-register sonority (for instance, mm. 121–38), or up a fourth from it, yielding a more strained, high-register brightness (for instance, mm. 139–50, stretching upward as high as the F_6 in m. 144, the apex pitch of the entire movement).

Coda (mm. 167–74)

Once the final bar of the exposition has been attained or replicated, the recapitulation is over. (The downbeat of m. 167 = that of m. 81, the end of the exposition.) Anything that remains is a *coda*, whose normal role is to confirm and/or wind down the preceding action in a contextually appropriate manner. In the most standard instances (within a Type 1 sonata) a coda begins with a reference to the opening of P (the *rotation initiator*), and that is what happens here. The two complementary P-based modules (mm. 167–70, 171–74, to be compared also with the P-based RT, mm. 81–84) present us with a simplified version of the theme's incipit, cleansed of its original shadowing imitation. (In its unadorned, ascending scalar steps one might retrospectively hear a gentle preparation for the vigorous scalar opening of the ensuing movement.) The coda's eight bars trace through a relaxed chord progression—a glowing benediction over the past proceedings—that brings us to the final bar's I:PAC, m. 174. (As edited in the *Neue Mozart-Ausgabe* critical score [1971, ed. Christoph-Hellmut Mahling and Friedrich Schnapp], the double-bar at the end is supplied with a fermata, presumably suggesting, at least in the context of later-eighteenth-century performance norms, a longer-than-usual pause before the music hurls us into the Allegro vivace finale.)

4

The Basics

Sonata Types 3 and 1

Having been introduced to some of the terminology and concepts of Sonata Theory in the preceding chapters, we are now prepared to look at the essentials of the system as a whole. In seminars I usually deal with this through regular readings from the *Elements of Sonata Theory*, asking the participants to move section by section through assigned parts of that book. For the most part, I use the seminar meetings to clarify and expand on that reading through the analyses of individual movements or sections of them to demonstrate the method and its results.

The analogue in this handbook is from time to time to interpolate summaries of Sonata Theory's most characteristic ideas. I began that in chapter 1, which provided an overview of the theory's conceptual principles: dialogic form and genre theory, the normative action zones within two-part expositions (the P TR ' S/C succession), trajectories toward generically normative cadences, tonal layout and cadential confirmation, the significance of themes and thematic rotations, openness to differing analytical methods, and an eagerness to complement music-theoretical analysis with historically responsible hermeneutic readings. We turn now to a closer look at Sonata Theory's standard toolbox of ideas and procedures.

This chapter will revisit many of the concepts that we have already encountered in the first three. The present intention is to gather together and re-experience those concepts in a more methodical context while also opening a more expansive discussion of the issues and problems to which those and other concepts might give rise. What follows is an attempt to package Sonata Theory's leading principles into a single chapter. It goes without saying that each of this chapter's points invites further elaboration and nuance, much of which is found in *EST* and in the individualized cases pursued in this book's analytical studies.

Five sonata types

Sonata Theory recognizes five interrelated sonata types, each of which is appropriate for certain kinds of musical projects. All five are variants of the sonata-form genre that integrates them as members of the same family. All are similar in their expositional conventions. Where they are most unalike is in what happens after the exposition.

A Sonata Theory Handbook. James Hepokoski, Oxford University Press (2021). © Oxford University Press.
DOI: 10.1093/oso/9780197536810.003.0004.

- The *Type 1 sonata*, housing only a nonrepeated exposition and a recapitulation (and no development), with no link or only a minimal link between them. As such, the Type 1 is a *double-rotational sonata*: its two rotations, exposition and recapitulation, are directly juxtaposed. Chapter 3 has dealt with an example of it: the slow movement of Mozart's Symphony No. 34 in C, K. 338. We'll revisit aspects of this sonata type at the end of this chapter, at the end of chapter 11, and in the whole of chapter 12.

- The *Type 2 sonata* (or "binary" sonata), typically consisting of an exposition followed by a P/TR-grounded developmental space (or episodic substitute for it), and a tonic return to S and C material (but no "recapitulatory" return to P in the tonic within sonata-space, though a tonic P might turn up as the beginning of a post-sonata coda). Like the Type 1, the Type 2 is a *double-rotational sonata*. The difference between them is that the Type 2's second rotation begins *off-tonic,* as a development of P and/or TR that eventually proceeds into the tonal resolution of S and C. Chapter 11 will be devoted to this sonata type.

- The *Type 3 sonata*, by far the most frequently encountered format. This is the "textbook" sonata form, featuring an exposition, a development, and a recapitulation beginning with P in (almost always) the tonic, as in the first movement of Mozart's Piano Sonata in B-flat, K. 333, discussed in chapter 2. The present chapter lays out the basic principles underpinning the Sonata Theory approach to the Type 3 sonata, and it concludes with a few brief remarks about the more abbreviated Type 1.

- The *Type 4 sonata*, encompassing differing realizations of the "sonata-rondo," with its recurrent P refrains. Though it occasionally appears in some slow movements, this sonata type is most characteristically found in lighter, rapid-tempo finales and is often subject to playful, diverse realizations. The first part of this book's appendix provides a brief overview of its most prototypical features.

- The *Type 5 sonata*, covering the concerto-sonata adaptations most characteristically found in the first movements of classical concertos. This type precedes the modulatory, "solo exposition" proper with an orchestral, multithematic ritornello (or tutti) that begins and ends in the tonic key—as we find, for instance, in all of Mozart's and Beethoven's concertos and in those of most of their contemporaries. The format also makes room for later recurrences of ritornello (tutti) material as well as for a solo cadenza near the end of the movement, in the center of the final ritornello. The Type 5 impression can be that of a Type 3 sonata (for solo and orchestra) made larger by means of "extra," interpolated ritornello passages for the orchestra alone. Dealing with the Type 5's myriad variants and options leads us into more specialized waters: the four concluding chapters of the *Elements* investigate this sonata type. As is the case with the Type 4 sonata, an overview of the Type 5 can be found in the present book's appendix.

The Type 3 sonata: mid-eighteenth-century origins and generic centering

The Type 3 format is the one normally found in Allegro first movements, in some slow movements, and in many finales. Along with the other sonata types, it was developed in the middle decades of the eighteenth century mostly through ongoing enlargements of binary form, apparently in pursuit of more expansive and variegated structures. Those middle decades (c. 1740 to c. 1760–65) saw a number of solutions to this issue. While general tendencies of formal layout and tonal resolution in all of this are certainly perceptible, many of the individual realizations strike us as less predictable or standardized than what we more commonly find in the last third of the century.

As Morrow summarizes the situation (following several wide-ranging studies of mid-eighteenth-century symphonic practice), "the first part of the century can be viewed as a period in flux, because several fundamental areas of musical style were undergoing change." Even though "many of the earliest binary/sonata movements can be understood in [Sonata Theory's terms] in general . . . their default levels do not always apply" (2012d, 780, 783). This is indeed the case, and, as is frequently pointed out, analyses of such earlier works should keep this uppermost in mind.[1] (Even at the simplest level: at what point in the historical expansion of the first part of a mid-eighteenth-century binary form does it become more analytically efficient for us to regard it as an "exposition"?) While one can question the degree of applicability of Sonata Theory's categories to the earlier, nascent sonata or symphony c. 1740–70, and while I would gladly participate in much of that questioning, that is not the burden of this book.

That said, as a genre, and not least in the hands of its greatest masters, post-1765 Haydn and Mozart, with Beethoven soon to follow, the sonata-form genre can heuristically be regarded as having become *centered* as a flexibly construed *regulative idea* guiding both composition and text-adequate hearing within the main lines of the long tradition that would follow (*EST*, 605–10). Morrow, too, notes this:

> Though the basic elements of conventional practice were mostly there by the 1760s, the details of the measure-to-measure and section-to-section techniques— how to create energy in the transition, when to expect S, etc.—took another decade or two to settle in. By the 1780s, however, one gets the sense that composers— particularly the good ones—were actively seeking ways to disrupt or tweak the conventional expectations of listeners without destroying the foundation that made such surprises piquant and desirable. (2012d, 788)

Sonata Theory primarily addresses those last-third-of-the century conventional options and the ways in which they were developed even further—disrupted or tweaked—in the decades to come.

The two-part exposition

The most widely reproduced page from *Elements of Sonata Theory* is that found on its p. 17, which contains two diagrams—the most normative layouts of the exposition and (Type 3) sonata movement as a whole. It is reproduced here as Figure 4.1a–b and includes a small but important correction to the one found in *EST*.[2]

Much of what follows in this chapter deals with Figure 4.1a, the schema of a typical *two-part exposition*, one in which the two parts are divided in the middle by a *medial caesura* (MC), a generically articulated break or gap. At the exposition's end is usually another break, a *final caesura* (not shown in the diagram)—often

(a) **Exposition only: the Essential Expositional Trajectory (to the EEC)**

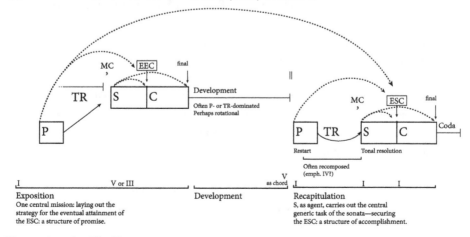

(b) **The entire structure: the Essential Sonata Trajectory (to the ESC)**

Figure 4.1a–b. The Type 3 sonata.

buttressed with an expositional-repeat sign—rhetorically closing off the exposition and separating it from the subsequent development. From the point of view of structural punctuation—a formal concern of several eighteenth-century theorists—these two articulations, medial and final, are the exposition's two *hard breaks,* its most generically displayed "resting points" of structural attainment and pause.[3]

Although both hard breaks became normative, they were not mandatory. Composers could disguise, smooth over, or erase either or both of them. Deciding not to produce an MC—composing through any presumed expectation of it, the lesser-chosen option by the last third of the century—results in not a two-part exposition but rather a *continuous exposition*, the important, alternative expositional type that lacks a clear mid-expositional break and new-theme relaunch. (Chapter 6 examines one of these by Haydn.) As for the final break at the end of the exposition, an earlier tradition of symphonic practice occasionally elided the final cadence of a non-repeated exposition with the beginning of the development—probably a holdover from earlier ritornello practice, as noted later in this chapter in the section on developments. And in later decades and into the nineteenth century, differing first and second endings at the end of the exposition would become a common way of modifying the final-caesura convention.

Figure 4.1a shows the four *action zones* of the two-part exposition, indicating them by letters. In part 1 (pre-MC), we have the *primary-theme zone* (P) in the tonic and the *transition zone* (TR) that drives toward the mid-expositional hard break, the MC. Following the medial caesura, part 2 opens with a renewed sense of initiation, a mid-expositional *relaunch*, in a non-tonic key. This is the *secondary-theme zone* (S). In an eighteenth-century, major-mode sonata its normative key is the major dominant (V); in a minor-mode sonata the norm is either the major mediant (III) or, less often, the minor dominant (v).

By the early nineteenth century, with only a few earlier precedents, Beethoven, Schubert, and others were exploring secondary keys other than those commonly inherited: iii, III, IV (!), vi, ♭VI, and so on. These alternative-key practices would become increasingly common in later decades. Additionally, some nineteenth-century expositions feature *tonally migratory S-space*: an S that begins in one key but ends in another. This is the *three-key exposition*, in which the second key (for the beginning of S) proves transient, unstable, and yields to a third key for the later modules of S, whose closure is usually attained in the expected dominant key. While Schubert was by no means the originator of this layout, it is one especially associated with some of his works.[4] The exposition of the first movement of his String Quintet in C, D. 956, for example, traces through the tonal plan, C major (I), E-flat major (♭III), and G major (V), effecting tonal closure in this last key. I set aside that three-key option for now, though it will recur in my discussion of the minor-mode sonata (chapter 8) and, especially, of the opening movement of Schubert's Quartet in D Minor, D. 810 (chapter 10).

As indicated by the curved arrow above Figure 4.1a's S-box, S's harmonic goal is to push toward and secure a perfect authentic cadence in the non-tonic key (normally,

V:PAC, III:PAC, or v:PAC). If this cadence turns out to be the conclusion of the exposition, or if the music that follows it presents new, essentially differing material (and not a repetition of all or part of S), we designate that V:PAC (or analogous-key PAC) as the point of *essential expositional closure* (EEC). That cadence is considered to be "essential" because with it the generically tonal goal of the exposition has been accomplished—perfect authentic cadential closure in the secondary key—even though there may be other textural, rhetorical, or narrative motivations to continue past this point with differing materials. The dotted arrow stretching from P to the EEC is the *essential expositional trajectory*, the vectored motion toward the generically expected non-tonic cadence in the exposition's part 2. Looking at the diagram again, we perceive, so far, an interplay of three trajectories: from P to the end of TR; from S to the EEC; and the broader arc from P to the EEC. Listeners or performers should feel the pull toward these genre-defining resting-points. Within an exposition nothing is inert, however temporarily calm, circular, or static any individual passage might seem.

Any new, differing material that follows the EEC belongs to the *closing zone* (C), whose tonal purpose is the further confirmation and stabilization of the secondary key. If the EEC occurs at the end of the exposition, there is no C. More often than not, though, a C-zone is present, especially in Allegro movements, and its length and style can be variable. It might consist of only a short codetta, or it might offer us one or more additional themes. When this latter option is taken, each thematic module can drive to a non-tonic PAC on its own, reinforcing the first one previously attained by the EEC, and the thematic portions of C may be narratively grouped with S as an *S/C thematic complex*—to be discussed later in this chapter.

Finally, a central claim of Sonata Theory is that the exposition's *ordered succession of thematic events* (the P TR ' S / C action zones) establishes a pattern that normally underpins the selective presentation of themes in later parts of the sonata, which usually "rotate" or cycle through some or all these thematic materials in the same order. Obviously, a recapitulation ordinarily traces through another P TR ' S / C succession (*rotation*); and—with some exceptions—the general tendency of developments is also to treat portions of expositional material in the order in which they had appeared in the exposition (for example, developments working first with features of P, then with those of S or C). This is why we refer to the exposition as the *referential rotation*, to which the sonata's later sections are a response.

Let's zoom in for a closer look at each of the exposition's four action zones.

Primary theme (P): initiating the sonata and the referential rotation

P is the sonata's point of departure. It establishes the piece's key and expressive tone, generically proposing that a sonata is to be made from it. P themes of this era are often what Caplin calls *tight-knit*: conventionally shaped, symmetrically grouped, tonally stable, efficient, and internally uniform and consistent (1998, 84–85; 2013, 263–64, 714). Most of the primary themes found in high-galant and early-romantic sonatas respond well to form-functional theory's system of theme classification: the sentence, the period, the hybrids, or their compound expansions (summarized on pp. 17–20 above). Quite apart from syntactic classification, we should also be responsive to a theme's texture and affective import. Does it evoke a standard topic or style (march, gavotte, fanfare, singing style, gigue, pastoral, tempest, and the like)? How does it move in musical space, and move us with it, in its determined vector toward a cadence: register, dynamics, contour?

At what point does P give way to TR? In most cases P will end with a cadence. More often than not—as with a complete period, sentence, or hybrid—the terminal cadence is a tonic-key PAC. Consequently, in approaching primary-theme music, one listens for the arrivals of I:PACs, of which there may be more than one. The last of these normally marks the end of P space. Any exposition with two or more I:PACs is considered to be *tonally overdetermined*, meaning that it produces more tonal affirmations than are needed to secure the key (*EST*, 73–77). The opening of the ensuing TR might react to such an overdetermination by trying immediately to wrest free of this reinforced tonal gravity.

When any first I:PAC gives way to a subsequent, differing theme that also ends with a I:PAC, we label the two different ideas P^1 and P^2. One notches the superscripted numbers upward only when new thematic material, still in the same action zone, follows a clearly articulated authentic cadence, usually a PAC. If P is merely repeated, even if varied, and proceeds to another I:PAC, both ideas are regarded as P^1, or simply P, unless one has chosen to indicate sub-modules within it with ad hoc *decimal designators*: $P^{1.1}$, $P^{1.2}$, $P^{1.3}$, and so on. In all cases, however, we should notice whether P is *non-elided* to TR, in which case there will be a clear break (a short rest) between P and TR, or whether P's I:PAC *elides directly* with the first bar of TR, jumping right into the sonata action. Both are common choices. In instances of the latter—P's I:PAC eliding with the beginning of TR—the impression often created is that of *P* as a broad, extended anacrusis to the more kinetic TR.

It is also possible for P^1 or P^2, if the latter is present, to be succeeded by a brief *post-cadential codetta*, extending beyond the last thematically generated I:PAC and inviting its own designation (P^{cod}).[5] This might consist of simple, non-thematic cadence reiterations: the first several phrases of Mozart's Piano Sonata in F, K. 332, give us a lucid example of this: they begin with P^1 (mm. 1–12), move on to a differing P^2 (mm. 13–20), and conclude with a cadential-reiteration codetta (P^{cod}, mm. 21–22). Two other common codetta types, both of which are elided with the final cadence of P^1, are: (1) a module sounded over a tonic pedal; or (2) a module not only over a tonic pedal but also circling through one or more cycles of middle- or upper-voice rotary $\hat{8}$-♭$\hat{7}$-$\hat{6}$-♮$\hat{7}$-$\hat{8}$ motion, the QUIESCENZA schema (see chapter 2, Figure 2.2). The role of each codetta type is to round off P with an "after-the-end" appendix that does not feature its own structural cadence. When a P-codetta is present, where does P end and TR begin? The general guideline is this: If a codetta comes to a full stop before launching a non-elided TR zone, it is always to be housed within P space. If it does not, and if the final element of, especially, a fully executed cadence repetition, tonic pedal passage, or QUIESCENZA elides or merges into obvious transition-like activity, we describe our experience by observing that what we had initially taken to be a codetta (P^{cod}) is retrospectively construed to have launched TR. As noted in chapter 1, the symbol for *retrospectively becomes* is ==>. Hence, when this reading of the situation seems intuitively correct, it can be regarded as P^{cod} ==>TR (or $TR^{1.1}$).

Another option is for P to end with a half cadence (I:HC), in which case P, ending with a short rest or gap, will not be elided with TR. This can happen with an antecedent or (perhaps sentential) compound antecedent. In this situation TR usually begins as a consequent (P^{cons}) but soon dissolves into TR activity (P^{cons} ==> $TR^{1.1}$). Since the P zone will not have sounded a I:PAC, it is considered to be *tonally underdetermined*: the tonic has been presented but not fully secured before moving into TR. It sometimes happens that P-as-antecedent is a rhetorically grand, much-extended idea that might even seem to enter TR-like rhetoric, to the point of extending its dominant-chord arrival with a dominant-lock and even a potentially viable I:HC MC, which "MC" is followed not by S (in V) but rather by a retention of the tonic key and the onset of TR as a dissolving consequent. Sonata Theory calls such a rhetorically broad P a *grand antecedent* (*EST*, 77–80).[6]

Still another possibility, especially in short-winded Allegro movements and in some slow movements, is for P to comprise only the presentation modules of a sentence ($\alpha\alpha'$) and to move into TR with the continuation (β; thus $P^{1.2}$==>TR or P^{cont} ==>TR). Since by definition a sentence's presentation is incapable of producing a structural cadence—one that brings a complete thematic idea to a secure conclusion—this situation, *TR of the dissolving-continuation* type, is one of the only cases in which the P action zone is considered not to end with a cadence.[7] A touchstone instance occurs in Mozart's familiar Piano Sonata in C, K. 545/i. P space is limited here to a mere four bars, which I read as $\alpha\alpha'$. The continuation (β) begins in m. 5 and is extended to a dominant-lock and I:HC MC in mm. 11–12, after which the secondary theme begins. In this case we are obliged to start TR in m. 5, even though m. 4 did not end with a I:PAC.

It sometimes happens that what seems to be the "real" P theme is preceded by a few bars that lead into it or that make an initial assertion that opens up tonal space before the theme proper begins (as happens, say, at the opening of Schubert's Fifth Symphony). We call such things P^0 (P-zero) *modules*, with the theme proper indicated as P^1. When such a gesture begins the movement, the analytical question is the following: Is this a P^0 module, or is it only a brief, in-tempo introduction that is not part of the ensuing sonata action? If those opening bars are included in the expositional repeat and also appear at the onset of the recapitulation (as with the first movement of Beethoven's Fifth), then we are dealing with a P^0. If they do not appear (as with Beethoven's *Eroica* Symphony and the Haydn Quartet movement examined in Chapter 6), they are regarded as a brief, in-tempo introduction.

Beginning the transition (TR): accepting P
and advancing toward the MC

Having just heard P's thematic proposal, the usual effect of the next action-zone, TR, is that of consenting to it and proceeding into the work of sonata-building. In many cases from the classical repertory, and especially in rapid-tempo movements, this means launching an energetic drive to attain the next expositional goal: the medial-caesura hard break (assuming a two-part exposition). Form-functional theory's "three primary functions" of a transition are also often in play: a *destabilization* of the initial tonic (though perhaps not its abandonment altogether); a *loosening* of the formal organization (away from what may have been a tight-knit P); and, toward the end of TR, a *liquidation* of motivic material (Caplin 1998, 125–38; 2013, 308).

Considered as wholes, TRs typically give the impression of accepting P with an enhanced textural, registral, or rhythmic fullness. This is most clearly the case in many symphonic expositions, where a *piano*-dynamic P is embraced at its final, elided, I:PAC with a strong, *tutti affirmation* (or *forte affirmation*) from the whole orchestra. Encountering this procedure is a strong cue (one among several) that we are leaping into the next action zone, TR. As already mentioned, such cases of P-TR elision can give the impression that the P action zone functions as a broad-space *anacrusis* to the more forward-vectored TR, where the sonata-action gets underway in earnest. Transitions, especially rapid-tempo TRs, normally convey a rhetorical *energy-gain*, even when some of their internal features momentarily feature more restrained gestures. Allegro-movement TRs that end quietly or are choked back in their final moments raise the questions, "why"? or "to what expressive effect"?

When does a transition begin? The simplest way into the question is to understand, first, when it does *not* begin. For Sonata Theory the rule of thumb—at least within expositions—is that it does not start in the middle of a cadential span, that is, in the middle of an ongoing flow between cadences.[8] We should not consider TR to start only where we perceive that the change of texture and function that we call "transitional activity proper" begins. Instead, having noticed such activity, we should back up our thoughts to where that cadential span had begun, even though it may have begun just as thematically as had P and not yet sounded like anything "transitional." We return, that is, to the cadential span's opening bar.[9] That TR-beginning can occur: (1) immediately following or occurring simultaneously with the last tonic-key cadence of P (either a I:PAC or a I:HC, though the latter cannot normally be elided to TR); (2) after any P-codetta that either has been fully completed or has come to a full stop; or (3) at the onset of a P-codetta (tonic pedal, QUIESCENZA, and the like) that we assess retrospectively to have launched a TR of the dissolving codetta type ($P^{cod}{=}{=}{>}TR$).

In some cases, TR starts with new material; in others, it takes modules of P-material as a starting-point for *Fortspinnung* elaboration; in still others, it begins with a recurrence of P material but dissolves away from it to become more fluid and free ("transitional"). Some of the most common TR types are:

- *The independent transition*: TR is launched with new material of its own (as was the case with the Mozartian slow movement discussed in chapter 3).
- *The developmental transition*: At least initially, TR elaborates modules from P. A continuum of possibilities exists between the independent and developmental types. Most seemingly independent TRs do share at least some aspects of P. The issue is one of degree. This is usually a judgment call. Which aspects of TR do you wish to emphasize? Its similarity to P or its differences from it?
- *The dissolving restatement*: P concludes with a I:PAC, and TR begins with the opening bars of P. A dissolving restatement usually suggests the onset of a *subrotation* of P (as we saw in Chapter 2 with K. 333/i).
- *The dissolving consequent (Pᶜᵒⁿˢ ==>TR)*: P has sounded an antecedent, and TR begins in the manner of a normative consequent.
- *The dissolving P-codetta (Pᶜᵒᵈ ==>TR)*: P has sounded a I:PAC but seems now to be entering into a codetta: repeated cadential units, or a tonic pedal, or perhaps one our two rounds of the QUIESCENZA figure. Instead of coming to a full stop, however, the codetta proceeds into transitional activity.[10]
- *The dissolving final element (reprise) of a larger, rounded structure*: Some P themes, especially in later sonatas, suggest the striving toward a larger rounded structure: the rounded binary format (aaba') or the ternary format (ABA'). When the final module (a' or A) begins, though, it does not complete itself with the expected cadence but shifts into typical TR activity.

Ending TR and part 1 of the exposition: the medial caesura

The medial caesura (MC), the dividing-moment of a two-part exposition, is a rhetorical sign of musical punctuation: a gap, a brief pause, a hard break, like a semicolon in a sentence. Its articulation is associated with the cadence or point of harmonic arrival (which often precedes the MC itself) toward which TR has been driving. More often than not, in galant and classical-era major-mode sonatas this harmonic moment will be a *half cadence* (HC) or *dominant arrival* in either the tonic or the dominant key, with that in the dominant key being more frequently chosen. For that reason, at least in the galant and classical eras, the latter is regarded as the *first-level default* or most commonly selected option offered by the genre to serve as TR's harmonic goal [*EST*, 25–26]).[11] In either situation the attained V will not be a tonic chord of the part-2 key (the key of S) but rather an *active V chord* (V_A) in either the tonic or the dominant.

Especially in rapid-tempo movements, the literal arrival moment of the V_A is frequently prolonged by means of a *dominant-lock*—a few energetic bars that sustain the dominant and drive onward to an emphatic end-point and the MC gap. (Form-functional theory refers to a dominant-lock as a "standing on the dominant.") One of the most recognizable features of many expositions, especially in rapid-tempo movements, the V-lock's generic implication is that TR's energetic activity, having grasped its goal-chord ($V_{A:}$), holds onto it as a harmonically controlling force and plunges forward determinedly with it toward the MC-gap that will bring TR, along with the exposition's part 1, to an end, perhaps emphasizing this rhetorically important moment with double or triple hammerblows. Scale degree $\hat{5}$ in the bass need not be literally sustained as a pedal point throughout the dominant-lock. While the V_A implication remains fixed, it is often elaborated through scalar motion or arpeggiation or decorated with neighboring chords.

It bears repeating: in V-lock situations *the time-point of the HC or dominant arrival proper is different from that of the MC.* Thus if the HC or dominant arrival is at m. X, the MC proper—the gap, the end of TR—can be articulated at m. X+1, X+2, X+2, X+3, or perhaps even a bar or two further down the road. A dominant-lock prolongs the HC's V_A up to the MC moment. For this reason a V-lock need not be construed only as a postcadential appendix (which in a literal sense it is), that is, as something that might carry the implication of playing only a subordinated structural role following the HC proper. On the contrary, the purpose of a dominant-lock is to keep alive the V_A that had been activated at the moment of the HC or dominant arrival and to drive it forward to its true goal: the medial caesura.

This is why we say that such an MC—the gap or breath—is *built around* a half cadence, in either the tonic or the incoming dominant key, even though the half cadence or dominant arrival proper occurs before the rhetorically articulated end of a V-lock. We notate these two familiar tonal options as I:HC MC or V:HC MC. (In many cases the closing portion of TR darkens stormily to the goal key's minor mode—producing a v:HC MC—thereby permitting the onset of S to unveil the major mode proper. Notice that in Sonata Theory's shorthand for any V_A MC, we do not distinguish between an HC proper and a dominant arrival.) The prototypical MC, such as the V:HC MC in K. 333/i (chapter 2), is a small gap of silence, a beat or two of rest before the fresh renewal of the exposition with the launch of S. In many instances, though, that gap is filled with a brief connective line or musical passage of *caesura-fill*, whose purpose is to bridge the gap between the MC and S, as happened in K. 338/ii (chapter 3).

Obviously, major-mode transitions that end with a I:HC MC do not modulate, even though the still-active dominant (I:V_A) that concludes any such TR may have been locally prepared by its own dominant (the applied dominant, V_A of V, which by itself is often not enough to signal a secured modulation). On the other hand, transitions that end with a V:HC MC will have modulated to the expected secondary key. The analogous options in minor-mode sonatas are the i:HC MC or either the III:HC MC or the v:HC MC, depending on the key of the subsequent S.

While the V:MC HC is more commonly encountered than the I:HC MC, within any given TR the normative expectations associated with the sonata genre make the I:HC option available for activation before that of the V:HC option. Once the opportunity for a I:HC MC has been passed by (perhaps by modulating away from the tonic, or perhaps simply by extending TR past a reasonable point where it might be offered), there is normally no going back to it; one needs to proceed onward toward the next available and more commonly selected option, the V:HC MC. *EST*, 36–40, refers to this as *the deployment sequence of medial caesura options*.

In some expositions a I:HC MC is set up normatively but is not accepted by the subsequent music. To be accepted, what follows an MC must be the opening of a genre-appropriate secondary theme (S) in a genre-appropriate new key. But this does not always happen. It might be, for example, that the immediately subsequent music rejects the MC offer by remaining in the tonic or veering off to a strange else-where, pursuing additional TR-like activity. These are instances of *MC declined*: not-withstanding the articulation of a clear MC, the music refuses to leave the TR action zone, perhaps, following an offered I:HC MC, in order to drive toward a V:HC MC down the road—the next available option in the deployment sequence (*EST*, 45–47). Analogously, a declined V:HC might lead either to a later-in-the-game V:PAC MC (see the later discussion of this option) or to a more expansive spreading of its wings to produce the effect of a continuous exposition, one that lacks both an ac-cepted medial caesura and an S-theme. Medial caesura declined is an alternative within the standard MC-treatment options offered by the genre. While always a striking compositional move, it is familiar enough to be regarded as a normative option readily housed within the existing generic system. It is not a deformation.

This is also the case with another relatively common situation in which an MC-to-come might be signaled but fail to materialize. One way for this to happen is for TR, midstream, to secure an unmistakable I:HC dominant-lock—in these contexts a strong predictor of an imminent MC—but then to shake loose from it before any anticipated MC is produced, as though the musical process changes its mind, or becomes "unfrozen," abandoning that lock to pursue more TR activity and even-tually coming to the next option down the road, a V:HC, perhaps itself seized onto as a lock. This is the *bait-and-switch tactic* within TRs: the circumstance in which music leads us to believe that it is preparing to execute one thing and then gives up the implication to pursue something else. Haydn often favored this procedure, and we shall see it illustrated in his quartet movement examined in chapter 6.

It is also possible, though considerably less frequent, especially after 1770, for TR to end with a perfect authentic cadence in V (V:PAC MC), a decisive sign of closure: full stop. How can we distinguish this from the point of *essential expo-sitional closure* (EEC), which is also articulated with a V:PAC? In order to come this reading, two conditions for it need to be optimally present. First, the V:PAC MC should occur reasonably close to the middle of the exposition, say, in the 50–75 percent range of it, not toward the last quarter of it, where we would more likely think of it as an EEC. Second, what follows it should be of a characteristic, familiar S-theme type, the recognizable style of S theme—"announcing itself as S"—that we normally expect from that composer in analogous situations where it would be preceded by the more common I:HC MC or V:HC MC. When these two conditions are met (and these are often judgment calls), Sonata Theory recognizes this V:PAC as an MC and the preceding TR zone as just that, and not as the broad center section of a continuous exposition.[12]

We are now in a position to summarize and complete the harmonic hierarchy of medial-caesura *defaults* (the most commonly available and selected choices) for MC production in the galant and classical eras, here c. 1750–1800, with Haydn and Mozart as the culminating figures of those decades of generic centering:

- In major-mode sonatas the medial caesura is usually articulated (in order of frequency of choice) by a V:HC MC (the first-level default), a I:HC MC (the second-level default), or a V:PAC MC (the third-level default). The HC MC options almost invariably conclude with the dominant chord in root position, though on rare occasions one might encounter an inverted dominant (or dominant seventh) chord before the hard-break gap as an obviously allusive variant.

- Two essential nuances bear repeating here. The first is that the MC-option *deployment sequence*—their order of availability as one moves more deeply into TR—differs from that of their default level, which registers only their relative frequency of appearance. The deployment sequence is I:HC MC, V:HC MC, V:PAC (*EST*, 36–40). The second is that TR's end is not infrequently darkened by collapsing into the parallel minor, thereby literally producing a i:HC MC or a v:HC MC that will immediately brighten into major with the onset of S, possibly via the mediation of a passage of caesura-fill.

- Within major-mode sonatas a far less frequently encountered *fourth-level default* is the I:PAC MC, in which a tonic-key PAC leads immediately (or perhaps through only a bar or two of caesura-fill) to the beginning of S. In most cases the impression given is that of omitting the TR action zone (*EST*, 29).

- In minor-mode sonatas the medial caesura is usually articulated by a III:HC MC or V:HC MC as strong first-level defaults, depending on the secondary key being modulated to, and the i:HC MC as a second-level default. In this last case, the i:HC MC is normally "obliged to yield at once—as a *quasi non sequitur*—to the tonic of the mediant major with the onset of S" (*EST*, 27).

To these c. 1750–1800 MC default hierarchies—the traditional generic hierarchies—should be added an important caveat once we move into later decades. In post-Mozartian decades, starting at least with early Beethoven in the 1790s, we find that the statistical logic of the earlier defaults no longer holds in the same way. The classical frequency-of-occurrence standard is no longer applicable, and the classically normative MC defaults are often rhetorically or harmonically overridden to produce striking effects.[13] Particularly from the often-eccentric Beethoven onward, one comes across what amount to transient "wrong-key" swerves and "wrong-key" MCs—"wrong," at least, in their purposeful veering away from the more standard practice of the generic tradition—along with other imaginative recastings of the MC hard-break convention. Many of these can be regarded as deformational alterations of the harmonic norm—deformational, that is, when read from the standpoint of the classical tradition's norms though not necessarily those of their own eras—but ones that nonetheless usually conjure up MC rhetoric (preparing and executing a hard break) and are followed by an "obvious" secondary theme that typically rights the tonal problem by eventually settling into the proper secondary key.)[14] In such cases rhetorical cues can trump harmonic ones.

Finally, we should note that some sonata expositions feature not merely one but two apparent but (usually) harmonically different MCs. The impression usually given is that a second MC is articulated in the middle of S space. When there is more than one half-cadence-oriented MC, the nearly invariable order is: I:HC MC, then V:HC MC.[15] When we have such *apparent double medial caesuras*, with each of them followed by music that is reasonably construable as post-TR (that is, as S-like), we have the special case that Sonata Theory calls a *trimodular block*, or *TMB* (*EST*, 170–77).[16] In prototypical cases a I:HC MC yields to an S-like theme that we retrospectively identify as TM^1 ($S ==> TM^1$). The TMB designation is invoked in those cases where what we have been regarding as S (soon to be reconstrued as TM^1) dissolves into TR-like behavior ($TM^1 ==> TM^2$) in order to produce a *second* MC (V:HC MC), which is then followed by a different, usually even *more* S-like theme, TM^3. While apparent double MCs are found in a considerable variety of expositions, the appearance of a TMB is especially common—almost *de rigueur*—in the first-movement solo expositions of Mozart's piano concertos.

The secondary theme (S) and the EEC

Not a few "new-*Formenlehre*" debates have centered around the question of the proper boundaries of an exposition's "secondary theme" (or "subordinate theme"). On what grounds can one determine where S begins and where it ends? Like many issues in formal analysis, one might initially imagine that such a question could be easily decided. But at present there is no consensus on this matter.

Let's turn first to the question of beginnings. Sonata Theory's view is that within normative classical-era practice the onset of S is usually to be determined when the following two conditions are met:

- It follows upon a clearly articulated MC (or its appended caesura-fill) and emerges in a generically viable non-tonic key. To qualify as a classical-era secondary theme, it should be recognized as a musical idea that *accepts the offer* of the preceding MC—the offer to step forward in a new key and begin a second phase of the exposition, the phase concerned with the stabilization and cadential securing of that non-tonic key.
- It is initiated with a fresh, mid-expositional relaunch: the onset of a new action zone, which in turn opens up the two-part exposition's second part (perhaps comprising both S- and C-space). It starts a new thematic process with a new musical phrase. Normatively this new thematic process contrasts with

the musical material that most immediately precedes it, that is, the concluding music of TR. It should give us the impression of something *freshly emergent and locally contrasting*, even in cases where it is initiated with the reinvigoration of P's basic idea (the *P-based S*, which is one of the most obvious ways of suggesting an initiatory relaunch).

To these I should add that, following a vigorously articulated, *forte* MC, many Allegro-tempo S themes begin with a drop to a *piano* dynamic and a *cantabile* texture, thereby initiating another textural or figurational build toward the close of the exposition.[17] While this is by no means always the case, when it does occur, it provides another signal that S-space is beginning.

One aphoristic wording of the onset-of-S guidelines set forth in *EST* turned out to be unexpectedly controversial: "If there is no MC, there is no S. If there is no medial caesura, we are confronting not a two-part exposition but a continuous exposition for which the concept of S is inappropriate" (117). Form-functional theory rejects that claim, along with the alternative format category of the *continuous exposition* (one without an MC and S), on the basis of a differing definition of "subordinate theme."[18] But the disagreement may be mitigated through a grasp of four different points. First, grounded in the generically centered practice of the late eighteenth century, Sonata Theory's claim is definitional, not ontological. This approach understands a normative S as that thematic zone which has been prepared by an immediately preceding MC, something that seems both intuitively persuasive and repeatedly demonstrated in classical-era repertory. Second, even though the MC + S guideline is an ultra-strong classical norm that should not be set aside lightly, it is not a rigid rule, nor should it be applied as one. One important feature of Sonata Theory is its conviction that "in free-compositional practice, *no default or norm is inviolable*. All are capable of being exceptionally treated, cleverly obscured or deformationally overridden" (Hepokoski 2016, 47, italics added here). Third, some exceptions to this guideline (a potential or obvious S that might not be prepared normatively), rare or almost nonexistent before 1800, are discussed and exemplified in both in *EST*, 48–50 ("Troubleshooting MC Identifications"), and in the 2016 article just cited.

And fourth—and to carry the question into later sonata repertories—while it is obvious that many works of the romantic and early-modern eras treat the classical MC + S convention and its alternative, the continuous exposition, with greater freedom—MC/S blurs, creative reshapings, and the like—the earlier guideline can usually be updated or nuanced to accommodate such things without too much trouble, and the resultant analyses can be helpful in perceiving not only such pieces' distance from classical practice but also their implicit connections with it.[19] Keeping the classical-era guidelines in mind (for those earlier norms also remained omnipresent in music-historical training, performance, and memory) puts us in a position to identify with precision just which features of later-era works were treating individual portions of the sonata in new or idiosyncratic ways. For this post-1800 music, even when some of Sonata Theory's guidelines are no longer as applicable as they had been in the Haydn-Mozart era, they remain a productive heuristic for analysis and interpretation.

Once S-space is entered, knowledgeable listeners and performers should hold themselves in an anticipatory readiness for its goal, the generic V:PAC (or analogous non-tonic PAC, the EEC), in order to experience *en route* how it is granted, thwarted, or withheld. In many cases the pathway from the onset of S to the EEC is laid out as a succession of thematic/tonal adventures. An S theme or one of its modules might temporarily be darkened into the minor mode, veer momentarily through a problematized chromatic patch, or lurch fleetingly toward a differing key. While simpler S-theme formats are certainly common enough (a sentence, a period, a hybrid, or a compound variant of one of these options), many S-zones are *multimodular* and feature a chain of differing ideas and expressive shadings as they course their way to the EEC. This is one reason that form-functional theory characterizes S as often "loosely knit" or "loosely organized" (as opposed to a "tight-knit" P theme; Caplin 1998, 97–123; 2013, 353–54, 709). In terms of tone and mood, the late eighteenth and early nineteenth centuries were familiar with a variety of different S types. Among them:

- *The bustling, staccato, energetic, or quirky S*: at *piano* dynamic, a much-favored S type of the midcentury galant.
- *The amorously lyrical, cantabile S*: a standard, graceful alternative to the preceding, commonly encountered in classical-era works.
- *The P-based S*: a preference, especially, of Haydn, the opening of S restates or recognizably varies the opening module of P (its basic idea) before taking that module in different directions. Steering away from the more generically typical production of something quite new, the P-based S implies an aesthetic grounded in the economy of materials, an ongoing treatment or processing of the all-generative P idea. This S type can be read as beginning a new subrotation complementing that begun in P.
- *S as a contrasting derivation of P*: while S may not literally return to the onset of P, analysis can demonstrate that the S theme is in some way motivically, intervallically, or rhythmically derivable from ideas set forth in P.
- *The forte S*: somewhat more unusual, the effect is that of an S that refuses to begin with a reduction in texture and dynamics but rather, for whatever reason, continues to bluster insistently onward in a *forte* dynamic.
- *The learned-style or fugato S*: a special-effect secondary theme, self-consciously evoking an older non-galant idiom; an often-strenuous display of compositional technique.
- Different types of S^0 *(S-zero) modules* preceding $S^{1.1}$ proper, of which three types might be mentioned here: (1) an accompanimental figure or vamp before the thematic onset of S; (2) an S theme that begins over the dominant, usually

righting itself onto more stable harmonies before too long ($S^0==>S^{1.1}$: what might be first heard as S^0—or is perceived to have a less-than-stable opening—is retrospectively understood as the "real" onset of the S theme); and (3) an S theme that begins off-tonic, perhaps arriving at the tonic only through a set of descending fifths (again, interpretable either, more simply, as $S^{1.1}$ or, if preferred, as $S^0==>S^{1.1}$). *EST*, 142–45 provides a discussion and examples of each type.

With regard to the question of when S ends, Sonata Theory's position is that the generic duties assigned to that action zone have been accomplished either with the single non-tonic PAC that closes the exposition or with the first satisfactory non-tonic PAC within S space that goes on to differing material. The reason for this is that "there is no generic requirement for a major-mode exposition to have more than one V:PAC, although many in fact do" (*EST*, 123). That is why this first PAC can be considered "essential" (the "EEC"): it is the single "essential" cadential task required to be done. The EEC concept resonates with Koch's later-eighteenth-century description of the galant exposition as a linear harmonic journey that, in a major-mode sonata, finally arrives at the last of its four potential cadential stations, an authentic cadence in the dominant (V:AC, usually a V:PAC). What Koch called the *Schlußsatz*, the passage of music designed to bring us to that cadence, is more or less equivalent to what Sonata Theory calls the S action zone.[20]

Since that first non-tonic PAC can, and often does, lead to additional ideas beyond the PAC, it is important to realize what is and is not claimed by the concept of essential expositional closure. The attainment of the EEC signals only that the generic cadential duties of the S action space have been fulfilled. *It does not mean that that cadence stops or closes any other ongoing successional thread that may continue beyond the EEC.* In the larger context extending to the end of the exposition, the EEC may turn out to be only the first in a number of thematically driven, obviously important PACs that produce closural effects of their own. Moreover, it may be that there is no explicit textural, rhetorical, or thematic disjunction between the S idea leading to the EEC and the differing thematic idea that immediately follows it. In such cases Sonata Theory's EEC serves as the first cadential moment in what is subsequently to be pulled together as the *S/C thematic complex*—a concept to be revisited in the ensuing section on the closing zone and illustrated in Figure 4.2. When one or more new themes and PACs are yet to come beyond the EEC, the only sense in which the EEC is granted a priority of "expositional closure"—considered in terms of the whole exposition all the way to its end—is that it accomplishes the first of these closures, the generically "essential" one. In such situations it can be helpful to distinguish between this *first-cadential closure*, the EEC, and a multi-thematic, rhetorically broader drive toward a later *expressive or narrative closure*. Nonetheless, the EEC is the cadence that satisfies the singular mission of the S action space and thereby

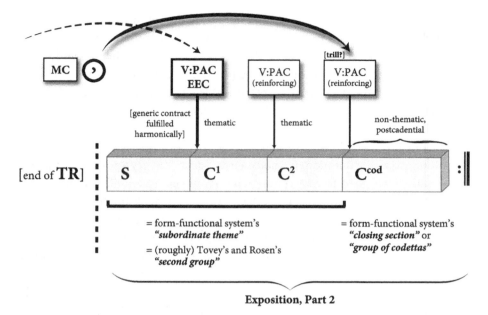

Figure 4.2. The S/C thematic complex.

brings it to a close, even though much more musical material can follow it.[21] Hence the caveat in the *Elements* (124):

> The EEC need not be—and often is not—the strongest cadence within the exposition. Stronger cadences . . . often occur as reinforcement-work in C-space. One should not determine an EEC on the basis of what one imagines an EEC should "feel" like in terms of force of unassailably conclusive implication. . . . Its "closure" may not in fact be absolute or "fully satisfying" from the perspective of the larger proportions or other telling factors within the exposition as a whole. This first PAC closing the essential exposition is primarily the attainment of an important generic requirement—nothing more and nothing less. (*EST*, 124).

This "first-PAC rule" is best understood as the *default starting-point* in determining what we are likely to consider as the conclusion of the S action space. Still, impressions of "closure" can be elusive things, and different analysts can mean different things by it. When we look at the analytical situation at hand more closely, it might happen, for any number of reasons, that we feel compelled to decide that this might not be the most persuasive or intuitive decision and should be altered. Nonetheless, the first PAC is at least the place that we first locate and identify as the most likely suspect, and in most cases there will be little need to change our minds about it.

While locating the first V:PAC in the secondary key usually presents us with no challenges (here, recall, "V:PAC" stands also for any structurally analogous non-tonic PAC), the larger question becomes: under which conditions might we *not* consider that V:PAC to be the EEC? Or: under which conditions might the execution of the apparent first V:PAC be either *attenuated* or perhaps so obviously surpassed in subsequent expositional V:PACs in such a way as to invite our questioning of its role in effecting a convincing S-space close? Analytically, this might not be so weighty a matter as might be supposed: at bottom, not much is at stake here. The larger point is to observe what is happening thematically and cadentially, not to insist upon definitive labels for these things. While not without some utility in helping us to reflect on what is set before us, debates about the proper location of the EEC under ambiguous conditions can devolve into speculations of not much import. We should note, however, that a first V:PAC, initially and locally imagined to be the EEC, can be retrospectively *undone* ("reopened") or *deferred* down the road under any of a number of commonly encountered conditions. Among the most obvious:

- The immediate repetition (perhaps varied) of either the S theme *in toto* or of the bars that had produced its cadence ("one more time"). This is the easy case for EEC deferral, and this is why the EEC is defined as the first V:PAC that goes on to differing material. The central guideline is that in most cases thematic material of what we choose to call C^1 should present a different theme from that of S. The obvious exception is that of the *"emphatically monothematic"* *exposition*, where P, S, and C are all initiated with the same basic idea (as in the finale of Mozart's Symphony No. 39 in E-flat, where P, S, and C all begin similarly).

- The revitalization of obvious S material beyond its first V:PAC, even when C^1 has begun as a new theme. This can happen when the apparent C^1 starts differently from S, only to incorporate (revisit) S material, usually S's cadential modules, toward its end. This might be regarded as a sign that S space has not been fully left behind: the revisited material might have recurred specifically to draw the seemingly new theme back into S-space, as a complementary S^2 idea. This situation can be represented as $C^1 ==> S^2$: what we first thought was C^1 turns out to be better regarded as S^2. Considering this option obviously depends on the degree of literal (or non-literal) resemblance of the back-reference to S material. Opinions can differ.

- The V:PAC is elided with a short, confirming passage shoring up that earlier cadence, and this short passage is then non-elided with fresh thematic material that follows. In other words, the confirming passage is more intuitively grouped with S^1 than with what follows it. Had there been no additional material after it, the S^2 would probably have been construed as C (another instance of $C ==> S^2$).[22] By extension, a clear separation of two C themes (say, a presumed C^1 and C^2 or even a C^2 and C^3) with a non-elided cadence, especially following one or more elided ones, might make us think twice about where the S action zone is best regarded as having been completed. At some point in our deliberation about this, the question becomes idle: little or nothing of telling analytical significance rides on this decision.

- The move to the V:PAC is attenuated, obscured, or called into question in one way or another: a sudden shift to minor, perhaps; or a drop to *piano*; or a pronounced shift of register; or the dropping out of an essential (but perhaps implied) voice, which might indicate that the expected cadential moment has been either attenuated or *evaded*; and so on. In all such ambiguous cases one weighs the contextual evidence surrounding the attenuated- or obscured-cadence effect and, with nuance and experienced judgment, makes a speculative assessment about the degree of closure that one wishes to assign to it. (We shall encounter such a case with Haydn's Symphony No. 100 in chapter 5.)

Finally, it is important to note that some expositions lack an EEC altogether: the generically mandated non-tonic PAC is absent. When this happens, the composer has staged the exposition as not realizing the normative, classical-era role that is expected within the genre. Such expositions typically convey narratives of cadential thwarting or frustration. Within classical-era practice (and probably within later practice as well), these expositions are most profitably treated as deformations. Sonata Theory refers to them as *failed expositions*, realizing, of course, that the "failure" in question refers not to a defect of composition but only to the dramatized outcome of the narrative plot that the composer is unfolding.[23] A touchstone can be found in the finale of Beethoven's Fifth Symphony, a C-major exposition that proves to be "unable" to produce a V:PAC/EEC, thereby forecasting that the recapitulation might well encounter the same problem in its drive toward an ESC (which in this case it does), resulting in a (tonally) *failed recapitulation*, and as such a (tonally) *failed sonata*. Needless to say, such expositions (and then recapitulations) are of special interest and invite our reflections about why the composer might have wished to produce them.

The closing zone (C)

From what has preceded in the discussion of S and the EEC—along with the Mozart analyses in chapters 2 and 3—it is clear how Sonata Theory understands the exposition's closing zone: C comprises all expositional material that we judge to occur after the EEC. While C material can be brief, as with a non-thematic codetta, it can also be quite expansive. It can include, for instance, two or more separate, melodically marked themes, each proceeding to its own V:PAC, with the whole C-complex capped off by a brief codetta. Reflecting on the mid-to-later-eighteenth-century galant "exposition," Koch referred to an additional theme that follows the *Schlußsatz* (Sonata Theory's S action zone) as an appendix (*Anhang*) or a "clarifying period" (*erklärende Periode* or *Nebenperiode*); in the early nineteenth century Reicha referred to such themes as "accessory ideas" (*idées accessoires*).[24] Such descriptions capture well Sonata Theory's concept of C-space.[25]

When we have a succession of differing C themes, each ending with its own V:PAC, each is given its own superscripted designation—C^1, C^2, and so on. An add-on codetta can be assigned either a number (like C^3) or a C^{cod} designation to distinguish it from thematic material proper. Any of the themes might be repeated, with or without variants or expansions. This might yield a succession like C^1, C^1 (again), C^2, C^{cod}, in which each of the units preceding the codetta can become increasingly intensified or cadentially emphatic as it brings us ever closer to the exposition's end. In some cases what seems to begin as a non-thematic codetta (music over a tonic pedal, for example, or the circling-round of a QUIESCENZA figure) can flower into a genuine theme with real harmonic motion. In such cases the designation can be something along the lines of $C^{cod} ==> C^2$.[26]

Following on the EEC cadence, C's traditional role is to confirm it, either with one or more additional PACs or with some other kind of tonal lockdown bringing us to the historically normative hard break that seals off the exposition. A situation in which C does not do this—a cadentially weakened or *nonconfirming* C, one, for instance, that begins thematically but proves unable to close with a cadence—can invite us to examine why that might be the case. To what extent might a C that proves incapable of confirming an EEC suggest that the latter's claim of tonal security has been unsettled? Can a *nonconfirming* C recontextualize what has already happened? These remain open questions. Confronting them depends on the local circumstances in which they emerge.

On the other hand, by 1800 and occasionally even before, the composer can convert the end of C-space into a *retransition function* (RT), sometimes under a first ending, leading back smoothly to the repeat of the exposition. Such an RT typically dispenses altogether with the generic hard break that had ended the classical exposition. The RT as a separable function can be especially unmistakable if it follows directly after a PAC at the end of a thematic C^1 or C^2 (a succession like C^1, C^2, RT). Situations where C (as a potential C^1) begins thematically but dissolves into RT before attaining a cadence ($C^1 ==> RT$) might imply a stance of ambiguity with regard to EEC confirmation.

C themes are not negligible add-ons. Post-EEC (and pre-codetta) themes have important rhetorical and expressive work to do and, as themes, they bear a structural complementarity to the similarly thematic S. Hence C themes are to be heard not merely for themselves but also in solidarity with the S that had preceded them, to which they display affinities as supplementary ideas or responses, important parts of an ongoing, quasi-narrative thematic chain. In that sense they can be conceptually construed as groupable with S. This brings up once again the question of what any analytical approach means by "closure" when faced with situations of multiple themes and multiple V:PACs, often of differing, perhaps increasing cadential strength. Since this often happens in Mozart's thematically prolific expositions, it is sometimes thought of as "the Mozart problem," which I introduced in chapter 2's discussion of the B-flat Piano Sonata, K. 333, p. 33, which might be reviewed here.

It is obviously possible for, say, the V:PAC that ends a C^1, a C^2, or a C^3 to trump S's V:PAC (the EEC) in terms of cadential flourish or strength, perhaps closing down the exposition's non-tonic thematic succession with a grand flourish or trill cadence, that unmistakable, classical-era sign of finality. As noted earlier (p. 67), from Sonata Theory's point of view such a final C^1, C^2, or C^3 cadence brings a different but no less important type of closure, *expressive or narrative closure*, to the full succession of non-tonic themes. One might suppose that the final, con-clusive closure of the exposition should intuitively be considered the EEC, but that is not Sonata Theory's position. The EEC and a fuller, more rhetorically com-plete sense of narrative closure often occur at two different expositional points. To label a theme as C^1 or C^2 does not mean that that theme and its cadence are expressively subordinated in significance to the one that had produced the EEC. Sonata Theory claims no priority for the EEC with regard to rhetorical force or expressive closure (or, for that matter, with regard to the Schenkerian *Urlinie* [*EST*, 147–49]). Instead, this approach proposes only that when considering themes, it can be helpful to use a labeling system that indicates whether or not we have already reached that first V:PAC. The label C^1 tells us at once that that has been accomplished, and that fact can be contextually useful and hermeneutically productive to know. But any C^1, C^2, or C^3 may well pursue and perhaps intensify a string of expressive ideas that are manifestly connectable with what had been begun with S.

To the vectors in Figure 4.1a–b at the beginning of this chapter, we can add an-other one (as suggested in the preceding section) to suggest a broadly arced trajec-tory from the beginning of S to the conclusion of the C themes, lasting, in principle, up to whatever might seem to be an obvious (*non-thematic*) codetta, winding down the accumulated tension. New to this handbook, this trajectory, the *S/C thematic complex*, is shown in Figure 4.2. It is essentially the same thing that other analytical systems refer to as the "secondary (or subordinate) theme group."

Normally differing from their preceding S, C^1 and C^2 or C^3 themes can appear in any number of thematic formats and styles, though certain kinds of closing themes are worth remarking upon. The *P-based C*, for instance (often sounded in a declar-ative *forte*), is a frequently encountered choice for C^1, suggesting that the opening of C space is marked by a return to materials from the opening theme. From time to time, in difficult-to-decide EEC situations, the strong reappearance of such P-based material can help us to decide when the closing zone is best regarded as starting.

On other occasions C^1 might return to materials from TR. And once again, while by definition (that of the EEC) C^1 and any subsequent closing themes should differ from S, an exception must be made for expositions in which P, S, and C^1 are all thematically based on the same material. Sonata Theory refers to this unusually strict procedure as the *emphatically monothematic exposition*. While one might automatically think of Haydn in such cases, it also crops up elsewhere. As already mentioned, one touchstone instance occurs in the finale of Mozart's Symphony No. 39. Moreover, in Haydn's so-called monothematic expositions, those featuring his commonly encountered P-based S, the composer often opens C space with a markedly contrasting, relaxed, rustic, or "simple" theme, as if registering the satisfaction of having strenuously attained the EEC. In Haydn such a strongly marked procedure—a sudden relaxation into more obvious thematic material in the last phases of the exposition—can help us identify problematically deformational EEC moments that are strongly attenuated, muffled, or obscured, as happens in the opening movement of his Symphony No. 100 in G (see chapter 5).

Let's turn now to the remaining sections of a Type 3 sonata movement: the development and recapitulation (Figure 4.1b).

Developmental space

The development is the freer, middle portion of the Type 3 sonata. Since a variety of things can happen within it, it is less suitable for generic diagramming. In prototypical cases it "develops" some of the exposition's themes or motives while tracking through different tonal colors and moods—pathways of tonal and affective instability. Some of these may be cadentially confirmed as secured modulations, though we might also encounter the insertion of a separate episode largely unrelated, at least on the surface, to the expositional materials (as we saw in chapter 2 with Mozart's K. 333/i). Since such post-expositional, pre-recapitulatory spaces do not always develop earlier material in the classic sense—cases abound in which the development is not self-evidently "developmental"—it can be helpful to think of that broad, central section, more inclusively, as the *developmental space*. In Mozart's Overture to *Die Entführung aus dem Serial*, for instance, the entire developmental space is occupied by a contrasting-tempo, lyrical episode based on one of the opera's early arias. In such cases "developmental space" means only the space where a normative development would be, if there were one.

One standard classical-era procedure (a *first-level default* with regard to tonality) is to begin the development by briefly setting forth in the key of the exposition's end (V) only to dissolve that tonal attraction by shifting elsewhere, not infrequently by a succession of descending fifths. When that is the case, the first lower fifth visited will be that of the movement's tonic, touched upon as a temporary way-station on the road to somewhere else. (Such a recurrence of the tonic key early on in the development, particularly when realized with the initial bars of the P theme, has led some commentators to speculate about the possibility of a "premature reprise," a concept that Sonata Theory does not endorse: "Early appearances of the tonic in the development normally carried few or no recapitulatory implications" [*EST*, 208].) Other developments introduce a new tonal color right at the start, either with a shock effect (as in the opening movement of Beethoven's Symphony No. 1) or with something more gradual.

Moving from the opening tonal area to others is usually accomplished through familiar harmony-and-voice-leading patterns: centralized *model-sequence procedures* grounded in fifth-oriented motion, ascending or descending 5–6 sequences, or other analogous operations. In the most straightforward instances Caplin's category of a developmental "core"—"that part of the development in which the traditional aesthetic sense of a 'working-out' of the material is most prominently expressed" (1998, 142)—is similar to Sonata Theory's concept of a development's *central action* or *central set of actions* (*EST*, 229–30). Major-mode movements often move toward minor-mode, distressed, or stormy passages in the center of their developments (in vi or iii, for instance) and can even provide a half cadence or authentic cadence in that key, as if momentarily swallowed up or captured by it.

Typically, the developmental space will end on a harmonically active dominant chord (V_A), most commonly V_A of the tonic (though there are other options, especially those leaning toward vi or iii), perhaps extended as a dominant-lock (a prolongation of the V chord) and often ending with yet another hard-break caesura (a harmonic interruption) before proceeding into the recapitulation. It is also possible—and common—for the development's end to be smoothed into the recapitulation through a brief passage of retransition (RT), not shown in Figure 4.1b. And at times it is difficult to avoid the impression that the development flows directly into the recapitulation with an elided authentic cadence in the tonic, though this should be taken as a local PAC, not a deep-structural one.[27] In practice, composers use a variety of means by which the development/recapitulation seam is traversed. Analysts should remain flexible in approaching them.

All such tonal observations are commonplaces in discussions of development sections. Where Sonata Theory differs from other accounts is in its attention to the ordered presentation of the development's thematic materials, all or most of which will usually have been derived from the exposition. While in some (misleadingly exaggerated) sense it may be true that "anything can happen," by far the most common thing to find is that the expositional materials selected for developmental treatment appear in the order in which they had been presented in the exposition. Recall that the exposition provides us with the movement's *referential rotation*, the succession of musical zones to which subsequent sections respond. Consequently, when analyzing developments we should determine the degree to which they too may be considered *rotational*. This is done by noting the leading thematic bases of the various developmental sections.

Most prototypically, the sonata's development begins by reverting to the exposition's part-1 (pre-MC) thematic material, most often P, the *rotation initiator*, thereby starting a second rotation. This P-onset may or may not eventually proceed to treat the exposition's part-2 (post-MC) materials (S or C) before the tonic-key onset of the recapitulation. Launching the development with P-materials is one of the sonata's many inheritances from galant practice and particularly from those realizations of binary form in which each of the two repeated parts starts with the same or similar head motive. Beginning a development with a clear, non-tonic reference to P may be regarded as a relatively strong *first-level default*, though like all first-level defaults it is by no means mandatory. (It can be enlightening, for instance, to observe how often Mozart steers clear of this norm in order to find another way to enter into his developments.)

A special case: the sonata-ritornello blend

While P-based developmental openings in the key in which the exposition had ended are legion, it is worth our while to single out a special version of it (not mentioned in *EST*) sometimes found in earlier, galant works from the 1730s, 1740s, and 1750s and occasionally, though more rarely, cropping up as late as the 1770s, though aspects of its influence lingered even longer than that. This is the situation in which at least two criteria are met: (1) *no repeats are indicated throughout the movement*, which means that our first sense of it occurs when the exposition is not repeated; and (2) *the exposition's final PAC elides with the extended return, in the same non-tonic key, of several bars of the opening of an energetic P*, providing a full or nearly full statement of that P. Under these conditions the concluding moment of the non-repeated exposition simultaneously pulls the trigger setting off a second rotation in that same key, and this initiates a non-tonic developmental space launched by a near-verbatim transposition of several of P's opening bars. Yust's observation regarding that procedure's impact is well taken: "Because the primary formal principle is repetition [as opposed to that, say, of form-defining hard breaks], caesura is generally avoided throughout, giving these forms a feeling of relentless forward momentum" (2018, 274).[28]

Specialists in the midcentury galant repertory have regarded this procedure as a lingering vestige of Baroque *ritornello form*, which with Vivaldi and others earlier in the century had become the mainstay of much concerto practice, one that was also "characteristic especially of the Italian overture" (Yust 2018, 269). And yet, "by the 1730s," as McClymonds reminds us, "the idea of composing all three movements [of the Italian overture] in non-repeating binary forms had quickly taken hold. First movements in particular bore unmistakable sonata characteristics," and their expositions were soon to include the "formal clarity . . . [of] functional areas clearly defined by means of cadences, tutti rests, contrasting melodic materials, dynamics, and textures" (2012, 117–19)—the emergence of what Sonata Theory calls the expositional action zones, P TR' S / C. In short, earlier ritornello practice was being crafted to sync with the emerging sonata format, only in this "Italian-Overture" case without the repeats associated with binary structures.

When that format is our "textbook," Type 3 sonata, the elided, quasi-verbatim P (the ritornello) will be sounded at least three times: in a major-mode work it opens the exposition in I, the development in V, and the recapitulation in I. Considering the resultant structure of sonata space, this is sometimes referred to as a *three-ritornello* structure, one that has been organized along Sonata Theory's Type 3 format; or, conversely, it can be regarded as a Type 3 sonata that adopts some distinctive features of earlier ritornello form. When an appended coda follows the recapitulation, that (post-sonata) coda, similarly, is likely to begin with a near-verbatim recycling of much of P, now in the tonic, bringing the movement to a close—in effect producing a four-ritornello structure to the whole. (Coexisting with the three-ritornello sonata-space version was a two-ritornello version, sometimes with a third ritornello appended as a post-sonata, half-rotational coda. The two-ritornello version syncs with Sonata Theory's Type 2 format or "binary" sonata, the topic of chapter 11, where we shall revisit the ritornello concept.)

What we should keep in mind, then, is that Type 3 sonatas that lack repeats and also elide the final cadence of their expositions with nearly verbatim statements of P in the same key are exemplars of this sonata-ritornello blend.[29] This is largely a midcentury practice, however, and as we get closer to the end of the eighteenth century there are ever-fewer instances of them. Yust calls attention to the "ritornello form" in the first movement of Mozart's Symphony No. 26 in E-flat, K. 184 (1773), a three-movement symphony that as a whole adopts the older Italian-overture format, since its three movements are connected without breaks (2018, 270). From our perspective this initial movement is a paradigmatic sonata-ritornello blend, with a return to the ritornello in the coda.[30] A more thematically complex blend is provided in the first movement of Mozart's Symphony No. 31 in D, "Paris" (1778), though there the coda (m. 284) begins not with P proper, but rather with a six-bar anacrusis-build to a brief return of P's head motive to conclude the movement (mm. 290–95).[31]

An instructive variant, leaning more toward Type 3 than ritornello practice, can be found in the opening movement of Mozart's Symphony No. 34 in C, K. 338 (1780). While lacking all repeats, this movement dispenses altogether with P-ritornello 2—a key indicator of ritornello influence. (In so doing it also steers clear of the normative first-level-default P-option at the beginning of the non-elided developmental space, which is introduced by the linking passage at m. 112 before moving into an extended episode). The movement continues by shortening P-ritornello 3 (at the recapitulation, m. 158, which is non-elided with the end of the development) and returning to a somewhat fuller version of it to start a cadentially elided coda (m. 237). And the idiosyncratic, ritornello-oriented structures of C. P. E. Bach's Hamburg symphonies from the 1770s are special cases altogether.[32]

Developmental space: common rotational options

Quite apart from the increasing infrequent situation of the sonata-ritornello blend, the larger point, once again, is that the first-level default for all Type 3 developments is to begin with at least an allusion to P. No extended or "full-ritornello" replication is necessary. It might suffice to start developing P's head motive. Nonetheless, once we perceive an aspect of P (or possibly TR) at the opening of a development, the question of rotational ordering is immediately called up. With regard to thematic rotations within developments, the following considerations apply:

- If part-1 materials (P or TR) eventually give way to a selection of part-2 materials (either S or C, or both), the development is *fully rotational*. In some cases one might even find a medial-caesura effect in the center of the development, followed by the onset of S in a key other than the tonic or dominant. From the standpoint of the rotation concept, how much of the development is occupied by part-1 material and how much by part-2 material is irrelevant, as are the keys and modes that those materials traverse.
- If only part-1 materials are developed, the development is *half-rotational*, and a new rotation will begin with the P-onset of the recapitulation.
- If a fully rotational succession of materials (for instance, P, then C) gives way to another onset of P (the rotation initiator) midway through the development, it may be that a new rotation within the development is starting. While infrequently encountered, some developments can be *double-rotational* or perhaps feature a full rotation and a subsequent half-rotation. The mid-developmental reappearance of an on- or off-tonic P can also lead to the complex, not easily resolved question of the *false-recapitulation effect*, which issue I defer here to *EST*, 221–28.
- When the development does not begin with part-1 materials (when its opening and much of what follows is S- or C-based), it can be regarded as *nonrotational*. This can invite the interpretive question of why this is occurring. What in the exposition—perhaps at its end—might have called for this kind of development? Why is the more normative P-onset not present? Was there an issue or problem suggested by either S or C in the exposition? Could the initial persistence of a telling unit of C, for example, suggest that the expositional rotation was not conceptually closed and that its rotation is spilling over in the developmental space, in a sense blocking out the more normative appearance of P?
- It is possible for a brief, inserted episode or link (new material) to precede the development's part-1 material, in effect pushing the onset of the developmental rotation or half-rotation forward in time.
- Sonata Theory also allows the possibility of rotational identifiers (themes) to be *written over* with differing material. A development might begin episodically with new material, for instance, only to proceed into TR, S, or C. Here, given the relative strength of the generic norm of beginning the development with P, one might suggest that P is being written over by the new material. P, that is, might be conceptually present but acoustically absent. Any such claims and their potential implications dive deeply into the conceptual underpinnings of Sonata Theory, and the interested reader is invited to pursue them in the *Elements* (212–15, 373–76).

Recapitulation (or recapitulatory rotation)

Recapitulation theory is not as simple a matter as might be supposed. The recapitulation's tonal/generic goal, of course, is to revisit and resolve at least the most marked elements of the exposition's non-tonic S and C, which, now in the tonic, comprise the sonata's *tonal resolution*. The equivalent of the exposition's EEC is the recapitulation's ESC, the point of *essential structural closure* (major I:PAC or minor i:PAC). Because S and C are so often sounded intact, or largely so, the recapitulation's ESC-moment will usually be the tonic-key equivalent of the exposition's EEC-point. Any exceptions to this are notable events. Normally, the exposition and recapitulation end with the same or very similar music. When the last module of the exposition's referential layout has been re-sounded in the recapitulation, the sonata structure is complete. Any significantly extended music after that is no longer in sonata space. Instead, it belongs to the coda, which Sonata Theory regards, along with any pre-sonata introductory music, as a *parageneric* space or *not-sonata space* (*EST*, 281–305).

Turning back to compare Figure 4.1b with 4.1a, we see that another, longer-range vector has been added. This is the *essential sonata trajectory*, the arc from the exposition's P to the recapitulation's ESC. It is only with the closure provided by the ESC that the tonic key proposed at the outset of the exposition is ratified and stabilized. The exposition's opening key had been offered only as a starting-point, one that would be left behind in its generically mandated branchings-out into other harmonic areas. Even the normative return of the tonic P at the onset of the recapitulation is not yet a moment where the tonic key is adequately secured. That will happen only at the ESC, the moment when it is finally clear, or at least implicit, that the tonic key has finally been fastened down and will no longer (one hopes) be lost, leaving only C space, if C space there is, to celebrate or confirm that security. With the ESC the sonata's harmonic journey has been brought to its generically mandated tonal goal.

Broadly conceived, the exposition, moving from an initial tonic to the non-tonic S and C, can be considered a *structure of promise*. Now that the sonata is underway in its harmonic and thematic journey, the promise is that of an eventual recovery and cadential affirmation of the tonic key after a tonal deviation away from it. This is why the recapitulation is a *structure of accomplishment*: it fulfills the promise of the exposition. That, at least, is what should happen, or, more precisely, what the prototypical constructions of the genre lead us to expect should happen. As all music analysts know, though, individual realizations of all aspects of the Type 3 sonata and of the other types as well frequently introduce moments of complexity, challenge, surprise, or nonconformity to the most common options (the generic defaults). It is with those deviations from the strongest classical-era norms where the theory of recapitulatory structures takes a turn toward the complex.

As has been observed in chapters 2 and 3, the first task of a Sonata Theory analyst in examining a recapitulation is to compare it, measure for measure, with its thematic-design model in the referential rotation. What is *thematically* the same, and what is different? (In this task, tonality is irrelevant. Obviously, the exposition's S and C will usually be replicated nearly verbatim, albeit now in the tonic, not in the original non-tonic key.) Bars that are thematically the same or very nearly the same as they had been in the expositional model are called *correspondence measures*. Bars that deviate further from their model but still clearly allude to them are called *referential measures*. Distinguishing between correspondence measures and referential measures is a matter of judgment and the connotative implications of terminology. The first term stresses their similarity to their expositional models, while the second notes the similarity but underscores their divergences from it. Thus I ask students to evaluate and notate into their scores which of the recapitulation's bars are the correspondence or referential measures. If, say, the recapitulation starts in m. 90, I ask them to write, in successive bars: 90=1, 91=2, 93=3 (or just =1, =2, =3), and so on.

At some point, typically toward the end of P or in parts of TR, the correspondence measures will stop, and the composer will "slip off track" and start to compose essentially new material. That moment, too, should be noted in the score. Of particular interest are cases in which the recapitulatory P and TR are fused into a single action zone—a commonly encountered situation. When this happens, P is not brought to its expositional close and instead merges *en route* with an interior portion of the expositional TR. In such cases of *P-TR compression* the composer erases the earlier, expositional border between the two action zones: two original spaces (CONTAINERS) become only one, on the way to the MC. The effect of is one of P-TR abridgment, telescoping.[33]

No matter where the correspondence measures had been abandoned, before too long the composer will "slip back on track," locking onto correspondence bars again. Most often this happens in the middle or near the end of the recapitulatory transition, though of course when the exposition's TR had ended with a V:HC MC, the analogous measures will need to be transposed down a fifth to prepare for S and C in the tonic.

The moment where correspondence bars resume is called the *crux*. The newly composed materials that preceded it (where the initial correspondence bars had ended) comprise the *pre-crux alterations*. Once the crux is reached, the composer has the option of simply filling out the rest of the exposition with correspondence measures, now in the tonic key. Compositional/creative thought could cease at this point and mere transposition take over, as considerations of symmetry and balance now outweigh the earlier imperative of setting down new ideas. Since no thematic-design changes are generically needed after the crux (the EEC, for instance, would now occur automatically), any such deviations from correspondence measures (*post-crux alterations*) are compositionally important. They represent creative interventions into what could have been an easier task. Each invites reflection and hermeneutic interpretation.

Mozart's, Beethoven's, and Schubert's recapitulations usually feature a large number of correspondence measures, with only small but expressively telling deviations from them. (The most commonly encountered deviations are located in the recapitulatory P, TR, or their merger: P==>TR. These occasionally blossom into churningly active expansions, though when they do, Sonata Theory does not use the term "secondary development" for them, but refers instead to the presence of quasi-developmental procedures that are sometimes found in the *recapitulatory transition* [*EST*, 236–37].) On the other hand, Haydn, especially in his fully mature works, often substantially rethought his recapitulations, which can feature a host of recompositions, expansions, compressions, and the like. While always singularly coherent within the ongoing processes or "internal logic" of the individual work—often in astonishingly clever ways—these unpredictable refashionings make it difficult to generalize about his recapitulatory practices: engaging surprises can occur all the way to the end.

Of the composers treated in this book, Haydn is the one who most consistently flies the flag of recapitulatory idiosyncrasy. Such rewritings are of an enhanced structural importance when they occur in the tonal resolution (S and C in a two-part recapitulation), which, according to a presumed but often much-exaggerated *sonata principle*, is generically expected to return largely intact ("resolved") in the tonic, but which in fact, and most particularly in Haydn, can be quite freely treated (*EST*, 242–45; Hepokoski 2002a). Though there are exceptions, for the most part Haydn adheres to the rotational principle, retaining at least the original expositional ordering of the thematic modules being presented or alluded to. This is normatively the case even when he recomposes much of this or that theme, touching, perhaps, on only its opening bars or basic idea (in what I have called the *synecdochic strategy* [*EST*, 233], in which a part of a theme is made to stand for the whole) or omits or alters thematic events within S or C space.[34] These ideas will be pursued in the analyses found in chapters 5 and 6.

With very few exceptions Sonata Theory uses the term *recapitulation* only to refer to full rotations launched by the rotation initiator, P, and normatively this means by its opening gesture $P^{1.1}$ (or P^0, if one is present). Thus from the Sonata Theory standpoint no "recapitulation" could begin with S, a claim that other approaches have sometimes made with reference to the Type 2 sonata (see chapter 11). $P^{1.1}$'s onset at the point of recapitulation is nearly always sounded in the tonic key, just as it had been heard in the exposition. This is the much-noted *double return* of the beginning of the theme and the tonic key, and it always brings with it the sense that a new, sonata-concluding rotation—a new cycle through the action zones—is being freshly launched. And with it we expect to move successively through identifying modules of the ensuing action zones, TR, S and C, the latter two of which are often traced through *in toto* as an extended, now-tonic-grounded end-rhyme with the exposition.[35]

When the double return occurs, we have no trouble identifying where the recapitulation begins. When it does not, we are faced with more challenging configurations that plunge us into areas of structural conceptualization that cannot be pursued at length here. Worthy of a glance, though, are situations in which the apparent recapitulation (one featuring what is clearly a rotation-beginning $P^{1.1}$) is not in the tonic key, but rather in IV. This is the case of the *subdominant recapitulation*, as in Mozart's Piano Sonata in C, K. 545/i. Normally such post-developmental $P^{1.1}$ returns are easily identifiable as onsets of recapitulatory rotations. This alternative has a history that stretches back into the earlier eighteenth century, and it carries with it a multifaceted set of implications that are dealt with in the *Elements* (262–68). I note here only that Sonata Theory's reading is grounded in the observation that "this penchant for the subdominant [recapitulation] could have arisen as an extension of the more common principle of moving toward the subdominant in recapitulations shortly after the initial re-sounding of P in the tonic" (*EST*, 265–66). When that common subdominant move is shifted further and further back in the direction of $P^{1.1}$, finally becoming identical with it, we have the subdominant recapitulation.

On occasion we find recapitulations that begin in the tonic but which sound P over a prolonged dominant pedal, blurring the normative seam between the development and the recapitulation, as in first movement of Beethoven's "Appassionata" sonata, op. 57, mm. 136ff. Such cases give the impression that the V_A at the end of the development is being prolonged into the recapitulation proper, coloring its onset and inviting us to inquire into why such a choice might have been made. Even more provocative are recapitulations that, following an obvious development, begin in keys other than the tonic or subdominant: in the submediant, perhaps, or even in the dominant—or in other keys (*EST*, 268–79). In some of these cases the apparent recapitulation begins off-tonic, then quickly readjusts back to the tonic, either by going back and relaunching $P^{1.1}$ in the tonic (the "back-up-and-redo" strategy, as in the first movement of Beethoven's Piano Sonata in F, op. 10 no. 2, mm. 118–37ff [*EST*, 271–75]), or by adjusting the tonality *en route*, with one or more corrective modulatory shifts to the proper tonic before too long (*EST*, 269–71). In all such cases—at least for Sonata Theory—the decisive point for judging where the recapitulation begins is not the eventual rejoining of the tonic but rather the onset of $P^{1.1}$ and what we should regard as the recapitulatory rotation. The principle of thematic ordering, in this case, trumps that of tonic recovery.

A differing set of issues emerges when what seems to be the recapitulation begins with a later module of P (say, $P^{1.2}$) or even TR, which latter becomes possible when the exposition's transition had begun in a manner similar to P, that is, as a dissolving restatement or dissolving consequent of P. The question then becomes: is this a genuine "recapitulation," or is there reason to believe that the recapitulatory *rotation* had been launched earlier, either within a Type 2 framework or embedded into some non-tonic developmental process toward the middle or end of the developmental space? Mounting an argument along these lines is always challenging, and in any case, such considerations are among the more rarefied aspects of Sonata Theory. I'll return to this issue in chapter 11.

There also exist what Sonata Theory calls *deformational recapitulations*. These are ones in which the generically mandated moment of closure—the I:PAC that marks the attainment of the ESC—is thwarted, blocked, or in one way or another not realized. Since these recapitulations lack an ESC, they do not accomplish their generic/harmonic purpose: the resolution of S with a perfect authentic cadence in the tonic. The suggestion would seem to be that, given the content of this particular realization and whatever expressive/narrative adventures it has led us through, the normative resolution expected within a sonata is being presented as something that cannot be brought about. In such a sonata narrative staged by the composer, the broad, dotted-line arrow in Figure 4.1b fails to land on its expected end-point, the ESC. It is left dangling, awaiting a resolution that does not happen in the recapitulatory space. In this scenario full closure (or the ESC) must be deferred to a coda, *outside of sonata space*, leaving the now-problematized recapitulation (and sonata) behind.

This is the situation of the *nonresolving recapitulation* (or the *failed recapitulation*, *recapitulatory failure*), which often, though not always, replicates in the tonic a problem that the exposition might have had in attaining the EEC. Three types of non-resolving recapitulation are:

- *S does appear in the tonic but does not manage to attain a I:PAC close (ESC)*. Here S's tonic orientation is on track but fails to secure cadential closure. As a result sonata space is left open, and the process flows onward, seeking the anticipated I:PAC (and ESC) in the coda. As has been mentioned before, the touchstone is the finale of Beethoven's Fifth Symphony, where the long-desired I:PAC is further deferred multiple times before being produced—finally—in the last stages of a long, rhetorically wrenching coda.
- *S (and whatever C implication there might be) is sounded completely in a non-tonic key (that is, the wrong key)*. A paradigmatic instance is found in Beethoven's *Egmont* Overture: P and S in F minor and A-flat major (the normative i and III) in the exposition, but returning in F minor and D-flat major (i and VI) in the recapitulation. There are surely programmatic reasons for this, and I have discussed them elsewhere (2001–2; 2009a and b). That *Egmont*'s complementary S-keys, A-flat and D-flat, are related by fifth is worth noticing, but the point remains that D-flat is not the tonic F (*EST*, 245; Hepokoski 2009b), and the sonata proper fails qua sonata, only to be bailed out in the post-sonata, F-major coda, the "Victory Symphony." In such cases the S theme is kept *tonally alienated* from the tonic in both exposition and recapitulation. It occupies an outsider status that is never integrated into the tonal resolutions expected of the sonata. In turn this can be read as carrying a tragic, wistful, or sorrowful implication, an expressive idea staged as incapable of assimilation into the reigning tonic, as we sometimes also find in Schubert. The wrong-key recapitulatory S appears more than once in later nineteenth-century repertory as an emblem of sonata failure.[36] The case outlined here must be distinguished from situations in which S *starts* in a non-tonic key but is soon readjusted back to the tonic (as in the first movement of Beethoven's "Waldstein" Sonata).

- *The truncated recapitulation* (suppression of the S-C block). Here the recapitulation closes down early, bringing back only the pre-MC music. Particularly when it is combined with the Type 1 sonata format (that without a development), this is a special sonata adaptation that occurs more often than was suggested in the *Elements* (247–49). As Martin (2015) notes, Mozart deployed this quasi-ternary design several times in his opera arias, where it is a familiar, frequently recurrent structure (P-S / P as a sonata-inflected variant of A B / A').[37] In high-classic music it is found most often in lyrical slow movements, such as that of Mozart's Piano Concerto No. 23 in A, K. 488, and Beethoven's Piano Concerto No. 1 in C, op. 15. The format also crops up here and there in earlier, mid-eighteenth-century practice (Morrow 2012b, 59–60, 73 n. 112).

Codas

Recapitulations are sometimes followed by codas. Some are brief and perfunctory, while others are prolonged, even multisectional, unfolding full or half-rotations in their own right. As addenda occupying *post-sonata* or *not-sonata space*, codas normally ground the recapitulatory securing of the tonic key, "confirming the reality of the fully secured tonic—celebrating it or basking in it—that it had taken the exertion of the sonata process to accomplish" (*EST*, 283). In earlier sonatas, those with both binary parts repeated (exposition and development-recapitulation), one sometimes finds that a (post-sonata) coda might also be included within the repeat of the second part, though that practice becomes rarer as we approach the turn of the century. In this case the large repetition includes, at the very end, a segment that is not a participant in the workings of the sonata proper.

Apart from their usual tonic-grounding function, codas can also serve a variety of other purposes within the larger movement. Sonata Theory refers to substantially extended codas as *discursive codas*. Produced as add-on tableaux beyond sonata space, discursive codas "can provide a challenge to the preceding sonata, as though the normative bringing of sonata space to completion at the end of the recapitulation were being arraigned as insufficient to the expressive task at hand" (283), as will be exemplified in the Beethoven and Brahms analyses in chapters 7 and 12. In some instances—such as that in the Brahms piece—codas are called upon to provide a satisfactory ESC when that cadential feature, for one reason or another, had not been attained in the ("failed") recapitulation.

Discursive codas often start out by returning to ideas laid out at the opening of the development, occasionally going further to give the impression of the coda as a compressed, tonic-key paraphrase of the development and recapitulation. (The allusion, it would seem, is to a once-common but now-missing "second-half-of-the-binary" repeat. In this respect the first-movement coda of Beethoven's *Eroica* Symphony is exemplary [*EST*, 285].) Or such codas might veer into problematic non-tonic patches or, in minor-mode sonatas, they might play a decisive, positive-or-negative role in the conflict between minor and major, the two oppositely affective modes (see chapters 7 and 8). Discursive codas often conclude with a more obviously coda-sounding set of modules that can be characterized a *coda to the coda*, wrapping up the whole work. Additional functions and options for codas are outlined in *EST*, 281–92.

Finally, it is worth underscoring the difference between a *codetta* and a *coda*. The former is an add-on extension that concludes an action zone *within* sonata space—a codetta, perhaps, to P, S, or C—whereas the latter is appended to the recapitulation, that is, to the whole piece, *outside of* sonata space, usually after the sonata proper, cadentially successful or not, has been brought to its end. The caveat "usually" may seem surprising to some readers, but it can happen that coda-like procedures are inserted into the concluding moments of the recapitulation, delaying the final C^2, C^3, or C^{cod} that will subsequently serve as both an end-rhyme to the exposition and the conclusion of the movement. (One might find, for instance, an end-of-recapitulation succession C^1–C^2–coda-like interpolation–C^3.) This situation, found, for instance, near the end of the first movement of Mozart's Symphony No. 40, K. 550, is what Sonata Theory calls *coda-rhetoric interpolation* (CRI). Along with similar expansion devices within recapitulatory C space, it is treated in *EST*, 288–92.

The Type 1 sonata and its expanded variant

By far the simplest format, the Type 1 sonata comprises only a nonrepeated exposition followed by an immediate recapitulation, though there may be a brief retransition (RT) connecting the two sections. The Type 1 thus lacks the Type 3's development section. This produces a *double-rotational sonata*, two similar rotations through the same material, with the second of them altered, usually in the recapitulatory transition (TR), to prepare a tonal-resolution statement of the secondary-theme and closing zones (S/C). In the literature the Type 1 sonata has been given various names, including "exposition-recapitulation" form, "sonata without development" form, "sonatina" form, and "slow-movement" sonata form, though the last two designations can be misleading. First movements of "sonatinas"—like Clementi's miniaturized, elementary C-major Sonatina, op. 36 no. 1, or either of Beethoven's two from op. 49, each called a *leichte Sonate* (easy sonata)—can be Type 3 sonatas, and while it is true that some slow movements are Type 1s (chapter 3 offered a close reading of one of these), one cannot claim that slow movements favor Type 1 formats.

The rapid-tempo Type 1 is a particularly appropriate format for some brisk, lighter overtures (Mozart's *The Marriage of Figaro* overture; most of Rossini's overtures). Its lightness, however, rules it out as a normative option for high-galant Allegro first movements,[38] and its straightforward form is only rarely found in finales. When no RT connects the exposition to the recapitulation, the former will proceed directly into the latter, and the initial return of P in the tonic can locally sound like the onset of an expositional repeat. This impression persists until the recapitulation deviates from the expositional model, at which point the listener, if not consulting a score, can realize that the format in play is that of the Type 1 sonata.

From time to time one comes across a Type 1 movement in which the recapitulation's primary theme (P) or transition (TR) is substantially expanded, producing a "developmental bulge" in either or both of those action zones, thereby effecting a proportional asymmetry between the exposition and the larger recapitulatory rotation. This is the *expanded Type 1* format. (*EST*, 349–50, cites several examples of it.) This more developed alternative renders it available for adoption in slow movements and finales, though not in first movements, at least not in late-eighteenth-century practice, though a few first-movement instances have been identified from the mid-to-later nineteenth century.[39] Particularly with regard to examples from Mozart, Beethoven, Schubert, and (especially) Brahms, the expanded Type 1 format has been explored by several scholars over the past decades, though not under that name (Pascall 1974; Green 1979; Daverio 1994; Galand 2008). Most recently, Peter H. Smith (2018) has provided a study of four expanded Type 1 movements from the 1880s and 1890s by Dvořák, two finales and two first movements, along with a review of the scholarship on that form.[40]

Analysts should take care to distinguish the expanded Type 1, whose second rotation begins in the tonic, in the manner of a recapitulation, from the similarly configured double-rotational Type 2, whose second rotation begins off-tonic, in the manner of a development. In most cases discerning the difference between the two presents no difficulties. When the second rotation's tonic-reference is only fleeting or brief, however (only a short incipit, perhaps, instead of a more extended sounding of P in the tonic), the Type 1/Type 2 distinction can be so slight as to be hermeneutically insignificant. At the end of chapter 11, focused on the Type 2 sonata, I'll revisit the Type 1/Type 2 differences and propose an expanded Type 1 reading of Wagner's *Tannhäuser* Overture, which, along with a few others, was mistakenly identified as a Type 2 in *EST*, 349.[41] And chapter 12 is devoted to a much more obvious example of the expanded Type 1, the finale of Brahms's First Symphony, a monumentalized realization encased within a grand introduction and climactic coda.[42]

5

Haydn, Symphony No. 100 in G, "Military," first movement (Adagio–Allegro)

After two or three sessions that introduce Sonata Theory through the analysis of works by Mozart, my seminars turn toward Haydn. Because of the latter's drive toward formal, thematic, and textural originality, economy of musical thought, densely woven motivic elaboration ("form as ongoing process"), and recapitulatory recastings, each of his compositions presents us with an array of challenges. All analysts of classical sonata form know that Haydn's works feature moves not readily housed under easy generalizations about standard practice. Yet, as noted in chapter 1, it is only against the background of the socially shared generic norms, still always implicit in Haydn, that one is able to register the idiosyncrasies of his compositional choices.

Once Sonata Theory has begun to accustom us to the Mozartian way of thinking, its application to Haydn sets the two composers' differences in relief. At the same time, it shows the adaptability of this analytical approach to one of the subtlest and most unpredictable composers of the era. To accomplish this, one might select almost any of Haydn's compositions. Here I have chosen one of his grandest and most familiar: the first movement of the "Military" Symphony.

Nicknames and paratexts

Beyond music-technical questions, of interest here is Haydn's practice of individualizing a work by stamping various points of it with entertaining, ear-catching gimmicks: late-eighteenth-century sonic, topical, or illustrative image-analogues that have given rise to the nicknames with which many of his works are associated.[1] In the case of the "Military" Symphony, as we shall see, the supplementary identifier was acknowledged by the composer himself. It's clear that Haydn intended certain moments of this very public music to be martially connotative for the audience for whom it was composed, or at least sufficiently so to encourage them to regard "Military" as an informally circulated paratext that could help to mediate their experience of the symphony as a whole.[2] In that sense the "Military" sobriquet has become part of the broader frame of reception for the "Symphony No. 100 in G," one that distinguishes it, say, from the "Clock" Symphony.

When we are dealing with works associated with an explicit or implicit paratext—which could range from a single title or nickname, as here, to a more

A Sonata Theory Handbook. James Hepokoski, Oxford University Press (2021). © Oxford University Press.
DOI: 10.1093/oso/9780197536810.003.0005.

detailed narrative "program"—we are invited all the more to advance beyond a technical explication of its musical structure (Hepokoski 2014). In addition to a formal/technical analysis, we are called to a broader interpretation of the piece's connotations. In turn these connotations can lead to reflections on aspects of its historical or cultural embeddedness. That hermeneutic impulse is central to the Sonata Theory project. To be sure, one cannot claim too much. Analytical and hermeneutic readings of a work are . . . well, only personal readings. As all students of hermeneutic theory know, interpreting texts responsibly is a complex endeavor, not a matter of projecting current fantasies onto cloud pictures. It entails a negotiation between our own, culturally limited horizons and the very different ones of past eras and cultures that we can only partially reconstruct. Our world would have been as unrecognizable to Haydn as his would be to ours. Yet the hermeneutic call asks us to tease out latent implications within individual moments of the work and to propose a coherent reading (an implicit "meaning") beyond the work's merely personalized significance-for-me.

How can we negotiate this distance? When moving beyond a self-contained technical analysis (an essential first step) into a more expansive hermeneutic reading, my own starting-points are threefold:

- The reading should be historically plausible. It should be a reading that the composer, so far as we can discern, might at least recognize as possible within the cultural horizon of his or her life-world. Situating the work in a sufficiently limned historical context is vital.
- The reading should not be so generalized as to be applicable to all comparable works of the period. Instead, it should be targeted to the musical facts of this or that particular piece. In this case, the reading should be "Military" specific, relying on features not readily transferable to the "Clock" Symphony or to any other work. As proposed as a general principle in chapter 1, what the two symphonies, and others, share in cultural ideology and baggage (which is a lot) belongs more to their common, socially shared *genre* than it does to the instantiation of that genre found in the individual work. Even so, since the individual work is also an exemplar of its genre, it will also take on the ideological burdens of that genre's enabling and constraining attributes.
- The reading, as a *close reading*, should be applicable to the musical details of the work as it unfolds in time. It should be mappable onto specific compositional choices phrase by phrase—or nearly so—rather than being applied, broad-brush style, to the whole without close attention to the piece's actual manner of unfolding: the thematic detail and structural processes of that work's microworld.

Even while analytical, then, this chapter also takes a few steps further into the hermeneutic interests that are intertwined with the Sonata Theory project.

Backdrop

One of the most impressive features of Haydn's music is its ability to mediate the yawning distance between its immediately appealing surface, much of which is so congenial to listeners at all levels of expertise, and the high density of the internal "logic" that generates its motivic-developmental growth. Citing comments from Arnold in 1810, who "heaps copious praise on Haydn's ability to make the difficult comprehensible," Dolan observes that "Haydn's music was celebrated in its time not for its esoteric complexity, but rather for the ease with which listeners could engage with it, and for its power to move them" (2013, 91). While the suggestion of "esoteric complexity" may stretch the point, what's clear is that supporting this music's affable surface is an uncommonly close-knit integration of compositional thought. Particularly in Haydn's more public offerings—the later symphonies and oratorios—he was crafting music that negotiated the growing gap between *Liebhaber* and *Kenner*, that is, between the general public and the connoisseur. The "Military" Symphony is a case in point.

Unlike Mozart's Symphony No. 34 in C (chapter 3), Haydn's Symphony No. 100 in G was an urban, much-publicized symphony. It appeared at a time when ever-grander symphonies and other works were emerging out of European courts and entering a more public sphere. A milestone in the history of the symphony, it was one of the highlights of Haydn's second visit to London (1794–95), where he was received as a musical celebrity of the highest order, probably the most prestigious living composer in Europe. (Mozart had died in late 1791, during Haydn's first trip to England.) First performed in London's Hanover Square Rooms on March 31, 1794, coincidentally Haydn's 62nd birthday, it was the highlight of the eighth of the 12 concerts that year sponsored by impresario and conductor Johann Peter Salomon. For this season, as with the other three Salomon/London seasons (1791, 1792, 1795), Haydn was to provide three new symphonies. In 1794 the three, in order of their premieres, were those that we now number 99, 101 ("Clock"), and 100 ("Military").

The "Military" nickname, or at least the general description of the work as such, was familiar in London immediately after its March 1794 premiere and may stem from the composer himself, who on May 4, 1795, in his fourth London Notebook, cited it as the "Military" Symphony (Webster 1991, 237).[3] This is not surprising. Schroeder reminds us (2005, 95) that "eighteenth-century commentators . . . were deeply concerned about the social or spiritual functions of symphonies," an observation that resonates with Griesinger's report that Haydn had remarked to him that "he had occasionally portrayed moral characters [*moralische Charaktere*] in his symphonies" (Webster 2005, 33).

All discussions of "the Military Symphony" agree that the designation alludes primarily to the sensational, noisy martial effects in the slow movement and finale. Haydn was plugging into an existing, and growing, musical tradition. Marches, military music, and "battle symphonies" were cropping up in those turbulent years and before long would become even more popular (Will 2002, 188–241). Landon and Jones (1988, 265) home in on a 1795 British context: "At a time when London was the haven for countless refugees from Robespierre's Reign of Terror in France, and England had joined Austria, Holland, [and] Spain in the war against that country, Haydn's clear intention [in those movements] was to evoke the terrifying sound of battle." The slow movement was the first of this work that Haydn had conceived, and Landon assures us that the symphony "was written, as it were, round the famous slow movement" (1976, 558). Since much of first movement is also suffused with march or march-like topics integrated into Haydn's symphonic style, it can be read as suggesting a preparatory mood or action in advance of the second movement.

The symphony splashed into London consciousness with grand *éclat* and soon made its way into wider Europe. In part this was due to its impression of immediate charm. As Schroeder put it, "after presenting the audience with two extraordinarily challenging symphonies at the beginning of 1794 [Nos. 99 and 101], Haydn decided to end the season with a highly accessible and popular work" (1990, 183). This echoes the remarks of Landon, who had written that this symphony was "the most celebrated piece of music Haydn wrote during the second London sojourn. . . . By now, [Haydn] was a supreme master of the popular style; in No. 100 he created his greatest triumph, at least as far as the European public of the day was concerned. Although it was later to be rivalled by the 'Surprise,' until 1805 or thereabouts the 'Military' was the most popular symphony ever composed" (1976, 558–59). Within only a few years, Landon noted, the instrumental parts for it would be published in Vienna, Augsburg, Berlin, Amsterdam, Paris, London, and elsewhere.

Living more than two centuries after all this, when Haydn's works have been settled into performance routine and potted-history textbooks, it is easy for us to overlook some fundamental things about the composer's most mature symphonies, at least from the grandiosity of the "Paris" Symphonies onward (Nos. 82–87, 1785–86). Looking backward, swayed by our knowledge of the gigantism of many subsequent works from the nineteenth century, we might regard such symphonies as modest in scope, as agreeable stepping-stones on the pathway to Beethoven's nine and beyond. But from the viewpoint of the 1780s and 1790s, Haydn's 25- to 30-minute works were monumental in size, complexity, sturdiness, and ambition. Each could be received as staking a claim to individual significance and a continued, esteemed performance life for decades to come. Consequently, they are properly heard as the full coming-of-age of the eighteenth-century galant symphony, a cultural development that had now attained a seemingly unsurpassable level of significance, durability, and quasi-"revolutionary" mastery of large-orchestral color and sonorous variety (Dolan 2013, 96).[4]

The modest *sinfonia*, sprouting across Europe as an elite entertainment genre in the 1740s and 1750s—light, energetic, stock-formula-governed, multiply manufactured, and ephemeral—had grown into something extraordinary, and all the more so in Haydn's masterly hands. Think, then, of Haydn's last two dozen or so symphonies as grand symphonies, as fully flowered culminations for their time,

magnificently realized end-points radiant with the exuberance of their own fullness, not as the beginnings of something else that would inevitably reset our perceptual scales of musical expanse, taste, and proportion.

Introduction: Adagio

Any pre-sonata introduction (or post-sonata coda) is a *parageneric space*: a space
existing outside the sonata genre proper. Introductions may be brief and in-tempo,
as with Beethoven's *Eroica* Symphony or Piano Sonata in F-sharp, op. 78, or they
may be slower and more extended, providing "a prolonged sense of anticipation
and formal preparation for a rapid-tempo sonata-to-come" (*EST*, 292). Substantial
introductions carry the implication of an enhanced importance for the piece as a
whole, while also laying out an initial mood or set of implications to which the subsequent sonata will respond.

Slow introductions of the galant era were attached initially to orchestral music,
not to chamber music or sonatas, and in the 1760s they were still rather uncommon.
Within Haydn's works two of the "Times of Day" symphonies from 1761—No. 6 in
D, "Le matin," and No. 7 in C, "Le midi"—begin with slow introductions, both of
them pictorial: the "sunrise" introduction to the former and the French-Overture
grandness at the onset of the latter, probably meant to suggest a sunny noontime
splendor (Sisman 2013, 58). Another introduction, though one apparently without
representational connotations, launches Symphony No. 25 in C, also from the
early 1760s.[5] Haydn began to write introductions somewhat more frequently, if
still sparingly, in the 1770s. Within a decade they would become a more attractive option: three of the six "Paris" Symphonies (1785–86) begin this way, and in
the mid-1780s Mozart provided three imposing examples with Symphonies Nos.
36 in C, "Linz" (1783), 38 in D, "Prague (1786), and 39 in E-flat (1788). Eleven of
Haydn's 12 London Symphonies (1791–95) begin with slow introductions, the only
exception being No. 95 in C minor, also the only minor-mode work of the set. As
Dolan put it, "slow introductions became effective ways to build up orchestral energy, transforming the opening of a symphony into a process of beginning, with its
own rhetoric. . . . The music does not simply begin, but thematizes the very act of
beginning" (2013, 105).

The era's typical introductions to major-mode works often pass through four
phases: (1) a *forte*, heraldic gesture or fanfare, a call to attention, sometimes
sounded in stark octaves; (2) a quieter, lyrical melody; (3) harmonic complications,
sometimes erupting with a dramatic *forte*, challenging the prior stability (a portentous modal darkening, an uneasy brooding, an unforeseen chromatic shift, or
searching sequences); and (4) the attainment of the dominant (sometimes in a
retained tonic minor) and a striding preparation for the Allegro to follow (*EST*,
297–99). In the "Military" Symphony Haydn omitted the first phase, starting directly with a trouble-free lyrical phase 2: a foursquare, modulating period (mm.

1–4, 5–8, ending on V), suggesting a pastoral mood or state of unruffled peace. (As will emerge, the Allegro P-theme-to-come will provide a responsive recasting of the antecedent; conversely, the antecedent can be understood retrospectively as providing some of the source material for the Allegro.)

Following the aa′ parallelism of mm. 1–8, m. 9 sets out with what initially can be taken for the b section of what seems to be unfolding as an apparent lyric-binary (or small ternary) format (aa′ba″). With disquieting inflections from the minor mode (F_5, $E\flat_5$), mm. 9–10 articulate a simple descending-fifth schema (Gjerdingen's FONTE schema in one of its characteristic roles) and return to the G-tonic, while also suggesting cautious steps forward, as if sensing a hidden menace. The tone of uncertainty increases with the foreshortened swaying of m. 11 and the suddenly alarmed leap and chromatic sigh, launched *forzando* in m. 12 and stifled at once. Something is afoot; the initial pastoral calm is encountering disturbances. Moreover, this presumed b-section fails to end on the active V (V_A) normative in a lyric binary. Instead, mm. 12–13 turn toward what is hoped will be an early but secure harbor: a premature, PAC in G major. But the anticipated G major is lost at m. 14 with the unexpected G minor that floods in like a dark shadow. (McClelland 2014, 298 n. 19, reads this as a deployment of the *ombra* topic.) Enhanced by the rumble of a timpani roll, the minor-mode intrusion swells ominously in the tutti orchestra. Should we consider m. 14 to be a i:PAC? Or was the expectant V⁷ in m. 13 cut short, blocked from its cadence with the F♯ upbeat in the bass at the end of the bar, initiating the minor-mode flooding in m. 14? Either way, it is not good news. The once-projected aa′ba″ is aborted, and "b"-related thematic material streams onward through the modal darkness.

The major-to-minor effect in m. 14 elaborates a typical "third available phase" of a slow introduction: harmonic divergences and complications. Try as one might to veer away from it, mm. 14–23 are sounded under the dystopic shadow of G minor, initially swelling toward the two hefty, C-minor thuds (iv), *fortissimo*, in m. 16. In m. 17 a gentler, quasi-processional start is made on E-flat major (locally III of the preceding C minor chord), an E-flat that some have read as having repercussions later in the movement.[6] But when the E-flat bass occurs in m. 18, Haydn colors it as an augmented-sixth chord in order to steer it, in crescendo, onto the dominant of G minor in the next bar. This dominant is locked onto (the final phase of the introduction) and prodded onward with timpani strokes and *forzando* pushes, as the upper voices groan above in mm. 19 and 20.[7] The persistent strides of the eighth-note momentum drop to *piano* throbs in mm. 21–22, then assert themselves once more at the introduction's end. We are left with a baleful, *fortissimo* dominant of G minor, held with a fermata and underpinned with the foreboding rumble of a timpani roll.

The G-major/G-minor decay enacts a familiar introduction scenario that Sonata Theory calls "the fall," in which "an initially confident, positive, or serenely pastoral, major-mode world [is] shattered by a sudden shift into the minor-mode negative . . . perhaps also with supernatural, *ombra* evocations" (*EST*, 301). Such an introduction implies that the subsequent sonata has work to do, namely, to overturn the minor mode not merely by sounding the tonic major at its Allegro opening but by securing it with unshakable confidence at the moment of the recapitulatory space's ESC, to which the whole sonata process points. Within the "Military" paratext framing the symphony, it is reasonable to imagine that what is being metaphorically suggested is a stable community initially at peace but now faced with the incursion of an outside threat that cannot be set aside. The Allegro that follows is tinted with the idea of the gathering-together of martial forces to restore G major, along the way encountering some skirmishes, all by way of preparation for the noisier battle-clash of the second movement.

Exposition: Allegro

As always with Haydn, a useful first step is to page forward in the score to determine whether an obvious MC is sounded somewhere in the exposition's middle, followed, perhaps, by an S whose opening gesture replicates or closely resembles that of P, only now in V (the P-based S, so often found in Haydn). In this case these things are easily located. M. 73 is a stereotypical V:HC MC, with two bars of flute/oboe caesura-fill, and the P-based S begins in m. 75. This is therefore a two-part exposition, not a continuous one, as we sometimes find in Haydn (and which will be illustrated in chapter 6).

Primary theme (P, mm. 24–39)

Tovey's observation about P is a useful *entreé*: "The allegro begins with a theme so typical of Haydn that we are apt to forget that in the whole range of classical music no other symphonic first theme has ever been scored in that way" (1981, 359). Tovey was referring to its first eight bars, where a solo flute chirps out the melody accompanied by two oboes, as if the middle and bass parts had dropped out altogether (see Figure 5.1). It has been common to characterize the theme as a dance, but given the "Military" paratext it might be better heard, as Dolan also notes (2103, 110), as the onset of a toy-like, fife-led march, conceivably the incipient stirrings of broader marches, assemblies, and struggles to follow.[8] Such a miniaturized march might allude to an earlier tradition of playfully parodied marches suitable for accompanying a "group of harlequins" (Haringer, 2014, 200, translating a phrase from Mattheson's 1739 *Der vollkommene Capellmeister*). This reading also invites a revised understanding of P's intervallic resemblance to the introduction's untroubled opening bars, P could be read as an initially diminutive, martial response to them (an instance of what Sonata Theory calls a *response module*), one whose intervals both identify with their original projection of security and take the first step on a course of action that, if successful, will bring about the restoration of a

Figure 5.1. Haydn, Symphony No. 100/i, mm. 24–39.

victorious, untroubled G major. That said, any such connotation is fused with the musical purpose of entering into the sonata process and the high aesthetic play of the symphonic genre qua genre. While the norms of the symphonic process hold the upper hand, some of its internal materials and compositional decisions are flavored with ideas that can be read as connotative.

P's simple 8+8 parallelism would seem to present no difficulties to either the listener or the analyst. It first strikes us as an easily recognizable compound period: a compound antecedent in the upper winds (mm. 24–31, readable as sentential, αα'β, 2+2+4) answered by a similarly structured compound consequent in the strings (mm. 32–39). But on closer inspection the apparent antecedent poses an analytical challenge. Because of the persistent sounding of D_5 in the lowest voice in mm. 29–31, the phrase's eighth measure (m. 31) does not close with a standard half cadence. In fact, once the melodic A_5 is reached in the third and fourth bars, over a dominant chord (mm. 26–27, the end of αα'), that A_5 and the D_5 below it seem frozen in stammering reiterations in what follows (mm. 28–31), emphasized especially by the double C_6-B_5-A_5 melodic descents in those measures. On the one hand, one can identify mm. 28–29, isolated as such, as a familiar half-cadential progression (I:HC in m. 29) and then observe that that V is followed by a two-bar prolongation that also sounds an upper-voice variant of the preceding two measures. On the other hand, such a reading should also observe that the half-cadential impression (mm. 28–29) occurs in the "wrong place"—prematurely in the phrase's sixth bar—within what we surely understand as a 4+4 antecedent. My own sense is that the returns to the dominant in the sixth and eighth bar (mm. 29 and 31) successively reinforce that earlier-sounded dominant to the point where a half-cadence effect, or a sufficient substitute for one, has been produced in the three-bar figuration of mm. 29–31. In sum, I regard mm. 24–31 as an unusually constructed compound antecedent. The 16-bar melody, the thematic proposal to build a sonata, retains its compound-period status.

Transition (TR, mm. 39–73)

This TR is prototypical for Haydn and for orchestral TR action zones more generally. As is common, P's final I:PAC elides directly into TR, m. 39, the exuberant entry of the full orchestra. This is the *tutti affirmation*, or *forte affirmation*, characteristic of many orchestral TR beginnings. With it TR joyfully accepts P's compound period as the start of a sonata, and the gears clench into forward motion. Depending on how one assesses the similarity of the figuration of some of TR's initial bars to aspects of P, this TR could be considered as either *independent (separately thematized)* or *developmental (EST, 95–96)*: the choice of category matters little. (I'll defer to the following chapter a discussion of the "organically" processual or developmental aspect of Haydn's approach to sonata forms.)

The TR also provides a good example of that zone's typical *energy gain and drive to the medial caesura*. It begins (mm. 39–49, TR$^{1.1}$) with vigorous activity over a tonic pedal (holding fast onto the tonic secured by the I:PAC at m. 39), then shakes loose of that pedal (TR$^{1.2}$, mm. 49–58) to gain steam with more rapid figuration in the first violin, driven ahead by multiple, short-winded pushes that turn toward the dominant via descending fifths (B^7-e-A^7-D) in mm. 53–58. With what can be regarded as TR$^{1.3}$ (mm. 58–62, a descending-thirds sequence), the D is increasingly tonicized in a tumble-down rush that plunges onto TR's harmonic goal, the dominant of D major (m. 62). This dominant arrival (not a half cadence) is clasped as a *dominant-lock* (TR$^{1.4}$, mm 62–73), while excited figuration above churns forward to the V:HC MC in m. 73. (As a reminder: although the dominant arrival in m. 62 occurs many bars before the MC, Sonata Theory still classifies m. 73 as a V:HC MC, here one to which a passing seventh has been added).[9] Two bars of anticipatory caesura-fill, like the opening of doors to a new space, bring us to the next action zone, S, and to the exposition's second part.

Secondary thematic zone (S, mm. 75–93?)

It is a commonplace observation that Haydn often begins his secondary themes by alluding to or restating the opening figure of the primary theme (the *P-based S*). When this happens, it reinforces one of the composer's central concerns: the creation of a network of internal interrelationships among the musical ideas of a piece, resulting in the impression of form as a process of ongoing motivic elaboration as it courses through the pre-given action zones. As Haimo put it, "Haydn constructs his compositions so that later events within a movement are related by repetition, transposition, derivation, or variation to earlier events" (1995, 4).

Notable in this case is the literalness of the back-reference. From m. 75 through the first three beats of m. 79, this S starts as a replication of its toy-march P-model, including its flute/oboe scoring, only now in the dominant, D major. Is this S to be nothing more than a blunt restatement of P, reverting back to the beginning of the exposition and its mini-martial connotation? As if reacting to the unimaginative rigidity of letting this happen, Haydn has mm. 80–85 stop the restatement in its tracks with a series of musical question marks ("Surely we're not going to do *this* again?"), followed by an attempted D-major PAC in m. 87 that instead darkens to D minor at its final-cadential moment. The aggressive D-minor phrase that follows, mm. 87–92/93, now shows that the thematic choice for P is to be utterly rejected—its neck wrung—by seizing its head-motive in the parallel minor (mm. 87–88, thereby keeping S-space open) and shaking it dead in a furious plummeting toward what is now expected to be a decisive cadence in D minor. Instead, the phrase empties out onto a D-*major* sonority in m. 93. Notice, then, that these two S phrases, mm. 75–87 and 87–92/93, are modally complementary: the first a major-mode phrase that turns minor, the second a minor-mode phrase that switches the lights back on to major.

But it is at the D-*major* downbeat of m. 93 and its subsequent release of new thematic material where the most challenging features of the exposition occur. These challenges are instructive in helping us to confront Haydn's original approach to sonata composition and to illustrate Sonata Theory's non-doctrinaire way of dealing with such situations.

Closing space (C) or S^C? (mm. 93–124)

In structural terms how should we read the downbeat of m. 93? Is this to be experienced as an attenuated "cadential" moment: a V:IAC? Or is it something else? And even if we were to conclude that it is best regarded as cadential, given the sharp melodic, dynamic, and textural corner turned here, should it be construed as an implicit but deformational EEC? None of this is clear. In all similarly blurred situations Sonata Theory's advice is to *explicate the ambiguities*.

On the face of it the downbeat of m. 93 seems not to end anything but rather, like a sudden change of mind, to shift without warning into something else. Yet, equally to the point, that something else sounds much like a typically Haydnesque C^1 theme. But to imagine m. 93 as an elided cadence *tout court* defies one's experience of it. However we think our way through it, it is certainly no PAC in V (or v). Instead, Haydn leads us up to the cadential moment, then pulls out the rug from under it. The glaring blankness of the first violins, oboes, and bassoon in mm. 93–94 is telling: a wiping-out of sonority at the expected cadential moment, leaving the preceding, emphatic A to hang unresolved in those parts, while the chordal seventh in the second oboe in m. 92 is similarly cut off from resolution, unless we decide, contra the evidence of timbre, that its G$\natural_4$ "resolves" in m. 93 with the F$\sharp_4$ rescue-operation in the second violins. (Notice also the awkward move from C$\sharp_4$ to F$\sharp_4$ in the second violins, mm. 92–93.) Try as we might, it is difficult to regard m. 93 as a dynamically attenuated V:IAC unless we are prepared to hang a host of qualifiers onto that assessment. More likely, it is better read as an *interrupted cadence*—that is, a cadence that is prepared normatively but stops short of closure at its final moment, leaving the cadence unrealized to turn impulsively toward something else.[10]

Thus we experience a radical disjunction between the hyper-decisiveness of the (D-minor!) cadential prediction, *forzando*, mm. 87–92, and the textural, registral, and dynamic otherness of the (D-major) *piano*, preparatory-rhythmic-stream figuration at m. 93, underpinned by the onset of delicate, downbeat *pizzicati* in the cellos and basses. This disjunctive moment deflates the acoustic realization of any kind of normative cadence, much less a PAC. The collapse is interpretable as a well-placed thrust of musical humor, conveying something along the lines of Kant's remark in the *Critique of Judgment* (1790) concerning jokes or witty tales: "*Laughter is an affect that arises if a tense expectation is transformed into nothing.*"[11] (Muffled, interrupted, or obscured cadences, typical of Haydn in this period, appear more than once at crucial late-expositional moments in the London Symphonies.)[12] But this "nothing" opens the pathway to what I read as the musically narrative goal of the exposition, the new, popular-style theme that starts to unroll at m. 95.

The deflationary non-cadence that appears at m. 93 and the galloping theme that follows it generate an engaging analytical problem. As Rosen rightly noted, along with many others, a familiar place for Haydn's "melodies with a marked popular flavor" is "towards the close of the expositions of the first movements," and their purpose is to "ground the tension previously generated" (1997, 333–35). In Sonata Theory terms, this most typically happens just after the arrival of the EEC, where such popular-style themes, contrasting in tone and style with the doggedly processual *Fortspinnung* that has preceded them, serve as a concluding space of relief, a celebration or affirmation of the now-secured secondary key.

Such themes nearly always launch closing space. They are C or, more precisely, $C^{1.1}$ themes. Consequently, we normally understand the sounding of such a theme as a Haydnesque signal both that the exposition's generic goal, a PAC in the secondary key (the EEC), has been secured and that we are now entering an expositional appendix, or what Koch called a "clarifying period" (*erklärende Periode*): Sonata Theory's C space. In most cases such a reading presents no problem, except in such situations as we find here, with the misfired (non-)cadence at m. 93. Since in this era the boundaries of action zones are usually clear, how are we to deal with this m. 93 blurring, along with the closing character of the new theme that arises in m. 95?

Sonata Theory offers two choices, either of which is viable (and less is at stake in the choice than the quasi-talismanic letters "EEC" might seem to suggest). One might wish to regard m. 93 as a rhetorical but deformational EEC, signaled in large part by the contrast that it initiates, as though the implicit closure in V were now assumed by the self-assured theme that ensues. That new theme, then, would be C^1. Bolstering this view is the modestly stronger (but still problematic) treatment of this "cadential" moment in the recapitulation (m. 226), though Sonata Theory is not eager to cite recapitulatory evidence to help make expositional decisions, particularly in Haydn, who often significantly recomposed his recapitulations.

On the other hand, one might conclude that m. 93's deflation cannot rise to the expected closural level of an EEC. This reading interprets the subsequent theme as a closing-style theme (C) that has been introduced prematurely, before the S action zone has been properly closed with a V:PAC. While infrequent, this situation does occasionally occur. Sonata Theory labels such themes as S^C, signifying the emergence of C-like material in the absence of an EEC, that is, in still-operative S space. (*EST*, 190–91, cites some examples.) While a definitive decision on this matter is imprudent—in such an ambiguous situation, opinions can differ, and any analysis should admit this up front—I lean toward the second option, considering the new material (93/95ff) to be an S^C theme. (Under this reading, mm. 93–94, the rhythmic stream would be an S^C "zero" module, similar in its path-clearing role to a C^0 module [*EST*, 187–90].)[13]

Zooming out for a broader view of this issue, this S^C theme (as I shall now call it) is destined to dominate much of the remainder of the movement: nearly all of the development and an outsized share of the recapitulation as well. Whatever this movement is about musically or connotatively, it is surely about the emergence and inexorably commandeering nature of this high-spirited theme. What might be its significance? Haydn may have styled the leading idea of S^C as a particular kind of late-eighteenth-century march, the quick march appropriate for a military parade or the even speedier display-march suitable for the parade gallop of cavalry, though this latter is normally in $\frac{6}{8}$ (Monelle 2006, 123). As Will notes, the topical effect of the late-eighteenth-century march, as with all marches, is to display "a military and social ideal of synchronized motion . . . soldiers subordinating their personal interests to the functioning of the whole" (2002, 193).

Such a reading can be reinforced with the long-standing observation (for instance, Geiringer 1968, 358) that Johann Strauss Sr.'s famous *Radetzky March* from 1848 resembles what we are calling Haydn's S^C theme—or perhaps draws upon the general category of Austrian quick marches that both melodies share.[14] Pursuing the topical metaphor, one might imagine that the exposition, while still governed by the action-zone expectations of the symphonic process, shifts from connotations of the small-scale rustlings of P's toy march to those, with S^C, of a formalized, imperial display-march, all in response to the modal disturbance encountered in the introduction. Such a reading is plausibly assimilable into the "Military Symphony" paratext and also suggests a reason for the expansion and spreading of this "proto-Radetzky" S^C theme throughout the development and recapitulation: signs of a swelling confidence in the face of soldierly encounters to come.

Whatever the topical connotation of S^C's initial stamp, the popular-style tune soon turns into a symphonic frolic to the exposition's close. In S^C proper an eight-bar, compound sentential antecedent, mm. 95–102 (ending with a locally tonicized dominant), leads to a foreshortened, six-bar continuation, mm. 103–108 (in form-functional terms completing a *compound hybrid 1* format, 8+6, thus with a compressed second part), closed off with what is likely to impress us as a strong PAC-effect bolstered by the elided *forte* entrance of the full orchestra and a firmly grasped new-tonic sonority for several subsequent bars. Sensing the continuation's foreshortening and resulting 8+6 asymmetry is important: it's as if S^C's continuation, compressed from an anticipated eight bars into six, speeds eagerly to secure the V:PAC that had been so blurred or muffled at m. 93. To be sure, to judge from the notation alone, the literal V:PAC status of m. 108 might be debated. If we read the first violin as the leading upper voice, its leap to F#$_5$ in that bar imperfects the PAC-effect. On the other hand, the formidable tutti reinforcement, with the flute's prolonged D$_6$ as the top voice of a commanding block of a now-sustained D-tonic provides the audible sense of a definitive point of arrival. (Spoiler alert: in the recapitulation this expositional PAC-effect at m. 108, about to be replicated in the tonic, will be treated differently, leading to unforeseen ramifications.)

Should m. 108 be considered the recovery of the "lost" EEC at m. 93? That is the reading that I prefer but would not insist upon. In metaphorical/narrative terms, finding itself tucked into still-open S-space (mm. 93–108), the closing-style S^C theme hastens to close the gap by rushing into the cadence that S should have produced on its own. On this reading the elided V:PAC at m. 108 triggers the affirmative onset of C proper, which proceeds in a *tutti* riot of now-secured D-major *Klang*, held fast and celebrated for several bars, while an enthusiastically festive adaptation of S^C's anapest rhythm is rolled out in the bass.[15] The sustained D-*Klang* persists from m. 108 to m. 113, loosened only in the next two bars to seek another decisive tonic cadence. Yet the upward leaps in m. 115's top voices do not allow the cadential door to be fully closed. Consequently, mm. 115–18 are called upon to shore up the weakened cadence ("one more time") with a stronger V:PAC—though again with a flyaway upper voice. Finally, the more emphatic mm. 118–21 ratify the close unequivocally ("yet *another* time! get it *right!*") with a definitive V: PAC. Had one decided not to grant m. 108 EEC status, the EEC might be deferred until m. 121. However one reads these passages, it is clear that the thematic vector that had begun with S at m. 75—the exposition's part-2 thematic-rhetorical trajectory diagrammed in Figure 4.2 of the preceding chapter—arrives at its final goal only at m. 121. Haydn rounds off the whole with a codetta, mm. 121–24, and the generic call for the expositional repeat.

Development (mm. 125–201/202)

As noted in chapters 1 and 4, developments in this era most commonly begin with an off-tonic sounding of a reference to P, thereby beginning a developmental rotation or half-rotation of the exposition's thematic array. Aware of this *first-level default*, one might expect the present development to begin with P-material. Instead, Haydn inserts two blank bars—two bars of "loud rest." What our familiarity with the genre expects to happen does not happen. It seems that P has missed its cue and failed to enter, and the result is two bars of question-mark emptiness. (Haydn is a master of provocatively placed silences and/or fermatas.) Into that yawning gap the ever-serviceable S^C theme resumes its onward trot, *piano*, only now on B-flat major, ♭VI of the preceding D major. Such sudden "third-relation" shifts are commonly noted as a favored device of wit or surprise in the later Haydn. (Neo-Riemannians would construe the D-to-B-flat juxtaposition as the product of a twofold PL operation [parallel and *Leittonwechsel*]: D major's third turned minor [P] and the fifth of resulting D-minor triad inflected upward to B♭ [L]).

Since the development begins with the "proto-Radetzky" S^C, heard only in the exposition's second (post-MC) part, it may be regarded as *non-rotational*. That is a reasonable conclusion, and one could leave it at that. Sonata Theory, though, also allows for an alternative, more abstract (even speculative) interpretation that S^C might be construed as *writing over* the absent P, or, more precisely, *writing over* the developmental space more normally allotted to P (or TR) material, in effect substituting for it (*EST*, 212–17).[16] Whatever the reason, Haydn based most of this development on S^C. From one perspective, this highlights a leading idea of this movement: the increasing emergence of that military-flavored quick-march that had also been the exposition's thematic goal. From another perspective, the theme's expositional connotation might be less relevant here, as its constituent parts may also be heard as being taken over by the generically musical, symphonic norms for developmental treatment.

Harmonically, the first part of the development, mm. 125–69, undergoes a step-by-step rise of implicit tonalities defined either by their dominants or by strong arrival $^6_4$ s over those dominants: from the opening B-flat entry (m. 127) to V/c (m. 134) to a twice-reinforced V/d (m. 140), to V/e (m. 153), then briefly to V/F (m. 157/158), and back to V/e (m. 165). Its central feature is an 11-bar, modulatory model (mm. 134–44) that is followed by an 11-bar sequence (mm. 147–57 = 134–44 up a step). The model begins with a *piano*, rocking figure on V^6_5 of C minor (m. 134, gaining rhetorical force with a mighty dynamic swell (mm. 137–38). Vehemently and *forte*, this propels into the next bar (m. 139), where the full orchestra enters with a chilly half-step drop in the bass from B♮ to B♭, which bass now underpins an imposing augmented sixth, unloading powerfully onto V^6_4 of D minor in m. 140. This is the inbreaking of the *tempesta* topic, perhaps the suggestion of a plunge into a brief but intense military skirmish. This $^6_4$ is prolonged for several *forte* bars in with a hectic, thrashing anapest figure in drum-beat octaves until, through another reference to the augmented sixth, it empties onto a half cadence in D minor at m. 146. The upbeat link at m. 146 (cf. m. 133) sets up the 11-bar sequence, up a step, mm. 147–57, through the thrashing "skirmish" figures now on the V^6_4 of E minor. Instead of moving to a half cadence, though, the frenzied figuration shifts up a step, to V^7 of F major, mm. 157/158), reinterpreted as an augmented sixth at m. 162 and pushing back to V of E minor at m. 165—which in turn is held as a six-bar dominant lock ending in a hammer-blow medial caesura (mm. 168–69), neatly dividing the development into two parts.

The strong mid-development MC at m. 169 produces a temporary respite in the action. Into that letup peeks a set of interrogative P-fragments, exchanged back and forth between the winds and the strings, mm. 170–77, as if inquiring whether it is safe to come out. The P-allusion, though, could be an allusion not to P itself but rather to the P-based S, under which interpretation the development begins to look more potentially rotational, with S^C writing over the absent P in the development's first half, up to the MC-effect of m. 169. Here a simple four-bar model (2+2, mm. 170–73) descends by fifths (e-A^7-D), and its sequence up a fourth (mm. 174–77, a-D-G) brings us squarely back onto the G-major tonic, perhaps anticipating some kind of imminent, double-return recapitulation.

But any such suggestion is dashed with the initially flickering return of S^C material (m. 178) and its anapests, heading for another run into the *forte* fray.[17] The frenetic diminished-seventh figuration at mm. 185–86 turns toward A minor, but any such implication is shattered with one of Haydn's characteristic developmental moves: an impetuous tumbling down a set of descending fifths (mm. 188–90). Here, the initially syncopated the fifths can be traced as: a, D^6, G, C^6, f$\sharp^o$, b^{6,} e, a^6, and D. Pulling free from the mad scramble, two further bars bring us to c$\sharp^{o7}$ (vii^{o7}/V, mm. 193–94) and finally to a closing half cadence on V of the tonic, G major (I:HC, m. 195). This is the harmonic-structural end of the development proper. Sounded over throbbing repetitions of V of G, several bars of anapest-echoing retransition-fill (mm. 195–201) dissipate the accumulated energy and provide a flowing anacrusis to the tonic return of P at the beginning of the recapitulation.

Recapitulation (mm. 202–end)

All commentators on the classical era observe that Haydn's recapitulations are less predictable, less generically regular, than those of Mozart, Beethoven, and many others. Spurred by his drive toward originality (attested to by his famous remark cited in chapter 1, p. 4), Haydn came to view his recapitulations as opportunities for the rethinking and recomposition of the expositional model. Haimo's "redundancy principle" conveys the thrust of the idea, albeit in characteristically late-twentieth-century, "modernist" terms: "Haydn regarded multiple statements of identical, or nearly identical, events as potentially redundant" (1995, 5). It would appear that habitual recourse to extended passages of literal repetition was something to be kept in check, presumably in order to keep the generative aspect of his creative thought flowing all the way to the end. And yet the signposts of musical structure and reprise were to remain sufficiently evident to clarify the arrival points of one's location within the ongoing form.

For this reason, normative-generic descriptions of "what usually happens" in classical-style recapitulations (as in chapter 4), when it comes to Haydn must be applied flexibly. While attempts have been made to establish guidelines that purport to explain Haydn's recapitulatory thinking within a reconstrued "sonata principle," the results have been overgeneralized and lackluster.[18] Although a sense of reprise and symmetry between Haydn's expositions and recapitulations usually remains in place, the latter's contents and implications can differ notably from those of the former—always in fascinating ways. Each recapitulation needs to be interpreted as a singularity, even as we keep in mind the more commonly encountered, external generic norms as a regulative guide for the interpretation of what we find. With each work Haydn approached the recapitulatory recomposition in a different, piece-specific way, ranging from mild variants (those with a regular ordering of the exposition's action zones and featuring relatively large groups of correspondence measures) to extreme ones (where the exposition's action-zone proportions and/or ordering, along with broad stretches of its music, are substantially altered). The present movement offers us an example of the extreme side of the continuum.[19]

In this recapitulation Haydn telescopes P, TR, and S space into a brief opening passage (mm. 202–26; TR is omitted altogether), and then expands the music around S^C, loading it with harmonic and other surprises. One's impression is that of the perfunctory touching upon stations marking the toy-march P and S, then elbowing them out of the way to let the more assertive S^C and its deformational consequences take over more of the remainder of recapitulatory space. While some commentators follow Landon's assessment that this theme's much-noted, sudden lurch out of the tonic (m. 239) is the start of "the biggest and most flamboyant coda of his symphonic *oeuvre* hitherto" (1976, 561), it is no coda at all (as also noted in Brown 2002, 280) but rather a spectacular digression inside sonata space.[20]

The recapitulation begins normatively, re-sounding P's eight-bar antecedent phrase as before, in the high woodwinds (mm. 202–9 = mm. 24–31). Close listeners will note that in mm. 208–9 the second oboe chirps out five steady quarter notes instead of only the three, alternating with rests, heard in the exposition, mm. 30–31. What follows (mm. 210ff) at first seems to be the start of the consequent, now played by the full orchestra, but it is here that Haydn makes the first of his startling recapitulatory decisions. Instead of corresponding to the exposition's P-consequent (mm. 32–39), the music leaps ahead to the P-based S (mm. 210–19 = mm. 75–84, now in the tonic), that are then altered to produce a different outcome. With this stroke Haydn deletes the consequent-end of the exposition's P and all of TR—some 43 bars (mm. 32–74). The expositional model's part 1 (P and TR) has been drastically shrunk to eight bars, the antecedent phrase, and its non-normative end is called into service as an operative MC. Thus m. 210 can be regarded as a crux, and from this point onward Haydn could have transposed the rest of the expositional model all the way to its end. But of course that is what he does not do.

Post-crux alterations of the P-based S begin in m. 220, where the ongoing theme unravels in another of Haydn's tumblings-down through a set of descending fifths (mm. 220–21), stubbing its toe (or worse) at the bottom with one of Haydn's familiar, *forte* "surprise" chords, a half-diminished vii/V. The surprise is sustained for two bars (mm. 222–23), before clarifying to an active dominant seventh (or ninth) chord in mm. 224–25, with evident intentions of a resolution in the following bar. We now arrive at a critical moment. The *forte* dominant chord does indeed lead to a tonic chord, m. 226, but that tonic is undercut with an abrupt drop to *piano*, a

marked change of orchestration to strings alone, a registral shift, and most important, the onset of the proto-*Radetzky*, S^C theme, only now starting directly on the
theme proper, shorn of its expositional two bars of rhythmic-stream preparation
(m. 226 = m. 95, not m. 93). Recall that m. 93/95 had been one of the problematic spots of the exposition, and it is hardly less so here. Is m. 226 an elided I:PAC?
Comparison with its model (its momentary analogue is m. 93, not m. 95) will show
that its cadential effect is stronger, and those analysts who had considered m. 93 as a
deformational EEC would read m. 226 as the corresponding ESC. The expositional
reading presented earlier, however, had chosen not to do so. Instead, the popular-
style theme was read as S^C (a C-like theme sounded in still-open S space), and one
of the principles of Sonata Theory is that what had been regarded as belonging to S
space in the exposition should be similarly regarded in the recapitulation. By those
lights m. 226 is not yet the ESC, and S space rolls onward with the quick-march tune
that will now lead to an expansion destined to take over most of what follows.

The onset of S^C marks another crux point settling into a 13-bar, newly
orchestrated set of correspondence measures (mm. 226–39 = mm. 95–108, now
in the tonic). The expositional model, though, had consisted of *14* bars, an eight-
bar antecedent followed by a six-bar continuation that had concluded with a tutti-
entrance V:PAC in m. 108. That V:PAC was my preference for the EEC, and it elided
directly into the tonic-sustaining, celebratory C^1. As the recapitulation replicates
the first 13 bars in the tonic, the V^7 in the thirteenth bar (m. 238) is primed and
ready to cadence as it had before, with a decisive I:PAC—and the ESC—in m. 239.
But this expected structural cadence is now subverted. In m. 240 we get instead a
hyper-emphatic deceptive cadence on E-flat (♭VI). Jumping in with full alarm, it is
sounded *fortissimo* by the full orchestra and sets the S^C's continuation-idea (which
had begun in m. 234) galloping off on an unanticipated musical adventure, a virtuosic, 37-bar interpolation.

The long, digressive jag of those extra measures on ♭VI of G has been much
discussed by commentators. Obviously, those bars lurch off-track from the expositional model and divert the recapitulation into a new space of vigorous expansion.
Those metaphorically inclined might imagine—by way of the structural homologies
shared between the music and the suggested image—a sudden command to charge
into battle or some similarly urgent, contextually plausible event that triggers a wild,
galvanic jolt to the proceedings just as they were beginning to settle.[21]

There are also musical justifications for this extraordinary insertion. First, the
recapitulation's telescoping of P, TR, and S invites a compensatory enlargement of
later material, if only to provide a roughly symmetrical sense of temporal expanse
between the exposition and the recapitulation—or, conversely, perhaps the opening
of the recapitulation had been radically abbreviated in order to create a sufficient
space for this later expansion. (As will also be noted in chapter 6, the mature Haydn
often abbreviates the opening portions of recapitulations, then responds to this
with extensions of the more popular-style, later portions.) Second, since E-flat is
more closely related to G minor than to G major, the jolt to E-flat might suggest a

back-reference to the brief tonicizing of E-flat in the introduction (m. 17), implying a late-in-the-game response to the introduction's G-minor clouding that had led to that E-flat.[22] Third, the jarring E-flat revels in the mature Haydn's fondness for local disruption and his love of quick harmonic color-shifts, often a third away from the ongoing tonic (to [b]VI or [b]III, the mediant relations). Haydn often places such shifts at unexpected points, such as in the later stages of the exposition or recapitulation. Fourth, this 37-bar interpolation takes on features that hark back to aspects of the development, as if those musical tensions were rising once again. Finally, as already noted, the entire movement has been characterized by a diminishing of the merely initiatory, toy-march P and a corresponding expansion led off by the popular-style, quick-march S^C. Setting the latter loose for one final romp not only accentuates that intention but produces an unexpected musical burst calculated to delight the attentive listener.

Mm. 239–46 plunge into the E-flat fray over a tonic pedal. In mm. 247–48 that E-flat bass is made to support an augmented-sixth chord with G-minor implications, perhaps recalling the similar harmonic events in the introduction, mm. 17–19. Amidst the galloping frenzy the G-minor threat is being re-confronted. When the augmented sixth resolves, however, it is to the dominant of *G major* (mm. 249–50). As this dominant unleashes a frantic scramble upward in the violins, descending chordal fifths tip us past the tonic G onto its subdominant: D^7, $G\sharp^7$, C (mm. 249–50, 251–52, 253).

And with that subdominant chord at m. 253 occurs the most anomalous event in the first movement, at least from the point of view of Sonata Theory. Unexpectedly— into the fraught center of the melee—Haydn plugs m. 253 into two sets of slightly altered correspondence measures with what I have called $TR^{1.2}$ and $TR^{1.3}$: mm. 253– 56 = variants of mm. 49–52, untransposed; and mm. 256–69 = mm. 56–69, now transposed to the tonic. Some analytical approaches would not regard this as an astonishing occurrence: after all, these measures restore passages from the transition that had been skipped over in the earlier part of the recapitulation. But what leaps out to the Sonata Theorist is that these linked passages appear *out of rotational order*. TR material is called into critical action within still-active S space. Moreover, it is to this material that the composer assigns the task of charging onward with maximal energy toward the ESC. To be sure, Haydn often recomposes his recapitulations in surprising ways, but although one can occasionally find reorderings of thematic pockets in them, they are infrequent, and Sonata Theory never takes them casually.

What could account for this swerve away from recapitulatory rotational order (P–S–S^C–*TR^{1.2-4}*)? Merely to note that the $TR^{1.2-4}$ thematic modules had been omitted earlier in the recapitulation does not suffice. As part-1, pre-MC music, events in the exposition's TR are under no obligation to reappear in the recapitulation (*EST*, 242–45; Hepokoski 2002a). While it might be gratifying to have them resurface here, their out-of-order recall might be the larger point. This disorder might suggest that by m. 253 the ongoing tumult has reached such a fever-pitch that normative considerations of modular/thematic order are cast aside: at a moment of peril one grasps at any weapon that seems available. On the other hand, TR's hyper-energetic figuration might be just the thing to push the frenzied interpolation all the way to the ESC. Or perhaps those TR modules had been passed over earlier to keep them in reserve for their more vital role here. Whatever the reason, after m. 269 (= m. 69, now in the tonic) the correspondence bars stop tracking their expositional TR-models, and the cadential mm. 271–72 lead to a decisive I:PAC in m. 273, which I read as the ESC. Not the least of the curiosities here is that the $TR^{1.4}$ interpolation (mm. 262–69) that steers the way to the ESC four bars later is a transposition of the same music (mm. 62–69) that in the exposition had led to the MC.

With that finalized structural securing of G major, the essential sonata trajectory has been successfully completed (chapter 4, Figure 4.1b). More than that, in the context of the whole movement this G major marks the point of victory over the G-minor threat that had precipitated the "fall" in the introduction. What remains is pure celebration. M. 273 returns the music to rotational order with a variant of C^1—that jubilant riot of now-tonic *Klang*. A seemingly helter-skelter but perhaps thankful allusion to the breathless surges of $TR^{1.2}$ is tucked in one last time (mm. 278–81, reappearing out of rotational order, as if by now fully licensed to do so) to bring us to the cadence at m. 282, and with it the varied return of the strongly ca-dential bars from near the end of the exposition, mm. 118–21, as "the last word" (mm. 282–85 = mm. 118–21). Echoing and slightly expanding the last four bars of the exposition to five, mm. 287–89 bring the whole to a celebratory close.

6

Haydn, String Quartet in G, op. 76 no. 1/i
(Allegro con spirito)

We now turn to a movement with a continuous exposition, the type that does not rely on a central break and relaunch by means of a successful medial caesura and a secondary theme. To introduce this topic, the most instructive classical-era illustrations are those pieces by Haydn whose processual aspects of motivic development and ever-churning *Fortspinnung* are so prominent that they drive through or steer away from any latent or predicted MC opportunity. My seminar choices for this have usually been the finale of Haydn's String Quartet, op. 33 no. 1 in B Minor (*EST*, 54; Hepokoski 2016, 58), the first movement of his Quartet in E-flat, op. 33 no. 2 (*EST*, 54–57), and the first movement of his Symphony No. 45 in F-sharp Minor, "Farewell" (*EST*, 316; Hepokoski 2016, 57). In this chapter I examine a different continuous exposition, the first movement of the String Quartet in G, op. 76 no. 1. This movement offers us a number of interpretive challenges, along with a few ambiguities. Along the way, these will invite further comments on the idiosyncrasies of Haydn's compositional approach, so different from that of Mozart, Beethoven, or Schubert.

Backdrop

This quartet is the first of a set of six composed in 1797, a set now tagged as the "Erdödy Quartets" after the name of the Count who commissioned them. They are late works in the career of "the father of the string quartet," vintage products of the most illustrious composer in Europe. No longer bound to the Esterházy service of the preceding decades, Haydn had installed himself in Vienna following his two trips to London (1791–92, 1794–95). (It is also worth noting that by 1797 his former pupil, young upstart Beethoven from Bonn, now 26 years old, was beginning to turn heads in Viennese aristocratic circles, starting to break into the world of prominent publication and attending to whatever new compositions the old master was producing.) While Haydn would compose no more symphonies, his attention was turning toward vocal works. "The commission from Erdödy," write the Graves (2006, 302), "came at a time when Haydn was otherwise occupied with vocal music," including the onset of annual masses "for Princess Maria Hermenegild Esterházy's name day" and ongoing work on his Handel-challenging oratorio *The Creation*. In addition to these six quartets' potential "connections to song, aria, and learned-style

A Sonata Theory Handbook. James Hepokoski, Oxford University Press (2021). © Oxford University Press.
DOI: 10.1093/oso/9780197536810.003.0006.

traditions," it is not difficult, with the Graves, to perceive a remarkable diversity and sophistication of musical invention that was advancing beyond any mere entertainment function into the realm of the connoisseur. In the op. 76 quartets Haydn was responding to the "growing sophistication among musical consumers by accommodating their thirst for novelty and acknowledging their familiarity with the idiosyncrasies of his art" and seeking to "inspire and instruct them through his many-faceted engagement of the musical resources at hand" (2006, 302–3).

By the 1780s and 1790s, and certainly in the hands of Haydn and Mozart, the string quartet was on its way to becoming one of the most advanced demonstrations of compositional art—a private genre aimed at a potential mix of professional and non-professional, "domestic" performers, but a genre particularly savored by connoisseurs. As Klorman has documented, from the late eighteenth century onward there has been a tradition of regarding chamber music as a *conversation*—not an "oration . . . delivered by a single speaker addressing a faceless public, [but rather] a conversation [that] takes place among a circle of friends, all of whom participate" (2016, 23). A prominent voice along these lines from the late twentieth century has been that of Carl Dahlhaus, who characterized high-galant chamber music's tendency toward the ideal of "the [utopian] spirit of conversation—under the aegis of humane education—which suspended class distinctions, at least until countermanded" (1989, 43).[1]

Noting some limits on certain construals of the concept of conversation, Klorman's study addresses more broadly the idea of chamber music as "social interplay" and has extended the conversation metaphor into a theory of *multiple agency*. "When chamber music is described as conversational (or, alternatively, operatic)," he writes, authors are usually

> refer[ring] to a way of experiencing a musical passage or composition as embodying *multiple, independent characters—often represented by the individual instruments—who engage in a seemingly spontaneous interaction involving the exchange of roles and/or musical ideas.* . . . A chamber music score is, above all, something to be *played*, an encoded musical exchange in which each player assumes an individual character, similar in many respects to a theatrical script. (2016, 122–23, italics in original)

Under such a view, one corroborated by the experience of the performers, say, of a string quartet, each of the four musicians is staged as an individual yet essential part of a closely knit, interacting group. The scenario is both fictive (as a musical narrative or action scripted "from above" by the composer) and actual (among the performers executing the script in real time). Each performer listens to the others, attends deeply, intimately, to them, taking cues from or responding to them, and also, at times, joining happily in the full, resonant "quartet texture" that is such a feature of the mature string quartet. No works better exemplify such an ideal than those of Haydn.

Brief, in-tempo introduction (mm. 1–2)

What we hear first are three assertive, multiple-stop chords, I-V^7-I, underpinning a top-voice $\hat{1}$-$\hat{2}$-$\hat{3}$ motion, G_5-A_5-B_5, all sounded in front of the repeat sign and before the main theme starts with the upbeat to bar 3. Preliminary gestures that precede a "real P" are not uncommon in this repertory. For analysts the question is: does that opening gesture belong or not belong to the exposition? To answer that question we ask two others: Is it included in the expositional repeat? And does it appear also at the start of the recapitulation? As observed already in chapter 4, if the answer to both questions is yes, we call that a P^0 gesture or theme ("P-zero"), preceding P^1 proper. The most familiar example of a P^0 gesture is heard at the opening of the first movement of Beethoven's Fifth Symphony, and one finds them in many other Beethovenian expositions as well. But that is not the case here. These two bars reappear neither in the expositional repeat nor at the start of the recapitulation (m. 140). (Their three-stroke, choppy rhythm, though, does recur here and there, most notably at the conclusion of the exposition [mm. 87–88], in the cello at the onset of the development, mm. 89–90, and at the end of the movement, mm. 224–25.) We therefore designate these opening two bars as a *brief, in-tempo introduction* that precedes sonata space proper (*EST*, 86–87, 292). Its role is at least fourfold: to set the preceding silence into sonic motion (that is, to open up the expectant silence of the external world into the differing, virtual world of music); to capture the attention of the listener with an arresting gesture; emphatically to throw open the sonata; and to declare the key of the work-to-come.

Beginning a work with a triple-stroke, annunciatory rhythm was a long-established generic option in the eighteenth century. (Beethoven's *Eroica* would shorten the gesture to two. Haydn's Quartet in E-flat, op. 71 no. 3 had truncated it to a single, abrupt chord, not unlike an urgent canine bark.) More generally, sounding three chordal, *forte* "hammer-blows" was a common rhetorical way to highlight major points of structural division, one not infrequently found at MC points and at the ends of expositions and recapitulations. Another question that might arise with mm. 1–2 is whether we wish to regard them as articulating a cadence. The answer is no. To borrow Caplin's distinction once again (2004, 81–85), while they house a *cadential content* (I-V^7-I), they do not serve a *cadential function*, that is, the function of ending something. (Among Haydn's generously stocked storehouse of clever incongruities is that of occasionally beginning an Allegro composition with a "cadential-content" closing formula—often as a brief, in-tempo introduction— that will have later repercussions in the piece. Other instances can be found in the opening bars of the Quartet in G, op. 33 no. 5; the Quartet in B-flat, op. 71 no. 1; and the Quartet in C, op. 74 no. 1.) In addition, a $\hat{1}$-$\hat{2}$-$\hat{3}$ rise in the upper voice, supported by I-V-I (or I-V^6-I) in the bass, is a standard *initiatory* move, one often presented more decoratively. This is the pattern that Gjerdingen christened the DO-RE-MI schema, "a favored opening gambit in the galant style" (2007, 78).

Exposition (mm. 3–88)

Once again, one of the first questions that we ask of an exposition is whether it articulates a medial caesura somewhere in its center, one followed immediately by a characteristic secondary theme (S) in an appropriate new key. An initial round of listenings to op. 76 no. 1/i, coupled with a glance or two at the score, will indicate that there is no obvious break or gap where we might expect an MC to be. Instead, the impression is one of a more or less unbroken flow. The most notable out-of-tonic, non-elided break occurs with the emphatic V:PAC at m. 72, surely too late to be taken for a V:PAC MC. (It occurs about 81 percent of the way through this exposition.) We preliminarily project that m. 72 is more likely to be the point of *essential expositional closure*, the EEC, followed by a typically unbuttoned, Haydnesque closing theme at m. 73. Consequently, our initial suspicion is that we are dealing with either a continuous exposition, with no MC and no S, or, much less likely, one featuring a masked or obscured medial caesura. This is to be determined by closer analysis.

Primary theme (P^1, P^2, mm. 3–32)

Mm. 3–18 present the leading idea of the movement in a manner that illustrates perfectly Klorman's concept of multiple agency, in which each performer is scripted as an individual voice interacting and responding to the other three members. Called to attention by mm. 1–2, the voices enter singly, one by one, rising in register from bottom to top: cello (mm. 3–6), viola (mm. 7–10), second violin (mm. 11–14); first violin (mm. 15–18). These are not imitative entries in the manner of a fugal exposition but rather a double-statement of an eight-bar theme, (4+4) + (4+4), each statement of which is an implicit, if skeletal, period. The two antecedents, mm. 3–6 and 11–14, end with implied half-cadence effects, while the two consequents, mm. 7–10 and 15–18, as compliant replies to the antecedents (each beginning with a modest variant of the antecedent's basic idea), end with implied perfect-authentic-cadence effects. The decorative turns in the lower voice in mm. 14 and 18 attenuate but do not undercut these cadential effects. With the successive entries of the second and first violin, the theme is repeated an octave higher and accompanied by an additional voice: initially second violin and cello, then first violin and viola. The complementarity of the voices' partnership could hardly be clearer. Each instrument sounds an essential phrase of the melody, joining into an agreement to build a sonata as partners before converging as a full, sonorous quartet in m. 19. What matters is not so much the theme itself as the idea of an emerging, participatory consent from all parties. That this initial gesture of invitation and inclusion is placed at the very start of the six op. 76 quartets is doubtless no coincidence.

    Here we might pause to reflect on a distinctive aspect of so much of Haydn's music. As was also the case in the first movement of the "Military" Symphony (chapter 5), the primary theme (P—or P^1, as will emerge) is a jaunty, comradely idea, unassuming in its presentation but proposing a *Gemütlichkeit* that speaks to the sociability of both the theme and the immediate occasion of quartet-playing. It's a clearly etched, matter-of-fact statement, a genial initial proposal, not brilliant on its own terms but one that plants a proposition to be unwrapped, worked upon, and elaborated in the ensuing sonata-work. The resonance of these opening ideas differs from that of many of Mozart's richly emotive themes, which can limn the subjective contours of a hypothetical, individualized (operatic?) personality.

This is to say neither that Haydn's characteristic opening themes carry little affective charge nor that they are not objects of aesthetic delight.[2] Considered from one angle, Haydn's themes are generic; considered from another, they are ear-catchingly quirky, unusual realizations of the generic. We are asked to find enjoyment in them as opportunities for later, unexpected elaborations. Haydn's sonata forms invite us to relish the manipulations that this connoisseur's entertainment affords in his hands. We often hear remarks about Haydn's witty or humorous character, but this shopworn trope must not be reduced to "wit" in the comic sense alone. Haydn's work is serious indeed, just as high play can be serious. One might more accurately construe his style as a constant striving for engaging originality, an animated cleverness, an agility of mind, or a festive joy in playing the sonata game at the highest levels of technique and mastery.

By m. 18 we have arrived at the second implicit I:PAC, the first having occurred at the end of the first statement of the theme. At m. 19 the four performers coalesce in a plush, four-voice texture to sound a new but obviously related idea grounded in the leading rhythm of the opening module. Above a sustained tonic pedal, the upper voices of mm. 19–20 and 21–22 lay out the presentation modules of a new sentence, αα, with β beginning in m. 23, and β itself, it might be noted, also has aspects of a second presentation. Have we now entered the next action zone, the transition (TR)? To answer this we look ahead to determine whether there are any additional tonic-key authentic cadences. And there are two of them: the quickly passed-through I:PAC at m. 28 and the more emphatic I:PAC at m. 32. (While observing this, we might also have glanced ahead to notice that the ensuing m. 33 veers off onto a very temporary E minor [vi].) Mm. 19–32 therefore remain in the primary-theme, tonic-key action space (P), which is sealed off at m. 32. Remembering our shorthand notational system, in which within any action zone superscript integers are notched upward for new material following a PAC, we can now regard mm. 3–18 as P^1 (more specifically, as P^1 and its varied repetition at m. 11) and mm. 19–32 as P^2 (or perhaps as P$^{2.1}$, with P$^{2.2}$ designating the cadential mm. 26–32). Noting the prolonged tonic pedal from m. 19 to m. 25, a feature often characteristic of tonic-confirming codettas, we also observe that what seems to have started off as a pedal-grounded codetta (P^{cod}) is unlocked at m. 26 (prompting an potential reinterpretation, P^{cod}==>P^2) to produce a I:PAC at m. 28 that is then reinforced in the ensuing four bars.

By m. 32 we have experienced four I:PACs, two implicit, mm. 10 and 18, and two explicit, mm. 28 and 32. The last of these stated is the most emphatic of the four: an expanded cadential progression (ECP) launched by the I^6 chord in m. 29. As we proceed through P, each I:PAC effect becomes stronger, more decisive. Why might Haydn have decided to include a second P idea, mm. 19–32—and not only a second P but one leading to two additional I:PACs, thereby producing what Sonata Theory calls an *overdetermined tonic* within P space? To understand this is to grasp what must have been the broad arc of the governing idea that extends from m. 1 to m. 32. Here we have the production of three separate musical ideas, mm. 1–2, mm. 3–18, and mm. 19–32. Mm. 1–2, the brief, in-tempo introduction (pre-sonata), opens up musical space, calls the proceedings to order, and prepares all parties for the sonata-to-come. But are the necessary participants in agreement to work together to build a sonata? In P^1, the answer, given by each performer separately, is yes: each is willing to play the cooperative role assigned to it—all of which is resonant with Klorman's view of chamber music as "social interplay" among the individual musicians. The fourfold handshake having been made in mm. 3–18 (with only implicit I:PACs), the four voices are now shown in a mutually supportive concord, mm. 19–32, striding forth toward two increasingly decisive cadences that will end the P action zone—and by implication will now be ready to move onward.

In sum, mm. 3–32 can be read as an ongoing process of growth and certainty, a local instance of *generative form* or *form as process*, a concept also often associated especially with much of Beethoven's, Brahms's, and Schoenberg's music ("organic" motivic ramification, "developing variation"). As mentioned in chapter 1, Sonata Theory does not regard the processual aspect of those measures—and of that which, similarly, follows them—as the central determinant of the movement's architectonic form. Rather, it understands the idea of a generically bounded P space as a given, as something conceptually prior to however a composer elects to realize it. In this case Haydn, characteristically, fills that generically pre-given space with a coherent flow of music designed to give the impression of a single idea in the process of steady growth toward a fuller texture and a decisive close—a single idea *in the process of becoming*. As Haydn told his biographer Griesinger, "Once I had seized upon an idea, my whole endeavor was to develop and sustain it in keeping with the rules of art. . . . This is what so many younger composers lack; they string one little idea after another; they break off when they have scarcely begun. Hence nothing remains in the heart after one has heard it" (as cited in Webster 2005a, 37).[3]

Transition (TR), beginning (mm. 33–c. 47–48)

Following a tonally overdetermined P space, it is not unusual to begin TR by veering off onto a differing tonal color, and that is what Haydn does here. Mm. 33–34 continue the music-as-process impression by sounding P's two-bar basic idea on vi, E minor. Mm. 35 and 36 further activate m. 34's rhythm and shift the music down two-fifths ([e], A^6, D), pointing toward an intended restabilization on D major (V), the normative secondary key area for a G-major exposition. But we are not securely there yet. As the music pursues its developing-process activity, two C naturals, mm. 37 and 38—the second starting a succession of downbeat *forzando* stings—generate the drop of another fifth to G^6 in m. 39. This comes to be interpreted as IV^6 of V, D major: once touched, this G-major chord starts to take on a half-cadential directionality through two chromatic alterations. First, the G-major subdominant chord darkens to G minor ($g^6 = iv^6$ of V, m. 40). And second, Haydn alters the G-minor chord into an augmented-sixth chord (m. 41), sounded *fortissimo* and driving strongly into a downbeat V in m. 42, an emphatic half cadence (V of D).

With mm. 42–43 we arrive at the moment of the exposition that is most challenging to interpret. Most obvious is the forceful dominant, A_2 in the cello, sustained as a pedal from m. 42 through m. 47. Such a dominant-lock normally signals the approach of an upcoming V:HC MC—a textural break after which a secondary theme will begin. But since there is no evident break or gap present in the area around mm. 45–50, that does not happen. By these lights, Haydn has baited us with the expectation of a V:HC MC, then switched strategies around mm. 47–48: the *bait-and-switch tactic* sometimes found in this composer's TRs.

On the other hand—and here is the ambiguity—since experienced listeners know that Haydn's secondary themes can be P-based (they frequently begin with P's basic idea, now in V), we should reflect on the viability of a different interpretation. This would be one in which a hypothetical P-based S is heard as beginning in the first violin at m. 43, albeit over that just-attained dominant-lock and starting off with a melody and second-violin/viola accompaniment that begin not on the tonic but rather on the supertonic, ii, of D, initiating what amounts to a ii-V-I-V progression over the V pedal, thereby sustaining its dominant-chord hold. On the face of it, such a reading is counterintuitive: one wonders how many competent listeners would register the music in this way, as opposed, say, to being argued into it after the fact. Nonetheless, pursuing the hypothesis, this reading would be obliged to accept three additional conclusions: (1) that m. 42, beat 3, must be interpreted as a hyper-abrupt MC that is not accompanied by a gap of silence (which is at least conceivable); (2) that the first four or five bars of such an "S," at best, are problematized by being sounded as an accumulative "sliding" over the sustained V in the bass (in Sonata Theory terms, it would start out as an S^0—"S-zero"—theme), even though such a sustained V is far more normatively the signal of a drive toward an upcoming MC; and (3) that there is no indication that this conjectural "S" makes the conventional drop from the preceding *fortissimo* (m. 41) to *piano* as the music streams onward.[4] To these qualms one might add yet another. It is strongly normative that S begin with material that contrasts with the music immediately preceding it. While Haydn's characteristic P-based S themes display an obvious affinity to P, they are often preceded by a clear MC and by TR music that is less obviously P-grounded. In this case the impression is that the ongoing music-as-process strategy is continuing onward, unbroken. The upbeat and first three beats of m. 43, for instance, replicate those of m. 33 under different harmonic lights.

Such an ensemble of caveats casts doubt on the viability of any such "S" reading, or at least on its intuitive persuasiveness. A subtler interpretation would be that at m. 43 Haydn presents us with a P-based-S option that might have been but that self-extinguishes above the dominant pedal amidst music-process conditions that imply something fluid and uninterrupted. On this reading, mm. 43–46 register an "S"-potential idea that cannot function as S in this environment, a once-imagined possible option that is now being left behind.[5] This P-based idea, underpinned by a doggedly sustained dominant, rises in anticipatory quasi-sequences, as if building toward something else, and the musical stream flows unstoppably onward. The more nuanced reading, then, is that unless this dominant-lock leads to a clear MC, growing more unlikely with every bar, we may be about to encounter a shift into a continuous exposition. And this is precisely what we find.

Transition continues (TR)==>FS, c. 47/48–72

The ingenious feature of the dominant-lock from m. 42 to m. 47 is that, instead of pushing through to a normative MC, it is gathered up into a prolonged anticipatory function, like the slow pulling-back of a bowstring or the slow tipping-over of a container of liquid. Far from leading to a medial caesura sealing off the TR zone, the sustained half cadence on V of V (starting at m. 42) undergoes a process of conversion into an anacrusis to the tonic downbeat at m. 48. It would be an error to read m. 48 as a V:IAC. Nothing closes here. In the first place, the V^7-I motion is replicated in mm. 49–50. Surely not closural themselves, as is clear from what follows, mm. 49–50 reopen any closural effect that one might mistakenly have attributed to m. 48. Moreover, taken together, mm. 47–48 and 49–50 can rhetorically imply the beginning of a new sentence (αα') propelled *en route* as a new forward impulse. The preceding HC transformation into V-as-anacrusis (mm. 42–47) has pushed the sonic stream through any putative cadential reading at m. 48, recharging the continuous flow.

At mm. 47–48, then, listeners can experience a *point of conversion* at which the more common two-part-exposition option is discarded. Reflecting back on what we have heard, our initial expectation at m. 33, however tentative, might have been that we were more likely to have started a TR that would lead to the more commonly encountered MC and then an S. But now, through mm. 47–48's persistent spinning-out (its *Fortspinnung*, FS), the exposition shows itself to be continuous. At the point of conversion the once-hypothetical P-based-S option is left behind, receding into the past as the music branches off into divergent, more intensely powered streams of ongoing process.[6] Moreover, at m. 47 the P-based motivic elaboration that has permeated the music through m. 46 relinquishes its grip. Mm. 43–46 provide us with a smooth shift of gears into the propulsive eighth-note activity that will dominate many bars to come. We can now perceive that m. 47 marks a moment of crossing that divides the music-elaboration process not into two standard, separable action zones (like TR and S) but rather into two distinct but continuous activity phases.

While the ongoing musical current has now tipped into D major (V), for the moment that key is held onto only tenuously. It bears repeating that a central tenet of Sonata Theory is that no key is fully realized until it is secured with a cadence, preferably a PAC. One may certainly enter into a key's unmistakable orbit, with the sense that the music is now controlled by that key's scalar content and characteristic harmonic progressions. But until that key is ratified with a cadence, it is present only as a *tonal color*—something that might be lost or something temporary or transient that one might be only passing through. We casually say that we are now "in D major"—understandable enough in shorthand-talk—but until that D major is cadentially confirmed, what we mean is that this key exists only as a proposition. When an exposition enters into dominant-key territory, that key remains an aspiration, something still to be ratified, and in many expositions the trajectory toward the cadence meets a number of obstacles along the way.

Following m. 48, the key-securing V:PAC is delayed until m. 72, far down the road, as Haydn leads the music through a field of textural struggles and modal- and tonal-color adventures. These stratagems of relatively late-in-the-game deflection and delay are typical of the composer, and they can be found in many of his other works. It is as though D major, into whose gravitational realm the composer has entered by m. 42, is only weakly in force, not yet fully subdued and susceptible to local, Haydnesque flat-side cloudings and decays. Haydn stages m. 72's eventual moment of essential expositional closure (the EEC, V:PAC) as the end-point of a turbulent process of harmonic and textural squabbles: through dark mini-skirmishes into the "earned" sunlight.

While mm. 47–72 enact a *Fortspinnung* narrative of the dominant key, D major, passing through a gauntlet of musical blows, it is one that is not difficult to trace. Following the hopeful confidence of mm. 47–50, the music stalls and stammers on a predominant chord, ii^6, mm. 51–53—a galant tarrying or lingering tactic that Gjerdingen dubs as the INDUGIO (2007, 273–83). Mm. 51–53's neighboring diminished sevenths suggest a potential eroding of D major, and, by mm. 54–55 the music collapses into the parallel D minor, as the running eighth notes take on a blustery tinge. The affective situation intensifies with the furious D-minor octave-drubbings of mm. 56–58.

How to escape this hailstorm of minor-mode pummeling? Solution: at m. 59 inflect D minor's fifth (A) up a half-step to the sixth (B♭): the familiar "L operation" (*Leittonwechsel* or 5-6 shift), producing the effect of "inflating" a D-minor sonority into a B-flat major one.[7] While the textural harangue is to be endured for an additional five bars (mm. 59–63), the musical process has at least transformed a minor chord (d) into a major one (B♭), albeit one still within D minor's orbit (♭VI of D major and/or D minor). We have encountered this B-flat before, as the bass of the g^6 in m. 40. There the exit had been through the augmented-sixth chord (m. 41). Analogously, at m. 64 the eighth-note hammerings suddenly give way to a held "augmented sixth," though in a different and uncommon inversion: it is D$_3$ that is the lowest chordal pitch, not B♭$_3$. The effect is that of a prolonged groan of pain: mm. 64–65, repeated and marked *forzando*, mm. 66–67, then moaning further with the descent, now with a sudden drop to *piano*, into the held c#^{o7} in mm. 68–69.

That c#^{o7} proves to be the corridor of passage out of the preceding turmoil. Interpreting it as vii^{o7} of D major, Haydn leads it to a tonic-major chord (m. 70), turning the corner to initiate a stock D-major cadential close. As if demonstrating that the just-heard clamor was little more than sound and fury signifying nothing— nothing at all—Haydn, with a nonchalant wave of his hand, pulls us out of it with the most blindingly naïve of major-mode cadential formulas, concluding with the V:PAC in m. 72. ("You weren't *really* worried, were you?") This PAC secures the now-"earned" D major and with it the point of essential expositional closure (EEC) that concludes the adventurous expansion section.

Closing zone (C, mm. 73–88)

With D major cadentially secured at m. 72, Haydn rounds off the exposition with a zone of trouble-free, relaxed satisfaction. Following an explicit or implicit EEC— often attained through ingeniously staged harmonic, contrapuntal, or textural struggles and delays—Haydn frequently celebrates that achievement with a congen- ially rustic, naïve-popular new theme (C^1) that immediately clarifies the preceding density of compositional thought with an air of insouciant ease. Those familiar with many of the composer's works can immediately recognize the "C-theme style."[8]

What we find beginning at m. 73 is a perfect example of such a theme, one that also restores the affective tone and congenial bounce heard in P^1. *Non-elided* with m. 72's EEC, the theme proper starts with the upbeat into m. 73, but the accompanying rhythmic stream, gently murmuring eighth-note figuration, has already been introduced to fill the gap in m. 72. Sonata Theory could regard the fill at m. 72 as one type of C^0 event—"C-zero"—that of introductory, rustling accompaniment preceding the theme itself. (Similar preliminary accompaniments can be found leading into the C^1 themes in the first movements, for instance, of Symphonies No. 99 [m. 71] and 100 [mm. 93–94, there perhaps an S^{C0}, as interpreted in chapter 5] and the Quartet in E-flat, op. 71 no. 3 [mm. 62–63].) M. 72 also sets in place the D$_3$ downbeat tonic pedal that will underpin C^1 and persist through m. 80. One often finds such tonic-grounding pedals in C-zones, serving as an unequivocal stabilizer of an already attained tonic.

One might construe the structure of what happens from m. 73 to the end of the exposition in either of two ways. Their difference will depend on how we interpret m. 80 and the music that immediately follows it. Is m. 80 the conclusion of a brief but self-contained thematic idea (mm. 73–80), or is it only the presentation of a larger compound sentence stretching from m. 73 to m. 86 or even to m. 88? The difficulty encountered by the first interpretation is that, since a persistent tonic pedal cancels out the possibility of a bassline $\hat{5}$-$\hat{1}$ motion, the strict view would insist that m. 80 cannot be regarded as a cadence, that is, as a closural gesture that ends a theme. And yet the 4+4 top-voice thematic layout clearly suggests that of a brief, rudimentary period. The closural "feel" at m. 80 would then be regarded as rhetorical, not literal. Moreover, what follows it are two statements of a contrapuntally elaborated and harmonized version of the QUIESCENZA schema, with the C naturals in mm. 80 and 81, then 83 and 84, initiating two rotary motions around the tonic, 8-♮7-6-♯7-8—each ending with a V:PAC. Such a double-QUIESCENZA, here at mm. 80–83 and the octave-higher repetition in 83–86, can be read as assuming their familiar late-expositional role of an appended codetta to a (here only rhetorically) cadentially completed theme. Under this reading, mm. 86–88 then round things off with another codetta.

On the other hand, it is also possible, though perhaps more strained, to construe mm. 73–80 as the presentation of a compound sentence, αα′, 4+4, with each α construed as a compound basic idea. This view would then read the harmonized double-QUIESCENZA in mm. 80–86 as β, the compound sentence's continuation (including its cadence). Under this interpretation, mm. 73–86 are to be heard as a single, compound-sentential theme with a foreshortened and repeated continuation. This certainly skirts the problem of the non-PAC at m. 80, and mm. 73–76 and 77–80. The difficulty comes with the cadence-effecting double-QUIESCENZA in the following bars. Again, at least in normative practice, such a double-QUIESCENZA typically serves as a post-thematic codetta, though under this reading it would be obliged to be regarded as the compound sentence's continuation.

As always, even while one might lean toward the one reading or the other, Sonata Theory prefers to include an explication of the ambiguities at hand. My own preference, perhaps responding to a more intuitive interpretation of this closing zone, is the first of them, whereby mm. 73–80 are heard as a rudimentary period over a tonic pedal. In any event, as already observed, the two V:PACs in mm. 83 and 86 are followed by a (second) brief codetta, mm. 86–88, which seals off the whole with stock V-I cadential flourishes, the last two bars of which might have been crafted to recall the triple-stroke rhythm of mm. 1–2, in part to prepare also for the expositional repeat, which begins again in bar 3.

Development (mm. 89–139)

Temporarily setting aside the question of keys and modulations, let's look first at which of the exposition's materials turn up in this section, and in what order. What we are seeking is a sense of whether the development is *fully rotational* (using selected expositional materials from different parts of the exposition and presenting them in their original order), *half rotational* (using materials only from the earlier parts of the exposition), or, perhaps, *non-rotational* (either relying on different materials or using the exposition's ideas out of order). As laid in chapters 1 and 4, any fresh introduction of P, following differing musical matter, suggests its role as a new *rotation initiator*, and developments often start with elaborations of P that go on to introduce a selection of other, later ideas from the exposition, but in their original order.

We see at once that mm. 89–96 are P-based: a *developmental rotation* begins here. In this case the triple-stroke underlaid in the cello in mm. 89–90 alludes to the rhythm of the introductory mm. 1–2, and the P-idea is accompanied by a running-eighth-note counterpoint above. But now the question is: does the P idea persist—and for how long? At m. 96 Haydn relinquishes the P idea, and the running eighths take on, initially, the spiky shape of mm. 61–62, and these and related arpeggiations carry on through m. 118. Considered as a whole, mm. 89–118 present an idea from the continuous exposition's Phase 1 (P) followed by an extract from its Phase 2 activity (jagged arpeggiations, as in mm. 60–62). Its materials are taken, in order, from the opening part and then the later part of the exposition. These observations are sufficient for Sonata Theory to group mm. 89–118 as a *full rotation*. That rotation ends at m. 118, for at m. 119 P material returns: another *rotation initiator*. Richly contrapuntal in all four voices, this return of P also marks a point of sonorous textural arrival, and contrapuntally rich P-variants pervade the remainder of the development: there are no more obvious references to the exposition's latter half. Consequently, mm. 119–39 constitute a *half rotation*, with the recapitulation setting off at m. 140. Conclusion: in terms of its selected thematic/rhetorical ideas, Haydn structured this development as a full rotation that is renewed and succeeded by a half rotation, with m. 118, beat 3, marking the boundary between them.

With a general sense of the development's thematic arrangement, we now glance at its harmonic plan. Beginning a development with P in the exposition's secondary key, as happens here, is a familiar procedure: the *first-level default*. Haydn first presents us with the antecedent phrase of P^1 in D major, mm. 89–92, as one of two voices unfolding in strict, two-voice counterpoint. In mm. 93–96, however, the consequent veers into E minor (ii of the local D, vi of the tonic G). That E minor, recalling the E-minor onset of the exposition's TR (mm. 33–34), will prove to be a tonal centerpoint around which much of the ensuing development will revolve. The jagged-arpeggiation figure steps forth at mm. 96–100, initially to sway through an E-minor tonic-dominant oscillation. In mm. 100–2 the E-minor chord is taken as the first element of a seventh-chord-enriched, descending-fifth chain (mm. 100–8), dropping by fifths every bar from m. 101 onward, away from and then back to E minor. Haydn prolongs E minor further for three more bars, mm. 109–11, before jostling it onto A minor (a fifth lower), mm. 112–15. Now taking mm. 111–15 as a broad model ($[e]-E_2^4-a^6-E_5^6-a$), Haydn leads it through two metrically compressed sequences, with the chords pushing forward twice as fast as those in the model. In the first sequence the model is replicated down a fifth, down to D minor, mm. 115–17 ($[a]-A_2^4-d^6-A_5^6-d$). Were this model to be mechanically replicated, the next key to be touched would be that down another fifth, G—the tonic key. Evidently not wishing to touch on the tonic at this point, Haydn elects instead for a variant of the FONTE schema (Gjerdingen 2007, 61–71) in order to notch the pitch level only a whole step lower, onto C (mm. 117–19 [d]–G_2^4–C^6–G_5^6–C).

But recall that m. 118, beat 3, is also a moment of rhetorical (thematic) disjunction. At that point we arrive at the end of the initial developmental rotation and are about to take off on a new one. Notwithstanding this moment of rhetorical conclusion, m. 118, beat 3, does not end a phrase. Instead, the ever-tightening sequences from m. 111 to m. 119 can be heard as an extended, urgent anacrusis that empties out, non-elided, onto the return of P at m. 119. In addition, the tense harmonic and metrical activity of those bars, extending into m. 119, sutures the dividing-point between the end of the initial, full rotation and the onset of the half rotation that follows. Retrospectively, we might go so far as to construe the entirety of the first developmental rotation as an even broader-scale preparation, more clearly vectored at its end, to the strong culminating downbeat on m. 119.

A new thematic rotation, now only a half rotation, starts off at m. 119 with the P-figure on C major, sounded in a richly textured, four-voice "quartet style." But the C-color proves to be transient. What follows is another set of anticipatory windups. Haydn ratchets the tonal level up by step twice, pushing it first through D minor (mm. 122–23), and, finally, back to the recurring tonal centerpoint, E minor (mm. 124/125–29). In turn, this E minor now descends by two fifths (A^6–D, mm. 130–31), finally shaking loose of E minor (interpreting it as vi of I) and arriving on V of the tonic (D, an active dominant, V_A, of I, m. 131). This active dominant is the goal of all of the preceding developmental activity, signaling that that section is near its end. The once-stable D at the end of the exposition and the start of the development has been converted into an active V of I. Sustained now as a dominant-lock whose upper line (whose first four bars advance melodically into the opening of P^2, mm. 19–22) strains dramatically up to the climactic ninth in m. 137, that D chord is preparatory to the onset of the recapitulation at m. 140. The V_A (mm. 131–39), of course, does not "resolve" to the initial tonic at the very beginning of the recapitulation: there is no cadence here. Instead, as almost always happens at the ends of developments, the V_A is harmonically interrupted—left hanging, albeit with a sense of anticipation.

Recapitulation (mm. 140–225)

The analytical procedure to be followed with all recapitulations is to compare them, bar by bar, to the exposition. Which measures are retained? Which are altered? As the previous chapter has already shown, with Haydn's recapitulations this is typically a more challenging task than with those of Mozart, Beethoven, Schubert, and others. Varied and unpredictable, Haydn's recapitulatory solutions customarily exhibit a reluctance to indulge in broad stretches of simple replication or transposition. On the contrary, he is more likely to continue the compositional impulse all the way to the end—the ongoing musical process of creative composition.

Given the regularized guidelines and expectations built into the mid-to-late-century sonata genre, Haydn must have developed early on an aversion to certain kinds of localized standardization. (Recall again his remark about his Esterházy decades: "Cut off from the world, nobody around me could upset my self-confidence, and so I had to become original.") True, he almost always retained the broadest features of that genre: the concept of expositional and recapitulatory internal action zones with their customary key plans, the rotational principle in the ordering of themes, the need for a relatively balanced tonal resolution in the second half of the recapitulation, and the like. And yet, with regard to how the local details were carried out, Haydn delighted in mixing ongoing regularities with ongoing surprises. Consequently, he steered clear of any extended reliance on commonplace practices, favoring instead his penchant for unceasing compositional play. Very little is routinized in his music. To grasp what Haydn is up to—the joy of the sonata as a dense, sophisticated connoisseurs' game—one needs to keep in mind a generalized backdrop of the normative, against whose more predictable aspects the composer's ongoing inventiveness can be perceived.

Here the recapitulation begins regularly enough, with a four-bar, tonic-key restatement of P¹'s antecedent (mm. 140–43 = mm. 3–6), now sporting that additional upper line that we had heard at the beginning of the development. But four bars of restatement is all that we get. Mm. 144–51 give us a new continuation, a passing dive into unanticipated canonic play. Led off by the first violin, P¹'s initial three notes ($\hat{5}$-$\hat{3}$-$\hat{1}$) are now isolated, climbing upward step by step in corkscrew fashion—in its rhythmic threes, metrically disrupting the *alla breve* meter—while the second violin and viola, in thirds, follow imitatively at the distance of two beats. Ratcheting upward, the canon breaks off at m. 148, and within a few bars we are led to a contentedly sanguine I:PAC (m. 151), as if nothing extraordinary had happened.

With the equivalent of exposition's P¹ now rounded off, m. 152 slips back on track to rejoin the norm of expositional restatement with several bars replicating most of the original P² (mm. 152–63 = mm. 19–30). This takes us through P²'s first I:PAC (m. 161 = m. 28), which in the expositional model had been followed with a related, reinforcing phrase producing another I:PAC (m. 32). Here, however, that reinforcing module gets only as far as its subdominant chord (m. 163 = m. 30), before being derailed elsewhere—initially onto a converging half cadence (I:HC) at m. 165.

Mm. 164–73 are completely new, a set of *pre-crux alterations* that will soon (at the *crux*) plug back into a near-literal tracking of the expositional model, only at a point where what had been sounded before in the dominant will then be transposed to the tonic. The half-cadential V at m. 165 is sustained as a dominant-lock for several bars, while above it the first and second violins resume their close-canonic interplay (mm. 165–68) now in a descending four-note pattern, all of which suggests an unspooling or winding-down that still—importantly—clings onto the tonic key.

Following the four bars of this dominant-lock, the cello sounds P^1's incipit, now in the tonic (m. 169), and three more connective bars hasten their way to the *crux* at m. 174 (= m. 51, now down a fifth, in the tonic, the start of the ii^6 prolongation).

Notice that in mm. 164–73 Haydn has kept P^2 away from the full closure that he had given it in the exposition. Instead, he has led it into a non-cadential else-where, only to rejoin the expositional model several bars into its TR (or ==>FS). We may therefore regard mm. 164–73 as a characteristic *recapitulatory P-TR merger* (*P==>TR*), in which the exposition's boundary between the two action zones has been erased. What had occupied 20 bars in the exposition (mm. 31–50) is replaced by 10 new bars here in the recapitulation. In sum, up until the crux at m. 174 the recapitulation, with its two passages of recomposition (mm. 144–51 and 164–73), has been foreshortened in comparison with the exposition—a not uncommon pro-cedure in Haydn's music. Such a foreshortening in the earlier stages of the reca-pitulation can suggest that a compensatory expansion might occur at some later recapitulatory point, which, as we shall see, is what does eventually happen.

Once the security of the crux is latched onto, Haydn replicates the expositional model in literal or near-literal correspondence measures for the next 28 bars (mm. 174–201 = mm. 51–78, now in the tonic). This well-mannered behavior covers a good stretch of structural ground. It takes us through the latter portions (FS) of the exposition's expansion section, bringing it to the point of essential structural clo-sure (the ESC, I:PAC [m. 195 = m. 72], the generically mandated cadential goal of the whole movement, fully securing the tonic) and from there into the first six bars (only) of the first statement of the more relaxed, "naïve-popular" C^1 (mm. 196–201 = mm. 73–78). Recall that in the exposition C^1's eight-bar format had been that of a rudimentary period, 4+4, sounded over a tonic pedal. Here in the recapitula-tion we hear the antecedent, mm. 196–99, but only two bars of the consequent, mm. 200–1. Instead of closing it, Haydn diverts the music into an extended, celebratory C^1 romp from m. 202 to m. 215: what had occupied only two bars (mm. 79–80) is now enlarged to 14—probably to be understood as a compensatory enlargement to balance the earlier recapitulatory foreshortening.

Having postponed the expected moment of C^1 closure, these 14 new bars start by interpolating six new bars of expectant anacrusis-buildup (mm. 202–7) that plunge into a second, now-complete statement of C^1 (mm. 208–15 = mm. 73–80, albeit with only an "IAC-effect" this time, at m. 215), probably with the conno-tation of a ecstatically satisfied, festive culmination.[9] Correspondence measures continue into the first statement of the C^2 modified-QUIESCENZA figure (mm. 216–18 = mm. 81–83), but what had been its repetition is now recomposed and modestly expanded (mm. 219–22) to produce a more finalized tonic PAC elided with the finishing-touches of the C^3 flourishes (mm. 223–25 = mm. 86–88).

Beethoven, Symphony No. 2 in D, op. 36/i (Adagio molto–Allegro con brio)

While my seminars in Sonata Theory begin with Mozart and Haydn, two different, historically "model" styles in which classical-era conventions in and around Vienna may be initially perceived or (with Haydn) at least inferred, they soon move onward to Beethoven and eventually into the later nineteenth century. And with Beethoven—even with young Beethoven of the 1790s, newly settled into Vienna—we encounter a composer eager to distinguish himself through dramatic treatments of these conventions: odd twists or attention-grabbing turns, not least around long-established structural markers in expositional and recapitulatory practice.

Those who seek to build a concept of "classically normative sonata form" from Beethoven's early works will find themselves frustrated, for, from the classical or Mozartian perspective, many nontraditional things occur in them. There can be no doubt that young Beethoven had absorbed the classical, action-zone conventions of his predecessors, but he proceeded to realize them in strikingly personalized ways. On the one hand, he often supercharged their inbuilt strength through a new dynamism and dramatic force. On the other hand, *en route*, he often subjected some of the most common aspects of the sonata-form inheritance, such as its standard defaults for medial-caesura treatment or normative key-choice, to provocative distortions, overridings, and deformations. Here, and in compositions from his later decades, one looks at one's peril for consistent exemplifications of the classically normative.[1] Norms and practices change with time, and in the sweep of the turbulent mid-1790s and early 1800s a new generation of composers was moving beyond the potential routinization of what we now call "the classical" in order to forge more personally customized styles.

This does not mean that once we arrive at Beethoven and beyond, Sonata Theory's outline of late-eighteenth-century, classical-era norms and defaults is rendered irrelevant. On the contrary, Beethoven sometimes powerfully reinforced them. But when he did not, it is an approach such as Sonata Theory's that immediately perceives Beethovenian difference as difference, serving as a heuristic filter to determine what is distinctive about his composition—what he brought to the table that is new, and what he brought to the table that would have a profound historical impact on later generations.

A Sonata Theory Handbook. James Hepokoski, Oxford University Press (2021). © Oxford University Press.
DOI: 10.1093/oso/9780197536810.003.0007.

Backdrop

Beethoven composed the Second Symphony over several years, from late 1800 to 1802, by which year at least an early version of it was complete. It was near the end of 1800 and in the initial months of 1801, around his 30th birthday, that he had begun laying out ideas for the first movement before setting it aside to compose the ballet *Die Geschöpfe des Prometheus* and a few other pieces.[2] In 1802 he resumed work on the symphony's succeeding movements, perhaps also modifying the earlier state of the first. In the absence of the autograph score's availability, dating the completion of the symphony's individual movements is difficult. One version of the work was heard in a benefit concert in Vienna's Theater an der Wien on April 5, 1803, flanked by other recent or new pieces (the First Symphony, the Third Piano Concerto, and *Christus am Ölberge*), but it would be another year before the symphony's publication in March 1804. Beethoven might have undertaken some further revisions in the interim.[3] Nonetheless, mid-1802 may be regarded as the time by which the first movement was essentially finalized, along with the rest of the symphony.

During that year, 1802, Beethoven became increasingly alarmed over his growing deafness. It was in the autumn of that year that he penned the confessional Heiligenstadt Testament. It was also the likely year in which he remarked to the violinist Werner Krumpholz that he was "not satisfied with what I have composed up to now. From now on I intend to embark on a new path" (reported by Czerny, here as cited in Lockwood 2003, 124). Commentators generally understand this as a fortified resolve in favor of an even greater compositional boldness, motivic integration, sharpness of contrasts, and formal experimentation, all of which can be found in such works as the op. 30 violin sonatas, the op. 31 piano sonatas, and others, above all in the *Eroica* Symphony from 1803–4. We may understand the Second Symphony as one of the works moving toward, or now onto, this "new path."[4]

By the early 1800s Beethoven was dramatizing the stylistic/generic norms of the era's Austro-Germanic musical production system. Seeking to make his mark, he was setting his music into dialogue with the system that he had inherited, one that had reached a pinnacle of development in the works of Haydn and Mozart. Convinced that such sonata structures were capable of being leveraged upward in dramatic content, Beethoven was ever more doggedly modifying an elite entertainment into something with substantially different claims. This was a risky gamble, all the more so since his self-conscious earnestness often exceeded the prior limits of the tasteful, balanced containment that had still been a prized factor in the works of Haydn, Mozart, and their contemporaries.

Beethoven set out to supercharge the sonata's built-in dynamism (trajectories toward cadences) both on its acoustic surface and in its larger tonal/rhetorical structure. Having assimilated sonata form's generous variety of norms, he was now determined to intensify them, to create a path through them that was more assertive, more decisively stamped, more eccentric, more extreme. Listeners around 1800 might have understood some of his noisier or rougher effects as new-century swerves

away from the *beautiful* in favor of the *sublime*—the sublime of fear, pain, sudden-ness, loudness, vastness, or darkness, whether construed in terms Burkean (stressing the terror that accompanies the experience of the sublime) or Kantian (the dynamic sublime, threatening to overwhelm us in its magnitude, yet remaining capable of being overcome.) To be sure, there were roots of all of this in eighteenth-century practice—*tempesta* or *ombra* effects in Gluck, Haydn, Mozart, and others—but in Beethoven's hands such effects were magnified. However they might have been interpreted, many of the results carried such resolute strength that listeners could imagine that something important and transformational was happening in them.

In a November 1801 letter to his friend Franz Wegeler, one reflecting his personal life, troubling health, and advancing deafness, he had written that he would "seize fate by the throat." The grip of the radical young composer's music was beginning to seize listeners in analogous ways. Such music made new demands on them, some-times channeling the unsettled political/revolutionary moods of the era and some-times suggesting exalted aesthetic moods that spoke in commandingly altered ways from the music of his immediate predecessors. With Beethoven a new, larger game was afoot. One of its axioms was to compose music with such personal force that it could be imagined to be exploring new expressive depths or staking out existential truth claims. This was also music that invited listeners to respond to it with a com-plementary reverence and to urge others to do so as well.

Readers of this chapter will benefit by keeping in mind chapter 5's discussion of Haydn's "Military" Symphony. Conceived only a few years apart, the two first movements share some broad-scale similarities. One is the "fall" into the minor mode in the slow introduction, though such an introductory collapse of major into minor is also found in several other symphonic works of the time. Another is the subsequent sonata's martial response to it. Yet such superficial similarities only accentuate the differences between the two composers. Haydn was 38 years Beethoven's senior. Old Haydn's largely settled worldview and young Beethoven's emergent, disruptive one stand in sharp contrast. To extend a remark made in chapter 5, it is a remarkable experience—a jolt—to hear Beethoven from the per-spective of the norms of Haydn and Mozart, as opposed to hearing his music ret-rospectively from our knowledge of, say, Schumann, Brahms, Bruckner, or Mahler.

Introduction: Adagio molto (mm. 1–33/34)

This slow introduction lays down the essential premise for the rest of the move-ment. It begins with an authoritative *fortissimo*, declared in tutti octaves and pinned in place with a fermata. The creative impulse: "Let this D-major world be!" The mu-sical image that emerges is idyllic, balanced, pastoral, a musical Eden before the fall. Mm. 1–8 lay out a parallel period, though one that divides (1+3) + (1+3). What impresses us as the lyrical period proper is the three-bar unit, in which the piercing sweetness of oboes and bassoons, mm. 2–4 (with upbeat), the antecedent, ending

I:HC, is complementarily replied to in the warm and lush strings, mm. 6–8, the consequent, ending I:PAC. Each of them, antecedent and consequent, is called into existence by *fortissimo* octaves, the second of which, shorn of a fermata, is fortified by its wind-cascade anacrusis in m. 4. This is a freshly created, innocent world in concord with itself, though in the consequent's m. 6 we briefly worry our way through a chromatic patch of crescendo, minor-mode mixture (a warning?). With a plucky *sforzando* resolve, we shrug through it and in m. 7 proceed with a strong *forte* of gamboling trills and frilly, carefree rhythms carrying us up to B$_5$ and thence to the cadential descent. For the present, all is well.

But then it happens—and in hyperdramatic fashion. The D major affirmed at the downbeat of m. 8 decays. In my workshops devoted to this movement I have referred to the crescendo upbeat to m. 9 and the subsequent downbeat *sforzando* as a "sag." In smooth, contrary motion to the upper voices, the bass droops to an alarming A♯ (V$_5^6$/vi), as though the music lacked the strength to sustain D major. (A similar sag, with different but eventually analogous consequences, is found in the introduction to Mozart's "Prague" Symphony, m. 4—which introduction may have been a model for this one.) From m. 9 through the last beat of m. 11, alternating winds and strings attempt to correct the sag through a series of hoists via chromatic ascending 5–6 sequences: (V$_5^6$/vi–vi; V$_5^6$/♯VII–♯VII; V$_5^6$/I–i), aiming at the recovery of D major. On the third beat of m. 11, however, the point of arrival turns out not to be the intended D major, but rather an alarming D minor.

With that trip-wire touch of D minor, the preceding D-major idyll collapses ("the fall"), plunging into a maelstrom of loss. Instead of its earlier sag to A♯, the bass drops through a passing but suddenly *fortissimo* V$_3^4$ to an enharmonic equivalent, B♭ (m. 12), sounded as the root of a forceful B-flat chord. Beethoven prolongs the B-flat shock as a bass pedal, with recurring *fortepiano* jolts. for the next five bars (mm. 12–16, enhanced every other bar by its own V^7), beginning sententially (αα, mm. 12–13, 14–15) and churning with interior rises and plummeting falls to heavy-downbeat accents. This B-flat passage can be reckoned as ♭VI of the initial D major, but in its immediate context it is VI of the new specter of D minor, into whose gravitational force we have been pulled. The remainder of the movement will be devoted to restoring the lost D major, which will be in continual threat of chromatic corrosion and modal collapse until it is heroically regrasped and restored in the final stages of the coda.

At this point, though, the imperative is to shake loose of that fixed B-flat sonority and to seek a potential escape from a D minor that looms just around the corner. As was the case with the earlier sag to the A♯ bass, the initial impulse is once again to rise by step through chromatic, ascending 5–6 sequences. But this strategy is not applied consistently, and the result is a sense of local tonal disorientation that dramatizes the "searching" phase of the era's typical slow introductions. There are two aspects to what ensues: harmonic and rhythmic/figurational. Let's first trace the course of harmonic changes. The B-flat in m. 16 gives way to G^7 (V^7/c, m. 17, thus accomplishing another chromatic ascending 5-6 shift, this time with the chords in root position and leading not to a pure triad but to a seventh chord) and from there up a fourth—or down a fifth—to C^7 (m. 18). The G^7-C^7 (ascending fourth/descending fifth) now drops another fifth, to F^7 (m. 19), as if pulling us back to B-flat. Another application of the chromatic 5–6 hoist (mm. 20–21, D^6_5 –g) brings us to iv of D minor (m. 21), which in turn leads to V^7 of the fateful D minor in m. 22. This V^7 functions as a crescendo-anacrusis that discharges into the imperious D-minor octaves in m. 23 (anticipating the Ninth Symphony of two decades later) and the stark i:HC-effect in m. 24. Here D minor is confirmed with a vengeance: a vicious undermining of the initial, idyllic D major.

Equally important in mm. 17–23 are its aspects of rhythm, orchestration, and internal figuration. Apart from the chordal changes, each bar's content is largely the same, starting out with a strong *sforzando-piano* push and sweeping string rises (and, usually, those "distant" horn-echo responses) and ending with wind-anacrusis figures tipping into the next measure. Here we lock into a fixed, bar-to-bar cyclical process, as though the narrative subject (the fictive "protagonist" implicit in this music) had relinquished a volitional shaping in order to submit to some larger regulating principle. Beethoven's control of hypermeter is as immediately audible as it is astonishing. Listen to mm. 17–23 as if the operative meter were suddenly thrice as slow, with each pulse occurring on the downbeat of the notated bars as each bar's music moves through emptier space. The effect is like one of zooming out from the action, taking a cosmic view of some mysterious procedure.

Once the dominant is attained in m. 24, it is held as a tense, prolonged dominant-lock, mm. 24–33 (generically, the final phase of a slow introduction), punctuated near the end with strong orchestral downbeat blows. Since most of this is governed by an implicit D major—though over V—we might hear this as an attempted re-covery of (or look back at) the lost tonic major.[5] And yet Beethoven treats it as a corridor of suspense, created in part by alternating references to both D major (whenever the pitch F♯ is touched) and D minor (the F♮s). Sonata Theory reads such a passage as a pondering of what we have heard and a projection of the need for the subsequent sonata as a corrective. It can be read metaphorically as the deliberation of a "thinking" music. We have experienced a staging of an existential "fall" from D-major security into D-minor peril—from Schiller's "naïve" mode, perhaps, into his "sentimental" mode, where a lost originary innocence can be regrasped only on different, more sophisticated terms through acts of individual creativity and will. In m. 33 the prolonged dominant converts to a powerful anacrusis, casting us into the sonata action.[6]

Exposition: Allegro con brio

As is usually the case in Beethoven's music from this period, a quick scan of the score can locate the MC that divides the exposition into two parts (m. 71, followed by two bars of caesura-fill), along with the obvious S that succeeds it (m. 73). Accordingly, presuming that we have the music of the whole movement vividly in our ears and memories, we may return to the sonata's first action zone, P, to start our analysis.

Before doing so, though, let's note that the leading imagery in this Allegro con brio is that of martial heroism, struggle, and victory. Its aim: the movement's eventual securing of the D major lost in the introduction. The sonata has modal work to do, something that can be generically accomplished only with the closure provided by the ESC. In this respect its broad-scale narrative is structurally similar to that of the first movement of Haydn's "Military" Symphony, but here the topical images are dramatically enhanced, their collisions and contrasts heightened. Phrase after phrase, the music presses more strenuously toward its goal, driving the narrative forward with single-minded conviction. As Lockwood notes, following a few observations on Beethoven's sketches for the movement (2003, 157), "The spirit of the military march was firmly established from very early on, and however expanded the first movement became, it never lost this spirit."[7] The masculine-oriented valor of the first movement had also been a leading idea of Adolph Bernhard Marx's 1859 reading of the movement—a "wonderful, joyful celebration of sound, to which end all of these heroes of the sound-world, the instrumental groups, are summoned" (227).[8] And as we shall see when we come to the secondary theme, Marx's reading—like Lockwood's and ours—reinforces the metaphor with more explicit soldierly imagery.

Primary theme (mm. 34–47)

The preceding anacrusis, m. 33, is a physical push of the exposition into action: a crescendo plunging to a downbeat *fortepiano*. Like a spring-loaded bolt, P shoots forth from below in the violas and cellos, outlining the D-major triad that will also be its eventual ESC goal, while above the violins shimmer nervously in eighth-note readiness. The 14-bar P theme is easily parsed as sentential and compound. The compound presentation modules, αα′ (mm. 34–37, 38–41, each with a two-bar basic idea and a two-bar contrasting idea), are sounded on I and ii$_5^6$, respectively, though with the G♯$_3$ inflection in the bass (V$_5^6$/V, m. 41) its final bar flows through the presentation phase and into the continuation, β. This continuation initially returns (mm. 42–43) to the contrasting-idea tiptoeing of the preceding two bars, as if recalibrating that figure, tilting it now, via ♭$\hat{7}$ (m. 42), toward the subdominant. It then proceeds with a determined sliding-downward of outer-voice parallel sixths (mm. 44–45, a variant of Gjerdingen's PRINNER schema [2007, 45–60])—here expanding to initiate the final phase, γ, a complete cadential progression that begins with the vii°$_5^6$/ii in the second half of m. 45 (sounding the cadence-triggering $\hat{3}$ in the bass) and pours out into the I:PAC at the downbeat of m. 47.

The closely managed dynamics and orchestration of all this are as important as its effects of harmonic motion and register. The big-push anacrusis at m. 33 and eruptive flare-crescendo of the hypermetrically weak m. 37—another anacrusis-push—give the impression that the *piano*-dynamic P begins the sonata action at an unnaturally quiet level. This is a furtive or cautious onset, waiting for an opportunity to break out. The flare-crescendo is absent from the complementary bar 41 as we move into the continuation's harmonic readjustment of the preceding figure. But following this, the dynamic can be suppressed no longer. Mm. 44–47 drive into the cadence with a resolute crescendo. Recall here the rather strong classical-era norm of *piano* P and elided, tutti/*forte* affirmation TR, a norm that we encountered in Haydn's "Military" Symphony. But with the hyper-dramatic Beethoven, caught up in the urgent currents of the new century, it's as if the impatient P cannot wait for TR's *forte* but surges on its own to provide maximal force onto the downbeat of m. 47. (The same "Beethovenian crescendo" into TR occurs in the outer movements of the First Symphony.) Throughout P as a whole we hear a parallel process of orchestral accumulation—a gathering of sonic forces—on the way to the white-hot tutti that marks the beginning of TR.

Transition (TR, mm. 47–71/73)

Since TR begins with the basic idea of P, this is a transition of the dissolving-restatement type. The dissolution occurs rapidly. The basic idea's $\hat{1}$-$\hat{3}$-$\hat{5}$ arpeggiation shoots aggressively up to $\flat\hat{7}$ (m. 49, re-sounding the $\flat\hat{7}$ from m. 42), tilting again toward the subdominant. This time it more clearly initiates a vigorous QUIESCENZA figure ($\hat{8}$-$\flat\hat{7}$-$\hat{6}$-$\flat\hat{7}$-$\hat{8}$, mm. 49–53).[9] Even more to the point, the B_2, $C\sharp_3$, D_3 hoist in the bass (IV^6-V^6_5 -I, mm. 51–53) revisits the introduction's corrective hoist following the latter's harmonic "sag" (mm. 10–11). TR recalls and responds to that moment, this time bringing the harmony back to D major (m. 53, instead of the "fall" to D minor in the introduction). Now thrashing about, the basic-idea-led QUIESCENZA begins again in m. 53 (Figure 7.1), but this time it drops not to IV^6 (a G-major chord) but to iv^6 (a G-minor chord), with B♭ in the bass (m. 55), re-experiencing the introduction's decay and modal "fall" (m. 12). Once again we hear a corrective attempt to hoist the bass upward through $C\sharp_3$ (m. 56) and thence to D (m. 57), but by this point D major has been lost to D minor, as it had been in the introduction, and it is immediately reinforced with yet another drop to the low B♭ (♭VI) in mm. 59–60. While within the genre it is not uncommon to find a major-mode TR that darkens midway through to its parallel minor or to the minor mode of the major key to come, Beethoven maximizes the drama of that norm through texture, rhythm, motivic figuration, and the crucial back-reference to the introduction.

And now with m. 61 and the G♯ in the bass: panic! The lurch from m. 60 into m. 61 is one of the exposition's most alarming moments, and it has caught the attention of more than one commentator. (Byros 2015 explicates its historical context.) Since it will also play a decisive role in the recapitulation, let's identify it by labeling m. 61 as $TR^{1.2}$. What happens here is a radical disjunction of normative harmonic practice. In the bass the move from B♭ to G♯ suggests a dialogue with

Figure 7.1. Beethoven, Symphony No. 2/i, mm. 53–64.

what Byros identifies as the LE-SOL-FI-SOL schema ($\flat\hat{6}$-$\hat{5}$-$\sharp\hat{4}$-$\hat{5}$), a move familiar from innumerable earlier works. The schema consists of a double-leading-tone circling round a target active dominant (SOL, $\hat{5}$). In mm. 60–61 Beethoven has omitted the potentially implicit dominant, leaving only its neighboring tones (B♭-[A]-G♯-[A]), and the G♯ is no longer a lower neighbor to A but rather the upper third of a different dominant chord: initially an E_5^6 chord (V_5^6 of A minor, V_5^6/v). Thus while the normative schema predicts a possible I:HC (with A as bass), what we find instead is a jagged, unprepared dominant arrival on that E_5^6 sonority, whose root, soon taking over in the bass, is treated as an already ongoing dominant-lock on the way to an MC—as though several connecting bars in between had been excised. As Byros put it, the unprepared new dominant in m. 61 is a "pronounced syntactic violation" or a "sublime intrusion" (2015, 232). Its effect is that of the sounding of an alarm bell.

Modally imperiled and in full panic, the minor-mode, dominant-lock music begun in m. 61 scrambles breathlessly toward the v:HC MC at m. 71. So intense, so unrelenting has the forward motion become that, far from being quelled at the MC, the energy spills over into the caesura gap (mm. 71–72, here sounded in commanding octaves) as a link to S (m. 73)—an instance of what Sonata Theory calls "juggernaut caesura-fill" (*EST*, 44–45). With its touching of the pitch C♯ the fill also accomplishes the crucial reversal of modal color back into major: the A major (V) expected for the exposition's part 2. It is this mm. 71–72 modal reversal on the dominant that A. B. Marx compared to the "sunny triumph on the [now-] luminous E♮," [the appearance of] "a hero in the splendor of his jeweled weapons" (1859, 229)[10]

Secondary thematic zone (S, mm. 73–112)

With the secondary theme, Marx continues (1859, 229), that hero strides in, "fanfare-like, as with a song of triumph sung at half-volume, [yet] splendid and filled with courage, sure of victory before the battle."[11] This is an apt metaphor, and along similar lines one can interpret mm. 73–76 as the march-like aspiration that steps forth in the winds, *piano*, to be received in mm. 77–80 with *fortissimo*, jubilant acclamations by a cheering crowd or fellow band of soldiers—an effect texturally replicated in mm. 81–84 and 85–88. At this point, all is eagerness and expectation. The head-motive of $S^{1.1}$ is rhythmically related to that of P, perhaps suggesting a more evidently martial response to or transformation of it (Figure 7.2a–b). The theme's goal, of course, is to secure the dominant key, A major, with a V:PAC (the EEC) so that the parallel passage in the recapitulation can replicate this in the tonic (the ESC), effecting with it (such is the generic hope) the definitive overturning of the threat of modal collapse initiated in the introduction.

With regard to thematic type, m. 73 marks the onset, to use Byros's words (2015, 232), of "a 40-bar, doubly-compound sentence (based on a 32-bar sentence norm)." This classification means that the sentence's presentation modules ($S^{1.1}$, αα′) are twice as long as those of the normative compound presentation ([2+2] + [2+2]), resulting in (4+4) + 4+4), mm. 73–80 + mm. 81–88, here for a massive, broad-shouldered effect. Each of the eight-bar presentational units concludes with a fleet-ingly tonicized half cadence (V:HC, mm. 80 and 88); one's initial impression is that of an eight-bar antecedent responded to not with the expected consequent but with an orchestrally reinforced repetition of itself.

Instead of articulating the normative point of momentary rest, m. 88's half ca-dence elides into a similarly broad continuation, $S^{1.2}$ (β), dashing headlong into the action under agitated syncopations in the second violins. Spurred onward by *sforzandi* first on the downbeats of every bar (mm. 88–91), then every half bar (mm. 92–95), the insistent rhythm (Figure 7.2c) is yet another transformation of that of P. Initially sounded in the violas and cellos/basses (mm. 88–89), it is immedi-ately picked up by the first violins, flutes, and oboes (m. 90). Its leading idea, man-ically tumbling $\hat{5}$-$\hat{4}$-$\hat{3}$-$\hat{2}$-$\hat{1}$ descents, seems ripe with cadential promise, yet is not ready to produce a cadence on its own. Instead, it hands over the cadential action

Figure 7.2a–b–c. Beethoven, Symphony No. 2/i, rhythm of P and $S^{1.1}$, $S^{1.2}$.

to the single-minded, blunt blows of mm. 96–99 ($S^{1.3}$). With mighty *fortissimi* m. 99 brings us to the cadential precipice (ii-V^7).

But that cadence does not happen. What seems inevitable is undermined by a deceptive move onto IV^6 in m. 100 and a breakdown onto an anguished $vii°^7$ in m. 101 (compare these bars with the "sags" of mm. 11–12 and 51–53)—followed by three mysterious beats of quizzical rest in m. 102, a musical question-mark, or what Kinderman has called "a rip in the form" (2009, 89). The heroic bravado of $S^{1.1}$, $S^{1.2}$, and $S^{1.3}$ has failed. Now collapsed, it has not brought about the EEC. What to do now?

The problem at hand involves what Sonata Theory calls the staging of "S failure": the inability of an ongoing S to produce the EEC, in extreme cases undergoing a total breakdown. One solution is to have different material—sometimes P-based—intervene in a rescue operation. Motivic material from P thus enters *pianissimo* (m. 103)—on A *minor*, no less!—then winds up cumulatively in a grand crescendo, dramatically seizing the *fortissimo* cadential $^6_4$ to reanimate A *major* (m. 110) and then pounce on the authentic cadence at m. 112, the EEC. In such situations "the impression [is] that the P-based material seemingly 'reserved' as a potential for C^1 [that is, the commonly encountered P-based C] is summoned to appear prematurely (in the space originally set aside for S-material proper) to direct the push to the EEC" (*EST*, 140). But is m. 112 literally a V:PAC? Yes. Since the structural voices are those in the first violin and basses, the PAC implication is clear; the $C\sharp_6$ in the flute may be regarded as a cover tone, or the upward-register transfer of an inner voice. There is little doubt that the strong cadence at m. 112 functions as the EEC, which is doubly confirmed when we hear the normative P-based C elided with and released by it.

A major, V, has now been secured. The question is to what degree it can be sustained for the rest of the exposition.

Closing zone (C) (mm. 112–131)

What remains of the exposition is vital to understanding the narrative of the movement. Elided with closing material (C), the EEC at m. 112 has just secured A major, bearing the promise of definitively restoring D major in the analogous spot of the recapitulation—the ESC. What occurs in C space, however, complicates the seeming victory of the EEC. The issues begin as soon as the P-based C material sets forth. In its second bar, m. 113, we hear the reintroduction of $G\natural_5$ in the second violins, $V^{\flat 7}/IV$ over a tonic pedal. Contextually, the $G\natural_5$ suggests the onset of a C-space QUIESCENZA, a figure that often reinforces a structurally secured tonic in a field of relaxation. The passage that it initiates can be read as an elaborate distortion of that schema. The QUIESCENZA's normatively expected $\hat6$ (F#$_5$), though, turns out to instead to be $\flat\hat6$ (F$\natural_5$, m. 114), and that F$\natural_5$ is engulfed by a *fortissimo* D-*minor* chord, mm. 114–15, the minor iv of A major (and the tonic minor of the movement).

This stops the acoustically literal realization of the implied QUIESCENZA in its tracks and hurls the music downward in a malevolent arpeggiation.[12] Mm. 114–15's gestural sign of D-minor-chord negation recalls the introduction's mm. 23–24 and its proclamation of "the [modal] fall" that has become the central problem of the movement. The implication is clear. While C-space is normally present to affirm the new key and mode secured at the EEC, in this case internal events within C undercut that stability. In this fallen world major modes can't be confidently sustained. As we had heard in TR and now hear again in C, the minor-mode corrosion from the introduction is still in effect.

The deformational QUIESCENZA modules of mm. 112–16 are repeated in mm. 116–20—the characteristic double-statement of that schema. Mm. 120–26, seeking to hold down a tonic pedal in the bass, grind home the point in an unstable *piano* dynamic stung with weak-beat *sforzando* shock-accents as the harmony flickers between the positive A-major chord (I) and the negative D-minor chord (iv) in a rapid-fire chiaroscuro. Mm. 126–31 finally pin A major to the ground not with a cadence but through a *fortissimo* act of will and a flurry of string figuration. In sum, even though the just-secured A major still predominates in the closing zone—and the whole of C is dominated by an implicit A pedal trying to hang onto it—the threat of internal modal decay has not yet been overcome. A short retransition under the first ending (RT) brings back the G♮$_5$ and tilts the music into the repetition of the exposition.

Development (mm. 138–215/216)

The second ending, m. 132[b], starts with the RT figure from the first ending, as if prepared to repeat the exposition still another time. But of course this is generically unacceptable. In mm. 134–35 Beethoven corrects this planted impression by backing up the music to modified versions of the A-chord punches from mm. 130–31 and revisiting that linking figure once again, mm. 136–38. This time, though, he inflects its course toward the fateful D minor—D major's worst nightmare and the recurring marker of this movement's modal decay. Although developments do not often begin with P on the tonic key, much less on the tonic minor, that is what occurs here.[13] P starts off warily in m. 138, soon plunging into a stressful round of developmental activity initially propelled by P's head-motive.

By mm. 144–45 the initial D minor *entry zone* has inflected to D♯^{7} (with F♯$_4$ in the second violins), and this precipitates "an extraordinary string of fifth-descents—a slippage downward desperately seeking a foothold to stop the sinking, all articulating P-material" (*EST*, 211). The first of these descents, onto G minor (mm. 146–47), triggers the *central action* of this first part of the development, laying down a *forte*, two-bar cell of turbulent double counterpoint: initially, upper strings against the lower, with sustained outcries from the winds. Upper and lower parts switch back and forth in two-bar units for the next six bars, each a fifth below (or a fourth above) its predecessor: thus to C minor (mm. 148–49), F (mm. 150–51), and B-flat (mm. 152–53). Thrashing about in a mighty struggle, this music is in dialogue with the strenuous-counterpoint variant of the long-established *tempesta* topic, a common feature of development sections in general but here musically intensified. At m. 154 Beethoven tightens the tension by doubling the speed of the descending fifths to one per bar: E minor (m. 154), $A^{(7)}$ (m. 155), D minor (m. 156), and $G^{(7)}$ (m. 157), finally landing on a ringing, open-string C-major chord, sustained and *fortissimo*, in mm. 158–59.

Turning away from the ongoing fifth-chain, this glaring C sonority initiates a more fearsome sinking of fortunes. A touchstone instance of Beethoven's "sublime" rather than his "beautiful," the extremity of the moment stares us in the face. We hear a broad chromatic descent in the bass (the negative *passus duriusculus* figure), C♮-B♮-B♭-A♮-A♭-G, mm. 158–66, while desperately whirling, P-based figures cry out in the upper voices. Driving ever-forward, a suspension-embellished, FONTE-related sequence ensues in mm. 166–67 (G^7-C) and 168–69 (E^7-a). The latter's ascending fourth/descending fifth (E^7-a) now drops another fifth to a D♯⁷ lock (mm. 170–81), racing up and down the chord's boundaries (D and C♯) in a frantic struggle, as if seeking a way out. Its final two bars, *pianissimo* echoes (mm. 180–81), are used as a mid-development (medial) caesura, followed by the onset of the secondary theme (m. 182), only now on G major, IV of the movement's tonic D.

The arrival of S marks this development as *fully rotational*, even divided, like the exposition, into two distinct parts separated by an MC. Reflecting on the exposition, we recall that this march-like S (Marx's "song of triumph ... splendid and filled with courage, sure of victory before the battle") had failed in its mission, having broken down before it could reach its intended cadence. The same is the case in the development. After a mere four bars (mm. 182–85) S's decay sets in, first threatening a move toward C minor (mm. 186–88) but steering clear of that to begin a series of chromatically ascending 5–6 sequences (Gjerdingen's three-part MONTE schema [2007, 92]), the arrival chord of each implying the dominant of a different key, first suggested as minor, then tweaked toward major: G (V/c, m. 186–89), A (V/d, mm. 190–93), B (V/e, mm. 194–96), swelling into a *forte* and finally lifting chromatically onto C♯ (V/f♯, m. 198, in effect a converging iii:HC).

While the first part of the development (mm. 138–81) had ended with an agitated struggle over a prolonged dominant-lock, D♯⁷ (V/IV), the second part ends with an even more desperate lock, this time on V/iii (V of F-sharp minor, mm. 198–214). Beethoven's violent treatment of the generically standard move to iii or its dominant toward the end of a development (*EST*, 198–205) illustrates once more the newly heightened tension that he brings to the Austrian symphony. Conceptually sustaining V/iii, this lock is a harmonic cage from which the narrative subject struggles to break free. On the one hand, in mm. 198–206 the first and second violins exultantly proclaim negative, lightning-bolt arpeggiations, recalling both the introduction's mm. 23–24 and the expositional C-space's mm. 114–16 and 118–20. On the other hand, in the same bars the manically racing violas and cellos adopt figuration from the exposition's crisis-moment in TR (mm. 61ff, TR[1.2], appearing here out of rotational order). What remains of the dominant-lock, V/iii, mm. 206–13, is thundering aftermath. Is there no escape? In m. 214 the horns glimpse a way out, sounding an A♮, *piano* and *crescendo* against the hanging C# in the strings, proposing a chromatic 5–6 shift that would convert the still-implicit C# chord (V/iii) into the "proper" A-major dominant (V/I). And in m. 215, in a burst of unexpected strength, that 5–6 shift is fully realized, *sforzando*, with the chordal-root A in the bass, vaulting the earlier C#-major sonority through V[7] of D and onto D major (m. 216)—and into the recapitulation.

Recapitulation (mm. 216–302/303)

Since so much of this recapitulation consists of correspondence measures with the exposition's *referential layout*—the opposite extreme from what we saw in Haydn's "Military" Symphony—our concern here will be only be twofold. First, we need to locate the crucial passage of recapitulatory divergence and recomposition, which occurs only within the pre-MC action zones. Second, we need to draw out the recapitulation's ongoing major-minor interplay and its crucial narrative implications.

The recapitulation begins with 13 bars of near-literal replication of the expositional model's P (mm. 216–28 = mm. 34–46, only with an added, queasily wobbling figure in the flute in mm. 223 and 225). At m. 229 the music slips off-track and into recomposition: the start of *pre-crux alterations*. Initially, the *piano*-attenuated I:PAC at m. 229 backs up to restate the cadence with intensified orchestration (mm. 230–31 = mm. 226–27), as if to reassure itself of its ultimate D-major goal down the road. In all such instances of backing-up, the structural consequence is to reopen the closural effect of the preceding cadence (m. 229). From that perspective we might momentarily suppose that we are still in P space. On the other hand, reinterpreting this after experiencing what is about to happen, we can retrospectively construe m. 229 to be in dialogue with *TR of the dissolving-cadential-reinforcement type* (reassessed as P[cod]==>TR), for at m. 232 Beethoven steers the music toward a converging half cadence, *forte*, attained in the next bar (m. 233). This not only initiates an end-of-TR dominant-lock on V of D (mm. 233–43) but also serves as the recapitulatory *crux*—the point where the music slips back on the track of correspondence measures (mm. 233–43 = mm. 61–71).

What has just happened merits a closer unpacking. What at first seemed to begin as a "one-more-time" repetition of the close of P (mm. 229–32) has, at the I:HC (m. 233), linked up with the closing phase of the exposition's TR space and continues with rhetorical correspondence measures up to the now-transposed MC (m. 243) and the two bars of caesura-fill (mm. 243–44) that bring us to S in the tonic (m. 245). Beethoven has thus foreshortened the exposition's P-TR complex. When P and TR are considered together (as pre-MC materials), we find fewer bars here than had been set out in the exposition, though in this case P is complete, and the omission of expositional bars occurs only within TR. Such a pre-MC abridgement is a common feature within recapitulations, always giving the impression of a hastening toward the denouement and the ESC-to-come.

In this case Beethoven omits the first portion of the exposition's TR (mm. 47–60). This was the portion that had replicated the introduction's "fall" or decay into the minor mode. Recalling that an overcoming of the minor-mode-collapse threat is the central problem of this movement, the implication is that the narrative subject ("the music") seeks to bypass such collapses in a more hopeful recapitulation. Equally telling, the moment of *crux* (m. 233, I:HC) rejoins the referential TR zone at that pivotal moment that I had labeled TR$^{1.2}$, m. 61 (Figure 7.1). The exposition's m. 61 had wrenched the proceedings onto an unprepared dominant-lock in the minor mode and an onrush of sudden panic. But in the recapitulation that moment is rejoined through a normative half cadence and recast, significantly, into the positive *major* mode, now racing forward with breathless excitement. But this major mode can't be sustained. At m. 237, as if struck down by a fatalistic blow, V of D major collapses to V of D minor and proceeds frantically from there to the MC in m. 243. This is musical drama at its highest. The two bars of caesura-fill (mm. 243–44 = mm. 71–72) tipping, as before, into the major mode, lead into the march-like S in the tonic (m. 245).

From S onward the recapitulation's materials continue to replicate those of the exposition, now in the tonic (mm. 245–302 = mm. 73–130). As such, we need not repeat our discussion of them here, though there are some points to observe with regard to the movement's major-minor narrative. The inability of the recapitulatory S$^{1.1}$ to produce the ESC, for instance, takes on a higher level of significance in the tonic. Its breakdown at mm. 272–73 (= mm. 100–1)—the "rip" in the form—is more ominous here, and the deceptive-cadence moment at m. 272 is portentously minorized as iv^6, not IV^6 as it had been in the exposition. Nonetheless, the music is pulled out of its local peril, as before, to arrive at the D-major ESC at m. 284 (= m. 112, the EEC).

In normative practice at this point, with the completion of the *essential sonata trajectory* (Figure 4.1b in chapter 4), D major should be fully realized—secured—for the remainder of the recapitulation. But in the exposition the closing zone had been shot through with internal modal decay, and that is what recurs in the recapitulation's C (mm. 286–87, 290–91, plus the major-minor flicker of the following bars). This is the equivalent of a mocking retort, corroding the ESC's D-major security at the moment that should have been its triumph. In turn this takes us back to the movement's central narrative problem, the haunting specter initiated by the introduction's modal "fall."

In sum, while the sonata proper does manage to recover and secure the D-major cadence signaling the ESC, it proves unable to sustain it in its purity through the end of the recapitulation. For all of the sonata's efforts, the major-minor problem is not overcome. Sonata Theory's way of expressing this is that while the sonata has succeeded *tonally*—it did attain and produce an ESC, behaving in that respect as a generically proper sonata—its processes of struggle have not managed to overcome the externally imposed, major-minor shadow that has been threatening the movement from the introduction onward. From that perspective we can say that we have experienced *sonata success but modal failure*. Sonata form, that quintessentially galant or Enlightenment machine, has proven inadequate to overcome this particular menace. There is still modal work to do. If we are not to give up altogether, D major needs to be strengthened into an incorruptible purity. That, now, can happen only beyond the sonata itself, in *not-sonata space*, the parageneric space of the coda. That coda will be obliged to bring us to the most important event of the movement: the exorcising of the possibility of minor-mode decay, thereby accomplishing what the preceding sonata could not.

Coda (mm. 304/310–360)

Beethoven's extended codas are always there for a reason. In this movement's discursive coda the task is to ramp up the energy to articulate a I:PAC sufficiently powerful to cleanse the movement of its persistent wiltings into minor. The conductor's and listener's role, moving with the music with open and expectant ears ("You are the music / While the music lasts"), is to be attentive to all signs of minor-mode mixture and ultimately to follow the pathway to that triumphant, now-impervious cadence—the narrative, expressive, and sonic goal of the first movement.

A transitional link to this coda (mm. 304–9/10) takes us from D to the subdominant G (m. 306) and into set of descending fifths: B^7, e (m. 308), A^7, and back to D (m. 310) to ignite the coda proper. Like the codas of many other composers, Beethoven's typically begin in a manner similar to that of the development, suggesting both a generically residual reflex to repeat the post-expositional music of the sonata (the once-normative repeat sign having fallen away) and a deeply entrenched rotational imperative. That this link recalls the music under the exposition's first and second ending and that the coda proper begins with a reference to the head motive of P is no arbitrary decision.

The drive to the decisive cadence occurs in two strong waves, the first almost successful, the second completely so. The first extends from m. 310 to the I:PAC in m. 322. The mounting windup into this cadence cannot be missed: a diatonically rising bass, $\hat{1}$-$\hat{2}$-$\hat{3}$-$\hat{4}$-$\hat{5}$, from m. 310–16, accented with recurring *sforzandi*. Up to this point all seems well. But in mm. 317 and 319, the mocking minor ninth—on P's tiptoeing figure—announces that minor-mode decay is still present. The dominant rages in protest (m. 318) and follows it up with a *fortissimo* vii^{o7}/V (m. 320)—more potential decay—winding itself up to push through that V and onto its I:PAC target (m. 322). But again the chromatic, mocking figure returns (mm. 323–25), annulling the major-mode cadence and suggesting a potential move toward iv. A stronger effort is needed if D major is to be sustained once and for all.

Thus the more powerful second wave, mm. 326–40, *fortissimo* and getting louder and more intense as it progresses, is called upon to accomplish the task. Prepared by its clenched-teeth, chromatically rising bass (more inclusive than the diatonic bass of the first wave), the I:PAC at m. 340 may have been the most forcefully prepared and executed cadence in the symphonic literature up to that time. Fully aware that this movement's overriding issue has been that of the impure intermixture of chromatic pitches into a pure D major, now, and with a mighty hand, Beethoven gathers up all the pitches of the chromatic scale (mm. 326–36) and hurls away the intruders in a grandly climactic expanded cadential progression—purely diatonic (mm. 336/37–40) and enriched with potent suspensions—landing monumentally on a now-unassailable I:PAC (m. 340).

Sensing a "choral grandeur" to this extraordinary climax, Tovey (1981, 42) was convinced that Beethoven's model must have been the chromatic close of the chorus at the end of Part 1 of Haydn's *Die Schöpfung* (*The Creation*), "Die Himmel erzählen die Ehre Gottes" ("The Heavens Are Telling the Glory of God").[14] However one might assess this claim, it's clear that each composer was using rhythm, orchestration, chromatic harmony, and intense sonic presence—reaching for the dynamic sublime—to articulate a hyper-conclusive cadence. And if Beethoven had indeed been making an intertextual reference to an exaltedly commemorative moment in *The Creation*, or (more likely) had even been determined to surpass it, it could serve to underscore a metaphysical, even quasi-biblical aspect of this movement, which, after all, had begun with a "fall." It may be that Haydn's enormously successful *Creation*, marked by its sharp antitheses of the pastoral and the dynamic sublime (Webster 2005b), was the indispensable backdrop behind this movement, if not the whole symphony. The remainder of the coda is an ecstatically resonant celebration of an "earned" D major, one substantially advanced from the naïve but lost innocence of the introduction's opening measures, to which this movement, at least, can never return.

8

The Minor-Mode Sonata

Sonata forms in the minor mode follow the architectonic norms of the major-mode sonata, those summarized in chapter 4 and diagrammed in Figure 4.1a–b. These include: the usual succession of expositional action zones (P TR' S / C, if we are dealing with a two-part and not a continuous exposition), the expectation of tonal resolution of S and C materials in the recapitulation, the trajectories toward generically anticipated cadences, and so on. Yet minor-mode sonatas bear an extra burden. This is the burden "of the minor mode itself, generally interpretable within the [high-classical and later] sonata tradition as a sign of a troubled condition seeking transformation (emancipation) into the parallel major mode," even though in many sonata movements such an emancipation does not occur: the movement may end in either the minor or (especially from the 1780s onward) the major (*EST*, 306). This chapter deals with some of the entailments of that burden.

The 2006 *Elements* devoted a chapter to the special features of the minor-mode sonata. Since then, new work on the minor-mode complications in galant and classical sonata forms has emerged. The most notable is Matthew Riley's 2014 monograph, *The Viennese Minor-Key Symphony in the Age of Haydn and Mozart*, an extension of Floyd Grave's 2008 and 2009 studies of Haydn's minor-key works into broader repertories. Riley's corpus study examines 54 minor-mode Allegro movements—first movements and finales—written mostly in the later 1760s, 1770s, and 1780s by a number of composers: Dittersdorf, Gassmann, Haydn, Hoffmeister, Koželuch, Mozart, Ordonez, Swieten, Vaňhal, Wagenseil, and Wranitsky (2014, 10–11).[1] While the remarks on the minor-mode sonata in the *Elements* remain accurate—indeed, they are bolstered by Grave's and Riley's work—it's prudent to revisit them here and incorporate into them some of these scholars' language and analytical observations.

Both Grave and Riley attend to the idiosyncratic conventions found in the minor-key works of the era. Riley, for instance, refers to the minor-mode symphony as a distinct *subgenre* of the larger sonata genre. His work places Haydn's and Mozart's symphonies (and by implication young Beethoven's) into a definable, localized tradition, albeit one that by the mid-1780s was undergoing transformations. While for practical reasons his study is specific to the rapid-tempo movements in Vienna's symphonic tradition, there is little reason to suppose that most of his observations are not also relevant to movements outside of his sample. As a modest caveat, we should be aware that omitted from his study are all non-Viennese composers, including such notables as Johann Stamitz and the other Mannheim composers, J. C. and C. P. E. Bach, Luigi Boccherini, and many others. Also lying outside his sample are chamber works, piano sonatas, and sonata-oriented opera and concert arias. That said, Riley's detailed report on the Viennese-symphony corpus lays a welcome groundwork for further examinations of eighteenth-century, minor-mode sonata movements.

The minor mode as a special-case affective mood

"A very small proportion of eighteenth-century symphonies are in minor keys," writes Riley at the onset of his study, "perhaps no more than 2 percent" (2014, 1). (With Beethoven's generation—and with the more urgent, "romantic" turn in composition—the minor-mode sonata would become more common and play a prominent role in nineteenth-century sonata-form pieces.) This is one reason why "the minor mode in late eighteenth-century music is semiotically 'marked'" (4). Riley provides three further justifications for this markedness. One is the artificiality and connotations of the minor mode itself, as noted by a number of the theorists of the day. (Riley cites remarks by Rousseau, Kirnberger, and Lacépède [4–5].)[2] For some in the eighteenth century the bottom line may have been that "contemporary rationalist thought about music . . . [was asserting that] the minor mode was imperfect and dissatisfying" (201). Another justification is the set of specific conventions consistently associated with minor-mode symphonies as a subgenre (to be noted later). And a third is the minor-mode sonata movements' frequent featuring of structural deformations, cueing the listener in advance to expect that "the ensuing experience will be extraordinary" (4–6).

Whether transiently intermixed within a prevailing major mode (Sonata Theory's *lights-out effect* within an ongoing chiaroscuro) or taking on the role of the governing modal tonic of a complete movement, the minor mode is a strong color on the harmonic palette, sometimes characterized as an ominous, darker minor as opposed to a positive, brighter major. Grave characterizes that era's minor mode as being "identified with images of rage, darkness, storm or underworld terror. . . . [It] offered a potential source of colour, theatrical intensity and narrative complication in the midst of otherwise unmarked major contexts." From the normative perspective of the major mode, minor tonality signified an "abnormal condition" (2008, 31, 34), one that "in general represented a troubled, parallel universe of harmonic sonority and relationship whose tonal centers were magnets for a host of associations and connotations that stood in opposition to major" (2009, 21).

Staging the minor mode as an oppositional field to the normative major can produce intensely dramatic effects. "Haydn, Beethoven, and Mozart," writes Haimo, "went beyond [the] conventional uses of minor, finding new ways to exploit the formal and dramatic possibilities of the minor mode. . . . In some cases . . . the appearance of the parallel minor at a point where the parallel major had been expected becomes a powerful, destabilizing force, one that actively frustrates closure and completion" (2005, 194). Such considerations, recall, lay at the heart of the preceding chapter's reading of the first movement of Beethoven's Second Symphony. By the high-galant/classical era, and surely some decades before this, the prevailing view was that the minor mode conveyed emotional states that were dysphoric, negatively valenced. But it will not do to collapse it merely into sadness or any such single attribute. Rather, we should think of the minor mode as capable of representing a broad range of differently nuanced moods. Composers plugged into this or that quasi-standardized mood through such rhetorical factors as tempo (minor-mode slow movements are a case study in themselves), texture, melodic shape, register, dynamic, and topical choice.

The eighteenth-century, minor-mode affective range might be imagined as a continuum of culturally sanctioned, sometimes overlapping stances. Its variety of moods can evoke: melancholy or melancholic wistfulness; doubt or hesitation; loss; weeping, lamentation, or mourning (dwelling within a ritualized grief); somberness; fatalistic external threat (as if pursued, toyed with, or trapped by a menacing force); high stress; desperate agitation; storminess (the *tempesta* topic); hard-pitched battles; rage (a transfer from the conventional rage aria); the grotesque, unnatural, or exotic; demonic realms (the *ombra* topic); or, in some situations, uncommonly sober earnestness in working through a difficult problem (as with the stern, minor-mode fugue or fugato). To these attunements Riley reminds us of two other options in eighteenth-century Viennese practice: the "contrapuntal chamber music of the imperial court, and Passion music," both sometimes associated with a largely eclipsed contrapuntal style that he calls the " 'untimely rhetoric' of pre-galant idioms" (2014, 5). Moreover, any of these moods might be subjected to parody through excessive treatment or other cueing strategies. The music of the nineteenth century would intensify and extend the range of the minor mode's expressive possibilities.

Characteristic styles and topics

One way of reading minor-mode themes is to understand, as Mirka put it, that "classical masterpieces were full of references to [the] eighteenth-century soundscape. . . . For listeners in eighteenth-century Vienna . . . [they] presented a colorful gallery of characters known from everyday musical life" (2014b, 1). Or, in the words of Allanbrook, "such music invokes . . . musical gestures that qualify as texts because they come already colored by rhythmic and melodic associations with the ordinary lives of human beings, their dancing, their music making, their worship, their protocol: the motions of daily human activities have stamped these gestures with meanings. . . . Late eighteenth-century instrumental music was a mimetic report, as it were, on the configurations of the composer's social cosmos" (2014, 108–9).

Consequently, many themes from this and other eras are semiotically identifiable as realizations of what have come to be called *musical topics*. In his pioneering work, *Classic Music*, Ratner had described topics as "a thesaurus of *characteristic figures*," a repertory of commonly evoked effects, some "associated with various feelings and affections," others projecting "a picturesque flavor (1980, 9)." [3] Thus Riley writes of "the well-known rhetoric of the *Sturm und Drang* style—driving rhythms, syncopations, wide leaps, unison opening gestures, dramatic pauses" (2014, 5). When the style is applied to final movements, we find the "relentless energy" and minimal "variation of texture" of the characteristic "'stormy finale'... a fast sonata form in duple or quadruple meter, usually notated as 2/2 ... sometimes in [common time]. Triple meter is avoided" (120–21).

Several of these features might be subsumed, as McClelland suggests (2014), under the broader topical categories of *tempesta* and *ombra*. With regard to the former, one result of this is that certain "stormy" P-theme openings can sound generically similar. The opening theme, for instance, of Haydn's Symphony No. 45 in F-sharp Minor ("Farewell") from 1772, probably the best known of his minor-mode, *Sturm und Drang* symphonies, closely resembles (and may even have been modeled on?) that of the "sheets-of-rain" descending arpeggios found at the opening of the finale of Dittersdorf's Symphony in G Minor (Grave g1) from around four years earlier. (Haydn would reuse the same idea as an unexpected F-minor interpolation into the center of the exposition of his Symphony No. 85 in B-flat, "La reine.")

Beyond the conventionalisms of *tempesta* and *ombra*, other minor-mode topics include: funeral music, most notably the ritual obsequies of the funeral march (often juxtaposed with a major-mode section of consolation, as in the *Eroica* Symphony); the often-spectral minor-mode siciliana; the simpler, more melodic "galant minor" theme, a "relatively subdued, well-domesticated manner" operating not disruptively but rather with "simplicity and reserve" (Grave 2009, 12); the later-eighteenth-century occasional taste for the contrapuntal or canonic minor-mode minuet; and the stylized exoticism of "Turkish" or "Hungarian/gypsy" music, for Viennese court and patronage circles the idiosyncratic music of a cultural Other that diverges from the elite-cultural norm and is consequently to be evoked with implications of bemusement or parody. Whatever the topic or standardized posture, there is no reason—at least in eighteenth-century music (and perhaps even in a few decades into the nineteenth)—to read any of them as confessional outpourings on the part of the composer. Rather, all such topics are better regarded as third-person, quasi-theatrical invocations of familiar expressive moods within varied, ever more complex musical discourses. They can be regarded as being more in line, say, with the ideas outlined in Diderot's essay on the "paradox of the actor" (1773), which observes that the great actor on stage is the one who does not personally participate in the emotions that he or she projects to the audience.

One should also be aware of two intervallic patterns commonly encountered in minor-mode passages of the era, both of which have extensive preceding histories of signification. One is the descending melodic-minor tetrachord in the bass, $\hat{8}$-$\hat{7}$-$\hat{6}$-$\hat{5}$ (in C minor, C-B♭-A♭-G), a figure often emblematic of adverse states including grief, lament, or other perilous situations. The descending tetrachord is sometimes intensified further by means of interior, descending chromatic half-steps: the

Figure 8.1. Some permutations of the pathotype figure.

frequently encountered chromatic fourth or *passus duriusculus*, inventoried in Williams (1997).The other comprises the melodic permutations of four scalar pitches in the minor mode, $\hat{1}$-$\natural\hat{7}$-$\flat\hat{6}$-$\hat{5}$, as a negatively valenced thematic initiator or set of registral boundaries toward the onset of a theme. This is what Kirkendale dubbed the *pathotype* figure, a "universal baroque formula" constituted by "the fifth formed by first and fifth degrees, and the diminished seventh which lies a semitone outside these notes. Characteristic is the leap of a diminished seventh, nearly always descending, with the leading note accented" (1979, 91). Figure 8.1 illustrates some typical permutations of the four scale degrees, notated here in C minor. An intervallic schema, the pathotype figure is prototypically deployed at the onset of minor-mode fugue subjects (as in the Ricercar—grounded in "the king's theme"—of Bach's *Musikalisches Opfer*, the finale of Haydn's String Quartet in F Minor, op. 20 no. 5, the Kyrie of Mozart's *Requiem*, and Beethoven's *Grosse Fuge*) but by no means limited to that genre. (It pervades many of Beethoven's Late Quartets, as with the onset of op. 132.) The figure is also sometimes perceptible as the topical-structural support of other, more florid minor-mode themes within sonata forms, as we shall see at the opening of Beethoven's Quartet in E Minor, op. 59 no. 2 (chapter 9).

Aspiration: escape from minor into major

One implication of inhabiting (or being inhabited by) a minor mode, in either local or more extended situations, is that the music (fictively, the narrative subject or "virtual agent") typically seeks ways to wrest itself away from it and into the refuge of a hopefully nearby major mode. In these scenarios the minor mode represents an existential condition from which the imperative is to flee. As a result, one common hope within a minor-mode sonata is to get free of that initial minor—often as soon as possible. Being attentive to such things is basic to Sonata Theory's style of reading minor-mode works.[4] This narrative-plot feature becomes more pronounced in the final third of the eighteenth century and becomes further entrenched in the nineteenth. Beethoven's C minors that seek transformation into C majors at their conclusions—not always with success—can be taken as broad-scale prototypes.

One should not imagine that only parallel majors will fill the bill, though only parallel majors have the capacity to stand for permanent solutions. Under the pressure of the minor mode, a temporary flight may also be made into a non-tonic major mode: any port in a storm. Many minor-to-major escapes are local and do not pretend to solve the problem of the minor mode's primacy, which is often returned to sooner or later, as if pulled back by the dark matter of a negatively gravitational force. A modally emancipatory solution standing for narrative success can be achieved only if three conditions are satisfied: (1) the initially governing minor-modal tonic key is converted into its parallel-major mode; (2) that major-mode key is secured with a perfect authentic cadence; and (3) that parallel major mode is sustained for the remainder of the movement.

Three of the most common escape-transformations of a dysphoric minor mode into a harbor of major-mode refuge are (Figure 8.2):

- A modulation to that minor mode's III (C minor to E-flat major; D minor to F major). In neo-Riemannian terminology, this is the R operation: the move to the relative major. Most obviously, one encounters it in the modulations to many S/C zones of minor-mode expositions (S/C in the mediant major), where III is a non-tonic, temporary placeholder, perhaps anticipating a major-mode tonic-key resolution in the recapitulation (which might or might not happen). Shifts from an actualized or implicit i into III, R operations, can also occur more locally, as transient flights from a patch of minor—any minor—on the way to something else, as can happen in development sections or elsewhere.
- A half-step-grounded slippage to the minor mode's VI (C minor to A-flat major; D minor to B-flat major). This is the *Leittonwechsel* operation, or L-operation, in this case the submitting of a minor triad in root position to a 5–6 shift and perhaps also underpinning the resulting major-triad chord with its implied root. One might imagine, for instance, a C-minor triad, C-E♭-G, whose G is inflected up a half step to A♭. This produces a major-mode A♭^{6} (a 5–6 shift), which may then be locally stabilized with an A♭ root. (Reversing the direction of the L operation will bring us back to the C-minor chord.) Plunges into the "purple-patch" or quasi-Arcadian VI (or ♭VI) carry with them a number of richly coloristic and structural implications, generated in part by ♭$\hat{6}$ as a tendency-tone seeking to resolve downward into $\hat{5}$. In all cases, however, the shift into VI is temporary—a slippage into a warm, local refuge that cannot last. I use the metaphors of *inflation* and *deflation* to characterize the expressive connotations of the L-operation, which always carries with it a coloristic modal shift, either from minor to major or the reverse, while holding two common tones between the two chords: a C-minor chord, for instance, can be

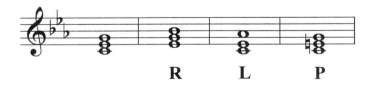

Figure 8.2. Three transformational operations of a minor tonic.

inflated to an A-flat one via the L operation; complementarily an A-flat chord can be *deflated* to a C-minor one.[5]

- A transformation of a minor tonic into its parallel major, the P-operation (C minor to C major, D minor to D major). This too can be a transient effect, to be read as a local "illusion" or "if only" moment within a more governing force-field of minor. The P-operation becomes narratively permanent and emancipatory, however, if secured with a I:PAC and held onto for the rest of the piece. And of course this does not happen in every minor-mode sonata. (See the later discussion of "tragic plot; comic plot.")

An illustration of all three maneuvers, at different levels of structure, may be found in Beethoven's Symphony No. 5 in C Minor. Here we encounter the normative R-operation in the exposition of the first movement's S and C (a broad passage of E-flat, III); the L-operation to provide the grounding tonic of movement 2 (A-flat major, VI); and the P-operation finally realized in the C-major finale, though secured with a I:PAC only late in the sonata form's coda, that is, in post-sonata space—the strenuously celebratory sonata proper that precedes it having been staged as unable to accomplish this.

The "mediant tutti"

A vivid illustration of the compulsion to leap out of an initial minor mode as soon as possible is found in the common practice of what Riley calls the subgeneric convention of the *mediant tutti* (2014, 12–24). He observes this convention within rapid-tempo, Viennese minor-mode symphonic movements and particularly in the cluster of those that were in vogue from the mid-1760s to the 1780s (Haydn, Dittersdorf, Vaňhal, Ordonez, and others). While the convention did not entirely disappear, it seems at least to have "subsided after the early 1770s" (20). In the years of its heyday, though,

> the large majority of minor-key fast movements in the familiar "stormy" style . . . allude to it. . . . Haydn's Symphony No. 39 [in G Minor] (1765) [*recte* 1767–68?] stands at the head of the tradition, with mediant tuttis in both of its outer movements. . . . The mediant tutti occurs at (or, occasionally, very soon after) the start of the second main paragraph of a minor-key fast movement, often (though not always) after a phase of dwindling energy, repeated figures or chords, a phase of motivic liquidation, or a pause. The final harmony of the preceding (first) paragraph is usually V/i. A loud, energetic gesture is then made, starting on a chord of the mediant. Although it is not always a literal tutti, it often comes as a sudden shock, and emphasizes the harmonic *non sequitur* . . . [usually expressing] the formal function of "initiation." . . . In other words, it sounds clearly like the start of a new section. (12–13)

All this may be heard at the opening of the first movement of Mozart's Symphony No. 25 in G Minor, K. 183 from 1773—a few years into this "stormy" tradition (Figure 8.3). The anxiety-ridden syncopations of the opening, along with the thematic P^0 (or P$^{1.1}$) in octaves (mm. 1–4)—not to mention the stark presentation of the pathotype figure—are all characteristic of the subgenre, as is the accented, clipped treatment of the dominant in m. 12 and the dramatically abrupt gap that follows it. A parallel consequent begins in m. 13 but, unable to sustain itself, it runs out of steam with "dwindling energy" and comes to rest, *pianissimo*, on V of G minor (V/i) in mm. 27–28—and is followed by another pause, as if questioning whether one has the energy or will to continue. What we hear next is a sudden, *forte* plunge onto B-flat major (m. 29), a prototypical instance of what Riley calls a mediant tutti. In this case the reinvigorating jolt of B-flat initiates the next action zone, the transition, into new motion. That TR will proceed onward with its energetic mission of producing the exposition-dividing MC, which it does at m. 58 (III: HC MC). Opening part 2, the drop to *piano* and perkily characteristic S will follow in m. 59, still in B-flat (III), along with the EEC (III:PAC) at m. 79, elided with a brief section of closing material.

Quite apart from noticing the important mediant-tutti production at m. 29, another thing to observe from the Sonata Theory standpoint is that *TR, mm. 29–58, is carried out entirely in B-flat major, the secondary-key area of the exposition.* Yet it is rhetorically clear that its role is that of a conventionally articulated transition. It appears at the normative part of the exposition (TR is the expected action zone that succeeds P), and it drives forward to produce a medial caesura and subsequent S. In K. 183/i the expositional layout's governing principle is the generically standard action-zone succession of P TR ' S / C, to which, in this case, the mediant tonality of TR is subordinated. The lesson here is that *tonality alone is not always sufficient to define where secondary themes begin*: conventionalized rhetoric and temporal/proportional placement need also to be taken into account.

On the other hand, one cannot claim—and Riley does not—that the impact of an early mediant tutti always marks the onset of TR. On the contrary, it sometimes happens that TR begins in the minor-mode tonic, perhaps as the start of a (grand) consequent, but soon plunges onto a mediant tutti. This is what we find in the first movement of Haydn's Symphony No. 39 in G minor (Figure 8.4, in which we also notice the varied pathotype figures within P$^{1.2}$, mm. 6–11.) In mm. 13–14 and 15–16, P$^{1.1}$'s (presentation) modules are revisited but then leap directly, and *forte*, into B-flat major in m. 17. What we had at first construed as a consequent within a perhaps ongoing P zone now shows itself, once the mediant tutti is produced, to have been the start of TR. This retrospective reinterpretation, then, can be indicated as: P^{cons}==>TR$^{1.1}$ (mm. 13–16), TR$^{1.2}$ (m. 17, the four-bar onset of which, mm. 17–20, traces through the descending-bass version of the ROMANESCA schema, I, V^6, vi, III^6), and so on. A more familiar example of the same thing, and on a grander scale, may be heard at the beginning of Mozart's Symphony No. 40 in G Minor, K. 550: P^{cons}==>TR$^{1.1}$ (mm. 21–27), TR$^{1.2}$ (m. 28).

Figure 8.3. Mozart, Symphony No. 25 in G Minor, K. 183/i.

Figure 8.4. Haydn, Symphony No. 39 in G Minor, movement 1, mm. 1–23.

Implications of expositional key choices, strategies of promise

As we know, the classical major-mode exposition normatively tonicizes the dominant (V) for its S and C action zones (part 2 of the two-part exposition, EEC in
V), though after 1800 composers began to experiment, at first intermittently and
infrequently, with the implications of visiting other keys for these zones (as with the
first movements of Beethoven's Piano Sonatas op. 31 no. 1 in G, with S starting in B
major, III, soon decaying into B minor, iii, for the remainder of the exposition, and
op. 53 in C ["Waldstein"], with S and C in E major, III). In major-mode expositions
the generic expectation was that all or most of the material in the part-2 action

zones would return in the tonic major in the recapitulation. It was in this tonal sense that the expositional keys of S and C in those expositions can be regarded as a *structure of promise*—the promise being that of a complementary *tonal resolution* and the attainment of the ESC in the recapitulation, thereby fulfilling a *structure of [tonal/generic] accomplishment* (Figure 4.1a–b in chapter 4). In the major-mode sonata, both P and S/C are normatively in the major mode, though some of them feature minor-mode patches, sometimes prominent ones (*EST*, 119, 141–42). In the generically standard situation the major-dominant key's structure of promise is revisited and resolved as the major-tonic key's structure of accomplishment. At the very least, the exposition's major-mode EEC is to be complemented with a major-mode ESC: a major-mode outcome for the ESC is almost never cast into doubt, and any exceptions should be considered deformational.[6]

With the minor-mode sonata we confront a different state of affairs. While P is grounded in the tonic minor (i), the normative choices for S and C before 1800 are the *relative major* (major-mode III, the *first-level default* or most common option) and the *minor dominant* (minor-mode v, the *second-level default*). *EST*, 310–17, refers to these generic alternatives as *the exposition with EEC in III* (or *an exposition of the i-III type*) and *the exposition with EEC in v* (or *an exposition of the i-v type*). In the first instance, i to III (as with C minor to E-flat major), a crucial affect pervading the exposition is that of modal contrast. A minor-mode first part (P) gives way to a major-mode second part (S/C). This situation may be represented with minus and plus signs: *a {– +} type of exposition*. In the second, i to v (as with C minor to G minor), the exposition is doggedly in minor all the way through: no modal contrast. Here we find *a {– –} type of exposition*. The differences between these two minor-mode exposition types determine the affective impact of the whole: one proceeds either from an initial negative condition to a space of modal relief (S/C in III, {– +}) or finds the modal-relief option blocked or closed off, thereby finding oneself trapped in a grim situation with no modal exit (S/C in v, {– –}). Either choice has strong implications for what can happen in the recapitulation, and these implications are central issues in minor-mode sonatas (as will be discussed in the next section, "Tragic plot; comic plot; structure").

On occasion we find an eighteenth-century, minor-mode exposition that makes an early feint toward its major-mode mediant (i-III) but falls short of attaining it for the onset of a secondary theme, lapsing into the minor dominant (v) shortly thereafter, either for the start of a negatively valenced S or for the concluding portions of a continuous exposition. This produces a i-(III)-v exposition, where the internal parentheses indicate a tonal area aimed for but lost before it can be thematically initiated as S[1.1]. A touchstone case is found in the first-movement exposition of Haydn's Symphony No. 45 in F-sharp Minor ("Farewell"). This is a continuous exposition that early on moves toward and *almost* produces a P-based S in A major (III)—or at least the frenetic musical process set into motion by P and TR leads us to expect this. At m. 38, though, that potential theme is not only blurted out prematurely (that is, it is not prepared by an MC and is therefore not an S) but also misfires by collapsing onto A minor (iii) and racing headlong onward from that unexpected event. With that modal collapse, III to iii, the opportunity to secure the mediant major is lost, leaving the exposition fated to move to the only other generically available choice of the era, the minor dominant (v). This is exactly what happens: following the m. 38 collapse, Haydn drives the music into C-sharp minor, eventually producing the EEC in the minor dominant (v, m. 65) and following it by a brief, EEC-reinforcing codetta in that key (C^{cod}). The result is a i-(III-iii)-v exposition; using plus-minus symbols, it may be represented as {– (+ –) –}.[7]

On other occasions, extending especially into the nineteenth century, we find that a secondary theme is successfully launched in the confident major mediant but proves unable to sustain that key all the way to the EEC. Instead, it decays within S space to the minor dominant and ultimately produces an EEC in that key. Thus we have a i-III-v exposition {– + –} with a clearly expressed but cadentially unsecured mediant key. Beethoven's *Coriolan* Overture (1807), for example, gives us a C-minor P (i), a "heroic" $S^{1.1}$ in E-flat (III, m. 52) that becomes tonally insecure and moves upward (through F minor) to settle onto G minor (minor v) for a later module of S (m. 72) and EEC (m. 102). In cases where S begins in one non-tonic key but moves to another to produce the EEC, we can speak of a *three-key exposition* (with a *tonally migratory* S). Most typically, this is one that gives us all three of the classically normative keys for the exposition's part 2: an initial i, an unstable III, and a more conclusive v. Such a pathway invites an obvious hermeneutic reading, all the more so in works with explicit or implicit illustrative content. In the case of *Coriolan* we have a quasi-programmatic situation suggesting an initially dire situation (limned by the grimly determined, accumulative tonic minor) responded to at first with a confident hope (the defiant, quasi-heroic stance of $S^{1.1}$ in III) that proves incapable of sustaining itself, soon crumbling into a fatalistic minor (v).

While Beethoven was by no means the only composer of his era occasionally to deploy a three-key exposition, and while such a triple-station layout is by no means limited to minor-mode sonatas, it would become a much-discussed practice encountered in Schubert, Brahms, and others. We'll revisit this situation head-on in chapter 11, in a close reading of the first movement of Schubert's Quartet in D minor, D. 810, whose exposition's principal keys are D minor, F major, and A minor (this last with unstable interior touches of A major): a more elaborately nuanced instantiation of the i-III-v schema found in *Coriolan*. On the other hand, and from a half-century later, the finale of Brahms's First Symphony, as we'll see in chapter 12, lays out a different three-key pattern (I-V-iii).

By the nineteenth century, composers of minor-mode sonatas sometimes explored S/C options other than III or v. One of the earliest to appear was an exposition that moved to the major submediant for S and the EEC, an *exposition of the i-VI type*, which by then could be regarded as a *third-level default*. Here we need cite only the first movements of Beethoven's Quartet in F Minor, op. 95 (F minor to D-flat major) and Ninth Symphony (D minor to B-flat major) and Schubert's Unfinished Symphony (B minor to G major). *EST*, 317, presents a brief history of the emergence of this type along with a listing of other examples. In terms of modally affective hue the i-VI expositional type again presents us with a {– +} contrast, though the move to the submediant is a coloristically darker move than the one to the mediant.

Tragic plot; comic plot; structure

Whatever the modal choice for S/C in the exposition, the crucial thing with regard to the movement's dramatic import is how it will recur in the recapitulation and be confirmed, or not confirmed, in the coda, if there is one. Will the movement end in minor or in major? Riley refers to the two narrative options as the *tragic plot* (a movement ending in the minor key with which the work began) and the *comic plot* (one ending in the parallel major) (2014, 36–38 and passim). The connotations of such matters lie at the expressive core of the minor-mode sonata, particularly those from the later Haydn onward.

Whichever choice is made for S/C, major III or minor v, those action zones still carry with them the sonata's generic *structure of promise*. That promise is grounded in tonal processes: the eventual goal of tonal resolution and a tonic-securing ESC down the road. The same tonal promise is also active in the minor-mode sonata and is almost always attained. But with the minor-key sonata a second factor is in play: *will the ESC be sounded in the major or in the minor*? More broadly, will the exposition's S and C both return in the tonic major or the tonic minor—or perhaps in flickering, chiaroscuro juxtapositions of both? And how might an extended coda, should there be one, play into this? The interplay of minor and major and their localized connotations can project a drama that carries enormous expressive weight, as various compositional means are staged either to escape momentarily from the pressing burden of the minor or, ultimately, to overturn it into the major.

Obviously, an exposition of the {– +} type (say, D minor, F major, i-III) can suggest that a complementary {– +} recapitulation (D minor, D major) is at least possible, under the hope that the exposition's major-mode S/C might be able to be retained as such in the recapitulation and into any coda that might lie beyond it. In such an exposition the normative tonal structure of promise associated with S/C can be conceptually coupled with a *strategy of hope*. When S and C do return completely in the tonic major mode, Sonata Theory reads such an outcome as *modally emancipatory*: Riley's *comic plot*; "one wins." Similarly, Grave had referred to such outcomes in Haydn's later minor-key instrumental pieces—accomplished in varied ways—as "modal reversals" along various "paths from minor to major," reversals construed as acts of "recuperation" from or "transcendence" of the minor mode and its connotations (2008, 2009). In these situations sonata form is deployed as a process-machine capable of transforming a dark, initial minor-mode situation into a brighter, confident major-mode one, all of which plays into the implicit narrative underpinning a particular sonata. One is lifted from an initial, oppressive condition into a victorious, positive one.

But of course things do not always turn out this way. As we shall see in the following section ("Comic plot; tragic plot; history"), Riley's work shows that before the 1770s it almost never happened at all but only emerged, and very gradually at that, and eventually into the mid-1780s and 1790s. The earlier norm was that the S/C that had been in a non-tonic major mode in a {– +} exposition would be recapitulated in the tonic minor: its original plus was now to be switched to minus, as if the dark hand of minor sweeps through each originally major-mode bar, moment by moment. "There is little more powerful or more affecting within minor-mode sonatas of the i-III type than the bleak realization that all of part 2 . . . might come back entirely in minor in the recapitulation . . . to cancel out the hopes raised in the exposition: a moving wave of despair passes through this music, inexorably reversing former hopes" (*EST*, 313–14). In such a situation—invariable in Mozart's minor-mode sonatas, though certainly not in later Haydn's and some of Beethoven's—we have Riley's *tragic plot*; "one loses." Sonata Theory reads such an outcome as *tonal success but modal failure*: the tonic is secured with the ESC, as presupposed by the genre, but the sonata has proved unable to liberate the initial minor into major.

Within this line of interpretation, *the add-on strategy of modal hope* implicit in {– +} expositions is not present in {– –} expositions. "We still encounter a structure of [tonal] promise—all expositions seek to forecast the procedures of their recapitulations—but what is promised here is an inescapable recapitulatory negativity. Typically, the remainder of the sonata experience unfolds as something to be endured or struggled against, grimly, determinedly, or stoically" (*EST*, 315), as in the first movement of Beethoven's D-minor "Tempest" Sonata, op. 31 no. 2, and several other movements, particularly finales (from the F-minor Piano Sonata, op. 2 no. 1, onward).

The modal options of how to handle major and minor in the recapitulation and coda can be quite varied. This is increasingly the case in the last two decades of the eighteenth century and into the nineteenth, when positive outcomes, {– +} recapitulations, became more entrenched as compositional options. Table 8.1 (from *EST*, 313) lists some of the possibilities for dark-light modal play in the high-galant/classical minor-mode sonata. If there is to be such a recapitulatory modal conversion, it is to be ratified at the major-mode I:PAC cadence that marks the ESC. That major-mode ESC is sometimes staged as being attained only through a struggle. Nonetheless, that crucial I:PAC can be modally lost, shown to be insufficient, if the ensuing C-space decays back into minor. In such cases the expressive connotation is that the gravitational force of the minor mode, representing a negative existential situation to which the sonata is responding, is so strong that even the potential minor-to-major mechanisms of sonata form prove insufficient to the task. After a seeming major-mode victory at the ESC, one can still be pulled back into the modal realm of the dysphoric minor. When this happens, the implication of the whole is

Table 8.1 Modal Options in Major- and Minor-Mode Sonatas

		Exposition	Recapitulation
1	*Major-Mode Sonata* I–V	{+ +}	{+ +}
2	*Minor-Mode Sonata* i–III option with positive recapitulation	{– +}	{– +}
3	*Minor-Mode Sonata* i–III option with negative recapitulation	{– +}	{– –}
4	*Minor-Mode Sonata* i–III option with mixtures in part 2: positive outcome within sonata space	{– [– +]}	{– [– +]}
5	*Minor-Mode Sonata* i–III option with mixtures in part 2: negative outcome within sonata space	{– [+ –]}	{– [+ –]}
6	*Minor-Mode Sonata* i–III option with mixtures only in recapitulatory space: positive outcome	{– +}	{– [– +]}
7	*Minor-Mode Sonata* i–III option with mixtures only in recapitulatory space: negative outcome	{– +}	{– [+ –]}
8	*Minor-Mode Sonata* i–v option	{– –}	{– –}

From *EST*, 313.
+ = major mode; – = minor mode.
The two signs within the braces refer to parts 1 and 2 of a two-part exposition: especially the onset of P and all of S/C.

that of exposing the normative generic claims of the ESC as weak or precarious. What is attained as generic conquest crumbles into dust a few bars later.

By the 1790s the minor-major drama need not be limited to sonata space alone (that action space comprising the exposition, development, and recapitulation). With Beethoven and later composers it can happen that the minor-mode sonata proper might succeed in overturning the minor in the recapitulation by sounding both S and C in the tonic major only to lose that major in a coda that tragically, menacingly, or viciously reverts back to minor, thereby restoring the *status quo ante*. The touchstone case occurs in the first movement of Beethoven's Fifth Symphony: a modally successful sonata, one with a ringingly victorious {– +} recapitulation, is shatteringly undercut by a collapse back into the tonic minor in the opening bars of the extended coda, reversing the sonata's modal claims—which had represented a willed human action against a negative condition—with its own gestures of gloating triumph, grinding the efforts of the preceding sonata under its heel. Such a coda can give the impression of a critique of sonata form itself, presented here as a facile Enlightenment solution not up to the task of facing this particular negative situation. As a result, the task of permanently overturning the C-minor mode and its implications will be pursued for the next three movements and conquered with a major-mode, now permanently secured I:PAC only late in the finale's coda.

On the other hand, it is also possible for a minor-mode sonata that ends in that minor mode—the norm before about 1775—to be modally emancipated in a major-mode coda. Here the modal victory occurs after the completion of sonata space, in a post-sonata *parageneric space* (*EST*, 312–17).

Comic plot; tragic plot; history

The discussion of the minor-mode sonata in the 2006 *Elements* treated the comic-plot variant of the minor-mode sonata, that with a recapitulation in which S and C occur in the tonic major, as though that had been a familiar option throughout much of the mid-eighteenth century. To that impression Riley's 2014 monograph provides a salutary corrective, showing that the tragic-plot sonata was the over-whelming norm for those few midcentury, minor-mode symphonies and, by exten-sion, for comparable mid-century sonatas and chamber works as well. Thus while the *Elements* had presented Mozart's seemingly pessimistic insistence on invariably minorizing his expositionally major-mode S and C ideas in the recapitulation as idiosyncratic, it is now clear that in doing so he was retaining what had long been the older norm and would remain as the predominant one until Haydn's innovations in the 1780s and 1790s, along with Beethoven's emergence in that last decade of the century. (It goes without saying that, even so, the fatalistic implications of Mozart's recapitulatory norm are no less striking.)

The heritage of ending minor-mode, binary-based forms in the same tonic minor of its beginning is one whose reach had gone back many decades. One need only recall the many minor-mode binary structures of J. S. Bach (dance movements), Domenico Scarlatti (*essercizi* or "sonatas"), or C. P. E. Bach (sonatas) whose first, repeated sections move from i to III (tonic minor to mediant major) and whose second section features a dogged return to the minor tonic, with or without a sig-nificant number of correspondence measures. This standard procedure appears to be a matter of returning at the end to the original tonic-modal color, whose mood and tone are projected as looming over the unfolding of the entire piece, governing its generic completion. By midcentury, when binary formats had expanded to the point where we might feel comfortable calling them "sonata forms," it is no surprise that the older modal practice was retained as the norm. Continuous expositions that had moved from the tonic to the mediant major brought back all or most of their later expositional modules in the tonic minor, and, similarly, two-part {– +} expositions, with an internal MC, did the same {– –} with the S and C material in the recapitulation.

When did this change? At what point did it occur to composers that ending a minor-key sonata movement with a *modal reversal* into major was something that might not only be generically modified but also turned into something with strong expressive connotations? Later than we might suppose.[8] As Riley notes (2014, 201–19), the history of minor-to-major reversals, whether within individual movements or within multimovement works considered as wholes (minor-key works with later movements or finales in major, for instance), is charged with numerous options and complexities. Among a few early examples of various adoptions of the idea, his study identifies a scattering of special cases from the 1760s in which a sonata-form finale (not a first movement) turns to the major mode only in its coda, that is, after the sonata proper had played out with a minor-mode recapitulation. This option produces a major-mode, post-sonata conclusion to a minor-mode multimovement work, sometimes only at the very end with the effect of an "extended *tièrce de Picardie*" (Riley 2014, 179 and the tabular list on 204). This procedure may be most familiar to us from the D-major *buffa* coda to the finale of Mozart's Piano Concerto No. 20 in D Minor, K. 466/iii (1785, a concerto variant of the Type 4 sonata).[9]

From the mid-eighteenth-century perspective, the issue of modal reversal touched problematically on the status of the minor-key sonata as a distinct subgenre. When the principle of modal reversal is in play, "by the end the minor-key symphony all but dissolves back into a major-key symphony . . . . The minor key symphony stands out as a reaction against the default entertainment function of so much instrumental music of the time. . . . The cheerful major ending trivializes the minor beginning. . . . [And for listeners today, it can seem that] the modal switch is achieved without much toil; it is, as it were, unearned" (Riley 2014, 202, 205). Or as Grave put it, the impression sometimes given is that "the composer could simply wave the magic wand of modal reversal at some point in the latter part of a movement, thereby dissolving minor-related imperfection in a major ending . . . suggesting some uplifting narrative about adversity overcome, yearnings satisfied or a state of impairment rectified by the restoration of wholeness and stability" (2008, 33).

Our main concern here, though, is the purposeful modal reversal of S and C or their equivalents in the recapitulations of minor-key movements. An early example, though an exceptional one because of the illustrative quotation of chant within it (an ecclesiastical S theme that would be inappropriate to minorize in the recapitulation, and cited in Riley as such [24]), occurs in the first movement of Haydn's Symphony No. 26, "Lamentation" (1768). Another is the first movement of a Dittersdorf Symphony in A minor from c. 1779 with the curious title, "Il delirio delli compositori, ossia Il gusto d'oggidì" ("The Delirium of Composers, or Today's Taste"), discussed, with examples, in Riley 2014, 217–18.[10] To be sure, a fully comprehensive corpus study of the larger repertory might bring to light one or more exceptions to the minor-mode-conclusion norm, but notwithstanding any such exception here or there, it's clear what that norm had long been: no modal reversal of S and C in the recapitulation.

It appears to be Haydn who, in the mid-1780s, began to treat as personally normative the practice of retaining the major-mode of S and C, or their equivalents, in the recapitulations of his minor-key sonata-form movements, accompanied by a key-signature change as well. This first occurs in the initial movements of his Symphonies No. 80 in D minor (c. 1783–84) and 83 in G minor (1785). From this point onward, as Grave observes (2008, 34), Haydn started "adopting major endings in minor-key works as a common practice," and a number of his subsequent works across several genres feature sonata movements whose recapitulations feature the {– +} modal reversal found earlier in their first-movement expositions: quartets (including op. 50 no. 4/i in F-sharp minor [1787],[11] op. 74 no. 3/i in G minor [1792–3] and others; several piano trios; and the Symphony No. 95/i in C minor [1791]) (2008, 34–35).[12]

Mozart would not be attracted to this innovation, while Beethoven, from the start, was determined to hyperdramatize modal conflict in his minor-mode movements, sometimes turning to the major in the recapitulation, sometimes not, and often projecting intense struggles of major-minor chiaroscuro in his recapitulatory S and C zones. Moreover, his recapitulatory major-mode strivings are often dashed with collapses back to minor at some point—particularly in his works in C minor. "Beethoven's sonata-form movements do not readily switch to major," comments Riley. "A sudden glimpse of the tonic major during a C-minor sonata-form recapitulation is always swiftly contradicted, as though revealed as a false hope or illusory consolation" (2014, 205). And Schubert's disturbing passageways through major-minor perils and fatalistic entrapments have been much commented upon. It is to an example of Beethoven's middle-period practice—though not one in C minor—that we turn in the next chapter, and we'll follow it with one of Schubert's minor-mode sonata movements in chapter 10.

9

Beethoven, String Quartet in E Minor, op. 59 no. 2/i (Allegro)

While in my Sonata Theory seminars I ask the participants initially to leaf through chapter 14 of the *Elements* ("Sonata Form in Minor Keys," 306–17), at the seminar table I present a more assimilable study to the principles of the minor-mode sonata through the analyses of individual works, commenting on the issues that arise in them at various points of their structures and then returning to the 2006 book to underscore specific passages. My analytical selections for this (at least the introductory ones, chosen from the 1770–1810 years) have varied widely, but they include the first movements of: Haydn's Symphonies No. 44 in E Minor ("Trauer"), 45 in F-sharp minor, "Farewell," and No. 95 in C minor; Mozart's String Quartet in D Minor, K. 421, Piano Sonata in C Minor, K. 457, and Symphonies in G Minor, No. 25, K. 183 and No. 40, K. 550 (including the latter's finale); and Beethoven's Piano Sonatas in C Minor, op. 13 ("Pathétique") and F Minor, op. 57 ("Appassionata"), along with the Symphony No. 5 and *Coriolan* Overture.

Since Sonata Theory is a hands-on method, best learned by being guided through multiple close analyses, not by reading about it, the group-discussion procedure is optimal. For the minor-mode sonata, though, this more informal procedure is not easily replicated in a book. In any event, with chapter 8 now behind us, we are now in a position to return to analysis proper—and to move further into the nineteenth century. In what follows, we zoom in on the first movements of two minor-mode works: in this chapter, Beethoven's String Quartet in E Minor, op. 59 no. 2; in the next, Schubert's String Quartet in D Minor, D. 810. (The close of chapter 11 and all of chapter 12, the last of this handbook, will bring us even further into the nineteenth century.)

Backdrop

By 1806 Beethoven's "new-path" compositional commitment was in full swing. This was the year not only of the three op. 59 quartets but also of his revisions to his 1805 opera, *Leonore*, along with the composition of the Fourth Piano Concerto, the Fourth Symphony, and the *Coriolan* Overture. His imperative was now consistent and clear: to recast inherited musical genres in idealized, hyperdramatized ways. One aspect of this was an enhanced projection of personalized force: musical metaphors of heroically masculine struggles of overcoming, of self-willed

A Sonata Theory Handbook. James Hepokoski, Oxford University Press (2021). © Oxford University Press.
DOI: 10.1093/oso/9780197536810.003.0009.

confidence and command. However one might interpret this in terms of political or biographical terms, it resonated with the turbulent military upheavals of the time, as the ongoing Napoleonic wars continued to rock battle-torn Europe, while shifting coalitions of nations formed, dissolved, and reformed again to confront the advances of French power. Beethoven was also mixing this "heroic-decade" sound with other expressive registers: poetic lyricism; implications of aesthetic devotion and musical depth; explorations of interiority; wryly ironic, sometimes puzzling twists of tone and process.

With the turn of the new century Beethoven was writing music that sought to be more self-consciously idiosyncratic—even eccentric. As such it invited new modes of attention adequate to its growing complexity and internal concentration. "It is around 1800 that the phrase 'understanding music' ('Musik verstehen') first appears in connection with listeners," writes Bonds (2017, 335). While music had always been there to enjoy or to astonish, it now seemed to be calling for something more from its most fervent listeners: reflection, interpretation, or explanation.[1] Around it was emerging the sense of a newly claimed depth or inwardness of expression and purpose (Watkins 2011). This music presented its listeners with a startlingly new, uncommon directness, calling for a more personalized involvement with it. While music in the past had usually been directed toward a more general public, it was not difficult to imagine that Beethoven's middle-period music complemented this traditional appeal with something more existentially personalized: the conviction "that this music is addressed, personally, to me; that somehow I am being asked to recognize myself in it or to help shape my identity around it."

In Vienna a circle of musically devoted aristocratic patrons, talented performers, and supportive friends sustained the attractions of this music's new aura. Such is the case with the op. 59 quartets, commissioned by and dedicated to Count Andrey Razumovsky, the wealthy Russian ambassador to the Habsburg court. Beyond Razumovsky's request, however, Beethoven would probably not have penned the op. 59s had it not been for the close availability of the quartet ensemble organized by the violinist Ignaz Schuppanzigh and the support of another of Beethoven's important Viennese patrons, Prince Lobkowitz. The Schuppanzigh Quartet (also destined to play a major role in the first performances of Beethoven's string quartets from the 1820s) was taking on the role of a stable, professional quartet. It was they who had launched a series of semi-public, subscription concerts in 1804–5, with Razumovsky's approval and support, probably taking place in the Lobkowitz Palace (Albrecht 2004, 10–11; Gingerich 2010, 452–53). Nancy November has recently speculated that the audiences for such concerts must have comprised "small circles of 'insiders'—skilled performers, composers, and often musically talented upper- and middle-class Viennese of Beethoven's acquaintance" (2013, 29).

Since quartet performances had usually been private (domestic or court affairs), these 1804–5 Schuppanzigh/Lobkowitz Palace concerts were innovative, and Beethoven's op. 18 quartets had probably been played on them. That precedent must have led Razumovsky to commission three new quartets from Beethoven, the op. 59s, with the intention of leading to similar Schuppanzigh performances. After some preliminary readings in 1806 by Schuppanzigh's group, the three quartets were probably first performed in January or February 1807. On the 27th of that month the *Allgemeine musikalische Zeitung* was able to report the performance of "three new, very long and difficult Beethoven String Quartets . . . [now] attracting the attention of all connoisseurs" (Albrecht 2004, 11–12).

The story of the Russian folksong melodies inserted into later movements of each of the three "Razumovsky Quartets" is a familiar one and need not be repeated here.[2] At any rate, our concern is with the first movement of the middle quartet, the E-minor Quartet, which sports no signs of inlaid Russianness. One point of what follows is to illustrate some of the characteristic issues that arise within individual minor-mode sonatas. Still another is to awaken aspects of the movement that could have struck the "1806 ear" (which we might imagine as being habituated to more generically normative things) as unusual, even bizarre—effects often lost to our own ears through a reception-historical process of the naturalization of middle-period Beethoven syntax. But this movement houses a number of unorthodox thematic and structural features, the most striking of which challenge analytical interpretation—action zones, for instance, that do not begin or end in prototypical ways, or normative cadential expectations that are left unsatisfied. In coming to terms with such music, we should insist on neither rigid definitions nor unyielding criteria—Sonata Theory's heuristic guidelines suggest nothing of the sort—but rather perceive the underlying norm with which any exceptional event is in dialogue.

Exposition

Primary theme (P^0, $P^{1.1}$, $P^{1.2}$, $p^{1.3}$, mm. 1–20)

Immediately evident in the opening material of this movement (Figure 9.1) is the absence of the normatively melodic, continuous flows found more often within P zones. Instead, we are more likely to be struck by a process of urgent motivic burgeoning and ramification, brusquely cut off at mm. 19–20, only to be resumed at m. 21. Not surprisingly, over the past century and a half the main lines of commentary on this movement have focused on this extraordinary beginning.

Mm. 1–8 confront us with three stop-and-go gestures. Two blunt, *forte* chords, I and V^6 in E minor, set these bars into motion, with the upper voice leaping a fifth upward, E_5-B_5—two imposing jolts of sound set into relief against a backdrop of silence.[3] This is a fatalistic, space-opening gesture, positing the grim E-minor chord as a premise, breaking it open onto its dominant and releasing it through m. 2's expectant emptiness into the world of all that is to follow. Such annunciatory gestures recall precedents in Haydn (see chapter 6), though Daverio, reflecting on the quasi-symphonic character of the op. 59s, also hears echoes of the *Eroica*: "a pair

Figure 9.1. Beethoven, String Quartet in E Minor, op. 59 no. 2/i, mm. 1–23.

of hammerstrokes with a [contrasting] *cantabile* response" (2000, 155). By contrast, Hatten regards m. 1 topically as a recitative cue, recalling an analogous opening to the "Tempest" Piano Sonata in D minor, op. 31 no. 2 (1994, 180–83).

As discussed in chapter 6, for Sonata Theory such pre-thematic starters raise the question, is this a brief, in-tempo introduction (not part of the sonata proper) or a P^0 idea that launches P-space? As always, the answer is found by determining whether it is included in the expositional repeat. At first glance, with the repeat sign following m. 1, the notation might imply that it is not, but when we turn to the exposition's first ending, mm. 69^a–70^a, we see that m. 70^a replicates m. 1 and cycles us back to the initial bar. Therefore—unlike the situation in Haydn's Quartet, op. 76 no. 1 and Beethoven's *Eroica* but like the situation in the Fifth Symphony to come—m. 1 is a P^0 module. It is part of the sonata proper, an essential part of its argument. This will also be confirmed through its presence in the development and at the onsets of the recapitulation and coda.

What follows, mm. 3–4, is a wispy, *pianissimo* response to those opening chords—call it $P^{1.1}$—tiptoeing further into 𝄴 musical space: a metaphorical question mark querying what m. 1 might imply.[4] M. 1's opening fifth recurs as an E_4-B_4 frame in m. 3, and m. 4 drops to B_3 and rises back to E_4: a modest melodic unfolding of the first bar's motivic kernel.[5] This is a touchstone example of a *reactive module*, one responding to what has just happened, even as it also suggests the onset of a process of "organic" germination forward in linear time. (Ever-insistent on form as process, Adorno jotted a note to himself urging "the analysis of [this] first movement . . . as the [unfolding] history of the opening fifth" [1998, 13]). In this first serpentine melodic sprouting, mm. 3–4, we also recognize the enframing outline of the minor-mode pathotype figure: E_4-B_4 [and B_3]-C_5-$D\sharp_4$. Additionally, the harmonic i-$V^{9/7}$-i sway outlines a brief opening gesture followed by an immediate close. Perhaps recalling some of Haydn's string quartets that begin with an epigrammatic closing figure, Beethoven gives us a terse acknowledgment of E minor by means of a fragment of cadential content isolated from a true cadential function. Nothing is closed or completed here. On the contrary, self-enclosed and sealed off by silence on each side, the "cadence" is posited as a brute sonic fact: a opening idea to be elaborated upon in what follows.

If all this were not strange enough, mm. 6–7 reiterate mm. 3–4 a half-step higher, on the Neapolitan F major. This notches up the impression of reactive puzzlement. P-theme tonal swerves are a familiar feature of Beethoven's "new-path" style, as in the openings of the Piano Sonatas op. 31 nos. 1 and 2 ("Tempest") and op. 53 ("Waldstein"). And as all commentators observe, this was not the first time that Beethoven had begun a sonata's first movement by immediately juxtaposing a brief, tonic-minor idea with its immediate repetition on ♭II. Its predecessor had been the F-minor Piano Sonata, op. 57 ("Appassionata"), from a year or two earlier. (Op. 57's finale had also swerved briefly onto the Neapolitan midway through its initial sentence.) A few years later he would revisit the effect with the clipped opening of the op. 95 quartet ("Serioso").

The larger question with regard to the opening of op. 59 no. 2, though, is: how are we to understand it? In a provocative reading of mm. 1–8, Gerd Indorf suggested that the blunt m. 1 chords might be heard as reopening the emphatic F-major cadential closure that had concluded the preceding quartet (Figure 9.2)—only now sounded a half-step lower (2004, 269–70). If we entertain this as a viable reading, two entailments follow. First, this would mean that the connotations of this quartet's opening reach beyond the boundaries of this individual piece, inviting us to read into it a linear continuity proceeding from the preceding work. By these lights, op. 59 no. 2 could be construed as a contrasting centerpiece of a quasi-narratively ongoing triptych. Second, the F-major Neapolitan gesture in mm. 6–7 might be heard as a backward-looking gesture to this quartet's predecessor, either asking us to reflect on where we had been at the end of the prior quartet or perhaps, urging us to feel the continued pull of its F-major tonic on the opening of this very different work.

When gauged against normative thematic prototypes, how are we to construe the shape of what we have heard so far? And where will the music proceed from here? $P^{1.1}$, mm. 3–8, has given us a cryptic musical idea and its out-of-tonic transposed repetition. From one perspective this can suggest an allusion to the two presentation modules of a sentence ($\alpha\alpha'$), though the harmonic plan and interpolated rests measure this music's distance from any normative model. This is my preferred reading, but nuance is everything. The point is to underscore what is exceptional about these bars, not to neutralize them by affixing onto them a label from a prefabricated analytical category. Applying the concept of dialogic form at the presentational level, mm. 3–8 could be heard as starting something deformationally "sentential" by means of a disjointed dialogue with the initiation function of a prototypical presentation. At the same time, their impression is that of a pair of reactive modules—looking both backward and forward—that also begin a process of germination that continues into the exposition as a whole.

Figure 9.2. Beethoven, String Quartet in F Major, op. 59 no. 1/iv, mm. 318–27.

What follows is the deformational presentation's expanded continuation. It begins with what I call $P^{1.2}$ (β, mm. 9–12), pursuing the process of motivic ramification in obvious ways. Here the motivic shapes set forth in mm. 3–8 are worried through in a patch of furrowed-brow anxiety. $P^{1.2}$ couples its sense of preparatory oscillation—two complementary diminished-seventh blurs, each leaning into a dominant seventh—with the rhetorically repetitive aspect of a new presentation: the a sentential, 2+2, αα′, subgrouping under β is self-evident. (Sentential continuations—internal portions of larger sentence chains or nested sentences—are not uncommon. They can, as here, have both a continuational function—"being-in-the-middle" via fragmentation and other characteristics—and a quasi-presentational function, leading to their own continuations.) $P^{1.2}$ is reactive to mm. 3–8 in still another sense. It advances the sense of disorientation by ratcheting up the tension of an ongoing upper-voice ascent. That ascent had begun in $P^{1.1}$, with the B_4 in m. 3, the C_5 in mm. 4 and 6, and the D_5 in m. 7. Now in $P^{1.2}$ the pressure rises to $D\#_5$, and $F\#_5$ in mm. 9–10 and finally peaks on A_5 in mm. 11–12, with some of the key pitches stung by *sforzando* accents.

At m. 13 $P^{1.2}$ releases onto a new melodic grouping, $P^{1.3}$ (γ). Over a static dominant, its first two bars, the repetitive mm. 13–14, register a whimpering recognition of being caught in the toils of a malicious E minor. At the same time they initiate a slide toward forward motion through a combination of means: a reintroduction of sixteenth-note motion; a more perceptible entrainment with the sinuously gliding $\frac{6}{8}$ meter; a melodically shaped, downward tending upper voice; and a sense of uneasy hesitancy provided by a single sigh, swelling dynamically onto the second beat, and its enriched restatement. Also central to these two measures' affect of pathos is their dividing of the pathotype figure among the three upper string parts: E_5 and $D\#_5$ in the first violin and C_4 and B_4 in the second violin, doubled an octave lower in the viola.

The troubled windups of mm. 13–14 flow into a stream of sixteenth notes whose initial i-iv motion (m. 15) signals the onset of an expanded cadential module. The running sixteenths not only disrupt our entrainment with the $\frac{6}{8}$ meter—an anxiety-riddled unsettling—but also suggest a sweeping acceleration toward what is expected to be a fatalistic E-minor cadence: we are being pulled into its darkness. With these octave-doubled runs Beethoven expands the predominant harmony, stretching it from the second beat of m. 15 through the first beat of m. 18 (vii°⁷/V). In mm. 15–17 he mutates the progression-initiating A-minor chord to an implicit F-major one: the more spectral ♭II⁶, mm. 16–17, to be construed over a still-understood but not literally present A_2 bass. The F♮ intruder recalls the Neapolitan swerve of mm. 6–7. In m. 18 the *crescendo* swell onto E minor's dominant, coupled with the $\hat{3}$-$\hat{2}$ descent in the melody, brings us to the brink of the inevitable. In a desperate refusal to submit, the cadence is subverted (m. 19) onto a vii°$^4_2$-V⁶ return to the *forte* P^0 chords from m. 1 and the blank silence of m. 2. (At the same time, in mm. 18–20 the cello's B_2-C_3-$D\#_2$ motion recalls touches on three of the four pitches of the pathotype figure. The fourth pitch, E_3, will be supplied in m. 21.)

As we soon find out, with that clipped abruptness the P-zone arrives at a non-normative end. In a mere 20 bars, Beethoven has led us through a concentrated process that remains disturbingly unsettled at its end. From the Sonata Theory point of view we notice, first, that there is no tonic cadence in P: we thus refer to the tonic in this first zone as *underdetermined* (not secured with a i:PAC; *EST*, 73–74). (In fact, we shall see that there is no unequivocal i:PAC until the coda.) And second, we have a deformational situation in which the P-zone is not closed with a cadence but remains hanging open on that V^6 chord. It is only in retrospect, once we have proceeded into an unmistakable TR, that we can conclude that that P's termination has been rhetorical, not cadential in the more normative manner.

Transition ($P^{1.3'}$==>TR, mm. 21–33/34)

In m. 21 Beethoven returns to $P^{1.3}$, the pathotype-saturated module from m. 13, only now over a tonic pedal, not a dominant pedal, and with some parts exchanged. In the first two bars what had been in the viola is now placed on top, two octaves higher, in the first violin, while m. 13's upper-voice melody is pushed down an octave into the second violin. With this double-counterpoint variant of the beginning of $P^{1.3}$ (mm. 21–24 return referentially to mm. 13–16) the music backs up to reapproach, and potentially this time to be captured by, the thwarted E-minor cadence, that sign of sinister finality from which the narrative subject is struggling to wrest free. In m. 25 the composer continues the octave-doubled runs, swerving away from the $P^{1.3}$ model and fleeing upward, *crescendo*, into a new and obviously TR-oriented *fortissimo* module in m. 26. It is only at this point that we realize that we are in the transition zone. What we had first heard as a variant of $P^{1.3}$ (m. 21, still potentially in the P-zone) can now be regrasped as $TR^{1.1}$ ($P^{1.3}$==>$TR^{1.1}$). (This zone is in dialogue with the *TR of the repeated cadential-unit type*, the oddity here being that the cadence in question had been emphatically blocked at the end of P.) The new, sequential material that starts in m. 26 can now be construed as $TR^{1.2}$.

The strenuous $TR^{1.2}$ unfolds as a high-energy, three-stage process that suggests how forceful the struggle must be to pull oneself away from the gravitational power of, at least, *this* E minor—and of the minor mode itself. Having now climbed all the way to $F\sharp^6$, the first gesture of $TR^{1.2}$ (mm. 26–27) bursts into *fortissimo* four-part harmony on V^7/c (minor? [given that preceding $A\flat_2$]; or possibly major?), with furious tremolos shuddering through the three lower voices. When the high F_6 plunges over two octaves downward in its resolution to $E\flat_4$ (m. 27)—like a wrestler hurling a combatant down onto the mat—whatever hope we might have had of a local escape to "C major" collapses to C minor. A modified sequence (mm. 28–29) then wrenches us to the tonal level to G minor; and a third (mm. 30–31), deploying an augmented sixth, produces a half cadence over a D bass, locally V of G minor.

The struggle away from E minor has proceeded by rising fifths, c, g, and D, this last as a dominant chord, V/iii. This is the proper dominant for the G-major S that will follow, albeit here in the parallel minor, as we so often find in the closing stages of TR. The dominant is now locked onto, while melodic lines swirl above into the iii:HC MC in m. 33. M. 34 is a bar of caesura-fill (CF), sustaining the low D_2 in the cello, with the viola wobbling an octave above it. This dissipates the accumulated energy in a stark *decrescendo* and links the end of TR to the beginning of S. The CF's dynamic pullback reins in the previously forward-vectored activity and drops the register down to the low D_2 in the cello, creating a mid-expositional gap: a dark-pit emptiness that permits the second part of the exposition to emerge and develop on its own terms.

Secondary theme (mm. 35–69/70)

Since mm. 35–39 hold onto the dominant harmony from the end of TR, what we find is a blurred entry into S-space. As a result, commentators have differed about where the secondary theme begins.[6] This problem can occur when S-themes start on or over the dominant, following an HC:MC in the key of S. Sonata Theory regards such an opening as one type of S^0 *(S-zero) or* $S^{1.0}$ *theme*: a new melodic idea, usually with a clear initiating function, but a theme that, at its opening, "retains the MC's active dominant, which continues to ring through the succeeding music as momentarily fixed or immobile . . . [rather like] a prolongation of the caesura-dominant itself" (*EST*, 142–43).

Emerging out of the low-register darkness and directed forward by the now diatonically inflected wobble in the viola, D_3-$C\natural_3$, the cello opens the exposition's part 2 in m. 35 with S^0. It begins with a triadic climb on the sustained dominant, D_2-$F\sharp_2$-A_2 ($\hat{5}$-$\hat{7}$-$\hat{2}$), mm. 35–36, releasing the preceding G minor into G major with the B♮ upper-neighbor at the end of m. 35. At the same time, it reanimates the cello's dotted-eighth-and-three-sixteenths rhythm from mm. 31–32 (traceable back to the $P^{1.3}$ melody in mm. 13–17), the task of whose pulsations is always to flow into the succeeding bar: it will recur throughout much of S. Recalling Adorno's suggestion that this movement may be heard "as the [unfolding] history of the opening fifth," we may be invited to hear a relationship between the D-F♯-A opening of S^0 and the blunt fifth-leap of P^0. As we shall observe, other aspects of the subsequent S-theme also suggest back-references to P, continuing the sense of this music as enacting a process of ramification and becoming. As so often in Beethoven, it is possible to hear S as an imaginative recasting of several of P's characteristic features: the prin-ciple, once again, of *contrasting derivation*. If one wishes to underscore this point, it is possible, with due cautionary nuances, to suggest that a new subrotation begins at m. 35. But to claim, with Adorno, that our task must be to show the "mediated *identity*" of P and S (my italics) is an ideologically grounded step too far (1998, 13).

The cello's D_2-$F\sharp_2$-A_2 is answered three octaves higher and in retrograde by the first violin, A_5-$F\sharp_5$-D_5, mm. 36–37. Continuing the process of S-emergence in the manner of a question or proposal, the cello climbs higher on the rungs of the V^7/

III chord, F#$_2$-A$_2$-C$_3$, mm. 37–38. The first violin responds with a reply that floats upward into the highest available register, sweeping the fog away into a patch of momentarily confident serenity, gliding along with the now-rolling $\frac{6}{8}$ meter. Triggered by the I^6 chord in m. 39 (reckoning now in G major), the seraphic mm. 39–40, with fluttering inner voices, sound a complete cadential progression and produce a seemingly trouble-free III:IAC on the second beat of m. 40. Mm. 35–40 can be grouped as a compressed, six-bar sentential phrase. Even while they prolong a V^7 harmony, mm. 35–36 and 37–38 suggest the onset of a rhetorical presentation (2+2, αα′). In this case, Beethoven omits the usual continuation idea (β) and proceeds immediately to the S$^{1.2}$ cadential unit (γ). Let's call the presentation, mm. 35–38, S$^{1.1}$ (S^0==>S$^{1.1}$) and attach the designator S$^{1.2}$ to the cadence, mm. 39–40.[7]

Grasping the import of this six-bar phrase, mm. 35–40, is critical to understanding all that follows in the exposition. Recall the menacing E-minor threat from P, remembering also that no E-minor PAC had been sounded in that zone: that chilling seal of negativity had been pushed aside, repressed in m. 19. The point now, in S, is to secure a major-mode III:PAC with the hope of resolving it into a I:PAC in the parallel spot of the recapitulation, whereby the mechanics of the sonata process would overturn the initial E minor into E major. While by no means providing terminal closure, sounding the serene, G-major IAC in m. 40 is the first step of this attempt. It could be understood, for instance, as a six-bar antecedent, naïvely hoping for a consequent.

But no consequent follows it. Instead, mm. 41 backs up to sound a variant of m. 39, a phrase-extension seeking to replicate the III:IAC with the melody now in the second violin. Near the cadential moment, m. 42, the predicted cadence falls apart on an f#^{o7} chord (vii^{o7}, with the cello also shifting momentarily into a higher register), slipping onto V$^6_5$ at the end of the bar. Nonetheless, gliding along on the $\frac{6}{8}$ metrical rails, the sense of local serenity spins onward in mm. 43–45, S$^{1.3}$, *piano* and *dolce*. These bars constitute another, similar cadential unit, I-ii^6-V$^{(7)}$-I, producing a second III:IAC at the downbeat of m. 45, again with B$_5$ in the topmost voice. As before, the IAC is not allowed to settle, but is immediately subjected to a variant of S$^{1.3'}$, mm. 45–46 (= mm. 43–44). This time the potential IAC-effect in m. 47 is softened through melodic diminution, and instead the tonic chord on m. 47 starts the gentle push of yet another cadential progression, mm. 47–48, this time clearly headed for a desired III:PAC downbeat and the hoped-for structural closure in 49. More than that, the V$^6_5$/V in the second half of m. 47 and, above all, the melodic descent in the first violin in m. 48 ($\hat{6}$-$\hat{1}$-$\hat{3}$-$\hat{2}$) recall and transpose m. 18 from P—the E-minor cadential moment whose seemingly inevitable i:PAC had been subverted. And similarly, Beethoven subverts the predicted G-major cadence in m. 49 with an unexpected *forte*, f#$^{o4}_2$—enharmonically the same diminished seventh that had thwarted the E-minor cadence in m. 19.

By now it has become clear that sounding that III:PAC (EEC) is not going to be an easy task. For all of its *dolce* serenity up to this point, S is now running the risk of being reduced to a string of failed cadential modules. The diminished-seventh bluster of mm. 49–50, $S^{1.4}$, not only blocks the expected III:PAC but also assumes the role of a two-bar anacrusis: a new, energetic windup gathering up strength to throw off a hopefully more secure approach to the anticipated structural cadence. Once again, the procedure in play—backing up to restate or refashion an earlier, unsuccessful cadential module—is the familiar "one-more-time technique" (Schmalfeldt 1992). Its first release, with the viola now in the upper voice, is in mm. 51–52, an $S^{1.3}$ variant now falling, with the viola's $\hat{6}$-$\hat{5}$-$\hat{4}$-$\hat{3}$-$\hat{2}$-($\hat{1}$) descent, toward a promised III:PAC. But again the cadence is blocked by an even more emphatic intervention of the $S^{1.4}$ anacrusis-windup, mm. 53–54, expanding outward in an aggressively strenuous wedge. This opens onto a climactic cadential $^6_4$ in m. 55, with registral extremes in the outer voices.[8]

At this point the S zone's "one-more-time" strategy changes. With the F$\natural^6$ in the first violin, m. 55, we abandon the quest for a straightforward cadential module. The three bars of mm. 55–57—at first a near-gravityless hovering, then a *dolce*, rapid plunging down to earth—close the wide-open wedge and signal a preparation for something new. They land on the downbeat of m. 58, where something different starts to generate. Call it $S^{1.5}$: a more decisive buildup, begun in a hushed, secretive *pianissimo*: *reculer pour mieux sauter*. If the soaring mm. 55–57 had struck us as a metrical expansion, unpinning our entrainment with the previously smooth-flowing $^6_8$ meter, the chromatic mm. 58–64 give us a different sense of metrical compression or disruption. The off-kilter rhythms and tied eighth notes set the notated meter into conflict with what soon locks into an implicit $^3_4$ displaced from the $^6_8$ barline by a half-beat: a metrically offset hemiola. While anticipated in m. 58, this becomes clearly apparent by m. 59, where the "misaligned $^3_4$" implications are more securely established with the second eighth note of the bar. Their metrical-clash tuggings, which Kerman characterized as "nervous . . . twitchy syncopation" (1966, 126), are unmistakable in the buildup occupying mm. 60–64.

Reinforcing the edgy tension of mm. 58–64 are the chromatic bass-line windings around the ever-strengthening dominant (notice the potent augmented-sixth approach to the $^6_4$ in mm. 62–63) and the inexorable homophonic *crescendo*. By m. 64 the now-supercharged V^7 is sounded *forte*, with ringing double-stops in the upper three parts. The import of all this could not be clearer: the drawing-back of the tensest possible bowstring in preparation for a potent downbeat-release. The arrow is shot forth with the *sforzando* tonic chord in m. 65, elided with and setting off a new, decisive thematic module. Notice also how Beethoven enhances m. 65's shooting-forth through a foreshortening of the last of the metrically displaced "$^3_4$" implications by an eighth note. Thus the ensemble's final bow-stroke in m. 64, marked *staccato*, becomes the trigger-moment that snaps the off-kilter syncopations back into realignment with the notated barlines, restoring our entrainment with $^6_8$ meter.

We now confront the most analytically challenging moment of the exposition, one that will shape any larger interpretive reading that we have of the movement.

M. 65 is certainly a point of strong tonic arrival: G major rings out with celebratory flourishes, and it is emphatically prepared by a preceding V^7. But does it qualify as a *structural cadence*? For Sonata Theory the question matters, since one of its central concerns is to attend to the manner of attaining, or not attaining, the generically mandated, non-tonic PAC near the end of any exposition: the completion of the *essential expositional trajectory* with the cadential production of the EEC. For all of the sense of euphoric arrival at m. 65, the notational evidence on behalf of an unassailably secured structural cadence is not complete, leaving open the possibility for two different understandings of this moment. In such cases Sonata Theory's maxim is to *explicate the ambiguities* rather than to insist upon only one right way to understand the situation.

Why might one hesitate before endorsing m. 65 as a structural cadence? What I'll call Reading 1 draws attention to its cadential complications. Here at the downbeat of m. 65 we first notice that the topmost voice is on $\hat{5}$, D_6, setting off an arpeggio cascade down to another $\hat{5}$, D_4. From that perspective m. 65 might heard as a III:IAC, not a III:PAC,[9] and that accented high D_6 continues to ring through mm. 65–68 as if sustained or frozen in that register. Moreover, at m. 65 Beethoven silences the second violin for two blank bars: its valenced leading-tone in m. 64, $F\sharp_5$, is kept from its predicted resolution onto G_5. Why? (As we shall see, in the parallel passage in the recapitulation this does not happen.) To be sure, the *sforzando* kickoff to the new thematic idea is forcefully accented, but the m. 65 reduction from the preceding double-stop thickness to a three-part texture is at least worthy of our notice. We might also observe that in m. 65 the downbeat G_2 in the cello is of the briefest possible duration, and the vigorous G_2-D_2 alternation in the cello keeps the D_2 dominant of mm. 63–64 in play through m. 68, albeit on metrically weak offbeats. This means that the thematic bolt shot forth in mm. 65–68 is registrally framed by a quasi-sustained D_6 on the top and D_2 on the bottom: the theme is encased within $\hat{5}$ above and $\hat{5}$ below.

To what degree does all this undercut, or at least attenuate, the impression of a structural cadence? Or, in extreme versions of Reading 1, is it conceivable to hear m. 65 as anything other than a cadence? The alternative would be to hear $S^{1.5}$, mm. 58–64, less as a cadential-function module than as a broad anacrusis that lands squarely on the tonic at m. 65 to set free a fresh, resolute thematic idea. (As noted in chapter 4, the music preceding elided PACs or PAC-effects, particularly when the thematic material of the cadential downbeat is vectored determinedly forward, can often take on the additional, preparatory function of an *extended anacrusis*, released at the point of tonic arrival.) But what would such a reading suggest? M. 65 surely marks an attainment of some sort. But it may be that m. 65's G major is insisted upon by a dogged force of will, not attained by a problem-free cadence: a hyperstrong downbeat prepared by a metrically conflicted, seven-bar anacrusis in mm. 58–64.[10] "If G major cannot be secured with an unequivocal cadence—if there is no literal PAC—we will at least proclaim G major to be sufficiently attained by fiat. *Plant the flag with fortitude even though the territory is not yet fully conquered.*" This would mean that m. 65 falls short of being read as an EEC.

And yet for all of these complications most listeners would probably find it more intuitive to hear an implicit cadential arrival at m. 65, especially in the immediate secondary-theme context of repeated cadential frustration through the several preceding "one-more-time" blockages, which are generically common toward the ends of secondary-theme zones. Those favoring a (quasi-) cadential understanding of m. 65—call it Reading 2—might suggest that the "PAC" resolution of the preceding V^7 is something to be conceptually understood, even though upon examination it is not literally present: the forceful, *sforzando* elision of the newly released theme blots the implicit PAC out of audibility. Listeners, the argument might go, will hear a *PAC-effect* at m. 65 even though a check of the notation does not provide the written evidence for one. Such a *PAC-effect*, in turn, could be understood as providing at least a locally credible *EEC-effect*. Within the flexibilities afforded by Sonata Theory practice, the argument would be that, given the strength of the m. 65 arrival and the manner in which it is prepared, it could be considered a *deformational EEC*—a contextually practical substitute for it—seeking to ground the G-major tonic by assertion, that is, by means other than the prototypically normative cadence.

In sum, Reading 1 (no structural cadence) argues that the generically expected III:PAC is so compromised at m. 65 that we should not conclude that the EEC has been satisfactorily accomplished. Reading 2 (implicit cadence-effect) allows for a sufficient EEC-effect via a cadentially attenuated but practicable stand-in for the EEC. Is it obligatory to choose either the one way or the other? Or might it be, in the reading that I prefer, that Beethoven has purposely composed these ambiguities into mm. 58–65 in order to unsettle our confidence in what, now mulling over the matter two centuries later, Sonata Theory regards as a normatively secured EEC? Perhaps the point is precisely that of its almost-ness, its combination of yes-and-no features, both of which play into the dramatic staging of the movement's larger {– +} drama of modal reversal or non-reversal. Any such conclusion would have to be a central part of one's hermeneutic reading of the movement.

What then do we make of the theme that begins in m. 65? Should we think of it as a closing theme (post-EEC) or not? It may sound like a characteristic C theme, or a C theme that could have been, but, again, the confidence of its C-status can be called into question through the multiple attenuations of the PAC-effect at m. 65. How to resolve this question? As I have also noted in chapter 5's discussion of the first movement of Haydn's "Military" Symphony, Sonata Theory refers to such a thing as an S^C *theme*: "the presence of a theme literally in precedential, S-space that in other respects sounds as though it is more characteristically a closing theme." This kind of theme seems "to bestride both the S- and C-concepts" (*EST*, 190–91). While regarding m. 65 as self-evidently precadential is a step too far, my preference is to call this an S^C theme, if only to remind myself of the problems surrounding the m. 65 moment. If you are convinced by the EEC-effect at m. 65 and wish to regard the new theme as C, that's also fine: substitute your C for my S^C in what follows.

In most cases S^C themes will lead to a clearer production of an EEC (and C themes will normally confirm the EEC with one or more cadences). That's not the case here. This S^C (or C) theme starts out as a confident sentence, with presentation αα′ (mm. 65–66, 67–68), but the sentence is cut short in m. 69^a. Its bluff bravado is redirected elsewhere; the theme is cut off at the knees. (The brutality of the truncation is not adequately captured by the benign connotation of the word "retransition," RT.) Even if we have considered m. 65 to mark a sufficient EEC, that G-major confidence cannot be reaffirmed with closing material. This leaves the exposition cadentially open. Under these circumstances m. 65's "EEC-effect" is at best left undersecured and uncertain. And with S^C's inadequacy now demonstrated, m. 70^a brings back the malevolent E minor with a vengeance. We are thrown back to m. 1 and the repeat of the exposition.

In sum, this {– +} exposition (E minor, G major, i-III) has produced at best a tenuous EEC-effect, one that has proved unable to be confirmed—and in fact is lost—in the brief music that follows, producing a non-closed exposition. Given m. 65's ambiguity, I suggest that this movement is at least in dialogue with the concept of what Sonata Theory calls a *failed exposition*, not at all in the sense that Beethoven has composed it poorly but rather in the sense that he has staged a musical drama of cadential ambiguity (an EEC almost but perhaps not quite attained) within an exposition that, by its end, is left open. The expositional tale told here is one in which the major mode (III), while very much present, has proven unable to produce and maintain an unequivocal, major-mode PAC close. In turn this means that the expositional hope of producing an unequivocal I:PAC/ESC in the recapitulation is cast into doubt. On the other hand, we should remember that there have also been no E-minor PACs in the exposition. A bitter struggle is brewing. But before getting to the recapitulation, we have to pass through the trials of the development.

Development (mm. 70^b–138)

Rotation 1 (mm. 70b–107)

In both the first and second endings Beethoven suppresses the once-normative hard break more typically found at the close of expositions. He effects these suppressions by the mid-course interruptions of S^C (mm. 69^a–70^a, 69^b–71^b): signs of its structural inadequacy with regard to expositional closure. In each ending the S^C theme disintegrates and swerves into a restatement of P^0. The second ending's treatment of this is more radical than the first's. Here S^C's G major collapses to G minor (m. 69^b) and immediately inflates from there into E-flat major (mm. 69^b–70^b, the L-operation escape described in the previous chapter, Figure 8.2). The *fortissimo* return of the P^0 idea (m. 70^b) lands on startlingly remote tonal territory, with the sudden impression of a "wrong" harmonic move: E-flat major (♭I of E minor, a half-step lower than the P^0 in m. 70^a).[11]

The immediately succeeding bars question that move and restate the P^0 idea on different tonal levels. Mm. 72–77 seek a way to unravel the immediate harmonic problem ("where to now?"). Reacting to the tonal surprise in mm. 70^b–71^b, m. 72 drops to *piano* ("Really?!") and the asserted E-flat major decays to the even more remote E-flat minor ($\flat$i,). M. 74 enharmonically reconstrues E-flat minor as D-sharp minor in order to pivot in the direction of B minor (d$\sharp$-a$\sharp$^{o6}, $\sharp$iii-vii^{o6} of B minor, minor v of the movement's tonic). Neo-Riemannian theory would recognize B minor (m. 76) as the hexatonic pole from the preceding E-flat major (m. 71^b): a chilling color-shift to a maximally "other," much darkened and mysterious place.[12] However Beethoven himself might have accounted for it, it's evident that he was seeking a fleeting harmonic move into a duskily brooding, estranged spot. Among its ironies is that a tonal color readily assimilable into the global tonic E minor's orbit—B minor as minor v—is locally produced as something eerily unfamiliar. And the negative gravitational force of the minor mode reasserts itself here: B minor is affirmed, *fortissimo*, in m. 76 ("no escape!") and holds its top F$\sharp$$_5$ through the next bar, poised and ready to pursue its malign intentions.

What follows is a set of *pianissimo*, minor-major tonal fluctuations, stagings of the musical process trying to slip free of the dysphoric minor's grip. The terse $P^{1.1}$ reappears on B minor in mm. 78–79 with a deceptive move at its end onto a G *major* chord (VI). That G is then interpreted as V of C minor for a restatement of $P^{1.1}$ a half step higher, mm. 81–82 (recalling the half-step dislocation from mm. 6–7), now with a deceptive move onto an A-flat major chord (VI). Beethoven then briefly sustains this A-flat major as a muted and mysterious dream-space, far afield from the movement's original E-minor tonic (indeed, the hexatonic pole of the global E minor). As if seeking temporary refuge on that tonal color, a hushed, $P^{1.1}$-based, fantasy-thematic sentence starts to glide forward in mm. 83–84, 85–86 (2+2, $\alpha\alpha'$)— a berceuse-like "if only!" But the A-flat major cannot last. In mm. 87–90 the continuation descends to the held-breath dominant of B-flat minor, a key a tritone away from E minor.

The nervous chromatic/enharmonic adjustments of mm. 91–96 serve as a corrective, lifting the brief dominant pedal of B-flat minor (mm. 88–90) onto that of B minor. At the same time, mm. 91–96's duple-vs.-triple dislocations and urgent *crescendo*—intensified through two scrapingly harsh bars of V^9 of B minor—recall the similar role of the exposition's $S^{1.5}$ (mm. 58–64, although here the moment of apparent arrival, m. 97's $^6_4$, is given an ominous, negative accent via a sudden drop back to *piano*). At this point we see that the musical material of the development so far has touched upon both pre-MC and post-MC material, our touchstone criterion for identifying a fully rotational handling of previous thematic ideas. As this passage proceeds, it becomes clear that mm. 97–106 are a complementary but recast variant of mm. 89–96, now lifting the music out of the minor-mode shadows and onto a resonantly proclaimed, *fortissimo* C major (m. 107, VI of E minor; globally construed, C-major can be read as the L-operation, "inflation-escape" key from E minor) and a contrapuntally treated variant of P^0—the start of a new rotation.[13]

The m. 65 question returns here: Is m. 107 a VI:PAC? Since cadential evasions and (far less often) realizations are central to this movement's narrative, this is no idle question. As with many such situations, it depends on one's definitions, and again it might be decided either way. Recall that, under one interpretation, the quasi-parallel moment of the exposition, m. 65, might not be regarded as a PAC but rather as the landing-point of an extended anacrusis. Do we have the same situation at m. 107? We might also remember that form-functional theory, with its strict criteria, is reluctant to call such a tonic arrival a PAC unless the V that precedes it is first sounded in root position,[14] and here the full V^7 of C is generated rung-by-rung in the descending bassline, $F\natural_3$, D_3, B_2, G_2, mm. 103–6. By those lights one can readily hear mm. 99–106 as another extended anacrusis to the strong downbeat at m. 107. This reading recognizes m. 107 as a forceful, new-tonic declaration but would filter that observation into the movement's generally non-cadential frustrations: a major mode asserted but not secured. On the other hand, there is no denying that the tonic-landing on m. 107 is stronger than that of m. 65: here we have $\hat{8}$ in the upper voice and a more firmly placed root in the bass. Those considerations might lead one to regard m. 107 as an elided VI:PAC, though the C major at hand is only transiently generated and soon decays: a red-hot burst of hopeful assertion.

Rotation 2, mm. 107–39.

Blazing ahead in a C-major *sempre fortissimo*, mm. 107–10 attempt to seize control of the originally minor-mode P^0 fifth-motive by wrenching it once again into the major, fortified by similarly motivic, now-cascading sixteenth-note runs. Through desperate force, the narrative subject seeks to commandeer the minor-mode P^0 and its rotation-initiating role in order to produce what might be read as a preemptive, *quasi-recapitulatory effect* on its own major-mode terms, albeit on VI of the global tonic, that is, on a perishable, non-tonic key.[15] The upheavals of its double-counterpoint repetition, with upper and lower parts exchanged (mm. 109–10) and P^0's fifth-leap now projected upward in the top voice, augment the impression of a vehemently erupted modal struggle. *Qua* actor in this tonal/modal drama, the minor mode parries with violence, wrestling down the asserted C major into a four-bar, *still-fortissimo* iteration on A minor (mm. 111–14). With that A minor now entered, a drop to *pianissimo* ushers in the whimperings of $P^{1.3}$ with a set of correspondence bars in that key (mm. 115–20 = mm. 13–18, down a fifth or up a fourth, with only a few variants). If one has entertained the reading in which m. 107 is heard as the futile and illusory C-major-P^0 start of a preemptive, off-tonic "recapitulation," we see here that this vain "recapitulation's" succeeding bars—the $P^{1.3}$ idea—have been captured by A minor, mocking whatever corrective pretensions the C-major outburst at m. 107 might have had.

This time, however, $P^{1.3}$ leads to a weak iv:IAC in m. 121—the first such minor-mode cadence in the movement. It is immediately elided with a restart of $P^{1.3}$, lowered now into the cello and begun with a clinging, two-bar *poco ritard* before slipping back into *a tempo* sixteenth-note runs. Apart from register and a few small variants, we start once again with four correspondence bars (mm. 121–24 = mm. 115–18 = mm. 13–16). At the end of m. 124 the running-sixteenths begin to "stick" in head-spinning, swelling *crescendo* reiterations, *all'unisono*, of a four-note figure, F-G-A-B♭ (mm. 125–26). This is still another anacrusis-buildup that blurs our entrainment with the 𝄌 flow by means of duple-vs.-triple metrical dissonance. In m. 127 it discharges onto B-flat, an arrival that triggers *fortissimo* variants of the viciously combative, sequential TR$^{1.2}$ (which also maintains the ongoing rotational ordering of modules). This time the ascending-sequential pattern is different, relying on the MONTE schema, the chromatic 5–6 shift (with half-step rises in the bassline), which hoists the tonal levels up by step: from B-flat (m. 127) to C (m. 129), to D minor (m. 131), and—most tellingly—to the goal of the whole procedure, the global tonic E minor, proclaimed by outer-voices with malevolent, *fortissimo* glee (m. 133).

With m. 133's return to the E-minor tonic, the development's modal struggle is finished. Prior attempts to seize a major-mode control of P^0—most notably that of the vainly preemptive C major of m. 107—are vanquished. Celebrating that negative victory, the brutally malign, *all'unisono* link into the recapitulation proper (mm. 133–39) grinds earlier major-mode strivings under E minor's heel and into the recapitulation proper. Harry Goldschmidt's description of this *Totentanz*-like passage cannot be improved upon: a "cruel, descending *unisono* with true catastrophe-trills" (cited in Wiese, 2010, 180).[16] While the link's expressive connotations could hardly be clearer, we should notice two things about it. First, it is a grotesque deformation of S$^{1.2}$ (mm. 39–40). This means that the pre-MC material that had started a new rotation with P^0 at m. 107 (and P$^{1.3}$ at m. 115 and TR$^{1.2}$ at m. 127) is followed here by a brief but important allusion to post-MC material. Thus Rotation 2 also meets the criteria for a full rotation. And second, Beethoven has presented us with the unusual situation in which the sonata process gains scale-degree 1̂ of the global tonic, E minor, in m. 133, several bars before the recapitulation, setting off a tumbling anacrusis into that subsequent rotational restart. This is not a case in which a clearly interrupted, root-position V$_A$ marks the end-point of the development.

Recapitulation (mm. 139–c. 209c)

As always, the goal of a recapitulatory analysis is to compare it, bar-for-bar, with the exposition's referential layout, noting any significant deviations from its rhetorical pattern: omitted or added measures, notable melodic variants, cadences added or suppressed—and, in the case of the minor-mode sonata, any changes in the interplay of major- and minor-mode ideas, particularly in and around the area of a potential (tonic-key) ESC.[17] In this case the {– +} exposition had been unable to produce and maintain an indisputable EEC. The two questions now are, will the recapitulation also provide us with a {– +} pattern—as usually happens by the time of Beethoven—and, more significantly, will the exposition's cadential problems be replicated in the tonic?

Primary theme and TR (mm. 139–69/70)

The enhanced, double-appearance of P^0 at the start of the recapitulation (mm. 139–40, 141–42, accompanied by fiercely rotary sixteenth-note figures) is locally referential not to m. 1 but rather to the development's P^0, C-major launch of its second rotation, mm. 107–8, 109–10. The onset of the recapitulation thus continues the process of reactive change and reorientation that has characterized the movement up to this point. The likely significance of the back-reference to mm. 107–10 is that Beethoven had staged the development's Rotation 2 as though it were beginning to imagine itself as a preemptive, major-key recapitulatory effect, seizing the minor-mode P^0 and recasting it into the major. As we heard, those futile C-major assertions had collapsed with the immediate fall into A minor (mm. 111–23) and with it the minor-mode capture of Rotation 2. Now, at the beginning of the recapitulation, the tonic E minor, by adopting the developmental Rotation 2's figuration at mm. 107–10, mocks the earlier, C-major "recapitulatory" pretensions and begins the real recapitulation on its own terms.

That four-bar statement made, P proceeds onward as in the exposition for several bars. Beethoven does rescore some of $P^{1.1}$ and $P^{1.2}$—dividing the parts differently among the four players—and he adds an extra tag in the cello to the F-major statement of $P^{1.1}$ (mm. 146–48), but mm. 143–52 are still referential to mm. 3–12. At mm. 153–54 $P^{1.3}$ corresponds both with mm. 13–14 (in figuration and melodic placement) and mm. 21–22 (since the sustained bass is now the tonic, not the dominant): recall that the first of these, mm. 13–14, had been in P space, while mm. 21–22 had begun TR space—which latter is now pursued here. Thus, as often happens in a recapitulation's early stages, a P==>TR merger (or compression) is in the offing. At m. 156 the music, now recomposed, diverges from that of the exposition: the start of *pre-crux alterations*. The running sixteenths stick first on a reiterative figure on A minor (mm. 156–57), chromatically altered and expanded on F major, *crescendo* (mm. 158–60). M. 161 plugs into the *fortissimo*-strained, $TR^{1.2}$ sequential figures, also recomposed but clearly referential to their expositional models—and now with an extra, added bar (m. 166) to provide an extra push onto the structural dominant, V of E minor, and the point of *crux* (m. 167 = m. 31, down a minor third and slightly varied), followed by a i:HC MC at m. 169.

From the m. 167 crux onward, Beethoven had the option of simply transposing the remainder of the expositional model for the rest of the recapitulation. And for the most part, aside from a notable expansion at the beginning of the now-E-major secondary theme, this is what he did. In that expansion—a *post-crux alteration*—the exposition's four "preliminary" S^0 bars (mm. 35–38) are stretched into eight (mm. 171–78) through a repetition and rescoring of the cello's triadic climb by the viola an octave higher. This is the preparatory passage where the minor mode that had ended TR turns into major. Now in the recapitulation this is not merely a major key but *E major*, the hoped-for {– +} transformation of the original E minor. The double length of its preparation both underscores the emergent E major's crucial role and provides a grander climb up to the seraphically soaring $S^{1.2}$ (m. 179). Following this, the remainder of the recapitulation consists of correspondence measures with occasional small variants here and there (mm. 179–209c = mm. 39–69), charged with all of the expressive complications of their model along the way.

At stake is the production of an ESC, a PAC in E major securing the tonic and thereby overturning the symbolic threat posed by E minor. But just as the exposition had fallen short of unambiguously completing its cadential mission, so too does the recapitulation. The crucial moment, analogous to that of the exposition, is m. 205 (= m. 65) and the onset of what I have called the S^C theme. The most curious thing about this potentially cadential moment is that the second violin's m. 205 is no longer blank, as it had been in its m. 65 model. Now in m. 205 the preceding bar's $D\sharp_5$ indeed resolves upward to E_5, and the double-stops of the preceding bar are also preserved. This bar has more of a sense of cadential completion than had its expositional model. Is this hermeneutically significant—perhaps as an even stronger cadential claim (or attempt) at this more crucial ESC spot? Be that as it may, the S^C (or C) theme still proves incapable of endorsing whatever cadential implication we might wish to assign to m. 205. In the recapitulation that theme, too, falls apart under the first ending—and then again under the second ending, where the ongoing E major decays to E minor.

What we have, then, is a sonata in which the E-major declaration at m. 205 is unconfirmed by what follows it. Even were we to regard m. 205 as an ESC (or sufficient ESC-effect), the process still unravels with the immediately following music. Within the generic {– +} plot of this E-minor sonata movement, the E-major goal-key has been dwelt in at some length but has not been sufficiently secured to project a successful, lasting outcome.[18] Heightening the stakes in op. 59 no. 2/i is the "extra-burden" premise of the minor-mode sonata, as outlined in chapter 8. In this quartet movement the sonata process, potentially a machine capable of converting minor into major, has been unable to secure permanently that parallel major in the recapitulation. To be sure, we have spent much recapitulatory time in E major, and this is obviously a {– +} recapitulation, but that S-zone, E-major stretch exists only as potential unless it is sealed off with a confirming PAC whose impact can be sustained.

In sum, in this musical narrative—in the musical "story" implied by the modular successions in this sonata—the sway of E minor has proven to be so strong that the sonata process, though it came very close to overcoming it, has been unable to do so. Its weak attempt at an E-major ESC could not hold. In turn this means that unambiguous structural closure—the arrival of the "real" ESC—is deferred into post-sonata space (or not-sonata space), that is, into the coda, where the minor-or-major outcome of the now-completed but cadentially insufficient sonata will be determined.

A note on the repeat of the development and recapitulation

Elements of Sonata Theory (*EST*, 20–22) surveys the history of sonata-form repeat conventions from c. 1750 onward. By the time of Beethoven, the more common convention within the first movement of multimovement works was to repeat the exposition but not the development and recapitulation, although that more structurally elaborate decision, producing a more symmetrically formalized, grander structure—and retaining that aspect of its binary-form ancestors—still remained as a lower-level default option. Beethoven's "new-path" decision in 1802 led him to experiment with the implications of various repeat options. In the three op. 59 quartets the composer adopted a variety of repeat schemes for first movements, and because he did so they must have been conscious decisions, not unreflective conventional defaults. Op 59 no. 1/i, for instance, features no repeats at all, for which Beethovenian precedents had existed in the first movements of the Violin Sonata in C Minor, op. 30 no. 2, and the Piano Sonata in F Minor, op. 57 ("Appassionata"). (Even more striking, the finale of the "Appassionata" does not repeat the exposition but does repeat the development and recapitulation.) And op. 59 no. 3/i repeats only the exposition. In the case of this E-minor quartet movement, being thrown back to repeat the entire development and recapitulation obliges us to re-experience the modal struggles and cadential failures of that broad stretch of music. Beethoven's repeat sign indicates that this is something that he wanted us to do.

Coda (mm. 210–55)

As often in Beethoven, the coda has specific things to accomplish beyond merely rounding off an already satisfactory sonata. And it requires more than just a few bars to accomplish them. Now on the other side of the sonata, the coda's main task is to produce what was lacking in the recapitulation: an unequivocal PAC in either E major or E minor. As we enter the coda, we don't know which it will be. This PAC will not only provide the generically expected tonal-structural closure to the piece but also, since this is a minor-mode movement, bring its narrative to a conclusion that is either emancipatory (liberated into the major, "one wins") or fateful (still locked into the minor, "one loses"). The watchword for such a coda: be on the anticipatory lookout for that structural PAC!

As a first-level default, the beginnings of codas, and particularly extended ones—discursive codas—most often return to music similar to that which had begun the development. (When the development had begun with the off-tonic P^0 or $P^{1.1}$, a tonic-P entry into the coda can of course also recall the opening of the piece.) In situations where the development and recapitulation had not been provided with their own repeat, such a P onset to the coda vestigially recalls that earlier practice. Here in op. 59 no. 2, with its first and second endings to the development-recapitulation complex, the impression given is that of recycling back to the musical ideas of that point yet again but varying what had occurred in the development's initial, ruminative passages to proceed elsewhere. Since this coda begins with the rotation-initiator P^0, now on C major (VI; cf. the C-major developmental breakout at m. 107), it also, like most codas, begins another rotational process, though none of the once hopefully proleptic, major-mode secondary material is permitted entry in this fatalistic, negative coda.

As is obvious, mm. 210–18 recall mm. 70b–78, now sounded on different tonal levels, leading from C major (VI) to an assertive P^0 sounded on the very remote G-sharp minor (♯iii, again the maximally darkened, mysterious hexatonic pole from that C major).[19] When the music drops to a reflective *piano* (m. 218), we enter a 10-bar, smoothly gliding passage (mm. 218–27) that features a series of chromatic/harmonic shifts with differing tonal implications, as the seesaw opening figure of $P^{1.1}$ is passed back and forth between the second violin and viola. The passage is characteristic of the mature Beethoven: following a problematized recapitulation, musical "progress" is momentarily stilled in a corridor of suspense that reflects on where we have been and what the tonal/modal outcome of the whole process might be: "How will this tale end?" Follow, then, the changing tonal colors and their implications. G-sharp minor (mm. 218–20) is first inflected to E^6 (via the L-operation, a 5–6 shift, m. 221). In the first of these chordal slippages, then, we get a transitory glimpse of the E-major sonority, the once-hoped-for emancipatory goal of this E-minor work, but it dissolves away from us as soon as it is touched. Reduced to the status of a local dominant (V/iv), the valedictory gleam of that E^6 gives way to an A minor chord (iv, m. 222). The slippages in mm. 223–24 attempt to treat the preceding A minor as vi of C major—that C major again!—and those two bars drift off to a delicious ii^6_5 and cadential $^6_4$ in a gesture toward that key. But that vision, too, fades away in mm. 225–28, first back toward A minor but then, treating A minor as iv of E minor, through the telling cadential $^6_4$ on the downbeat of m. 227, which then slides into the murk of E minor's vii^{o4}_2. The recapitulation's claim on E major is in the process of being extinguished.

On that vii^{o4}_2, now in a hushed *pianissimo*, m. 228 begins another cumulative, duple-vs.-triple passage (recalling $S^{1.5}$, particularly in its rhythmic configuration from the development's first rotation, mm. 91–96, 99–106). In m. 230 Beethoven drops the cello's pitch a half-step, which places a dominant-root, B_2, under the diminished seventh. This sets off a rapid *crescendo* that sustains the resultant V^9 of E Minor in an expansively dissonant, post-sonata wail of anguish. It peaks registrally at m. 232, *fortissimo*, with the completed climb to C_6 in in the first violin, and proceeds to grind in the discordant pain of the V^9 for several bars, becoming even more intense in mm. 236–39, where double-stops in the top three voices, jamming together the diminished-seventh pitches, C, A, F♯, and D♯ of the dominant ninth, cry out in a sonorous thickness of texture unprecedented in this movement. As Hatten observes, the telescoped pitches are no mere happenstance: "the V^{m9} implied by arpeggiation in m. 4 . . . and hinted by the 6-5 voice leading in the bass in m. 12 . . . becomes the crux of an intensification in the coda" (1994, 192). In mm. 237–40 the fadeout *decrescendo* back to *piano* interrupts the stalled V^9 and brings the coda's brief first rotation to a decayed end.

Now shorn of its former hopes for modal transformation, the *pianissimo* return of the mournful $P^{1.3}$ in m. 241 begins a reactive, valedictory second rotation *in medias res*—no P^0, $P^{1.1}$, or $P^{1.2}$ this time. Mm. 241–45 retrace mm. 13–17 with correspondence bars—and yet at the same time the rotational aspects of the coda remain relatable to those of the development, where $P^{1.3}$ had appeared in a second-rotational process (m. 115). This time, though, m. 246 spins off to what we now realize is fated to be the inescapable denouement: an inexorable process of structural-cadence generation—call it *the final capture*—in E minor. Two features mark this event. The first is the double-touching of the i^6 chord in mm. 247 and 249: that generic trigger for an expanded cadential progression, with the telltale $\hat{3}$-$\hat{4}$-$\hat{5}$ ascent in the bass. And the second is the icy chill of the Neapolitan ♭ii^6 above the soundings of $\hat{4}$, recalling, of course, the "F-major" unsettling of $P^{1.1}$ back at the sonata's start, mm. 6–7. The reiterative mm. 246–47 and 248–49, *crescendo*, provide a double-windup to the dominant at m. 250. And finally—finally!—E minor produces its only unequivocal i:PAC in m. 251.

I read m. 251, then, as the announcement of the movement's real ESC, the more effective, terminally secured ESC that the recapitulation, striving toward the major, had proven incapable of providing. Yet even here there is one last twist of the knife. The landing on m. 251 is elided with a concluding, declarative statement of $P^{1.1}$, insistently *fortissimo* and in octaves, mm. 251–52. (One could regard it as either a P-related displacement within the second coda rotation or the start of a new half-rotation.) While previous utterances of $P^{1.1}$ had been set forth as nervously *pianissimo* questions—fearful apprehensions—it is now presented as the minor-mode victor. As with $P^{1.1}$'s first appearance, the figure is a self-enclosed hieroglyph, sealed off within itself and at least proto-cadential. But I prefer not to regard the second beat of m. 252 as a second, reinforcing cadence that is the better choice for the ESC. Since the *fortissimo* $P^{1.1}$ is an obvious extension of its PAC downbeat—to be heard as a single idea, a single thing—a more nuanced reading would propose that the i:PAC/ESC implication of m. 251 is extended through m. 252's second beat. From that perspective the ESC is spread over the bars 251–52 and attains its finality only with the landing on the octave E's on the second beat of m. 252. This ESC is not reducible to a single time-point (the downbeat of m. 251) but rather to a four-beat $P^{1.1}$ figural complex spanning mm. 251–52. The remainder of the movement is given over to brief, resounding $P^{1.1}$ aftershocks, an E-minor, codetta-like close to coda space.

Multimovement sonata cycles as complete gestures

What we have dealt with here is only the first "chapter" of Beethoven's four-movement "novel," and this opening narrative is one of defeat and loss. That the Molto Adagio second movement will continue the modal quest with the reactive, parallel-major prayer-mirage of E major is relevant to the narrative processes of the quartet as a whole—as will be the return of E minor in the limping scherzo (with its brightly E-major, *thème-russe* trio), and its hectic E-minor finale (with its C-major, off-tonic start on VI), driving home the negative minor mode all the way to the end. The modal struggles begun in the first movement remain in play all the way to the quartet's fatalistic end.

Such observations touch on another central aspect of Sonata Theory: the consideration of a multimovement work as a whole. Chapter 3, dealing with a non-tonic slow movement from a symphony by Mozart, introduced some of the issues in play, as did chapter 8 on the minor-mode sonata. Any time that we are concerned with a single movement, we are likely to focus on its particular microworld of properties, dealing with it as if it were a stand-alone work. In those circumstances it is easy to set aside how it appears to us when we reflect on its role within the composition's movements as a connected whole. From that perspective any single movement that we look at individually is not only just one of a set of (probably) three or four movements meant to be heard in succession, but it is also situated in a particular place in that succession: in what Sonata Theory calls *first-movement position, second-movement position,* and so on.

From at least early Beethoven onward, if not also with Haydn, Mozart, and perhaps a few of the era's comparable others, the issue at stake is "the idea of seeking to grasp successive movements as a coherent whole rather than as a string of dissociated contrasts" *(EST, 318). Elements of Sonata Theory* devotes a chapter to this issue (318–42), proposing roles and norms for each movement and reflecting on the implications of their various key-choice options and their orderings within a multimovement work's three- or four-movement trajectory. (What difference does it make, for instance, if the second and third movements are ordered, say, as non-tonic slow movement and tonic minuet/scherzo as opposed to tonic minuet/scherzo and non-tonic slow movement? [*EST,* 337–40]).

For Sonata Theory the heart of the matter lies in the phenomenological experience of the complete work as we move through it (or it through us). This is predicated on attending to *the role of the listener* in making the effort to perceive a multimovement work as an intelligible, internally interconnected singularity in its own right (like the complex display object that we call "the op. 59 no. 2 quartet"). To encourage that to happen, we should start by "foreground[ing] our awareness that individual movements of the music do not die away into loss once they have been replaced by the next audible module. They continue to exist in our memory, creating an ongoing string of contexts, the conditions for the existence of what is currently being sounded" (*EST,* 342). This is another principle of the Sonata Theory approach: the phenomenological involvement applies not only to the local details of piece as we experience them in ever-elapsing time but also, more broadly, to our journey through several movements.

> Entering the acoustic surface of a second movement, we can draw the memory of the first into it: the first movement's ideas and grounding tonalities remain present as a tacit backdrop against which the otherwise self-contained processes of the second movement can be read. . . . Entering the third movement, we can draw the first and second into it [and so on into the fourth, as a response and re-action to all that has preceded it]. . . . Throughout all phases of the work, we can trace an ongoing conceptual narrative—a master thread—not so much in what we literally hear as in our reconstructions of the work's ongoing dialogue, moment by moment, with a pre-existing, flexible, and constellated network of generic norms—norms not only for individual zones and individual movements, but for multimovement works as a whole. (*EST*, 342)

10

Schubert, String Quartet No. 14 in D Minor, D. 810/i (Allegro)

Schubert and sonata form: a strange combination? A puzzle to be solved? A divergent practice to be analytically reconfigured on new terms? Or if not, how should we characterize its often elliptical relationship with the inherited norms of sonata construction? In the past three decades few analytical topics have been pursued more vigorously. The result has been a cascade of recent studies, articles, and books cycling around the same analytical issues and seeking to come to terms with Schubert's difference from the sonata practice of Haydn, Mozart, and Beethoven, with their more purposeful drives toward tonal resolution and cadential completion.

With Schubert, many have argued, we are invited into worlds of musical otherness that call for a new orientation in order to construe them according to the terms that they appear to set for themselves. The unhurried lyricism of many passages in his sonata movements, their unstable, chromatic slippages, their drawing forth of the sonic presence of radiantly glowing moments, their pools of stasis, circularity, or obsession: all these contribute to the sense of difference frequently experienced in this music—sometimes sensuously luminescent, sometimes disturbingly chilling.

By the time of Schubert some of the classical-era norms of sonata construction no longer carried the binding force that they once had. To what extent is the Sonata Theory way of thinking, so at home with Haydn and Mozart, a productive approach to Schubert's sonata movements? Or more to the point, as was the case already with Beethoven, how can our awareness of the classical-era system and its traditional norms be flexibly used as a heuristic guideline to recognize, and then to interpret, the often-unusual happenings that we find in Schubert's sonata movements? This chapter provides some suggestions by looking at a single first movement, that of Schubert's String Quartet in D Minor, D. 810, nicknamed "Death and the Maiden" because of the second movement's variations on Schubert's song of the same name—though most writers agree that musical premonitions of death pervade all four movements. Before setting out on that analysis, however let's take some time to consider the larger challenges at hand when we confront Schubert's sonata-form works from the standpoint of Sonata Theory. Following that, we'll look at D. 810's backdrop and biographical context and then move on to the analytical reading proper.

A Sonata Theory Handbook. James Hepokoski, Oxford University Press (2021). © Oxford University Press.
DOI: 10.1093/oso/9780197536810.003.0010.

Sonata Theory and Schubertian sonata form

Any analyst looking into the architecture of Schubert's sonatas will immediately recognize that while the overarching concept of "sonata form" is very much in play, the feel and style of sonata composition is being realized in highly individualized, unusual ways. Our charge here is that of reading the intensity of D. 810's first movement through the interpretive lens of Sonata Theory, a mode of analytical thinking concerned with retracing individual exemplars' pathways through action zones and toward sonata form's generically expected cadences, the EEC and ESC. Schubert's way of getting there typically features internal repetitions, hesitancies, blockages, and harmonic/syntactic deviations that can give the impression of a disinclination to proceed onward at all. This is not a defect, as once declared by strait-laced "classical-style" guardians, some dying echoes of which are still readable in Rosen 1997, 517: "a degenerate style" of mere "classicizing." Sonata Theory rejects this kind of language. Schubert's way of inflecting the potential of sonata structures is one of his music's most imaginative, most cherished attributes.

Setting aside sententious evaluations as a matter of principle (especially negative ones), our concern is only to inquire into how Schubert and so many others adapted the ever-changing historical genre for their own aesthetic and cultural purposes. From the standpoint of the core axiom of Sonata Theory, *dialogic form*, we need to explore how individual composers created personalized, often idiosyncratic works *in dialogue with* the more traditional norms of the genre—and, increasingly, with the newer models provided by an emerging canon of exemplary works from the past—as they understood them in their own historical circumstances. As analysts we should be eager to embrace the suppleness and expandability of the sonata genre as it underwent a process of historical dissemination through differing musical minds in differing decades, places, and cultural conditions.

In close readings of Schubert's music our task is to embrace compositional difference at the action-zone level while never losing sight of the generically inevitable EEC and ESC goals. It is his internal treatment of the zones that attracts so much analytical attention. So extraordinary can this be that it can seem as though "the hierarchy of formal components of the classical sonata is dissolved into a democratic juxtaposition" (Godel 1985, 242, translated in Fisk 2001, 274). What we find are successions of semi-independent, self-justifying zones or tableaux often freed from the usual tugs of the normative diatonic system by means of local chromatic escapes. This results in sonata expositions exemplifying not so much the process-of-becoming approach typical of Haydn and Beethoven—developing motivic webs spun over the four action zones of an exposition—but rather a succession of reactive or contrasting "existential states" (Gingerich 2014, 204), each with its own, often extended, textural or harmonic "expressive resonance" (Hatten 2016; 2018, 164). While aspects of motivic interrelationships may be discerned among Schubert's action zones, their structures are not so tightly wound as those in Haydn's or Beethoven's sonatas. Instead, he tends to regard the main thematic action zones,

P and S, as psychological separate spaces in which to dwell and within which to explore obsessions—not infrequently dreamlike, quasi-hallucinatory, or nightmarish. As we shall see, the S-space of D. 810/i is a perfect illustration of this.

Schubert's expositions can house extended spaces of stasis, circulatory modulations (which conclude where they began), striking tonal fluctuations, and coloristic digressions. These last include affectively charged modal switches from major to minor or the reverse: the deflationary darkness of a "lights-out" switch or the impression of a glowing but ephemeral "lights-on." (Beach 2017, 12, puts it nicely: modal mixture is "an integral feature of much music of the classical period, but [for Schubert it becomes] . . . a defining feature of his style.") Beyond effects of modal mixture, we also find the unmooring of local tonal or modal security: once-secure ground sways under one's feet. Not holding firm, governing keys can slip into spectral elsewheres before submitting to course corrections that bring them back onto the generically normative track, as if returned to pre-assigned generic duty.

Such procedures are commonly assessed as the weakening of the traditional tonic-dominant axis, sometimes in favor of "three-key expositions" (perhaps some variant of tonic, mediant, and dominant, as will be the case in D. 810/i),[1] passing slippages onto enharmonically inflected or third-related key areas (Hinrichsen 1988; Clark 2011),[2] occasionally extreme "usage[s] of equal-interval cycles, to the point of setting in motion mechanical cycles, and cycles within cycles, that threaten to spin out of control, far beyond the norms of its time" (McCreless 2015, 36, in a close analysis of D. 887 that concludes that in this last quartet Schubert "pushed the limits of harmonic rationality" in a "riot of equal-interval cycles" [35]), or patches here and there governed by an alternative, non-diatonic system, such as that described by neo-Riemannian hexatonicism (Cohn 1999, 2004, 2012).

All such features have given rise to colorful ways of describing the impression given by many Schubertian expositions: as lyrical, paratactic episodes or fantasy-sonata blends (Mak 2010; and 2016, 282–84, citing also earlier claims along these lines; Rusch 2016); as products of a "wanderer" through established forms, moving perilously close to "the edge of the precipice . . . [yet] with the assurance of a sleep-walker," yielding music in which, "more often than not, happiness is but the surface of despair" (Brendel 1990, 86); as disoriented, "potpourri" excursions through alien sonata landscapes (Adorno 2005: "sonata form" as a now-broken given, to be traversed through as once-familiar but now-alien territory);[3] as a sensuous, conflicted, "dream-laden" music of "delicacy and stillness-in-motion," "fragmentary imaginary narrations of his own life, as a Fremdling" (Fisk 2001, 273, 278, 269).[4]

Under these lights, Schubert's expositions and recapitulations have led some to imagine that what Sonata Theory regards as the essential expositional and essential sonata trajectories are to a large extent either disabled or rendered beside the point.[5] But that is not the case. While Schubert's lingerings through successive existential states are remarkable, while his indulgent pools of sound catch us up in their heightened sonic presence, and while such behavior sets his approach to sonata construction in contrast to that found in the tight networks of Haydn and

Beethoven, their arc eventually bends toward the cadential resolutions mandated by the guidelines of the genre (EEC, ESC). Not to understand this is to miss the point of the delays and postponements. While *en route*, Schubert's cadential trajectories may seem to be temporarily placed on hold, but they are still there. In the end the genre exerts its force. The narrative subject is finally obliged to submit to it, yielding to the norm predetermined by the then-traditional rules of the game, an effect especially unsettling in minor-mode movements.

Backdrop

While Schubert had written a number of quartets and sonatas, along with six complete symphonies, before 1823–24 (by age 26), he had published none of them, apparently considering them not yet ready for it. To the extent that any of them were known at all, it was only to a private circle of supportive friends. At the time his public profile in Vienna was largely that of a composer of Lieder, sacred music, and lighter, entertainment or domestic music for piano.[6] All that would change in 1823. This was a year of grave alarm for Schubert, though one poignantly coupled with emerging Viennese opportunities.

In *Schubert's Beethoven Project* (2014) John M. Gingerich documented this aspect of Schubert's life and what seem to have been its compositional consequences. "The first hint that Schubert was seriously ill is a letter from 28 February 1823 in which he excused himself because 'my health still does not allow me to leave the house.' . . . All the clues point to syphilis as the cause of Schubert's illness and as the cause of his death not quite six years later" (83). Unsightly symptoms kept Schubert from public view for much of that "year of crisis," and the young composer, who had been looking toward an ever-expansive future, was now facing the specter of a death sentence. Yet Gingerich notes that it was in early 1824 that Schubert turned to writing and promoting new, ambitiously large-scale instrumental works, most notably chamber music and symphonies. These were elevated genres associated with the stature of Beethoven, whose works Schubert revered. (In 1823–24 Beethoven was completing the Missa Solemnis and the Ninth Symphony.) This newly determined "Beethoven project," as Gingerich dubs it, began in early 1824 with the composition of the Octet, D. 803 (February), and two string quartets of a projected three: the A minor Quartet, D. 804 (February), and most of the D minor Quartet, D. 810 (through the end of March), our concern in this chapter. The third quartet, the G major, D. 887, may have been begun in late May, though Schubert completed it only in 1826.

Another factor in Schubert's ambitious turn—what Gingerich calls "the divide of 1824" (22)—was the violinist Ignaz Schuppanzigh's innovative chamber-music enterprise launched in 1823. We recall from the preceding chapter that the same Schuppanzigh had played a central role in Beethoven's composition of his op. 59 quartets. He would again be decisive not only in Schubert's turn to more expansive quartet composition, but also to "late Beethoven's" turn to quartets in 1825–26. In the summer of 1823, by which year the new fashion of Italian opera, with Rossini's works in the lead, was sweeping over Vienna, much to the concern of some of those who feared the decline of Austrian instrumental music,[7] Schuppanzigh had established a series of six public subscription chamber-music-only concerts and had followed them up with six more in December and a further set of six that began in February 1824—and more after that. One should not underestimate the significance of these concerts. They took an Austro-Germanic genre associated with privileged, private performance and presented curated sets of them to the public, appealing to an emerging audience of connoisseurs. This was a profound "break with prevailing concert practices . . . [that] in turn transformed the status of chamber music, most particularly that of its leading genre, the string quartet. . . . Schuppanzigh's series demanded and thereby created a new kind of listening, of concentration on musical processes without the aid or distraction of text, sustained through the course of a whole concert." (Gingerich 2014, 122).[8]

Schubert wrote the A minor and D minor Quartets in February 1824 with Schuppanzigh performances in mind. The A minor, D. 804, received just that on March 14 (Schuppanzigh seems to have been unimpressed with it), while the D minor, D. 810, languished. It was first heard in private read-throughs in late January 1826 and a single, private performance by the Schuppanzigh group a day or two later, on February 1. Its first movement (only) may have been presented publicly at a benefit concert for Schubert on March 26, 1828—the last year of his life. D. 810 as a whole was published by Joseph Czerny in 1831, three years after Schubert's death. Two more years would pass before the quartet's first complete public performance, in Berlin, on March 12, 1833, now by a quartet led by Karl Möser.[9]

Exposition (mm. 1–140)

Primary theme (P⁰, P¹)

"Mm. 1–14 burst forth at their outset, then recede into *pianissimo* and before long into stasis (fermata on V, m. 14), as if parting the curtain for the main theme proper, P¹." This is the description of this movement's opening gesture in *EST*, 89, which cites it as a touchstone of a thematically elaborated P⁰ theme, a preliminary statement extended "beyond the brief formulaic flourish" to serve as an initial gesture drawing us into the ensuing drama. Its generic roots lie in the tradition of minor-mode, negative-stamp P⁰ mottos, heard in such works as Haydn's Symphonies No. 44 and 95 and Beethoven's Fifth Symphony and *Coriolan* Overture (*EST*, 87–89; Hepokoski 2010a). Here in D. 810 the opening pronouncement, mm. 1–4 (P$^{0.1}$, a presentational αα′) could hardly be more negative: it resounds with stark, open-string resonance; it is framed by tonic D's above and below; its zigzag interior line of two descending fifths, $\hat{8}$-$\hat{4}$-$\hat{5}$-$\hat{1}$, suggests a tonic-predominant-dominant-tonic fate while also producing vertically a grinningly empty fourth and fifth (mm. 2–3);[10] and it stamps the whole with a commanding triplet that will dominate the subsequent P^1 and TR. This is a fatalistic summons, an illuminated motto or seal of fate. It is probably to be read as a metaphorical representation either of one's hailing by death or of one's immediate, shuddering reaction to such a beckoning.

It is to the threat of mm. 1–4 that the entire movement—indeed, the entire quartet—will react. Starting at m. 5 ($P^{0.2}$, β), the first reaction is a cautiously *pianissimo* drawing-back: "can it be? how are we to respond to this?" The expanded predominant iv^7 in mm. 5–8 predicts the inevitability of the D-minor dominant to follow, but when that A_2 arrives in the cello (m. 9) it supports a $^6_3$ chord, F^6. This is a fleeting illusion of potential escape into the relative major, one sustained through the weary sigh in m. 10. But illusion it was: m. 11 returns us to m. 7's "inevitable" iv^7 of the reality tonic, D minor, and into the foreboding dominants of mm. 13–14, V^{6-5}_{4-3}. While none of this is difficult to read in terms of affect ("can this death sentence be escaped?"), three additional aspects are worth noting. First, a central feature of mm. 1–14 is its coordination of rhythmic motion and dynamics: the tense, *fortissimo* compression of mm. 1–4 is followed by a gradual expansion of note-values, through its quiet, quasi-hymnic center and into the ominous stillness of its final bars, mm. 13–14—in effect a notated *ritardando*. Second, in this rhythmic deceleration, the three-quarter-note figures of mm. 8 and 12 can be regarded as brooding augmentations of the earlier triplet. And third, notice the frozen fixity of the second violin and viola for much of this music from m. 5 to the fermata in m. 14. The second violin's D_4 departs from that pitch only at the "F-major" fantasy-moment of mm. 9–10, where it descends to C_4, and in the final bar, where it finally settles to a poised-and-ready $C\sharp_4$; the F_3 in the viola is similarly immobile throughout most of mm. 5–13.

Are mm. 13–14 to be regarded as a phrase-ending half cadence? Or perhaps only an ominous settling on the dominant? Or, despite the stoppage implied by the m. 14 fermata, might the emphatic landing on the preceding bar, m. 13, along with the four-beat sustaining of its chord, suggest a "cadential $^6_4$" impression that in turn invites us to imagine an implicit chordal motion through that fermata into an implicit, if attenuated i:PAC in m. 15 (attenuated because of its non-triadic octave D's on beat 1)? Might such a "i:PAC" simultaneously complete the process of mm. 1–14's radical deceleration (tumbling off the cliff of mm. 14's dominant and into the clutches of the tonic) and jump-start the Allegro-motion proper of P^1? These are not easy questions, and the matter might be decided in any of these ways. In D. 810/i a number of Schubert's motions toward or into a tonic are cadentially ambiguous, which contributes to the air of troubled uncertainty that pervades this movement.

However one reads the implication of its onset, m. 15's $P^{1.1}$ is the narrative subject's second reaction to mm. 1–4. The gears clench, and $P^{1.1}$ initiates a more forward-driving vector, vainly hoping, one might imagine, to overturn its D-minor threat by means of the sonata process itself (Chapter 8). Consider the signs of anxiety that Schubert packs into its first module, mm. 15–18 + m. 19. Shot through with the negativity of the triplet motive and stung by impulsively accented lashes,[11] the

D-minor Allegro bolts forward, intensifying as the melody churns upward from $\hat{1}$ to $\hat{5}$ (D_4 to A_4). The implicit norm is that of a 2+2, four-bar module (mm. 15–16, 17–18). Given the melody alone, one might expect that the chromatic sequence implied by the second two-bar unit, mm. 17–18, would be harmonized as V^7/iv–iv–V^7/V–V (D^7–g–E^7–A, a variant of the traditional MONTE schema [Gjerdingen 2007, 98]). Instead, suggesting a boxed-in struggle to wrest free from this, Schubert replaces the expected iv with $\flat II^6$ ($E\flat^6$, an alarm-bell Neapolitan) and the "final" V with III^6 (F^6, recalling the fantasy of escape from mm. 9–10). Following the 2+2 unit, he now appends an extra measure (m. 19), snapping m. 18's "wrong-chord" F^6 back to the "right-chord" dominant, A^7—revisiting the similar corrective procedure heard in the final bars of P^0. (Notice also the coloristic dab of non-diatonic hexatonicism: F^6 and A^7 are juxtaposed by the LP operation.) In turn, the extra measure (m. 19) is now made to serve as a determined anacrusis casting us back to a *forte*, higher-octave repetition of mm. 15–19 in mm. 20–24.

Assessing the thematic shapes presented thus far, we can see that the struggles of mm. 15–19 and 20–24 mark the presentational onset ($\alpha\alpha'$) of a compound sentence. Its continuation at m. 25, $P^{1.2}$ (β), begins with a drop back to *piano*, initiating a succession of resistances to the prevailing D minor. The first is a four-bar unit, mm. 25–28, whose threat of a half cadence (or perhaps an active dominant, V_A) decays at its end, with chromatic groans in the first violin and viola, to a diminished seventh. Clouded over by that same diminished seventh, the second is foreshortened to three bars, mm. 29–31, and manages via an internal VI-iv^7-V progression to resecure the dominant chord. The third, mm. 32–40, begins as a *pianissimo*, varied repetition of the second (m. 32 recalls m. 29) but immediately spins off into the longer, chromatic "parenthetical insertion" of mm. 32–40 (Beach 2017, 163).[12] Roving far afield from D minor and mounting in a fearsome *crescendo*, its chromatic slippages are generated by an expanding "omnibus" wedge in the outer voices: the first violin rises from $E\flat_5$ (mm. 32–35) to the maximal tension of A_5 (m. 40), while the cello descends from A_2 (m. 32, initiating what at first seems to be a sinking *passus duriusculus*) to the open-string C_2 (m. 38), then leaps an octave to continue the descent from B_2 (m. 38, beat 3) to the electrifying reseizure of D minor's active dominant, A_2 (m. 40). Along the way, with the second violin and viola shuddering in tremolos, the chromatic wedge passes through such far-flung chords as $A\flat^7$ (m. 33), a passing c_4^6 (34), $A\flat_2^4$ (35), $D\flat^6$ (36), and so on. The chromatic intensification finally produces an augmented-sixth approach (m. 39) to a climactic V_{4-3}^{6-5} (m. 40), which shouts its fateful i:PAC resolution at m. 41, eliding with TR in a blazing, *fortissimo* return of the initial summons, $P^{0.1}$.

Transition (TR, mm. 41–60/61; de-energizing type)

Since there are no further i:PACs in what follows and since D minor is left behind within a few bars, we soon realize that this is the start of TR. We recognize it as a transition of the dissolving-reprise type: mm. 41–44 are an intensified variant of mm. 1–4, expanded registrally and with the original silence-gaps filled in by frenzied triplets hanging on for dear life. The P^0 return also confirms it as part of the sonata proper, not as a brief, in-tempo introduction to it. Mm. 41–44 pounce with full force on m. 45, which begins a precipitous slide down the chute of descending fifths: two dissonant ninth chords, E^9 (mm. 45–46) and A^9 (mm. 47–48), are followed by a glimpse of D_4^6 (m. 49—now suddenly *piano* but sounding the global-tonic-major chord, darkening at once to d_4^6 (m. 50–51). At the same time, the descending-fifth sequence supports a chromatic descent in the upper voice, from A_5 down to F_5 (mm. 44–50): an additional sign of high distress. Deflating that which had just been pumped up, that A_5-F_5 descent reverses the upper-voice F_5-A_5 ascent produced at the end of P, mm. 36–40.

As we approach the end of TR—mm. 52–60/61—the Sonata Theory analyst will notice four interrelated, Schubertian factors that differ from what classical-era norms usually offer as concluding procedures for this zone. First (leaping ahead a few bars), while at first glance m. 60 might look notationally like a plausible MC—with gap—it is difficult to hear that measure's V^7/III (C^7) as a satisfactory interrupted dominant or terminal chord of TR. Notwithstanding the blank spots in mm. 59 and 60, it is better to hear m. 60 as an active V^7/III chord that floats through the m. 60 gap to empty out into an F major accompanimental pattern at m. 61, in the manner of a much-attenuated PAC. To be sure, one needs to nuance the III:PAC suggestion at m. 61: it is at best underarticulated, and not all listeners will agree on the strength of its implication. The larger point is to underscore the boundary-blur that this weak moment of S-entry offers us—a blur not uncharacteristic of Schubert.

Second, notice the harmonic color-shift from the d_4^6 at the beginning of m. 51 to the F^6 on the downbeat of m. 52, along with the "premature" F-major module that it launches. The F major in which this passage dwells is an unearned tonic: it is produced not through its dominant but by the second violin's chromatic slippage, D_5-$D\flat_5$-C_5 in mm. 51–52—as if pretending to wish away the D minor and hurrying onward toward a major-mode S (and of course also recalling the momentary F-chord escapes of mm. 9–10, 18, and 23, now finally left "uncorrected" to V of D minor). The *pianissimo* mm. 52–61 do sound a separable thematic module "in F," but one that should not be taken for the beginning of a secondary theme. In part, this is because of Sonata Theory's conception of a normative S: a characteristically new idea nearly always set up by a preceding MC. Additionally, while in some respects m. 52 does initiate a new thematic module, it is one that is prepared by and sprouts directly from the omnipresent triplet-motives that immediately precede it. From the Sonata Theory point of view mm. 52–60/61 end TR. They are not to be housed in the S action zone.

Third, and supporting this reading further, a closer look at that m. 52 material shows us that it comprises a short-winded, five-bar idea—quietly pattering steps in F major—leading to a weak III:IAC in m. 56 elided with a varied and expanded repetition from mm. 56–61. This reiteration climbs to a climactic precipice with the *forzando* diminished-seventh predominant in m. 59 and then draws back to settle the preceding IAC (m. 56) into the weakly sounded III:PAC implication at m. 61. In its brevity, the mm. 52–56 / 56–61 double-module fails to display characteristic S-onset behavior. Quite apart from its elided internal repetition, its concluding m. 61 draws open the curtain to unveil a completely different, more S-like thematic idea, one that commentators have intuitively, and correctly, heard as the start of S.

And finally, from the *piano* in m. 49 onward we find a flagging of dynamics in the latter stages of TR. Despite some internal dynamic swells in what follows, this is different from the energy-gain that more typically marks the overall impact of most TRs. Considering this along with the factors cited earlier, what we have here is a somewhat exceptional but occasionally encountered instance of a *de-energizing transition* (*EST*, 31, 44, 48–49, 116). Such a TR can feature a blocked or suppressed MC proper in favor of a broad passage "with reduced dynamics or sounded in *diminuendo*, non-normative by earlier, eighteenth-century standards. In most cases a de-energizing transition falls to a PAC in the new key, thus unlocking the secondary-theme zone" (*EST*, 48).[13]

Secondary thematic zone (TMB, mm. 61–134)

With m. 61 and the *pianissimo* start of its new-thematic, F-major excursions we enter an idiosyncratic yet characteristically Schubertian secondary theme zone: a contrasting existential state responding to the dark ultimacy laid out in P and TR. Here we dwell in an estranged, obsessive, otherworldly space, a realm of illusory refuge or a still-haunted grasping for consolation. Its gentleness is one of the most unsettling things about it. In this context the gliding richness of the harmoniously linked first and second violins, floating as a yoked pair through sonic space, could hardly be more incongruous. Moreover, Schubert now subdues the P and TR death-triplets into a persistently rocking figure in the viola and underpinned by complementary, tonic-pedal-oriented oscillations in the cello. Might there be a suggestion here of a berceuse, or perhaps a longed-for regression back to the security of a now-lost cradle-world?

The tonal goal envisioned is the production of a conclusive III:PAC/EEC (in F major). If realized, that would establish an expositional structure of hope—the hope that one might attain a I:PAC/ESC (in D major) in the recapitulation, thereby reversing the negative D-minor premise of the opening. As outlined in chapter 8, this is a fundamental feature of minor-mode sonata expositions that move to III, from minor to major {– +}, whether or not that recapitulatory potential is fulfilled. Everything that follows in the exposition should be understood with this in mind. What we shall find, though, is that each attempt to secure that III:PAC is either locally thwarted or immediately undone. And before long it will be completely lost, as the positive F-major goal is overtaken by the negative alternative, A minor

(minor v), thus completing a three-key exposition that blots out the second key's major-mode hopes.

Above all, notice the recursive thematic behavior displayed in S^1, mm. 62–83. What we have is a single, brief phrase—seeking closure in the major mediant—heard in four different variants, none of which is cadentially conclusive. As if pretending to be the consequent to an unsounded antecedent, the model, mm. 62–66, is an asymmetrical, five-bar phrase (2+3) that drifts toward a weak cadential gesture in its final two bars. But is m. 66 a III:IAC? Is it a cadence at all? One of its problematic features is the bass motion, or near-lack of it, throughout mm. 62–66. Form-functional theory, for instance, would deny IAC-status to m. 66 on the basis that the implied dominant chord in both mm. 64 and 65 appears first in inversion before being sounded in root position (Caplin 2004, 70). And even within those two bars the sense of dominant-chord strength is diluted: the first two beats of m. 64 momentarily sound a melancholic a_4^6 chord ("iii$_4^6$," clarifying into the "proper" V_5^6 in beats 3–4), echoed in the a_4^6 on beat 3 of the following bar (where the A_4 in the second violin, yoked once again in parallel thirds with the first violin, is likely heard as an upper neighbor to its resolution onto G_4 at the end of the bar). All this colors the "III:IAC" impression with a yearningly sensuous, A-minor glow (as also noted in Black 2016, 92), estranging it from the cadential norm while simultaneously suggesting the tonal color, A minor, to which the local F major is fated to succumb.

With this established, one can make quick work of the ensuing three variants. Mm. 67–71 begin as a repetition, now with the first violin an octave higher and melodically altered in m. 70 in hopes of a $\hat{3}$-$\hat{2}$-$\hat{1}$ descent into a weakened "III:PAC" in m. 71. Those hopes disintegrate with the F#$_5$ in m. 71 and the concomitant diminished seventh chord. Mm. 72–76 give us a distorted S^1 variant that decays rapidly to F *minor* (over its V), then seeks a quick escape to F minor's III, A-flat major (mm. 74–75), again decaying onto a diminished-seventh chord at the cadential moment (m. 76). Mm. 77–83 begin as an intensified repetition of the preceding phrase but now with the potential ♭V:PAC (!) cadential moment blocked at m. 81 ("No! you can't go there!"), correcting the tonality back to F major, with two added bars, and restating the now-cloying III:PAC-effect at m. 83.

That measure's cadentially anemic resolution might tempt some to imagine that the EEC has been secured. But when the same measure spins off, *forte*, into a now-imitative, destabilized variant of S^1's basic idea—entering the lower voices as well, below a scrambling first violin—it is clear that we have not left S-space behind. Instead, charged with a new burst of energy, S-material converts into a busy double-counterpoint complex that unspools into divergent harmonic directions. (Recall that the normative EEC is the first-secured new-key PAC *that goes on to differing material*, particularly in an exposition's central portions.) Yet because the texture is so strikingly altered and because the pseudo-cadence at m. 83 does lay down a gesturally weak end-point to an initial S-phase, it is convenient to consider this new section as S^2.

At the downbeat of m. 83 Schubert reinterprets the F-tonic as VI of A minor, leading to a brief touching of its V, the E-major sonority on the downbeat of m. 84. This is a potentially calamitous tonal swerve. F major had represented a positive outcome for this exposition; the exposition's alternative outcome, however, is A minor. Should the preceding F major be unable to hold firm and give way to A minor, the result would be the conversion of a modally positive exposition into a negative one {− + −}. The contrapuntally active sequences that immediately follow suggest an attempted flight away from that potential A minor. Once A minor's E-major dominant darkens to E minor (m. 84, beat 2), a harmonically shifting pattern is set into motion that lowers the tonal level to D (m. 85), then to G (m. 87), and then once again to F (m. 88). (Note also the linear bass motions F-E-D, mm. 83–85, and A-G-F, mm. 86–88.) This return to F is the fatal step: it recycles us back to the state of affairs at m. 83, where that F had given way to V of A minor in the following bar. And that is what recurs here: the F is again treated as VI of A minor and leads, now, to its V^7 (m. 89), which rushes in a manic accumulation to a furiously *fortissimo* PAC in that key (m. 90). This signals the permanent loss of F major and the reality, now, of the negative {− + −} expositional pattern. (An added feature of the move to A minor is the completion of the fatalistic descending tetrachord, A_4 [and A_3], G_3, F_3, E_3 [mm. 86–89].)

And yet the agonistic struggle persists. While the v:PAC at m. 90 posits a decisive A-minor capture, the continued churning of double counterpoint reopens it by leaping back to the *status quo ante* at m. 86. This undoes the v:PAC by returning to material that precedes it: mm. 90–93 = mm. 86–89, only now with upper and lower parts exchanged. This time, though, the penultimate dominant chord is wrestled to the ground in mm. 93–97 and stopped from proceeding to the v:PAC, and m. 93's E-chord arrival is soon converted into a half cadence at m. 97—a temporary reprieve from full A-minor closure. The v:HC at m. 97 is then sustained by a dominant-lock punctuated by three brusque impulses in the cello, the final one of them *pizzicato* (mm. 97–99), and followed by three bars of caesura-fill (mm. 99–101). The half cadence, dominant-lock, and caesura-gap keep the sonata-game alive: A-minor closure is at least temporarily forestalled. At the same time, mm. 97–101's opened window signals that it is cognizant of the loss of the once-fantasized F major and the inevitability of eventual, negative A-minor expositional outcome.

Both harmonically and rhetorically, m. 99 articulates an unmistakable medial caesura (v:HC MC). But this is an MC within still-open S-space. Any such MC-effect triggers the concept of the *trimodular block* (TMB), a format normally signaled by the presence of *apparent double medial caesuras* (*EST*, 170–77), of which the second occurs somewhere between the onset of S and the securing of the EEC. But in D. 810/i where is the first MC? Normally this would have occurred at the end of TR, just before the start of the S that that MC makes possible. In this case, though, that terminal MC had been overridden by the alternative of the de-energizing transition, whose non-MC conclusion substitutes for the more usual practice, thus conceptually standing in for the first MC. In short, by m. 99 and the caesura-fill that follows, it is clear that the post-TR portion (part two) of the exposition is in dialogue with the TMB principle. Accordingly, we can now relabel S^1 (mm. 61/62–83) as TM^1, S^2 (mm. 83–101) as TM^2, and what follows at m. 102 as TM^3. We are on the way to the EEC-to-come, now presumably destined to be in the minor dominant.

As if in denial of that now-inevitable A minor, TM^3 sets forth in *A major*—the major dominant—with a *pianissimo*, troubled variant of TM^1. The closely packed, middle-register texture of the three lower strings projects a richly sonorous yet disquietingly hallucinatory impression. Now it is the second violin and cello that glide through the *pianissimo* theme, with ruffled accompanimental figures in the first violin and viola, the former featuring a nervously repeated upward leap, the latter returning again and again to a frozen dominant pitch, E_4. By this point, if not long before, we realize how strange this music has been from TM^1 onward. What we have been hearing are reiterations of the same musical module, always in pursuit of cadences that are either undermined or subsequently reopened. It is just such procedures that have given rise to the characterization of much of Schubert's music as metaphors of alienation, wandering, sleepwalking, suffering, or reiterative or delusional obsession—in this case, all in reaction to the D-minor threat staged in P and TR.

Equally unsettling is the unreality of m. 102's A major. From Sonata Theory's point of view, major V is not a concluding-key option within a minor-mode sonata. By the 1820s the normatively available keys were the traditional major III and minor v, along with such more recent possibilities as major VI (*EST*, 317, this last key choice occasionally deployed by Beethoven, Schubert, and others). But moving to *major V*—here, A major—was not a default option. Within the generic system it was an illicit tonal choice. Going there, and staying there, is a deformation of the norm suggesting flights of delusion or denial (*EST*, 315, n. 18). On the one hand, major V seems to pretend that the initial key had not been D minor but D major, in which case the major-dominant S-key would have been the strong norm; on the other hand, it masks the dysphoria of the long-traditional minor-dominant option by coloring it with a prolonged, but modally false, "Picardy" major-mode hue.[14]

In mm. 105–6 TM^3 traces through the pseudo-cadence of TM^{1}'s mm. 65–66— even more weakly now, in this estranged, "if-only" world of A major, since there is no V-I motion in the bass, while far above the first violin replicates its earlier ascent to A_6 heard in mm. 89–90. The theme's repetition swerves cadentially toward C major (m. 109), and for the moment we seem tonally adrift, though since C major is III of A minor, there is a suggestion of the persistent pull of that latter key, conceptually (though not acoustically) still present. At m. 110 the C-drift is corrected: the music resets back to the modally false A major, in which it produces the now-familiar pseudo-PAC at m. 112, whose bass motion is provided by the viola—while the first violin again rushes up to A_6. One might hear the subsequent, *forte* and *forzando* octaves (mm. 112–13) as seeking to cling to the A-major deception. In context, though, rather than being a gesture of affirmation (for example, of a conceivable major-mode EEC), the sixteenth-note torrent is more likely to strike us as a gesture of rejection imposed by the conceptual A minor, which extinguishes the major-mode delusion at the end of m. 113, yanking us back to A-minor reality.

What follows is a cruel drama of tonal and modal struggle. Panicked at the touch of A-minor color, the cello leaps in, *fortissimo*, at m. 114 (TM$^{3.2}$, trying to divert the narrative back to F major, TM^1's now-long-lost key.[15] The upper three voices ring out a strident variant of the obsessive module's incipit in parallel $^6_3$ chords, but, choked dynamically back to *pianissimo*, the cry dissolves away, and the music returns to the inevitable A minor (mm. 118–19; though notice that the chord above the cello's C$_3$ in m. 118, launching the cadential schema, is C major [III], not the expected i$_6$). Once again the cello blocks that cadence with *fortissimo* F-major resistance (m. 120), and the upper strings cry out even more intensely, an urgent two beats earlier than before. But this last gasp of F major cannot be sustained. With m. 124 all hope fades away. As a sign of futility, the rhythmic contour of the familiar theme's incipit is retained but is now emptied out in a characteristically Schubertian chromatic passage (eerily marked with a *diminuendo* to a dynamic even lower than the *pianissimo* of m. 123), sinking downward mostly in half steps until it reaches the vii^{o7} of A minor at m. 128. When the E$_3$ in the cello is added to this, we have a sustained V^9 supporting a nastily reiterative winding figure in the first violin and viola (TM$^{3.3}$): no escape, now, from the A-minor web.[16] (Notice also in TM$^{3.3}$ the anguish of the repeated G♮-G# cross relation.) The fall into the A-minor cadence is finally sounded in mm. 132–34. Completing the process, m. 134's v:PAC is maliciously pounced upon with shock-dynamics: a sudden, *fortissimo* relish.

Closing zone (C, mm. 134–40)

I regard m. 134 as the EEC, even though what follows is not new material. What was the cello's eruptive, F-major protest-figure (mm. 114 and 120) is now turned into an A-minor seal of doom (m. 134), and the keening wails in the upper voices are ones re-sounding the obsessive TM^1 motive that we have been hearing for some time. But most of mm. 134–40 is sounded over a tonic pedal, a typical codetta treatment of closing space (C^{cod}), and its impact is one of a negative affirmation of finality. Mm. 134–40 provide an example of what Sonata Theory calls "C as S-aftermath," an exception to the "non-S-ness of C" guideline—only here sounded *fortissimo*, not in its more usual *piano* dynamic (*EST*, 182–83). With m. 140 the exposition door slams shut on minor v. With it the recapitulation-to-come is foreordained to a tragic, D-minor conclusion. The expositional repeat—an essential but often disregarded feature of this movement—obliges us to re-experience the drama of these initial 140 bars, registering once again the gravity of their thematic and tonal obsessions before Schubert sends us into the continued anxieties of the development.

Development (mm. 141–186; 187–98)

The expositional door having been vehemently closed—twice—the development begins with an attempt to spring it back open. The *fortissimo* return of the TM$^{3.2}$ rejection-figure, now in the second violin and on C major (m. 141, leaping onto III of m. 140's A minor, reverts to the modular state of affairs at m. 120, preceding the exposition's A-minor conclusion. This gesture overrides the more common way of launching a development, that of returning to P (or TR) to begin an off-tonic second rotation or half-rotation. As we soon learn, this development will continue to be dominated by TM$^{3.2}$ and TM$^{3.3}$ material, ideas that themselves had been grounded in variants of the TM^1 module. The obsessions of the exposition's second part continue to reverberate past its decisive close. Because this development is neither launched by the rotation-initiator (P or P-based TR) nor written over by differing music that substitutes for it, we cannot consider it to be rotational in the normal sense of that term. What we have instead is a half-rotation of a different kind and one that presents challenges to the normative rotational principle.

Reflecting on S- or C-dominated developments, *EST* (217) suggests that they

> might be understood as backing-up and recapturing the expositional rotation's part 2, which may have been problematic in some way [which is certainly the case in D. 810]. If so, then the putative half-rotation grounded in S keeps alive certain features of the expositional rotation in developmental space. Alternatively, we might imagine that within the development all of the more normative part-1 materials have been subjected to an ellipsis and missed out altogether. . . . All of these things remain open questions. Whatever our preference, the sheer presence of a dominating S [or here, TM^3] is the central thing. . . . [And we should recall that within any sonata] S is a specially privileged zone, one that has an important burden placed on it [that is, that of serving as the agent that executes its genre-specified tonal motions to the EEC and ESC].

Complementing the TM^3 modules' omnipresence is the tonal drama through which they move. The initial C-major declaration cannot hold. By m. 143 it swerves onto V of D minor: the global tonic and the key of the existential threat. In mm. 144–45 this specter of D minor slithers a half-step lower, onto the dominant of C-sharp minor (V_{4-3}^{6-5}, m. 145), but this potential key dissolves into a prolonged e♯°⁷ (mm. 146–49) that launches a variant of the hushed, static, and sinuous TM$^{3.3}$. Schubert then interprets the e♯°⁷ as vii°⁷ of F-sharp minor, though with curious consequences: it first resolves as a common-tone diminished seventh onto a D chord (m. 150), which is then made to function as VI of F-sharp minor (which tonal process recalls that of mm. 83–84, 88–89, and 144–45). This permits mm. 150–51 to re-sound mm. 144–45 down a fifth and project a cadence onto F-sharp minor, now leapt upon, *fortissimo* in m. 152 (♯iii:PAC), replicating the shock-dynamics of the

EEC. Responding to this is a five-bar, closing-zone-based codetta (enhanced with accompanying triplets from P and TR),[17] that reinforces F-sharp minor with another decisive ♯iii:PAC at m. 156. We see, then, that the development's mm. 141–56 have recycled elements of the exposition's close, mm. 120–40. The earlier developmental attempt to go back in time (m. 141 seeks to recapture the vigor of m. 120) is brought to a differing but no less negative conclusion.

And that conclusion, too, is immediately reopened. Schubert now recasts and expands the preceding F-sharp-minor codetta (mm. 152–56) into a modulating eight-bar phrase (mm. 156–63) that moves via descending fifths from V of F-sharp minor (m. 157), through V of B minor (m. 159), and onto E minor, *fortissimo* (m. 160), solidifying that tonal level at m. 163 with a suddenly *pianissimo* ii:PAC. This is elided with a four-bar codetta featuring TM$^{3.3}$ over a triplet-throbbing tonic pedal. Mm. 156–66 are then treated as a model for sequential reiteration down a whole step, lowering its cadence and codetta onto D minor (mm. 156–66 = mm. 166–76, with a much-altered final chord).

D minor! The tonic key of the movement—and the whole quartet. Within the sonata genre it is rare to encounter a strong tonic landing and codetta in the center of a development. For tonal-resolution reasons it is almost unthinkable. It is as if the sonata's final goal (the recapitulatory ESC cadence) is secured too early, threatening to shut down the whole process long before anyone might have anticipated. But the whole development up to this point has been a succession of strange occurrences. Quite apart from its obsession with TMB motives (especially TM^3), the development has produced three minor-mode PACs *complete with reinforcing codettas* (the first of which supplies yet another PAC). Moreover, the three PACs and codettas descend by whole step, lowering the tonal levels down to the tonic: ♯iii:PAC (m. 152, echoed in m. 156), ii:PAC (m. 163), and i:PAC (m. 173). By mm. 173–75 one finds oneself in the darkest tonal pit imaginable: a stabilized tonic minor, a premonition of the ESC-to-come, the chill of a premature brush with death.

Small wonder, then, that the narrative subject, finally aware of that into which it has fallen, responds in m. 176 with the *fortissimo*, terrified squawk of a thickly scored D$^9_7$ chord. In utter panic, mm. 176–81 claw their way upward, violating all norms of chord-succession with chord-roots succeeding one another by half steps[18]—D, E♭^{6}, E, F^6, on F♯, and G^6—finally emptying out via an augmented-sixth chord onto a half cadence in D minor (m. 182), sustained as a dominant-lock and driving to a forceful, end-of-development caesura after the second beat of m. 186. In this development Schubert has staged a relay of motivic and cadential catastrophes, a claustrophobic nightmare with no exits in sight. Mm. 187–97 serve as a (post-developmental) retransition (RT), continuing the dominant-lock from the preceding bars but converting them into an 11-bar, creeping-*crescendo* anacrusis that swells unstoppably to the re-entry of P^0 and with it, presumably, the start of the recapitulation, into which it discharges, *fortissimo*, at m. 198.

"Recapitulation" (mm. 198–297/298)

Schubert's normative recapitulations are heavily reliant on correspondence measures with the exposition, as if fated to trace mechanically through its referential pattern bar-for-bar, only with telling harmonic shifts interpolated here or there to accomplish tonal swerves desired for coloristic effects or for eventual resolution into the ESC. Those harmonic twists, along with any other deviations from the exposition's referential rotation (such as added or excised measures), are of crucial importance.[19] The task of resolving a *three-key exposition* presents an added complication, particularly with regard to its second key (since the third will always be resolved into the tonic). Will the exposition's second-key material (here, TM^1 in F major) return in the tonic or will it recur out-of-tonic, remaining a thematic module that proves to be unassimilable to the tonic key—a situation that Sonata Theory calls *tonal alienation (EST*, 245; Hepokoski, 2009b)? A minor-mode sonata, bearing its "extra burden," intensifies such questions. How will this movement's {– + –} modal qualities be treated in the recapitulation?

A scan through D. 810/i's apparent "recapitulation" shows that from m. 198 onward all bars except one (m. 240, an added bar) map directly onto those of the exposition, although the tonal levels in which they appear are affected by four tonal wrenches (mm. 208, 241, 254, and 272). Since so much of D. 810's "recapitulation" consists of correspondence measures, we need to focus on only those portions that illustrate Schubert's compositional interventions (as opposed to his copying out untransposed or transposed replications). The initial curiosity, though, is that m. 198 jumps into the expositional layout with the TR statement of P^0 (m. 198 = m. 41, not m. 1). The P-zone proper is left out altogether. That issue needs to be dealt with first.

Transition (mm. 198–218)

Should the fact that the "recapitulation" begins with TR be a stumbling block for formal analysis? Most would say no. Indeed, I would be surprised to learn of any prior commentators who did not consider m. 198 to be the start of the recapitulation. And it is not difficult to conjure up any number of generically viable justifications for it: common recapitulatory refashionings of P and TR; normative P-TR compressions; and so on. What is clear in this case is that Schubert wished to rejoin the "recapitulatory" battles and correspondence measures at a point of maximal exclamatory tension: at the TR-point, not the P-point. In the exposition one role of P had been to build up to TR's strong-downbeat onset with the P^0 restatement. But here, deep into the sonata, that preparatory role has been supplied by the RT *crescendo* in mm. 187–97.

And then we have the curious situation in which the tonic D minor had been prematurely arrived at, and even cadenced in, back in m. 173—in what surely seemed to be developmental space. Is it outlandish to wonder whether that earlier D-minor music might be read as taking on the tonic-minor role of the seemingly absent P^0 and P^1? If we entertain that line of reasoning—and for many readers it may be a stretch—it would mean that the tonic-launched recapitulatory rotation is inlaid into the concluding portion of developmental space. On the one hand, one might suggest that at m. 173 the ongoing developmental procedures are still so active as to inhibit a conventional setup for the tonic return and correspondence measures that signal a normative recapitulatory beginning, and, on the other hand, that m. 173's sequential landing on the tonic D minor harmonically triggers the onset of a process that we more conventionally associate with recapitulatory beginnings. Mm. 173–97 may be read as dwelling uneasily in two overlapping spaces: ending a development and (harmonically) beginning a new (tonal) rotation that will soon prove to be the recapitulatory rotation.[20] With that caveat, I'll remove the scare quotes around m. 198's "recapitulation."

The dramatic arrival of $P^0/TR^{1.1}$ at m. 198 triggers the arrival of correspondence measures: mm. 198–207 = mm. 41–50. At m. 208 (referential to m. 51) Schubert effects the first of the recapitulation's four tonal swerves. By altering the model's harmony to V^7 of D (minor) instead of slipping, as before, toward F major, he remains in the tonic. (Notwithstanding its potential PAC-effect, m. 209 is not a structural cadence; also construable as the final bar of a dominant-lock that has now, with the *decrescendo*, been converted into an anacrusis, m. 208 serves primarily as a serviceable gateway into D major.) As a result, at m. 209 (the crux) what had been heard in F major before is now shifted a minor third lower, onto D major. Modifying the recapitulatory TR to remain in the tonic is standard procedure. Notable here are two additional things: (1) like its expositional model, mm. 209–18 (= mm. 52–61) serve as the final bars of a *de-energizing transition*, leading to the much-attenuated "I:PAC" in m. 218 that deposits us on the doorstep of secondary-theme space; and (2) one must keep in mind that securing D *major* is the grand hope of this sonata-plot (the modal reversal of the initial D *minor*). The question now is whether—and for how long—that D major can stay in place.

Trimodular Block (mm. 218/219–298)

With the gently rocking TM^1 in the tonic major at m. 218/219, we once again enter its dream-space of longed-for security. D major is precisely where we wish to be and where we wish to conclude. In the exposition, though, TM^1 had proved to be a troubled theme not only because of its compulsive reiterations and problematized cadence gestures but also because its expositional F major (III) had been shown to be incapable of being sustained: it was a major-mode key that would soon drift away and fall back into the minor (there, A minor, v). Here in the recapitulation, then, TM^1's D major is precarious. It is a locally false tonic major, foreordained to be lost, not least because of the Schubertian practice of remaining fatefully locked into broad stretches of literal correspondence measures in his recapitulations. Given the fixity of those correspondence-blocks, the heart of the recapitulatory drama lies in Schubert's efforts *en route* to alter the tonal levels through intermittent, single-bar interventions that steer the subsequent thematic blocks onto different tonal colors. The effect of any such tonal shift is either that of being pulled closer to an ultimate tonic resolution or that of veering away from that tonic-pull for reasons that can be assessed only in its immediately local context. Reflecting on the expressive implications of these shifts is a central analytical task. What had happened at the analogous points in the exposition? What now happens here? And what are the immediate implications of each tonal wrench vis à vis the sonata's ongoing musical/narrative plot?

Most to be feared in this movement's minor-mode narrative is the inevitable gravitation toward a D-minor ESC, the key of the initial death-summons. This is the disturbing import of the only new bar added to the recapitulation: while mm. 218–39 are correspondence bars (= mm. 61–82)—which resume in m. 241 (= m. 83)—m. 240 is an interpolated bar that punctures the TM^1 dream, collapsing in a stroke to the "reality-key" of D minor. This produces m. 241's weak "cadence" on D minor. Recall that the expositional TM^2 had modulated from its downbeat F chord (m. 83) to A minor—that is, up a third. Therefore, if the recapitulatory TM^2 were to proceed as a mere transposition, the key would shift similarly, thereby escaping the immediate clutches of its D-minor onset. But in the second half of m. 241 Schubert applies a second tonal twist to the recapitulation—down another third from the expositional model. Having shifted downward twice by thirds (mm. 208 and 241), we now track the exposition's music with correspondence measures a fifth below (or a fourth above) the model (m. 242 = m. 84, and so on.) As we enter the TM^2 flurry of double counterpoint, the result is that we remain in D minor, a key that appears to be exerting more and more control over the recapitulation. This brings us to the grim i:PAC in m. 248 (cf. m. 90, v:PAC), which, analogously with the exposition, is immediately reopened, though soon varied, with contrapuntal parts exchanged.

If we assess the state of play at m. 251, it is clear that if no further tonal shifts are made, the music will continue in D minor and proceed to a i:HC MC several bars down the road (by m. 257, which would replicate m. 99's v:HC MC down a fifth). In that scenario, even while reopening the i:PAC at m. 248, the music would nonetheless remain captured by D minor, and that is just what it is trying to avoid. Accordingly, Schubert intervenes in m. 254 (referential to m. 96) to apply a third transpositional wrench, jamming the music down another third, from the D-minor to the B-flat major tonal level. This is an act of tonal/modal denial. Refusing to consent to the D minor and all that it represents, the narrative subject resorts to one of the familiar off-tonic escapes from an unwelcome minor tonic—an off-tonic, L-operation shift {– +} onto its submediant major (illustrated in chapter 8, Figure 8.2). Now on the B-flat plane, m. 255 snaps back onto literal correspondence measures. This results in a VI:HC (V of B♭) at m. 255, prolonged by the expected dominant-lock to a VI:HC MC (m. 257 = m. 99) and three bars of caesura-fill (mm.

257–59 = mm. 99–101). This brings TM^2 to an expectant end in the submediant and sets the stage for the entry of TM^3 in that "wrong key."

In the exposition TM$^{3.1}$ had sought to cover up the A-minor (v) conceptual reality with A-major, "Picardy" coloring. In the recapitulation the delusion—the denial of D minor (i)—plays out a half-step higher, in B-flat major. How long can this escape-key be sustained? Correspondence bars bring us to a "weak" VI:PAC at m. 270 (= m. 112's "V:PAC") and the subsequent two bars of sixteenth-note scrambling. In the exposition the mirage of A major had collapsed to A minor on the final beat of the second of these bars (m. 113). Here in m. 271 there is no such modal collapse: through a fourth tonal twist at the mm. 271–72 seam, B-flat major is pushed through to its end and is even celebrated, as if in triumph, with the defiant cello figure at m. 272 (TM$^{3.2}$). But that very celebration triggers the cruelest of ironies. The cello's vibrant, B-flat "Yes!" in m. 272 replicates its deceptive-cadence "No!" from m. 114, now up a fourth. The delusional affirmation at m. 272 is simultaneously the agent of its undoing. It unwittingly accomplishes the final tonal swerve, that which now transposes the expositional model down a fifth (or up a fourth) from the exposition's A minor to the recapitulation's D minor.

The inevitability of that key and mode now seems clear, and strict correspondence bars bring us to a tragic close: the D-minor cadential attempt at m. 278 (= m. 120, undermined by a deceptive cadence via the cello's now-more-pathetic "No!"); the slippage onto the nastily winding TM$^{3.3}$ (mm. 286–89 = mm. 128–31); the structural cadence, i:PAC/ESC at m. 292 (= m. 134); and the closing zone (C), an anguished set of cries, now locked into D minor (mm. 292–98 = mm. 134–40). While the exposition had concluded with two final chords, V-i in A minor (mm. 139–40), the recapitulation omits them, or rather replaces them with the bludgeoned stillness of the held D$_2$, fading away in the cello (mm. 297–98). Schubert has brought the sonata movement to a dark, tragic close. The drama has been played out.

Coda (mm. 299–341): desolation

In this coda-space there will be no turns to D major, no shafts of light—only mourning and reminders of lost hopes. It unfolds in three phases. The first (mm. 299–311) brakes the previously active rhythm into a bleak, ashen cortège. Mm. 299–302 sustain a $^6_3$ chord ("B♭$^6_3$," recalling the B-flat delusion of TM$^{3.1}$) over a throbbing D-bass, doubled several octaves above in the first violin. Suggesting a slowly pulsating augmentation of the rhythms of P^1's head motive, the outer-voice D's in mm. 299–302 encase death-triplet reiterations in the second violin and viola. Suppressed grief bursts forth with the *fortepiano* outcry at m. 303: vii°^{7} of "B♭" over the low D$_2$. The next four bars bring us to up to the brink of a D-minor cadence in m. 307, which is evaded by a second dissonant pang on the same chord (m. 307 = m. 303), now reduced to a triple-*piano* whimper. Four bars more bring us to a fateful i:PAC, with mm. 309–10 not only replicating mm. 305–6 but also eerily reminding us of mm. 13–14—the original "fall" in to P^1.

The coda's second phase (mm. 311–26) reanimates the opening figure of P^1, now *più mosso* (mm. 311–15 = mm. 15–18): the return of that theme, a reminder of the past now hastening toward a conclusion. Because this P^1 idea was omitted from the recapitulation (which had started at TR), it has not been heard since the exposition. It may be that its presence here is in some sense compensatory for its absence in the recapitulatory rotation.[21] An altered upbeat at the end of m. 315 flips the tonal center onto B-flat major—best heard here as a cruel irony—and by m. 318 the music begins a set of mounting ascents to differing levels. Flying by quickly now and swelling in an unstoppable *crescendo*, the chord-to-chord harmony is that of MONTE schema subjected to wild dislocations: notice especially the unmoored jolt from Bb^7 to Ab in m. 318 (sounding locally like a V^7 moving to its IV), then yanked to the same pattern a step higher, C^7 to Bb in m. 319, and followed by a giddy mount to the dominant of D minor in m. 321.[22] At m. 324 the now-violently *fortissimo* cadential drop is decisive, and it is reinforced by multiple repetitions that hammer it firmly into place (mm. 324–26).

Obviously, the movement could have ended there, or perhaps with a pair of additionally reinforcing chords. The coda's third phase is thus unanticipated: extra music added as a final tag, mm. 326–41. This is an appended "coda to the coda" that flashes us suddenly, and *ritardando*, into a very different place.[23] This is another example of what Sonata Theory calls a *response module*, one whose expressive sense is dependent on our understanding it as a reaction to what has just happened. In this case the reaction is clear. The combination of the minor mode and the repeated dotted rhythm unmistakably mark this as a funeral march. Its extraordinary harmonic swerves suggest an uncommon extremity of grief. The cello's D_3-Bb_2-Gb_2-Bb_2 line opens a yawning chasm of heartache, with the Gb_2 supporting an "unthinkable" eb^6 chord—the minor Neapolitan—before passing through an augmented-sixth (m. 329) that brings us to the cadential $^6_4$ of D minor (m. 330) and, pushed onward by weary triplets, to the cadence at m. 332. Its *pianissimo* repetition, now with the first violin down an octave, cadences in m. 338. Three bars later the movement dies away to silence.

11

The Type 2 Sonata

Flourishing especially c. 1740–75—though scattered realizations of it persist well beyond these years and, indeed, into the early twentieth century—the Type 2 sonata is the "binary"-format sonata, one that lacks a full recapitulation beginning with P in the tonic. Examples can be found in the same kinds of movements as those of the Type 3: first movements, slow movements, and finales, along with some overtures.[1] Its most prototypical realizations follow a stretch of modulatory development with a return to the tonic key and a locking onto correspondence measures with the exposition not with P but shortly before or at the onset of S. This means, first, that the S/C block (the two action zones comprising the *tonal resolution*) will normally be the only post-developmental zones sounded in the tonic and, second, that that S/C block *continues a rotation already in progress*, one that had begun with treatments of a non-tonic, modulatory P/TR (or, less often, an episodic substitute for them) filling out the preceding developmental space. Thus the Type 2 sonata is a *double-rotational sonata*: Rotation 1 is the exposition; Rotation 2 is the development plus the tonic-return of the S/C block.

Primed to expect a Type 3 sonata through the frequency of their numbers in the standard repertory, present-day listeners can be inclined to feel a lack at the moment that a P-launched recapitulation has been expected. It is as though only the second half of the (two-part) exposition has been "recapitulated," with much or all of P and perhaps much of TR left out altogether. What happened to them? Several twentieth-century analytical systems have assumed that in such cases the recapitulation begins with the second theme. But as we shall see, from the current approach's point of view this is a misuse of the term "recapitulation." It is useful to remind ourselves at the outset that no evidence suggests that Type 2s were historically derived as compact variants of Type 3s nor that we should regard Type 2s as incomplete structures that grew inexorably to become Type 3s; rather, they were two coexisting, alternative sonata options.[2] Particularly at midcentury, both were equally available, though Type 2s, as noted earlier, would become far less common in the last third of the century, nearly elbowed out altogether (but never completely) by the grander, more rhetorically expansive Type 3 format.

With its complications, variants, and occasionally imaginative or deformational treatments, the Type 2 has turned out to be the most controversial of the five sonata types. Sonata Theory's appeal to it, particularly in nineteenth-century instances, has sometimes been contested. This is in part because of the sharp decline in its use after about 1775 and in part because most nineteenth- and twentieth-century discussions of sonata form either overlooked it or failed to deal with it adequately.

A Sonata Theory Handbook. James Hepokoski, Oxford University Press (2021). © Oxford University Press.
DOI: 10.1093/oso/9780197536810.003.0011.

In my seminars I have found that the clearest pathway to understanding Sonata Theory's concept of the Type 2 sonata is to build a historical case for it, step by step, from the relatively simple, early-to-mid-eighteenth-century, "pre-sonata" binary structure and its related ritornello variant (suitable for some orchestral movements) through the often more complex, later-eighteenth-century exemplars and deformations and eventually into the nineteenth's as well. (Since Type 1s and Type 3s have been always been more familiar options, making such a case for them is less of an issue.)

For that reason this chapter proceeds differently from its predecessors and is devoted to constructing an argument, that on behalf of the Type 2 sonata, its variants, and its corresponding entailments. Modeled on the Type 2 sessions in my seminars or workshops, I start with elementary examples from the 1750s and 1760s, let their principles settle in through a summary of the "takeaways" from each, and then move on to more complex or challenging pieces from later decades. What follows here, then, is a succession of analytical overviews of several individual movements, most of which are by Mozart, whose output (unlike Haydn's or Beethoven's) displays a generous array of prototypical Type 2s. Toward the end of the chapter, I'll have reached the point of examining two deformational Type 2s (the much-discussed first movement of Mozart's Piano Sonata, K. 311, and his Overture to *La clemenza di Tito*). To conclude it, I'll lay out an argument on behalf of Sonata Theory's case for the persistence of the Type 2 and double-rotational sonatas into the nineteenth century (these include both Type 2s and expanded Type 1 sonatas, which under some conditions are almost indistinguishable) and respond to some specifics cited by critics of the Type 2 concept, along the way presenting an overview of Wagner's Overture to *Tannhäuser* (strictly considered, an expanded Type 1 sonata that, morphologically congruent with the Type 2 layout, addresses the same issues).

Following some preliminary comments about historical predecessors, our first two Type 2 examples, drawn from the child Mozart's small-scale symphonies K. 16 and K. 22, are crucial to the more general argument. The first illustrates the simplest realization of the Type 2 format; the second, a touchstone Type 2/"ritornello-form" blend, incorporates some variants into the elementary prototype—common modifications that can crop up in other sonatas—that can be grasped only with the foreknowledge of the elementary schema exemplified in K. 16/i. Together, the first two analyses provide the foundations that enable one to progress to subsequent levels of complication without lapsing back to alternative, mid-twentieth-century readings. Should this slippage back happen at any later level, as it certainly can, one needs to return to the beginning—here, K. 16/i and K. 22/i—to rebuild the foundations once again.

I invite you to join me in this discussion by first considering a brief overview of the format's history and then following the logic of each movement discussed: getting each piece into your ears, consulting the score (though the initial few pieces are easily analyzed by ear), and solidifying the takeaways to be absorbed at each step along the way.

Historical considerations: binary form

The step-by-step approach is historically informed: to understand the Type 2 sonata is to understand how that format came to be. The place to begin is with late-Baroque and early-galant binary form, a central aspect of which is that each half is repeated. The Type 2's roots, like those of the Type 3 sonata, reach back to the earlier option of composing binary-form structures (originally, dance movements) in which the second section's conclusion rhymes with that of the first by replicating the first's final bar or two, now in the tonic. (This option was not always followed. Quite often, most of the second section was freer and did not display much by way of correspondence measures.)[3]

In time, and certainly in some binary-formatted works from the 1720s, 1730s, and 1740s, the length of that end-rhyme came to be expanded to several bars, perhaps as many as a half-dozen or more. In such cases both the first and second sections end with a similar set of stabilizing measures. The impression given is that at a certain point midway through its course the second section locks into a stretch of correspondence measures with the first, providing a rhyming *tonal resolution*. Also notable in several binary structures of that era is that the second section can begin with an allusion to the same head-motive (HM) as the first, though not in the tonic. When this occurs, the result can be diagrammed along the lines shown in Figure 11.1, which assumes a major-mode work. *Elements of Sonata Theory* (*EST*, 355–62), provides some examples from those decades as found in the keyboard sonatas of Domenico Scarlatti, where this proto-Type-2 format is common, and C. P. E. Bach. (In what follows, one should bear in mind that Figure 11.1 schematizes

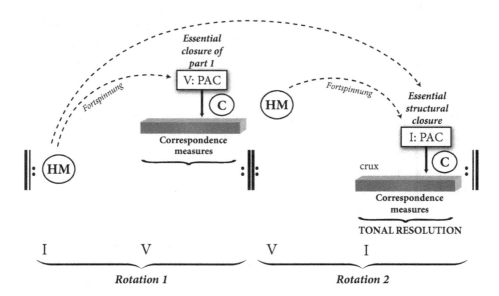

Figure 11.1. One type of binary structure, c. 1720–50 (D. Scarlatti, C. P. E. Bach, etc.).

only one possibility among a few others. Another variant of binary format, for instance, anticipates the Type 3 sonata.)[4]

In Figure 11.1's binary p 1 proceeds via *Fortspinnung* from the head-motive in the tonic to a PAC in the dominant ("essential closure of part 1"). This cadential arrival may or may not be reinforced with a brief closing tag (C). Section 2 reverses the tonal motion: starting with a head-motive allusion in V and then probably modulating elsewhere, it soon locks into correspondence measures with the latter stages of section 1 (at the *crux*), replicating, now in the tonic, the final stages of the earlier section's music. It therefore concludes with a complementary I:PAC ("essential structural closure," ESC) and closing tag, if one had been present in section 1. Since each section begins with HM and ends with the same stretch of correspondence measures, we consider the whole structure to be *double-rotational*, in which the first section is the *referential rotation* against which the second is to be compared.

In the 1740s and 1750s the idea began to emerge of dividing the first section of an ever-expanding binary form into two parts by means of a prominent half cadence or medial caesura and subsequent new-thematic launch. When this was the case, it was reasonable to conclude that the enlarged end-rhyme should embrace all of the material after the MC: what we now call the S and C zones. The result would be that diagrammed in Figure 11.2: the simplest, most mechanical realization of the mid-century-galant Type 2 sonata. Now imagining this schema as an early, small-scale sonata form, in Figure 11.2 I have changed Figure 11.1's HM designation to P, subdivided each of the two repeated sections in terms of action-zones, P TR' S/ C, and included EEC and ESC designations at the appropriate points. We can then

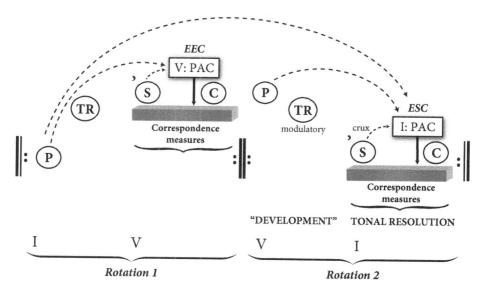

Figure 11.2. From binary form to the Type 2 sonata (here, without coda).

decide to recognize Rotation 1 as an exposition, but for obvious reasons it would not be correct to call Rotation 2 a recapitulation. Instead, Rotation 2 comprises two separate portions: a freer, modulatory space, probably anchored in P and possibly TR material (an embryonic "development"), and the tonal resolution provided by S and C.[5]

Mozart, Symphony No. 1 in E-flat, K. 16/i: the simplest Type 2 prototype

Featuring no internal complications and exemplifying the schema diagrammed in Figure 11.2, the Molto allegro first movement of eight-year-old Mozart's Symphony "No. 1" in E-flat, K. 16/i (London, 1764–65), serves as an ideal starting-point. As in the diagram, both halves of binary structure are marked with repeat signs, and discerning the exposition's action zones is an elementary matter: P ($P^{1.1}$ and its *piano* $P^{1.2}$ reply, mm. 1–11, and their repetitions, mm. 12–22), TR (mm. 23–30, concluding with a I:HC MC), S (mm. 31–45, including a repeated $S^{1.2}$ cadential module, mm. 42–45, with EEC at m. 45) and C (C^1, mm. 46–49 and 50–53, and C^2-C^3 mm. 53/54–58 and mm. 57–58, the latter two bars replicating the end of TR, mm. 29–30).

Following the expositional repeat, Mozart—probably with Papa Leopold looking over his shoulder—began the second rotation in m. 59 with P sounded in V: here P returns in full (mm. 59–69). He then replicated P, still intact, in vi, C minor (mm. 70–80). In mm. 81–92 he modestly expanded TR to set up the return to the tonic and the tonal resolution, ending again with a I:HC MC (m. 92, led into at the *crux* in m. 91 [mm. 91–92 = mm. 29–30]). S then returns intact in the tonic at m. 93 (leading to the ESC at m. 107), as does C at m. 107/108. The final bar of the tonal resolution, m. 120, ends the second section (which is then repeated) and corresponds to the final bar of the exposition, m. 58.

Takeaways

- Once the exposition of a Type 2 sonata is completed, the most common move, as is also the case with a Type 3, is to start the second rotation with a P-reference in V (assuming a major-mode exposition) or other non-tonic key. In K. 16/i the P idea is completely presented, including even its immediate restatement, here in vi, though in many other instances the off-tonic P-reference is made through only its head-motive or opening bars.
- In this case a strongly articulated caesura—the hard-break final caesura at the end of the exposition, along with a repeat sign—separates the end of the exposition, C^3, from the ensuing P and the "rebeginning" onset of Rotation 2. The

procedure's rotational aspects are clear: the whole sonata is a *double-rotational* structure.

- Given a P-TR-based developmental space, until the moment of the crux (m. 91) and, especially, the beginning of the tonal resolution (S at m. 93), we cannot know whether we are hearing a Type 2 or a Type 3 sonata.[6] Still learning the ropes, the child composer could have brought back P in the tonic at m. 93, in which case this would have been a Type 3 sonata, featuring a recapitulation that follows a half-rotational developmental space grounded in P and TR. Only when the tonic key is returned to not with P, but rather with S, midway through the ongoing rotation, do we realize that this is a Type 2 sonata.

- It follows that as we move through any sonata, a developmental appearance of either S or C would immediately suggest that a Type 2 format is not in play. Why? Such an appearance would make the development *fully rotational* (containing both pre-MC and post-MC material). In a prototypical Type 2 sonata the developmental-space portion is normally *half-rotational*, occupied with P and TR. Completing the rotation, S and C are reserved for the correspondence measures of the tonal resolution.

- Underscoring the point: In a Type 2 sonata the tonic return of S at m. 93 begins the second part of an ongoing thematic-modular rotation that had started with P (m. 59) and TR. It does not function as a fresh beginning but rather pursues its role as the continuation of something already underway, namely the second rotation. To be sure, S does launch the tonal resolution (as it also does in a Type 3 sonata), but it does not begin a "recapitulation," which for Sonata Theory can happen only with generically expected rotation-initiator materials, nearly always P. Hence we do not use the term "recapitulation" in our descriptions of Type 2 sonatas. While Rotation 1 is an *exposition*, Rotation 2 is the *tonal-resolution rotation*, meaning the rotation that in the course of its progress produces the tonal resolution. In a Type 2 sonata the tonal-resolution rotation is separable into two parts: the *development* (or *developmental space*, if "development" seems to claim too much) and the *tonal resolution*.

- In the simplest Type 2s, as in K. 16/i, P appears in the tonic only at the beginning of the sonata. That P does not return in the tonic later in the piece is to be regarded neither as a lack nor as something that "ought" to happen. To construe it as such is to interpret it through the Type 3 norm, which is not applicable here.

- As K. 16/i shows us, a double-rotational, Type 2 sonata is complete in itself. *There is no obligation to append a (P-based) coda to it*, and several other, similar examples without codas from the era are not difficult to find.[7] Type 2's sonata-space ends with the tonal resolution's correspondence-measure completion of C (assuming that there had been a closing idea present in the exposition). Nothing more is required, even though a subsequent coda is often found in other examples—as in K. 22/i, to which we now turn.

Mozart, Symphony No. 5 in B-flat, K. 22/i: an alternative, ritornello-style Type 2 prototype

The divergences from the K. 16/i pattern that we find the first movement of nine-year-old Mozart's Symphony No. 5 in B-flat, K. 22/i (The Hague, 1765), offer us an alternative Type 2 schema that helps us to approach more complex examples in historically grounded ways. On the one hand, this movement's double-rotational sonata format shares several Type 2 aspects that we have seen in K. 16/i. On the other hand, this vigorous, Allegro movement presents us with three important features not found in the earlier example:

- Unlike K. 16/i, K. 22/i has *no sectional repeats*.
- The final V: PAC of the exposition elides with the verbatim replication of P in the same dominant key. There is *no hard-break caesura* separating the end of the exposition from the opening of the second half of the binary/sonata format.
- The same thing happens at the end of rotation 2's tonal-resolution portion (S and C), which is now similarly elided with a post-sonata coda-return of a verbatim P, now back in the tonic.

These features are historical earmarks of concerto-style *ritornello form*, now tailored at midcentury to merge seamlessly into what Sonata Theory calls the Type 2 format to produce a relentless, ongoing stream of music. Recall that chapter 4's section on developments in Type 3 sonatas introduced us to the concept of early- and mid-century orchestral *sonata-ritornello blends*: pp. 75–76 may be useful to review at this point. While the Type 3 version, with exposition, development, and full recapitulation, effects a merger with *three-ritornello form* presenting the fully or nearly fully stated P at the beginning of each of these sections (with a possible fourth return of P as the onset of a brief coda), the Type 2 version, lacking a full recapitulation, merges with *two-ritornello form*, with that P beginning each of the two rotations (often with a third P-return or a smaller version thereof as coda). Specialists in earlier, midcentury symphonies and Italian-style overture movements sometimes refer to this commonly encountered format—a "continuous structure without repeats"—as a blending of ritornello and "binary" structures.[8] As befits its concerto-influenced, "Italian-overture" origins in the 1730s, this Type 2/ritornello merger, like its Type 3/ritornello sibling, is primarily suitable for rapidly paced orchestral movements (and not, for example, for keyboard works). As such, it crops up with some frequency in orchestral movements from the 1730s through the 1770s—K. 22/i is a touchstone example—with lingering vestiges of it turning up here and there in later works.

As was the case with K. 16/i, parsing this movement's exposition is an easy task. A persistent, *Trommelbass* tonic pedal underpins all of P (mm. 1–9) and the *crescendo*-swelling TR[1.1] (mm. 10–15). Mozart unlocks the B-flat pedal bass at TR[1.2]

(m. 15) and leads it promptly to a I:HC MC (m. 18.) The secondary theme begins in V as $S^{1.0}$ (over a dominant pedal, m. 19), becomes increasingly active, and within a few bars produces the EEC (m. 31). C and its slightly varied repetition occupy mm. 31–35 and mm. 35–39 to complete the exposition.

Our attention should be drawn to what happens in m. 39. Had the young composer decided to follow the K. 16/i pattern (the simplest option), he could have filled that measure with three quarter-note F chords (the generic three-hammerstroke articulation) and a quarter rest, along with a repeat sign that would bring us back to m. 1 and a second run through the exposition. Instead, the exposition flows directly into developmental space: the final bar of the exposition (m. 39) elides with the start of Rotation 2, the tonal-resolution rotation, which begins with nine bars of P (the *rotation initiator*) in the dominant. The effect is striking: the bustling, galant energy driving the exposition continues to sizzle onward, having no time for the more normative hard-break pause, or punctuation-breath, typically found at this point. As noted, this is characteristic of the influence of *ritornello form*, a blending of ritornello principles with those of (here) the Type 2 sonata.

It is important not to construe mm. 39–47 as still housed in expositional space, for instance, as yet another closing idea or a P-based C.[9] They are not. In this era's binary forms and more obvious "sonatas" with repeats (whether of the Type 2 or Type 3 versions) it is common behavior for the second part, following the repeat of part 1, to begin with several bars of P sounded in the same key as that in which the exposition ends. The rotational situation in K. 22/i is identical with that of K. 16/i, which had also begun a second rotation with a full repetition of the P-idea in V.[10] Similarly, in the two- and three-ritornello/sonata blends discussed here and in chapter 4, one function of each ritornello is to *begin* a new section. In the Type 3 (three-ritornello) version the second ritornello begins the development; the third begins the recapitulation. Ritornellos of this sort are *section-initiating gestures*. By no means, then, does the fact that mm. 39–47 persist in V, F major, disallow them from beginning the developmental space. On the contrary, K. 22/i's mm. 39–47 launch a second rotation with a full repetition of P in the dominant, characteristic of all versions of major-mode sonata-ritornello blends, before moving into "development" proper.

More characteristically developmental activity ensues from m. 48 to m. 65. It is based on P figuration (along with a touch of TR, since mm. 53–54 refer to mm. 15–16) and includes a shift to C minor that drives to a ii:PAC (m. 57) and reinforces that key further with a full restatement of P in ii (mm. 57–65), anchored by the now-familiar *Trommelbass* pedal. At m. 65 the C-minor statement of P merges seamlessly (without a preceding medial caesura)[11] into $S^{1.0}$ modules and a twofold set of falling fifths, first onto F minor (over its V, mm. 65–68), then on the tonic, B-flat (over its V, mm. 69–72). This is an uncommonly smooth entry into the tonal resolution, and these bars are referential to mm. 19–22, which they slightly vary—as something of a near crux. M. 73 is a clearer crux (= m. 23), locking onto correspondence bars for the rest of Rotation 2. This brings about the ESC in m. 81 (= m. 31) and the ensuing C material (mm. 81–89 = mm. 31–39), which concludes Rotation 2 and sonata space proper.

Just as the exposition had ended with an elision into P in V to begin Rotation 2, the tonal resolution ends by eliding into P's opening bars in the tonic—another characteristic of the sonata-ritornello blend. As in the Type 3–ritornello blends, this P begins a *coda outside of sonata space*: the onset of an almost immediately aborted new rotation. Just as the P-in-V, mm. 39–47, did not belong to the exposition, so now this P-in-I, mm. 89–97, does not belong to the sonata proper. (The classic twentieth-century misreading was to regard such tonic-P returns as the concluding portion of a "reversed recapitulation," that is, as something still part of sonata space [*EST*, 382–83].)

When such a P-based coda does occur, as in K. 22/i and many other Type 2 sonatas—setting aside the ritornello-influenced features of this particular example—one might make the argument that its reappearance also serves a *compensatory* purpose, bringing back a tonic-key P reference in the coda to round out the work (*EST*, 384–86). Should we wish to do so, we can regard it as a *compensatory coda*, even though in the Type 2's historically earliest exemplars, as K. 16/ i and earlier examples can show us, *there was no need to think of a Type 2 sonata as lacking anything for which such later compensations would have to be made.* Figure 11.3 recasts the formatting of the earlier two diagrams to show the rotational structure of K. 22/i.

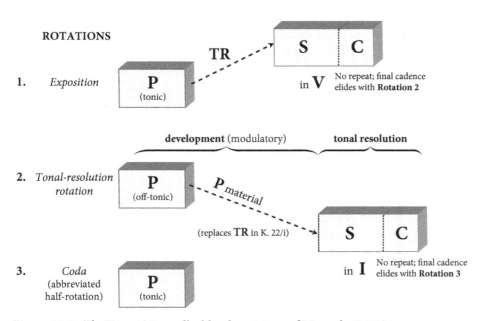

Figure 11.3. The Type 2/ritornello-blend prototype of Mozart's, K. 22/i.

Takeaways

- While a Type 2 sonata usually features an expositional repeat preceded by a hard-break caesura—typically replicated in the tonal-resolution rotation—some Type 2s, particularly orchestral movements, omit these repeats. When this happens, Rotation 1 can conclude with its final cadence elided to the onset of Rotation 2, as in K. 22/i. This feature is a sign of a common, midcentury blending of earlier ritornello-form principles with those of sonata form, producing a *sonata-ritornello blend*.

- The off-tonic return of P in the middle of such a movement should not be construed as the conclusion of the exposition. On the contrary, in a Type 2 sonata that is the way that Rotation 2 usually begins, a feature more immediately evident in Type 2s that include an expositional repeat. That off-tonic P marks the entry into developmental space, which is also the normative way that most developmental spaces begin in these decades.

- A similar line of reasoning governs how we should regard the elided tonic P-reference at the end of the movement. This added P is not part of the sonata proper: it is not in sonata space, much less part of a "reversed recapitulation." Instead, it is the start of an appended coda. Whether we are dealing with a Type 2 or a Type 3 sonata, it is standard coda behavior to begin with a P-reference in the tonic. And when we are dealing with a sonata-ritornello blend, this P-reference can be quite literal, replicating much of the original P^1. More precisely, as has been suggested in earlier chapters, codas in both sonata types usually begin by alluding to the thematic material that had begun the development, as if returning to its opening gesture, only now in the tonic (*EST*, 281–92).

Stamitz, Symphony in D, op. 3 no. 2/i: reinforcing the K. 22/i sonata-ritornello-blend prototype

In every Sonata Theory seminar that I have led, I have paired Mozart's K. 22/i prototype with the similarly structured first movement (Presto) of Johann Stamitz's Symphony in D, op. 3 no. 2 (1757), whose score I make available as either a PDF or a hard-copy handout, though its Type 2 layout is easily followed without a score.[12] (At the time of this writing, this movement was accessible for listening on the standard internet streaming services.) Stamitz's movement is laid out in one of the prototypical formats of the midcentury Mannheim composers, and in light of the clarity of its differentiated P TR' S/C zones and more expanded development, it is a particularly lucid example of this ritornello-blended version of the Type 2 schema.

Analogously with K. 22/i the Stamitz movement: (1) lacks repeat signs; (2) elides the concluding cadence of the exposition (Rotation 1) with the return of P in V, marking the onset of Rotation 2, which here comprises a P-TR-based development and an S-C correspondence-measure tonal resolution; and (3) elides the concluding cadence of the tonal resolution (simultaneously the end of C, the end of Rotation 2, and the end of sonata space) with the coda, which begins with a return to the initial bars of P, now in the tonic, and soon self-extinguishes as it brings the movement to a close with its final chords. As in K. 22/i, the coda starts a third rotation but winds up being only half-rotational. Initiating a coda, this final statement of P is not part of sonata space.

J. C. Bach, Symphony in G Minor, op. 6 no. 6/i: Type 2, no repeats, no coda, and no dialogue with ritornello form

From the preceding the reader might have gotten the impression that Type 2 or-chestral sonata movements without internal repeats are invariably in dialogue with earlier ritornello practice. But as with Type 3 orchestral sonatas that is not the case: we do encounter such Type 2 sonatas for which the appeal to P-ritornello returns has little or no purchase. The opening Allegro of J. C. Bach's Symphony in G Minor, op. 6 no. 6 (1769), is a case in point. Its double-rotational, Type 2 format is easily traced, another prototypical example of that schema. Rotation 1, the exposi-tion, modulates from G minor to B-flat (III), spans mm. 1–65, and is not repeated. A perfunctory, three-bar link leads us to the remainder of the movement, Rotation 2, the development and S/C tonal resolution. This spans mm. 68–143 and concludes in a strongly reinforced tonic G minor. Rotation 2 does indeed begin with develop-mentally treated, P-related motives (the modulatory mm. 68–95 are grounded in figuration from mm. 4–11), but its second rotation differs from Mozart's K. 22/i and the preceding Stamitz example in four ways: it is not elided with the exposition; it does not begin with very opening of P (mm. 1–3 had been a *forte* flourish probably best regarded as P[0]);[13] it does not treat its P-zone material in anything resembling the "verbatim" ritornello manner; and it does not open its developmental space by remaining in the exposition's III (instead, it moves at once to IV, C minor). Finally, there is no coda: once past the exposition, P-material never returns in the tonic—reminding us once again that such a coda was not an obligatory feature of the Type 2 sonata.

Mozart, Divertimento in E-flat, K. 113/ii: binary format with repeats, episodic writing-over of P in Rotation 2

Now 15 years old, Mozart composed the E-flat Divertimento in Milan in 1771. Its second movement, a brief binary structure in B-flat (V), provides a convenient way to introduce an important Type 2 variant: the replacement of P in Rotation 2 with differing material. This unassuming Andante movement is so slight, its action zones so underdeveloped, that we might ask whether we wish to grant sonata-status and its accompanying terminology at all to this binary structure. One might decide this either way: little is at stake here, except for its embryonic illustration of a procedure that we sometimes find played out in larger, more sonata-proportioned structures. While Rotation 1, construable at least as a proto-exposition, gives us a touchstone illustration of Koch's eighteenth-century description of the successive harmonic goals of the first part of a binary structure,[14] it is also subdivisible into short phrases that correspond to features that we find in more expansively realized action zones. Thus we find rudimentary instances of: P (mm. 1–4, 5–8), TR (mm. 9–12, ending with a "weak" dominant-arrival V_5^6 -V^7 of V MC), S (mm. 13–17, now in V, a cadential module and its elided repetition), and C (mm. 17–18), ending with a hard-break caesura and a repeat sign.[15]

For our purposes the central point is what happens at the onset of the binary form's second section. Instead of beginning with the more usual P-in-V, mm. 19–26 sound *new material*. This consists of non-thematic, standard-issue galant filler designed to tilt us back to V of I, which is attained as a I:HC in m. 24 (a "tonicized half cadence"), which cadence is lingered upon in the *pianissimo* echo of mm. 25–26. At m. 27 we hear the slightly varied tonic return of TR (m. 27 is a near-crux; mm. 27–30 are referential to mm. 9–12), and the remainder of the movement, S and C, consists of stricter correspondence measures (mm. 31–36 = mm. 13–18, though Mozart weakens the expected "ESC" moment, m. 35, into a I:IAC, not a I:PAC, holding back a stronger closure, effectively the ESC, until the two-bar return of C material, where the structural voices providing the PAC-effect are best regarded as being articulated in the string parts).[16] It is important to notice that Mozart has added no coda to this movement: its final bar, m. 36, corresponds to that of Rotation 1, m. 18.

In sum, what we might have expected to be a normative Rotation 2 consists of eight bars of non-P material (replacing the eight bars of Rotation 1's P), followed by a standard tonic-key return to TR, S, and C. As a whole, the movement traces through the schema diagrammed in Figure 11.2, with the exception that in Rotation 2 the usual P-zone has been taken over by something else. Sonata Theory describes such a situation as a *writing-over*: the case in which new material replaces a generically customary element. That we are still dealing with "Rotation 2" is clear, but Mozart has *written over* the expected non-tonic P, the usual rotation initiator, with something else that serves as a stand-in or proxy for P. When such a proxy occurs in a developmental space, we usually refer to it as an *episode*. Thus Rotation 2 can be described as: *episode and TR' S/C*.

In such cases the Sonata Theory (*dialogic-form*) approach encourages us to proceed to a further interpretive step. Because of the regulative strength of the genre at hand, the double-rotational binary or proto-Type-2 format shown in Figure 11.2, we can regard the missing P as *conceptually present but acoustically absent*. P is not literally realized in sound but has been placed behind an acoustic curtain by the substitutive episode that hides it from our auditory perception. At this point the question becomes: do we sense traces of the absent P pressing through the acoustic fabric of mm. 19–26's episodic curtain? Perhaps: one might, for instance, read mm.

20 and 22 as related to the descending figure of m. 3. Still, for the most part, the otherwise unremarkable mm. 19–26 seem quite new. By and large, Rotation 2's P has been moved out of earshot.

Takeaways

- Type 2 sonatas need not begin Rotation 2 with P (the normative rotation initiator). P might be replaced by new, episodic material that *writes over* P's more usual reappearance—in effect substituting for the missing P. Once past the episodic material, however, the rotation will get back on track and proceed in regular order (with TR or S).
- We have seen in two of the preceding cases (Mozart's K. 22/i and Stamitz's Symphony op. 3 no. 2/i), both exemplars of sonata-ritornello blends, that a Type 2 sonata might end with what might be construed as a "compensatory" coda-return of P-referential material in the tonic. The presumed compensation is that for the absence of a tonic-key P at the opening of Rotation 2, where P had been sounded in V. On the other hand (as is shown by in K. 16/i, J. C. Bach's G-minor Symphony, op. 6 no. 6/i, and numerous other works), no such compensation is generically obligatory. What K. 113/ii's lack of a coda shows us is that *even when P is absent from Rotation 2, there is still no obligation to bring it back in an appended coda.*
- A general principle is emerging for Type 2 sonatas: in the developmental-space portion of Rotation 2, pre-MC material (P and/or TR) need not appear as such: either P or TR, or both, may be written over by something else. On the other hand, in the tonal-resolution portion, post-MC material (S and C) is obliged to appear, nearly always intact.

Mozart, String Quartet in D, K. 155/ii: binary format with repeats, episodic writing-over of P in Rotation 2, P returns as coda

The previous example, K. 113/ii, is productively paired with another unassuming, brief-binary slow movement (again, hardly qualifying as a "sonata" proper), this time the Andante in A from Mozart's Quartet in D, K. 155 (Bolzano, Verona, 1772). Mm. 1–4 house a diminutive P (a sentence presentation $\alpha\alpha'$), and mm. 5–8 a TR of the dissolving-continuation type ($P^{cont} ==>TR$), ending with a I:HC MC. The remainder of Rotation 1 (the exposition, mm. 9–20) is occupied with S (with a V:IAC at m. 16 and a V:PAC/EEC at m. 20). There is no closing material, and the exposition (or, simply, part 1) concludes with a hard break and a repeat sign.

At the beginning of Rotation 2, the expected four-bar P is written over by an eight-bar episode, mm. 21–28, ending with a I:HC. M. 29, the crux, slips back on track at TR: mm. 29–32 = m. 5–8, at their original pitch-level and leading to the same I:HC MC. At m. 33 Mozart shifts the expositional model down a fifth to bring S to the tonic-key level to begin the tonal resolution, and what follows consists of correspondence measures (mm. 33–44 = mm. 9–20), but with one exception. He alters the expected I:PAC/ESC at m. 44 into a I:IAC, undercutting the sense of full closure at Rotation 2's "final-bar" moment. Thus in K. 155/ii the tonal-resolution correspondence bars are kept from producing a satisfactory ESC. In turn, that lack of closure opens the door to a "compensatory," P-referential coda, mm. 45–50. Sonata space having been concluded, though not closed, the coda begins with the 2+2 presentational modules of P, now differently harmonized, and concludes with two bars of cadential finality, mm. 49–50. The final bar rhymes with that of Rotation 1 and provides the needed I:PAC/ESC, here deferred into coda space. The presence of the repeat sign after the coda should not tempt us to deny it coda-status. As is well-known, in this period codas (in both Type 2 and Type 3 sonatas) could be tucked in before such a repeat (*EST*, 282).

Takeaways

- A Type 2 sonata in which Rotation 2's P is written over with an episode may or may not have a P-referential coda following the close of sonata space. In K. 155/ii it does, and it is smoothly led into with the I:IAC at m. 44; in the previous example, K. 113/ii, it does not. While such "compensatory" codas became more common as the century moved into its final decades—perhaps recalling residues of sonata-ritornello-blend practice—the Type 2 format never required them.
- Even with the I:IAC in m. 44 (concluding Rotation 2), it is inappropriate to call mm. 33–50 (or perhaps 29–50?) a "reversed recapitulation." In Sonata Theory, by definition, a "recapitulation" cannot begin with S. What we have instead is the familiar pattern of a double-rotational sonata (a Type 2) with a half-rotational, P-referential coda. This is the pattern shown in Figure 11.2, to which a coda has been added, though here preceding the Rotation-2 repeat sign.

Mozart: Piano Sonata in E-flat, K. 282/i

After having examined the preceding pieces, the Type 2 first movement of Mozart's E-flat Piano Sonata, K. 282 (Munich, 1775) should present us with no significant analytical problems. The double-rotational structure is clear, conforming to the pattern illustrated in Figure 11.2, including the repeat signs. The composer starts Rotation 2 with an off-tonic allusion to the first bar of P, then leads it into briefly elaborated, differing material. Following the I:HC caesura-effect at m. 21 he guides the music onto a "first crux" at m. 22, a varied, affectively enhanced version of TR

(= m. 4, at the original pitch-level), submits some of it to expressive recomposition, and moves toward a "second crux" around the end of m. 25), fully stabilized by the I:HC MC at m. 26 (= m. 8, up a fourth).[17] The ensuing correspondence measures, mm. 27–33 (= mm. 9–15, now in the tonic), constitute the tonal resolution, S and C, with the ESC at the downbeat of m. 33. For Sonata Theory, though, the central thing to notice is what happens in mm. 34–36, following the Rotation-2 repeat sign. Not only is this a now-quite-common (but never obligatory) P-referential coda, but Mozart also wrote the word "Coda" above it.

Mozart, Violin Sonata in D, K. 306/i

Having mapped out the Type 2 fundamentals with a number of briefer pieces, we now turn to a high-galant work of full-scale proportions: the Allegro con spirito first movement of Mozart's Violin Sonata in D, K. 306 (Paris, 1778). Apart from providing us with a classic instance of a Type 2 sonata in full flower, the movement contains other instructive features that are worth noting along the way.

With their initial ideas launched by stiff, marchlike rhythms, the exposition's two pre-MC zones are clear and normative. Mozart built P (mm. 1–12) as a sentence (2+2+4, $\alpha\alpha'\beta$, with varied β-cadential repeat, mm. 9–12). As the violin begins to emerge more thematically, TR (mm. 12–25) is also crafted as a sentence that soon moves through a standard $\hat{4}$-$\sharp\hat{4}$-$\hat{5}$ bassline to a converging half cadence in m. 20 (I:HC). This dominant is then sustained as a figurationally decorated lock through m. 25/26. Its final bars give us an uncommonly high-polished fashioning of the medial caesura. Notice especially the sudden drawback from its energetic clatter to the *piano* whisper in mm. 24–25: a handing-over of the melodic role to the solo violinist, who now steps to the fore with a bar of caesura-fill before starting the secondary theme proper.

The two post-MC zones in mm. 25/26–74 offer us a few more challenges. S consists of a chain of contrasting modules: this is a situation where Sonata Theory's *decimal designators* come in handy. While it is easy to perceive mm. 26/27–31, $S^{1.1}$, as the rhetorical presentation of a new sentence ($\alpha\alpha'$), we also notice that the A-major theme (V) begins harmonically off-tonic, on $F\sharp^7$ (m. 27, V^7/ii) and settles onto m. 31's A major through a set of FONTE-related descending fifths: V/ii, ii, V^7, I.[18] The $S^{1.2}$ continuation, mm. 32–38 (β, a delicious realization of the INDUGIO schema [a lingering or tarrying around scale-step $\hat{4}$ in the bass: Gjerdingen 2007, 273–74]) is also sentential, $\alpha\alpha\beta$, once again deploying the $\hat{4}$-$\sharp\hat{4}$-$\hat{5}$ bassline, now in the dominant, to arrive at an internal half cadence in m. 38 (V:HC). Spinning its wheels in mm. 38–45, $S^{1.3}$ prolongs that dominant by alternating it with the tonic (4+4, another, now broader sentence presentation), and then merges into the plush, descending-fifths cascade of mm. 46–48, $S^{1.4}$, and finally into the cadential $S^{1.5}$, mm. 48^{b}–52, ending with a decisive V:PAC in m. 52.

Since the V:PAC in m. 52 articulates a full break with the differing, non-elided theme that follows, our initial assumption is that m. 52 must be the EEC, flush-juxtaposed with the onset of C. Moreover, that "C" seems normative, moving into its first V:PAC at m. 57 and through a repetition to another at m. 62. But with that repeated V:PAC, Mozart unexpectedly shifts the music back to a recovery of a now-expanded $S^{1.5}$ (compare mm. 62–68 to mm. 48–52). When "assumed" and "obvious" C-space gives way in this manner to unmistakable S-material, Sonata Theory interprets that as *reopening S-space* (*EST*, 152–59), thereby incorporating what we had initially assessed to be C into that S-space. The effect is as if having entered into normative closing space, the music changes its mind and returns to S-space in order to close it one more time. We now reinterpret the once-presumed "C," mm. 52–62, as part of S. Notwithstanding its prototypical C-behavior, it now becomes understood as S^2 (C==>S^2). This resituates the EEC to m. 68; the "real" (or "replacement") C^1 follows at mm. 69–72, and it is elided with a C^2 codetta-tag to close the exposition in mm. 72–74. The final bar is stamped with the three-beat march rhythm to facilitate its return with the expositional repeat.

As often happens in Mozart's works, the development, setting off in V, begins not with P but with new material, 4+4 (αα, mm. 75–78, 79–82). While its trilled chirps may recall those of mm. 40–41 and 44–45 and its Alberti bass might be heard as a simplification of that in mm. 1–4, its overall effect is that of something new—and not-P. When TR material is introduced in m. 83 and proceeds to be thrashed through a much-extended set of harmonically coloristic sequences, we conclude that mm. 75–82 should be regarded as a developmental episode writing over P: instead of the more rotationally orthodox P-TR we have Episode-TR. Still caught up in the TR harangue, the V^7-of-D dominant arrival in m. 97 is prolonged with a six-bar lock. Its last two bars (mm. 101–2) collapse the preceding $^6_4$ of D major (mm. 99–100) into $^6_4$ of D minor—a not-uncommon, darkening feature near the ends of TRs that projects an implication of unexpected peril. Mm. 103–4 rush into the common escape strategy by shifting the D-minor sonority to a B-flat chord ($\flat$VI, via a variant of the familiar L-operation [d^{5-6}_{3-3}], though sounded here in differing inversions). In mm. 105–6 that B-flat converts into an augmented-sixth chord that pulls the harmony back to the fatalistic dominant of D minor, mm. 107–12. Its final four bars, though, replicate mm. 22–25—TR-concluding MC figures from the exposition, though here implying D minor, not D major.

At this point Mozart could have returned to P for a full, Type 3 recapitulation. But instead, using m. 109 as the crux (= m. 22) and m. 112 as the MC (= m. 25), he proceeds directly into the single bar of solo-violin caesura-fill and, through a registral shift up a fourth (or down a fifth), into $S^{1.1}$ in the tonic (m. 113 = m. 26). With this return of S and its beginning of the tonal resolution, we now realize that this is a Type 2 sonata, whose development had been rotationally filled not with P-TR but rather with Episode-TR. We now understand, that is, that we are midway through a developmentally expanded, ongoing Rotation 2. And so far the only sounding of P has been at the opening of the exposition.

As is typical of Mozart's tonal resolutions, an extended stretch of correspondence measures follows: mm. 113–58 = mm. 26–71, now in the tonic. This brings us through the ESC (m. 155 = m. 68) and into C^1 (mm. 155b–58 = mm. 68b–71). At m. 158 what is expected is a continuation of the correspondence bars to conclude the movement: the transposed equivalents of the tag-codetta C^2 (mm. 72–74). And those bars are indeed brought back to conclude the movement several bars later, in mm. 168–70, elided with their enhanced repetition in mm. 170–72. In the gap between C^1 and C^2, however, Mozart interpolates nine bars, which begin as a *non sequitur* jolt or surprise interruption. Filling them are the thematic presentation first heard in P (αα, mm. 159–62 = mm. 1–4) and a few P-based cadential bars (mm. 163–68). This added passage exhibits typical P-referential, Type 2 coda behavior of the sort discussed earlier in this chapter. The difference here is that the coda-style music does not appear after the completion of Rotation 2—and the sonata proper—but is relocated into a space opened up before the tonal resolution's C^2 completion. Mozart has held C^2 in reserve to round out the entire movement.

This is a not uncommon occurrence within sonatas of all types. Sonata Theory refers to this technique as *coda-rhetoric interpolation* (CRI): "a passage of coda-rhetoric material . . . before all of the final [tonal-resolution] modules have been sounded" (*EST*, 288). In K. 306/i, mm. 159–67's P-referential CRI steps outside of sonata space and then steps back into it at mm. 168–72 for C^2 and its emphatic reiteration. The return of P$^{1.1}$ in m. 159—unheard since mm. 1–4 (and written over at the opening of the development)—is not part of a presumed "reversed recapitulation." Indeed, it plays no "sonata" role within this movement's sonata space proper. Instead, it functions as a (perhaps compensatory) coda, and once having sounded it, Mozart plugs back into Rotation 2's C^2 codetta to provide an elegant end-rhyme to the exposition's close.

A structural deformation (1): Mozart, Piano Sonata in D, K. 311/i.

The initial Allegro con spirito of Mozart's D Major Piano Sonata, K. 311 (Mannheim, 1777) is one of the most unusual of his sonata forms. It has given rise to a number of different explanations, most of which have fallen back on the "reversed recapitulation" (or "mirror" form) claim (*EST*, 368). As we shall see, even within the flexible guidelines of the Type 2 sonata, K. 311/i presents us with a challenge. The central complication is that its developmental space, the first half of Rotation 2, does not follow the norm of being entirely grounded in P (or an episodic substitute) and/or TR (pre-MC material) but instead, midway through, swerves into a strong thematic module from S (m. 58), presented off-tonic (in IV) but with nine bars of strict correspondence measures (mm. 58–66 = mm. 28–36), sounding momentarily like a premature (but "wrong-key") tonal-resolution effect.

And a touch of C-related material even follows it, all before the "real" tonal resolution, which begins normatively by locking onto the end of TR and moving into the tonic-key onset of $S^{1.1}$ (m. 79).

Before dealing with that, let's review the exposition's action zones. P spans mm. 1–7: a variant of the period format in which the antecedent's descent from scale degree $\hat{5}$ to $\hat{3}$ produces a I:IAC (m. 4), which downbeat elides with the beginning of the consequent, whose $\hat{5}$ now descends to $\hat{1}$, I:PAC (m. 7). (It's worth noting that this is a rare occurrence of an antecedent *elided* with its consequent.) The sentential TR, mm. 7–16, is non-problematic: Mozart sustains the converging I:HC in m. 13 via a dominant-lock (designating it as $TR^{1.2}$ will prove useful) and leads it to a I:HC MC in m. 16. The S that follows is a normative, eight-bar period: antecedent, mm. 17–20 (V:HC), consequent, mm. 21–24 (V:PAC). Our initial impression is that m. 24 is likely to be the EEC, and that reading is certainly feasible. On the other hand, the staccato eighth-note figure that dominates the next four bars (mm. 24/25–28) can be heard as wheel-spinning reverberations of a rhythm that had dominated the melody of S. If one hears that aspect as decisive—my preference—m. 24 would not be characterized by new material but would rather be construed as the start of an S^2 codetta. Under that reading, mm. 17–24 would be reconstrued as S^1.

The static reverberations of mm. 24/25–28 release into a genuinely new thematic idea in mm. 28/29–32 (V:PAC), repeated in mm. 32–36. Thus mm. 24/25–28 become $S^{2.1}$ and mm. 28–36 $S^{2.2}$. (It is the thematically salient $S^{2.2}$ that will bring about the potential confusions in the development.) The V:PAC at m. 36 marks the EEC, and Mozart elides it with the arpeggios of C^1, mm. 36–37, a standardized tag-codetta (C^{cod}). C^1's familiar rhetoric signals that m. 37 ought to be the end of the exposition. Instead, in mm. 38–39 the composer appends a *non sequitur*, *piano* cadential figure, C^2, an after-the-fact confirmational bow or *remarque sur l'escalier*. Among other things, it settles the high-energy A_5 in m. 37 down to a more relaxed A_4, the goal pitch of all of the S-space PACs.

Up to this point, while by no means ruling out the Type 2 possibility, the listener has no reason not to suppose that this sonata movement will proceed as a Type 3, far and away the more common Mozartian format at this time. Those suspicions seem confirmed as we move into the development. What is striking at its outset is that mm. 40–54 are taken over by modulatory sequences anchored by C^2: the *non sequitur* tag from the end of the exposition now spills over into developmental space and begins to multiply. A C-based opening to the development typically implies "the presence of a strong 'final' [expositional] idea that captures and arrests our attention, one whose forcible gestures, still echoing, override the more standard appearance of P at this point" (*EST*, 215). Any such development-opening C-idea might be regarded as a writing-over of the more common P, particularly if what follows confirms that reading—for instance, if the music soon shifts to the rotationally succeeding TR or S material. The C^2 sequences at the beginning of this development touch upon shifting tonal colors, and in m. 55 C^2 empties out into a normative, if worrisome, PAC in B minor (vi:PAC)—and a quarter-rest hard break, echoing that at the exposition's end, as if recasting that earlier conclusion into the minor mode. A quizzical two-bar link follows, mm. 56–57, leveraging the key toward G major: "What next?"

Unexpectedly, out bursts a full-throated, *forte* replication of $S^{2.2}$ in G major (IV, mm. 58–66 = mm. 28–36, including two IV:PACs, mm. 62 and 66). This literal restatement of $S^{2.2}$ brings the Sonata Theory–oriented listener to two observations. First, given the sense in which the preceding m. 55, the vi:PAC, had returned to the end of the exposition, only now saddened into the minor, the sudden subdominant blurting of $S^{2.2}$ in m. 58 seeks to shift the thematic material to an expositional point before C^2, in a sense, to turn back time, albeit now in the developmental IV, in order correctively to reapproach or perhaps even rid itself of that now-problematic C^2.[19] In addition, notice that at the conclusion of this subdominant $S^{2.2}$ (m. 66, IV:PAC, the developmental analogue of the m. 36's EEC), what follows is an expanded variant of the opening of C^1, coming ever closer to the C^2 potential moment.

Second, apart from the development's initial C^2 expansions (which could be read as a writing-over of the more conventional P), the subsequent developmental presence of $S^{2.2}$ and C^1 rules out any lingering sense that we might have had that what has happened so far could be part of a Type 2 sonata. Recall that the developmental space of a Type 2 is normally to be anchored only with P, or TR, or an episodic writing-over of one or both, since S and C materials are to be reserved for the crux and the correspondence measures of the tonal resolution. Once a P-launched development, midway through its course, proceeds to sound S or C material, it becomes fully rotational, not half-rotational, and the Type 2 possibility is set aside. With the appearance of $S^{2.2}$ and C^1 materials, mm. 58–c. 71, we are being led to expect that we are dealing with a Type 3 sonata, and we anticipate the full recapitulation that must be about to appear.

For the moment, though, the point seems to be to avoid releasing that pesky C^2 *non sequitur* once again, which any conclusive ending of C^1 material seems to invite. Accordingly, near the development's end Mozart does not allow C^1 to close. Instead, at mm. 71–74 he adds new, modulatory material that steers us through the familiar $\hat{4}$-$\sharp\hat{4}$-$\hat{5}$ bassline into a half cadence in D at m. 75 (I:HC). M. 75 also serves as a crux, locking onto correspondence measures with the exposition's $TR^{1.2}$ and its drive to the I:HC MC (mm. 75–78 = mm. 13–16, at their original pitch level). From the now-supposed Type 3 perspective, this is a curious move. It appears to be *yet another rotational backing-up* to a spot ($TR^{1.2}$) before the exposition's S-point.

Notwithstanding the crux at m. 75 and the apparent rotational disorder at hand, one might still imagine a full recapitulation starting at m. 79, which, though odd, would at least confirm our ongoing Type 3 assumption. Instead, the correspondence measures begun in m. 75 continue at m. 79 into a full, tonic-key restatement of S^1 and the multimodular S^2 (mm. 75–99 = 13–36, with the exception of mm. 83–86, to which we shall return). But by m. 79, lacking the return of P^1, we are now dealing with Type 2 behavior, in which the tonic key and correspondence measures return just at or slightly before the tonal resolution. The sonata that in the development had unequivocally displayed Type 3 behavior—by its prominent internal inclusion of S and C material—is now staged as changing its mind and insisting on converting into a Type 2. All in response, it would seem, to avoid running once again into that unwelcome C^2 *non sequitur*, which has proven to be a disruptive agent in the sonata's structure.

At m. 79, then, a cheekily playful movement, Mozart overturns normative sonata-type expectations by mixing Type 3 and Type 2 principles. Such mixtures are rare but not nonexistent. Sonata Theory refers to instances of them as "Type 3==>Type 2 conversions." These conversions are nearly always the result of an S- or C-based development that at the crucial moment throws away the expected P-recapitulation to proceed instead into the tonal resolution in the Type 2 manner. "This option probably belongs more to a theory of Type 2 structural deformation than to a theory of standard practice" (*EST*, 376, which proceeds with a further discussion of these mixtures, of which K. 311/i is the touchstone example).

The m. 79 surprise yanks the text-adequate listener out of the self-evident Type 3 assumption into a new Type 2 reality—a structural jolt. Doubtless as a reaction to this, m. 83, in the midst of S^1, deflates unexpectedly from the preceding D major into a fleetingly troubled D minor. At the same time, the music detaches itself from otherwise strict correspondence measures in order to lead to a D-minor half cadence in m. 86. This internal half cadence not only erases the "early-PAC-problem" that had occurred in the analogous spot of the exposition, m. 24, but also produces (yet another surprise) a second MC-effect in dialogue with the trimodular-block (TMB) option. This alteration more clearly keeps what I had called $S^{2.1}$ in the exposition within secondary-theme space in the recapitulation. $S^{2.1}$ locks back onto correspondence measures (m. 87 = m. 24), and $S^{2.2}$—whose earlier, subdominant surfacing in the development has occasioned so much analytical puzzlement—appears intact in the tonic (mm. 91–99) to secure the I:PAC ESC in its final bar.

At m. 99 one expects an elision with the arpeggiations of C^1, as had occurred in the exposition. One problem with that, though, might be that such an elision would bring us even closer to the non-integrated C^2, the source of the structural disruption in the first place. Accordingly, another surprise: at m. 99, instead of C^1, Mozart brings in the shiny-bright P theme, unheard since mm. 1–7. As we have seen, *in a Type 2 sonata such a return of P at this point always signifies the start of coda behavior* (an incipient Rotation 3). And once P has been fully sounded, its expected cadence in m. 105 is evaded with a I^6 chord that triggers more obviously coda-like rhetoric in mm. 105–109. The issue here is that we have not yet heard the conclusion of the tonal resolution (the conclusion of Rotation 2). C^1 and C^2 have not yet appeared, but they will do so at the very end, mm. 109–12. As had happened in K. 306/i, mm. 99–108/109 are a classic instance of *coda-rhetoric interpolation* (CRI), to be understood as momentarily stepping outside of sonata space, only to return to it in the final four bars.

Mozart's last touch to this unusual movement happens in those last four bars. Instead of closing C^1 with a strong tonic chord, he brings it up short with an expectant halt on vi, keeping the figure open. (M. 110 does not correspond harmonically with m. 37.) In the final two measures, what had been "C^2" before, in mm. 38–39, is integrated more securely into closing space. Even while still being granted the last word, its *non sequitur* aspect has been absorbed into a more functional role.

A structural deformation (2): Mozart, Overture to *La clemenza di Tito*, K. 621

Two of Mozart's last overtures, those to *Così fan tutte* (1790) and *La clemenza di Tito* (1791), feature notable structural deformations.[20] Of the two, *Così*—a Type 3 sonata—is the more complex, in part, one presumes, to display through dizzyingly multiple subrotations and modular redundancies the perpetual, quasi-licentious mixing and remixing of the same whirligig thematic modules, setting up an instrumental analogue to what will follow in the opera's plot. Within the context of this chapter, however, we turn instead to the structure of *Clemenza*, which presents us with Type 2 issues similar to those in K. 311/i but recasts them with different connotations.

A glance at this latter overture's exposition sets the narrative scene. Its action zones are clear, though from a cadential point of view the first two of them are unusually concluded—a feature to which I shall return. These zones are: a C-major, imperiously "Jupiterian" P, mm. 1–16, subdivisible into P^0 (mm. 1–8, an initial entrance punctuated by dramatic fermatas), and a double-statement of P^1 (mm. 8–12, 12–16), in which each P$^{1.}$ ends with a "soprano clausula," V$^6_5$-I; a tonally static but dynamically accumulative TR, mm. 16–29, eventually shifting to the MC sounded on a V$^6_5$/V chord, probably to be heard as complementary to the V$^6_5$/I in mm. 11 and 15; S, a contrasting, compound-period wind dialogue in V (G major), mm. 30–45; and a P^1-based C, mm. 45–55, featuring two stormy outbursts sounded over a G-tonic pedal.

Considered only by itself, the developmental space, mm. 58–112 (preceded by a two-bar anacrusis-link, mm. 56–57, shifting to E-flat), at first appears normative. It is fully rotational, dominated first by P^1-material, mm. 58–86, that eventually gives way to a double-statement of the stormy P-based C, mm. 87–112, with an internal, modulatory link (mm. 94–101) separating the two statements. The curiosity here, though, is that the latter's second statement, mm. 102–12, replicates the exposition's P-based C, mm. 45–55, *at the original pitch level*: what had been a pedal-grounding of G major in the exposition is now recontextualized as a dominant-lock, V of C (m. 102 is a converging I:HC)—followed by a question-mark fermata close (m. 112): "What next?"

Up through the point of this fermata, the listener should suppose that we are dealing with a Type 3 sonata. Any development that has sounded thematic material of both parts of a two-part exposition—a fully rotational development, as occurs here—will always imply this (as had also been the case in K. 311/i). What we expect is a tonic return of the grand-style P⁰ at m. 113. Instead, Mozart gives us the tonal resolution of S, mm. 113–31, in the manner of a Type 2 sonata, leading to the ESC at m. 131. Even more astonishing, the next referential-layout module in line, the P-based C, now expected in the tonic, is omitted altogether. Instead, the ESC dovetails with an extended, literal restatement of P and much of TR (mm. 131–56 = mm. 1–26). Citing Tyson's 1975 work on the chronology of the opera, Heartz tells us that, rushed for time before the Prague premiere, Mozart did not write out this return of P and TR. "Instead, he indicated to the copyist 'D.C. 26,' directing him to write out again at this spot the first twenty-six measures" (1978, 32, copied into 1990, 321). Following this, Mozart returned to the manuscript to complete the final 12 bars with grand, P/TR-related flourishes.

By the end of the overture and its thematic reorderings we have been presented with a number of structural challenges. Heartz read the late return of P and TR in the then-usual manner, as part of a "recapitulation . . . in reverse order" (1978, 32; 1991, 321). His reading of the protracted literalness of P and TR at the end—one apparently borrowed from A. B. Marx, as we shall see—is that it solved an apparently unforeseen difficulty posed by internal issues within the sonata's progress. "By using [a] figure associated with the first theme so extensively at the end of the Development, Mozart found himself in a situation where a normal reprise would present a problem: his imperial flourishes and fanfares were used up for the moment. . . . The result [of the shifting of P and TR to the end] was rather similar to what Stamitz and other Mannheimers had done many times in the opening Allegro movements of their symphonies" (1978, 40; 1991, 331). Similarly, in 1991 Rice also found the presumed "reverse recapitulation" to have been structurally curious, even suggesting that it may have been "another product of Mozart's haste," since it "allowed him to keep connecting material to a minimum" (69).

From the Sonata Theory perspective, though, the elided, literal return of P and TR need not be accounted for through appeals to either imagined earlier structural difficulties or the rush of the compositional moment. More likely, it is to be consigned to post-sonata coda space, thereby owing a debt to midcentury (Type 2) *sonata-ritornello-blend* practice, in which elided coda-returns to a literal or near-literal statement of all or most of P were common. We have seen earlier instances of this in the first movements of Mozart's Symphony No. 5, K. 22, and Stamitz's Symphony in D, op. 3 no. 2 (a product of the "Mannheimers"). To be sure, in the *Clemenza di Tito* Overture the extent of the P *and* TR coda-recurrence is striking, and while one might pursue this on its own terms, by itself it does not challenge the more fundamental reading of its structure as an adaptation of the sonata-ritornello blend.

Approaching the matter more recently from another angle and questioning the later viability of the Type 2 sonata as a genuine nineteenth-century option, Vande Moortele (2017, 237), noted that "from our modern point of view, [the overture is] a 'Type 2 sonata' by any standard"; to support his view, however, he added that toward the middle of that century A. B. Marx read the piece's structural anomalies as "cleverly and strikingly" divergent with regard to what he then regarded as the norm (seemingly a Type 1 or 3 format). According to Marx, the composer "begins his third part ['Marx's term for the recapitulation,' notes Vande Moortele] with the subordinate theme; only after this theme, which is too weak to achieve closure, does he come back to the beginning."[21] It should be noted, however, that Marx did not indicate explicitly that the concluding P/TR return is still part of a "recapitulation" (or even of a still-persisting "third part," however freely he might have been using that term), only that they bring the overture to a "close" [*Schluss*], nor does the concept of the "reversed recapitulation" or "coda" appear in his discussion either literally or by implication. What does seem clear, though, is that Marx was either unaware of the Type 2 sonata practice or, for whatever reason, decided not to allude to it in the brief, single paragraph that he devoted to this piece as part of a broader survey of sonata form within overtures.

How might a Sonata Theorist work one's way through this thicket of problems? It's clear that because of its fully rotational development (P and P-based C) the *Clemenza di Tito* overture is, like K. 311/i, no touchstone example of a Type 2 sonata. Our first step is to remind ourselves of a central principle of dialogic form—that the "real form" of any piece rests not in its acoustic surface alone (what is printed on the page and what one hears), to be reflected on in isolation as a purely self-generating phenomenon, but rather in the particulars of how that piece carries out its implicit dialogue with generally prototypical norms (*EST*, 605). One consequence of this is Sonata Theory's insistence in such hard cases that the question is not the reductive one "*Is* this piece a Type 2 sonata?", as if a simple yes or no answer could brush away the challenges of the structure with a catch-all category. Rather, the question should be, "To what extent did Mozart set this piece into a *dialogue* with aspects of the Type 2 format, with which format we know he was familiar?" Or, put another way, from the interpretive side of things, "Is it appropriate for us to use the Type 2 norms as a ready-to-hand conceptual schema to interpret, indeed even to help us *perceive*, what the actual structure of this piece is?" In this case there is no other generic option: using a Type 1 or Type 3 lens for a piece lacking a full recapitulation starting with P is self-evidently less relevant.

As with K. 311/i, we might conclude that we are dealing with the deformation of the Type 3==>Type 2 conversion: Type 3 signals by the end of the development are overturned by Type 2 ones at the critical point where one would normally expect a recapitulation. This is tenable so far as it goes, but it still doesn't get to the heart of this piece's narrative connotations. What is most structurally curious about the movement is its literal replication of the exposition's P-based C material at the end of the development, mm. 102–12 (there heard as an active V of I, not as a tonicized V, as before), coupled with the absence of that material where it would customarily be expected, following S in the tonal resolution. One consequence of this is that this C material is never stabilized into the tonic (except as expressing its dominant at the end of the development).

This leads us to a larger rhetorical issue. From m. 86 through m. 156, Mozart gives us four thematic modules presented in literal, extensive correspondence measures, succeeding each other in lockstep but *out of rotational order*, with the onset of the tonal resolution beginning only after the first of them: C (mm. 86–112), concluding as V of I, ending the development; S (mm. 113–31) resolved into the tonic to begin the tonal resolution; and P and much of TR in the tonic (mm. 132–46 and 146–56). From the dialogic Type 2 perspective, the P/TR music from m. 132 onward is all coda, occupying post-sonata space—or, more precisely, it is in dialogue with the coda tradition of the Type 2 sonata. And yet it's clear that more is going on than is explicable by the magic-wand invocation of the Type 2 format.

Whatever else the piece is about, it is also about the disruption of rotational convention through the explicit reordering of statically fixed thematic modules. That must have something to do with the plot of the opera that follows it, one that demonstrates the eventual clemency of a monarch in the face of a web of amorous tangles that have been generating luridly conspiratorial betrayals and plots against him. It's not difficult to imagine that the immobile, Jupiterian P^0 and P^1, largely over a tonic pedal, convey the magisterial topic of unshakeable order and authority, in this case, a representation of the Emperor Titus and "the power and stability of absolute monarchy" (Rice 1991, 66).[22] This authority, it seems, is reluctant even to bring itself to an end with an authentic cadence. Hence the soprano clausulas, V_5^6-I, mm, 11–12 and 15–16. The impression of granitic immobility is sustained throughout most of TR—another formulaic-gesture prolongation of the tonic until the jostling that produces the V_5^6/V MC in mm. 28–29, as if the static C major had just noticed, *de haut en bas*, an "other" in its presence.

In this context the utter contrast of the S's lyrical wind-dialogue can be read as a shift away from the emperor to the non-tonic otherness of what will eventually turn out to be the schemes surrounding him. Mozart represents that sense of difference benignly, by a formally simple, square-cut, even naïve (hardly "conspiratorial") wind-march, which contrasts the neutralized, "middle style" of S, operating outside of the emperor's key of C major, with the obdurate, absolute-power "high style" of the preceding P and TR. The EEC (m. 45) elides directly with P-based C modules (mm. 45–55), concluding the exposition. This closing music returns to the authoritative motives and pedal bass characteristic of P's lofty, imperial style, now convulsed by two *forte* diminished-seventh outbursts, theatrical rage-tremors, over a G-tonic pedal: a registering of the perils at hand, anticipating what is expected to be Tito's fury upon becoming aware of what the otherness of this S has been plotting behind its innocent mask.

The point of the opera's plot is that notwithstanding the many betrayals of Tito, he eventually grants the conspirators mercy. Things change. With that in mind, it must have been clear to Mozart that the tonal resolution's S-music, producing the ESC (m. 131), should not be followed once again by an image of the emperor's rage—or the fear of that rage. This realization probably generated the piece's formal oddities. The P- and P-based-C grounded development is dramatically accumulative, beginning with restrained, tiptoe-like figuration moving stealthily from one tonal center to another (the growing of plots against the emperor?) and ending, from m. 86 onward, with Tito's P-based-C outbursts. Placing the P-based C at the end of the development (instead of after S, as in the exposition) at least allowed that expositional material to return in a programmatically viable place, albeit out of rotational order and, in its second statement, mm. 102–12, expressing V of I.

Immediately after this last P-based-C statement, Mozart brings in the tonal resolution (S, m. 113) and with it the second appearance of the deceptively benign other, now marched up before him in "his" tonic C major. The moment of the ESC (m. 131) may be read as the emperor's grant of pardon, effecting "la clemenza di Tito" by assimilating that other back into the order of his C-major authority. Following that, the extensive, ritornello-like P-TR appendix that follows as the coda suggests a restoration of the emperor's initial state of C-major grandeur, as, now exiting the scene, the overture's connotative drama has been resolved.

In sum: overlaid onto the Type 2 deformation (the non-normative dialogue with orthodox Type 2 norms, or the Type 3==>Type 2 conversion), the *Clemenza di Tito* overture features a clever, quasi-programmatic game of thematic permutation among what Mozart has crafted as essentially static modules. Realizing, this, one's thoughts might move in the directions of the eighteenth-century theorist Joseph Riepel's musical dice games, and the more general appeal of the *ars combinatoria* (Ratner 1980, 98–102). On the other hand, as Byros has reminded us (2013, 213–14), from nearly the beginning of Mozart's mature career—and especially in the 1770s—the composer amused himself with linguistic permutations, inversions, or reversals of spellings (referring to himself as "Trazom," for instance) and normal word orders, and similar manipulations of orthodox sense. It may well be that in several of his much-later works, including the *Così fan tutte* and *La clemenza di Tito* overtures, this spirit of combinatoriality and permutation, now swayed also by plot-anticipatory aims, reared its head once again.

Seeming Type 3 "recapitulations" that do not begin with P^0 or P^1: dialogues with the Type 2 format

In chapter 10 we saw a case—Schubert's D-Minor Quartet—where a presumed "recapitulation," with correspondence measures, seemed intuitively to begin at TR, not with P. Yet in that movement a strong aspect of standard P-behavior, the emphatic return to the tonic key, had been inset into the end of the development, where it apparently launched tonal features of a recapitulatory rotation while still in developmental space. What do we make of analogous cases in which a presumed "recapitulation" begins several bars into the rotation, either with a later module of P or with TR (usually of the dissolving-restatement type), but where a new but initially *off-tonic* thematic rotation within a still-ongoing developmental space had been started shortly before it? This would be a situation where a development ends by reintroducing P material in still-developmental ways—beginning a new thematic rotation, though not in the tonic and not necessarily through correspondence measures—and the subsequent "recapitulation" (tonic key and correspondence measures) begins several bars into that rotation.

Cases like these can be construed as hybrids, intermixing features of both Type 3 and Type 2 sonatas. This can happen when a sonata's development section seems to rule out Type 2 behavior (for example, by pursuing S or C material or at least departing from P's head-motive) but toward its end, while still developmental (and off-tonic), swerves into a newly thematic, P-initiated rotation. And that new rotation—the return to P material—soon brings the development proper to an end, setting up an apparent, tonic-key "recapitulation" that begins later in that rotation. Let's touch on a few examples:

- *Haydn, Symphony No. 95 in C Minor, first movement.* One's initial impulse is to place the start of the recapitulation at m. 120, where, after an expectant pause (though not following a root-position dominant), the tonic key is returned to, a prominent P-theme is sounded, and correspondence measures with the exposition are briefly locked onto. But m. 120 is the start of the P^1 theme, and in the exposition that theme had emerged only in m. 4, following a typical, minor-mode motto-emblem P^0 statement (mm. 1–2). Backing up from P^1's return at m. 120, we notice that at m. 98 the final phase of the development had brought back a variant of the declarative P^0 motto, the actual rotation initiator, initially elided with an IAC in E-flat. Moreover, prior to m. 98, the development had been fully rotational: it had featured treatments of P^0 (m. 62), P^1 (m. 76), and S (m. 88). Merging with lingering patterings of the preceding S, the non-tonic resumption of P^0 at m. 98 begins a new rotation, setting off within still-developmental space, though seeking its way back to its original C-minor home. (Notice the end-of-development dominant-lock at m. 113 and its evaporative fading in mm. 116–19.)

  The rhetorically marked return to P^1 and correspondence measures at m. 120 continue a rotation already in progress. On the one hand, m. 98's P^0 can be regarded as entering the final phase of the development: its rapid shifting of non-tonic tonal levels is self-evidently "developmental." On the other hand, from a purely thematic/rotational point of view, it provides us a "developed" version of the initial module, P^0, that may be read as starting a tonal-resolution rotation. Its next module in line, that is, and the second thematic module within the rotation, is the P^1 that starts the presumed "recapitulation" at m. 120. The sonata as a whole, however, is a *triple-rotational sonata* (in the manner of a Type 3), not a double-rotational sonata (in the manner of a Type 2). Haydn has blurred the customarily clear seam between a Type 3's development and recapitulation with aspects of the Type 2 prototype.
- *Beethoven, Leonore Overture No. 3.* Listeners not aware of tonal levels and recapitulatory norms might assume (with Tovey 1981, 138) that the "recapitulation"

begins at m. 330, with the fully prepared return of P in the flute (a preparation that includes the two time-stopping, trumpet-signal caesuras and the subsequent, stunned reaction to them) and the brief run of correspondence bars that it initiates. The analytical problem is that this P-return, along with the beginning of a new thematic rotation, is in G (V), not in the tonic, C. Accordingly, this off-tonic P is swallowed back into development to set up the supercharged, tonic return of the P theme at m. 378. But m. 378 corresponds to the exposition's beginning of TR in m. 69, a *sempre fortissimo* affirmation of P. What seems tonally to be the "real recapitulation" begins with TR. As with the situation in Haydn's Symphony No. 95/i, we have a Type 3/Type 2 blurring of the normative (Type 3) development-recapitulation seam. From the Type 2 perspective, the tonal-resolution rotation begins back in m. 330. Yet this is more emphatically a Type 3, triple-rotational sonata. (See also the discussion in *EST*, 278.)

A somewhat related situation arises when we find three features in play: (1) the exposition begins with a preliminary, P^0 idea that sets up a more obviously thematic P^1; (2) the development is based entirely on a much-expanded P^0; and (3) the "recapitulation" begins with P^1 correspondence bars. This results in a *double-rotational sonata* (each rotation starts with P^0, then moves on to P^1). Most listeners would probably hear such instances as Type 3 sonatas (exposition-development-recapitulation), though they are actually Type 2 sonatas that have been rhetorically fashioned to "sound like" Type 3 sonatas, bridging the gap between the two formats. The first movements of two well-known Schubert symphonies provide the touchstones. In the Symphony No. 5 in B-flat, P^1 (m. 5) is preceded by the anacrusis figure P^0 (mm. 1–5); the development (mm. 118–69) is dominated by P^0 material; and the "recapitulation" starts with the "thematic" P^1 (beginning in IV, E-flat, m. 171—a "subdominant recapitulation" [see p. 81]). And in Schubert's Symphony No. 8 in B Minor, P^1 proper (m. 13) is preceded by *two* zero-modules, which can be designated as $P^{0.1}$ (initial ominous motto, mm. 1–8) and $P^{0.2}$ (rhythmic stream, mm. 9–12). Schubert devotes the entire development to an expansion of $P^{0.1}$. As in his Fifth Symphony, the onset of the developmental space (m. 114) doubles as the start of the second rotation of the whole movement, one in which $P^{0.1}$ is expanded into the development and only empties out, in this case, into the recapitulatory effect with the sounding of the rhythmic-stream $P^{0.2}$ in the tonic at m. 218. From one perspective, m. 218 certainly does "feel" like a clearly marked point of recapitulation and at one level of analysis might even be regarded as such. On the other hand, $P^{0.2}$ is an interior module of an ongoing second rotation, one that had started at the opening of the development. From that perspective this movement is a double-rotational sonata in dialogue with the Type 2 format, whose second rotation of materials normatively starts off-tonic at the beginning of the development.[23] Several decades later, the same structural plan, only with a generative, much-expanded P^0 section, occurs in the first movement of Bruckner's Symphony No. 9.[24]

Type 2 and expanded Type 1 sonatas

The end of chapter 4 noted that in terms of their morphologies Type 2 sonatas can seem much like expanded Type 1s: as Smith has also observed, they are indeed "closely related parallel-binary forms" (2018, 256). In Sonata Theory terms both are *double-rotational sonatas* whose second rotations feature a developmental/modulatory expansion of P or TR followed by an S/C tonal resolution. In light of this similarity, it might be prudent in the present, Type 2 context to call attention once again to the differences between them:

- In the Type 2 sonata the second (post-expositional) rotation does not begin in the tonic. It therefore cannot be taken for the start of a recapitulation. If what follows the exposition does begin with P in the tonic, though, replicating the opening of the exposition—however brief that replication might be—it is an expanded Type 1.
- The strong, virtually inviolable norm for any Type 1 sonata, normal or expanded, is to do away with all internal repeats. Therefore if one finds a repeat sign at the end of an exposition, one can be assured that one is not dealing with a Type 1 sonata. Type 2s, however, may or may not feature repeat signs. The only regulative guideline is that an overture in the Type 2 format will always omit them. The overriding rule is that overtures in sonata form—whether they be Type 1s, Type 2s, or Type 3s—always omit expositional (and other) repeats.
- In the eighteenth century and well into the nineteenth (where only a handful of examples have turned up),[25] the expanded Type 1—unlike the Type 2—seems never to have been an option for first movements of multimovement works. Instead, in the classical era its appearances are largely confined to slow movements and finales.

The Type 2 sonata in the nineteenth century

By the last quarter of the eighteenth century the Type 2 format was increasingly set aside as composers turned more and more to the Type 3 schema. But it never disappeared. *Elements of Sonata Theory* (*EST*, 364) provides a list of some nineteenth- and early-twentieth-century Type 2s,[26] some of which can be cited here, along with a few additions: Weber's Overture to *Der Beherrscher der Geister* (*Ruler of the Spirits*); Schubert's *Quartettsatz* (a deformational Type 2 featuring a number of challenging tonal and action-zone curiosities);[27] the first movement of Beethoven's B-flat Quartet, op. 130;[28] the slow movement of Mendelssohn's String Octet (Smith 2019) and Overture to *Athalie*; the first movements of Chopin's Second and Third Piano Sonatas and Cello Sonata (Davis 2014); Verdi's overture to *Luisa Miller*; the finale of Schumann's Fourth Symphony; Liszt's *Les préludes*; the first movement of Tchaikovsky's Fourth Symphony; the finale of Bruckner's

Seventh Symphony (Darcy 1997) and the first movement of his Ninth;[29] the first movement of Dvořák's String Quartet in E-flat, op. 51 (Smith 2019); and, even later, the first movement of Sibelius's Fourth Symphony—a particularly clear instance. Additionally, the first movement of Dvořák's Cello Concerto is an ingenious—and unusual—hybrid between a Type 5 sonata (the high-galant/classical-concerto format) and a Type 2 thematic arrangement.[30] There is little reason to doubt that further inquiry into the nineteenth century would locate dozens, perhaps many dozens, of more examples.

From Sonata Theory's point of view the case for the persistence of a Type 2 tradition among some nineteenth-century works is compelling, regardless of under what terms that format might have been understood at that time. Still, there remains resistance to the Type 2 approach to those works, even among those who concede its relevance to the mid- and later eighteenth century. As noted in *EST*, 365, a sticking-point is that no descriptions of it seem to have appeared in nineteenth-century *Formenlehre* textbooks or guides (A. B. Marx and others), while descriptions of what Sonata Theory refers to as Types 1, 3, 4, and 5 abound. On this basis some have maintained that the Type 2 concept ought not to be applied to nineteenth-century works, all the more so to those from the 1830s onward. The dismissal of the Type 2 claim is typically coupled with the idea that these Type 2s were probably not understood in this way by their composers but rather as individualized variants of the Type 3 format in which internal considerations within each work prompted the start of a "recapitulation" with S in the tonic, which in turn—though only sometimes—was extended by means of an added P-reference at the end, resuscitating once again the concept of the "reversed recapitulation," whereby the added P is to be housed in recapitulatory space, not in coda space.

Since these objections continue to linger at the time of this writing (though Sonata Theory's view of this has also gained traction)[31] and since they should neither be rejected out of hand nor dismissed as minor, it might be helpful to present Sonata Theory's position more clearly. The matter is worth pursuing not only for the sake of the immediate question but also because it bears on the larger debate concerning the utility (or not) of Sonata Theory's conceptual approach, modified with appropriate historical nuances, to romantic works more generally, an issue that I take up again in an early section of chapter 12. With regard to the Type 2 matter, let's start with some general observations and then look at some of the details of one of the most widely noted, recent arguments against the Type 2 interpretation.

The first thing to note is that compositions displaying what Sonata Theory regards as a straightforward Type 2 format can be found in virtually each decade of the nineteenth century. Whatever it might have been called, or however composers or textbook theorists of form might have thought of it, a Type 2 tradition persisted as a continuity from the later eighteenth century far into the nineteenth. Yes, there is a sharp decline in Type 2 usage in the 1800s, but there is no clear break in the chain of that tradition—as maintained, for example, by one of Sonata Theory's harshest critics, Paul Wingfield, who declared that "the so-called Type 2 sonata was one of

the casualties of the 'stylistic revolution of the 1770s'" (2008, 160).[32] It seems im-
probable, though, that around 1800 or 1810, or shortly before, such a full erasure
of one of the standard options of fairly recent compositional history could have
occurred. More to the point, it strains credulity to suppose that, independently and
on their own, numerous nineteenth-century composers just happened from time
to time to start composing works in the format that replicates in all of its double-
rotational details both of the two versions of the eighteenth-century Type 2: that
without a P-based coda and that with that coda. At least as Sonata Theory sees it, the
rotational features in play are the features distinguishing Sonata Types 1, 2, and 3,
and rotational procedures remain a central aspect of nineteenth-century composition (and of some twentieth-century composition as well).

But the question lingers: how were nineteenth-century composers themselves
thinking of that "Type 2" double-rotational structure when they had recourse to it?
Until more evidence emerges, we cannot know. Still, even if some Type 2 composers
were not cognizant of its roots and history, as could well be the case, they were nonetheless plugging into a historically continuous tradition, not reinventing afresh
an earlier format that was now to be construed under totally different terms. Not
only did they plug into it, but they also produced pieces that followed its double-
rotational aspects in exemplary fashion. To be sure, some of the more historically
aware composers might have regarded it as an older and largely "anachronistic"
form that, nevertheless, could still be pressed into occasional service in the nineteenth century for certain kinds of "compressed" sonata movements (from the far
more familiar, Type 3 perspective). No matter how composers might have regarded
such sonata "compressions," however, when considered from a broader, more dia-
chronic sense of historical convention, they were nonetheless reanimating the Type
2 schema.

What does Sonata Theory mean when it refers to a nineteenth-century work as
a Type 2 sonata? Only that the piece was participating in a dialogue with the *Type
2 tradition*, one that we as historians can reconstruct as stretching back into the
eighteenth century, when its usage was more common. To identify a nineteenth-
century work as a Type 2 sonata does not discount that work's other ("romantic")
differences from eighteenth-century practice, all of which should be pursued in
analysis. Sonata Theory's "Type 2" is a terminological convenience from the standpoint of a more synoptic, twenty-first-century mode of theorizing—one, however,
that is grounded in a historical understanding of the varieties of the sonata genre
and its potential for modifications to suit different places and eras but that does
not assume that many nineteenth-century composers grasped (or even much cared
about) the history of that kind of sonata.

This is not an argument that seeks to bolster a modern-day "reframing" of the
Type 2 concept as "frankly presentist," as Peter H. Smith has suggested, while also
noting that, even so, any such reframing would "only put it in the good company
of other influential theories widely recognized as heuristically beneficial, such as
Schenkerian analysis and William E. Caplin's theory of formal functions" (2019,

107). On the contrary, although some might be inclined to use the Sonata Theory apparatus in a largely "presentist" way—within which its analytical benefits are still strong—that theory proper seeks to be historical through and through. Pursuing the discussion, however, Smith also acknowledged that "it does not seem implausible that earlier eighteenth-century conventions may have been a source for some of the alternatives to the 'textbook' type 3 form, especially in light of the emerging historical consciousness of nineteenth-century composers" (107). While Sonata Theory's terminology is not that of the eighteenth and nineteenth centuries, it nonetheless carries the conviction that musicians of those centuries would at least have recognized the concepts that it believes must have underpinned their ever-changing, ever-expanding sonata practice.

Apart from Wingfield's 2008 remarks, the most direct objection to the Type 2 concept to describe certain pieces from the 1800s is found in Steven Vande Moortele's 2017 study of *The Romantic Overture and Musical Form from Rossini to Wagner*. Disavowing such readings, Vande Moortele places much weight on the absence of the Type 2 concept among nineteenth-century theorists, citing especially A. B. Marx's description of Mozart's *La clemenza di Tito* overture, which I have treated at some length earlier. In any event, as Smith also put it, as theorists and historians we should be cautious in the way that we deal with "the lack of recognition of the parallel binary sonata [the Type 2 sonata] in nineteenth-century *Formenlehre* [treatises]," the danger being a "precipitous" impulse to grant "too much authority [to these writings] to dictate how we interpret the contemporaneous repertoire, and in ways that would go well beyond the type 2 paradigm" (2019, 107).

"Strong subordinate themes" in two overtures: *Le carnaval romain* and *Tannhäuser*

An extended aspect of Vande Moortele's argument points to the presence in some romantic overtures of what he calls "strong subordinate themes," which result not in the usual "turning inward" characteristic of many S themes but rather in a "turning outward" to produce an end-accented exposition.[33] In such works "it is the main theme [P] that is 'subordinate' to [S] . . . not the other way around" (2017, 154).[34] One certainly understands the rhetorical evidence behind this claim, though in this context the qualifier "subordinate" is used to refer to expressive impact, weight, or memorability, not to a specific action-zone space. But when his discussion extends to pieces where the Type 2 concept might be invoked, he conflates the two meanings. His prooftexts in this regard are two overtures: Berlioz's *Le carnaval romain* and Wagner's *Tannhäuser*, both of which feature emphatic, even explosive S themes.[35] Once again the argument is that such a strong, expositionally climactic S "eclipses or overrules the preceding main theme," becoming "the more fundamental entity, to which the main theme is [now] subservient" (2017, 148). Accordingly—and here is the key move—such a strong S now becomes capable of beginning what he wants to interpret as a recapitulation. And so when considering each of these two overtures,

> the "Type 2 sonata" is not the appropriate lens. The return of [such a strong] subordinate theme after the development is more than just the tonal resolution it would constitute in a "Type 2" reading. It is most emphatically a thematic return. . . . The subordinate theme appeared as the highpoint of the exposition, and it is the only theme that is capable of launching the recapitulation. In that sense, the strong subordinate theme assumes main-theme function . . . [one that] reacts in real time to the internal workings of the earlier portions of the piece. (190)

From Sonata Theory's point of view this line of argument is unpersuasive for a number of reasons, of which three can be cited here. First, in a Type 2 sonata the return of S to begin the tonal resolution is "most emphatically a thematic return" as well. There is no need to propose that by virtue of the strength of its thematic profile it can, in certain cases, not only assume "main-theme function" but also become "the only theme that is capable of launching the recapitulation." Second, the moment when Vande Moortele's readings start to claim that an S of any kind can start a "recapitulation" is the same moment when he turns his attention away from the sonata's rotational aspects. Within a Type 2 sonata S's correspondence measures and tonal resolution always appear in the latter portion of an ongoing rotation. Apart from wishing to endow a "strong S" with an *ad hoc*, counter-generic honorific status (that of supplanting P), there is no explanatory advantage to be gained by doing so. While "strong S" expositions need not lead to Type 2 sonatas, it is evident that the double-rotational format, where the second rotation normally consists of a P/TR developmental space and an S or S/C tonal resolution, is well-suited to pieces with a "strong" secondary theme. A more cogent argument would seek to pursue the happy synchronization of the Type 2 format-tradition with a specific kind of "romantic" expositional content, one that strives to make the S-led tonal resolution a particularly satisfying choice, as if it had been auto-generated by internal musical processes.

And finally, at least from the Sonata Theory perspective, his alternative readings of *Le carnaval romain* and the *Tannhäuser* overtures, while ingeniously argued, are less satisfactory than the more straightforward, rotational readings. Since at first glance—under the initial assumption that we are expecting a sonata form—the post-introduction, *Allegro vivace* portion of *Le carnaval romain* (starting at m. 78) provides us with a written-out, *repeated exposition*, something rarely if ever found in overtures (*EST*, 20), it is far and away the more eccentric of the two compositions. In an earlier discussion of Berlioz's overture, Stephen Rodgers had demonstrated that it is most profitably understood as an unusual strophic-song/Type-2 sonata hybrid, one that leans more toward the conventions of strophic song than toward those of the sonata (2009, 63–84). On that reading, the overture's "strong" S (from the sonata perspective) serves more generically to produce frenetic, strophe-ending refrains in V, V, and then I (mm. 128, 225, 344). The piece is elaborated not so much as a sonata as it is the presentation of three verse-refrain strophes in which the much altered third strophe's verse leads to a tonal resolution of the initially off-tonic refrain.[36] (An additional tonic-key statement of the refrain is found toward the end of what might be regarded as a quasi-"fourth-strophe" coda, m. 413.) Following a link from the second strophe to the third verse proper, that differing verse (mm. 300–44) is modulatory and cumulative, and it also brings back multiple treatments of the incipit of the love-song theme from the overture's introduction before bursting onto the refrain (which is then abruptly cut short at m. 356). All this makes for an impulsively carnivalesque, bizarre "sonata," but to the extent that one is dimly yet dialogically perceptible behind the more compelling strophic design, it would have to be regarded as a deformational Type 2—deformational because of the non-normative repeated "exposition" (strophes 1 and 2), which produces not the usual double rotation but rather an unusual triple-rotational offshoot.[37]

In the second case, the central, sonata portion of the *Tannhäuser* overture, the double-rotational structure could hardly be clearer. While one might at first think that it is a Type 2 sonata (and indeed, this is how *EST*, 364, lists it), it is probably better understood as an *expanded Type 1 sonata*, since the second rotation sets forth (violas, mm. 180–81) with a flickeringly brief, *tonic-key* (E-major) pointing toward the beginning of the exposition (mm. 81–82), whereas an off-tonic start for the second rotation would have suggested instead the Type 2 reading. On the basis of this E-major, P-based start, m. 180, strictly considered, is the launch of a *recapitulatory rotation*. In this case, though, the tonic-key reference is so evanescent—a mere two bars, and we should also note that the exposition's opening had also been tonally volatile, hardly stable on E major—that distinguishing between a Type 2 and an expanded Type 1 does nothing by way of analytical work. The central thing to notice is the double rotation of materials.

Let's pursue this larger point through an overview of a Sonata Theory reading of the overture's interior sonata.[38] Beginning in the tonic E major, Rotation 1 (P, TR, S), spans mm. 81 to around m. 172. Wagner built the "Venusberg/Bacchanal" P/TR block as a succession of four segments, beginning in mm. 81, 96, 112, and 124. The usual cadential separators are absent, though, with the result that by classical-prototype standards the point at which P ends and TR begins is blurred. Because m. 112 returns to the opening motive of m. 81 and m. 124 marks the onset of new material, I have regarded P as extending through the third segment. Thus: $P^{1.1a}$ (m. 81), $P^{1.2}$ (m. 96), $P^{1.1b}$ (m. 112), and the motivically different TR (m. 124), *un poco ritenuto*. In the context of this exposition, the S that follows is generated as the emphatic *end* of an expressive/narrative process kindled and rendered ever more incandescent throughout the expositional music that precedes it. The "strong" S in B major (V) soars forth at m. 142—Tannhäuser's song, "Dir töne Lob!" from Act 1, Scene 2—but instead of producing a V:PAC EEC, it disintegrates into frenzied sequences without producing an EEC.[39] Initially *fortissimo* but rapidly suffocated by a *diminuendo*, the disintegration proper serves as a link to the beginning of Rotation 2, m. 180.

The second rotation presents us with the same order of thematic materials, only with the seductive *Liebesbann* episode (mm. 195–219), interpolated between selections from P and the return of TR (m. 220 = m. 124), leading into the "strong" S as the E-major tonal resolution (mm. 242–73). Once again, the tonic-key opening of Rotation 2 gives us only the briefest of impressions that an expanded Type 1 format is the governing schema with which the piece is in dialogue. That opening, mm. 180–81, gives us both an ephemeral return to the tonic E and a return to P-motives (P$^{1.1a}$ in the violas, referential at pitch to mm. 81–82; P$^{1.2}$ in the winds, referential at pitch to m. 96). Immediately following these two bars, the music swerves into non-tonic, P-based directions (compare mm. 188–95 with mm. 92–95, the last bars of P$^{1.1a}$, but also with mm. 135–40, a touch of TR's preparation for S, though now fading away in this second rotation, *un poco ritenuto*) in order to settle into the *Liebesbann* episode (mm. 195–219). (Interlude-like developmental episodes are frequently encountered, particularly among illustrative or programmatic works.)

With m. 220 Wagner jolts the music back onto a close, transposed tracking of the exposition's TR. This means that m. 220 is the *crux*, the point at which a recapitulatory rotation (or a Type 2 sonata's second rotation, were this sonata an unequivocal example of one) locks onto correspondence measures with the exposition's model. And with the crux the thematic aspect of the second rotation is now back on track. The literal correspondence measures last, initially, for 10 bars: mm. 220–29 = mm. 124–33, only down a fourth, not the expected fifth. In order to regain the tonic, a tonal adjustment will have to be made. That adjustment occurs in mm. 230–c. 237, a set of intensified *post-crux alterations* that steer this sequentially mounting music to the forcefully anticipatory, proper dominant, the *forte* V$^{[9]}$ of E, m. 237. Mm. 235–37 are increasingly referential to mm. 134–36, and with m. 238 we rejoin correspondence measures for three bars: mm. 238–40 = mm. 137–39, now transposed to the proper pitch level. M. 241, another post-crux alteration, compresses mm. 140–41 into a single, maximally powerful dominant push onto the strong downbeat of S, m. 242, where correspondence bars once again resume, now at some length. Concluding Rotation 2, this now-tonic S produces the ESC on the downbeat of m. 273, which simultaneously ignites the manic onset of the coda, *molto vivace*, and the return to P materials—here P$^{1.2}$, suggesting the beginning of a third rotation, as so often in codas.[40]

Apart from the completion of the double-rotational-sonata layout preceding the *molto vivace* at m. 273, we might recall that *più mosso* codas were anything but uncommon in the operatic repertory of the time, particularly, though not exclusively, as add-on concluding sections in Italian or French solo pieces or rapid-fire ensembles, typically to end a scene or to bring down the curtain with maximum vigor. Such a freshly energized, *più mosso* coda sometimes made its way into overtures as well, as at the ends of Rossini's overtures to *Il barbiere di Siviglia* and *La gazza ladra*, and Wagner himself had provided one to dig the spurs into the conclusion of the *Rienzi* overture.

Finally, a double-rotation-plus-coda reading can also be supported by an appeal to Liszt's 1849 description of the *Tannhäuser* overture. At one point, addressing the overture as a whole, Liszt tells us that it should not be regarded as a *poëme symphonique*, since it "conforms more to the rules of classic form [*la coupe classique*]" and consequently displays a "perfect logic in the *exposition, développement*, and *dénouement* of [its] propositions."[41] Was Liszt's *dénouement* the equivalent of a Type 3 "recapitulation"? Not necessarily. He may well have been referring instead to the block-like, near-literalness of S's transposed reprise, mm. 242–72, that marks the E-major tonal resolution. Along these lines, it is worth noting that he recognizes the preceding, post-episodic shift into m. 220 (Sonata Theory's return of TR) as joining the same "transition"—*la phrase de transition*—that we had heard before in the exposition, and with the tonic-key arrival of S he indicates nothing about that return to suggest that it is the beginning of a new, recapitulatory section.[42] Nor do we hear anything from Liszt about either any presumed "reversed recapitulation" or any kind of reversal in the ordering of the exposition's thematic succession. On the contrary, his description may be folded comfortably into a double-rotational reading of the sonata structure.

Most important to our discussion, immediately following his description of the return of S, Liszt identifies the m. 273 return of P material ($P^{1.2}$, *molto vivace*) as the start of the coda: "the coda takes up once again the principal themes [*dessins*] of the beginning of the Allegro and [soon] brings them to the highest point of frenzy, [and] to a chromatic descent over the pedal on B [m. 296]."[43] While Liszt of course knew nothing of Sonata Theory's twenty-first-century term, "expanded Type 1" (or its double-rotational sibling, the "Type 2"), his identification of what he was hearing as a coda suggests that that is precisely what he was describing. Quite differently from A. B. Marx's comments on Mozart's overture to *La clemenza di Tito*, Liszt's remarks on the *Tannhäuser* overture help to confirm the potential, at least in some professional quarters, for a mid-nineteenth-century awareness of the double-rotational sonata format with back-references to P-material as coda.

12

Brahms, Symphony No. 1 in C Minor, op. 68/iv, finale (Adagio; Allegro non troppo, ma con brio)

In the several Sonata Theory seminars that I have led, as with our journey through this book, most of our time is spent with the music of Mozart, Haydn, Beethoven, and, toward the end, Schubert. This is because the clearest introduction to Sonata Theory is that which seeks both to codify the "norms, types, and deformations" of the late-eighteenth-century *centering* of the principles of Austro-Germanic sonata-making, at least as historically construed in the hands of its most influential composers, and to provide a suitable entry into the often dramatically eccentric, early-nineteenth-century music of Beethoven and Schubert, where striking twists away from the older defaults become more frequent. In every seminar, though, the question of the theory's relevance to even later sonata repertories inevitably emerges.

As a flexible, conceptual system, Sonata Theory is by no means meant to apply only to sonata composition before, say, 1820 or 1830. (On the contrary, back in the 1990s what was soon to grow into the Sonata Theory project began with an inquiry into recurring patterns of what I was calling *sonata deformation* in nineteenth- and early-twentieth-century composition.)[1] For that reason, in each of my seminars I have always concluded with a few close looks at later-nineteenth- or early-twentieth-century late-romantic or early-modernist works. Common choices have included: the first and second movements of Brahms's Second Symphony; Tchaikovsky's *Romeo and Juliet* and the first movement of his Sixth Symphony; the outer movements of Mahler's Second Symphony; and the outer movements of Rachmaninoff's Second Piano Concerto.[2] In this final chapter we'll look at the concluding movement of Brahms's First Symphony, chosen in part because of its lucid exemplification of the expanded Type 1 sonata. The main Sonata Theory questions at hand are: which aspects of the theory still hold?; what new challenges and strategies can we expect to find in these later works?; which older norms have withered away or been sidelined in favor of new and different structural possibilities? Before entering this massive finale—filled to the brim with connotative intricacy—let's set the stage properly.

A Sonata Theory Handbook. James Hepokoski, Oxford University Press (2021). © Oxford University Press.
DOI: 10.1093/oso/9780197536810.003.0012.

Sonata Theory and "romantic" sonata form

As we advance the clock by a half-century for our encounter with Brahms, we find ourselves in a different musical world from the one where we've been. The 1870s were more complex times, increasingly urban and fraught with social, political, cultural, technological, and musical contexts that Haydn, Mozart, Beethoven, Schubert, and their contemporaries could scarcely have imagined. Fortified by its crystallizing canon of consecrated masterworks with a nearly deified Beethoven at its center, this music's tradition was on its way to becoming an administered business. Now in the process of consolidation and furthering its interests in a competitive world of alternatives, the "institution of art music" promoted and sustained large swaths of repertory, some reverentially old, some aspiringly new, in a bureaucratized network of mutually supportive enterprises.[3] These include civic opera houses, orchestras, conservatories, societies, publishing houses, academic textbooks, journalistic commentaries and reviews, and biographical and critical-edition projects. All of this was bolstered by the emergence of the university-centered discipline that would come to be called *Musikwissenschaft* ("musicology")[4]—not to mention the spread of the high-prestige art-music tradition to the national peripheries surrounding Western Europe. Such cultural shifts have deep implications both for the practice of musical composition and for what we should bring to the table in our encounters with it.

We are concerned here with how Sonata Theory's way of thinking retains its utility when adapted to deal with romantic or early-modern repertory. By the last two-thirds of the nineteenth century the sonata-form tradition had become an arena of change, teeming with the potential for individualized adaptations. It admitted far more flexibility and diversity of structure, key choice, and thematic transformation than had been the case with the preceding decades' composers. (Already by 1839 young Schumann had suspected that tradition to be in danger of having "run its course.")[5] Nonetheless, while past sonata practices were still honored—and drilled into budding musicians in conservatory and university training—composers, in varying degrees, felt less constrained by the classical-era defaults. Not a few regarded them as formalistic shackles from which to be freed.

Particularly in the hands of flamboyantly progressive composers (of whom Brahms was not one), the effect of this was to encourage a much broader range of possibilities for sonata-form-oriented works. By midcentury both the concept of sonata form and a number of its classical-era conventions had been unraveling under a number of loosenings, often in the service of an illustrative program or the search for heightened sonic drama, coupled with a ready-to-hand supply of era-appropriate topical norms and standardized expressive postures. Compositional choices that would have been experienced as strikingly deviant in the classical era (Sonata Theory's "deformations") could become familiar defaults, menu-available sonata-choices, in the post-Beethovenian world, whose composers were exploring new kinds of sonata treatments and deformations—which in turn could become flexible models offering new ideas for subsequent compositions. What we are dealing with is an ongoing feedback loop within an increasingly self-referential, internally ramified, and "autopoietic" cultural subsystem.[6]

The Sonata Theory approach is aware that nineteenth-century works, especially as we advance further into that century, were not bound by all of the same traditions and/or constraints that had been more or less intact (though flexibly so) in the high-galant era of Haydn, Mozart, and their contemporaries. Nor does the elementary task of observing that this or that nineteenth-century work deviates markedly from the norms systematized in *EST* for an earlier, albeit highly influential era undercut the conceptual underpinnings of the method. On the contrary, a crucial aspect of its application to later works is a heightened awareness that mid- and late-nineteenth-century sonatas were cultivating new norms that encouraged deviations from those of the classical tradition in striking ways. Many generalized aspects of the sonata-form tradition remained, while some of its specifics fell away or were overridden by other, more idiosyncratic options.

One advantage of classical-era Sonata Theory is that it is readily updatable when it looks at works from later decades. Built into the method is the expectation that several of the localized procedures, styles, and aesthetic tones that drove normative compositional practice at or before the turn of the nineteenth century would be differently handled by later composers working under differing cultural and institutional conditions. Applying the Sonata Theory "filter" to them is a productive way to ferret out those differences in order to set them in high relief. What is new, transgressive, or experimental in these later works has its impact maximized when read against the backdrop of the classical tradition deployed as a persistent, serviceable interpretive code, even though several of those once-vigorous norms, merely stale if perpetuated as reflex, academic conventions, were no longer binding in current practice. Given the honorific burden of the still-present past, newly composed works implicitly relied on the foil of historically generic orthodoxies—fundamental knowledge within the field—in contrast with which their own imaginative singularities could be perceived as both building upon and boldly diverging from.[7]

This position has proven to be controversial in some quarters, and at the time of this writing a pressing question is emerging within the new *Formenlehre* with ever-greater urgency: just how relevant is "sonata form," much less the principles of Sonata Theory as laid out in the *Elements* (or those of its complement, form-functional theory, as laid out in Caplin's *Classical Form*), in approaching such works? Particularly in extreme cases the dazzling variety of later-nineteenth-century sonata realizations can tempt us to suppose that each example is better regarded as unique or self-generating—that by the century's middle and end the sonata tradition had lost so much of its force that appeals to central generic aspects of the classical-form conventions should no longer be relevant to their analysis.

To emphasize singularity to this extent would be to move toward the philosophical position of nominalism, that is, toward the idea that only individual realizations exist as such—this or that work construed as an *unicum*—as opposed to the appeal to categories or concepts (like era-appropriate adaptations of Sonata Theory) that seek conceptually to organize and explicate the historical trends and tendencies still perceptible in their composition.[8] While acknowledging that opinions on this will differ, Sonata Theory maintains that to move too far in this direction gives up too much that is analytically and hermeneutically productive in coming to an understanding of many of these *unica*. In mid- and later-nineteenth-century sonata-form-oriented works some aspects of once-normative composition become increasingly open to substantial modification, while others do not.

What matters in the application of Sonata Theory to such works is historically informed nuance. While some compositional procedures in these later works can be described as deformational, at least from the culturally constrained Mozartian point of view, some of those procedures became quite common in the later era and culture for which they were written.[9] To regard these new and recurring features as *sonata deformations*, sortable into recognizable *sonata-deformation families* that organize and group them conceptually, is largely a matter of convenience—a shorthand way of registering their divergences from the touchstones of earlier practice, which is being kept heuristically in mind as a conceptual backdrop. They are deformational, that is, not necessarily in themselves or with regard to the altered norms of their era but rather in comparison with the once-centered but now enervated classical tradition. Most important: that tradition was by no means forgotten. On the contrary, it was the mainstay of the concert and recital tradition perpetuated and celebrated repeatedly in the concert hall and salon—the classical canon—performed cheek to jowl with challenging new works. It was also the tradition passed down in compositional training as community-shared historical knowledge. The honored past was part of that present's living history. "Classical" models and precedents were omnipresent before one's eyes and ears.

While *EST* does focus on the inherited (and flexible) norms at work in the Haydn–Mozart–(early) Beethoven era—the historical *centering phase* of sonata practice—an essential aspect of Sonata Theory is its ability to perceive and accommodate change in compositions from later eras. Perceiving change is possible only when one grasps which earlier norm has been overridden or creatively modified. It is no surprise to find mid- and later-nineteenth-century works with blurred (but not abandoned) action-zone boundaries, blurred or harmonically adventurous medial-caesura allusions, new ways of ending TR and introducing S, *ad hoc*, sometimes highly chromatic treatments of keys, substantially recrafted recapitulations, and the like. To observe these divergences is not to destabilize the relevance of Sonata Theory to these works. On the contrary, it is to affirm it as an analytical standpoint that enables us to recognize these moments of difference as difference and then to confront them on updated and appropriate terms. That is what renders the concept of *dialogic form* still relevant and hermeneutically productive in this era.

When approaching a later sonata-form work, a Sonata Theory reading continues to be attentive to how its most central concerns are handled. What most obviously persists of this conceptual approach in those readings are its broader, more generalized underpinnings:

- the principle of dialogic form, now expanding in this "historicist" era of the solidification of the art-music canon to include the work's dialogues with and allusions to not only older (and current) sonata traditions but also to specific moments of strongly valenced individual pieces of music, whether they be past ones reverentially consecrated by the institution of art music or newer ones that are thought to be profitable in displaying one's allegiance to aesthetically partisan, ideological factions;
- the presence of expositional action zones—the now highly individualized ways in which P TR' S / C, those traditional CONTAINERS, can be filled—and their trajectories toward once-generically-normative cadences (though the once-traditional, localized norms for MC and S-key and thematic treatment are often much altered, and recapitulatory practice can be quite free);
- the attainment or non-attainment of significant cadential points, most notably the EEC and ESC within sonata space (the distinction between the stagings of tonally successful and failed sonatas);
- the distinction between two-part and continuous expositions;
- the rotational principle, which remains ever-strong, often decisive;
- the realizations or adaptations of the varying sonata types (Types 1 through 5);
- and the potent expressive/narrative import of the minor-major binary.

Backdrop

But again, to bring us back to the case at hand, Brahms was by no means one of the extreme cases. In the polemically divided musical world of the 1860s and 1870s, the Brahms/Clara Schumann circle had taken up the banner of the curatorial or "absolute-music" faction, epitomized by the more abstract chamber music of the classical and early-romantic heritage. The Brahmsians pitted themselves against the showy virtuosity of the innovators: Liszt, Wagner, and their partisans. In the balance, each side believed, was nothing less than the historically appropriate continuation of the Austro-Germanic tradition—and ultimately its survival.

The story of Brahms's agonizing over the composition of a symphony from the early 1860s through the First Symphony's premiere, in Karlsruhe, on November 4, 1876, is a familiar one, and it need not detain us here. (He composed most of the work, and certainly its finale, in the last two years, while the first movement, though without its introduction, had been fully drafted by June 1862.) The most provocative aspect of it, Brahms's postcard birthday greeting to Clara Schumann from Switzerland on September 12, 1868, bearing a texted version of what would become the melody of the horn-call from the finale's introduction, will be dealt with in the analysis that follows.

As Brodbeck put it in his monograph on the work, the key point is that "there can be little doubt that as a symphonist Brahms remained encumbered by the imposing example of Beethoven" (1997, 11). And every commentator on the First cites Brahms's October 1871 remark to the conductor Hermann Levi in Karlsruhe: "I will never compose a symphony! You have no idea how it feels to one of us when he continually hears behind him such a giant." Nor was this a purely individual matter. Multiplying the strain was the broader problem of the viability of the Austro-Germanic symphony after Beethoven's death in 1827, and above all after the game-changing monumentality and innovations of his Ninth. By the 1840s, 1850s, and 1860s the thought had arisen that the symphony itself, as an instrumental genre of "pure music," had been exhausted. Indeed, in *Opera and Drama* (1851), as Dahlhaus reminds us, "Wagner [had] pronounced the death of the symphony, viewing the post-Beethovenian efforts as a mere epilogue with nothing substantially new to say" (1989, 265). It was during the 1850s that the prestige of the symphony qua "absolute music" was being supplanted by that of such progressive alternatives as the Lisztian symphonic poem and program symphony and the Wagnerian music drama.

Despite some important attempts by Mendelssohn and Schumann, starting in the early 1840s, to recharge the genre, the symphony had entered a midcentury fallow period that would last more than two dozen years. The posthumous publication of symphonies by Mendelssohn and Schubert in the 1860s only underscored the issue. Table 12.1 dates the appearances of historically durable symphonies in Austria and Germany between 1839 and 1876. I have included Bruch's two from 1868 and 1870 since they were likely spurs to Brahms's work, as Frisch suggests (1996, 20–25). And while I have included the premieres of early, then still unpublished versions of Bruckner's first two symphonies—the First in Linz, 1868, the Second in Vienna,

Table 12.1 Appearances of Major Austro-Germanic Symphonies, 1839–76

Year	Symphony
1839	Discovery and performance of Schubert's C Major Symphony (No. 9, "Great")
1840	Mendelssohn, "Symphony No. 2, '*Lobgesang*'"
1841	Schumann, Symphony No. 1 ("Spring") and the first version of what would become Symphony No. 4
1842	Mendelssohn, Symphony No. 3 ("Scottish")
1846–51	Schumann, Symphonies 2, 3, and 4
1851	Posthumous publication of Mendelssohn, Symphony No. 4 ("Italian")
1865–67	Premiere and publication of Schubert, Symphony No. 8 ("Unfinished")
1868	Publication of Mendelssohn, Symphony No. 5 ("Reformation")
1868	Premiere of Bruckner, Symphony No. 1
1868–70	Bruch, Symphonies 1 and 2
1873	Premiere of Bruckner, Symphony No. 2 (performance of revision, 1876)
1876	Brahms, Symphony No. 1

1873—it's difficult to assess the degree to which their single, isolated performances were yet capable of producing a lasting imprint on the resuscitation of the symphony. That would happen only in the later 1870s and 1880s, triggering the politically heated battles between the Brahmsians and the Brucknerians.[10]

To be sure, in this trough a number of other symphonies continued to be produced and commented upon. Frisch tabulates dozens of them composed "in the Austro-German sphere" from 1851 to 1877 ("the period between Schumann's Third and [the publication of] Brahms's First"), several with programmatic or illustrative tinges, by Gade, Spohr, Anton Rubinstein, Raff, Svendsen, Reinecke, and others (Frisch 1996, 7–10). While these now-little-known works were certainly well composed and doubtless contain much of interest to today's historians, they were destined not to make a lasting historical mark. Brodbeck's 2013 discussion of these midcentury symphonies concludes that while they did indeed represent a still-breathing tradition, many of them had been composed under "aesthetic demands" that had been "reduced," yielding to "a concept of the genre as *mittlere Musik* (music of an intermediary *niveau*)" and responding to comfortable "market demands" and "simpler pleasures" in an enterprise in which "originality was not essential" (73).

For a composer of Brahms's reputation to undertake the composition of a symphony was no small matter. Especially in the context of Wagner's and Liszt's rising statures, this was a make-or-break prospect. Doing nothing could be read as a resigned gesture of defeat. If a symphony by Brahms were to be worth anything at all, it would have to be a music-historical event, monumental in scope and effect. It would have to be something that one could proudly hold up to the unsurpassable Beethoven standard. It would have to be an act of reclamation, a bid to revitalize the idea of the "great symphony" as a viable genre for current, modernizing times.

To raise the stakes further, the season of the First's initial performances, November and December 1876 (it would be published, after a few more revisions, in October of the next year), witnessed the squaring-off of the two reigning musical ideologies of the era. On the one side was Brahms and—finally—his hyper-earnest C-minor symphony, whose mere appearance and obvious success served as a manifesto by example and played a prominent role in ushering in what Dahlhaus assessed as "the second age of the symphony," in which that genre, certainly by the 1870s and 1880s, "had regained its apparently long-lost position in the minds of audiences and composers alike" (1989, 265). On the other side, and to great fanfare and publicity, Wagner's Festspielhaus in Bayreuth had opened just three months earlier, in August 1876, with an inaugural performance of Beethoven's Ninth Symphony, followed by the first complete public performance of all four music dramas of *Der Ring des Nibelungen*. The two sides' aesthetic clash could hardly be more stark.

While by no means staid or structurally unadventurous, Brahms's works often have an autumnal aura about them. Yet that retrospective glow was in sync with the twilight ethos of much of the post-1870 Viennese world. Many of his pieces are also charged with a stern sense of duty, standing firm as proud holdouts against inevitably changing fashions. With Brahms we find a purposeful display of technical madeness, to be staged and received within the context of a once-magnificent tradition now past its prime: the once-grand tide now at ebb. Moreover, Brahms frequently intermixes his networks of ever-ramifying motives with a conspicuous density of counterpoint. (His progressive critics disparaged such displays as fussily academic.) Agawu sums up the complexity of Brahms's musical language nicely. It may be traced to a "triple heritage: the . . . Viennese classical school; a contemporary 'romantic' sensibility; and an archaising or perhaps 'archaeological' manner" (1995, 135).

Again and again Brahms produced music that was "remembering," and often alluding to, past greatness as he saw it: the achievements of past Austro-Germanic master composers, of whom he surely regarded himself not only as the legitimate heir but also as one of the last links in the historical chain. As Brinkmann notes, "the earliest reactions of Brahms's contemporaries to his First Symphony already underlined the point that its internal musical logic reflected a 'course of ideas' (Robert Schumann's 'Ideengang'), whose origins could, furthermore, be defined in terms of the history of the genre" (1995, 33). Tracing a work's *Ideengang* and interpreting some of its connotative implications is a primary aim of Sonata Theory. As might be expected, it will be a central point of the analysis of the First's finale that follows.

Descriptions of the finale's music have tended to concentrate on one or both of two features: (1) the interrelatedness of the themes and thematic figures, seeking to demonstrate the movement's motivic economy and hence "unity" (an analytical practice reflecting the Schoenberg-school concern with developing variation, the process of motivic growth from a few basic intervallic shapes [*Grundgestalten*] not only within the movement but also reaching back to earlier movements); and/or (2) possible thematic allusions to musical moments within historically prior works, ranging from Bach to Beethoven to Schubert to Schumann to Bruch (as noted generally in Brahms, and problematized in Knapp 1997, 81–141). While the reading in this chapter will deal with some of those aspects, though perhaps not as single-mindedly as others have treated them, my larger concern is to demonstrate the continued value of the Sonata Theory approach to such a work.

The finale of Brahms's First Symphony—and the symphony as a whole, for that matter—is rich in potential but underdetermined connotative implications, not a few of which point to things outside the piece itself. Chief among these signifiers are: the introduction's important horn call (m. 30), with its demonstrable Clara-Schumann-greeting associations; and the obviously intentional similarity of the sonata's hymnic P idea (m. 62) to the "Ode to Joy" finale theme of Beethoven's Ninth Symphony—and perhaps to other themes as well. Readings of these two ideas have ranged widely over a number of possibilities: the dialectic of "nature" and "history" (Brinkmann 1995, 33–53); the conclusion of a symphony that as a whole traces out "a *Bildungsgeschichte* . . . a playing out of the Christian drama of suffering and redemption [though] in ordinary [secular] human experience" (Brodbeck 1997, 78);

the C-minor-to-C-major grappling with Beethoven's Fifth Symphony; dialogues with the rising tide of Austro-Germanic nationalism; and others.

What follows is only one of several viable readings for this polysemous work, though it is one for which Sonata Theory is especially suited. Its larger context: I want to read the whole of Brahms's First Symphony as a statement about itself as a historical achievement. The signifying gestures and musical processes of the symphony, and certainly those of its monumental concluding movement, point toward themselves or, what is much the same, to Brahms as the agent setting them into motion. The finale's successive events thematize the strain and anxiety of their own making and then, in its jubilant coda, celebrate the labor of having accomplished the Herculean task. From this perspective the finale is about the weighty issues surrounding the writing of a symphony in the mid-1870s; about the conceptual effort required, in alliance with the Clara-Schumann circle of traditionalists, to fulfill this mission of revitalizing a waning Austro-Germanic heritage; and about the composer's self-doubting struggles to bring this work into life, which had started with the high-stress, pounding heartbeats of the first movement's opening bars ("dare one even *try* to do this"?). In this reading the master trope of the finale is: at this deep-eleventh hour of the genre's history, is it truly possible to bring this symphony to a successful completion?

The finale: structure and framing

Because this finale is not a Type 3 sonata, some commentators have misconstrued its overall form, and a few have proceeded to ground dubious hermeneutic readings on that analysis.[11] From the Sonata Theory point of view its overall format is clear. Like the finale of Brahms's C-minor Quartet, op. 51 no. 1, and his *Tragic* Overture (and like the finale of Schubert's C-major String Quintet), the First Symphony's finale is an *expanded Type 1 sonata*: a non-repeated exposition followed immediately by a recapitulatory rotation (starting with P in the tonic) that before long swells out into substantial developmental activity, then rejoins correspondence measures around S, now in the tonic, to accomplish the sonata's tonal resolution.[12] While retaining the exposition's rotational order, Brahms expands the recapitulation's pre-MC zones, P and TR, to create a developmental "bulge" before resuming the post-MC process of tonal resolution (*EST*, 349–50). Because of this bulge the recapitulatory rotation occupies many more bars than does its expositional model. As noted near the end of the previous chapter, the double-rotational procedure resembles that of a Type 2 sonata, with this difference: following the exposition, an expanded Type 1 will immediately re-sound P in the tonic (in the manner of recapitulation), while a Type 2 presents P, or an episodic substitute for it, in a non-tonic key.

But Brahms adds another important structural feature to this finale: he encases its expanded Type 1 sonata within a heavy-duty *introduction-coda frame*.[13] *Elements of Sonata Theory* (*EST*, 304–5) discusses the introduction-coda frame as a generic option and provides a number of examples from the late eighteenth century onward, noting along the way that "the framing introduction-coda combination becomes more common in the later decades of the nineteenth century."

> Whenever we find an introduction-coda frame the interior sonata space seems subordinated to the outward container. The introduction and coda represent the higher reality, under whose more immediate mode of existence—or under whose embracing auspices—the sonata form proper is laid out as a contingent process, a demonstration of an artifice that unfolds only under the authority of the prior existence of the frame. Metaphors of narrativity are not inevitably implied—the external narrator and the tale told—but in some cases they can spring to mind and appear to be hermeneutically relevant. (305)

In Brahms's finale the introduction and coda are of substantial proportions and share important, memorable materials. It is their music that, first, establishes the conditions under which we are to grasp the interior sonata and, then—after the sonata's tonally successful but modally failed resolution (a positive C-major sonata ending in a negative C minor)—brings the movement to a climactically brilliant C-major close. In addition, the incipit of the introduction's semiotically charged horn call is inserted into each of the two rotations' interstices (preceding and preparing S), perhaps as reflective reminders, perhaps as sonata-renewing impulses to keep the process going. In the reading presented here the introduction and coda convey the movement's import more vividly than does the internal sonata. This will be the point of view in the analytical discussion that follows.

Introduction (mm. 1–60)

Section 1: Adagio, C minor (mm. 1–29)

Is there a more heavy-hearted sigh in music than that sounded in the opening three measures of this finale? In the octave-doubled bass, mm. 1–2, the ground sinks from under one's feet, $\hat{8}$-$\hat{7}$-$\hat{6}$-$\hat{5}$ in C minor—that fatalistic tetrachord, descending, *crescendo*, onto the ready-and-waiting dominant pitch with a portentous *forte-piano* accent. Far above, in mm. 2–3, with the first violins in the lead, doubled in lower octaves by the second violins and first horn, a melodic push swells to leap a fifth upward, from C_6 to G_6 with a *fortepiano* pang. The weary exhale traces out a minor-mode melodic line, $(\hat{1}$-$)$ $\hat{5}$-$\sharp\hat{4}$-$\hat{5}$-$\hat{3}$-$\hat{2}$—a permutation of the traditional pathotype figure's intervals (see chapter 8, figure 8.1), here reckoned around $\hat{5}$. At the same time, a third, chromatic line of middle-register, sinuous winds, mostly in thirds, curls back into itself with shriveling anxiety. Notice that the m. 2 chord, on the weighty *fortepiano* downbeat, is not the expected $^5_3$ or $^6_4$ but an electrifying $E\flat^6_3$, perhaps pointing toward a similar harmonic jolt in m. 9 of Haydn's "Representation of Chaos" (*The Creation*), and here setting off a string of chromatic chords before settling on V of C minor at the end of m. 3.

We are thus cycled back to the C-minor stress of the symphony's global and modal tonic. As Brinkmann put it, "at its commencement the finale . . . takes up the initial conflict of the entire symphony, clearly forming an arch with the first movement" (1995, 35). We recall, though, that the first movement (with C-minor ESC in m. 458) had at its very end relaxed its iron grip, at the close of the *Meno Allegro* final limb of its coda, in order to release into a C-major conclusion. The first movement's Picardy ending had conveyed a glimmer of hope that in the finale we might be led into the modal reversal of the symphony's C minor into C major. That's the tonal/modal issue at stake in this finale. Beginning it with such C-minor earnestness places it squarely in front of us.

But much more is also implicit in these opening three bars. As numerous commentators have been quick to point out, the opening bars' resolute sigh is simultaneously the birth of the creative impulses that will be given the duty of bringing this symphony to its end: a casting-up of motivic figures, a wellspring-burst of particles, from which much of what follows is to be assembled. The bass's descending tetrachord will reappear as a *basso ostinato* figure cycled a dozen times, 11 of them in major, at the beginning of S (S$^{1.1}$, mm. 118–32). The six-note rhythmic and melodic line above it, turned into C major, will become the head-motive of P (mm. 62–63, where the scale degrees will then be $\hat{5}$-$\hat{8}$-$\hat{7}$-$\hat{8}$-$\hat{6}$-$\hat{5}$). And the curling wind-line foreshadows any number of similarly twisting figures in the subsequent sonata (for instance, the violins' lines at mm. 106–10, to be labeled TR$^{1.2}$).

One of the broader conventions at work in this opening is what Sonata Theory calls the *generative introduction*, the type that "spawns, nurtures, or otherwise generates" the basic material of the sonata proper, most often its P theme (*EST*, 303). Particularly in some nineteenth-century works—and the introductions to both the first movement and the finale of this symphony are illustrations of it—one connotation of this convention can be to imply that the pre-sonata material can be read as a "representation of the 'narrator' . . . or the animating force . . . of the tale told in the sonata" (*EST*, 304). Such introductory material can invite a reading that points back to the composer in the act of composition, weighing problems, alternatives, and potential choices. The most familiar examples are from Beethoven, in the theme-searching introductions to the finales of the *Hammerklavier* Sonata and the Ninth Symphony, though I would extend the workshop-brooding image to the openings of the String Quartets op. 127, 132, and 130 as well. I read Brahms's introduction similarly: the composer's self-projection as he faces the gravity of this challenge, in solidarity with his aesthetic supporters at this point in the tradition's history: "Once more unto the breach, dear friends, once more; / Or close the wall up with our [symphonic] dead."

Proceeding through the remainder of the introduction's first section, mm. 1–29, is relatively straightforward. A fading reverberation of the preceding sigh sounds over the dominant in mm. 4–5, *diminuendo*, while the dynamically and harmonically erratic pizzicatos of mm. 6–12 suggest a fearful knitting-together of the composer's will, a nervous prodding-forward that rushes ahead, *stringendo*, but hits a brick wall of doubt—a *pizzicato-fortissimo* Neapolitan sixth on the downbeat of m. 12—and draws back at once. Mm. 1–12 lay out the first of the three subrotations that will occupy mm. 1–29, the C-minor first half of the introduction. A second subrotation follows in mm. 12–19. In mm. 12–15 its rescored and varied return to the opening sigh and *diminuendo* reverberation, *a tempo*, is both a thematic rebeginning and a continuation. It leads to a varied revisiting of the *stringendo* pizzicatos, this time mounting to the "stuck" pitches of a remote F♭ major triad (mm. 18–19).

With the third subrotation (mm. 20–29) the composer's will to stream ahead is more determined. In m. 20 the preceding bar's F♭ is respelled as E (at first suggesting V of a) to launch a sweeping, *arco* bass figure, and the descending third above, the oboe's E♮$_5$-D$_5$-C$_5$, foreshadows the first three pitches of the horn-call-to come (m. 30). By m. 22 we return to C minor (initially with V in the bass), where a melodic line in the winds, mm. 22–23, sounds an anticipation of the theme to be heard in the second part of the exposition (S$^{1.4}$, m. 148). Retrospectively, we realize that mm. 1–29 lay out fragmentary ideas of themes, and in roughly the same order, that will become fully developed expositional actors in their own right. Thus we have anticipations of P (mm. 1–2, 13–14), TR$^{1.2}$ (mm. 2–3, 4–5, the twisting dyads), S$^{1.1}$ (mm. 1–2, bass), and S$^{1.4}$ (m. 22): embryonic ideas flashing in the composer's mind. The introduction can be considered proto-rotational, a Rotation 0, perhaps, preceding the exposition's role as the normative Rotation 1.

By m. 24 the sweeping lines fracture into worrisome diminished-seventh indecision, shot through with erratic *forte* and *piano* dynamics. The crisis mounts to the upper-voice gasping figures in mm. 27–28—full panic—and the *sforzando*-battered diminished sevenths break off abruptly with the shattering timpani roll begun *fortissimo* in m. 28: *timor et tremor*. By this point Brahms has given us three anxiety-ridden attempts, three subrotations, to get started in this finale but has broken off each try. In m. 28 his compositional will collapses for a third time, stymied in an inescapable C minor.

And yet . . .

. . . dovetailed with the moment of deepest alarm, mm. 28–29, the bass line again starts its initiating descending tetrachord, C-B♭-A-A♭, and locks onto G in m. 30, suggesting that yet another subrotation has already begun. This subrotation will be transformative, giving the impression of entering into the discourse from somewhere else.[14] With the arrival of that bass G (a tremblingly expectant V$_4^6$ of C *major*) everything changes. "A moment's darkness and terror," writes Tovey, "and then day breaks" (1981, 196).

Section 2: Più andante, C major (mm. 30–61)—dedication emblem and consecration

The reversal of perspective at m. 30 could not be more striking. It operates on multiple levels: modal, textural, rhythmic, dynamic, expressive, and connotative. So impressive is the moment that one is compelled to reach for metaphors adequate to describe it. The preceding bars' frenetic anxiety—their gasping, rhythmic compression and body-rattling timpani roll—releases into a maximally contrasting space, *più andante*, turning a corner to open onto an expansive vista. In an epiphany of C-major clarification, deep, fresh breaths of cool air rush in. Tovey once more: "the horns give out a grand melody that peals through the tremolo of muted violins like deep bells among glowing clouds" (1981, 196). Similarly, Brinkmann: "pure C major appears in the noble sound of the trombones, which are heard for the first time in the symphony at this point, along with string tremoli, the whole passage pianissimo—a completely new configuration, a previously unheard tone which, being so out of the ordinary, encases the central event of this focus of attraction: the great 'alphorn' call on the first horn" (1995, 36), sounded over shimmering strings, now muted and *pianissimo*. How we read this impressive moment, along with the introduction's C-major section 2 as a whole (mm. 30–61) conditions our understanding of all that follows.

Any reading of it must start with Brahms's September 12, 1868, postcard from Switzerland, a birthday greeting sent to Clara Schumann that, along with an underlaid text, contained the melody that was later to be written into mm. 30–38 of this introduction,: "Also blus das Alphorn heut: 'Hoch auf'm Berg, tief im Thal, grüß' ich dich viel tausend mal'" ("Thus blew the alphorn today: 'High on the mountain, deep in the valley, I greet you many thousands of times.'") When this alphorn theme resurfaced in the symphony, its implications would not have been lost on Clara Schumann. In its initial performances, long before Brahms's postcard became publicly known, it would have been a private, even intimate communication addressed to her. (The well-known personal and professional close relationship between Brahms and Clara Schumann need not be rehearsed here.) Now knowing the theme's genesis, though, alters our grasp of its potential significance.

The alphorn theme carries a number of connotations. Obvious to most commentators is its allusion to the *plein-air* sound of an alphorn echoing through the vast mountains: an escape from the artificial confines of a merely urban genre—standard symphonic practice—into a romanticized, folklike evocation of a healthy, uncorrupted nature, in the sense of the Schillerian naïve, momentarily reanimated as a reinvigorating agent. Still another potential connotation—perhaps fortuitous—is suggested by what Tovey noted, with some skepticism, as the British late-nineteenth-century penchant for hearing the similarity of the alphorn theme's first seven notes to the bell chimes of the "Westminster Quarters" ["Westminster Chimes"], a connection that on first glance seems implausible, although, as I'll note later, the topic of bells might be suggested in another of the movement's themes.[15]

That such an alphorn image was historically addressed to Clara Schumann steers it in an additional direction, especially when linked contextually both with the enervated state of the Austro-Germanic symphony in the 1860s and 1870s and with Brahms's own apprehension about trying to produce one at all. Under these lights, the symphonic reanimation of the 1868 Clara-greeting whisks away C minor and all that it represents. As envisioned here, that reanimation makes C major possible and with it the continuation and completion of the finale.

This alphorn music can be construed as a dedication of this work to Clara—a *dedication emblem*—suffused with the affection that Brahms felt for her and merged with the historical charge of producing this symphony. Recalling the text on the composer's postcard, he was staging both his affection and his symphony as *hoch* ("elevated") and *tief* ("deep") attributes worthy of being repeated *viel tausendmal* ("many thousands of times"), like the dissemination and subsequent performance life of the symphony). One can think of Clara Schumann as the designated recipient of a Brahmsian gift: the symphonic work, of which her spirit and encouragement were foremost among the enablers. Without her—nothing.

And it is surely relevant that at m. 30 Brahms marked the first horn's theme *f[orte] sempre e passionato. Passionato?* This is not an adjective that one would expect to accompany a topical *Naturlaut* (sound of nature). More likely, it suggests an only slightly concealed, yet *sempre forte* outpouring of an idealized devotion. Nor is that all. The nine-bar dedication emblem, sent out (to Clara) in the tenor register, mm. 30–38, is echoed—responded to in the manner of dialogue—by the purity of the flute two octaves higher, mm. 38–46: the imagined "she" echoes and reaffirms his dedication and affection, while in the varied reprise of the theme a few bars later, especially in mm. 52–55, the two voices are doubled and intertwined, now in full concord, preparing to start the business at hand, arranging the pieces on the board before the real game begins: the exposition of a sonata.

The eight-bar horn theme is almost entirely pentatonic on C (another "natural" signifier) except for the F#$_4$ in m. 34. This gives the prevailing pentatonicism a fleetingly Lydian hue at the same time that a chiaroscuro, chromatic inner-voice descent begins to move in the shimmering accompaniment (for instance, in the first violins, mm. 34–38, C$_5$, B♭$_4$, A$_4$, A♭$_4$, G$_4$, F$_4$, E$_4$). The bass underpinning all of this also invites our attention. The initial G-bass, launching the expectant V$_4^6$ of C major, shifts to C a fourth higher midway through m. 33. That C is sustained for the remainder of the theme and its repetition in the flute—through m. 46. Thus the theme's cadential effect (V^7-I, mm. 36–38, 44–46) takes place over a pedal tonic.

Brahms fashioned mm. 30–61 to flow into a familiar, songlike CONTAINER, aa′ba″ (the "lyric binary" or "rounded binary" format, which form-functional theory calls "small ternary form"). The contrasting "b" section (mm. 47–51) shifts to a hushed wind chorale, marked *dolce* and led by darkly voiced trombones doubled by the bassoons. Invoking the solemnity of a sacred affirmation, like a self-crossing, it suggests an act of masculine-toned *consecration* both of the sincerity of the dedication emblem (something on the order of "I swear this to you from the depths of my being") and of the *hoch* and *tief* task of what lies ahead, the completion of the symphony—a renewed *Weihe des Hauses*. (It is also preparatory for its ecstatically climactic return in the coda, as the now-renovated "house" is being successfully brought to its close.)

Following immediately after the prolonged C major (mm. 30–46), the chorale's opening A-chord (V/ii, m. 47) provides a sense of lift, both spiritual and harmonic. With that A chord Brahms deploys the harmonic apparatus of the common MONTE-family schema (a chromatic 5–6 shift, here with bass-support A) in an uncommon way. Instead of having it occur, as it normally does, in the middle of a phrase, as the hinge between two levels of a sequence, he deploys the MONTE's chromatic leverage to start a new, sharply contrasting phrase. This phrase lifts first onto ii of C (the D-minor chord, m. 48), then proceeds to ii's relative major (F) with the IV:PAC in m. 50. The apparent close on IV, though, is immediately recast as a normative IV of C leading to the V in m. 51, whose role is both that of a readjusted close to the "b" phrase, canceling out the preceding IV:PAC, and that of an anacrusis to the varied alphorn reprise that follows. One thread through this "b"-phrase chorale that contributes to its impression of uplift is the quasi-chromatic hoist moving from one voice to another in mm. 47–51: [C♮, m. 46, then] C♯-D-E♭-E♮-F-G.[16]

I have already dealt with the interlaced voices in the alphorn theme's a″ reprise. It remains only to note that instead of closing with a I:PAC, this final subsection of the introduction ends, *diminuendo*, on an anticipatory V^7 (m. 60). Now fading away, the introductory material draws back behind the curtain, out of view, in order to display that which has been made—the sonata proper. The giver withdraws in order to present the gift.

Exposition: Allegro non troppo, ma con brio (mm. 62–183)

Primary theme (P, mm. 62–94)

That mm. 62–94 constitute P is self-evident. Sounded and then repeated, the broadly lyrical, hymnic theme sounds numerous I:PACs, a feature that, had it occurred in music of the classical era, Sonata Theory would regard as a massively *overdetermined* tonic (*EST*, 73–77, and chapter 4, p. 57). The most structurally telling of these I:PACs occur in mm. 78 and 94, each of which closes off a single strophe or stanza of a complete theme. The apparent start of a third stanza, m. 94, not only gives us a TR's characteristic *forte-* (here *fortissimo-*) affirmation launch but also proceeds to modulate away from C major. From the action-zone point of view none of this is problematic. More telling are the multiple connotations that the primary theme bears. These include its expressive and motivic relationships to the introduction, the theme's thematic structure, and the implicit topic family and historical precedents to which it points.

Following such an emotionally fraught introduction, P strides onto the sonata stage with a newly attained, relaxed confidence, now *senza sordino* and full-throated once again, very much resembling, as Frisch has noted (1996, 24–25), the similarly placed P in the finale of Bruch's Symphony No. 2, op. 36 (1870), which must have counted among its models. Since it has been preceded by the dedication-emblem alphorn theme, it is reasonable to conclude that P, and hence the will to begin a sonata and thereby to complete this symphony, can be understood as enabled only by the alphorn's memory-laden C-major presence. Not only was P's head motive anticipated in the finale's opening bars, but one also can hear the expansiveness of the alphorn theme's head motive blowing through it like an animating breeze: compare the intervals of mm. 30–33 to those of mm. 62–65.

Brahms channeled the songlike P theme into a small binary format, a a' || b c.[17] Its first two limbs are emphatically square-cut (4+4), while the final, cadential limb, mm. 70–78, stretches out to a gratifying nine bars, whose I:PAC in m. 78 elides with a rescored P-repetition. The theme's shape may also be construed as a late-romantic example of what form-functional theory designates as a compound sentence. One potential issue here, though, is that mm. 62–65 and 66–69 articulate an unmistakable period (I:HC, I:PAC), while, as we have noted earlier, form-functional theory maintains that, at least in the classical era, a presentation, even a compound presentation, does not end with a cadence. That said, it remains clear that from the broader, generic perspective of the theme, the I:PAC at m. 69 closes only the first part of an implicitly larger structure that is to conclude more decisively at m. 78.

The larger point is that Brahms (like Bruch in his Second Symphony) decided to fill P-space with a non-texted strophic song. And not merely with a song (in two tonally closed stanzas), but with a specific type of song, a type that helps to clarify its much-noted resemblance to Beethoven's stanzaic "Ode to Joy" melody.[18] That type, also shared by the "Ode to Joy" (and for that matter by the similar, concluding song of Beethoven's Choral Fantasy, op. 80) and perhaps by the opening theme of Brahms's own B-major Piano Trio, op. 8, is that of the *communal anthem*, a vocal genre, as in various national-anthem-oriented songs ("God Save the King" or Haydn's melody influenced by it, "Gott, erhalte Franz den Kaiser," also sounded in "Emperor" Quartet in C, op. 76 no. 3 [Buch 2003, 1–65]).

Perhaps more pointedly, it calls up the genre of the Germanic "sociable" or companionable song, the *geselliges Lied*, the sort of hearty music-making that had flourished among amateur clubs or other fraternal groups for many decades.[19] In a helpful study of that genre from several decades ago, F. E. Kirby informed us that such communities' *gesellige Lieder* were typically shared between a soloist and a chorus, and that "many of these songs were occasional or topical. . . . They celebrate the seasons of the year, engagements, weddings and anniversaries; or they are didactic and moralizing; many are also drinking songs celebrating good fellowship. . . . The musical style reflects the fact that these songs are to be sung by amateurs: the phrase structure of the melodies is regular and simple, the declamation syllabic, the harmonies simple" (1966, 119).[20]

It is not sufficient merely to identify a musical topic for Brahms's P theme—communal anthem or *geselliges Lied*. Rather, we need to ask why the composer crafted such a P theme in the first place. As the sonata's *Hauptgedanke* (principal idea) this is the theme that is to set the terms and tone for the sonata that it launches. Because one of P's most obvious allusions is to Beethoven's "Ode to Joy" melody, it is easily read as an act of solidarity and renewal, a faith-keeping gesture. The implicit claim, as well as its peril, could hardly be clearer: "Remaining true to the cause, I clasp the master's hand."

Equally significant are the communal connotations of the *geselliges Lied* as a type. Brahms's suggestion of an alliance with Beethoven is not solely a matter between two individual composers from two different generations. Brahms's P is a performative act of comradeship, a fantasy of community, with those musical factions that in his view have held true to the aesthetic and moral seriousness of the Beethoven Project, amidst midcentury decades of erosion, commercializing institutionalization, and self-promoting extremism. Not unlike Beethoven's, Brahms's theme summons up a *Bruderbund* of true believers. The composer offers us a hearty yet sober *geselliges Lied*, an act of song binding together those who share the Austro-Germanic tradition's highest aims, as Brahms saw them. One need not restrict the theme's implied community to the Brahms/Clara Schumann circle and its supporters, though it is clear that for Brahms that group constituted its devotedly earnest, central core: "And so, it is we—*you and I*—who raise our voices together in this shared song as we step into the task of building this symphony's concluding sonata form."

Transition (mm. 94–118)

Mm. 94–95 initially seem to begin a third stanza, now vigorously *animato* and *fortissimo*, with added horns, trumpets, and bassoons—a textural intensification, once again, that recalls the classical *forte affirmation* option for the onset of an energy-gaining TR. Plunging into this new action zone, the theme at once fragments into vehemently repeated rhythmic diminutions of its first four notes, with each four-note set's first note prodded by *sforzando* accents. While mm. 94–97 remain in C, their mm. 98–101 variant lurches toward E minor, spinning away from the governing tonic. (Here the E minor is only a fleeting tonal color, though in what follows it is one that will prove of central importance.) The immediate goal is to prepare and lay claim to G major, the traditional secondary key, V. To that end mm. 102–05, with their wedge-like inward-plunges in the outer voices and descending F-E bass (d^6 and a passing a_4^6), aim squarely at the intended arrival point, m. 106's pounced-upon D^7 in m. 106, V of G. Brahms's TR thus far suggests a compound sentential structure: presentation (4+4), continuation (2+2), and, in this case, an emphatic dominant arrival seized upon with G major firmly in mind (m. 106).

Once touched upon, the D^7 chord in m. 106 snaps into a higher level of activity. Since its reworking will have a significant role to play in the development, it is useful to identify m. 106 as $TR^{1.2}$ (with all that precedes it in the zone as $TR^{1.1}$). $TR^{1.2}$ unfurls wind-whipped, sixteenth-note contrapuntal exchanges among the voices; as noted earlier, the sixteenth-note contours are grounded in a five-note curling figure traceable back to intervallic shapes found in mm. 2–3 and 4–5.[21] What ensues is a skirmish between the claims of G major (modally positive) and, once again, E minor (modally negative). G-major dominance seeks to sustain itself amidst the flurry but time and again drops onto E-minor coloration: the end of m. 108 going into m. 109; m. 110, beat 4, going into m. 111, beat 1; and the downbeat of m. 112. Even while touched by E-minor harmonic colorations, the rising bass line that brings TR to an end, mm. 111–17, soon wrests free of them: G-A-B-C-C♯-D, or, reckoned in G major, $\hat{1}$-$\hat{2}$-$\hat{3}$-$\hat{4}$-$\sharp\hat{4}$-$\hat{5}$.

The exultant attainment of scale degree $\hat{4}$ (m. 113–14), the C-chord that is locally IV of G major, not only touches on the sonority of the global tonic, C major (as IV of V) but also triggers one of the characteristic bass-linear motions, $\hat{4}$-$\sharp\hat{4}$-$\hat{5}$, historically associated with half-cadential initiations of a medial-caesura process. Added to this MC allusion are the triple impulses on the D bass, mm. 116–17, recalling the hammerstroke reiterations of earlier MC practice. Yet the dominant chord proper does not clarify until the third of these impulses (m. 117, V^7 of C); that dominant contains a seventh; mm. 114–17 are sounded in a sudden *diminuendo*, choked off or dying away in a manner that recalls aspects of a de-energizing transition (*EST*, 48, 116); and the unflagging violin figuration plunges through m. 117 onto the G chord at m. 118, setting off what is clearly the secondary theme. While all of this blurs the normative sense of half-cadential arrival, and while little of what happens here suggests the articulation of a prototypical MC in the classical manner, it's clear that Brahms is at least making a gesture toward that tradition. If pressed to locate an "implicit" MC, one would probably point to the final arrival of the V^7 at m. 117— synchronized with the third touching of D in the bass—though the central thing to observe would be how cleverly Brahms smooths over the sense of a classical MC gap while sufficiently gesturing toward one to give us an adequate sense that we have indeed arrived at a rhetorical conclusion to TR.

In addition, in these final bars of TR, we hear, like the momentary lifting of a veil, the fleeting allusion to the alphorn-theme dedication emblem's head motive (mm. 114–18), imported from the introduction to help fill this dynamically fading, end-of-TR interstice. Here Brahms inlays into the sonata proper something *external* to it, an outside signifier from not-sonata space. The re-sounded horn greeting serves no functional role but rather suggests a flickering-back to a memory. We might read it as a glance back at Clara Schumann ("remember: this is for you"), suggesting a renewal of determination, having made it this far, to continue onward in this *hoch* and *tief* mission. On the other hand, it is worth noticing that the dedication-emblem fragment is again sounded in dialogue between the flute and the horn. And this time it is the flute that leads and the horn that gratefully responds. On this reading we have the fantasy-projection of a feminine voice—*her* feminine voice—imagined to be sending a sign of encouragement: "Splendid, Johannes, splendid! Keep going!"

Secondary thematic zone (mm. 118–83)

Entering the exposition's part 2, the music takes on a now-*animato*, "down to business" character. As is the case with all secondary theme zones, that business is that of pushing onward toward the securing of the EEC, often encountering a series of musical adventures along the way. The generic question always is: how easy or how difficult will it be to accomplish this? Because the secondary theme's varied content and EEC material will be largely replicated bar-for-bar in the recapitulatory rotation, as is Brahms's customary practice, the key and mode of that EEC, presuming that it is attained at all, will be an important predictive feature for the tonal and modal success of the sonata proper. Since the preparation for S has opened the door to G major, and since S begins in that normative key, we enter part 2 with every expectation that the EEC down the road will be a V:PAC. As we find out, though, that is not to be.

Like many secondary-theme zones, Brahms's is a *multimodular* S: it proceeds through several different, contrasting modules as it plows ahead, intent on closing S space with the desired PAC. Tracing the secondary theme's adventures on the way to that cadence, these modules can be identified by the usual decimal designators: $S^{1.1}$, $S^{1.2}$, $S^{1.3}$, and so on (remembering that the decimals after the numeral 1 indicate that we have not yet attained a PAC). As is commonly noted, the opening of the $S^{1.1}$ melody, mm. 118–19, is related to the incipit of the alphorn theme that we have just heard in the preceding bars. If the alphorn theme can also be construed as a dedication emblem, that would imply that the external impulse to keep going, mm. 114–18, gives us the spur needed to cross the boundary into the secondary-theme zone and continued sonata progress.

Quite apart from its veiled allusion to the dedication emblem, most of $S^{1.1}$, mm. 118–32, is taken up with a set of differing upper-voice realizations over a rapidly moving, four-note linear-ostinato bass, always pressing metrically across the bar line: beats 2, 3, 4 → 1. (Here we recall that its tetrachordal intervallic source had been generated in the first and second bar of the movement, though there in C minor.) Ten of the 12 bass repetitions are identical, C, B, A → G; the eleventh, m. 128 into m. 129, coinciding with a *crescendo*, shifts the ostinato up a fifth, G, F♯, E → D, as the locally implicit key deflates to G minor; and the twelfth, m. 129 into m. 130, registers this modal decay further by inflecting the third note with a flat, G, F♯, E♭ → D, suggesting a weak half cadence in G minor.

But more can be said about the ostinato that underpins $S^{1.1}$. For one thing, it initially sounds scale degrees $\hat{4}$-$\hat{3}$-$\hat{2}$-$\hat{1}$ on G major. In other words, $S^{1.1}$ begins on a IV chord, a C major chord, and C, of course, is also the sonata's global tonic. (Beginning an S—or any theme—on IV is unusual, though it can happen that some classical

S themes begin off-tonic with a set of descending fifths to the tonic (as we have seen in Mozart's K. 306/i).[22] In this case the bass suggests the voice-leading schema that Gjerdingen termed the PRINNER (2007, 45–60). The PRINNER's prototypical formulation—whose skeletal pitches, of course, allow imaginative realizations—presents scale degrees $\hat{6}$-$\hat{5}$-$\hat{4}$-$\hat{3}$ in parallel thirds or tenths over a descending bass $\hat{4}$-$\hat{3}$-$\hat{2}$-$\hat{1}$ (or, to use Gjerdingen's upper-voice/lower-voice symbols, ❻❺❹❸ over ④③②①). Accordingly, I call S[1.1] the "PRINNER ostinato," and although Brahms provides much-embellished skirtings around the schema's traditional upper-voice pitches (E$_5$-D$_5$-C$_5$-B$_4$), we can readily locate its embedded traces in the first two and last two notes of the melody in mm. 118–21. Beginning S with a PRINNER is unusual: it runs counter to the schema's nearly invariable use as a "musical riposte" or reply to a schematically different "opening gambit" (Gjerdingen 2007, 45–47).[23] Also curious is the "nose-to-the-grindstone" circularity and four-note brevity of the ostinato bass. This, too, seems uncommon, since ground-bass patterns normally move at a slower pace and span more bars. There are early-music instances of similar short grounds, sometimes with topic-family annunciatory or celebratory bell connotations, but they, too are infrequent, and it is far from clear that Brahms would have known about them.[24]

Another aspect of S[1.1] is that the composer stages it as tonally and modally unstable. The traditional tonal goal of a C-major exposition is G major. But the G major at m. 118 is not securely tethered. While mm. 118–21 posit it, mm. 121–24—over the same ground bass—slip onto E minor, recalling the G-major/E-minor tension in TR, mm. 98–101. In mm. 124–25 there follows a two-bar "overcorrection" (on V[7] of C), whereupon Brahms reasserts the desired G major in mm. 126–28. But in mm. 128–30, with the pitch-shift in the ostinato bass, the music decays to G minor. With the v:HC at m. 130 (led into via an augmented-sixth chord) the ostinato cannot proceed further: the now-wobbly grindstone slips off its axle. With jagged rhythms and syncopations, the cadential span begun at m. 118 sputters to a halt at 132.

Sonata Theorists will notice that m. 130's v:HC, a pronounced half cadence in the center of S-space, is sustained by a dominant-lock featuring a triple-hammerstroke bass on the downbeats of mm. 130–32. These three bars display the earmarks of medial-caesura behavior (v:HC MC). What we have is a *second MC-effect* (the second in a case of *apparent double medial caesuras*—even though the first of them, as noted earlier, had been blurred). The presence of a second MC-effect in already-launched S-space—a *postmedial caesura* (PMC)—is typically the feature that announces the presence of a *trimodular block* (TMB; see p. 64 and *EST*, 170–77). What would normally follow is a melodically pronounced new theme (TM³, here with m. 118 recast as TM¹ merging into TM² around mm. 128–30) providing a fresh relaunch or renewal of S-space. What follows at m. 132, though, while thematically different from what precedes it, seems more like a reactive attempt to shore things back up than a new launch proper. Confronting equivocal signals, Sonata Theory is content to explicate the ambiguity of the situation. We do in fact have a second MC-effect at m. 132. If one is struck by the newness of m. 132, one might consider the upbeat of m. 133 to be the start of the TM^3 module of a trimodular block. But I am less convinced by that newness. I hear that module as more recuperative than initiatory. Accordingly, I call it S$^{1.2}$—following an MC-like internal half cadence.[25] However we decide the issue, the larger point is that the first-launch attempt at a G-major secondary theme (S$^{1.1}$) has fallen apart.

Dolce and *piano*, the recuperative S$^{1.2}$, mm. 132–42, seeks to re-stabilize the lost G major, though the passage is shot through with corroding residues of G minor. Although the syncopated dominant of G in the violas tries to keep a steady bead on a G-tonic, that dominant fizzles, *diminuendo*, in a cloud of descending, dissonantly embellished $^6_3$ chords, mm. 136–42. With them the music resettles momentarily on B^6, V^6 of E minor (m. 142), S$^{1.3}$, pointing toward the same E minor that had colored mm. 98–101 (in TR) and mm. 121–24 (in S$^{1.1}$). As is becoming clear, the anticipated G major is proving unsustainable. When it appears it either deflates to G minor or decays onto G major's relative minor, E minor. At stake is the viability of the generically traditional, modally positive outcome of a C-major exposition: this would be the production of a G-major EEC, a sign of bright promise for a C-major ESC down the road, which later point will have been the realization of a tonally and modally successful sonata, bringing this final movement (and with it, the whole symphony) to a positive close. But here, midway through S-space, this G major is in trouble.

Brahms devotes the remainder of the exposition to the staging of a struggle between the threats of an ever more assertive E minor {–} and an aspirational but weak G major {+}. Beginning *piano*, the *marcato* bustling of the next module, mm. 142–47, S$^{1.3}$, gives us a rekindling of dynamic forces, but the negative pulls of E minor are now in the ascendant. Its *crescendo* prolongation of the dominant of E minor (with its third, D♯, in the bass), is a coiled windup that casts us into the E-minor squalls at the *fortissimo* downbeat of m. 148. This is the onset of S$^{1.4}$, whose swirling fatalism in the top voice realizes the implications of its thematic forecast back in the introduction, mm. 22–23 (there in a chilled, foreboding C minor). With that onset, underpinned by four striding half notes (mm. 148–49), E minor now claims dominance—and G major's hopes fall into despair.

It is not difficult to read the implications of what follows. Three bars into S$^{1.4}$, mm. 150–51 try to wrest the music's course back into the major mode {+} with a twice-repeated, *sforzando* cadential swerve onto D major, an antechamber of the preferred G major. Mm. 152–55 recast mm. 148–51 in the manner of a negative-image reply and darken back onto V of E minor {–}. As the internal motion grows more animated with urgent triplet-jabs, m. 156 begins a varied repeat of S$^{1.4}$, with vigorous D-major cadential swerves again in mm. 158–59, followed by a fallback onto E minor in mm. 160–61. In mm. 162–63, though, an unexpected change of direction flows into a suddenly hushed G$^6_4$ sonority at m. 164: the beginning of S$^{1.5}$, a last-ditch hope for G major, though the immediately following, breathless music is corroded by intermixture with G minor. But the bold, *forte* arrival of the tutti, C major chord at m. 168 carries the stronger implication of VI of the now-inevitable E minor, onto whose cadential $^6_4$ the music drops in bars 170 and 171. All is now lost.

We hear another shouted outcry from the C-major *tutti* chord, VI of E minor, in m. 172: a desperate hope from the G major side of things, grinning triumph from the side of E minor. But Brahms seals the exposition's fate with a perfect authentic cadence in E minor, iii:PAC, in m. 176. And even here the iii:PAC seems resisted. It is followed at once by reactive convulsions—as if trying to restore that C-chord—that only invite the pounding in of the negative cadence twice more, at m. 178 and, savagely, m. 183. Mm. 176–83 may not strike us as a normative codetta, which would place them into a conceptual C-space; rather, they seem more to be emphatic reiterations of the E minor PAC at m. 176, twice more slamming shut a reopened door. Accordingly, we might either understand the EEC as triply hammered in over the entire eight-bar cadential passage (an "EEC complex"), mm. 176–83, or place it at m. 183 (iii:PAC), which, here at the end of S-space, closes out the exposition with a vicious succession of emphatic quarter notes.

To conclude in minor an exposition that had begun in major (and here, C major no less) is dialogically negative with regard to the tradition.[26] What had been expected to be a normative two-part exposition, major-major {+ +} has collapsed into a major-minor one {+ −} or, to suggest more accurately the process of hopes dashed, {+ (+) −}. Probably recalling precedents in Schubert, Brahms has given us a three-key exposition. But in a major-mode three-key exposition in which the tonic, the mediant, and the dominant are in play, the order of presentation is usually that of ascending by thirds: tonic, then mediant (perhaps flatted), then dominant (major) (as tallied in Hunt 2009). That more standard tonal sequence suggests the traditional dominant major's overcoming of the interloping mediant, which is often unsecured with a cadence. In this finale, however, the order is: tonic, dominant (major), mediant minor. This sequence stages the collapse of the positive dominant (major), here G, and its fall into, or its capture by, its relative minor.[27] Notwithstanding the presence of a "successfully" attained EEC (one that at least closes the exposition cadentially), Brahms has dramatized a narrative of expositional failure, ending, dialogically, in the "wrong key" (as opposed to the one that we are to understand is striven for) and in the "wrong mode."

When we recall the reading of this finale presented here—an 1874–76 struggle to reanimate the declining Austro-Germanic symphony, a high-stakes enterprise with pitfalls and possibilities for missteps lurking around every corner—we can understand E minor's snuffing out of G major as portentous with regard to the sonata as a whole. An exposition, after all, presents us with a strategy of promise: a prediction about how the sonata is likely to be completed in its tonal resolution. An E-minor EEC virtually guarantees a minor-mode ESC—perhaps in the tonic C minor, though that remains to be seen. At least in this movement, from the EEC onward the finale's sonata form seems predestined to move from its initial, communally hearty C major to a recapitulatory conclusion in minor, resulting in a tragic narrative of modal failure that bodes ill for the success of the arduous symphony project that the composer has undertaken. The specter of potential failure hovers over all that follows.

(Expanded) recapitulatory rotation (mm. 186–367)

Primary theme and transition (mm. 186–302)

Following the exposition's concluding E-minor PAC, a three-bar retransitional link (RT, mm. 183–85) pulls us back to C major and another tonic-key onset of P (m. 186). In that link we hear once more the e-chord/C-chord juxtaposition that has been in play since at least m. 168, now with C major overturning the turbulence of E minor's expositional takeover. Though mediated by a modulation (the tilt to $V^7/$ I in m. 185), the quick turn back to C major suggests an inflating of the preceding E minor through the inflection of the latter's $\hat{5}$ (B) up to $\hat{6}$ (C, the *Leittonwechsel operation*, L) and the support of the conceptually resultant ${}^6_3$ ("C^6_3") with a chordal root below (producing C^5_3).[28] Coupled with this, one reading of the immediate return of the communally hearty *geselliges Lied* can be read, despite the exposition's drastic conclusion and its dire prediction for what is likely to come, as projecting a sturdy group-reassurance, a reassurance that control of the whole is being kept in hand. If this reading seems overly sanguine, we might alternatively understand the *volte-face* of its sudden return to tonic-key, lyrical relief as a hoped-for reboot of a sonata process that has taken a bad turn.

Even though P returns in the tonic and intact for 15 bars (mm. 186–200 = mm. 62–76), close listeners can realize that this is no expositional repeat, since it is an orchestrationally reinforced version of what we had heard at the exposition's beginning. Similarly, one need not be misled into thinking of it as the return of a rondo-like refrain (of a Type 4 sonata—see the appendix): the broadly paced theme bears no trace of an Allegro-tempo "rondo character" (*EST*, 398–99), and in the exposition it had begun as a straightforward strophic song. On the other hand, especially when we soon learn that it will dissolve into developmental activity, we might imagine it to have been the start of the developmental space that, following a non-repeated exposition, begins by making a tonic-key feint to a return of P (in the manner, say, of the first movement of Beethoven's String Quartet in F, op. 59 no. 1). This hypothesis can be kept alive until, many bars later, we find out that P does not return, post-development, to launch the recapitulation of a Type 3 sonata: in this case the development proper will lead only to a crux-resumption of correspondence measures with the ground-bass ostinato of $S^{1.1}$ at m. 302 (= m. 118). At that point we reassess what we have been hearing since the end of the exposition and realize that at m. 186 Brahms deploys the tonic return of P as the beginning of the *recapitulatory rotation*: a full rotation of expositional materials that begins in the tonic and moves through the successive zones to arrive at the tonal resolution and ESC. In short, Brahms is shaping the sonata portion of the finale as an expanded Type 1 sonata.

Within an expanded Type 1 sonata (as is also the case with a Type 2 sonata), the developmental expansion takes place in the earlier portions of the rotation, that is, in the P/TR zones. To facilitate the discussion that follows, Figure 12.1 provides an

Exposition: P to the onset of S

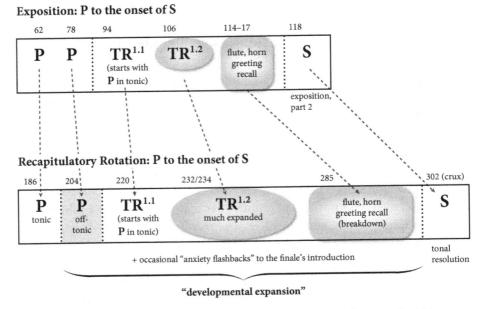

Figure 12.1. Brahms, Symphony No. 1, finale: rotational parallels, mm. 62–118, 186–302.

overview of the rotational parallels between the exposition's and the recapitulatory rotation's P and TR zones.

The recapitulatory rotation's developmental expansion proper (from mm. 201–04 to the crux at m. 302) may be heard as a narrative of struggle, a chiaroscuro tableau of lights and darks. On the one side are the optimistic, buoyantly hopeful forces of the major mode, seeking to maintain confidence in the finale's sonata project and a presumed expectation of an ultimately major-mode outcome. On the other are those of its negative, minor-mode shadow: a lurking anxiety that repeatedly cancels out recurring lights of optimism with images of conflict or collapse. This light-dark contestation has lain at the expressive core of the symphony from its opening bars.

From Sonata Theory's point of view, the key to interpreting this developmental narrative lies in the era's operative principles of major-minor interplay, particularly those outlined in chapter 8's section, "Aspiration: escape from minor into major." Following a fall into an unwelcome minor, "the music," qua fictive protagonist, often seeks to escape from it as quickly as possible. As noted in Figure 8.2, three different ways to do this are especially attractive: (1) flipping into the presumably safe harbor of the minor's relative major (the R-operation); (2) activating the process of a *Leittonwechsel* inflation (the L-operation) to shift to a major-mode tonal level a major third lower; or (3) annulling the minor by reverting back to its parallel major (the P-operation). Once any of these three processes has been effected, the question is whether the resultant major-mode level can be sustained or whether it is fated to decay once again or, perhaps, to be thwarted by some other negative process.[29]

Notice, then, that Rotation 2's tonic-key onset of P (m. 186) cannot bring the theme to its C-major conclusion. At the end of its cadential module, m. 201, C major threatens to decay to C minor—C major's antithesis, the ultimately negative key in this symphony. Once that possibility is touched upon, Brahms immediately stages the music as fleeing from it with an easy escape to its relative major, E-flat (m. 204, the R-operation), to begin the second stanza of the *geselliges Lied*, corresponding to the exposition's second-stanza start at m. 78. But the melody has scarcely rebegun before it withers at m. 207 into E-flat minor gloom, enhanced by a horn-fifth darkening of orchestration and a plagal plunge onto a local B-flat minor (mm. 208–10) This second developmental fall into minor triggers the m. 208 onset of the first of the development's "anxiety flashbacks" to the introduction (here recalling the edgy *pizzicati* of mm. 6–11 and 16–19). Mounting in an urgent *crescendo*, the B-flat minor color reverts back onto an E-flat minor bar (m. 211) that Brahms's application of the L-operation immediately inflates to a bright B major and another attempt to restart P (m. 212). Mm. 208–12's narrative import is clear: "Why can't I continue? Perhaps, as I had initially feared, I cannot succeed; still . . . let's pull ourselves together and try again."

Mm. 212–20 are that retry, now on a different pitch level (up a sixth or down a third): the chordal pattern of mm. 204–12, including a second anxiety flashback in *crescendo*, is replicated in 212–20. At its end, though, Brahms harmonically alters this second flashback to arrive at an E minor bar in m. 219, which he then inflates (L-operation) to effect the move back to the bright tonic C major (m. 220). The whole tonal process out of C major (m. 200/201) and back into it (m. 220) has been densely chromatic, brooding, troubled. Throughout it "one stumbles through the darkness, eventually blundering into the light of C major, blinking and disoriented" (Cohn 2012, 194). However one characterizes its affective import, Brahms has led us through a darkly ominous corridor before putting us back onto the C-major tonal center for what is now the fourth attempt to start the P theme.

What we have had so far is a modally "fallen" first stanza of P, followed by two off-tonic, undercut starts to a second stanza. With the *animato* return to the P-incipit in the tonic at m. 220, we leave the idea of completed stanzas behind and reconnect with the exposition's TR$^{1.1}$: mm. 220–31 = mm. 94–105, at the original pitch level (with an only slight adjustment of the bass in mm. 230–31). This stretch of correspondence bars stays on track until that crucial moment when the exposition's music had set its initial sights on G major by locking onto its dominant at m. 106, TR$^{1.2}$, which had also initiated a brief but energetic contrapuntal complex. Any similar locking onto V/V here in this developmental space within the recapitulatory rotation, however, would be an inappropriate move. Instead, at m. 232 an unexpected lurch onto B^7 derails the correspondence measures, and the texture shifts abruptly into a jagged set of descending thirds alternating with their ascending-sixth inversions. Here everything changes, as with the flip of a switch. The turn into a dense thicket of double counterpoint pitches us into a new narrative phase of alarm. And from the rotational point of view (Figure 12.1) this plunge magnifies and intensifies the exposition's contrapuntal onset of $TR^{1.2}$, recalling most notably the activity in mm. 106–10.

M. 232 unleashes the full force of the light-dark tension that has been infiltrating the development. We now have a sudden shredding, a sustained *forte* scattering of any momentary security to the four winds. The brutally emphatic quarter-note triple upbeats (2, 3, 4 → *1*) repeatedly recall those that had pounded in the minor-mode EEC (mm. mm. 180–83, themselves a negative recasting of the 2, 3, 4 → *1* upbeats that had pervaded $S^{1.1}$, the PRINNER ostinato). Here the triple-note upbeats are leveraged into power-springboards catapulting upward to land on apex pitches that then reverse direction to fall in sheet upon sheet of cascading sixteenths overlapping with the same two-bar motive flung forth sequentially in an upper-voice/lower-voice exchange. We have been thrust into the clamor of battle. Tonal/chordal levels fly about like straws in the wind. By m. 235 the furiously churning descending-third/ascending-sixth intervallic pattern sets off a chain of descending fifths: A major, D minor, G minor, C major, finally arriving on an F major chord at m. 239. Here Brahms switches the harmonic strategy into ascending 5–6 sequences, which push up the chordal level by whole steps for three bars of intensification: m. 239, F major, m. 240, G minor, m. 241, A major. The composer then seizes upon that A chord, wrestling it down to the earth (m. 242) and pinning it there with triple hammerblows, mm. 243–44 (caesura-like behavior), in order to interpret it—more properly, to subdue it—as a dominant of D minor.

This opens up a reactive breathing-space at a *piano* dynamic, mm. 244–56, an attempted recovery resembling an expanded caesura-fill. While the sixteenth-notes continue to swirl in the strings, the ear is more likely attracted to the smooth floating in the wind-choir above them. The 13-bar passage is governed by three sequential glide-paths, each thwarted at the point of potential cadence. The first, mm. 244–49, leads off with plangent motivic pleas for relief exchanged between the oboe and the flute, each sounding a four-note variant of the P-incipit motive (mm. 244–45).[30] From a still-sustained V of D minor, the passage begins to modulate away from that key in m. 246, and in mm. 247–49 a gentle descent by fifths—A, d, $G^{(7)}$—points at a quasi-cadential landing on C at m. 249. (Keep in mind that a sustainable C major cadence is the desired outcome of not only this movement but also the entire symphony.) That C chord, however, is immediately treated as V of F minor to launch the second glide-path, largely a replication of the first a third higher. This sets the music in motion for a quasi-cadential landing onto E minor (yet again), which we expect to occur at m. 254. Instead, the composer steers away from it to shift the music back to where it had been in m. 246 (mm. 254–56 = mm. 246–48), seeking to grasp once again that earlier, C-major tonic-chord outcome. But this is a vain hope, thwarted at once by a "loud-rest" empty downbeat (m. 257) followed by a stern, *forte* rebuke. And with that we are cast into a second round of the $TR^{1.2}$ contrapuntal harangue, set off once again with the descending-third/ascending-sixth set of upbeats.

With this return of the contrapuntal assault, the manic intensification can no longer be quelled. The violence redoubles at m. 264, where motivic compression tightens the ongoing motives, thrashing them upward and downward. In mm. 264–67 the winds toss about sixteenth-note wails, while the strings plummet rapidly down a set of thirds, alternating spikily, as always, with ascending sixths—and feeling every bounce along the way. By the end of m. 267 the music has reached an explosive point. Reactively, the winds howl out the four-note P-incipit previously sounded at m. 244, now at full-volume *fortissimo* anguish. At this point we understand that the process of mounting crisis and reaction has been proceeding through two developmental *subrotations*. The referential subrotation spans mm. 232–56; the second begins at m. 257, varying and intensifying the first and driving inexorably toward a catastrophic climax.

Thunderously reinforced by rumbles in the now-added timpani, the sequential paroxysms of mm. 268–73 hurtle us first onto C^6_5 (V^6_5 of F minor, mm. 268–69), then onto D^6_5 (V^6_5 of G minor, mm. 270–71), and finally, leaping up a fourth, onto G^6_5 (V^6_5 of C minor, mm. 272–73). C minor! By m. 273 we are pointing at the very key and mode that the music has been so desperately trying to exorcise. Worse, once its dominant has been touched upon, the music locks onto V of C minor (m. 274, seen especially, though not only, in the timpani's pounding heartbeats), while the upper voices twice mount chromatically upward in a panting, vertiginous frenzy. The mounting pressure channels into the sheer panic of mm. 279–84, a succession of syncopated, convulsive shudders, *fortissimo*, *marcato*, and reinforced in its first two bars with the powerful entrance of the trombones to complete a maximally thick tutti.

This is another flashback to the anxieties of the movement's introduction. Referenced here are the similar syncopations from the introduction's mm. 27–28—the gasping, C-minor passage of maximal *Angst* that we had heard just before the C-major entrance of the alphorn theme. Here too, in mm. 279–84, the specter of C minor flares before us. The struggle may be mapped by noticing the concluding chord of each bar. Mm. 279 and 280 drive to V/c (continuing to prolong the dominant-lock from the prior measures); as the bass now starts an ominous descent, mm. 281 and 282 drive to a desperate, darkly shadowed C-*major* $^6_4$; m. 283 drives to C minor's Neapolitan sixth ($\flat\text{II}^6$); and m. 284 drives to c^6. Mm. 279–84 bring us to the culmination of all of the composer's doubts about the historical task of composing this symphony: "Having come this far, is the whole process now doomed to shut down?; has it all been for naught?; how can we possibly proceed from this crisis of self-confidence?"

Mm. 285–86: utter despair, exhaustion—breakdown. This pivotal moment brings us the much-discussed return of the alphorn theme's four-note incipit, *fortissimo* and tutti. Unlike its appearance in the introduction, it first sounds not in the emancipatory C major but rather in an A-minor-tinged, tragic variant: A minor's $\hat{3}$-$\hat{2}$-$\hat{1}$-$\hat{5}$ cast downward in the melody (and simultaneously, in augmentation, in the bass, mm. 285–87). Its first three notes are colored by a diminished-seventh-chord outcry of anguish (m. 285) that releases in the next bar onto a desolate a^6 chord (m. 286) whose energy at once depletes in a stark *diminuendo*. All seems lost.

Most bitter of all, this is registered with a minor-mode version of the opening of that once-cherished *hoch* and *tief* dedication emblem, one probably also suffused with images of Clara and her hopes for Brahms and this symphony. The narrative plunges into a heartbreak of failure, collapse, and the potential abandonment of this symphonic project. For an instant, we are crushed, thrown down under the task at hand.

But then at m. 287 the miracle happens. Perhaps because the horn greeting has just been touched upon, like a talisman that retains its power even in the pit of despair, the A minor sonority of the preceding measure (a^6) transforms into C major (C^6, via the R operation). It is one of the wonderful moments of this finale. As if touched by some unbidden power, the darkness of A minor lifts, clarifies into the luminous brightness of C major. Mm. 285–289 repay study, not only because of the overlapping nestings of the alphorn incipit, with the augmentation version in the bassline steering us confidently onto the dominant of C major at m. 289, but also because of the sonority of its extraordinary orchestration. (Notice the telling $\hat{1}$-$\hat{3}$-$\hat{5}$ ascent, reckoning in C major, in the horns and trumpets, *diminuendo*, in mm. 285–88.)

With that magical C-major transformation, Brahms is able to move into a slightly varied but intensified recall of the final, dissolving limb of the introduction's alphorn melody: essentially, mm. 289–296 = mm. 52–59 (though we should absorb the resonance of the steadfast tonic pedal held from m. 293 through m. 300). It was at this point where the introduction, in a dwindling *diminuendo*, had given rise to the first impulses of the sonata proper: P at m. 61. Here at the end of the development it is conceivable that Brahms could easily have led the music into a full, P-led recapitulation around mm. 297 or 298. In that case we would be dealing with the more familiar Type 3 sonata—and a very long sonata movement. Instead, he interpolated the *calando*, subdominant-leaning mm. 297–302, a masterstroke of coloristic shading, to lower the music into the IV chord that begins S$^{1.1}$ and the PRINNER ostinato—setting it carefully in place.

It is at the onset of S$^{1.1}$ that we realize Brahms has chosen the expanded type 1 format for this movement. Why this format? Or, more properly, what is the role of the expanded Type 1 schema in this narrative? The easy answer would be: to shorten a movement that was already in danger of becoming overlong. While this might be part of the explanation, there must be more to it than that. Reflecting on these matters under Type 3 assumptions, Brinkmann (1995, 37–44) posited the idea that the alphorn theme's return at m. 285, and especially its re-stabilizing on C major, takes on the role of the start of the finale's recapitulation. For Brinkmann its appearance here effects an "effacing" or substituting for the presumably absent P in "an ambiguous, yet unequivocal game with the formal conventions," the result of formal thematic processes that reach their "structural culmination" at m. 285, regarded as "the dynamic climax of the evolution of the entire form." What was then needed was an account of why P itself had been "repudiated" as unsatisfactory. This led Brinkmann into speculations about the supposed antithesis between the ideals of humanist, fraternal freedom (P) and those of a sacralized nature (the alphorn theme), which latter are finally embraced as superior around m. 285 (and then once more in the climactic coda).[31]

But once one understands the availability of the expanded Type 1 format—not only Brahms's attraction to it elsewhere, but also the history of its usage in preceding eras (*EST*, 349–50 and pp. 84–85 and 225 above), such argumentation dissolves away. There is no reason to think that P, as *geselliges Lied*, has been repressed at all. It appeared exactly where it should have, that is, at m. 186, the beginning of the second (here, recapitulatory) rotation. Nor do we have to confront the idea of a replacement or substitute for P at the beginning of a presumed recapitulation, much less the fact that this presumed substitution proceeds immediately into $S^{1.1}$ (m. 302) and a prolonged set of correspondence measures. All these events are accounted for within the expanded Type 1 format. Another glance at Figure 12.1 can help to clarify where we are in the structure as we approach the $S^{1.1}$ crux in m. 302.

That said, there is no denying that the powerful recurrence of the alphorn theme at mm. 285–96 is an event of real importance in this movement, and it calls for an interpretation. In the reading proposed here, I have been regarding the alphorn theme as a dedication emblem that carries the memory of a once-private communication from Brahms to Clara Schumann. Under those lights, while the dedication emblem does appear twice in the midst of the Type 1 sonata, just before $S^{1.1}$ in both the expositional and recapitulatory rotations, its fragmentary recall is external to the processes of the sonata form itself. It surfaces as a flashback-memory, recalling the *raison d'être* for undertaking this project in the first place, an impulse that includes an imagined or real Clara-inspired spur to composition.

Consequently, when we find the alphorn idea embedded in the interior of the sonata, it is staged as an interpolation, not as part of the sonata process. Thus I do not regard the alphorn recall as a participant in the otherwise normative rotational order of thematic presentation, nor do I consider its set of correspondence measures with the introduction to be a genuine crux within the sonata. Instead, it exists conceptually above and apart from the sonata. On the reading presented here, I interpret Brahms as thematizing both himself (for instance, in the introduction) and the making of the sonata-product, which gets underway only with the onset of P. The listener can imagine Brahms "watching himself"—or perhaps inviting you to watch him—in the process of composing a sonata-grounded finale. The maker and the thing being made: the two aspects proceed on simultaneous but separable conceptual planes, with the latter, the presentational object, subordinated to the former.

In sum: the recapitulatory rotation's developmental space brings us to a point of acute distress, a musical crisis. Hence the "A minor" alphorn cry of despair at m. 285, which is immediately buoyed up by a tonic-major sounding of the alphorn theme's final limb guiding the composer, as if supported and led by the hand, into the secondary-theme zone and the remainder of the sonata. Just as the external alphorn recall had encouraged the composer to proceed into $S^{1.1}$ in the exposition, so too here, it is the minor-mode breakdown and its immediate C-major overcoming that gives the composer renewed encouragement and sets him on his way to continue into S$^{1.1}$ and the sonata proper's completion.

Secondary thematic zone (mm. 302–67)

Since the multimodular secondary theme zone is largely a transposition of its model in the exposition (with a single requisite wrench midcourse to keep it on the C-tonic track), it presents us with few analytical problems. For the most part, mm. 302–67 = mm. 118–83, with only a few deviations: the composing of new musical ideas stops, and the process of transposition takes over. To be sure, Brahms rescores some of this music, especially that of S$^{1.1}$ and S$^{1.2}$ (notice, for instance, that the PRINNER ostinato, $\hat{4}$-$\hat{3}$-$\hat{2}$-$\hat{1}$ on C major, is now shared and alternated between the lower strings and the winds high above, mm. 302–10), but nonetheless its transposed music corresponds bar-for-bar with that of the exposition. This sonata-crux rejoining of an extended set of correspondence measures has its point within the broader narrative. Once the breakdown at the end of the development has been overcome, the path is cleared for a resumption of the sonata, now coursing onward toward its end with businesslike efficiency.

Since S$^{1.1}$ now begins on C major (m. 302), this transposes the exposition's G-major S$^{1.1}$ up a fourth (or down a fifth). Had the exposition's S-modules remained in G all the way to the EEC, Brahms could have retained this transposition level throughout. But the exposition's S-space had housed a conflict between G major and its relative minor, E minor, and ultimately the latter had prevailed. Were Brahms to adhere to a harmonically strict transposition of S, it would begin on C (as it does here) but wind up with an off-tonic "ESC" in A minor (vi), a fourth higher or a fifth lower than that of the exposition's EEC, resulting in a tonally nonresolving recapitulation. While that deformational option had a few precedents within the tradition, and while it appears in a later work of Brahms, the Cello Sonata No. 2 in F, op. 99/i, the composer decided to forgo it here. [32] In order to divert the music away from the A-minor outcome, he needed to effect a harmonic shift somewhere *en route* so that the ESC could occur in the tonic.

That decisive twist occurs in mm. 324–25, which Brahms alters to empty out on a G sonority (V of C minor) on the downbeat of m. 326. By contrast, the referential measures of the exposition, mm. 140–41, had emptied out in m. 142 onto a B^6 chord (V^6 of E minor), whose root is a third higher than that of the G chord at m. 326. Thus from m. 326 onward, the transposition level is no longer that of a fourth higher (or fifth lower) than the exposition but rather that of a third lower. Whereas the exposition's tonal conflict in S-space's latter stages had been between G major and E minor, the tonal resolution's analogous conflict is now between E-flat major and C minor. The music courses on in this altered transposition level and brings us to the steel-fisted, C-minor ESC cadences in mm. 362–67 (= mm. 178–83), which bring the sonata proper to an end.

A C-minor conclusion for a sonata that had begun in a confident C major implies a catastrophic narrative both for the sonata as a whole and for Brahms's historically perilous, four-movement symphonic project, insofar as it had implied the quest for a C-major emancipatory conclusion. Such a conclusion, one might have initially supposed, was to have been accomplished via a sonata process presumed to be adequate to the task. In this movement, though, the composer staged the sonata process as *modally failing.* In Sonata Theory terms, while the sonata proper has succeeded tonally (that is, it has brought us to a C-tonic conclusion for the ESC), it has fallen short of securing a major-mode ESC. Instead, it has fallen prey to the negative pulls of the minor mode. The sonata has fallen short—failed—modally. In so doing, it reverses the familiar minor-to-major trajectories often encountered in the repertory (not to mention the C-minor-to-C-major precedents, most notably in Beethoven's music). If C-major emancipation is to be obtained at all, it will have to be secured in post-sonata space, and in such an emphatic way as to trump the minor-mode ESC of the preceding sonata.[33] C-major closure will have to be accomplished by sheer force of will.

Coda (mm. 367–457)

As we saw in Chapter 4 ("The Basics") and Chapter 7 (on the first movement of Beethoven's Second Symphony), Sonata Theory regards codas of substantial length as *discursive codas.* These are usually subdivisible into separate subsections or phases, the last of which is usually a "coda to the coda." Such is the case here. Brahms's coda passes through four phases, each with its assigned task: the first two are preparatory, the third activates the charge toward and finally produces the desired tonic-major PAC (m. 447), and the fourth, in a burst of joy, celebrates the symphonic achievement in a concluding coda to the larger coda that brings Brahms's historical project to a successful end.

Phase 1, mm. 367–74, begins the coda with eight *piano* bars of reactive backwash that swirl in the rhythmic currents that had produced the preceding ESC. As if stunned, lacking a solid tonal footing, we are given a succession of four non-diatonic chords, each spanning two bars, that reflect a battered, temporary disorientation: C minor (mm. 367–68), E-flat minor (mm. 369–70), F major (mm. 371–72), and D-flat minor (mm. 373–74). While the move from C minor to E-flat minor is certainly shadowy, that from F major to D-flat minor—in neo-Riemannian terms, the shift to F major's hexatonic pole—is darker still, immersing us into a moment of otherness that we cannot currently comprehend. We are passing through a murky threshold into a mysterious process that we cannot yet foresee.

Phase 2, mm. 375–90, initiates the process of regeneration: 16 bars that bar-by-bar, like a coiling spring, load into increasing power, energy, and anticipatory excitement. While we begin far afield, on E-flat major (mm. 375–78), the return of the P-incipit in the groaning bass (though ominously inflected with $\flat\hat{6}$) signals a new stirring of the seeds of that theme. Fortified by tellingly placed *sforzandi*, the P-incipit figure is replicated a half-step higher, on E minor (mm. 379–80). This sets off a dynamically accumulative harmonic rise, gaining in tension and tempo (with the tightening of the *stringendo* at m. 383). All of this is aimed directly at rising to and securing the dominant of C major, which dominant has been sounding as a pedal in the horns and timpani since m. 375 and is enhanced by the trombones in m. 384. The pitches of that V^7 are in place by m. 387 and are vigorously reiterated as the now-sure-footed bassline marches downward to the chordal root, which is attained at the end of m. 390 and discharges as an anacrusis (not a cadence) onto the C-major opening of phase 3, m. 391.

Within the coda the role of phase 2 is not merely to reattain the dominant of C major but to *supercharge* it. This escalating, "Beethovenian" buildup must be made so powerful, so determinedly pointed toward a "new" C major, that it reaches that higher level of intensity required to vault the music's narrative beyond the modally failed sonata and onto a higher, transcendent plane embracing and transfiguring the whole. One might read this transformational phase in either of two ways. On the one hand, it might signify the composer gathering together a renewed strength following the modally failed narrative in order to summon up the will sufficient to overcome it ("I will seize fate by the throat"). On the other hand, one might imagine it as the intervention of some externally generated process, like a *deus ex machina* or the command of history itself, ratifying the historical necessity of bringing this grand but risky symphonic project to a successful, C major completion.

The coda's third phase, mm. 391–447, opens into that transcendent C-major world, *più allegro* and fully confident of victory. The C-major PAC that will bring the movement and the symphony to full narrative closure is now in sight. All commentators observe that the music that begins at m. 391 is a transformation and displacement of the initial notes, 8̂-7̂-8̂-6̂-5̂, of the preceding sonata's P, with the 6̂-5̂ appearing in the upper winds. (This is especially clear in mm. 391–93 and 393–95.) More to the narrative point, though, this music, in its forward bolt, might be read as in dialogue with the topic family of the *gallop*: the metaphor of a noble steed charging its way past all obstacles toward certain C-major triumph.

Before reaching that C:PAC, the gallop to the cadence pauses to look back in retrospect to what has been achieved, not only in the finale, but in the whole symphony. This happens, of course, with the climactic chorale, mm. 407–16, replicating at pitch that interior phrase from the introduction's dedication emblem, mm. 47–51. There it had been intoned *piano*, *dolce*, and *più andante* by trombones and bassoons, carrying connotations of a solemn, devotional vow or a consecration of the project-to-come. In contrast, it is now rung out thrillingly, *fortissimo*, like a bright, blazoned image, in the strings and brass. (The *alla breve* time signature and *più allegro* tempo require a doubling of the original notation values to approximate the speed at which it was first heard.) This is an ecstatic declaration of accomplishment, bearing connotations of both celebration and valediction. Brahms's climactic return to that external dedication emblem shifts the focus one last time to the motivation and inspiration for wagering all to compose this symphony in the first place: "and now . . . now . . . *I have done it!*" In this C-major context the piercing brilliance of its initial, densely packed (and MONTE-generated) A-major chord, filling sonic space from top to bottom, could not be more spectacular. Like its model in the introduction, the ensuing phrase provides an impression of uplift, whose proclamatory half notes rise to the strongest possible C-major dominant (mm. 415–16)—a further supercharging within an already supercharged space.

Seizing upon that dominant, the gallop forward resumes in m. 417.[34] (Probably intentionally, its sense of giddy delight recalls that in Beethoven's coda to the Ninth Symphony's finale.) Three mighty windups, mm. 431–34, 435–38, and, most emphatically of all, 439–46, finally bring us to the long-sought C-major PAC in m. 447 with as decisive a finality as Brahms could muster. From the point of view of the sonata, this is not the moment of essential *structural* closure (the essential closure to the sonata had occurred, problematically, in C minor at m. 367) but rather that of the higher authority of essential *narrative* closure, at which point the C-major PAC at m. 447 can be understood as overturning the C-minor ESC of the preceding sonata. As discussed earlier in this chapter (and in *EST*, 304–5), in certain kinds of situations where a sonata movement is encased within an introduction-coda frame, Sonata Theory regards that external frame as the higher reality, one that subordinates the sonata as contingent, merely as a thing made or an inset narrative, generated and set into motion by the maker of that thing or narrator of that tale, represented in the introduction and coda.[35]

Elided with that commanding C:PAC, the coda's final 11 bars, mm. 447–57, can be regarded as the discursive coda's fourth and final phase, a *coda to the coda* (*EST*, 286). Such a coda typically reinforces or reaffirms the structural cadence that precedes it. Striking here is that rather than providing us with one or more additional I:PACs, these 11 bars instead articulate two plagal cadences (technically *postcadential* gestures) initiated by potent subdominants in mm. 448 and 450–52. This is how Brahms brings his arduous symphonic project, shot through with peril at every step, to an end. The implication of the two plagal cadences could hardly be clearer: "It is finished. So be it. Amen."

Sonata Types 4 and 5

In this book's chapters I have not dealt with Sonata Types 4 and 5—sonata-rondo and concerto-sonata—for two reasons. First, these two types introduce theoretical complications that steer us into more complex conceptual and analytical waters. Often playful by their very nature, Type 4 sonatas can be extraordinarily variable, even peculiar, in their realizations. And classical-era Type 5s, with the added ballast of their orchestral tutti (or "ritornello") framings that, from one point of view, encase a smaller-scale internal "sonata," stir up theoretical challenges that need to be explicated at length. (Stretching out over 170 pages, the four concluding chapters of *Elements of Sonata Theory*—the Type 5 chapters—can be regarded as a separate study, a book within a book.) And second, in order to deal adequately with Type 4 or Type 5 sonatas, at least from the Sonata Theory point of view, one needs to have a secure grasp of the principles that ground Sonata Types 1, 2, and 3. Still, in a practical *Handbook*, Types 4 and 5 should not go unmentioned. What follows are outlines of each that, while insufficient, at least point in the direction of the broader, more nuanced studies found in *EST*.

The Type 4 Sonata

The Type 4 sonata is the sonata-rondo, a blend of the sonata format proper (usually that of a Type 3 sonata, with exposition, developmental space, and recapitulation) with the recurrent refrains characteristic of a rondo. Some textbook accounts designate the sonata-rondo with such letter schemes as ABACAB'A, in which A is the refrain and B and C are considered as episodes, with the recapitulatory B' resolving an originally non-tonic B into the tonic. This string of letters is inadequate. First, it does not distinguish between the AB complex as a simple juxtaposition of two themes in differing keys and that complex as a fully realized sonata exposition. In order to be considered a Type 4, the movement should unfold in relatively grand proportions, and the AB and AB' sections should be laid out in the manner of an exposition and a recapitulation, passing through their normative action zones, P TR ' S / C—noting especially the action-zone presence of a TR. Second, even if one wished to retain the ABACAB'A letter-string for the sonata-rondo (which Sonata Theory does not), it would be better to divide it up with dashes in order to acknowledge the implicit rotations, each starting with A, thus producing AB–AC–AB'–A. (In such a designation AC is considered a full interior rotation, with C providing an alternative digression to the original B.) That string is how Sonata Theory designates the simpler, *symmetrical seven-part rondo* (*EST*, 402), which, even with its sonata-like effect of tonal resolution in B', does not normally rise to the level of a Type 4 sonata proper.

   In the most elementary Type 4 layout the rondo theme opens the exposition, opens the developmental space (which might then proceed to be either an episode or a development, or both), opens the recapitulation, and opens the post-recapitulatory coda as well. This theme fills out P-space and, at least in the classical era, its recurrences are almost always sounded in the tonic.[1] While variants of the general plan abound, Figure A.1 illustrates a prototypical way of realizing the Type 4 sonata. This schema can be useful to keep in mind, even when confronting the many Type 4s that alter or deviate from it. In Type 4 sonatas, P is labeled as P^{ref} ("P-refrain") because of its regular recurrences, and each recurrence is almost always prepared by means of an explicit retransition (RT), smoothing the path back into it. In Sonata Theory seminars, the initial Type 4 example that I have used is the exuberantly witty finale of Mozart's Symphony No. 35 in D, "Haffner," K. 385, in which the developmental space is fully rotational, referring to both P^{ref} and a (non-tonic) S.

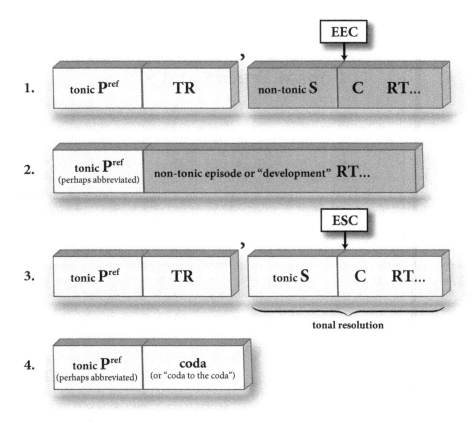

Figure A.1. A prototypical schema for the Type 4 sonata (four rotations).

As Figure A.1 indicates, this prototypical Type 4 schema is *quadri-rotational*: four rotational cycles, each beginning with the P-refrain, the rotation initiator, typically in the tonic, though the last cycle is customarily an incomplete or *half-rotation*, not proceeding beyond P^{ref} material into a contrasting idea. Here in Half-Rotation 4, one notices an engaging ambiguity. On the one hand, from the Type 3 perspective that rotation is coda-like in the sense that it is post-recapitulatory: the tonal aspects of the sonata have been fulfilled, and this last return of P^{ref} carries the sense of an after-the-end appendix (not to mention the fact that codas in Type 3 sonatas not infrequently start with a reference to at least the incipit of P). On the other hand, from the Type 4 perspective the duties of that schema—to display the recurrences of the "rondo" theme, the essence of which is its obligation to return—are not completed until P^{ref}, or at least a notable homage to its initial phrase, has been made. The concluding coda to Half-Rotation 4, then, might be construed as either (from the Type 3 perspective) a coda to the coda or (from the Type 4 perspective) a coda more properly to the last sounding of P^{ref} and by extension all that it has led to in the preceding structure.

The rondo and Type 4 format emerged as post-1760 vogues that were especially appropriate for witty, amusing finales, though they, or abbreviated variants of them, are sometimes found in slow movements. Rondo-oriented structures are never available for first movements or overtures. In the Type 4 sonata the rondo refrain, P^{ref}, is often a recognizable melodic type, usually distinguishable as a theme of "rondo character" or, as occasionally suggested, "*contredanse* character" (*EST*, 398): light, playful, and not infrequently disposed in some sort of closed form, such as a rounded binary (a a′ b a″) or other binary format, sometimes with internal repeats indicated (for example, ||:a a′:|| and ||:b a″:||).

Notwithstanding the possibility of internal repeats within P^{ref}, the Type 4 sonata's exposition is never repeated. This lack of an expositional repeat is one way of distinguishing between the Type 3 and Type 4 sonata in Haydn's finales, in which many of his Type 3s (featuring a repeated exposition) also begin with a P of the "rondo-character" type. What P sounds like, in other words, does not by itself classify the movement as a sonata-rondo—at least not from our present-day, structuralist point of view.

Complicating this last claim, though, is that the late eighteenth century used the term "rondo" freely, sometimes more to indicate thematic character than structural format *per se*. Mozart, for instance, labeled the finale of *Eine Kleine Nachtmusik* as a "rondo"—and the insouciant P theme certainly does crop up repeatedly, and wittily, in the subsequent structure, like a shiny token of irrepressible *buffa*-spirits—but he laid out the movement as an unambiguous Type 2 sonata. The same is true of his Rondo in D (for piano), K. 485, which from our perspective is formatted as a Type 3 sonata. This suggests that defining a rondo or Type 4 too closely can be misleading. It is also the case that many Type 3 finales lean strongly toward the Type 4 format and style, just as many Type 4 finales lean toward aspects of the Type 3. Some of this might be attributable to the influence of mid-eighteenth-century *sonata-ritornello blends*, with their recurring P themes, as discussed in chapters 4 and 11.

A number of other factors add further complications, many of which are dealt with in Chapter 18 of *EST*. One is that both the rondo proper and the Type 4 sonata (with full exposition) can appear in abbreviated formats. The (non-sonata) rondo, for instance—a straightforward juxtaposition of themes—can also appear in an AB–AC–A framework, not a "seven-part" but a "five-part" rondo, which itself can be subjected to freer variants. Additionally, the Type 4 sonata can be blended with the Type 3, the Type 1, and expanded Type 1 sonata; *EST*, 405–12, differentiates the different formats as Type 4^3, Type 4^1, and Type 4^{1-exp}, and cites examples of each. And Mozart's idiosyncratic blend of Type 4 procedures with concerto rhetoric in most of his concerto finales is a separate study in itself: "While certain broad principles are shared among them, his creative reshapings of the Type 4 concept from piece to piece remain a challenge to anyone who seeks to generalize about them" (*EST*, 417).

The larger point is that the mere adoption of a rondo or Type 4 format (or even to stylize P as a theme of "rondo character") seems to have been an invitation for playful experiments with form and tonality. From time to time, and particularly in Beethoven's rondos and Type 4s, the rondo-refrain can appear in an impudently "wrong key," demanding some sort of subsequent reaction or adjustment. On other occasions, an expected rondo-refrain (perhaps P^{ref}) will be omitted, thus running two episodes together. And Haydn's many rondo and Type 4 finales offer dozens of examples of surprises and unpredictable turns, sometimes resulting in *ad hoc* structures that diverge from presumably prototypical realizations of the Type 4 schema, even while remaining in a high-spirited dialogue with them (*EST*, 413–17). In some instances, Haydn's Type 4 finales suggest dialogic hybrids with other structural formats, as when P^{ref} returns are subjected to notable variation (as in his String Quartet in D, op. 71 no. 2/iv [Grave 2006, 290]). In short, the affable lightness of the Type 4 tone is frequently accompanied by clever, *ad hoc* treatments and alterations of what we might wish to imagine as any idealized type of the form. The rondo and sonata-rondo invite protean, mercurial realizations: the delightfully wry moment or exception always lurks around the corner.

The Type 5 Sonata

The Type 5 sonata is that found in classical-concerto first movements, which juxtapose formalized tutti passages (or ritornellos) for orchestra alone with extended passages in which the soloist steps forth front and center. This sonata type is found in the opening movements of all of Mozart's and Beethoven's concertos, along with those of their contemporaries and immediate successors. For those engaged with classical and early-romantic form, the most heuristically helpful way to begin the study of the Type 5 sonata is to absorb Mozart's thematically bountiful realizations of it. It is on his distinctive practice that this summary focuses, as do the four chapters devoted to it in the *Elements*.

To be sure, one finds divergences from the Mozartian customizations in the opening concerto movements of Beethoven and others. (Some of the Beethovenian ones will be mentioned in passing later.) These usually consist of differing ways of treating the thematic profiles of the action zones, though the outer shell of the format—the tutti and solo blocks' schematic alternations—remains quite consistent. Nonetheless, I should emphasize at the start that other composers of the later eighteenth and early nineteenth centuries treated the local details of the format somewhat differently than did Mozart—C. P. E. Bach, Joseph Haydn, Giovanni Battista Viotti, John Field, Carl Maria von Weber, Johann Nepomuk Hummel, Fryderyk Chopin, and others (as noted in Horton 2011 and 2015). In confronting all of these, though, Sonata Theory's (Mozart-oriented) model remains a helpful prototype. If that model is kept in mind—ready to perceive varying treatments of it—it is a relatively easy matter to turn to the often diverging, and often simpler, Type 5 realizations of other composers.

The Type 5 format persisted into the mid- and later nineteenth century, though by midcentury and beyond mostly as a self-consciously academic or classicizing option (as with Brahms's concertos). From at least Mendelssohn's concertos onward, concerto first movements could be written as sleeker, Type 3 sonatas, sometimes preceded either with a brief solo statement or flourish as an entrée (Schumann's and Grieg's Piano Concertos, Rachmaninoff's Second) or a more extended, full-blown introduction (Tchaikovsky's Violin Concerto and First Piano Concerto).

Tutti/Ritornello and solo blocks

In order to accommodate the solo and orchestra interplay, the Type 5 sonata has a number of distinguishing features. Most notably, to the Type 3 sonata format the movement adds (at least traditionally) four conspicuously separate orchestral passages that we designate as *tuttis* or *ritornellos*. (Either term will do.) Within the larger form, these are prominent *structural pillars* for the orchestra alone. One of their most obvious roles is to demarcate the main sectional divisions of the piece, either introducing or reinforcing the extended sections of the movement in which the solo leads and participates. The solo-led exposition, for instance (which Sonata Theory calls the *solo exposition*), is bracketed off by a broad orchestral tutti/ritornello that precedes it and a second, briefer one that follows it and separates it from the development.

One way to think of the most commonly encountered Type 5 sonata is to regard it as a Type 3 sonata (with solo and orchestra) interlarded with non-solo orchestral padding or commentary at certain generically preordained points.[2] This in fact was Georg Joseph Vogler's 1779 recipe for producing a concerto: one first writes "an ordinary sonata," that is, our Type 3 sonata, and then adds to it a "prelude, postlude, and interlude" for orchestra alone (*EST*, 435). Heinrich Christoph Koch's much-discussed 1793 descriptions of the formal plan of a concerto are more sophisticated than Vogler's, and apart from some of young Mozart's earliest experiments with concerto production in 1767 and 1772 ("concerto arrangements" or "pastiche concertos," some of which were adaptations of keyboard sonatas of J. C. Bach), the evidence suggests that he did not write his mature concertos in the manner that Vogler had described but instead began by drafting the movement in order, that is, with its opening orchestral ritornello (*EST*, 435–40, 449 n. 63).

The diagram in Figure A.2 sketches out the broad sections of a prototypical Type 5 sonata, particularly with those of Mozart in mind. Once again, while this diagram should not be taken a square-cut template to apply inflexibly to other composers, the Mozartian model is a convenient place to start in one's analyses of classical concertos.

Sonata Theory's shorthand designations for the tutti/ritornello pillars are R1 ("Ritornello 1"), R2, R3, and R4. In the classical style, though, R3 is the least pillar-like of the four. While it had been historically situated either at the end of the development or at the onset of the recapitulation, in practice it can be much abbreviated or omitted altogether. And R4, at the end of the movement, splits into two distinct parts, R4^1 and R4^2, surrounding the obligatory solo cadenza. The

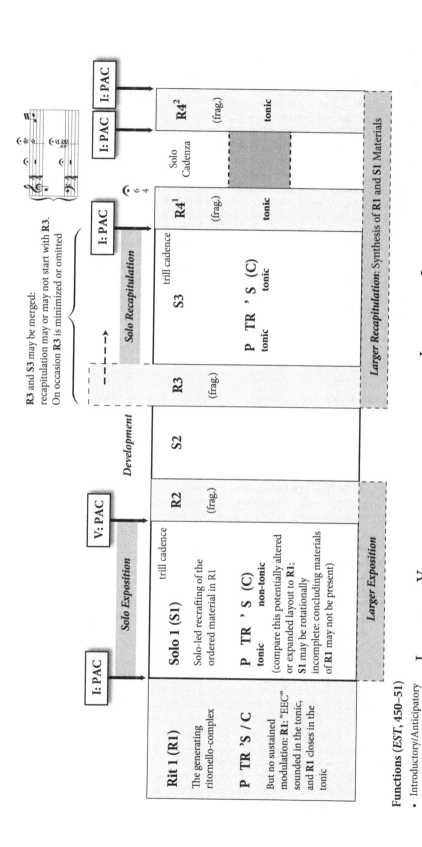

R3 and **S3** may be merged: recapitulation may or may not start with **R3**. On occasion **R3** is minimized or omitted

Rit 1 (R1)	Solo 1 (S1)	R2	Development S2	R3	Solo Recapitulation S3	R4¹	R4²

Rit 1 (R1)

The generating ritornello-complex

P TR ' S / C

But no sustained modulation: **R1**: "EEC" sounded in the tonic, and **R1** closes in the tonic

Solo Exposition

Solo 1 (S1)

trill cadence

Solo-led recrafting of the ordered material in R1

P TR ' S (C)
tonic   **non-tonic**

(compare this potentially altered or expanded layout to **R1**; **S1** may be rotationally incomplete: concluding materials of **R1** may not be present)

Larger Exposition

I: PAC   **V: PAC**

R2

(frag.)

Development

S2

R3

(frag.)

Solo Recapitulation

S3

trill cadence

P TR ' S (C)
tonic   tonic

I: PAC

R4¹

(frag.)

tonic

Solo Cadenza

I: PAC

R4²

(frag.)

tonic

I: PAC

Larger Recapitulation: Synthesis of **R1** and **S1** Materials

I   –   V

I   –   I

Functions (*EST*, 450–51)

- Introductory/Anticipatory   I
- Action-Zone Rhetoric
  (P TR ' S / C)
- Referential Rotation

Figure A.2. A prototypical schema for a Mozartian Type 5 sonata.

sonata-like sections in which the soloist plays are notated as S1 (solo exposition), S2 (development), and S3 (normally, beginning either at the start of the recapitulation or at that part of it that continues the recapitulation when the latter is begun with a brief R3).

The eighteenth-century Type 5 sonata arose as a hybrid between the older, Baroque ritornello concerto (alternating tutti sections—ritornellos—with solo sections) and the later-eighteenth-century, high-galant expectations of what we now call sonata form. Over the last half century, that conjoining of the stately old (the four R blocks) and the flexibly new (the three S blocks) has given rise to massive rounds of commentary and speculation about the relationship (or not) of these separate sections, especially the orchestral ritornellos, to more efficient sonata practices. Sorting one's way through these arguments is no easy undertaking.

When schematized into such a diagram as Figure A.2, the format is deceptively simple. Despite the Type 5's apparent rigidity of format, Mozart's realizations of it abound in imaginative variants. This gives rise to what the *Elements* characterizes as "the paradox of Mozart's concertos," at the heart of which lies the tension between the old-world formality of the ritornello pillars and the interactive freedom in the way its materials are handled or modified by the solo passages.

> The expressive core of these concertos resides in the charged gap between these contradictory pulls. On the one hand . . . Mozart's Type 5s are encumbered by the task of fulfilling certain quasi-archaic (or at least traditional) stations of concerto practice. . . . On the other hand, faced with these generic constraints, Mozart took every opportunity to realize them in surprising and inventive ways. . . . Paradoxically, the more calcified requirements seem to have enabled a more supple response, or at least to have encouraged one by way of a challenge. . . . As a result, each work is a world unto itself, with multiple internal interactions and conceptual threads binding together each whole as a unique utterance. (*EST*, 470–71)

This is why the *Elements* devotes four chapters to the Mozartian Type 5 sonata and why we must be content to provide only a cursory overview of it here.[3]

Tutti/Ritornello 1 (R1)

Beginning and ending in the tonic key, the opening orchestral tutti/ritornello, R1, plays a critical role in the architecture of the whole. In Mozart and Beethoven concertos it can last for two or more minutes before the soloist enters. (In three prominent piano concertos the soloist is given a brief role at the opening of the piece, an exceptional practice in each case: interleaved with the opening theme in Mozart's No. 9 in E-flat, K. 271; as the unexpected sounding of R1's opening phrase in Beethoven's No. 4 in G, op. 58; and as a ringingly resonant, expanded display-anacrusis to R1 in Beethoven's No. 5 in E-flat, op. 73.) R1's succession of musical ideas is typically laid out in the manner of an exposition's four action spaces: P TR ' S / C. Nonetheless, *since R1 normatively begins and ends in the tonic key, it should not be considered an exposition.* To qualify as a true "exposition," the S and C zones should have been secured with one or more final cadences in a non-tonic key: V:PAC in a major-mode work, III:PAC or v:PAC in a minor-mode one.

In the prototypical, Mozartian initial ritornello (R1), S and C are sounded completely in the tonic. On some occasions, though, a move to a non-tonic key might be made at some point in R1, usually at or around S, "as if" R1 were being initially imagined as the exposition of a symphony. When this happens, we soon find out that the contrasting key cannot be sustained, since R1 will shortly thereafter revert back to the tonic and conclude there. Such internal tonal swerves can be found, for instance, in Mozart's Piano Concertos in D minor, K. 466 (where the first bars of R1:\S are initiated in III), and in C, K. 503 (where R1:\TR ends emphatically in V). And the opening movements of the Beethoven's First, Second, Third, and Fourth Piano Concertos make a point of visiting non-tonic key areas somewhere in Ritornello 1 for a "wrong-key," non-tonic start to R1:\S before being pulled back into the tonic key to conclude R1 "correctly."[4] Similar R1 tonal moves can be found in several of the proto- or early-romantic piano concertos of Field, Hummel, Moscheles, Ries, and Kalkbrenner, which sometimes present all or nearly all of the entirety of

R1:\S in a subordinate key before returning to the tonic to complete R1 (Horton 2011; Hepokoski 2012, 248–49 nn. 38 and 44).

Even while R1 begins and ends in the tonic key, there is no denying the unmistakably exposition-like, four-action-zone layout of the classical-era Ritornello 1 (P TR ' S / C). Different composers, of course, fill these four rhetorical zones in individualized ways. Mozart's opening tuttis (and often his subsequent solo expositions as well) are thematically prolix, built as concatenations of contrasting thematic modules While his multiplicity of themes can be readily housed within the standard rhetorical zones, their abundance typically produces the impression of a spontaneous, plentiful bouquet of quasi-improvisational thematic ideas, whose succession is yet, somehow, held in a perfect balance, with each "new" theme reacting to or commenting on its predecessor(s). On the other hand, Beethoven's opening tuttis (and his solo expositions) are tauter—even sternly so, as if duty-bound to a conviction of economic principle. Quite different from Mozart's R1s, they are less thematically extravagant, more concentrated on the processual development and growth of the initial theme's melodic or rhythmic profile.

However this or that composer decides to realize it, R1 provides the *first referential layout* of the movement—the *referential rotation* of ordered thematic materials to which all subsequent ones should be compared and understood. One might imagine Ritornello 1 as making an initial proposal of thematic ideas that may then, in the subsequent solo exposition, be revisited, added to, or adapted (with the proper expositional modulation) in a variety of ways. Thus arise what *EST* describes as "the three structural functions of Ritornello 1" (449–51), although the degrees to which any one of them might be emphasized can vary, usually according to the length of R1 and the grand-scale ambitions (or not) of the movement. These three functions are:

- the *introductory-anticipatory function* (anticipating the entry of the soloist);
- the *expositional-rhetoric function* (the four-zone, P TR ' S / C rhetorical layout of most R1s);
- the *referential-layout function* (providing an initial rotation of musical ideas to which later, diverging ones are to be compared).

Because some of the thematic material of the solo exposition can differ from that of R1—especially but not only in Mozart's concertos—a central challenge in the analysis of Type 5s is to keep track of the themes and to remember whether or not they were first presented in the orchestra's thematic statement in R1. It is because of this potential profusion of themes that Sonata Theory has recourse to the most complex of its shorthand designators. With concertos, though, this complexity can't be avoided; tracking the courses of the themes is an analytical imperative. That some of the movement's themes are first introduced in R1 while others appear first in S1 is the cause of the many theoretical complications that we find in Type 5s.

EST identifies all the Ritornello 1 themes and all their later recurrences with the prefix R1:\ (R-one-colon-backslash). By contrast, any theme newly introduced in the solo exposition is marked with the prefix S1:\ (S-one-colon-backslash). Thus the action-zone succession in Ritornello 1 (Tutti 1) is: R1:\P, R1:\TR, R1:\S (leading to R1:\EEC), and R1:\C, while the succession found in Solo 1 will contain both R1 material (such as R1:\P or R1:\S$^{1.1}$) along with any S1 material first introduced there (such as, say, S1:\S^1, which would indicate that the soloist presents "its own," new theme, S^1, at the onset of the solo exposition's S-space [S1]). Further complications crop up when we use decimal designators of individual modules (such as R1:\S$^{1.2}$ or R1:\C$^{2.2}$).

Of these shorthand designators, the most conceptually problematic is R1:\EEC, which in the tonic-grounded R1 is almost always a I:PAC. The problem, once again, is that the "EEC," by definition (a term coined to refer to *expositional* practice), is the first *non-tonic* PAC after the onset of S (usually a V:PAC or a III:PAC) that goes on to differing material. This means that within the R1, with its *tonic-key* context, the label R1:\EEC is only an efficient way of saying two things: that this would be a "real EEC" if it were in V or III, as in an exposition; and that in the narrative fiction of the piece Ritornello 1 is proposing that this be the analogous moment of the essential expositional closure in the solo exposition to follow (S1:\EEC). But in that subsequent exposition this might or might not be the case. The S1:\EEC need not be congruent with that of the R1:\EEC, most obviously when the S1:\EEC is produced by a non-R1 theme introduced by the soloist, an issue to which we shall return.

The solo exposition (S1)

Once R1 has run its course, the time has arrived for the soloist to enter. This is a dramatically charged moment. While from time to time the R1-S1 seam might be unusually negotiated, there are two normative options for how to do this: the soloist can take up R1:\P at once, thereby initiating the *solo exposition* (S1); or the soloist can enter with a brief, warm-up passage of new material—perhaps a modest link, a bridge, or a *thematic preface*—soon finding its way, in most cases, to R1:\P (initiated by either the soloist or the orchestra) and the solo exposition proper.

Think of the solo exposition, S1—whether by Mozart or anyone else—as a staging of the soloist's adaptation of (or personalized commentary on) the thematic succession offered in R1. While much of the R1 material will surface in S1—R1:\P, for instance, is sure to appear at or near the opening—the soloist may well replace or add to some of R1's proposed ideas, taking them into new directions. The analyst's task is to compare the material of S1, bar for bar, theme for theme, with R1's referential layout to determine how they differ: what narrative is each telling? When several of the solo exposition's thematic materials differ from those of R1, the S1 response to R1 will have produced an *alternative referential layout* to that proposed in R1. By the end of the solo exposition, then, we will have had two separate layouts, two differing paths through the normative succession of action zones: that in R1 and that in S1. It will be the task of the recapitulation to reconcile or synthesize these two thematic paths.

R1 and S1 may be quite similar thematically, as in Mozart's Piano Concerto No. 23 in A, K. 488. More often, though, at least within Mozart's concertos, the solo exposition differs from R1 at a number of spots. The most common divergences occur when:

- the soloist replaces the music of R1:\TR with newly introduced, thematic, and solo-led S1:\TR material (which Sonata Theory refers to as a *sujet libre* [*EST*, 525–28]);
- the soloist begins a solo-led version of R1:\S but before long provides it with a substantially different continuation;
- Solo 1's S space is expanded into a *trimodular block* (TMB, *EST*, 537–40, and chapter 4 of this volume, p. 64), in which the soloist presents both its own, new S theme and that heard earlier in the opening tutti. The result is the impression of "double S themes," one new theme (to be understood as the soloist's more personalized statement) and one already heard in R1. Most often, though not invariably, the new theme is presented first, as a "fresh start" to S space. Instead of leading to its own PAC, though, this theme will usually dissolve into TR-like behavior to set up *a second MC* in the center of S-space (the first will have preceded S space), whereupon the opening tutti's S theme will then emerge. The appearance of this *second MC + S effect* is what turns Solo 1's S space into a *trimodular block*. In this scenario we have: S1:\TM^1 (the soloist's new theme), dissolving into TM^2 (==>TM^2, setting up the second MC), and TM^3 (R1's originally proposed S theme). On other occasions, though, one might find the order or themes switched, with R1's S theme heard before the soloist's new one.
- somewhere during or after S-space, the soloist launches into the generically expected practice of concluding the solo exposition with a *display episode* (DE) of virtuosic but non-thematic figuration—rapid-fire scales, runs arpeggios, sequences, or invertible counterpoint—rounding off the whole with an emphatic *trill cadence* (V:PAC or, in a minor-mode concerto, III:PAC) that elides into the *forte*, affirmative orchestral entry of Ritornello/Tutti 2 (R2).[5] (On very infrequent occasions, as noted in *EST*, 548, the onset of R2 might begin by diverting the soloist's trill cadence into a deceptive resolution—a stern, ♭VI refusal—as in Beethoven's Triple Concerto and Violin Concerto, which latter's hyper-expansive R2, retracing much of the previously heard music, is unusual in a number of respects.)

It should be added that the obligatory display episode might be situated either *within* Solo 1's S space or *beyond* it, in C space. That is determinable, as always, by locating the first appropriately non-tonic PAC within S space that goes on to differing material. In Mozart's first movements one might find any of three different situations:

- the S1:\EEC might occur *within* S space, which happens when the "thematic" portions of S space do not bring us to their own PAC but instead merge into a non-thematic concluding display episode (DE) that finally brings S space to a close with the emphatic trill cadence that elides with the downbeat of R2; in this last case the non-thematic display episode is folded into R1:\S space as its virtuosic final feature, and Solo 1 will house no C modules (and certainly none of those that had been proposed in R1), which will have to be pushed forward into the orchestral R2;
- the S1:\EEC might occur as a cadential *elision* into the moment of the stylistic switch into the display episode, relegating all of the latter (S1:\DE) to S1:\C space and thus still awaiting the arrival of R1:\C material, which will have to be fully or partially recovered in R2.
- the S1:\EEC might be placed *prior* to or elided with the sounding of one or more the obviously thematic C modules that had first been heard in R1, now similarly confirmed as C modules within S1; in this case the shift into the display episode will emerge at some later point in C space, either after a previously heard C theme or shifted into within one (R1:\C==>S1:\DE).

From the Sonata Theory perspective the only caveat is that the S1:\EEC may not be placed at a rotational point earlier than that at which the R1:\EEC had occurred. If one finds, for instance, that a new theme in Solo 1 leads to a strong V:PAC but then, following this, the music proceeds into the R1:\S theme, that latter theme should be considered as remaining within Solo 1's S space. The basic principle is that material initially presented within one action zone in Ritornello 1—the most foundational determiner of the rotational succession—should not normally be shifted to a different action zone in Solo 1.

The role of Ritornello 2 (R2): solo exposition and larger exposition

In Mozart's concertos it is usually the case that the solo exposition's music will not have traced its course all the way to the last of R1's C modules. The result is a *rotational incompleteness*, a lack or a falling-short. This invites a drive toward rotational completion through the sounding of some or all of R1's concluding modules in the orchestral music, R2, that follows the concluding trill cadence of S1. At least some of those R1:\C modules unattained in S1, then, might be presented, in order, in the orchestra's ensuing, briskly efficient R2.

And yet Mozart's most normative opening of R2 presents us with another issue. In most of his concertos R2 begins with a re-sounding of the *forte*, vigorous onset of initial tutti's transition zone (R1:\TR[1.1]), declaratively placed at the onset of Ritornello 2 to affirm the soloist's emphatic, concluding trill cadence in the secondary key. Once that has been done—once we hear the R1:\TR[1.1] cadential affirmation at the beginning of R2 in III or V—R2 usually merges into a non-tonic statement of some, but perhaps not all, of the R1:\C modules to which the solo exposition's rotational journey had not yet arrived. In other words, once past its generically normative but *rotationally inert* R1:\TR[1.1] opening move, and using the concluding modules of R1 as a referential guide, R2 *can continue the rotation left incomplete in S1.*[6] And even here in R2 the rotation might also be left incomplete, saving that full completion for the R4[2] statement at the end of the movement.

Understanding the rotational practice within concerto movements is such a central feature of Sonata Theory's Type 5 concept that it bears restating and leads to an important distinction. When the solo exposition is rotationally incomplete (lacking one or more final modules of R1:\C), the latter part of R2 often sounds some or all of the missing modules, as if trying to make its way to the end of R1's rotation. For this reason S1+R2 is considered to be a *larger exposition*, as shown in Figure A.2, since it will still be seeking to complete final material not heard in the solo exposition. This means that in a Type 5 sonata, following the opening orchestral music, the proto-expositional R1, we have both a *solo exposition*—in some senses S1 is a "complete" exposition considered only on its own terms—and the add-on to it, R2, that, recalling what had happened at the end of R1, expands the solo exposition into a *larger exposition*. This double-structural effect will recur in the recapitulation, as also shown in Figure A.2. When R2, the final section of the larger exposition, does not succeed in finding its way to the thematic end of R1 (the most fundamental referential layout), it will be R4^2's final touch of synthesis that accomplishes this.

Solo 2 (S2): developmental space

R2 may or may not be cadentially closed. If it is not, it will merge into S2 and the soloist's "take-over." However it ends, it is immediately followed by Solo 2, S2, fashioned in the manner of a modulatory development, though that developmental space may well contain one or more new ideas that can impress us as thematic episodes. "In general," though, "Mozart's solo-dominated Type 5 developments . . . [tend to] pursue material only loosely related to expositional material, if related at all, although several of them do take up an idea or two that had been sounded [in Ritornello 1 or Solo 1]. In nearly all such cases one can find some connection to earlier music: a characteristic rhythm or a small feature of figuration" (*EST*, 563). Most typically, Mozart hands S2 over to sequential patterns of solo-virtuosic figuration.

Ritornello 3, Solo 3, and Ritornello 4 (R3, S3, R41, R42): solo and larger recapitulations

As already mentioned, Ritornello 3, R3, is the most difficult of the tuttis to characterize. By the time of Mozart and Beethoven it may be little more than an orchestral passage at the end of the development leading into the recapitulation, in which case it might be hardly perceptible as such. In some cases it may seem either to be omitted altogether or to consist of only a few orchestral bars that lead off the recapitulatory rotation with the R1:\P theme (heard as it had been sounded at the beginning of R1) before yielding to soloist participation.

Solo 3 (S3) is the *solo recapitulation*, usually folding back into itself any R1:\S thematic modules that might have been omitted in S1 and nearly always producing its own S3:\ESC while not yet finding its way to the end of R1's modular succession. Reaching that end-point will be the task of R4—more precisely, of R4^2, following the solo cadenza. Considered together, then, the [R3] + S3 + R4^1 + R4^2 grouping constitutes the *larger recapitulation*. It will be the task of the larger recapitulation to serve as the agent of *synthesis*, collecting, bringing back, ordering, and sounding in the tonic key all of the thematic material heard *after the medial caesuras* of both Ritornello 1 (what occurs in Ritornello 1 after R1:\MC) and the solo exposition (what occurs in Solo 1 after S1:\MC). This is what most commands our analytical attention: the way in which all the post-MC themes are returned to and thus synthesized in the larger recapitulation—like the final fitting-together of previously separated puzzle pieces, thereby embellishing and complementing the satisfaction of their tonal resolution.

As already noted, Ritornello/Tutti 4, R4, is split into its two halves divided by the solo cadenza. R4^1 begins at the point of the solo recapitulation's concluding trill cadence. It may or may not begin similarly to R2. However it begins, it will soon lead to an emphatic $^6_4$ chord, sustained by a fermata, to lay out a platform for the soloist's cadenza. The cadenza was originally conceived to be improvised, though written-out cadenzas are common today, and in his Fifth Piano Concerto Beethoven famously integrated cadenza-like material into this portion of the score itself: *non si fa una Cadenza, ma s'attacca subito il seguente*. The traditional, classical cadenza is regularly disposed to sound like a free recasting of some of the movement's themes (as it happens, often in rotational order). Its concluding, hyper-flashy trill cadence, V^7-I, dovetails with the onset of the orchestral R4^2, whose burden is to sound any remaining closing modules, some of which might not have been heard since the end of R1. Once this has happened, this final synthesis-rotation will have been completed, and the movement is brought to its close.

Notes

Epigraphs

1. Frye, *The Secular Scripture: A Study of the Structure of Romance* (The Charles Eliot Norton Lectures, 1974–75) (Cambridge, MA: Harvard University Press, 1976), 166.
2. Jauss, "Sketch of a Theory and History of Aesthetic Experience," in Jauss, *Aesthetic Experience and Literary Hermeneutics*, trans. Michael Shaw (Minneapolis: University of Minnesota Press, 1982), 31.
3. Felski, *The Limits of Critique* (Chicago: University of Chicago Press, 2015), 12
4. Adorno, "The Essay as Form," in *Notes to Literature: Volume One*, ed. Rolf Tiedemann, trans. Shierry Weber Nicholsen (New York: Columbia University Press, 1991), 11.

Chapter 1

1. Cf. Yust's quasi-phenomenological description of experiencing music as a "temporal structure" in which one travels step by step through a "musical landscape" to arrive successively at various "points" generically predefined to posit "a definite temporal ordering of those points. . . . As we listen, we look ahead . . . seeing proximate and more distant goals, and some of those in between. . . . The composer shapes a musical landscape to, above all else, carefully control the temporal experience of traversing that landscape" (2018, 3–5)—all of which recalls aspects of Husserl's concept of protention, now effected over longer spans of time and prepared in advance with the experiences and expectations of prototypes of the present state of the relevant genre kept in mind, as posited in Huron 2006 and elsewhere.
2. On embodied cognition, see, e.g., Cox 2016 and Korsakova-Kreyn 2018. From another perspective, engaging with music is particularly susceptible to our bracketing out the sense of externally elapsing time and slipping into what Csikszentmihályi called the "optimal experience" produced by "flow," "a state in which people are so involved in an activity that nothing else seems to matter; the experience is so enjoyable that people will continue to do it even at great cost, for the sheer sake of doing it" (1990, 4). Becker's ethnomusicological study of "deep listeners" to music describes them as experiencing "a nearness to trance" (2004, 2) that is cognitively enmeshed with emotional response, and she treats the phenomenon of "becoming the music" (141–44) in terms of Damasio's concept of "core consciousness" (1999, 82–106).
3. Levine's formulation, though with respect to "forms" rather than genres, is helpful: "*Forms do political work in particular historical circumstances*. . . . Forms matter . . . because they shape what is possible to think, say, and do in a given context" (2015, 5).
4. Cf. Hatten, 2018, 286: "Formal functions in the Classical style, when manifested in prototypical structures (e.g., sentences or periods) and forms (e.g., sonatas or sonata rondos) may also create virtual backgrounds against which more salient events can be interpreted as actorially agential," which in turn can suggest a "virtual agential freedom in their (willful) transcending of implied structures."

5. Transferring the point to a higher level, we might also suspect that while a genre is responsive to and enabled by its situatedness within specific cultural circumstances, it would be similarly reductive to collapse a genre into nothing more than a symptom of those circumstances, which were always more culturally complex, more culturally fraught, than our simpler characterizations of them today.

6. In this formulation the "implied listener or performer"—a construct "prestructured" by the details of the individual text itself, along with those of its genre—is an adaptation of the idealized, phenomenological concept that Iser 1978, 20–38, proposed for readers of literature, based on his earlier study, *The Implied Reader* (trans. 1974). Obviously, "real" listeners or performers—then or now, each with his or her own historical or personal constraints also in play—might or might not strive to attain such an "implied" status.

7. Byros 2009, 2012, and 2015, 217–28, provide additional overviews of "schema" and "subschemata" as systems of "replicated patterning" or "predetermined ... sequence[s] of action," with particular reference to Koch's late-eighteenth-century description of "sonata form."

8. What might be the entailments of my references in the preceding paragraphs to the concepts of normativity, schema, generic guideline, or prototype? As Horton points out, one might appeal to any of "three notions of normativity." Norms (such as the classical-era medial-caesura norms offered by Sonata Theory that are Horton's immediate concern) "can be understood *quantitatively*, as conventions that are statistically verified; *sociologically*, as concepts regulating social praxis; or *prototypically*, as cognitive types permitting the assimilation of diverse information" (2017, 153). A prototype, then, is not the same thing as a compositional norm: a prototype need not be statistically predominant, only more salient cognitively. At least for Mozartian-era composition, Sonata Theory's perspective might be helpfully construed from any of these three perspectives, though the *Elements* does order several of its "default" choice-levels in a way that implies (at least for Mozart and Haydn) a statistical frequency. Such defaults do not always apply in the same way from the norm-transgressing Beethoven onward—which is what Horton seeks to demonstrate. (Some nuances in Sonata Theory's concepts of norm and deformation are provided in chapters 4, 7, 9, 11, and 12.)

9. Waltham-Smith's observation is thicker, more provocative than the preceding paragraph suggests. Among other things, she explores questions of the presumed "ownership" of musical works and styles and their potential appropriations or "exappropriations" as "property"; and of the act of listening to music as an "interplay of production and consumption" (18). On her reading such moments in Haydn harbor a critical moment in that they can call attention to the artifice of the given system's "conventionality," obliging listeners to notice it as such, as "*convention used unconventionally*" (6), "hear[ing] convention *as* convention" (67). In turn, this precipitates reflections "on own existence as style" (20), on "its own condition of possibility [as residing] in conventionality" (27). This "conventionality" is not reducible to a set of conventions or devices. "We get closer to the idea of conventionality when we consider what happens when conventions are misused, as is often Haydn's wont. Recognizing the application or misapplication of a norm leads to the recognition of shared recognition" (17). Only this "misapplication" of a norm—its fragmentary brokenness away from familiar usage— draws forth that usually unnoticed norm to be perceived as such and thereby as a purely contingent aspect of style. On the one hand, such lines of argument recall those of Adorno on the "alienated" aspect of late Beethoven; on the other hand, they can recall Heidegger's distinction between two modes of being: the "ready-to-hand" (*Zuhandenheit*, as of our "unseen" awareness of tools when they are put to their conventional uses) and the "present-at-hand" (*Vorhandensein*, as of our gaze and at tools when they become broken or useless, enabling us to note their existence as such).

10. The time-space conversion suggested here synchronizes with now-familiar conceptual-metaphor theory, as in, e.g., Lakoff and Johnson 1980, Lakoff 1993, Fauconnier and Turner

1998 and 2002, and others. Within music cognition, a recent and convenient discussion is provided in Cox 2016, which treats such target-source domain mappings as: TIME IS SPACE; TIME IS A CONTAINER; TEMPORAL LOCATIONS ARE SPATIAL LOCATIONS, and so on.

11. I elaborate the idea of the conceptual priority of generic action spaces in Hepokoski 2010, paragraphs 18–20.

12. The strictest current view, still a pragmatically clarifying one for current analysis of classical-style and early-romantic art music, is that of form-functional theory, elaborated in Caplin 1998, 42–45; 2004; and 2013, 4–5. Recent responses to it, though, have demonstrated that cadence theory is historically complicated and at some level incapable of settling comfortably into non-period-specific definitive assertions—or even, at times, into all situations found in the ca. 1780–1810 era (Caplin's years of "the core repertory of the high Viennese classical style" [1998, 3]). From the eighteenth-century theoretical point of view, cadential or quasi-cadential approaches to the tonic from V (or an inversion of V) exist in a continuum of closural strengths. The closural decisiveness of each depends on such factors as: the number of chords included, and beats traversed, in the "cadence" proper; a leap of a fourth or a fifth in the bass to the tonic (our PAC or IAC, surely the strongest cadential move) as opposed to a weaker, stepwise bass approach to the tonic (V^6 to I or V^4_3 to I); the existence, or not, of a 4-3 suspension above the V; the presence, or not, of an additional, enhancing $^6_4$ chord above scale degree $\hat5$ in the bass before resolving to V; and the appearance, or not, of a predominant chord or other progression preceding the V. Some key texts investigating the situation include: Gjerdingen 2007, 139–76; Holtmeier 2011; Diergarten 2011 and 2015; Sanguinetti 2012, 105–10; Burstein 2014; Neuwirth and Bergé 2015; and Harrison 2019.

13. The cadence types applied in this book are those summarized in Caplin 1998, 27–29, and 2013, 4–5.

14. The term "journey" is from Burstein 2016, who contrasts it with the CONTAINER concept of action spaces, arguing that for earlier, mid-eighteenth-century works the concept of a journey can seem more appropriate. While in certain situations this is clearly the case, my response is provided in the preceding and, more extensively laid out, in 2016, 49–53. Cf. Yust's concept of traversing a "musical landscape" in order to arrive at certain pre-established "points" along the way (2018, 3–5; see also n. 1 in this chapter).

15. Music-scholarly calls for a return to the surface have been made most urgently by those advocating semiotic or topical approaches in the analysis of this repertory, as with Hatten's sustained attention to the "irreducible significance of the surface," that is, "to the deep expressive import of those events that in purely structural analyses are too often quickly bracketed off—for example, by interpretations that unwittingly depreciate nonharmonic tones as mere ornaments or diminutions elaborating a more fundamental structure" (2018, 184; cf. Hatten 1994, 160, 278, where the "irreducible" claim was initially made). One of the most tenacious appeals along these lines, to the point of the near-sidelining of structural aspects that can be uncovered by other, more technically oriented analytical approaches, has been that of Allanbrook 2014, an advocate of Ratner's topical and terminological approach to discussions of classical-era music: "It is time to sing the praises of superficiality. . . to ask of music analysis that it at least attempt an account of the palpable, of the *phainomena*. . . . Most of the analytical methods used in the twentieth century have taught us to withdraw from the surface in the belief that deeper truths lay concealed beneath. . . . Modern theories of musical depth take for granted the existence of a surface, but only as the plane from which, paradoxically, one must immediately descend in order to transcend" (85–86).

It is within the field of literary-critical studies that the return to the pleasures and enticements of the surface has been most elaborately theorized. With a prehistory in writings of such writers as of Barthes, Sontag, and others, the twenty-first-century concept of "surface reading" has been introduced and debated in an entire issue of *Representations* entitled "How We Read Now" (2009 [108 (1)]), led off by the much-noted manifesto of Best and Marcus: "We take surface to mean what is evident, perceptible, apprehensible in texts; what is neither hidden nor hiding. . . . A surface is what insists on being looked at rather than what we must train ourselves to see *through*" (9). Cf. also the reasoned discussion of Best and Marcus, and much else of relevance, in Felski 2015, 52–56 and passim, along with the collection edited by Anker and Felski 2017—all of which can be complemented by the essays advocating the recovery of variously inflected types of "new formalism," beyond the older, narrower concept of it in the approach to literature, as in the *Reading for Form* collection edited by Wolfson and Marshall 2006, or the expansive reconfigurations of "formalism" as found, e.g., in Levine 2015.

16. Allanbrook 2014, 109–11, lists many dozens of these topics (or "musical commonplaces" of the late-eighteenth century) in her provisional "map of the known musical cosmos . . . [one] amenable to infinite extension. . . . Jumbled together are characteristic styles, social dances, vocal and instrumental effects, textures, and so on. . . . [Successions of these commonplaces are] what is most immediately palpable to the listener—on the surface, where listening takes place."

17. Brody 2016 reflects helpfully on the variety of form-theoretical positions (including that of Sonata Theory) regarding the claims of harmonic vs. thematic processes in the determination of formal types.

18. The quotation is a paraphrase of a remark by Jean-Paul Sartre (*What Is Literature?*), as reconfigured in Iser 1978, 207. It is cited as a leading idea of *EST*'s Appendix 1, "Some Grounding Principles of Sonata Theory" (605).

19. Wittgenstein, *Philosophical Investigations* (rev. 4th ed., 2009), "Part 2" or "Philosophy of Psychology," section xi, no. 113.

20. Whitney Davis 2011 argues that our seeing or valuing "formality" in an artwork (as a result of a conviction of the vital importance of "form" and "formalism"), itself a practice leaning toward the ahistorical, is the product of concrete historical and social moments: "Formality is not an inherent property of artifacts or works of art. Rather, formality is an aspect of an object recognized by the human subjects who perceive it. . . . If anything, formalism should be an intensive study of the *subjects* who look closely at artifacts or works of art" (53).

21. Caplin 2004, 254–55 describes formal function as "the specific role played by a particular musical passage in the formal organization of a work. It generally expresses a temporal sense of beginning, middle, end, before-the-beginning, or after-the-end." A fuller elaboration of the concept is presented in Caplin 2009.

22. What follows here is only a quick overview. In seminars I not only assign readings from Caplin but also provide students with a fuller summary, "The Classification of Theme Types: Period, Sentence, Hybrid," that provides more elaborate considerations of these matters. I have currently made that paper available in the "unpublished writings" section at jameshepokoski. com. In it I offer a way of approaching the form-functional analysis of most themes of this era by following what I call a *four-step method*—essentially an ordered screening process. I also provide some caveats to the form-functional classifications and suggest alternative ways of construing some of the theme types that we encounter in this repertory.

23. In cadential terms such a situation presents us with what amounts to a repeated consequent (or "consequent-styled phrase"), each ending with the same authentic cadence—that is, as two hearings of a "consequent" that is not responding to a preceding antecedent. Yet in situations where encountering thematic period structure at this point of the piece is the strong norm, the second phrase might still be heard as responding to or complementing the first, though this may be a more common practice in the decades after the classical period. (See, e.g., the first eight bars of Chopin's Nocturne in E-flat, op. 9 no. 2.) Given the relative infrequency

of this situation and the strength of the antecedent-consequent norm—and departing here from form-functional theory—I suggest by way of nuance that the first "consequent" (the first four bars, ending with a PAC) might be heard as being situated "in antecedent position," that is, as in dialogue with the periodic norm (antecedent + consequent), yet departing from it in its uncommon, early PAC-closure at the end of the first phrase. (Lawrence 2020 offers an alternative view of this situation.)

24. For Caplin, the aa′ initiating function of a *presentation* (b.i. + b.i′) should also be supported by a prolongation of tonic harmony. While this is often the case, Sonata Theory does not insist on the harmonic point. This throws the emphasis more on the b.i. + b.i.′ melodic configuration, coupled with a sense of its thematic-initiation role.

25. For two instructive examples of adaptations of the QUIESCENZA see: the [compound] consequent phrase, mm. 9–16, of the recurrent ritornello theme in the third movement of Bach's Violin Concerto E, BWV 1042; and the opening two bars of the Adagio molto introduction to Beethoven's Symphony No. 1 in C, where the opening chord, V^7 of IV, is the second harmonic element of the standard QUIESCENZA (the first element is absent), and the final element, in the second half of m. 2, is supported not by a tonic chord but rather by the "deceptive" submediant chord.

26. The broader conceptual backdrop for Sonata Theory—its grounding principles of dialogic form, hermeneutic theory, and more—is laid out more formally in the sixteen propositions found in Appendix 1 of *EST*, 603–10 ("convictions and conclusions that helped to generate the theory").

Chapter 2

1. "A hallmark of the galant style was a particular repertory of stock musical phrases employed in conventional sequences. Local and personal preferences among patrons and musicians resulted in presentations of this repertory that favored different positions along various semantic axes—light/heavy, comic/serious, sensitive/bravura, and so on.... [The] 'galant' [was] a code of conduct ... an eighteenth-century courtly ideal (adaptable to city life), and ... a carefully taught set of musical behaviors.... The galant composer necessarily worked in the here and now.... The art of galant music, like the art of figure skating, is replete with compulsory and free-style 'figures,'" standard musical/contrapuntal formulas that we now classify as "schemata" (Gjerdingen 2007, 6–7). From another perspective, Allanbrook reads much late-eighteenth-century instrumental music as combining and recombining stock topical signifiers whose origins lay in comic opera. Her view of the high galant style, especially in Mozart's hands, is one grounded in "comic mimesis," the product of successions of "concise mimetic units," all tending "toward thematic multiplicity and contrast in the application of those expressive modes" (2014, 90).

2. "Module" can therefore mean something as small as what form-functional theory calls an "idea" ("minimally, a 2-m. unit. A constituent member of a phrase" [Caplin 1998, 255; 2013, 708])—such as "basic idea," "contrasting idea," and "cadential idea"—but it can also suggest the modestly extended joining-together of form-functional "ideas." Sonata Theory, however, would not refer to longer expositional stretches (such as P and TR together, or even a complex TR) as modules.

3. Allanbrook 1992 hears in these measures a topical combination of "singing style" (*cantabile*) with "the arpeggiated-music-box style" and compares this opening favorably to that of the mechanical, "music-box" onset of K. 545/i (147–49). Her topical reading of the entire movement, K. 333/i, is based on the claim that "the music-box-appoggiatura and virtuoso-brilliant

styles are juxtaposed ['worked out, developed, *ausgearbeitet*'] to be treated speculatively in comparison and contrast, their oppositions assimilated, and then separated again . . ." (169), or, as she put it in more recent writing, the movement is informed by "the interchange between a singing-style *empfindsam* motive in music-box register and a brilliant-style topos" (2014, 127).

4. Another argument with regard to the proper placement of expositional closure might come from Schenkerian theory: the point at which the "linear-fifth progression" (or *Zug*) in the key of the dominant (or other relevant non-tonic key) is completed. *EST*, 147–49, considers that interpretation and notes that the EEC and the completion of this *Zug* need not be identical.

Chapter 3

1. Cf. Hatten's "virtual-agency" characterization and discussions of musical gestures as "significant and affective energetic shapings through time" (2018, 21 and passim; and 2004, 97–176); and Monahan's theory of agency (2013).
2. Compare this with the similar continuational moment in K. 333/i's P, discussed in chapter 2.
3. One might imagine other instances in which we find a more extensively expanded RT. When this happens, the question can arise of whether we are not dealing with an RT but rather with a (short) developmental space, thus more appropriately construing the whole as a Type 3 sonata without an expositional repeat. No absolute guidelines can be provided for this decision. This is a judgment call, and in nearly all such dilemmas nothing significant is at stake one way or the other.

Chapter 4

1. For detailed summaries of the symphonic practice of that era, c. 1730–60, see Morrow and Churgin's anthology of individual regional- and composer-oriented studies (2012), which makes much, albeit sporadic, use of Sonata Theory terminology.
2. In *EST*, 17, the lower of the two diagrams was misprinted in such a way that it implied that the recapitulatory space extended into the coda. The recapitulatory bracket should have stopped, as here, at the end of C, the closing-zone box directly above it.
3. The eighteenth-century view of musical pauses and/or cadences as comparable to the effects of punctuation within an oration has been often noted: see, e.g., Hepokoski and Darcy 1997, 115–16 (citing several others); Gjerdingen 2007, 155–57; and Mirka 2010, 238–39.
4. The classic overview of this procedure for Schubert is Webster 1979, and the matter is confronted and interpreted in virtually all subsequent literature on Schubertian sonata forms.
5. This is an updated designation not mentioned in *EST*.
6. Examples of the grand antecedent occur at the beginning of the expositions of Mozart's Symphony No. 40 in G Minor, K. 550/i (I:HC at m. 16; V-lock, mm. 16–20, concluding with an MC-effect) and Symphony No. 41 in C, K. 551/i (I:HC [or dominant arrival], m. 19; V-lock, mm. 19–23, with MC—and fermata—at m. 23).
7. On the lack of a structural cadence at the end of a sentence's presentation, see the discussion of the sentence in chapter 1, pp. 18–20. At this point it might be useful to remind ourselves of the vexed issues surrounding the classification of cadences in the eighteenth century (ch. 1, n. 12). In m. 4, for instance, the motion in the outer voices (with $\hat{5}$-$\hat{4}$-$\hat{3}$ motion in the upper voice and $\hat{7}$- $\hat{1}$ [$\hat{7}$-$\hat{8}$] motion in the bass, m6→M3) qualifies as one of the long-established *clausulae*

or ways of implying some sort of formulaic, conventional close. In this m. 4 case the implication is that of a weakly rhetorical effect of a mild pause or light conceptual break, as if for a breath within an ongoing thought. Gjerdingen calls such a $\hat{7}$-$\hat{1}$ clausula a *comma* (2007, 155–56, using m. 4 of K. 545/i as an example) and likens it to the usage of a comma in a prose sentence. In the early eighteenth century some theorists referred to it as the *clausula cantizans* (Gjerdingen, 140), a *soprano clausula*, the one with the usual soprano voice ($\hat{7}$-$\hat{8}$) now in the bass. Complicating the matter—and also commenting on K. 545/i—Diergarten (2015, 77–78) describes mm. 2, 4, and 8 as "simple minimal cadence[s]" in the eighteenth-century sense, that is, traditional, formulaic ones with only weak closural strength, approaching the tonic either by ascending or descending step. Some theorists today would not regard any of these "minimal cadences" (or clausulae) to be marks of sufficiently strong closural punctuation to effect a structural end (or to have a sufficiently assertive "cadential function") to a section of music in this period of repertory. In that sense, largely for pragmatic reasons, one would be hesitant today to call them "cadences" without qualification. A useful summary of the historical and contrapuntal issues surrounding the concept of "cadence" can be found in Harrison 2019.

8. The caveat "at least within an exposition" is included here because within recapitulations, P and TR are sometimes merged as a single cadential span. This occurs when a perhaps shortened P is not closed with a cadence but flows directly into portions of the exposition's TR or a recomposition thereof.

9. Note that, as observed earlier in the discussion of P, the principal exception to this guideline (remembering that no "rule" or guideline is inviolable) is the "TR of the dissolving continuation type," following the αα' of a sentence presentation: $P^{1.2}$==>TR.

10. Form-functional theory's term for this is a "false closing section" to the main theme (Caplin 1998, 129). Dissolving P-codettas that begin with a double-statement of its initial figure can give the impression of a presentational beginning of a new sentence.

11. *EST*, 608, characterizes *defaults* as "hierarchies of choices, hierarchies of norms that we may consider to have been [conceptually] arranged into first-level defaults (the most common options, the most standard choices pre-made by the genre unless they were overridden), second-level defaults, and so on."

12. Form-functional theory does not acknowledge the possibility of a V:PAC MC, that is, one that occurs before the first S theme (Caplin and Martin 2016). Construed from other points of view, however, the evidence suggests otherwise (Burstein 2010; Hepokoski 2016).

13. Arguing on behalf of the post-1790 decline of the more traditional, eighteenth-century MC default levels, Horton 2017 inventories a number of Beethovenian and later works and clarifies a point perhaps not made strongly enough in the *Elements of Sonata Theory*. The closing portion of chapter 11 and the opening portions of chapter 12 of the present volume make the larger case of how galant and classical-era norms are to be appealed to and nuanced in later, nineteenth-century works.

14. A prototypical example is found in the first movement of Beethoven's Violin Sonata in A, op. 12 no. 2. Here we find a "wrong-key" vi:HC MC in m. 30, the result of a TR staged as "suddenly going wrong" (mm. 27–30), plunging abruptly toward the submediant, F-sharp minor. All the MC rhetorical signals are in place at m. 30, including a bar of standard fill; what is deformational is the implicit key. A viable, tarantella-like S begins on F-sharp minor in m. 31, and soon is lifted to G, then, sequentially, to E minor (v) and F, and eventually to the proper S-key, E major (V, mm. 44ff).

15. In extraordinary thematic circumstances, one might be persuaded to consider a V:PAC as the second MC. While this might seem counterintuitive (why is the V:PAC not an EEC?), it sometimes happens that there are other thematically compelling reasons to consider what follows that V:PAC to still be housed within the S action zone. This situation sometimes arises in Schubert, whose MC treatment is at times very free.

16. Caplin 1998, 115–17, construes the situation differently, as an *internal* cadential division within S, one in which the rhetorical issue of a second MC articulation, *qua MC*, is not treated as the key factor. As he also puts it in 2013, 354, "a subordinate theme may initially lead to a half cadence (or dominant arrival) as a temporary structural goal.... [It sometimes happens that] an internal HC articulates the end of the first part of a *two-part subordinate theme*." Caplin's second part of his two-part S corresponds to Sonata Theory's TM³.

17. These might be compared with Richards's list of the "the seven contributing signals for second-theme beginnings" (2013a). Richards is concerned with situations in which a secondary theme might be inferred in the absence of one or more of these criteria. "One may therefore understand the initial ST of a movement to be a synthesis of musical signals which, taken together, allow a passage to be perceived as the first syntactically complete set of formal functions (at the very least, a beginning and end) which centres on the secondary key of the movement. Thus, an ST is not merely a full-fledged theme set in the new key, but rather a theme in the new key that is articulated by one or more reinforcing signals which render that theme perceptible" (3).

18. The debate is laid out in Caplin and Martin 2016 and Hepokoski 2016.

19. Smith's 2014 discussion and analysis of two-part and continuous expositions by Schumann can serve as a model example.

20. Helpful accounts of Koch's "expositional" *Sätze* may be found, e.g., in Burstein 2010 and 2016.

21. More broadly: the larger problem of defining S-space is that it might be understood from two different perspectives, each of which is justifiable. Assuming a classical-era, major-mode sonata exposition, one might maintain, with form-functional theory and a number of other approaches, that it is to be understood as one or more thematic/syntactic units, each of which proceeds to a V:PAC. By these lights, the secondary (or "subordinate") activity can be a *group* of themes that extends all the way to the last of them. The "S theme group" will therefore end only with the last of the V:PACs, which might then give way only to a nonthematic codetta, if one is there at all. The alternative, preferred by Sonata Theory, is to decide the matter generically and historically, along the lines of Koch's description of the role of the exposition's *Schlußsatz*, with which Sonata Theory's first-PAC guideline resonates. Any remaining themes—leading to their own V:PACs—are considered to be C¹, C², and so on. As noted earlier (and in the subsequent discussion of the closing zone), Sonata Theory comes to terms with the concept of a successively coherent "subordinate theme group" by construing it instead as an *S/C thematic complex*.

22. A touchstone: Mozart, Symphony No. 40 in G Minor, K. 550/i: S¹ (mm. 44–51), S¹, varied repetition (mm. 52–66) and the *elided* S² appendix (mm. 66–72), *non-elided* with P-based C material that follows (mm. 73ff). See *EST*, 163–66.

23. On the complex question of music and narrativity—with internal conflicts and/or disruptions yielding either comic or tragic outcomes—see., e.g. Almén 2008 and Millard's recent overview (2018) of recent claims and counterclaims surrounding this issue.

24. See, e.g., *EST*, 132, 180, and Burstein 2010.

25. This is a point of terminological difference between Sonata Theory and form-functional theory. Again, what Sonata Theory would designate as themes C¹ and C², when they are present, would be regarded as additional themes still housed within a broader S group. But as happens so often, the differences between the two approaches can seem larger than they are. Both systems perceive the same thing on the ground and differ only in their zone-categorization preferences.

26. Caplin 1998, 123, and 2013, 389–90, refer to such cases a "false closing section." Cf. n. 10 in this chapter.

27. Examples from Beethoven include the first movements of his Violin Sonata in A, op. 30 no. 1 (m. 150) and (emphatically) Piano Concerto No. 4, op. 58 (m. 253), as well as the second movement of his Symphony No. 2 in D, op. 36 (m. 158).

28. In Yust's view the primary determinants of the larger concept of musical "form" (considered as an "independent modality" from that of tonal or rhythmic structure) are "melodic similarity and difference and grouping" as instantiated by "repetition (similarity), contrast and fragmentation (difference), and caesuras, which are breaks, either literal (i.e., rests) or expressed by marked changes of texture" (2019, 60). On this account sonata form is only one subspecies of this more encompassing concept.

29. This is a frequent observation in several of the essays anthologized in Morrow and Churgin 2012. In an important and wide-ranging study from 2008, Galand argues for an even broader historical influence of what he calls "ritornello scripts"—essentially the tendency for a work to begin its major sections (such as Sonata Theory's rotations) with references to P—as a central principle threaded through many different kinds of sonata and sonata-rondo structures, whether or not such a structure also features repeats along with cadential elisions into P-returns. "I generally use 'ritornello,' " he writes, "to identify an opening thematic block and its recurrences," rather in the manner of a refrain that helps to anchor longer structures. (242). Galand proposes that "the ritornello idea" might well have operated as a formative, background principle within the development and subsequent history of sonata form and, noting the work of Eugene K. Wolf (from the 1980s and 1990s) and others with regard to the importance of the ritornello principle to origins of the symphony, that "the common notion that sonata form evolved out of the binary suite movement has come under fire. It may be more convincing to argue that the confluence of repetition patterns and tonal schemes in the classical symphony developed rather out of the ripieno concerto" (244).

30. Curiously, Yust seems to disregard the normative Type 3 + coda structure, tonal and thematic, that is also apparent in K. 184/i, instead regarding that movement as demonstrating Mozart's "full awareness of ritornello form as an alternate formal procedure in the genre" (270). This assessment appears to be a consequence of Yust's larger desire to regard ritornello form as a quite separate format from that of sonata form, largely on the basis of its lack of repeats "reinforced by rhyming closing material" and corresponding caesura-separators, which he regards as central to sonata form proper (269; cf. n. 28). Thus in the context of the larger argument of his book, he is reluctant to embrace the sonata-ritornello blend without qualification. With regard to K. 184, it may be worth noting that the finale, also lacking internal repeats, also shares some but not all features of a such a blend. Ritornello 2, however, is lacking (the development is taken over by TR-figuration), and Ritornellos 3 (recapitulation) and 4 (coda) are probably best regarded as not being elided with a PAC.

31. The "Paris" Symphony's finale also lacks repeats but otherwise shares no significant features of this concept of ritornello form.

32. Yust also tells us that ritornello form had become "the standard design for north German [symphony] composers J. G. Graun and C. P. E. Bach," noting in addition that the latter's Hamburg symphonies from the 1770s, sometimes featuring four or more ritornellos, present sometimes awkward, sometimes even impassable challenges if one tries to approach them only from the sonata-form perspective (2018, 269, 275–82). He also lays out specific objections to Sonata Theory's 2006 glancing summary of Bach's four-ritornello Symphony in G, Wq. 182/1/i (*EST*, 265), which movement, he concludes, "stubbornly resists description in traditional sonata-form language" (278). Morrow, too, while generally sympathetic to the Sonata Theory approach, concludes that while some of Bach's "distinctly odd " first movements can sometimes be "shoe-horned into some variety of sonata practice, they generally lack the internal rhetoric and distinctions that make a sonata movement compelling

and thus make more sense when analyzed as exploiting the rolling structure of the ritornello" (2012a, 283–85).

33. Guez 2018 offers a novel take on the potential implications of omitted and/or added recapitulatory bars, which can result in expositions and developments of notably differing length. Similarly, Guez 2019 examines various types of recapitulatory "tonal alterations"—most notably in Schubert—which range from the generically necessary (one or more that are required to produce the proper tonal resolution) to those which are deployed for other, nongeneric tonal effects.

34. In a recent study of Haydn's altered recapitulations, one proposing a recasting of the "sonata principle," Riley 2015 essentially confirms and amplifies, at least to this reader, *EST*'s passing mention of the synecdochic strategy.

35. Its historical emergence within binary form is helpfully traced in Greenberg 2017.

36. Cf. Monahan 2015, 16: "Nonresolving recapitulations are rare in the eighteenth century and appear only sparingly, and to striking effect, in early and middle-period Beethoven. But the technique turns up increasingly throughout the Romantic era; for Bruckner it even became a default strategy, a means of prolonging tonal/dramatic tension deep into the coda (Darcy 1997)." Monahan also discusses a specific instance of it in Mahler's Symphony No. 6/i (2015, 101–15, 124–25).

37. A more extensive categorization of Mozart's "aria-sonata" forms will be available in Hunt (forthcoming). I thank Graham Hunt for providing me with a preliminary copy of that article.

38. Exceptions to this are rare, though one may be found in the opening movement of Mozart's Symphony No. 23, K. 181, where the recapitulation follows the nonrepeated exposition after a brief, seven-bar link. With its run-on three movements, the symphony shares affinities with the older "Italian opera *sinfonia*" tradition.

39. "Brahms's op. 25/i is extraordinary [for its era] in employing this format for a first movement; Beethoven's op. 131/ii aside, rapid-tempo expanded Type 1s are much more commonly found as finales" (*EST*, 349–50).

40. Smith's four examples from Dvořák are: String Quartet in C, op. 61/iv; Piano Quintet in A, op. 81/iv; Piano Quartet in E-flat, op. 87/i; and String Quartet in A-flat, op. 105/i. The question of Dvořák's models for his deployment of the expanded Type 1 format (Mozart, Schubert, Brahms—or perhaps all three) is discussed in 2018, 276–77.

41. The potential confusion regarding the difference between the expanded Type 1 and the Type 2 sonatas is illustrated in the publication history of the *Elements* itself. In the first printed editions of *EST*, both the finale of Brahms's C Minor Quartet, op. 51 no. 1 and his *Tragic* Overture were identified, in separate chapters, as examples of the expanded Type 1 (p. 350) and the Type 2 (p. 364)—the latter being the lingering residue of an earlier, mistaken analysis that we had corrected before the book was published (hence their appearances on p. 350). Shortly after the first printing the erroneous double-listing of the *Tragic* Overture was called to our attention, and we deleted the Type 2 reference to it (p. 364) from subsequent printings. Unfortunately, the same cannot be said of the op. 51 no. 1 reference on p. 364, which we failed to notice. At the time of this writing the error remains on that page.

42. For the present, following up on the preceding note, we need only note that the expanded Type 1 and variants of it show up elsewhere in Brahms's output, as in the finale to the C-minor Quartet, Op. 51 no. 1, and the *Tragic* Overture, op. 81. In the *Tragic* Overture, for instance, the expanded recapitulatory rotation is launched in m. 185, aggressively hurtled into at the end of the exposition and signaled by a return to the D-minor tonic and the initiating P^0 hammerblows first heard in m. 1. This hyper-declarative rotation initiator is subjected to a stunned, *pizzicato* echo (m. 187) and followed by P^1 proper in mm. 189–92 (= mm 3–6),

which thereafter unravels into an expansive development. The crux and tonal resolution is joined only much later, with the onset of S at m. 300.

Chapter 5

1. For one view of Haydn's "interest" during his London travels in both the musical and the non-musically "interesting," see Mathew 2018. Cf. Waltham-Smith 2017, 5–10, 58–68.

2. The classic discussion of paratexts is that of Genette 1997. If the "text" of Haydn's Symphony No. 100 is considered to be the music itself (or its notational carriers), its *paratexts* are those verbal indicators that surround the text proper (title, composer's name, dedication, nickname, placement within a published series of works, and so on) in order to mediate the presentation of that musical text to its performers or listeners. A paratext that operates as "a *threshold* . . . as Philippe Lejeune put it, 'a fringe of the printed text which in reality controls one's whole reading of the text'. . . a zone not only of transition but also of *transaction*. . . . Limited to the text alone and without a guiding set of directions, how would we read Joyce's *Ulysses* if it were not entitled *Ulysses*?" (quoted in Genette 1997, 2).

3. Webster provides us with a caveat on this point (237): "No. 100 was widely known as the 'Military' Symphony while Haydn was still in London: he listed it thus in the (lost) fourth London Notebook. This title too however seems not to have been original; the autograph and other authentic musical sources do not transmit it." Will 2002, 9, n. 30 agrees, though without the subsequent caveat.

4. Dolan proposes that "Haydn's breadth of expression stemmed, in large part, from his colorful instrumentation; indeed, the notion that Haydn was the father of instrumental music refers in part to his orchestration and to his innovative treatment of the sonorities of his instruments." Haydn's music, then, was the culmination "of a more general process of [orchestral expansion and] consolidation that unfolded over the course of the eighteenth century . . . ultimately making possible a new musical technique: orchestration. . . . Haydn's music demonstrates some of the crucial aspects that make orchestration modern, and separate it from instrumentation" (2013, 92, 97).

5. Still another early example from the same period—though an unusual case—is the first movement of Haydn's Symphony No. 15 in D, which features an interior Presto sonata movement framed by similar opening and closing Adagios.

6. Haimo 1988, 343, amplified in Mastic 2015. These discussions will be noted further once we come to the second half of the recapitulation.

7. In this chapter my source-score is the H. C. Robbins Landon critical edition, which, along with several other small differences, alters some of the *forte* dynamics found in other scores to *forzando* or *sforzando*.

8. Cf. Landon, 1976, 560: "It is a fascinating sound, looking forward to the 'toy' music of Rimsky-Korsakov and the ballet music of Tchaikovsky."

9. Additional comments on the articulation of this MC and the seventh above the dominant are provided in *EST*, 26.

10. What I call an *interrupted cadence* is analogous to classical rhetoric's *interruptio* or, possibly, *aposiopesis*: instead of cadencing as expected, the thought advances at once beyond the (unsounded) cadence to the next thematic module in line. What we find here in Haydn is the clearest type of it, where the interruption (the "lost" cadence) merges with the onset of the subsequent musical idea. (Another, less analytically challenging variant is an interrupted cadence that leads instead to a "loud rest," such as the one pointed out in chapter 3, in the slow movement of Mozart's Symphony No. 34 (p. 48). My own touchstone reference for an

interrupted cadence—a technique related to the evaded cadence—is that in the first movement of Mozart's Piano Sonata in A Minor, K. 310, mm. 8–9. Some analysts have regarded m. 9 as an implicit I:PAC; others as a I:IAC. In my view it is neither. Instead, Mozart breaks off the drive to cadence at the end of m. 8—*interrupts* it at the bar-line—to return to a restatement of the theme ("one more time") begun in m. 1. As it happens, m. 9's "one more time" initiates TR (of the dissolving-restatement type). Thus in this case P does not close with a cadence proper.

11. The translation, from the work's Section 54, is that of Kant, *Critique of Judgment*, translated by Werner S. Pluhar (Indianapolis: Hackett, 1987), 203. The italics are those in the original.

12. As noted in *EST*, 215 n. 20 (which outlined our 2006 view of the m. 103 moment and subsequent theme of Symphony No. 100), "Notice the almost perfectly parallel case in the first movement of Symphony No. 99 in E-flat, m. 71; and cf. that of Symphony No. 103 in E-flat, 'Drumroll' (with a continuous exposition), m. 80."

13. Mastic 2018, paragraph 3.2 n. 12 and Example 5, suggests a Sonata Theory–oriented reading of all this that differs from what I have proposed in the preceding. In brief, Mastic reads mm. 75–108 as a trimodular block (TMB), an interpretation that requires the locating of double medial caesuras. Mastic locates the first at m. 73 and the second at m. 93, regarded as "MC^2 (V:IAC elided)." Accordingly, this means that TM^1 starts at m. 75, TM^2 at m. 82, and TM^3 at m. 95. Construing m. 93 as an elided V:IAC MC, though, is problematic, not only because the IAC status of m. 93 is questionable but also because of the voice-leading and dynamics in play at this point. As noted in *EST*, 44, an elided authentic-cadence onset of S (or TM^1 or TM^3) is possible within the style, but usually as the conclusion of what Sonata Theory calls a *de-energizing transition*—perhaps relatable to the idea of expanded caesura-fill—displacing the more normative MC option. Chapters 10 and 12 of this volume, on Schubert and Brahms, will propose localized readings along these lines. (Cf. also the alternative option of the *blocked medial caesura* followed by an expanded fill figure that ends with an elided authentic cadence [*EST*, 47–48], which seems not to be the case here in the "Military.")

14. Landon advances a similar idea with some caution: "Our idea of military music is . . . quite different from that of the late eighteenth century as well as the period up to 1848 known to Austrian history as the *Vormärz* ('pre-March'). But if Strauss sounded military in his day perhaps Haydn's theme sounded military to the public of 1794 et seq. At any rate [as in No. 99/i], it certainly sounded like a popular tune . . . with a tap-room accompaniment over a pizzicato bass" (1976, 560).

15. On this reading mm. 108–15 would be an instance in which the closing zone proper does not present us with differing material, but only with a refashioning of the musical ideas that had produced the EEC.

16. *EST*, 215, lays out some of the issues at stake regarding developments that begin with C material (analogous to the S^C music in play here). "If initial C-material eventually gives way to a succession of post-P$^{1.1}$-themes that would otherwise be considered rotational, C writes over P. In that case we confront a curious overlapping of rotational implications. . . . At the moment of the development's C-launch we experience the presence of two conceptual rotations—the 'normal' developmental one and the one produced by the trespassing of C-cadential material onto a space not its own, an encroachment beyond its customary borders."

17. Pursuing the potential rotational implication for the whole development, we have: S^C (writing over P)–P-based S–and S^C again (now in its proper rotational place).

18. Two examples are Haimo, 1995, 3–4, and Riley 2015.

19. Noting the extremity of this "altered recapitulation," Haimo 1988, 342, provided a diagram of the bar-to-bar "correspondences between exposition and recapitulation in Symphony No. 100, first movement," along with a second one interpreting (in pre-Sonata-Theory terms)

their "correspondences of motivic function." Building on Haimo's discussion and expanding it (see n. 22), Mastic 2015, Example 5, produced a more detailed and interpretive version ("formal analysis") of the former's initially proposed diagram.

20. Landon might have been recalling Tovey's somewhat different (but influential) remark: "The recapitulation is, as always in Haydn's mature works, very free and more like Beethoven's larger codas than like any more formal procedure; but [this theme] is too strong a personality to be suppressed or cut short, and so the final effect of the movement is nearer to orthodox ideas than is usual with Haydn" (1981, 359). Cf. Schroeder 1990, 185: "an unusually long coda of over fifty bars."

21. On metaphor theory and the structural homologies, sharable features, or enabling similarities between the source domain and the target domain, see Lakoff and Johnson 1980; Lakoff 1993; Fauconnier and Turner 1998 and 2002; and Cook 2001, mentioned in chapter 1 n. 10. For some historical and contextual constraints on the proliferation of metaphor, see Hepokoski 2014, 75–79, and chapter 7 of this volume.

22. Such, at least, was the claim in Haimo 1988, 343, proposing a characteristically modernist ("unity") argument on behalf of the large-scale "integration" of the movement: "The seemingly anomalous turn to the ♭VI in the recapitulation functions . . . to integrate the introduction into the remainder of the movement by relating the dominant elaboration of the recapitulation to the dominant preparation in the introduction [mm. 15–16]. No other D-E♭-D progression occurs anywhere else in the movement." (Note, though, that bassline E♭ in m. 16 is the third of a C-minor chord.) Pursuing Haimo's discussion of long-range integration in Haydn's "altered recapitulations," Mastic 2015 adopts the former's reading in order to advance the argument to long-range structural "connections" (as opposed to relying on the concepts of purposeful disruption, mere surprise, or amusing wit) by noting a few other emphases on ♭VI in this movement, including mm. 14–18, mm. 87–92, and, especially, the D to B-flat shift at the onset of the development: "I would argue, however, that the main function of the surprising appearance of ♭VI in the recapitulation is to create a feeling of connection across different parts of the work—not just to the introduction, as Haimo points out, nor even just within the first movement itself" (paragraph 3.7).

Chapter 6

1. Adorno's similar view claimed more for this sonic image of spirited conversation among equals, though, as usual, he couched it more tartly, in polemical, culture-critical terms. In chamber music "the relation of social purposes is sublimated into a purposeless esthetic in-itself. . . . Art and play are in accord: chamber music is an instant. . . . The spiritualization of competition, its transposition into the realm of the imagination, anticipates a state of things in which competition would be cured of aggression and evil. Ultimately it anticipates the state of labor as play. . . . The price is that it does not intervene in reality, that it does not help" (1989, 87–88).

2. Schroeder notes that their relaxed, sometimes folklike tone can recall appealing flavors and rhythmic moves of Lower-Austrian dances (1990, 144–51).

3. About such thematic *Entwicklung* in Haydn, Waltham-Smith (alluding to a similar observation by Burnham about Beethoven's middle-period works [*Beethoven Hero*, 1995], notes: "In contrast with Mozart's predilection for thematic groups with sharply contrasted characters, Haydn's monothematicism allows the listener to accompany the theme on its journey not just as a bystander but also through a process of *identification*" (2017, 59). On music's more general capacity to encourage such identification, see also chapter 1, pp. 1–2.

4. My descriptions of the dynamic markings in this movement refer to those found in the Urtext Henle (Munich) edition, edited by Horst Walter. In the 2003 preface, p. vi, Walter notes that "many details of dynamics and articulation were either self-evident . . . or were left to the discretion of the players. As a result, Haydn is very sparing in his use of dynamic marks." The commonly available Dover edition of the opp. 74, 76, and 77 quartets collects and reprints a set of earlier, separately published Eulenberg (London) editions, edited by Wilhelm Altmann, that interpolated additional dynamics, including an interpolated *poco forte* at bar 43. (Might Altmann have been reading m. 43 as a suggested S?)

5. Some of Haydn's other continuous expositions make conspicuous feints at potential P-based secondary themes that, in one way or another, the composer keeps from materializing as such: situations of the *almost-but-not-quite S*. A touchstone case occurs in the opening movement of Symphony No. 45, "Farewell" (Hepokoski 2016, 57).

6. The form-functional approach, which axiomatically disallows the concept of a continuous exposition leading to a V:PAC, would seek to locate a "subordinate theme function" that is identifiable within the continuous flow, perhaps locating it with the sentential onset at mm. 47–50. The differences between form-functional theory and Sonata Theory on this matter are laid out in Caplin and Martin 2016 and Hepokoski 2016.

7. On the metaphor of "inflation" and the minor-to-major L-operation, see chapter 8, ex. 8.2 and surrounding commentary.

8. One can recognize the style even when other complicating factors—harmonic or cadential—might lead us to wonder whether S-space has actually been left behind. Ambiguities of zone can arise in cases in which Haydn launches a manifestly "C^1-style" theme at the proportionally proper spot of the exposition, even though he has not decisively closed off S-space with a clearly articulated V:PAC (EEC). This is the case in the "Military" Symphony, discussed in the preceding chapter.

9. While the Altmann-Eulenberg edition (reproduced in the Dover score) adds a *piano* dynamic to the upbeat of m. 208 (not to mention the inserted *forte* at the upbeat to m. 206), the Henle Urtext contains no such dynamic. It is possible that Haydn conceived this last sounding of C^1 to be played at a full-blown *forte*.

Chapter 7

1. As observed also, e.g., in Richards 2013b (on "the obscured medial caesura" in Beethoven) and Horton 2017.

2. Marston (1994, 147) summarizes the situation thus: "Recent scholarship has established that the composition of the whole symphony extended over a considerable period of time: sketches for the first movement in Landsberg 7 probably date from around the winter of 1800–01." Cooper (2001, iii) claims more: "Around the end of 1800, work on the symphony was abruptly halted, with the first movement more or less complete but the remainder hardly begun."

3. As noted, e.g., in Marston 1994, 128, who observes that the finale seems to have been especially problematic, and in Lockwood 2003, 156–57, who writes, "Beethoven often revised his works after their first performances, especially orchestral works, which took time to publish, and he often kept on revising as long as he possibly could, that is, until the work was actually in print. Thus the final touching-up of the Second Symphony, which was extensive, must have taken place while he was in the midst of working on the Third."

4. While not a universal view, it is one shared by others, e.g., Marston (1994, 147–50, though concerned primarily with the finale) and Kinderman (2009, 61).

5. More normatively within slow introductions, such a "fall" into the tonic minor would not revert back to major before the onset of the exposition. Beethoven's troubled—or clouded—return to it here, albeit over the dominant, is unusual.

6. I prefer the anacrusis reading to that of an implicit or actual PAC-effect at m. 34, though an argument could be mounted for either. Cf. the windup anacrusis linking the slow introduction of the First Symphony to its Allegro con brio sonata. Jonathan Del Mar's critical edition of the Second Symphony for Bärenreiter (2001) includes the indication, *attacca subito l'Allegro*, under m. 33.

7. Considering Beethoven's sketches for the movement, Lockwood notes (2003, 157), "The early ideas for the introduction include a slow-tempo version of the march theme that he later transferred to the Allegro exposition as the main second-group theme." More than that, an early sketch for P had been "a simple triadic figure (1-3-1-5-1-3-1)" . . . [whose] interval sequence is nearly identical to the one that Beethoven later used for the opening of the first theme of the *Eroica*."

8. "Ein Tonfest zu begehn in Herrlichkeit und Freudigkeit, und dazu all' diese Helden des Tonreichs, die Schaar der Instrumente herbeizurufen." Marx initially regards the Second Symphony's "general idea" to be similar to that of the First, only now everything has become "broader, larger . . . warmer," suggesting the "intensified power" of its composer ("die Kraft des Bildners gesteigert"). All translations from Marx are my own.

9. A much-elaborated QUIESCENZA schema (or perhaps merely an allusion to one) might also have been noticed in the preceding mm. 42–47: beginning in the bass, D, C♯, B, and completed with the first violin's C♯$_5$-D$_5$ in mm. 46–47. Notice that, if we do discern a QUIESCENZA suggestion lurking in those bars, it is one that occupies the full continuation portion (β or β + γ) of a compound sentence and one whose interior is also inlaid with a PRINNER and closes with a complete cadential progression. Schema families, or allusive suggestions of ones, are capable of highly free, creative treatment.

10. "Um sich dann im sonnigen Triumph auf dem leutchtenden E zu vollführen, ein Held in der Pracht seines Waffenschmiedes."

11. "Eben so glanz- und muthvoll, wie Triumphlied, siegsgewiß vor dem Kampfe noch mit halblauten Sang angestimmit, tritt der Seitensatz einher, fanfarenhaft."

12. A completed QUIESCENZA that decays to ♮6̂ as its third event would proceed in an 8̂-♮7̂-♮6̂-♯7̂-8̂ pattern: A-G♮-F♮-G#-A. There is no sounded G# in mm. 112–16, however, though we might imagine one as possible—perhaps implicit—on the last quarter note of m. 115 (as part of a vii°7 neighbor to the A-major tonic). Under these lights one could consider mm. 112–16 as a deformational, anything-but-relaxed QUIESCENZA, immediately repeated in mm. 116–20. Notice that the G# that is acoustically "missing" from each of the two QUIESCENZE is sounded multiple times after their completion, in mm. 120–25, repeatedly stung by *sforzandi*.

13. As already noted, the most common high-galant opening for development—the first-level default—is to sound P or a variant thereof in a non-tonic key, most typically that in which the exposition had ended. For issues surrounding an early, *tonic-key* appearance of P in the development—claims of a "premature reprise" and the like—see chapter 4, p. 73, and *EST*, 206–12. It is worth noting that this symphony's second movement, Larghetto, also begins the development with P in the tonic minor (m. 100).

14. Following Tovey, Webster 2005b, 155, is similarly convinced: "[The ending of] 'The Heavens Are Telling' . . . made a great impression on Beethoven, who 'troped' it at the end of the first movement of the Second Symphony." Haydn's *Die Schöpfung* had received its first public performance—with enormous impact—in Vienna in March 1799, only a year or two before Beethoven drafted the Second Symphony's first movement.

Chapter 8

1. Along the way Riley notes the importance of Johann Baptist Vaňhal as having "a central role in the story of the Viennese minor-key symphony. . . . Vaňhal and Haydn dominated the vogue for minor-key symphonies in the late 1760s and early 1770s, and together they defined the styles of the stormy fast movement and the contrapuntal minuet. When other composers adopted the stormy style or revived it in later years, it was to Vaňhal as much as to Haydn that they alluded. Vaňhal himself knew Haydn's compositions well and often took them as models" (2014, 70).

2. Grave 2008 and 2009 also devotes much attention to eighteenth-century theoretical views of the problematic status of minor, and the topic has been explored by other writers as well (*EST*, 307–10).

3. Lowe 2014, 602, summarizing an argument from Lowe 2007, speculates on the "high degree of topical competency among the lay listeners that made up the late-eighteenth-century public concert audience," going so far as to suggest that "this competency allowed for an immediate perception and understanding of musical structure and form. . . . Topical competency was the springboard for the construction of meaning among the musically uninitiated."

4. As will be suggested later, it is uncertain whether this guideline—this drive to wrest free of the minor—can apply as normative for minor-mode works written in the middle third of the eighteenth century. In earlier repertories it may be that minor-mode saturation of a movement (say, a minor-mode, binary dance movement of J. S. Bach or a minor-mode keyboard sonata movement by C. P. E. Bach from the 1740s) is more concerned with applying the consistency of the minor-mode color and its technical implications rather than trying to stage strategies of escape from it. If so, the emergence from such a point of view was doubtless gradual.

5. I introduced the inflation-deflation metaphor—in relation to a different repertory—in 2008, 185–86.

6. An instructive example, generically deformational in a number of respects, though not in this one, is found in the first movement of a sonata mentioned earlier in this paragraph, Beethoven's Piano Sonata in G, op. 31 no. 1. This is Beethoven's first rapid-tempo sonata to move not to the dominant but to the mediant for the secondary thematic zone. After the G-major opening, S is first sounded in a bright B major (m. 66) and drives to a III:PAC in m. 73. The theme is immediately repeated, and much expanded, in B minor (mm. 74–98), producing a minor-mode iii:PAC EEC in m. 98. It is followed by an "aftershock" C zone with a momentary but failed attempt to restore B major (mm. 100–1). In the recapitulation S is much altered. It is begun in VI, E major, m. 218, even producing a VI:PAC in that key (m. 225), but is eventually corrected to the tonic G major, m. 234, where the theme is restarted—a characteristically Beethovenian "back up and redo" procedure. From this point onward S's correspondence measures, now sounded in the major, bring it to a I:PAC ESC in G major in m. 256. The following C zone reverses its model's modal flicker by suggesting a momentary flicker of G minor in mm. 268–70, but G major is immediately restored to close the exposition.

7. I discuss the exposition of the "Farewell" more closely in 2016, 37.

8. Viewing the modal question broadly, Grave suggests that this modified concept of the minor mode—away from the "less haunted" mood of the earlier eighteenth century, grounded more in major-minor "compositional "equivalence" or "equality" of treatment, and toward a more theatrically grounded, exceptional mode of coloristic instability and intensity—emerged around the 1750s and 1760s (2008, 28–32).

9. *EST*, 419, classifies the form of the K. 466 finale as one of several following a Type $4^{1-\text{exp}}$ design: a hybrid of the Type 4 sonata (sonata rondo, adapted to the concerto), and the expanded Type 1 sonata—a complex but frequently encountered option in Mozart's concertos.

10. Riley also notes two examples from the finales of two minor-key movements by Vaňhal in the 1770s in which the entire recapitulation, starting with P, is played out in major (2014, 179, 194–98, 204).

11. Commenting on "the unusual and problematical aspects of the key of F-sharp minor," employed famously in the "Farewell" Symphony," Webster noted (1991, 332) that Haydn "composed two additional works in F-sharp minor, the String Quartet Op. 50 No. 4 (1787) and the Piano Trio Hob. XV:26 (1794–95). . . . Both later works are unusual in one relevant sense: they are Haydn's only post-1781 works which *end* in the minor. [Op. 50 no. 4's finale is fugal.] . . . Thus Haydn does seem to have regarded the key of F-sharp minor as exceptional— as calling for special treatment."

12. The table provided in Webster 1991, 220, is a helpful listing of the key and mode choices in the various movements of Haydn's minor-mode symphonies, quartets, and piano trios.

Chapter 9

1. Cf. Dahlhaus's more extravagant claim: "Beethoven, virtually in one fell swoop, claimed for music the strong concept of art [*der emphatische Kunstbegriff*], without which music would be unable to stand on a par with literature and the visual arts. . . . Beethoven's symphonies represent inviolable musical 'texts' whose meaning is to be deciphered with 'exegetical' interpretations" (1989, 9; for a discussion of more current views of such claims, see Hepokoski 2013).

2. One of the most recent studies of it can be found in Ferraguto 2014.

3. Cf. what seems to be an obvious allusion to these two chords at the opening of Brahms's *Tragic Overture* from 1880.

4. A number of commentators, stretching back to Nottebohm, note that an early sketch for this brief idea, mm. 3–4, had been more compressed, taking up only three beats, not four. In the sketch the B_4 in what is now m. 3 had not been sustained but went directly into a variant of the running sixteenth-note figure in m. 4: thus the second half of the bar (m. 1 of the sketch) and its final note in the next bar read B-C-B-A-G-F♯-|E. This figure, mm. 1–2 of the sketch, is then repeated on the Neapolitan, F major, in mm. 3–4.

5. Cf. the melodic shape and four pitches of the famous *Basso del tema* that had grounded the variations of the *Eroica* finale from only a few years earlier.

6. In part this issue arises when analysts wish to identify themes or zones as beginning in the middle of an ongoing thematic stream, a conclusion that Sonata Theory avoids.

7. While the decimal designators are arbitrary choices, unlike the integers that precede the decimal point (which indicate whether a structural PAC has been attained), Sonata Theory tries to remain consistent in affixing the 1.2 designator to that which follows a sentential presentation (i.e., normally a continuation), even when the presentation is best characterized as a zero-module. To help alleviate this seeming inconsistency, one might imagine that the zero-module at some point comes also to imply a "point-one" function (here, $S^0 ==>$ functionally $S^{1.1}$).

8. In a reading that differs from the one presented here, Hatten regards m. 55 as the "expressive climax" of the S-zone (1994, 128).

9. That reading, III:IAC, is presented in Hatten 1994, 128: "a strong imperfect cadence with 5-1 bass in mm. 64–65, accompanied by a shift to metrically stable cadential material [that] signals the actual close of this section."

10. The metrically dislocated buildup recalls that in the first movement of the *Eroica*, mm. 29–37—the end of P and the strenuous dominant anacrusis to the powerful downbeat of m. 38, launching a TR of the dissolving-reprise type. Presumably no listener would take m. 38 of the *Eroica* for a cadence. The reprise aspect of m. 38 is also a powerfully conditioning element in the *Eroica* that is lacking in op. 59 no. 2/i.

11. Neo-Riemannians will recognize that E-flat's relation to the E minor tonic (e.g., as returned to under the first ending) is that of the slide operation (S), in which two triads a half-step apart share the same third.

12. Discussions of hexatonic poles within non-diatonic, chromatic harmony—why they are labeled as such and what their expressive impact can be—can be found in a number of essays by Cohn (e.g., 1999, 2004), as well as, more technically, in Cohn 2012, 17–32.

13. Recall the basic principle: unless there are overriding contextual reasons to decide otherwise, if P/TR material is left for post-MC material and then $P^{1.1}$ (or P^0, if it exists) returns decisively—the rotation initiator—that can usually be taken as an indication of the start of a new rotation.

14. Caplin 2004, 70: "A central tenet of my concept of cadence is the requirement that dominant harmony occur exclusively in root position prior to the moment of cadential arrival (or, in the case of a half cadence, just at the moment of arrival). So essential is this harmonic condition that if the dominant first appears inverted (say as V^6_5) or becomes inverted after initially being in root position, then either no sense of cadence will be projected or else a potentially cadential situation fails to be fully realized as such."

15. The narrative reading here should not be confused with a reductive one on behalf of an off-tonic "false recapitulation." Regarding the latter—or any more nuanced suggestion of the potential for the effect of the latter—I note that, in principle, the general question can emerge with any such Rotation-2 start (P^0 or $P^{1.1}$) that follows a preceding round of development. (While some analysts insist that "false recapitulations" must start in the tonic, others have admitted the possibility of an off-tonic onset.) Fraught with controversy and terminological squabbles, this whole issue is vexed, and it is treated at some length in *EST*, 221–28. For a clear impression of such a *false-recapitulation effect*, as it is called in the *Elements of Sonata Theory*, the initiating P^0 or $P^{1.1}$ needs to follow a set of clearly laid-out criteria with regard to temporal placement (how far into the developmental space it is situated) and should replicate that module's appearance at the beginning of the exposition.

16. Goldschmidt's original German is better: "grausam niederfahrendes Unisono mit wahren Katastrophentrillern."

17. The Henle critical edition of this quartet numbers the bars under the first ending as 208a, b, c, and d. The first bar under the second ending is m. 209. See also n. 19.

18. While given the impression provided in m. 205 it is probably too strong to insist that this is a *cadentially failed recapitulation* (one type of nonresolving *recapitulation*), the open-endedness of the E-major assertion places this movement in dialogue with that concept. From this perspective of non-attainment, Beethoven has staged this narrative as one in dialogue with that of a *failed sonata*. "Failed sonatas" (not, of course, a compositional defect but rather one important kind of sonata-plot) are those whose narratives present structural situations in which "the exposition fails to produce an EEC, and, complementarily, the recapitulation, even though it unfolds wholly in the proper key, is kept from producing the tonic closure of the ESC, the principal goal of any sonata form" (Hepokoski 2001–2, 152; cf. *EST*, 177–79, 245–49).

19. I cite the bar numbers here as provided in the Henle critical edition, where the single bar under the second ending is m. 209 and the *fortissimo* P^0 motto is reckoned as m. 210.

Chapter 10

1. Or even "four-key expositions" in some pre-1823 works, as in the first movements of the Symphony No. 2 in B-flat, D. 125, and the Piano Sonata in B, D. 575, and the second

movement of the Trout Quintet, D. 667, as noted in Rusch 2014. Approaching these early works from the standpoint of form-functional theory, Rusch makes a case for their fusion of fantasia and sonata.

2. As in Clark's noting of "cyclic chains" of thirds, and "the mediant and submediant [as a] repositioning of fifth-space." "Third relations are . . . Schubert's most common choice for his remote secondary themes" (2011, 228). Cf. Beach 2017, 26: "chains of descending major thirds. . . . A progression in major thirds—for example, C major—A-flat major—E major—C major—is not tonal. It does not exist within the major-minor system." McCreless 2015 is also relevant here.

3. A sample from Adorno 2005, 10: "These are the signs of Schubert's landscape, dried flowers are its mournful bloom; the objective symbols of death trigger the images, and the feeling of those images reinforces the symbols of death. There you have the Schubertian dialectic: it absorbs with all the force of subjective interiority the fading images of an objective presence in order to rediscover them in the smallest cells of any musical realization. The allegorical image of Death and the Maiden evaporates along with it not in order to sink into individual feelings, but rather to resurface in the solace of musical form. Musical solace brings a qualitative change as a result of this dialectical process: but it is a qualitative change only at the level of smallest detail; at the highest level, death."

4. These aspects of Schubert's music have seemed an open invitation to those recent analysts eager to read it, and sometimes to identify with it, as a musically coded construct in sync with current Anglophone views of gender and sexuality: a feminine or gay sensibility, non-teleological as opposed to the presumed masculine trajectories of traditional sonata practice (e.g., McClary 1994; Brett 1997; Fisk 2001; Clark 2011).

5. For a recent argument along these lines see Clark 2011, 204–21. Preferring an anti-teleological account of Schubert's sonata forms, Clark is critical of the forward-vectored, "masculinist" arcs found in both Schenkerian analysis and Sonata Theory. The latter is characterized as "an apparently old-style version of sonata form," readily reducible to a "privileged teleological, masculine paradigm that has been the subject of sustained feminist critique" (204). Particularly troubling is Sonata Theory's terminology of generic "deformation," along with the concepts of generically "wrong keys," expositional and sonata "success and failure," and the like (204–6). For Clark these are ineradicably negative terms, which can perpetuate critical attitudes toward Schubert's handling of sonata forms. In reality, nothing could be further from the aims of Sonata Theory. Since trajectories toward generically mandated cadences are an offending issue here (219–21), one presumes that Clark would similarly arraign cadentially oriented accounts of binary dance forms (the roots of "sonata form") from at least the early seventeenth century onward, if not earlier, or perhaps the very concept of cadential resolution. The argument on behalf of the implicitly gendered features of the tonal system is worth pondering, and Clark's reflections, when applied to the whole history of the genre system in which Schubert and so many others were enveloped, may well be persuasive in the final analysis. But that is not the fault of Sonata Theory, which seeks only to explicate individual realizations within a historically given cultural practice, not to pass judgment on a now-obsolete genre system.

6. Notwithstanding a prodigious collection of works completed before 1823–24, among them chamber music, sonatas, and symphonies, one senses with young Schubert a notable reluctance to publish. His opp. 1 and 2, for instance, had been "Erlkönig" and "Gretchen am Spinnrade," published in 1820 though composed in 1815 and 1814, respectively. The larger instrumental works of Schubert before 1824 were published only after his death in 1828—in some instances many decades later.

7. Six of Rossini's operas had been presented in Vienna in early 1822 and were received with widespread enthusiasm, as was Rossini's visit to Vienna at the same time. One telling document from two years later is the February 1824 letter to Beethoven from numerous of his supporters,

urging that the premieres of the Ninth Symphony and the Missa Solemnis be given in Vienna rather than in Berlin: "It is Austria which is best entitled to claim [you] as her own. . . . All the more painful must it have been for you to feel that a foreign power has invaded this royal citadel of the noblest . . . that shallowness is abusing the name and insignia of art, and unworthy dalliance with sacred things is beclouding and dissipating appreciation for the pure and eternally beautiful" (Thayer-Forbes 1967, 897). Splitting open in the Viennese early 1820s, the Beethoven-Rossini dichotomy would haunt future generations of music historians: a collection of essays on this historiographical issue is found Mathew and Walton 2013.

8. Cf. the assessment of Bonds 2017, 335, on the emerging goal of "understanding music," cited in chapter 8, p. 155.

9. Cf. the similarly worded (and Gingerich-oriented) summary of the composition of these three quartets in McCreless 2015, 2.

10. Cf. the similar opening of Haydn's Quartet in D Minor, op. 76 no. 2, though there the two opening fifths ("Quinten") instead outline $\hat{5}$-$\hat{1}$-$\hat{2}$-$\hat{5}$ and begin the P-theme proper, not a P^0 module.

11. The late-nineteenth-century critical edition (reprinted, e.g., in the familiar Dover-score series) marked the mm. 15–18 lashes as *forzandi*. The 2009 Bärenreiter score, Urtext der Neuen Schubert-Ausgabe, ed. Werner Aderhold, however, contains only accents here, not *forzandi*.

12. On p. 163 Beach's bar numbers for the "parenthetical insertion" are mm. 32–46. As is clear from the surrounding context and the Schenkerian graph on p. 164, "46" is a printer's error for "40."

13. The passages from the *Elements* cited in the text also suggest the origins of the de-energizing TR in the concept of expanded caesura-fill and provide some examples from Mozart and Haydn. We also note that the alternative of the de-energizing TR—settling quietly onto the new tonic of the secondary key—becomes more common in the nineteenth century, as in the first movements of Schumann's Fourth and Brahms's Second and Third Symphonies.

14. This is not the first time that Schubert had moved to major V in a minor-mode exposition: the same implication of "impermissible" escape can be found in his Piano Sonata in A minor, D. 784/i (*EST*, 315 n. 18).

15. The cello outburst's sixteenth-note figure has been long in the making, grounded in persistent accompanimental motivic play since TM^2. In mm. 102–14 one might also notice the coloristic move from A major to A minor to F major, tracing out a PL hexatonic operation. (Cf. the LP operation mentioned earlier with regard to mm. 18–19.)

16. As was pointed out to me by Liam Hynes, the sustained V^9 above the E-bass may be intended to recall the same chord in TR, mm. 45–46, the point at which TR begins to diverge from P. If the present V^9 is read as connecting back to that earlier moment, revisiting it, it could fortify further the idea that the F-major escape of the end of TR and most of TM^1 was foreordained to be non-viable as a permanent goal.

17. I do not regard the presence of the P-related death-triplet in the cello at mm. 152–54 as sufficient to suggest a rotational initiation. Its role is that of an unsettling reminder within a development that is more obviously governed by TM^3 references. The same assessment applies at the reappearances of these triplets at mm. 163–65 and 173–75.

18. One might describe the chord succession more vividly: while the chord-roots ascend by half-steps, the presence of alternating first-inversion chords produces a jagged bass-line motion that suggests a harmonically deformational dialogue with the otherwise familiar MONTE schema. Cf. mm. 17–19.

19. Incorporating aspects of Sonata Theory, Guez 2015, 2018, and 2019 treat Schubert's recapitulatory practices *in extenso*.

20. For Type 2 sonata analogues to this situation, see the section in Chapter 11, "Seeming Type 3 'recapitulations' that do not begin with P^0 or P^1: dialogues with the Type 2 format."

21. The general idea of a *compensatory coda*—in various types of sonatas—is touched upon in *EST*, 249, 286, 362, and especially 384–86.

22. This extraordinary passage is worth considering more closely. In mm. 318–20 the chromatic ascent in the topmost line (D_5–$E\flat_5$–$E\natural_5$–F_5–$F\sharp_5$–G_5–$G\sharp_5$–A_5) suggests—even demands—a harmonization via a normative MONTE schema (or chromatic 5–6 sequence), a rising-sequence pattern that cranks the harmonic levels up by step (Gjerdingen 2007, 89–106). As noted before, that schema is grounded in a repeated two-chord pattern in which the first chord—with its root a third below that of its predecessor—carries a local dominant or dominant-seventh implication (as here, $B\flat^7$, C^7, D^7, E^7) and the second chord that of its resolution. Had that norm been followed in mm. 318–20, it would have produced "second-chord" triads on $E\flat$, F, g, and A (the latter two on beats two and four of m. 320). But instead Schubert—radicalizing his MONTE alterations in P^1 (mm. 22–23)—dislocates the normative resolutions of each of the four implied dominants. Thus we hear instead: $A\flat$ (instead of $E\flat$); $B\flat$ (instead of F); $E\flat^6$ (instead of g); and F^6 (instead of A). Even at the music's whirlwind pace, the impression given is that of a tonal system spinning out of control.

23. On the "coda to the coda" option—the final stages of what Sonata Theory calls a *multisectional* or *discursive coda*—see p. 84 above.

Chapter 11

1. A few vocal numbers in Mozart's operas are also cast in the Type 2 format. Examples include the Quartet, "Andrò ramingo e solo," from *Idomeneo*, and Osmin's Rage Aria, "Solche hergelauf'ne Laffen," from *Die Entführung aus dem Serail*. In both, the text for the exposition is fully recycled in the Rotation-2 development and tonal resolution: the textual delivery and the musical structure are mutually reinforcing. See Martin 2015 for an overview of sonata and non-sonata structures in Mozart's arias.

2. Comments along these "non-evolutionary" lines are frequent in the various essays on the early symphony found in Morrow 2012. Particularly emphatic on this point is the overview found in Morrow's essay on the "Historiography of the Eighteenth-Century Symphony," 2012c, 30–31. Cf. Morrow 2102e, 430: "One can certainly not argue for a general progression of the 'more primitive' Type 2 to the 'complete' Type 3."

3. Greenberg 2017 provides a useful corpus study of such matters, ranging from the 1670s to the 1750s, which has helped to inform the discussion immediately following.

4. Scarlatti's keyboard sonatas display a variety of binary-form realizations, of which the general contour schematized in Figure 11.1 (an embryonic Type 2 sonata) is the most common. On occasion, though, one can find more expansive sonatas that return to the tonic with HM midway through section 2 in the matter of an embryonic Type 3 sonata. Such sonatas include a "recapitulatory" or "reprise" rotation at that point. One example can be heard in Scarlatti's well-known C-major sonata, K. 159.

5. While Figure 11.2 assumes a two-part layout in each section, it was of course also possible to compose each section as continuous, without an MC. Such examples would represent an expansion of the Figure 11.1 scheme either via more extended *Fortspinnung* or by the concatenation of a string of diverse modules.

6. One might suppose, however, that with the arrival of the crux at mm. 91–92 (= mm. 29–30, the end of the exposition's TR), it is becoming clear that the normative next move would be into S in the tonic.

7. For another, slightly more complex example of an Allegro, Type 2 sonata—with both halves repeated—whose P does not return as a coda, see the first movement of Mozart's Symphony

No. 6 in F, K. 43. As with K. 16/i, P appears in the tonic only at the opening of the exposition. Still another example, easily traceable by ear alone, can be found in the finale of Mozart's Symphony in D ("No. 45"), K. 95/iv.

8. The term "binary" for Type 2 structures and their ritornello blends is found frequently in the several essays dealing with early symphonic traditions in Morrow 2012. Particularly helpful is the tabular listing of format-options in Rober 2012, 228–29, which summarizes the options found in the 1731–47 symphonies of Johann Gottlob Harrer.

9. As a reminder: the P-based C is most often the sign of the *beginning* (or near-beginning) of C-space, not its end. A P-based C does not normally succeed a clear and distinct early C theme. (See p. 72 along with *EST*, 184–85.)

10. While K. 16/i's repeats disallow it from being a true sonata-ritornello blend, the example of K. 22/i—not to mention numerous similar Type 2 orchestral structures of the era—it may be that the decision fully to restate P in the dominant after the repeat sign (mm. 59–69) was influenced by models of sonata-ritornello-blend practice.

11. Thus while we have been given a two-part exposition (Rotation 1), the tonal-resolution rotation (Rotation 2) is continuous.

12. For the score, see the 1902 collection, *Denkmäler der Tonkunst in Bayern*, iv, Jahrgang iii/i, which is the volume entitled *Symphonien der Pfalzbayerischen Schule: Mannheimer Symphoniker* (ed. Hugo Riemann). At the time of this writing, the volume was downloadable as a PDF at http://imslp.org/wiki/Sinfonien_der_pfalzbayerischen_Schule_(Riemann%2C_Hugo).

13. Bach inlays variants of the figuration from mm. 2–3 of P^0 as a short but energized Rotation 2 interpolation (or post-crux alteration) toward the end of the tonal resolution, mm. 132–39, though this shares none of the features of a ritornello.

14. The brevity of the musical ideas in this movement suggests that the analytical description might be more helpfully carried out in Kochian terms, even though those terms are readily translatable into (here, proto-) Sonata Theory descriptors. Along those lines, Rotation 1 may be parsed as follows: *Grundabsatz* (motion to an authentic cadence in I, mm. 1–4); *Quintabsatz* in I (motion to a close on an active V of I, mm. 5–8); *Quintabsatz* in V (motion to a close on an active V of V, mm. 9–12, here first touched upon as a V_5^6 before settling into root position); *Schlußsatz* (motion to an authentic cadential closure in V, mm. 13–17; *Anhang* ("appendix," confirming the arrival in V, mm. 17–18).

15. Alternatively, because of the quarter-rest pauses, one might be tempted to read m. 8 as a I:HC MC and m. 12 as a second MC in dialogue with the V:HC type. The presence of apparent double MCs would suggest an embryonic version of an exposition with a trimodular block (TMB), in which proto-TM^1 and proto-TM^2 have been telescoped into a single four-bar gesture over V/V (mm. 9–12), and TM^3 would occupy mm. 13–17. But such a reading may seem gratuitously to presuppose a grander structure (the more expansive TMB) that has been consciously compressed into the miniaturized phrases that we find here.

16. Because the oboe and clarinet in m. 36 sound a $\hat{4}$-$\hat{3}$ descent above the $\hat{2}$-$\hat{1}$ in the first violins, one might be tempted to regard this final cadence as an IAC. My preference, though, is to regard the wind lines as decorative enhancements of the structural voices in the strings, noting also that Mozart's rhetorical positioning of this cadence—as the final gesture of the movement—helps to bolster its effect of adequate closure. This ambiguity is not present at the end of the exposition, whose m. 18 is an unequivocal V:PAC supported in all of the voices.

17. "Double-crux" possibilities are mentioned in *EST*, 240.

18. By no means does K. 306/i provide us with the only instance of starting an S via such descending fifths. Other examples include: Mozart's String Quartet in C, K. 157/i, mm. 21–24, Piano Sonata in C, K. 279/i, mm. 17–20, and Violin Sonata in C, K. 303/i, mm. 20–23; and *Magic Flute* Overture, mm. 58–64; and Beethoven, Piano Sonata in E-flat, op. 7/iv, Symphony

No. 1 in C, op. 21/ii, mm. 27–30. (Cf. the P theme of Haydn, Symphony No. 94/i, "Surprise," and Beethoven, Cello Sonata in F, op. 5 no. 1/iv.) At the time of our writing of the *Elements*, we considered the descending-fifths opening of such an S theme as one type of S^0 theme (*EST*, 145). I now prefer to regard as a special type of $S^{1.1}$ theme (or perhaps, reconciling both options, $S^0 => S^{1.1}$).

19. M. 58 is not, as claimed in Irving 1997, 102, "the start of the 'Reprise' . . . with an unusual subdominant restatement of a theme originally sounded at bar 28." Notice that Mozart will re-sound $S^{2.2}$ in its proper location and in the tonic in the later tonal resolution, mm. 91–99. From the Sonata Theory point of view, m. 58's $S^{2.2}$ is backward-looking, seeking to recapture a thematic module from the exposition that precedes the anomalous C^2.

20. Overtures appear to be more open to such deformations—surely for quasi-programmatic reasons—than do individual movements of more abstract, multimovement sonatas. I have dealt elsewhere, for instance, with the truncated recapitulation found in Mozart's overture to *Idomeneo* (2009a, 75–77; *EST*, 248). Cf. Vande Moortele 2017.

21. The relevant portions of this passage are worth reproducing here (Marx 1860, 405): "Sie hat Sonatenform, weicht aber wieder in geistreich treffender Weise ab." Following the development (occupying "einen zweiten Sonatentheil"), which is concerned largely with the principal theme and ends with a prolonged dominant pedal, Marx's view is that it would have been unwise to bring back a recapitulatory P immediately: "Allein nun darf Mozart nicht wagen, denselben sofort wiederzubringen. Folglich beginnt er seinen dritten Theil—mit dem Seitensatz; erst nach diesem, der zu unkräftig ist, einen Schluss herbeizuführen, kehrt er auf den ersten Anfang zurück, wiederholt die Intrade, den Hauptsatz, knüpft auch den Gang an, führt ihn aber nun zum breiten glänzenden Schlusse." In a Type 1 or Type 3 sonata, Marx's "third part" would be the same thing as a recapitulation, and it is easy to conclude that that is what is meant here. But is that unmistakably its implication? Perhaps so, but it may be that in such anomalous cases Marx, by "third part," might have meant only whatever comes after the end of the "second part," that is, after the development.

22. Rice also notes the similarity of this overture's opening to that of the Symphony No. 34 in C, K. 338 (1780) and adds that its continuation in the next several bars is also "closely related to the opening measures of the overture to *Idomeneo* (1781)" (1991, 68).

23. Obviously related are those "Type 3" sonatas whose developmental space concludes with material refashioned from an introduction that had preceded the sonata proper. Here the layout consists of (1) introduction + exposition; (2) development ending with materials taken from the introduction, which then leads into the recapitulation. Examples can be found in the first movements of Mozart's "Posthorn" Serenade in D, K. 320, and Schubert's Symphony No. 1 in D. The development of Beethoven's *König Stephan* Overture is based completely on the introduction, as is the first movement of Bruckner's Symphony No. 5 (see n. 29).

24. See also n. 29.

25. Some post-1840 exceptions to this in two works of Dvořák are noted at the end of chapter 4, n. 40. An interesting test case, however, is found in the first movement of Smetana's Quartet No. 1 in E minor. At the start of the second rotation, violin 1 brings back the melody of P at pitch (implying a thematic E minor), while the chord supporting it is a half-diminished seventh—in second inversion—on C sharp (which incorporates the E-minor triad). Is this a situation of beginning Rotation 2 "in the tonic"? Smith cites it as a Type 2 sonata (2019, 133), and there is a case to be made for that reading. The movement, though, seems to straddle the line between the expanded Type 1 and the Type 2 sonata, probably tilting more toward the former.

26. As noted earlier (p. 000), the list in *EST*, 196, contains three errors—pieces that are better regarded expanded Type 1s: two by Brahms (the finale of the C-minor Quartet, op. 51 no. 1, and the *Tragic* Overture, though this last appeared in only the earliest printings of

the *Elements*), and Wagner's *Tannhäuser* Overture, which last will be dealt with later in this chapter.

27. Schubert's C-minor *Quartettsatz* is complicated through an unusual treatment of medial caesuras, a deformational example of a trimodular block, an episodic development, and the tonal alienation of TM^1 and TM^2 in the tonal resolution. The three-key exposition in brief: P^1 (m. 1, multiple descending-tetrachord whirlpools of fate); P^2 (codetta, mm. 13) and $P^2 ==> TR$ (m. 19); the theme best regarded as TM^1 (through arriving "too early" and in A-flat, m. 27); TM^2 (m. 61, darkening to A-flat minor); TM^3 (starting in the "modally false" G major [not the expected G minor], m. 93); EEC (in G major, m. 125), elided with a closing zone. The development opens by suppressing P, writing over it with a TM^3-related episode (m. 141). The return of TM^1 at m. 195 would normally signal the start of the tonal resolution, but the major-mode theme returns not in the tonic C but in B-flat. The wistful TM^1 never returns in the tonic: it is "tonally alienated," lost, a permanently unassimilable fantasy or hope, as often happens in analogous moments of other Schubert movements. Similarly, TM^2 (m. 229) begins off-tonic, in E-flat minor. It is only with TM^3 (m. 257) that the Rotation 2 resolves into the tonic C, only here into the modally problematic C major. Still in C, the ESC is attained in m. 289 and continues with the expected closing-zone correspondence measures, closing Rotation 2 and Type 2 sonata space. Schubert snuffs out the sonata's major mode close, however, with the chilling, C-minor return of P as coda, m. 305.

28. The P-zone of Beethoven's Op. 130/i extends from m. 1 to m. 37 (I:"IAC"). It features two contrasting tempi, inlaying aspects of a stop-and-go slow introduction into P proper. The slow portions, Adagio ma non troppo, may be regarded as zero-modules: $P^{0.1}$ (mm. 1–4), $P^{0.2}$ (mm. 4–7), $P^{0.3}$ (mm. 7–14). The fast portions, Allegro, may be regarded as P^1 modules, first shooting forth in mm. 15–20. P^0 returns in mm. 21–24, and P^1, getting underway in earnest, in mm. 25–37. Now looking ahead, most commentators would regard the "recapitulation" as beginning with P^1 in the tonic at m. 132. But two other factors are decisive here. First, the apparent referential measure with m. 132 is m. 25, the second appearance of P^1 in the exposition—that is, well into the expositional rotation—and the next several referential measures reinforce this association. Second, the development, beginning in m. 94 is anchored in P^0 intermixed with by P^1 material that probably alludes to P^1's first expositional appearances. In sum: the development is readily heard as dealing with material from m. 1 to m. 24, and the "recapitulation" then shifts into the tonic and referential measures (though not yet quite correspondence measures) that relate most clearly to m. 25. That's classic Type 2 behavior—that of a double-rotational sonata. In Sonata Theory terms, m. 132 is not a "recapitulation" but instead continues an ongoing rotation whose preceding music had been treated developmentally. Or, more nuanced, it is a Type 2 sonata that is also contrived to give the impression of a "recapitulatory" return at m. 132.

29. A word of caution is warranted here: Bruckner's massive, sonata-grounded structures, especially those from the Fifth Symphony onward, have been much discussed—and debated—in the past quarter-century. Not least has been the question of the degree to which several of these movements, along with those in other Romantic works, may be (or may not be) considered to be "deformations" of some still largely shared concept of sonata form, a concept that some have disputed (e.g., Horton 2004, 154). Some of the earlier chapters of the present *Handbook* have dealt with such concerns in general terms; the remainder of this chapter and the beginning of the next address them more directly. Sonata Theory, of course, by no means proposes a rigid, inelastic definition of the form. Rather, it construes "classical" sonata procedures as a historically situated constellation of flexible options with ample opportunities for individualized variants, overrides, and later-decade updates. With regard to Bruckner, and allowing for the possibility of loosely conjoined, internal diversions within the structure's large-scale, governing format—brief, individual passages that can appear "out of order"— that composer produced, in addition to some Type 3 structures, three types of closely related

double-rotational structures. The first is the *Type 2 sonata*, e.g., Symphonies No. 7/iv and No. 9/i. These two differ only insofar as the latter's exposition begins with an extended, generative P^0 that prepares a more declarative P^1 proper, while the developmental space is largely given over to an expansion of P^0, with a strong tonic return (and "recapitulatory" effect) only with P^1. The second, nearly identical with the first in this case, is the *expanded Type 1 sonata* with only a brief touching of the tonic at the beginning of Rotation 2, e.g., Symphony No. 6/iv, in which Rotation 2's onset, mm. 177–84, initiating the developmental space, replicates *at pitch* that of Rotation 1, mm. 3–10, though in a lower octave. The third, is the sonata-related type in which a generative but more separable "Introduction" (pre-sonata) is the basis for the entire developmental space, e.g., Symphony No. 5/i. In this last case the contents of each of the two rotations exceed that of sonata space proper: the two rotations are: introduction, exposition; and introduction (= development), recapitulation.

30. The Dvořák example was called to my attention in a 2008 term paper by Paul Sherrill, "Dvořák Cello Concerto in B Minor, Op. 104, *Allegro*," written as the concluding project for a Sonata Theory seminar. "The overall form is not merely a typical Type 5 sonata … but the much rarer Type 2 variation on the Type 5 design: it consists of only three full rotations through the sonata layout [Tutti 1, Solo Exposition, and Development-Tonal Resolution], the last of which begins as a developmental space but reaches a crux point just in time for the second theme."

31. Galand 2008 and Smith 2019 provide extended studies that reinforce the idea of referring to the concluding, post-sonata reference to P as a coda. In a companion study, Smith 2018, in particular, applies the same reasoning to concluding coda-returns of P or P material in expanded Type 1 sonatas.

32. The larger context from Wingfield, 2008, 160: "It is difficult to identify a single work in the nineteenth-century repertoire where a Type 2-orientated reading is richer and more compelling than a Type 3-based one. Indeed, in all of these cases, a Type 2 interpretation seems to marginalise much that is of central importance. … The more pragmatic alternative is that nineteenth-century theorists neglected the Type 2 model simply because it was a historical curiosity at the time they were writing. Perhaps, then, we should apply Occam's razor to sonata categorisation and conclude that the so-called Type 2 sonata was one of the casualties of the 'stylistic revolution of the 1770s.'"

33. While introducing the concept of the strong subordinate theme (which is by no means always associated with potential Type 2 formats), a key criterion for Vande Moortele is that S be more memorable, often broadly laid out and songlike, in contrast with a relatively fluid or unstable, preparatory P/TR. Here his initial examples, in order, are taken from Mendelssohn's *Hebrides* Overture, Wagner's Overture to *Der fliegende Holländer*, Berlioz's Overture to *Les francs-juges*, and Auber's to *La muette de Portici*.

34. In this citation Vande Moortele is commenting on the "strong" S in Mendelssohn's *Hebrides* Overture—a Type 3 sonata. Within his larger discussion, though, it's clear that he extends the claim to several other pieces as well.

35. The *forte*, decisive S was already a familiar though less frequent secondary-theme option in the late eighteenth century (*EST*, 136–37).

36. As I have pointed out in a separate treatment of strophic songs within French and Italian operas, "When a third stanza exists, it became common to alter the music of its verse section—indeed, to treat it quite freely—before returning to more familiar music from the refrain space" (1997, 163). Vande Moortele's dismissal of the strophic reading of the third stanza on the grounds that it is not a "variation" of the verses that had preceded it (2017, 177) may be too hasty.

37. Even while admiring some aspects of Rodgers's reading, Vande Moortele adduces questionable caveats to it (questionable, that is, from the point of view of Sonata Theory)—the presence of the lengthy introduction, the much-altered verse portion of the third strophe—in

order to maintain instead that the "strong," carnivalesque, and tonic-key S (m. 344) "launches the recapitulation. . . . The strong subordinate theme now finally assumes the role it was supposed to play all along: that of main theme" (2017, 180).

38. Wagner's 1852 "programmatic commentary" of the various events from the opera represented in the *Tannhäuser* Overture is helpfully provided, with corresponding bar numbers, in Grey 1988, 15, though Grey, in the then-standard manner of late-twentieth-century analysis, also reads the sonata structure as an "arch-like modification of the sonata form [with a] reversed order of themes in the recapitulation" (16). For a larger context of Wagner's prose essays, see Grey 1995.

39. This secondary theme and all that precedes it, as is the case in *Le carnaval romain*, also share the setup and execution features of a strophic song's climactic refrain. *Tannhäuser*'s S is taken from Act 1, Scene 2 of the opera. Having resolved to leave Venus and her seductive realm, Tannhäuser sings this melody at three different points (in D-flat, D, and E-flat). Wagner thus casts it as a strophic song. (The overture quotes only that song's first, more square-cut and positive half.) Within an otherwise fluid operatic scene, the triple-recurrence of Tannhäuser's melodic pleas to Venus provides the listener with stable, refrain-like anchors. The song itself, though, is not a "refrain." (Indeed, the second half of each stanza of his song—the portion that does not appear in the overture—features at the end its own rhyming, two-line refrain, an appeal for permission to depart.) Still, what this suggests is that Wagner might have crafted the overture's exposition to be in dialogue with certain principles of strophic song, as Berlioz had done in *Le carnaval romain*. From a formal standpoint this structural feature also helps to account for the emphatic arrival marking the secondary theme's "strong" onset, though as a whole this overture's sonata/song generic hybrid tilts far more decisively toward the sonata than does Berlioz's *Carnaval romain*.

40. In one of Vande Moortele's two readings of the overture (2017, 184–87) he notes the schematic, symmetrical arch form of the whole piece, a sonata portion with "reversed recapitulation" enframed and subsumed on each side by the Pilgrim-Chorus introduction and coda. To be sure, if one observes only the ordering of the themes apart from either the rotational principle or the themes' action-zone participation, such an arch is perceptible, with the *Liebesbann* episode in the development, *un poco ritenuto*, as its center-point. On the other hand, any presumed double-rotational sonata (an expanded Type 1 or a Type 2) with a P-based coda—not to mention a central episode—produces such an apparent arch. And if such a sonata is better regarded as double-rotational, the thematic-arch design becomes a secondary by-product of that generic format. The arch is still significant but not to be regarded as the primary determinant of the sonata's form.

41. Franz Liszt, *Lohengrin et Tannhäuser de Richard Wagner* (F. A. Brockhaus, 1851, orig. 1849), accessed in October 2019 at https://fr.wikisource.org/wiki/Lohengrin_et_Tannh%C3%A4user_(Franz_Liszt,_1851). "Ainsi, pour ne parler encore que de l'ouverture, nous ferons remarquer qu'on ne saurait prétendre d'un poëme symphonique, qu'il soit écrit d'une manière plus conforme aux règles de la coupe classique, qu'il ait une plus parfaite logique dans l'exposition, le développement, et le dénouement des propositions. Leur ordonnance est aussi claire, aussi précise, quoique plus riche, que ceux des meilleurs modèles en ce genre."

42. The relevant sentence begins with his description of the return of TR at m. 220: "Elle fait place à la phrase de transition qui avait amené la mélodie en *si* [the exposition's S], phrase de brâme lamentable et qui, cette fois sur la pédale de *fa-dièze*, aboutit par une progression chromatique au retour de cette même mélodie [S], sur la tonique."

43. Liszt's crucial line is also quoted in *EST*, 383 n. 54: "La Coda résume les principaux dessins du début de l'Allégro, et arrive à son plus haut degré de frénésie, par une descente chromatique sur la pédale de *si*, opérée par la dernière répétition de la phrase corollaire."

Chapter 12

1. The deepest roots of sonata-deformation theory—hence to an incipient Sonata Theory—reach back, at least in terms of published material, to Hepokoski 1992, esp. 143–52, and 1993, 19–30. More central, but unpublished—the actual seedbed of Sonata-Theory-to-come—is a rudimentary, bound draft from 1993 that I prepared in conjunction with a Sonata Deformation graduate seminar at the University of Minnesota, Twin Cities: "Three Documents on Analysis." The three were: a broad outline of numerous types of "Sonata Deformation Families"; "Principles of the Symphony in the Period of its Centering Phase, c. 1780–1820"; and "One Approach to Musical Hermeneutics: Thoughts on Music Analysis." All of these unpublished papers are available on jameshepokoski.com.

2. For some published discussions of Sonata Theory or rotation-grounded analysis of post-1850 structures, see Hepokoski 2006, 2007, and 2012, and Monahan 2015. Additional remarks on deformation theory can be found in my articles 2002b, 2010b (concerning Richard Strauss), and 2010c (concerning Claude Debussy). On my use of the term "early modernism," see, e.g., 1993, 1–5; 2002b, 456–57; 2006, 7.

3. For the concept of the "institution of art" (which, if focused specifically on "the institution of art music," I regard as a central feature of the European elite-music system from c. 1830 up through much of the twentieth century), see, e.g., Bürger 1984 and 1992, and Hohendahl 1988. I have integrated the concept into much of my own writing on the late-nineteenth and early-twentieth centuries, e.g. 2002b, 455; 2006; and many others. Cf. n. 6 for Luhmann's slightly differing concept of "autopoiesis."

4. Within nineteenth-century universities—most notably those located in Austro-Germanic cities—the academic transformations from broadly based philological inquiries into a diverse set of more narrowly focused, scientifically minded subdisciplines (specialty areas, especially within the humanities, which would eventually lead to the initial projects of *Musikwissenschaft*) are brilliantly outlined in Turner 2014.

5. *Neue Zeitschrift für Musik*, April 20, 1839, quoted in Hepokoski 2002b, 427, which also deals with the problems surrounding the continuation of the Austro-Germanic musical tradition in the decades after Beethoven's death.

6. The term is from Niklas Luhmann 1990. Striving toward ever-increasing complexity and self-referentiality (or "autonomy"), autopoietic subsystems "produce the elements, of which they consist, by means of the elements of which they consist. It is thus a question of self-referential closed systems, or more exactly of systems that base their relation to their environment (*Umwelt*) on circular-closed operational connexions. . . . The [functionally differentiated] structure of modern society makes it possible to form autopoietic subsystems." One issue explored by Luhmann is the emergence of "some problems that arise when this [sub]system [of art] achieves autonomy over the determination of its elements, strives for self-referential closure. . . . As against Adorno, it is a question here not of 'autonomy vis-à-vis society,' but of *autonomy within society*; we see the social nature of art not in negativity, in an 'oppositional position towards soceity,' but in the fact that emancipation for a specific function is only possible within the society" (191–93). Cf. the broader discussion in Luhmann 2000.

7. I develop these ideas further, and from different angles, in 2002b, 424–30 and 447–58; and in 2006, 28–31.

8. The devoted nominalist would doubtless make the same claim for all compositions, including those of the classical era. While acknowledging the aspect of uniqueness of every singularity (every token of the type or genre), genre theory and dialogic form take a very different point of view, as noted in chapter 1.

9. One obvious case is the emergence of the *two-dimensional* or *double-function sonata* (*multimovement form within a single movement*) (Vande Moortele 2009). That and others are noted in Hepokoski 2002b, 447–54.

10. In the early 1870s Bruckner, recently appointed as a professor of harmony and counterpoint at the Vienna Conservatory, was known primarily as an organist of considerable distinction and a composer of church music—though his devotion to Wagner and large-scale Wagnerian effects were starting to become controversial in some more conservative quarters.

11. The classic case is that of Brinkmann 1995, 32–53, to be revisited later in this chapter. Other analysts have mistakenly concluded that rondo elements are a factor here. On the other hand, Frisch 1996, 61, identifies the finale's form correctly, essentially following the reading provided in a critical edition of the score by Giselher Schubert: *Brahms 1. Sinfonie c-Moll, op. 68*, Einführung und Analyse von Giselher Schubert mit Partitur (Munich and Mainz: Piper/Schott, 1981, 69). Brodbeck 1997, 68–74, is also on the right track, though his determination, albeit cautiously, to fold in and expand on some of Brinkmann's hermeneutic observations may not seem convincing to all.

12. See the note on Brahms's C-minor Quartet finale and *Tragic* Overture, chapter 4, n. 41, which corrects an error found in the *Elements*.

13. Brodbeck 1997, 70, also notes "the growing impression of a subordinated sonata form by the creation of an encasing 'introduction-coda frame.'" The reference to that concept here, along with the specific language in which it is conveyed (e.g., "encasing"), is that found in Hepokoski 1993, 6, which also mentions the finale of Brahms's First Symphony as one among several other examples.

14. This could be regarded as one of the few Brahms examples of the formal technique that Adorno (following Bekker) characterized as a *Durchbruch*—a breakthrough.

15. Big Ben's "Westminster Chimes" were originally devised in 1793 for the clock chimes of Saint Mary the Great, the University Church in Cambridge. Mentioning the alphorn theme, Tovey reports that "when this symphony was first performed at Cambridge, this passage excited special comment from its resemblance to Dr. Crotch's well-known clock-chimes. These chimes are, foolishly enough, alleged by Crotch himself to be derived from a figure in Handel's 'I know that my Redeemer liveth'" (1981, 196). The claimed Handelian figure, from *Messiah*, occurs in mm. 5–6 of the introduction to the aria, where it sounds in E major, identical intervallically and in scalar terms to the first four notes of Westminster Chimes ("Westminster Quarters"). However tempting it may be to speculate on potential connotations of historical time and temporality at this moment in the finale, I know of no evidence that Brahms could have been aware of any of this.

16. Knapp 1997, 82–84, surveys a number of musical allusions or ciphers that may or may not have been embedded in this chorale phrase (for instance, the F-A-E cipher, *Frei aber einsam*, as had been initially suggested in Musgrave 1983, 131).

17. Like the alphorn theme that precedes it, P's structure traces through a well-known song-form type. Similarly formatted as they might seem, for the analyst their two patterns are worth distinguishing. As noted earlier, the alphorn theme is laid out in what I have called the "lyric binary" format (the "rounded binary" or form-functional theory's "small ternary" form), *a a' b* || *a"*, with a harmonic interruption on V at the end of *b*. Beethoven's "Ode to Joy" theme from the Ninth's finale—so obviously relevant to Brahms's P theme here—provides a familiar example. One variant of this form replaces the final *a"* with a new melodic idea, yielding an *a a' b* || *c* pattern, while still retaining the harmonic interruption at the end of *b*. Also distinguishable, however, is another type of *a a' b c* structure, which is what one finds in this finale's P theme. Here *b* flows into *c* without a harmonic interruption, which suggests that it should be counted among form-functional theory's "small binary" forms. (One of several earlier examples of this: the opening theme of Schubert's G-flat Impromptu, D. 899.) For an

extended discussion of the "lyric binary," the "small binary," and their variants in Italian opera and song, see Hepokoski 1997, a discussion updated and terminologically nuanced with regard to Chopin's nocturnes in Hepokoski (forthcoming c. 2020–21).

18. As always noted, its explicit recall of Beethoven's theme occurs in its "b" phrase (of the aa || bc format), mm. 70–73. Perhaps not surprisingly, commentators have claimed other allusions embedded both in the theme and in its general style. Not mentioning its similarity to the finale-theme of Bruch's Second Symphony, Brodbeck, for instance (1997, 67–68, 71–73), also wants to derive, in the manner of a "significant 'double allusion' " (Beethoven's theme being the other), P's hymnic head motive (in minor) from the ground bass in the second movement of Bach, Cantata No. 106, "Gottes Zeit ist die allerbeste Zeit," and argues the case at some length. Brodbeck also noted (66–67) that in 1877 Adolf Schubring associated the theme not only with that in Beethoven's Ninth Symphony but also with Schumann's apparently well-known song from 1840, "Der deutsche Rhein [Patriotische Lied]," WoO 1, a setting of Nikolaus Becker's poem, "Rheinlied." Knapp 1997, 88–91, suggests other "allusive webs" woven into Brahms's theme: "authentic folk tunes, Beethoven's 'Ode to Joy,' and predecessors in Brahms's own finale theme provide a rich allusive background for the main theme" (91). On the other hand, elsewhere Knapp provocatively suggests that "the famous evocation of Beethoven's 'Ode to Joy' theme . . . generally taken for a fairly straightforward *homage*, may just as easily be construed as a pointed rejection of its model" (81, a comment elaborated upon on p. 103).

19. Schumann's patriotic song, "Der deutsche Rhein," (see the preceding note) may also be considered a *geselliges Lied*.

20. See also the extended commentary in Parsons 2002 on Schiller's text, "An die Freude," which Beethoven (and many others) set as music—of the *geselliges Lied* type—in the Ninth's "Ode to Joy."

21. Harking back to practices in Schumann, Musgrave, some years ago, wanted to read a "Clara" cipher into this five-note curling figure. "It will not have escaped the attention of readers familiar with Schumann's musical language that [this intervallic] motive . . . is identical with C-B-A-G♯-A which has widely come to be regarded as representing Schumann's personal cipher for Clara. Although no single piece of evidence irrefutably confirms the shape's significance, the coincidence of factors makes it hard to dismiss; every example of concentrated use gives it added credence" (1983, 128). Whatever we might make of such a suggestion, we might note *en passant* that those exact pitches are heard at the transposition level found, for instance, in beats two and three of the second violin in mm. 108 and 110.

22. See chapter 11, n. 18.

23. It is difficult to find examples of a PRINNER taking on this theme-initiating role, though two precedents, each projecting a much different affect, may be found at the P^1-theme proper in the first movement of Beethoven's String Quartet in E-flat, op. 127 (mm. 7–22, multiple, slightly varied PRINNERS) and the opening of the S theme in the finale of Schubert's String Quintet in C, D. 956, mm. 46–49. (Could Schubert's uncommon PRINNER S-opening have been on Brahms's mind here in the finale? Schubert's finale is also an expanded Type 1 sonata.)

24. One striking instance of a short ground with carillon allusions is the insistently repeated F-E-D ostinato in Marin Marais's "Sonnerie de Sainte-Geneviève du Mont de Paris" (1723). Others include: the C-D ground in William Byrd's keyboard work, "The Bells" (probably before 1600); the relatively brief ground in Antoine (or perhaps Jean-Baptiste) Forqueray's "Le carillon de Passy" (early 1700s?); and the four-note bell-ostinatos in such organ works as Nicholas Lebègue's "Les cloches" (c. 1670?) and his pupil Pierre Dandrieu's similar "Carillon ou cloches" (c. 1700?), both grounds of which are remarkably similar to Brahms's. But even given Brahms's well-known interest in past musical styles, could he have been aware of such

a tradition? Or was the tradition (possible an organ tradition) still present in some German-speaking regions? Even more provocative is the recurrence of potential bell metaphors to describe certain moments in Brahms's finale. See, e.g, Tovey's remark about the bell-like aspect of the alphorn theme, p. 245, and the related discussion in n. 15.

25. More abstractly, one might wonder whether such an analytical category as "PMC declined" might be considered as a compositional possibility, though that might stretch the credulity of more than one reader.

26. Two precedents in Beethoven might be mentioned: the first movements of the String Quintet in C, op. 29 (C major to A minor), and the Piano Sonata in G, op. 31 no. 1 (G major to B minor). The recapitulations of both works, however, end in the tonic major. Note also that Brahms would also conclude the first-movement exposition of his Symphony No. 3 in F major in A minor.

27. Brahms would revisit the I-V-iii expositional scheme in the first movement of Cello Sonata No. 2 in F, op. 99 (1886). As Hunt 2009 confirms, there are few if any precedents for this tonal pattern among the major composers, although we should note the unusual I-V-♭III (tonic, dominant, flatted mediant major in Beethoven, Piano Trio in G, op. 1 no. 2/ii discussed in Hepokoski 2001–2) and Schubert, String Quartet in E, D. 353/iv (labeled as a "Rondo" but also in dialogue with what Sonata Theory calls the Type 4¹ sonata [*EST*, 407–9]).

28. On the metaphor of INFLATION and DEFLATION, see the discussion in chapter 8, pp. 141–2, concerning the transformations shown in Example 8.2.

29. Cohn 2012, 191–94 provides a chord-transformational, *Tonnetz*-oriented analysis of the tonal shifts encountered in mm. 186–221, correctly interpreted as "the opening of the recapitulation."

30. Brodbeck 1997, 76, wants to hear back-references in mm. 246–48 of this module, where he calls attention to "a subtle 'combined reference' to both the alphorn theme (recalled by the descending pattern E-D-C) and head-motif [of P] (represented by the incomplete neighbor-note pattern C-B♮)." While not discounting the possibility, I'm less inclined to hear such references.

31. Brinkmann's conclusion: "It is no longer the humanist fervor of freedom and brotherliness [as sounded in the Lied-like song of P] but nature and religion that resolve the issue for Brahms" (1995, 45). See also Brodbeck's discussion of Brinkmann, leading down a path of tenuous allusions to the music of Schumann and Bach (1997, 70–78). Frisch (1996, 63–65) notes the "considerable force" of Brinkmann's idea but ultimately rejects much of it as "too extreme," largely favoring instead what Sonata Theory would call the expanded Type 1 reading.

32. In the opening movement of the Cello Sonata No. 2, the exposition material from S onward moves from C (V) to an EEC in iii (A minor). This music returns in the recapitulation as F to D minor (I to vi), and the return to F is accomplished only in the coda.

33. Cf. Hepokoski 2001–2, 152–54: "What Counts as a Nonresolution? Differing Strengths of 'Failed' Recapitulations"; and *EST*, 254.

34. Citing the *Johannes Brahms Breifwechsel*, XVI, 146, Brodbeck 1997, 24, tells us that mm. 417–18 were last-minute additions to this passage, penned around October 14, 1876, before he sent the movement to the copyist. Thus the original plan had been to follow up the chorale's final dominant (mm. 415–16) with the music that now begins at m. 419.

35. This might prompt the question, was not this also the case in the first movement of Beethoven's Second Symphony (treated in chapter 7), in which a substantial introduction and solution-bearing coda also surround an internal sonata? Perhaps to some extent, but not in the same sense as we find it in the Brahms finale. In the Beethoven, the introduction presented us with a modal problem, the decay of D major into D minor; the sonata was staged as a strategy that failed to solve that problem adequately, and the coda completed the task of exorcising the minor-mode infiltration that the sonata had only partially fulfilled. One might say that

the Beethoven movement was more *processual*—linear, start to finish—than the Brahms finale, where many of the pivotal events of the introduction and coda are separable from the sonata process proper. The procedures of Sonata Theory, at least, encourage us to pose such questions as these.

Appendix

1. Later eighteenth-century exceptions to the principle of tonic return—most notably in some of C. P. E. Bach's rondos—are mentioned in *EST*, 403. See also the remarks in the following text on Beethoven's often "wrong-key" rondo-theme entries.

2. Note, however, that "ritornello formats in concerto first and second movements may [also] be in dialogue with Type 1, 2, or 3 sonatas. The Type 5 adaptation of the Type 1 sonata (no developmental space) is found primarily in slow movements. . . . The infrequent adaptation of the Type 2 sonata ('binary' without a full recapitulation) may be found [in the first movement of Mozart's Violin Concerto No. 4 in D, K. 218]" (*EST*, 431). A much later instance of the Type 2/Type 5 dialogue, as noted in chapter 11, can be found in the first movement of Dvořák's Cello Concerto.

3. *EST* provides a close look, especially, at the first movement of Mozart's Piano Concertos No. 17 in G, K. 453. See also the reading of the Type 5 first movement of Brahms's Piano Concerto No. 1 in D Minor, op. 15, in Hepokoski 2012.

4. The Third Concerto's R1 has been especially commented on in this respect. Within a C-minor tonal context, its treatment of R1:\TR—an emphatic "mediant-tutti" leap into E-flat (m. 24) leading to its MC-preparation for a decisive launch into R1:\S in the same key (m. 50)—gives the impression that what is being composed is the exposition of a symphony, not a concerto. The "correction" of the non-tonic start of R1:\S back into C—C *major* at this point, m. 62—reasserts the "concerto-ness" of this opening R1. Tovey, for instance, made much of this in his commentary on Piano Concerto No. 3/i, among other observations referring to "the one feature (the sudden shift back to the tonic during the announcement of the second subject) by which Beethoven rectifies something that dangerously resembled a mistake" (1936, 70–71). Probably in the wake of Tovey, Plantinga, too, is uneasy about this moment and the non-tonic transition that precedes it (1999, 138–39). My own view is that the major-mode mediant feint dramatizes the impulsive urgency with which the narrative subject seeks to "escape" from the tonic minor (as described in chapter 8, pp. 140–2).

5. While some writers have used the term "display episode" to refer to virtuosic or figurational passages in Type 3 keyboard sonatas, especially those toward the end of the S/C thematic complex, Sonata Theory uses the term only with regard to its generically specific role and function within Type 5 sonatas.

6. On the potential problems associated with the claim of "rotationally inert" modules in Type 5 sonatas—most notably at an R1:\TR[1.1] beginning of R2—see *EST*, 552–56.

Bibliography

Adorno, Theodor W. 1989. "Chamber Music." In Adorno, *Introduction to the Sociology of Music*, translated by E. B. Ashton, 85–103. New York: Continuum.

Adorno, Theodor W. 1998. *Beethoven: The Philosophy of Music*, edited by Rolf Tiedemann, translated by Edmund Jephcott. Stanford: Stanford University Press.

Adorno, Theodor W. 2005. "Schubert (1928)," translated by Jonathan Dunsby and Beate Perry. *19th-Century Music* 29 (1): 3–14.

Agawu, Kofi. 1999. "Formal Perspectives on the Symphonies." In *The Cambridge Companion to Brahms*, edited by Michael Musgrave, 133–55. Cambridge: Cambridge University Press.

Albrecht, Theodore. 2004. "'First Name Unknown': Violist Anton Schreiber, the Schuppanzigh Quartet, and Early Performances of Beethoven's String Quartets, Opus 59." *The Beethoven Journal* 19 (1): 10–18.

Allanbrook, Wye J. 1992. "Two Threads through the Labyrinth: Topic and Process in the First Movements of K. 332 and K. 333." In *Convention in Eighteenth- and Nineteenth-Century Music: Essays in Honor of Leonard G. Ratner*, edited by Wye J. Allanbrook, Janet M. Levy, and William P. Mahrt, 125–71. Stuyvesant, NY: Pendragon Press.

Allanbrook, Wye J. 2014. *The Secular Commedia: Comic Mimesis in Late Eighteenth-Century Music*, edited by Mary Ann Smart and Richard Taruskin. Oakland: University of California Press.

Almén, Byron. 2008. *A Theory of Musical Narrative*. Bloomington: Indiana University Press.

Anker, Elizabeth S., and Rita Felski, editors. 2017. *Critique and Postcritique*. Durham, NC: Duke University Press.

Artemeva, Natasha. 2004. "Key Concepts in Rhetorical Genre Studies: An Overview." *Technostyle* 20 (1): 3–38.

Beach, David. 2017. *Schubert's Mature Instrumental Music: A Theorist's Perspective*. Rochester, NY: University of Rochester Press.

Becker, Judith. 2004. *Deep Listeners: Music, Emotion, and Trancing*. Bloomington: Indiana University Press.

Best, Stephen, and Sharon Marcus. 2009. "Surface Reading: An Introduction." *Representations* 108 (1): 1–21.

Black, Brian. 2016. "The Sensuous as a Constructive Force in Schubert's Late Works." In *Rethinking Schubert*, edited by Lorraine Byrne Bodley and Julian Horton, 77-108. New York: Oxford University Press.

Bonds, Mark Evan. 2017. "Irony and Incomprehensibility: Beethoven's 'Serioso' String Quartet in F Minor, Op. 95, and the Path to the Late Style." *Journal of the American Musicological Society* 70 (2): 285–356.

Bonds, Mark Evan. 2020. *The Beethoven Syndrome: Hearing Music as Autobiography*. New York: Oxford University Press.

Brendel, Alfred. 1990. "Schubert's Last Sonatas." In Brendel, *Music Sounded Out: Essays, Lectures, Interviews, Afterthoughts*, 72–141 New York: Farrar Straus Giroux.

Brett, Philip. 1997. "Piano Four-Hands: Schubert and the Performance of Gay Male Desire." *19th-Century Music* 21 (2): 149–76.

Brinkmann, Reinhold. 1995. *Late Idyll: The Second Symphony of Johannes Brahms*. Cambridge, MA: Harvard University Press.

Brodbeck, David. 1997. *Brahms: Symphony No. 1*. Cambridge: Cambridge University Press.

Brodbeck, David. 2013. "The Symphony after Beethoven after Dahlhaus." In *The Cambridge Companion to the Symphony*, edited by Julian Horton, 61–95. Cambridge: Cambridge University Press.

Brody, Christopher. 2016. "Parametric Interaction in Tonal Repertories." *Journal of Music Theory* 60 (2): 97–148.

Brown, A. Peter. 2002. *The Symphonic Repertoire*, vol. 2: *The First Golden Age of the Viennese Symphony; Haydn, Mozart, Beethoven, and Schubert*. Bloomington: Indiana University Press.

Buch, Esteban. 2003. *Beethoven's Ninth: A Political History*, translated by Richard Miller. Chicago: University of Chicago Press.

Bürger, Peter. 1984. *Theory of the Avant-Garde*, translated by Michael Shaw. Minneapolis: University of Minnesota Press, 1984.

Bürger, Peter and Christa. 1992. "The Institution of Art as a Category of the Sociology of Literature." In *The Institutions of Art*, translated by Loren Kruger, 3–29. Lincoln: University of Nebraska Press.

Burstein, L. Poundie. 2010. "Mid-Section Cadences in Haydn's Sonata-Form Movements." *Studia Musicologica* 51 (1–2): 91–107.

Burstein, L. Poundie. 2014. "The Half Cadence and Other Such Slippery Events." *Music Theory Spectrum* 36 (2): 203–27.

Burstein, L. Poundie. 2016. "Expositional Journeys and Resting Points." In *A Composition as a Problem VII: Proceedings of the Seventh International Conference on Music Theory: Tallinn, Pärnu, January 8–11, 2014*, edited by Mart Humal, 5–16. Talinn: Eesti Muusika- ja Teatriakadeemia.

Byros, Vasili. 2009. "Towards an 'Archaeology' of Hearing: Schemata and Eighteenth-Century Consciousness." *Musica humana* 1 (2): 235–306.

Byros, Vasili. 2012. "Meyer's Anvil: Revisiting the Schema Concept." *Music Analysis* 31 (3): 273–346.

Byros, Vasili. 2013. "Trazom's Wit: Communicative Strategies in a 'Popular' Yet 'Difficult' Sonata." *Eighteenth-Century Music* 10 (2): 213–52.

Byros, Vasili. 2015. "'Hauptruhepuncte des Geistes': Punctuation Schemas and the Late-Eighteenth-Century Sonata." In *What Is a Cadence?*, edited by Markus Neuwirth and Pieter Bergé, 215–51. Leuven: Leuven University Press.

Caplin, William E. 1998. *Classical Form: A Theory of Formal Functions for the Instrumental Music of Haydn, Mozart, and Beethoven*. New York: Oxford University Press.

Caplin, William E. 2004. "The Classical Cadence: Conceptions and Misconceptions." *Journal of the American Musicological Society* 57 (1): 51–117.

Caplin, William E. 2009. "What Are Formal Functions?" In *Musical Form, Forms, & Formenlehre: Three Methodological Reflections*, edited by Pieter Bergé, 21–40. Leuven: Leuven University Press.

Caplin, William E. 2013. *Analyzing Classical Form: An Approach for the Classroom*. New York: Oxford University Press.

Caplin, William E., and Nathan John Martin. 2016. "The 'Continuous Exposition' and the Concept of Subordinate Theme." *Music Analysis* 35 (1): 4–43.

Churgin, Bathia. 2012. "The Symphony in Italy." In *The Symphonic Repertoire*, edited by Mary Sue Morrow and Bathia Churgin, 103–16, [vol. 1 of] *The Eighteenth-Century Symphony*. Bloomington: Indiana University Press, 2012.

Clark, Suzannah. 2011. *Analyzing Schubert*. Cambridge: Cambridge University Press.

Cohn, Richard. 1999. "As Wonderful as Star Clusters: Instruments for Gazing at Tonality in Schubert." *19th-Century Music* 22 (3): 213–32.

Cohn, Richard. 2004. "Uncanny Resemblances: Tonal Signification in the Freudian Age." *Journal of the American Musicological Society* 57 (2): 285–323.

Cohn, Richard. 2012. *Audacious Euphony: Chromaticism and the Triad's Second Nature*. New York: Oxford University Press.

Cook, Nicholas. 2001. "Theorizing Musical Meaning." *Music Theory Spectrum* 23 (2): 170–95.

Cooper, Barry. 2001. "Introduction" to *Beethoven: Symphony No. 2 in D Major, op. 36*, iii–v. Cassell: Bärenreiter.

Cox, Arnie. 2016. *Music and Embodied Cognition: Listening, Moving, Feeling, and Thinking*. Bloomington: Indiana University Press.

Csikszentmihályi, Mihály. 1990. *Flow: The Psychology of Optimal Experience.* New York: Harper & Row.

Dahlhaus, Carl. 1989. *Nineteenth-Century Music,* translated by J. Bradford Robinson. Berkeley: University of California Press.

Dahlhaus, Carl. 1991. *Ludwig van Beethoven: Approaches to His Music,* translated by Mary Whittall. Oxford and New York: Oxford University Press.

Damasio, Antonio. 1999. *The Feeling of What Happens: Body and Emotion in the Making of Consciousness.* New York, San Diego, and London: Harcourt Brace.

Darcy, Warren. 1997. "Bruckner's Sonata Deformations." In *Bruckner Studies,* edited by Timothy L. Jackson and Paul Hawkshaw, 256–77. Cambridge: Cambridge University Press.

Daverio, John. 1994. "From 'Concertante Rondo' to 'Lyric Sonata': A Commentary on Brahms's Reception of Mozart." In *Brahms Studies,* vol. 1, edited by David Brodbeck, 111–38. Lincoln: University of Nebraska Press.

Daverio, John. 2000. "Manner, Tone, and Tendency in Beethoven's Chamber Music for Strings." In *The Cambridge Companion to Beethoven,* edited by Glenn Stanley, 147–64. Cambridge: Cambridge University Press.

Davis, Andrew. 2014. "Chopin and the Romantic Sonata: The First Movement of op. 58." *Music Theory Spectrum* 36 (2): 270–94.

Davis, Whitney. 2011. *A General Theory of Visual Culture.* Princeton, NJ: Princeton University Press.

Deutsch, Otto Erich, ed. 1958. *Schubert: Memoirs by His Friends,* translated by Rosamond Ley and John Nowell. London: Adam and Charles Black.

Diergarten, Felix. 2011. "'The True Fundamentals of Composition': Haydn's Partimento Counterpoint." *Eighteenth-Century Music* 8 (1): 53–75.

Diergarten, Felix. 2015. "Beyond 'Harmony': The Cadence in the Partitura Tradition." In *What Is a Cadence?,* edited by Markus Neuwirth and Pieter Bergé, 59–83. Leuven: Leuven University Press.

Dolan, Emily I. 2013. *The Orchestral Revolution: Haydn and the Technologies of Timbre.* Cambridge: Cambridge University Press.

Fauconnier, Gilles, and Mark Turner. 1998. "Conceptual Integration Networks." *Cognitive Science* 22 (2): 133–87.

Fauconnier, Gilles, and Mark Turner. 2002. *The Way We Think: Conceptual Blending and the Mind's Hidden Complexities.* New York: Basic Books.

Felski, Rita. 2015. *The Limits of Critique.* Chicago: University of Chicago Press.

Ferraguto, Mark. 2014. "Beethoven *à la moujik*: Russianness and Learned Style in the 'Razumovsky' String Quartets." *Journal of the American Musicological Society* 67 (1): 77–123.

Fisk, Charles. 2001. *Returning Cycles: Contexts for the Interpretation of Schubert's Impromptus and Last Sonatas.* Berkeley: University of California Press.

Frisch, Walter. 1996. *Brahms: The Four Symphonies.* New York: Schirmer Books.

Galand, Joel. 2008. "Some Eighteenth-Century Ritornello Scripts and Their Nineteenth-Century Revivals." *Music Theory Spectrum* 30 (2): 239–82.

Geiringer, Karl. 1968. *Haydn: A Creative Life in Music.* Berkeley: University of California Press.

Genette, Gérard. 1997. *Paratexts: Thresholds of Interpretation,* translated by Jane E. Lewin. Cambridge: Cambridge University Press.

Gingerich, John M. 2010. "Ignaz Schuppanzigh and Beethoven's Late Quartets." *The Musical Quarterly* 93: 450–513.

Gingerich, John M. 2014. *Schubert's Beethoven Project.* Cambridge: Cambridge University Press.

Gjerdingen, Robert O. 2007. *Music in the Galant Style.* New York: Oxford University Press.

Godel, Arthur. 1985. *Schuberts Letzte Drei Klaviersonaten.* Baden-Baden: Valentin Koerner.

Grave, Floyd. 2008. "Recuperation, Transformation and the Transcendence of Major over Minor in the Finale of Haydn's String Quartet op. 76 no. 1." *Eighteenth-Century Music* 5 (1): 27–50.

Grave, Floyd. 2009. "Galant Style, Enlightenment, and the Paths from Minor to Major in Later Instrumental Works by Haydn." *Ad Parnassum* 7 (13): 9–41.

Grave, Floyd and Margaret. 2006. *The String Quartets of Joseph Haydn.* New York: Oxford University Press.

Green, Douglass M. 1979. *Form in Tonal Music: An Introduction to Analysis.* 2nd edition. New York: Holt, Rinehart, and Winston.

Greenberg, Yoel. 2017. "Of Beginnings and Ends: A Corpus-Based Inquiry into the Rise of the Recapitulation." *Journal of Music Theory* 61 (2): 171–200.

Grey, Thomas S. 1988. "Wagner, the Overture, and the Aesthetics of Musical Form." *19th-Century Music* 12 (1): 3–22.

Grey, Thomas S. 1995. *Wagner's Musical Prose: Texts and Contexts.* Cambridge: Cambridge University Press.

Guez, Jonathan. 2015. "Schubert's Recapitulation Scripts." PhD dissertation, Yale University.

Guez, Jonathan. 2018. "The 'Mono-Operational' Recapitulation in Movements by Beethoven and Schubert." *Music Theory Spectrum* 40 (2): 227–47.

Guez, Jonathan. 2019. "Toward a Theory of Recapitulatory Alterations." *Journal of Music Theory* 63 (2): 209–29.

Haimo, Ethan. 1988. "Haydn's 'Altered Reprise.'" *Journal of Music Theory* 32 (2): 335–51.

Haimo, Ethan. 1995. *Haydn's Symphonic Forms: Essays in Compositional Logic.* Oxford: Clarendon Press.

Haimo, Ethan. 2005. "Parallel Minor as a Destabilizing Force in the Abstract Music of Haydn, Mozart, and Beethoven." *Tijdschrift voor Muziektheorie* 10 (2): 190–200.

Haringer, Andrew. 2014. "Hunt, Military, and Pastoral Topics." In *The Oxford Handbook of Topic Theory.* edited by Danuta Mirka, 194–213. New York: Oxford University Press, 2014a.

Harrison, Daniel. 2019. "Cadence." In *The Oxford Handbook of Critical Concepts in Music Theory*, edited by Alexander Rehding and Steven Rings, 535–76. New York: Oxford University Press, 2019.

Hatten, Robert S. 1994. *Musical Meaning in Beethoven: Markedness, Correlation, and Interpretation.* Bloomington: Indiana University Press.

Hatten, Robert S. 2004. *Interpreting Musical Gestures, Topics, and Tropes: Mozart, Beethoven, Schubert.* Bloomington: Indiana University Press.

Hatten, Robert S. 2016. "Schubert's Alchemy: Transformative Surfaces, Transfiguring Depths." In *Schubert's Late Music: History, Theory, Style*, edited by Lorraine Byrne Bodley and Julian Horton, 91–110. Cambridge: Cambridge University Press.

Hatten, Robert S. 2018. *A Theory of Virtual Agency for Western Art Music.* Bloomington: Indiana University Press.

Heartz, Daniel. 1978. "Mozart's Overture to 'Titus' as Dramatic Argument." *The Musical Quarterly* 64 (1): 29–49. Rev. Heartz 1990.

Heartz, Daniel. 1990. "The Overture to *La clemenza di Tito* as Dramatic Argument." In Heartz, *Mozart's Operas*, 318–51. Berkeley: University of California Press.

Hepokoski, James. 1992. "Fiery-Pulsed Libertine or Domestic Hero? Strauss's *Don Juan* Reinvestigated." In *Richard Strauss: New Perspectives on the Composer and His Work*, edited by Bryan Gilliam, 135–75. Durham, NC: Duke University Press.

Hepokoski, James. 1993. *Sibelius: Symphony No. 5.* Cambridge: Cambridge University Press.

Hepokoski, James. 1997. "*Ottocento* Opera as Cultural Drama: Generic Mixtures in *Il trovatore.*" In *Verdi's Middle Period, 1849–1859: Source Studies, Analysis, and Performance Practice*, edited by Martin Chusid, 147–93. Chicago: University of Chicago Press.

Hepokoski, James. 2001–02. "Back and Forth from *Egmont*: Beethoven, Mozart, and the Nonresolving Recapitulation." *19th-Century Music* 25 (2–3): 127–54.

Hepokoski, James. 2002a. "Beyond the Sonata Principle." *Journal of the American Musicological Society* 55 (1): 91–154.

Hepokoski, James. 2002b. "Beethoven Reception: The Symphonic Tradition." In *The Cambridge History of Nineteenth-Century Music*, edited by Jim Samson, 424–59. Cambridge: Cambridge University Press.

Hepokoski, James. 2006. "Framing Till Eulenspiegel." *19th-Century Music* 30 (1): 4–43.

Hepokoski, James. 2007. "Gaudery, Romance, and the 'Welsh Tune': [Elgar's] *Introduction and Allegro*, Op. 47." In *Elgar Studies*, edited by J. P. E. Harper-Scott and Julian Rushton, 135–71. Cambridge: Cambridge University Press.

Hepokoski, James. 2008. "'Un bel dì? Vedremo!' Anatomy of a Delusion." In *Madama Butterfly: L'orientalismo di fine secolo, l'approccio pucciniano, la ricezione: atti del convegno internazionale di studi, Lucca-Torre del Lago, 28–30 maggio 2004*, edited by Arthur Groos and Virgilio Bernardoni, 219–46. Florence: Leo S. Olschki.

Hepokoski, James. 2009a. "Sonata Theory and Dialogic Form." In William E. Caplin, James Hepokoski, and James Webster, *Musical Form, Forms, & Formenlehre: Three Methodological Reflections*, edited by Pieter Bergé, 71–89. Leuven: Leuven University Press.

Hepokoski, James. 2009b. "Response to James Webster." In William E. Caplin, James Hepokoski, and James Webster, *Musical Form, Forms, & Formenlehre: Three Methodological Reflections*, edited by Pieter Bergé, 106–10. Leuven: Leuven University Press.

Hepokoski, James. 2009c. "Approaching the First Movement of Beethoven's *Tempest* Sonata through Sonata Theory." In *Beethoven's* Tempest *Sonata: Perspectives of Analysis and Performance*, edited by Pieter Bergé, 181–212. Leuven: Peeters.

Hepokoski, James. 2010a. "Formal Process, Sonata Theory, and the First Movement of Beethoven's 'Tempest' Sonata." *Music Theory Online* 16 (2) (May–June 2010), http://mto.societymusictheory.org/issues/mto.10.16.2/mto.10.16.2.hepokoski.html.

Hepokoski, James. 2010b. "The Second Cycle of Tone Poems." In *The Cambridge Companion to Richard Strauss*, edited by Charles Youmans, 78–104. Cambridge: Cambridge University Press.

Hepokoski, James. 2010c. "Clouds and Circles: Rotational Form in Debussy's 'Nuages.'" *Dutch Journal of Music Theory* 15 (1): 1–17.

Hepokoski, James. 2012. "Monumentality and Formal Processes in the First Movement of Brahms's Piano Concerto No. 1 in D Minor, op. 15." In *Expressive Intersections in Brahms: Essays in Analysis and Meaning*, edited by Heather Platt and Peter H. Smith, 217–51. Bloomington: Indiana University Press.

Hepokoski, James. 2013. "Dahlhaus's Beethoven-Rossini *Stildualismus*: Lingering Legacies of the Text-Event Dichotomy." In *The Invention of Beethoven and Rossini: Historiography, Analysis, Criticism*, edited by Nicholas Mathew and Benjamin Walton, 15–48. Cambridge: Cambridge University Press.

Hepokoski, James. 2014. "Program Music." In *Aesthetics of Music: Musicological Perspectives*, edited by Stephen Downes, 62–83. New York: Routledge.

Hepokoski, James. 2016. "Sonata Theory, Secondary Themes and Continuous Expositions: Dialogues with Form-Functional Theory." *Music Analysis* 35 (1): 44–74.

Hepokoski, James. Forthcoming. "Aspects of Structure in Chopin's Nocturnes." In *The Integration of a Work: from Miniature to Large-Scale. Warsaw 2018*, edited by Zofia Chechlińska and Jim Samson. Warsaw: Narodowy Instytut Fryderyka Chopina.

Hepokoski, James, and Warren Darcy. 1997. "The Medial Caesura and Its Role in the Eighteenth-Century Sonata Exposition." *Music Theory Spectrum* 19 (2): 115–64.

Hepokoski, James, and Warren Darcy. 2006. *Elements of Sonata Theory: Norms, Types, and Deformations in the Late-Eighteenth-Century Sonata*. New York: Oxford University Press.

Hinrichsen, Hans-Joachim. 1988. "Die Sonatenform im Spätwerk Franz Schuberts." *Archiv für Musikwissenschaft* 45 (1): 16–49.

Hohendahl, Peter Uwe. 1988. "Introduction." In *A History of German Literary Criticism, 1730–1980*, edited by Hohendahl, 1–11. Lincoln: University of Nebraska Press.

Holtmeier, Ludwig. 2011. Review of Gjerdingen, *Music in the Galant Style*. *Eighteenth-Century Music* 8 (2): 307–26.

Horton, Julian. 2004. *Bruckner's Symphonies: Analysis, Reception and Cultural Politics*. Cambridge: Cambridge University Press.

Horton, Julian. 2011. "John Field and the Alternative History of First-Movement Concerto Form." *Music & Letters* 92 (1): 43–83.

Horton, Julian. 2015. "Formal Type and Formal Function in the Postclassical Piano Concerto." In *Formal Functions in Perspective: Essays on Musical Form from Haydn to Adorno*, edited by Steven Vande Moortele, Julie Pedneault-Deslauriers, and Nathan John Martin, 77–122. Rochester, NY: University of Rochester Press.

Horton, Julian. 2017. "Criteria for a Theory of Nineteenth-Century Sonata Form." *Music Theory & Analysis* 4: 147–91.

Hunt, Graham. 2009. "The Three-Key Trimodular Block and Its Classical Precedents: Sonata Expositions of Schubert and Brahms." *Intégral* 23: 65–119.

Hunt, Graham. Forthcoming. "Aria-Sonata Forms? Taking *Formenlehre* to the Opera Once More." In, *Analyzing Mozart's Operas: External Stakes, Internal Challenges*, edited by Nathan John Martin and Lauri Suurpää. Leuven: Leuven University Press.

Huron, David. 2006. *Sweet Anticipation: Music and the Psychology of Expectation*. Cambridge, MA: MIT Press.

Indorf, Gerd. 2004. *Beethovens Streichquartette: Kulturgeschichtliche Aspekte und Werkinterpretation*. Freiburg im Breslau: Rombach Verlag.

Irving, John. 1997. *Mozart's Piano Sonatas: Contexts, Sources, Style*. Cambridge: Cambridge University Press.

Iser, Wolfgang. 1978. *The Act of Reading: A Theory of Aesthetic Response*. Baltimore, MD: Johns Hopkins University Press.

Kerman, Joseph. 1966. *The Beethoven Quartets*. New York: Norton.

Kinderman, William. 2006. *Mozart's Piano Music*. New York: Oxford University Press.

Kinderman, William. 2009. *Beethoven*. 2nd edition. New York: Oxford University Press.

Kirby, Frank E. 1966. "Beethoven and the 'Geselliges Lied.'" *Music & Letters* 47 (2): 116–25.

Kirkendale, Warren. 1979. *Fugue and Fugato in Rococo and Classical Chamber Music*, translated by Margaret Bent and Warren Kirkendale. Revised edition. Durham, NC: Duke University Press, 1979.

Klorman, Edward. 2016. *Mozart's Music of Friends: Social Interplay in the Chamber Works*. Cambridge: Cambridge University Press.

Knapp, Raymond. 1997. *Brahms and the Challenge of the Symphony*. Stuyvesant, NY: Pendragon Press.

Korsakova-Kreyn, Marina. 2018. "Two-Level Model of Embodied Cognition in Music." *Psychomusicology: Music, Mind, and Brain* 28 (4): 240–59.

Lakoff, George. 1993. "The Contemporary Theory of Metaphor." In *Metaphor and Thought*, 2nd edition, edited by Andrew Ortony, 202–51. Cambridge: Cambridge University Press.

Lakoff, George, and Mark Johnson. 1980. *Metaphors We Live By*. Chicago: University of Chicago Press.

Landon, H. C. Robbins. 1976. *Haydn: Chronicle and Works*, vol. 3: *Haydn in England 1791–1795*. Bloomington: Indiana University Press.

Landon, H. C. Robbins, and David Wyn Jones. 1988. *Haydn: His Life and Music*. Bloomington: Indiana University Press.

Lawrence, John Y. 2020. "Toward a Predictive Theory of Theme Types." *Journal of Music Theory* 64 (1): 1–36.

Levine, Caroline. 2015. *Forms: Whole, Rhythm, Hierarchy, Network*. Princeton, NJ: Princeton University Press.

Lockwood, Lewis. 2003. *Beethoven: The Music and the Life*. New York: Norton.

London, Justin. 1993. "Loud Rests and Other Strange Metric Phenomena (or, Meter as Heard)." *Music Theory Online* 0 (2) (April), http://www.mtosmt.org/issues/mto.93.0.2/mto.93.0.2.london.html.

London, Justin. 2012. *Hearing in Time: Psychological Aspects of Meter*. 2nd edition. New York: Oxford University Press.

Lowe, Melanie. 2007. *Pleasure and Meaning in the Classical Symphony*. Bloomington: Indiana University Press.

Lowe, Melanie. 2014. "Amateur Topical Competencies." In *The Oxford Handbook of Topic Theory*, edited by Danuta Mirka, 601–28. New York: Oxford University Press, 2014a.

Luhmann, Niklas. 1990. "The Work of Art and the Self-Reproduction of Art." In *Essays on Self-Reference*, 191–214. New York: Columbia University Press.

Luhmann, Niklas. 2000. *Art as a Social System*. Stanford, CA: Stanford University Press.

McClary, Susan. 1994. "Constructions of Subjectivity in Franz Schubert's Music." In *Queering the Pitch: The New Gay and Lesbian Musicology*, edited by Philip Brett, Elizabeth Wood, and Gary Thomas, 205–33. New York: Routledge.

McClelland, Clive. 2014. "*Ombra* and *Tempesta*." In *The Oxford Handbook of Topic Theory*, edited by Danuta Mirka, 279–300. New York: Oxford University Press, 2014a.

McClymonds, Marita Petzoldt. 2012. "The Italian Opera Sinfonia 1720 to 1800." In *The Symphonic Repertoire*, edited by Mary Sue Morrow and Bathia Churgin, 117–34, [vol. 1 of] *The Eighteenth-Century Symphony*. Bloomington: Indiana University Press, 2012.

McCreless, Patrick. 2015. "Probing the Limits: Musical Structure and Musical Rhetoric in Schubert's String Quartet in G Major, D. 887." *Music Theory & Analysis* 2 (1): 1–36.

Mak, Su Yin. 2010. *Schubert's Lyricism Reconsidered*. Saarbrücken: Lambert Academic Press.

Mak, Su Yin. 2016. "Formal Ambiguity and Generic Reinterpretation in the Late Instrumental Music." In *Schubert's Late Music: History, Theory, Style*, 282–306, edited by Lorraine Byrne Bodley and Julian Horton. Cambridge: Cambridge University Press.

Margulis, Elizabeth Hellmuth. 2014. *On Repeat: How Music Plays the Mind*. New York: Oxford University Press.

Marston, Nicholas. 1994. "Stylistic Advance, Strategic Retreat: Beethoven's Sketches for the Finale of the Second Symphony." *Beethoven Forum* 3: 127–50. Lincoln: University of Nebraska Press.

Martin, Nathan John. 2015. "Mozart's Sonata-Form Arias." In *Formal Functions in Perspective: Essays on Musical Form from Haydn to Adorno*, edited by Steven Vande Moortele, Julie Pedneault-Deslauriers, and Nathan John Martin, 37–73. Rochester, NY: University of Rochester Press.

Marx, Adolf Bernhard. 1859. *Beethoven: Leben und Schaffen*. Vol. 1. Berlin: Otto Janke, 1859.

Marx, Adolf Bernhard. 1860. *Die Lehre von der musikalischen Komposition, praktisch-theoretisch*. 3rd edition, 4 vols., vol 4. Leipzig: Breitkopf und Härtel (Orig. 1847).

Mastic, Timothy R. 2015. "Normative Wit: Haydn's Recomposed Recapitulations." *Music Theory Online* 21 (2) (June), http://www.mtosmt.org/issues/mto.15.21.2/mto.15.21.2.mastic.html.

Mathew, Nicholas. 2018. "Interesting Haydn: On Attention's Materials." *Journal of the American Musicological Association* 71 (3), 655–701.

Mathew, Nicholas, and Benjamin Walton, eds. 2013. *The Invention of Beethoven and Rossini: Historiography, Analysis, Criticism*. Cambridge: Cambridge University Press.

Millard, Russell. 2018. "Telling Tales: A Survey of Narratological Approaches to Music." *Current Musicology* 103: 5–44.

Mirka, Danuta. 2010. "Punctuation and Sense in Late-Eighteenth-Century Music." *Journal of Music Theory* 54 (2): 236–82.

Mirka, Danuta, ed. 2014a. *The Oxford Handbook of Topic Theory*. New York: Oxford University Press.

Mirka, Danuta. 2014b. "Introduction." In *The Oxford Handbook of Topic Theory*. edited by Danuta Mirka, 1–57. New York: Oxford University Press, 2014a.

Monahan, Seth. 2011. "Sonata Theory in the Undergraduate Classroom." *Journal of Music Theory Pedagogy* 25: 1–65.

Monahan, Seth. 2013. "Action and Agency Revisited." *Journal of Music Theory* 57 (2): 321–71.

Monahan, Seth. 2015. *Mahler's Symphonic Sonatas*. New York: Oxford University Press.

Monelle, Raymond. 2006. *The Musical Topic: Hunt, Military and Pastoral*. Bloomington: Indiana University Press.

Morrow, Mary Sue. 2012a. "Carl Philipp Emanuel Bach." In *The Symphonic Repertoire*, edited by Mary Sue Morrow and Bathia Churgin, 280–98, [vol. 1 of] *The Eighteenth-Century Symphony*. Bloomington: Indiana University Press, 2012.

Morrow, Mary Sue. 2012b. "Eighteenth-Century Viewpoints." In *The Symphonic Repertoire*, edited by Mary Sue Morrow and Bathia Churgin, 40–74, [vol. 1 of] *The Eighteenth-Century Symphony*. Bloomington: Indiana University Press, 2012.

Morrow, Mary Sue. 2012c. "Historiography of the Eighteenth-Century Symphony." In *The Symphonic Repertoire*, edited by Mary Sue Morrow and Bathia Churgin, 18–39, [vol. 1 of] *The Eighteenth-Century Symphony*. Bloomington: Indiana University Press, 2012.

Morrow, Mary Sue. 2012d. "Sketch for a History of the Eighteenth-Century Symphonic Repertoire." In *The Symphonic Repertoire*, edited by Mary Sue Morrow and Bathia Churgin, 779–92, [vol. 1 of] *The Eighteenth-Century Symphony*. Bloomington: Indiana University Press, 2012.

Morrow, Mary Sue. 2012e. "The Symphony in the Austrian Monarchy." In *The Symphonic Repertoire*, edited by Mary Sue Morrow and Bathia Churgin, 411–71, [vol. 1 of] *The Eighteenth-Century Symphony*. Bloomington: Indiana University Press, 2012.

Morrow, Mary Sue and Bathia Churgin, eds. 2012. *The Symphonic Repertoire* [vol. 1 of] *The Eighteenth-Century Symphony*. Bloomington: Indiana University Press.

Musgrave, Michael. 1983. "Brahms's First Symphony: Thematic Coherence and Its Secret Origin." *Music Analysis* 2 (2): 117–33.

Neuwirth, Markus. 2011. "Joseph Haydn's 'Witty' Play on Hepokoski and Darcy's *Elements of Sonata Theory*." *Zeitschrift der Gesellschaft für Musiktheorie* 8 (1): 199–220.

Neuwirth, Markus, and Pieter Bergé, eds. 2015. *What Is a Cadence?* Leuven: Leuven University Press.

Nottebohm, Gustav. 1887. *Zweite Beethoveniana: Nachgelassene Aufsätze*. Leipzig: C. F. Peters.

November, Nancy. 2013. *Beethoven's Theatrical Quartets: Opp. 59, 74 and 95*. Cambridge: Cambridge University Press.

Parsons, James. 2002. "'Deine Zauber binden wieder': Beethoven, Schiller, and the Joyous Reconciliation of Opposites." *Beethoven Forum* 9 (1): 1–53. Urbana-Champaign: University of Illinois Press.

Pascall, Robert. 1974. "Some Special Uses of Sonata Form by Brahms." *Soundings* 4: 58–63.

Plantinga, Leon. 1999. *Beethoven's Concertos: History, Style, Performance*. New York: Norton.

Ratner, Leonard G. 1980. *Classic Music: Expression, Form, and Style*. New York: Schirmer Books.

Rehding, Alexander, and Steven Rings, editors. 2019. *The Oxford Handbook of Critical Concepts in Music Theory*. New York: Oxford University Press.

Rice, John A. 1991. *W. A. Mozart: La clemenza di Tito*. Cambridge: Cambridge University Press.

Richards, Mark. 2013a. "Sonata Form and the Problem of Second-Theme Beginnings." *Music Analysis* 32 (1): 3–45.

Richards, Mark. 2013b. "Beethoven and the Obscured Medial Caesura: A Study in the Transformation of Style." *Music Theory Spectrum* 35 (2): 166–93.

Riley, Matthew. 2014. *The Viennese Minor-Key Symphony in the Age of Haydn and Mozart*. New York: Oxford University Press.

Riley, Matthew. 2015. "The Sonata Principle Reformulated for Haydn Post-1770 and a Typology of his Recapitulatory Strategies." *Journal of the Royal Musical Association* 140 (1): 1–39.

Rober, R. Todd. 2012. "Johann Gottlob Harrer." In *The Symphonic Repertoire*, edited by Mary Sue Morrow and Bathia Churgin, 227–39, [vol. 1 of] *The Eighteenth-Century Symphony*. Bloomington: Indiana University Press, 2012.

Rodgers, Stephen. 2009. *Form, Program, and Metaphor in the Music of Berlioz*. Cambridge: Cambridge University Press.

Rosen, Charles. 1997. *The Classical Style: Haydn, Mozart, Beethoven*. Expanded edition (original ed. 1971). New York: Norton.

Rusch, René. 2016. "The *Four-Key* Exposition? Schubert's Sonata Forms, the Fantasia, and Questions of Formal Coherence." Presentation, Society for Music Theory (November 4, 2016, Vancouver, BC).

Sanguinetti, Giorgio. 2012. *The Art of Partimento: History, Theory, and Practice*. New York: Oxford University Press.

Schachter, Carl. 2016. *The Art of Tonal Analysis: Twelve Lessons in Schenkerian Theory*, edited by Joseph N. Straus. New York: Oxford University Press.

Schmalfeldt, Janet. 1992. "Cadential Processes: The Evaded Cadence and the 'One More Time' Technique." *Journal of Musicological Research* 12 (1–2): 1–52.

Schmalfeldt, Janet. 2011. *In the Process of Becoming: Analytic and Philosophical Perspectives on Form in Early Nineteenth-Century Music*. New York: Oxford University Press.

Schroeder, David P. 1990. *Haydn and the Enlightenment: The Late Symphonies and Their Audience*. Oxford: Clarendon Press.

Schroeder, David. 2005. "[Haydn's] Orchestral Music: Symphonies and Concertos." In *The Cambridge Companion to Haydn*, edited by Caryl Clark, 95–111. Cambridge: Cambridge University Press.

Schubert, Giselher. 1994. "Themes and Double Themes: The Problem of the Symphonic in Brahms." *19th-Century Music* 18 (1): 10–23.

Sisman, Elaine. 2013. "Haydn's Solar Poetics: The *Tageszeiten* Symphonies and Enlightenment Knowledge." *Journal of the American Musicological Society* 66 (1): 5–102.

Sisman, Elaine. 2014. "Symphonies and the Public Display of Topics." In *The Oxford Handbook of Topic Theory*. edited by Danuta Mirka, 90–117. New York: Oxford University Press, 2014a.

Smith, Peter H. 2014. "Schumann's Continuous Expositions and the Classical Tradition." *Journal of Music Theory* 58 (1): 25–56.

Smith, Peter H. 2018. "Form and the Large-Scale Connection: Motivic Harmony and the Expanded Type-1 Sonata in Dvořák's Later Chamber Music." *Music Theory Spectrum* 40 (2): 248–79.

Smith, Peter J. 2019. "The Type 2 Sonata in the Nineteenth Century: Two Case Studies from Mendelssohn and Dvořák." *Journal of Music Theory* 63 (1): 103–38.

Solomon, Maynard. 1995. *Mozart: A Life*. New York: HarperCollins.

Thayer, Alexander. 1967. *Thayer's Life of Beethoven*, revised and edited by Elliot Forbes. Princeton, NJ: Princeton University Press.

Tovey, Donald Francis. 1936. *Essays in Musical Analysis*, vol. 3: *Concertos*. London: Oxford University Press.

Tovey, Donald Francis. 1981. *Symphonies and Other Orchestral Works* (selected reprint from *Essays in Musical Analysis*, 1935–39). Oxford: Oxford University Press.

Turner, James. 2014. *Philology: The Forgotten Origins of the Modern Humanities*. Princeton, NJ: Princeton University Press.

Tyson, Alan. 1975. "'La clemenza di Tito' and Its Chronology." *The Musical Times* 116 (1585): 221–27 (reprinted in Tyson 1987, 48–60).

Tyson, Alan. 1987. "The Date of Mozart's Piano Sonata in B-flat, K. 333 (315c): The 'Linz' Sonata?" In Tyson, *Mozart: Studies of the Autograph Scores*, 73–81. Cambridge, MA: Harvard University Press.

Vande Moortele, Steven. 2009. *Two-Dimensional Sonata Form: Form and Cycle in Single-Movement Instrumental Works by Liszt, Strauss, Schoenberg, and Zemlinsky*. Leuven: Leuven University Press.

Vande Moortele, Steven. 2017. *The Romantic Overture and Musical Form from Rossini to Wagner*. Cambridge: Cambridge University Press.

Waltham-Smith, Naomi. 2017. *Music and Belonging between Revolution and Restoration*. New York: Oxford University Press.

Watkins, Holly, 2011. *Metaphors of Depth in German Musical Thought: From E. T. A. Hoffmann to Arnold Schoenberg*. Cambridge: Cambridge University Press.

Webster, James. 1978–79. "Schubert's Sonata Form and Brahms's First Maturity." *19th-Century Music* 2 (1): 18–35, and 3 (1): 52–71.

Webster, James. 1991. *Haydn's 'Farewell' Symphony and the Idea of Classical Style: Through-Composition and Cyclic Integration in His Instrumental Music*. Cambridge: Cambridge University Press.

Webster, James. 2005a. "Haydn's Aesthetics." In *The Cambridge Companion to Haydn*, edited by Caryl Clark, 30–44. Cambridge: Cambridge University Press.

Webster, James. 2005b. "The Sublime and the Pastoral in *The Creation* and *The Seasons*." In *The Cambridge Companion to Haydn*, edited by Caryl Clark, 150–63. Cambridge: Cambridge University Press.

Webster, James. 2009. "*Formenlehre* in Theory and Practice." In William E. Caplin, James Hepokoski, and James Webster, *Musical Form, Forms, & Formenlehre*, edited by Pieter Bergé, 123–39. Leuven: Leuven University Press.

Wiese, Walter. 2010. *Beethovens Kammermusik*. Winterthur: Amadeus Verlag.

Will, Richard. 2002. *The Characteristic Symphony in the Age of Haydn and Beethoven.* Cambridge: Cambridge University Press.

Williams, Peter. 1997. *The Chromatic Fourth: During Four Centuries of Music.* Oxford: Clarenden Press.

Wingfield, Paul. 2008. "Beyond 'Norms and Deformations': Towards a Theory of Sonata Form as Reception History." *Music Analysis* 27 (1): 137–77.

Wolf, Eugene K. 1966. "The Recapitulations in Haydn's London Symphonies." *The Musical Quarterly* 52 (1): 71–89.

Wolfson, Susan J., and Marshall Brown, editors. 2006. *Reading for Form.* Seattle: University of Washington Press (Orig. a collection published in a special issue of the *Modern Language Quarterly* 2000).

Wollenberg, Susan. 1998. "Schubert's Transitions." In *Schubert Studies*, edited by Brian Newbould. Aldershot, UK: Ashgate, 16–61.

Wollenberg, Susan. 2011. *Schubert's Fingerprints: Studies in the Instrumental Works.* Farnham, UK: Ashgate.

Yust, Jason. 2018. *Organized Time: Rhythm, Tonality, and Form.* New York: Oxford University Press.

Zaslaw, Neal. 1989. *Mozart's Symphonies: Context, Performance Practice, Reception.* Oxford: Clarendon Press.

Index of Names

These references identify appearances of names within the text and endnotes as well as contextual discussions of the five main composers treated in this book (Mozart, Haydn, Beethoven, Schubert, and Brahms). Passing mentions of those five, ubiquitous in this book, are not listed. For individual compositions, see the Index of Works; for discussions of individual concepts within Sonata Theory and related fields, see the Index of Concepts.

Adorno, Theodor W., 158, 162, 180, 277 n.4, 278
  n.9, 289 n.1, 295 n.3, 303 n.6, 304 n.14
Agawu, Kofi, 240
Albrecht, Theodore, 155, 156
Allanbrook, Wye J., 138, 279 n.15, 280 n.16,
  281 nn.1, 3
Almén, Byron, 283 n.23
Auber, Daniel-François-Esprit, 301 n.33

Bach, Carl Philipp Emanuel, 76, 136,
  151, 200, 270, 285 n.32, 292 n.4,
  307 n.1
Bach, Johann Christian, 208, 210, 240, 270,
  298 n.13, 306 n.31
Bach, Johann Sebastian, 140, 151, 281 n.25,
  292 n.4, 305 n.18
Beach, David, 180, 184, 295 n.2, 296 n.12
Becker, Judith, 277 n.2
Becker, Nikolaus, 305 n.18
Beethoven, Ludwig van, 3, 53, 85, 105, 151,
  179, 181, 199, 234, 236, 238–9, 240,
  249, 278 n.9, 290 n.3, 291 nn.7, 14, 294
  n.18, 295–6 n.7, 303 n.5
  "Beethoven crescendo," 126
  "Beethoven-Rossini dichotomy," 295–6 n.7
  codas, 83–4, 134–5, 173–4, 289 n.20
  concertos, 52, 269, 272, 272–3, 276
  default procedures, overriding, 6, 55, 63,
    120–22, 154–6, 178, 233, 278 n.8, 283
    nn.13, 14, 290 n.1, 291 n.5, 292 n.6
  form as process ("organic" growth), 9–10,
    110, 179, 306–7 n.35
  hyperdrama, 121, 126, 153–5
  introductions, 243, 291 n.5
  minor mode, 137–8, 140, 142, 147, 149, 150,
    153, 189, 263
  "new path" (1802), 121–2, 154–6, 158, 293 n.1
  recapitulations, 79, 81, 82, 100, 117, 301
    nn.36–7

rondos, 269
  "sublime," 122, 127, 131, 135
  three-key exposition, 147
Bergé, Pieter, 279 n.12
Berlioz, Hector, 228–9, 301–2 n.37
Best, Steven, 280 n.15
Black, Brian, 187
Boccherini, Luigi, 136
Bonds, Mark Evan, 26, 155, 296 n.8
Brahms, Johannes, xiii, 85, 110, 122, 147,
  234, 237–41
  aesthetic convictions, 237, 239–40
  allusions to others' works, 240, 248–9, 265,
    304–5 nn.15–18
  changed musical/cultural world, 1870s,
    234, 237–41
  concertos, 270
  expanded Type 1 sonata, 241–2, 260, 286
    nn.40–2
  form as process, 9, 110
  three-key exposition, 147, 254
  Wagner, contra, 237–9
Brendel, Alfred, 180
Brinkmann, Reinhold, 240, 243, 245, 260–1,
  304 n.11, 306 n.31
Brodbeck, David, 238, 239, 240,
  304 nn.11, 13, 305 n.18, 306
  nn.30, 31, 34
Brody, Christopher, 17, 280 n.17
Brown, A. Peter, 41, 101
Bruch, Max, 238, 240, 248, 305 n.18
Bruckner, Anton, xiii, 122, 238–9, 286 n.36,
  299 n.23, 304 n.10
Bürger, Peter, 303 n.3
Burnham, Scott, 289 n.3
Burstein, L. Poundie, 279 nn.13–14, 283 n.12,
  284 nn.20, 24
Byros, Vasili, 4, 126–7, 128, 222,
  278 n.7

Index of Works

Index of Concepts

This index locates discussions of individual concepts within Sonata Theory and related analytical and conceptual fields. It does not locate every occurrence of the entries listed below. (Several of the terms recur regularly throughout the book.) Instead, it's a guide to their initial or central discussions, along with other explanatory appearances. Definitional and other key passages are indicated in italics. Tables and Figures are indicated by an italic *T* and *f* following the page number.